Patrícia Zovella

16⁹⁵

The "Underclass" Debate

SPONSORED BY THE COMMITTEE FOR RESEARCH ON THE URBAN UNDERCLASS
OF THE SOCIAL SCIENCE RESEARCH COUNCIL

The "Underclass" Debate

VIEWS FROM HISTORY

Michael B. Katz, Editor

PRINCETON UNIVERSITY PRESS

PRINCETON, NEW JERSEY

Published by Princeton University Press, 41 William Street,
Princeton, New Jersey 08540
In the United Kingdom: Princeton University Press, Chichester, West Sussex

Library of Congress Cataloging-in-Publication Data

The "Underclass" debate : views from history / Michael B. Katz,
    editor.
        p.   cm.
    "Sponsored by the Committee for Research on the Urban Underclass
of the Social Science Research Council."
    Includes bibliographical references and index.
    ISBN 0-691-04810-X (cl : acid-free paper) — ISBN
0-691-00628-8 (pb : acid-free paper)
    1. Urban poor—United States—History.   2. Afro-Americans—Social
conditions.   3. Afro-Americans—Economic conditions.   4. Urban
policy—United States—History.   I. Katz, Michael B., 1939-   .
II. Social Science Research Council (U.S.). Committee for Research
on the Urban Underclass.
HV4044.U56   1993
362.5'0973—dc20   92-24994
                                                        CIP

Publication of this book has been aided by the Committee for Research on the Urban Underclass
of the Social Science Research Council

This book has been composed in Linotron Berkeley

Princeton University Press books are printed on acid-free paper
and meet the guidelines for permanence and durability of the
Committee on Production Guidelines for Book Longevity of the
Council on Library Resources

Printed in the United States of America

10 9 8 7 6 5 4 3 2

Contents

Preface

SINCE its preliminary meeting in 1987, I have served as archivist to the Social Science Research Council's Committee for Research on the Urban Underclass. Listening to the discussions and reading the material, I was struck by the role of history in the way scholars, journalists, and politicians formulated the issues in the "underclass" debate. Almost every major claim they made included either implicit or explicit assumptions about the past. Yet very few of them knew of the recent historical work related to their arguments, and what they said or implied about history often was incomplete, uninformed, or wrong. Over and over again, it seemed to me that historians could clarify many of the most important issues, and I wanted to find a way to bring the best in contemporary historical scholarship into the debates. Therefore, I developed a plan for a historical volume and proposed that the committee sponsor it. Its members agreed. Because we wanted to attract the most able authors writing on the subject, regardless of academic status, we conducted a national competition, open to everyone from graduate students through full professors, to write chapters. We succeeded in attracting a remarkable and diverse set of applicants. Three scholars—Michael Frisch of the State University of New York at Buffalo, Ira Katznelson of the New School for Social Research, and Viviana Zelizer of Princeton University—joined me and Robert Pearson, SSRC staff to the committee, to evaluate the proposals and select the authors. In the course of writing their chapters, the authors met twice in New York for memorable seminars, once to share chapter proposals, and once to share drafts. It has been my privilege as editor to work with them. Collectively, the chapters of this book present a stunning synthesis of recent social history related to urban poverty; they also represent a sustained, and unprecedented, application of historical scholarship to a great and urgent issue of public policy.

The violence in Los Angeles that erupted in the spring of 1992 has suddenly thrust the state of inner cities and urban poverty into public consciousness and onto the political agenda. In the rekindled debate, most of the competing interpretive frameworks remain incomplete because they fail to ground their explanations in social history. The events in Los Angeles and their threatened echoes elsewhere cannot be understood apart from the history of urban America. They result from the processes that have shaped the configuration of race, poverty, and space. This book is, in part, that story. Although it was written before recent events in Los Angeles, it provides historical evidence with which to explain the roots of violence in America's inner cities.

The authors owe individual thanks to many people who assisted them with their chapters. They will acknowledge these debts privately. Collectively, we would like to thank the three scholars listed above for evaluating proposals and the staff of the SSRC's Committee for Research on the Urban Underclass, especially Martha Gephart, Alice O'Connor, and Robert Pearson, who were unfailingly helpful, supportive, and efficient.

The "Underclass" Debate

The Urban "Underclass" as a Metaphor of Social Transformation

Michael B. Katz

THE TERM *underclass* offers a convenient metaphor for use in commentaries on inner city crises because it evokes three widely shared perceptions: novelty, complexity, and danger. Conditions within inner cities are unprecedented; they cannot be reduced to a single factor; and they menace the rest of us. The idea of an underclass is a metaphor for the social transformation embedded in these perceptions. Nonetheless, writing about the underclass does not convey the qualitative differences between past and present, for it echoes the oldest themes in American discussions of urban poverty and rests on assumptions about history, which usually remain implicit and unexamined. The purpose of this volume is to raise these assumptions to the surface, to subject them to scrutiny with evidence from recent historical research, and to identify the ways in which past experience has shaped America's contemporary urban underclass.

In his novel *The Dean's December*, Saul Bellow exposes the tangle of ideas and emotions embedded in responses to the underclass. When a young black man murders the graduate student who had invited him home from a Chicago bar, responsibility for the university's reaction rests with the novel's protagonist, Dean Albert Corde. As his investigation of the case draws him into its context in the inner city, Corde's despair grows, and he reacts with an incendiary article in *Harper's* about the erosion of civilization and society in his native city. When he meets the public defender assigned to the accused, Corde tries to explain why he believes the emergence of an underclass signifies the destruction of a people:

> Your defendant belongs to that black underclass everybody is openly talking about, which is economically "redundant," to use the term specialists now use, falling farther and farther behind the rest of society, locked into a culture of despair and crime—I wouldn't say a culture, that's another specialists' word. There is no culture there, it's only a wilderness, and damn monstrous, too. We are talking about a people consigned to destruction, a doomed people. Compare them to the last phase of the proletariat as pictured by Marx. The proletariat, owning *nothing*, stripped utterly bare, would awaken at last from the nightmare of history. Entirely naked, it would have no illusions because there was nothing to support illusions and it would make a revolution without any scenario. It would need no historical script because of its merciless education in reality, and so forth. Well, here is a case of people denuded. And what's

the effect of denudation, atomization? Of course, they aren't proletarians. They're just a lumpen population. We haven't even conceived that reaching it may be a problem. So there's nothing but death before it. Maybe we've already made our decision. Those that can be advanced into the middle class, let them be advanced. The rest? Well, we do our best by them. We don't have to do any more. They kill some of us. Mostly they kill themselves.[1]

By the late 1970s, the specter of an emergent underclass permeated discussions of America's inner cities. Corde's reaction mirrored these discussions' fear, pessimism, and confusion. The word *underclass* conjured up a mysterious wilderness in the heart of America's cities; a terrain of violence and despair; a collectivity outside politics and social structure, beyond the usual language of class and stratum, unable to protest or revolt. Was it the result of great economic forces consigning ever larger swatches of the population to a scrapheap of useless people? Did it reveal the birth of a new culture that reproduced itself by feeding on its own pathologies? Did it have a future beyond self-destruction? By its withdrawal and willful negligence, had the rest of America nurtured the underclass it now feared and despised?

ORIGINS OF THE DEBATE

Open debate on the underclass accelerated in 1977 when *Time* magazine announced the emergence of a menacing underclass in America's inner cities. Drugs, crime, teenage pregnancy, and high unemployment, not poverty, defined the "underclass," most of whose members were young and minorities. "Behind the [ghetto's] crumbling walls," wrote *Time*, "lives a large group of people who are more intractable, more socially alien and more hostile than almost anyone had imagined. They are the unreachables: the American underclass. . . . Their bleak environment nurtures values that are often at odds with those of the majority—even the majority of the poor. Thus the underclass produces a highly disproportionate number of the nation's juvenile delinquents, school dropouts, drug addicts and welfare mothers, and much of the adult crime, family disruption, urban decay and demand for social expenditures."[2]

With the publication in 1982 of Ken Auletta's *Underclass*, the word secured its dominance in the vocabulary of inner-city pathology. Auletta reinforced the image emerging in the mass media. For him, the underclass was a relatively permanent minority among the poor who fell into four distinct categories: "(*a*) the *passive poor*, usually long-term welfare recipients; (*b*) the *hostile* street criminals who terrorize most cities, and who are often school dropouts and drug addicts; (*c*) the *hustlers*, who, like street criminals, may not be poor and who

---

[1] Saul Bellow, *The Dean's December* (New York: Harper and Row, 1982; reprint, Pocket Books, 1983), pp. 228–29.

[2] "The American Underclass," *Time*, August 29, 1977, pp. 14, 15.

earn their livelihood in an underground economy, but rarely commit violent crimes; (d) the *traumatized* drunks, drifters, homeless shopping-bag ladies and released mental patients who frequently roam or collapse on city streets."[3] A new social stratum, identified by a set of interlocking behaviors, not primarily by poverty, dominated the wastelands that were all that remained of America's urban-industrial heartland.

Few would question the multidimensional quality of inner-city problems, although their specification and interaction remain contested. Nor would many disagree that they are dangerous, even though they would define their source and consequences differently. But no consensus exists as to their novelty. Critics worry that arguments for the existence of a new underclass represent a resurgence of old images of the undeserving poor, an attempt to mask recurrent poverty with an argument that blames the victim.

The division of poor people into moral categories represents one of three enduring preoccupations in discussions of poverty and welfare. The others are the impact of welfare on work motivation and family (does welfare destroy the will to work and erode family stability?) and the limits of social obligation (what do we owe each other?). Together, these preoccupations underlie the constellation of issues around which debates on urban poverty have swirled for centuries. Those issues not only animate contemporary mass media commentaries on the underclass, they also drive the research of the social scientists who have tried to appropriate the underclass from the media by defining it clearly and subjecting it to careful analysis. The major issues in the debate are these:

1. The extent to which individuals are responsible for their own poverty, or the balance between individual agency and structural forces
2. The role of culture (defined as the influence of sets of attitudes, values, and group behaviors) on perpetuating poverty and dependence
3. The contribution of family structure, organization, and modes of child rearing to developing and reproducing social pathologies
4. The influence of ecology, or environment, on behavior (put another way, how neighborhood characteristics contribute to crime, welfare dependence, low school attendance, and premarital pregnancy)
5. The capacity of institutions to counteract the influence of family and neighborhood, and why institutions so often fail to fulfill their missions
6. Why poverty persists despite public policy and whether policy has, in fact, made matters worse

These remain complex, consequential, and persistent issues. Even when they are interpreted in a similar manner, the resulting conclusions may at different times be classified as either liberal or conservative. Why these issues have persisted, what form they have assumed in different periods, how the cluster of

[3] Ken Auletta, *The Underclass* (New York: Random House, 1982), p. xvi.

ideas and practices surrounding them in the past have influenced the present—these are subjects for history.

THE EMERGENCE OF THE UNDESERVING POOR

Attempts to divide poor people into categories and to distinguish invidiously among them go back centuries. Before the late eighteenth and early nineteenth centuries, poor-law officials tried to distinguish between the "able-bodied" and "impotent" poor. The distinction reflected the need to distribute scarce resources rather than the attempt to make a moral judgment. In practice, however, no one could draw the line with precision. An 1821 Massachusetts legislative report advocating poor-law reform argued that all the "evils" associated with current practice resulted from "the difficulty of discriminating between the able poor and the impotent poor and of apportioning the degree of public provision to the degree of actual impotency."[4]

Nineteenth-century writers moralized the old distinction between the able-bodied and impotent poor into the worthy and unworthy or deserving and undeserving. In the 1820s, the Philadelphia Guardians of the Poor asserted, "The poor in consequence of vice, constitute here and everywhere, by far the greater part of the poor." In the terminology of the time, paupers, those individuals dependent on charity and public assistance, became synonymous with the undeserving poor.[5] In 1834, the Reverend Charles Burroughs reminded an audience of the distinction between poverty and pauperism. "The former is an unavoidable evil, to which many are brought from necessity, and in the wise and gracious Providence of God. It is the result, not of our faults, but of our misfortunes. . . . Pauperism is the consequence of willful error, of shameful indolence, of vicious habits."[6] Less than a decade later, another minister pointed out that the "popular mind" regarded poverty "solely as the product of him or of her who has entered its dreadful, because dishonored, uncared for, or unwisely cared for, service. Let me repeat it, the causes of poverty are looked for, and found in him or her who suffers it."[7]

By the second quarter of the nineteenth century, the vocabulary of poverty had acquired two of its lasting features: the division of the poor into categories of merit and the assumption that the roots of poverty lay in individual mis-

[4] "Report of the Committee on the Pauper Laws of this Commonwealth [1812]," reprinted in David J. Rothman, ed., *The Almshouse Experience: Collected Reports* (New York: Arno Press and New York Times, 1971), p. 4.

[5] Philadelphia Board of Guardians, "Report of the Committee Appointed by the Board of Guardians of the Poor of the City and Districts of Philadelphia, to Visit the Cities of Baltimore, New-York, Providence, Boston, and Salem [1827]," in Rothman, *Almshouse Experience*.

[6] Charles Burroughs, "A Discourse Delivered in the Chapel of the New Alms-House, in Portsmouth, N.H. . . ." (Portsmouth, N.H.: J. W. Foster, 1835), p. 9.

[7] Walter Channing, "An Address on the Prevention of Pauperism" (Boston: Office of the Christian World, 1843), p. 20.

behavior. Writings about poverty by the political Left as well as the Right frequently reflected these ideas. Marxists talked about the "lumpenproletariat," and even reformers in the Progressive Era who began to criticize individual explanations of poverty in the 1890s used the old distinctions.[8] Insofar as it is described in moral terms, the underclass falls within this tradition.

Concern about the impact of welfare and the use of "workfare" as social policy also share a very long history. Early nineteenth-century legislators tried to balance their obligation to care for the helpless and deserving poor with their fear of promoting dependence. Although relief could discourage work and encourage reliance on the public purse, to refuse all help remained unthinkable, for few questioned communities' obligation to prevent their members from dying of starvation or exposure. The preferred policy became refusing help to people in their homes and forcing them into institutions. In practice, this meant the substitution of poorhouses for outdoor relief (what we would today call public welfare). Although states deployed new networks of poorhouses, outdoor relief nonetheless persisted everywhere, until some cities finally abolished it temporarily in the third quarter of the nineteenth century.[9]

Poorhouses were supposed to be unpleasant. Their sponsors expected their very existence to deter all but the most desperate from applying for help. Within them, work requirements would keep existence harsh, and inmates' work would pay part of the cost of their upkeep. More important, however, work was a form of both punishment and moral training. In the 1820s, the managers of Philadelphia's almshouse replaced their horses with treadwheels operated by inmates. Later, when a committee pointed to the system's inefficiency and recommended the substitution of steam engines, the managers demurred. They cared more for the impact of the treadwheel on inmates than for increased economy and productivity. In the 1850s, an informed New Yorker, lamenting the failure of work requirements to take hold in New York's poorhouses, praised the almshouse in Providence, Rhode Island. Even when no profitable work was available, poorhouse managers set inmates "at something which is not profitable, at all events they must be kept employed." He had seen "a party of men carrying wood from one corner of the yard to another and piling it there; when it was all removed it was brought back and piled in the old place."[10]

By itself, idleness became synonymous with crime and poverty. In 1851, new rules for the Philadelphia police pointed out, "As a general thing, any idle, able-

[8] For example, see Robert Hunter, *Poverty* (New York: Macmillan, 1904; reprint, New York: Harper and Row, 1965), pp. 3, 63.

[9] I discuss poorhouses at length in *In the Shadow of the Poorhouse: A Social History of Welfare in America* (New York: Basic Books, 1986).

[10] Priscilla F. Clement, "The Response to Need: Welfare and Poverty in Philadelphia, 1800–1850" (Ph.D. diss., University of Pennsylvania, 1977), pp. 172–73, 307–9; "Letters to the Secretary of State on the Subject of Pauperism," first published in the *Columbia Republican*, in the fall of 1853, in New York Secretary of State, *Annual Report on Statistics of the Poor, 1855* (New York State Senate Documents, no. 72, 1855), pp. 103–4.

bodied poor man has no right to complain, if the eye of the police follows him wherever he roams or rests. His very idleness is an offense against all social laws."[11] Later in the century, when poorhouses had fallen into disfavor, willingness to work remained the touchstone of merit, and philanthropic societies opened woodyards and laundries. In his *Handbook of Charity Organization* (1882), Buffalo's Reverend S. Humphreys Gurteen admitted the difficulty of distinguishing "between worthy and unworthy cases." The answer was a labor test: "*in all cases . . . let the 'labor axiom' be the test, i.e., whether or not the applicant is willing to do as much work as his condition will allow.*" For this reason, he decreed, every Charity Organization Society should operate a woodyard or place to break stone. Others advocated laundries as a work test and form of work relief for women. Only those men willing to chop wood or break stone and those women ready to scrub clothes for less than prevailing wages deserved help.[12]

Poorhouses had other purposes, too. Their sponsors considered them humane replacements for the common practice of auctioning the care of the poor to the lowest bidder or of contracting it out; they expected poorhouses to curb public expenses for relief; and they hoped to break the cycle of dependence within families. Indeed, as in the late twentieth century, worries about the creation of a culture of dependence within poor families alarmed nineteenth-century reformers, who believed pauper parents incompetent and irresponsible. They expected institutional care to offer children a healthier, more well regulated, more educative environment. The report that persuaded New York State's legislature to call for the creation of poorhouses observed that pauper children raised outside almshouses were "not only brought up in ignorance and idleness"; their "health" remained "precarious," and they often died "prematurely." Later in the century, when poorhouses proved miserable places for children, reformers turned to the same arguments to advocate breaking up families and placing children in special institutions.[13]

Stripped of their period features, nineteenth-century discussions of inner cities also sound remarkably contemporary. Nineteenth- and early twentieth-century writers portrayed the undeserving poor as clustered in inner cities, where they formed slums that threatened to infect both the respectable poor and the middle classes. Observers worried about the consequences of social isolation and the growing concentration of poverty. In 1854, in his first annual report as head of New York City's Children's Aid Society, Charles Loring Brace argued

[11] *Act of the Legislature Establishing the Uniform System of Police for the Philadelphia Police District (3 May 1850) and Rules and Regulations of the Police Department* (Philadelphia, 1852), pp. 34, 36, quoted in Allen Steinberg, *The Transformation of Criminal Justice: Philadelphia, 1800–1880* (Chapel Hill: University of North Carolina Press, 1989), p. 153.

[12] S. Humphreys Gurteen, *Handbook of Charity Organization* (Buffalo, N.Y.: Published by the author, 1882), p. 141. Italics in original.

[13] "Report of the Secretary of State [of New York] in 1824 on the Relief and Settlement of the Poor," reprinted in Rothman, *Almshouse Experience*, pp. 1060, 955.

that the growing density of America's cities had eroded the character of their inhabitants. "The very *condensing* of their number within a small space, seems to stimulate their bad tendencies." He defined the "greatest danger" to America's future as the "existence of an ignorant, debased, and permanently poor class in the great cities. . . . The members of it come at length to form a separate population. They embody the lowest passions and the most thriftless habits of the community. They corrupt the lowest class of working-poor who are around them. The expenses of police, of prisons, of charities and means of relief, arise mainly from them."[14] As a consequence of altered urban ecology, contact between rich and poor had decreased, and the well off increasingly abandoned their responsibility for those left trapped by poverty within America's cities. In 1882, S. Humphreys Gurteen pointed to "a terrible chasm already existing between the rich and the poor; a chasm which is becoming wider and wider as the years roll by, and for the existence of which the well-to-do of the country are largely responsible."[15]

Housing reformers of the nineteenth and early twentieth centuries argued that the unsanitary, congested housing of the poor bred immorality, crime, and disease. Slums, they contended, were viruses infecting the moral and physical health of the city districts that surrounded them. In their writing, urban poverty acquired its lasting association with disease, embodied most recently in the melding of drugs, AIDS, and poverty into metaphors of epidemics threatening to leap the boundaries of the inner city.[16] "We must deal with [pauperism]," claimed New York City's Charity Organization Society in its fourth annual report in 1886, "as we would with a malarial swamp, draining and purifying it instead of walling it about, or its miasma will spread and taint neighborhoods like a plague."[17]

By the latter nineteenth century, poverty, crime, and disease blended to form a powerful, frightening, and enduring image. As is the case today, its dimensions were novelty, complexity, and danger. Among the urban poor, an undeserving subset, dependent on account of their own shiftless, irresponsible, immoral behavior, burdened honest taxpayers with the cost of their support, threatened their safety, and corrupted the working poor. Increasingly concentrated within slum districts, they lived in growing social isolation, cut off from the role models

---

[14] *Second Annual Report of the Children's Aid Society of New York* (New York, 1855), p. 3.

[15] Gurteen, *Handbook*, p. 38.

[16] Thomas W. Langfitt and Rebecca W. Rimel, "Suffer the Little Children," and "In Philadelphia There's Suffering Enough," *Philadelphia Inquirer*, June 25, 1989; Vicki Maloney, "America's Shame: Inner-City Ghettos Are Our Berlin Wall," *Philadelphia Inquirer*, June 4, 1989; Charles Rosenberg, "What Is an Epidemic? AIDS in Historical Perspective," *Daedalus* 118, no. 2 (1989): 1–17.

[17] *Fourth Annual Report of the Central Council of the Charity Organization Society of the City of New York, January 1st 1886* (New York Central Office, 1886), p. 14; David Ward, *Cities and Immigrants: A Geography of Change in Nineteenth-Century America* (New York: Oxford University Press, 1971); Roy Lubove, *The Progressives and the Slums: Tenement House Reform in New York City, 1890–1917* (Pittsburgh: University of Pittsburgh Press, 1962).

and oversight once provided by the more well-to-do, reproducing their own degradation.

Social policy had failed to prevent the emergence of the late nineteenth century's version of the underclass. Poorhouses, for instance, had met none of their sponsors' goals. Despised, neglected, they moved to the backwaters of social policy, increasingly transformed into public old-age homes by the removal of special classes of inmates (children, the mentally ill, and the sick). Public school systems, once the hope of urban reformers, had developed into huge, unresponsive bureaucracies that, critics argued, delivered education less effectively than had the smaller schools of the past. Riddled with graft, outdoor relief (public welfare) demoralized the poor and fueled a meteoric rise in taxes.[18]

As reformers and legislators cast about for new policies, they did not abandon the distinction between the deserving and the undeserving poor. Nor did they redefine its dimensions. The deserving poor fell into two classes: the first, clearly helpless and pathetic people who on account of age or infirmity could neither care for nor support themselves. The other met dual criteria: they had suffered circumstances beyond their own responsibility (the death of a husband or a seasonal layoff, for instance) that had rendered them dependent, *and* they proved themselves willing to work for whatever small support public and private charity might offer. Most deserving were widows who kept their children clean, taught them manners, sent them to school, managed their tiny incomes effectively, and spent hours every day sewing or scrubbing for tiny wages. The other able-bodied poor were family men out of work, sober and responsible, willing to chop wood or break stone. However, they remained, always, slightly suspect because they had failed to save for the episodes of dependence that predictably punctuated life among the working class.[19]

FROM THE UNDESERVING POOR TO THE CULTURE OF POVERTY

In their emphasis on race, gender, and culture, the great themes in late-nineteenth-century discussions of urban poverty also resemble those in contemporary writing about the underclass. In popular impressions (although not in fact), the color of the underclass is black. Despite the continuing racism that has scarred American history, this association of urban poverty with race is relatively new, a product of the massive migration of African Americans into Northern and Midwestern cities after World War II. Before then, of course, most African Americans lived in rural areas, and racial ghettos within Northern cities re-

---

[18] I discuss the transformation of the poorhouse and the problems with outdoor relief in *Shadow*, chaps. 2 and 4, and the criticisms of urban school systems in *Reconstructing American Education* (Cambridge: Harvard University Press, 1987), chap. 3.

[19] My conclusions here rest on reading case records of nineteenth-century philanthropic agencies.

mained relatively small. At the time, the most visible extreme poverty occurred within the vast tenement-house districts inhabited by second-generation whites and new European immigrants. Nonetheless, observers, fearful of cultural differences, which they equated with inferiority, very often framed discussions of poverty in racial terms and applied them to nationality groups. This scientific racism culminated in the eugenics movement of the early twentieth century and in immigration restriction. In this way, stigmas of cultural difference, race, and poverty blended very early in images of the undeserving poor. Of course, the objects of racial stigma have altered with time. Because racism directed toward African Americans is so powerful, the contemporary fusion of race and poverty remains the most resilient and vicious in American history.[20]

Images of alcoholic, immoral, incompetent mothers unfit to raise their children also extend far into the past. Nonetheless, throughout most of American history, widows remained the quintessential deserving poor. Most despised and distrusted have been unmarried men unable to support themselves. Public officials and charity reformers waged long, tough, and only partially successful campaigns to drive them from the relief rolls and out of poorhouses. (Today, they try to purge them from the rolls of General Assistance.) In the 1870s, as a new noun, *tramp,* entered the language to identify this most visible element among the era's equivalent of the underclass, commentators invariably referred to them as men.[21]

When the first federal welfare program for women with children, Aid to Dependent Children, entered public policy as part of the legislation creating Social Security in 1935, its sponsors assumed it would apply to a relatively small group of widows, and it carried no stigma. Nor had its predecessors, the widows' pensions enacted by several states in the early twentieth century. In the 1950s, as the recipients of ADC (later AFDC, Aid to Families with Dependent Children) increasingly became unmarried and black, public attitudes shifted. Race and sexuality fused with the usual stigma attached to welfare, and African-American women raising children by themselves became the new undeserving poor.[22]

[20] Mark H. Haller, *Eugenics: Hereditarian Attitudes in American Thought* (New Brunswick, N.J.: Rutgers University Press, 1963); Donald K. Pickens, *Eugenics: Hereditarian and the Progressives* (Nashville, Tenn.: Vanderbilt University Press, 1968); Daniel Kevles, *In the Name of Eugenics: Genetics and the Uses of Human Heredity* (New York: Knopf, 1985); Oscar Handlin, *Boston's Immigrants, 1790–1865: A Study in Acculturation,* rev. and enl. ed. (Cambridge: Harvard University Press, 1959); Oscar Handlin, "The Horror," in Oscar Handlin, ed., *Race and Nationality in American Life* (Garden City, N.Y.: Doubleday Anchor Books, 1957), pp. 111–32.

[21] Michael B. Katz, *Poverty and Policy in American History* (New York: Academic Press, 1983), pp. 157–81; Erik H. Monkkonen, *Walking to Work: Tramps in America, 1790–1935* (Lincoln: University of Nebraska Press, 1984); Paul Ringenbach, *Tramps and Reformers: The Discovery of Unemployment in New York* (Westport, Conn.: Greenwood Press, 1973).

[22] Susan Tiffin, *In Whose Best Interest? Child Welfare Reform in the Progressive Era* (Westport, Conn.: Greenwood Press, 1982), pp. 130–34; Roy Lubove, *The Struggle for Social Security, 1900–1935* (Cambridge: Harvard University Press, 1968), pp. 91–112; Winifred Bell, *Aid to Dependent Children* (New York: Columbia University Press, 1965).

Sentiment, however, did not shift in favor of dependent men, unless they were white. Increasingly, males divided into two groups, adults out of work because of plant closings and economic restructuring, and young minority men, unskilled, unwilling to work, and dangerous. What defined them was not poverty or welfare receipt (they received very little) but behavior, especially their alleged responsibility for crime and irresponsibility to the children they fathered. Together with African-American women supported by welfare, they became the core of the underclass.

In the 1960s, writers who tried to interpret the growth and persistence of poverty formalized long-standing arguments about behavioral pathology into a theory of culture, which, despite shifts in its political connotation, has proved remarkably tenacious. Anthropologist Oscar Lewis injected the concept of a "culture of poverty" into academic social science and popular commentary. Like the underclass, the culture of poverty did not mean simply economic deprivation. Rather, it referred to a "way of life . . . passed down from generation to generation along family lines." Lewis viewed the culture of poverty as adaptive, a way of coping "with feelings of hopelessness and despair which develop from the realization of the impossibility of achieving success in terms of the values and goals of the larger society." In his definition, "the lack of effective participation and integration of the poor in the major institutions of the larger society," along with a long list of behavioral pathologies, characterized the culture of poverty.[23]

The culture of poverty echoed old ideas and prefigured future debates. It also meshed with developments in social psychology. It reflected the assumption, widespread among liberal intellectuals, of the helplessness and passivity of dependent peoples, who needed the assistance of outsiders to break the cycles of deprivation and degradation that reproduced it from generation to generation. It offered a more palatable explanation than false consciousness of why very poor people failed to revolt, or even protest, and why so many remained unmoved by the rising tide of postwar affluence.[24]

Lewis and others who adapted the culture of poverty to particular issues, such as education, where "cultural deprivation" enjoyed a short vogue as an explanation for learning problems, hoped to put the idea to liberal political purposes as a force energizing activist, interventionist public policy. They did not intend to

[23] Oscar Lewis, The Children of Sanchez (New York: Random House, 1961); La Vida: A Puerto Rican Family in the Culture of Poverty, San Juan and New York (New York: Random House, 1966); "The Culture of Poverty," Scientific American 215 (1966): 19–25; "The Culture of Poverty," in Daniel P. Moynihan, ed., On Understanding Poverty: Perspectives from the Social Sciences (New York: Basic Books, 1969), pp. 187–220.

[24] Lee Rainwater, "The Problem of Lower Class Culture," Journal of Social Issues 26 (1970): 133–37; Handlin, Boston's Immigrants, pp. 51, 120–21, 125; Stanley M. Elkins, Slavery: A Problem in American Institutional Life, 3d ed. (Chicago: University of Chicago Press, 1976); David C. McClelland, The Achieving Society (New York: Free Press, 1961), pp. 36, 43, 205.

reproduce the old distinction between the worthy and unworthy poor. None-theless, others with more conservative agendas turned the concept's original politics on its head. The culture of poverty became a euphemism for the pathol-ogy of the undeserving poor, an explanation for their condition, an excuse, as in the writing of Edward Banfield, for both inaction and punitive public policy.[25]

The culture of poverty fused with racial politics in 1965 with the leak of a confidential report to President Lyndon Johnson by a young assistant secretary of labor. Daniel Patrick Moynihan's *The Negro Family: The Case for National Action* did not use the phrase "culture of poverty," but its language, especially its metaphor, "tangle of pathology," seemed to reflect the same ideas. Moynihan actually grounded his analysis of the development of single-parent black fam-ilies in the unemployment of black men, a fact most of his critics overlooked. Nonetheless, he identified the fundamental problem within black communities as "family structure" (meaning out-of-wedlock births, female headship, and welfare dependence) and warned of the grave consequences of the dominance of a black "matriarchy." "Ours is a society which presumes male leadership in public and private. The arrangements of society facilitate such leadership and reward it. A subculture, such as that of the Negro American, in which this is not the pattern is placed at a distinct disadvantage."[26]

Moynihan's report coincided with the crest of the civil rights movement. Indeed, Johnson drew on it for his famous Howard University speech of June 4, 1965, in which he lashed out at the persistence of black poverty. However, civil rights leaders and others found Moynihan's analysis, as reported in the press, offensive, empirically flawed, denigrating, deflecting blame from the sources of poverty to its victims. The furor over Moynihan's report, in fact, drove black families off the agenda of social science for nearly two decades. Similar attacks discredited the culture of poverty. Scholar after scholar pounded at its politics, theoretical foundations, and methodology. Among social scientists it, too, en-tered a deep, if temporary, eclipse.[27]

Black scholars drew from a different intellectual stream to explain the per-sistence of poverty. Around the globe, previously dependent people were assert-ing their right to liberation. As they fought guerrilla wars, organized against dictatorships, or, in the United States, struggled against racism and segregation, they revealed the bankruptcy of ideas that portrayed them as passive, incapable of self-assertion, unable to generate indigenous leadership. Their leaders devel-oped theories of dependence and internal colonialism to explain poverty and underdevelopment in the Third World. In radical American writing, the ghetto

[25] Frank Riessman, *The Culturally Deprived Child* (New York: Harper and Row, 1962); Edward Banfield, *The Unheavenly City* (Boston: Little, Brown, 1970).

[26] The full text of the report, "The Negro Family: The Case for National Action," is in Lee Rainwater and William L. Yancey, *The Moynihan Report and the Politics of Controversy* (Cambridge: MIT Press, 1967), pp. 39–125.

[27] Rainwater and Yancey, *Moynihan Report*, reprints many of the criticisms.

became a colony, and exploitation and racism the explanation for persistent black poverty. Neither the culture of poverty nor the undeserving poor made sense, other than as mystifications that hid the dynamics of power and subordination. This alternative to long-standing themes in American writing about poverty flourished only briefly. Its association with the Black Power movement, location outside the academic mainstream, lack of intellectual polish, and the diminishing energy of the civil rights movement all contributed to its failure to alter the framework that constrained discussions of poverty.[28]

SOCIAL SCIENCE AND URBAN POVERTY

For the most part, the assumptions underlying the War on Poverty during the same years fit within the prevailing framework. Only community action, the emphasis on the participation of the poor in the design and implementation of programs to serve them, rejected conventional approaches. The most controversial portion of the poverty war, community action, challenged the power of state and local politicians, who quickly goaded Congress and the president into blunting its impact and denaturing its meaning. For the most part, the War on Poverty rested firmly on supply-side views of poverty. It emphasized opportunity, not through focusing on the labor market, as the Department of Labor at first advocated, but by improving individual skills through education and job training.[29]

The War on Poverty and the expansion of related government programs created poverty research as a field in social science because legislation mandated evaluation. Leadership fell to economics, which alone among the social sciences seemed to offer the necessary tools, theories, and prestige. The aftermath of the culture of poverty still tarnished sociology and anthropology, which had failed to develop compelling alternative perspectives or ways of answering legislators' and administrators' questions about the results of programs. Policy research itself became a new field, grounded in economics, located within new schools in universities and in the new world of independent centers and institutes. Poverty research developed sophisticated new methods, especially large-scale social experiments, applied most notably to tests of income maintenance programs, but it contributed few new ideas and little in the way of theory.[30] It revolved, in

[28] Michael B. Katz, *The Undeserving Poor: From the War on Poverty to the War on Welfare* (New York: Pantheon, 1990), pp. 52–65.

[29] Margaret Weir, "The Federal Government and Unemployment: The Frustration of Policy Innovation from the New Deal to the Great Society," in Margaret Weir, Ann Shola Orloff, and Theda Skocpol, eds., *The Politics of Social Policy in the United States* (Princeton: Princeton University Press, 1988); "Poverty and Urban Policy: Transcript of 1973 Group Discussion of the Kennedy Administration Urban Poverty Programs and Policies" (Kennedy Archives, Boston, Mass.); Katz, *Undeserving Poor*, pp. 79–123.

[30] Robert H. Haveman, *Poverty Policy and Poverty Research: The Great Society and the Social Sciences* (Madison: University of Wisconsin Press, 1987).

fact, around one of the oldest preoccupations in the history of poverty and welfare: the results of relief. Did welfare hurt the labor market by weakening the willingness to work? Did it erode family life? Did it demoralize the poor? These questions drove the poor-law debates of the late eighteenth and early nineteenth centuries; they energized the research into income maintenance and other experimental programs in the late 1960s and early 1970s; and they fueled the evaluations of "workfare" in the 1980s. Both the political Left and Right accepted them as the key questions; only their answers differed.

By and large, academic economists of the time did not consider the implications of their research for assessing the distinction between the deserving and undeserving poor and its relation to the existence of a culture of poverty. By the early 1980s, however, conservative writers drew the connection. The questions, asked in the conservative political climate of the era, were these: Why, despite all the new social programs of the War on Poverty and Great Society, had poverty worsened? What explained the explosive growth of female-headed African-American families, the unemployment of African-American men, and the crime, violence, and social disorganization within inner cities? Spending on social welfare had risen dramatically; segregation and other barriers to African-American economic and political advancement had lowered; and the country had enjoyed unusual prosperity and economic growth. Given this context, what could account for the rise in social pathology, especially among inner-city African Americans?[31]

In *Losing Ground*, Charles Murray gave the most widely cited answer, although many others offered similar arguments. The culprits became the social programs themselves. Well intentioned though they were, they had eroded the will to work and the incentives for stable family life. Murray and other conservative writers fueled renewed interest in the culture of poverty and the undeserving poor. Social programs had fostered a new, demoralized way of life among minorities clustered within inner cities. They reproduced welfare dependence between generations. They reinforced values and behaviors that varied from those of the rest of American society. They were the source of a new culture defined by behavior rather than income. They were the roots of the underclass.[32]

Other conservative writers took the argument in another direction. Murray's dependents were clever and rational. They understood how to work the welfare system to advantage; they knew they earned more by not working. Lawrence Mead's, by contrast, lacked competence. Victims of a culture of dependence spawned by well-meaning but misguided liberal policy, they had lost the capacity to work and to carry out the ordinary duties of citizens. Cutting off their welfare would not send them back to work. Small government, as Murray

[31] Charles Murray, *Losing Ground: American Social Policy, 1950–1980* (New York: Basic Books, 1984); George Gilder, *Wealth and Poverty* (New York: Basic Books, 1981).

[32] Murray, *Losing Ground*.

advocated, was an illusion out of touch with the late twentieth century. Only strong, authoritarian government could solve America's greatest social problem. As a consequence, the state should force its dependents to work. Only work, regardless of its conditions, rewards, or prospects, would reenergize the lost populations of the inner cities.[33]

Social scientists counterattacked by showing how Murray and others were wrong. Critics have subjected the evidence and methods of few books to such withering and authoritative criticism as they meted out to Losing Ground. But Murray and the conservatives had tapped the issues that troubled many Americans and then had offered clear answers. Many remained predisposed to believe them, despite evidence to the contrary. Indeed, for the most part, liberal social scientists failed to move beyond criticism of data and methods. They addressed themselves to the same questions about the results of welfare and offered different answers. But they could say little in answer to the basic questions posed by conservatives.[34]

THE UNDERCLASS DEBATE

When the "underclass" surfaced in Time, other magazines, and Auletta's book, few liberal social scientists objected. They had no alternative framework. With no other language in which to describe or comprehend what had happened within inner cities, underclass became a new neutral ground on which to debate. What were its characteristics? Its sources? Its prognosis? As leading liberal social scientists tried to appropriate the concept from both the media and conservative commentary, they faced one especially delicate obstacle. How could they reinsert culture and the African-American family onto the agenda of social science without conceding the argument to the conservatives? No realistic analysis of inner-city poverty could ignore family, which, in fact, had emerged as a key concern within African-American communities. But in politics and social science, conservatives had appropriated family and culture in the 1960s.

Indeed, most subsequent commentary on the underclass used imprecise definitions that stressed family and individual behavior and rested on implicitly moral concepts of class structure. For instance, in two long and widely read 1986 articles in the Atlantic, Nicholas Lemann revived the culture of poverty thesis to describe and explain the emergence of an isolated underclass. The rise in out-of-wedlock births—"by far the greatest contributor to the perpetuation of the misery of ghetto life"—most accurately captured the distinction between the underclass and the rest of American society.[35]

---

[33] Lawrence Mead, Beyond Entitlement: The Social Obligations of Citizenship (New York: Free Press, 1986).

[34] Robert Greenstein, "Losing Faith in Losing Ground," New Republic, March 25, 1985, p. 14; Christopher Jencks, "How Poor Are the Poor?" New York Review 32 (May 5, 1985):41.

[35] Nicholas Lemann, "The Origins of the Underclass," Atlantic Monthly 257 (June 1986): 31–61,

The major liberal response came in 1987 with William Julius Wilson's *The Truly Disadvantaged* (1987), which tried to incorporate family and culture into a social-democratic analysis of inner-city poverty and the underclass. *The Truly Disadvantaged* quickly became the most influential scholarly book on contemporary American poverty.[36] Wilson was not the first contemporary social scientist to write about the underclass. In 1963, in *The Challenge of Affluence*, Gunnar Myrdal commented on an "under-class" cut off from the labor market; in 1969, Lee Rainwater connected the emergence of an underclass to the intensification of poverty that accompanied the otherwise successful operations of American capitalism; and in *The Black Underclass* (1980), Douglas Glasgow, writing about the young men who had participated in the great Watts riot of 1965, called attention to the emergence of an underclass as a "permanent fixture of our nation's social structure." By "underclass," Glasgow meant "a permanently entrapped population of poor persons, unused and unwanted, accumulated in various parts of the country." Glasgow, however, wrote only about men and scarcely mentioned African-American family structure.[37]

Despite his concern with African-American family structure, Wilson located the origins of the underclass in African-American male joblessness. He asserted that neutral terms, such as *lower class* or *working class,* did not evoke the recent transformations in America's cities that resulted in increased concentrations of poverty. African-American middle- and working-class families, he argued, had abandoned inner-city ghettos to "a heterogeneous grouping of families and individuals who are outside the mainstream of the American occupational system." They were the underclass: "individuals who lack training and skills and either experience long-term unemployment or are not members of the labor force, individuals who are engaged in street crime and other forms of aberrant behavior, and families that experience long-term spells of poverty and/or welfare dependency." For him, underclass signified "the groups . . . left behind," who were "collectively different from those that lived in these neighborhoods in earlier years."[38]

Those collective differences in behavior and outlook signified the emergence of a distinctive culture. Wilson understood culture as an adaptation, however, "a response to social structural constraints and opportunities" that would change with the transformation of the structural conditions that had generated it.

and 258 (July 1986): 54–68. Lemann offers a more nuanced interpretation in his subsequent book, *The Promised Land: The Great Black Migration and How It Changed America* (New York: Knopf, 1991).

[36] William J. Wilson, *The Truly Disadvantaged: The Inner City, The Underclass, and Public Policy* (Chicago: University of Chicago Press, 1987).

[37] Gunnar Myrdal, *The Challenge of Affluence* (New York: Pantheon Books, 1963); Lee Rainwater, "Looking Back and Looking Up," *Transaction* 6 (February 1969): 9; Douglas G. Glasgow, *The Black Underclass: Unemployment and Entrapment of Ghetto Youth* (New York: Random House, 1980), pp. 3–8. I am indebted to Herbert Gans for early references to the use of the term *underclass.*

[38] Wilson, *Truly Disadvantaged,* p. 41.

"Concentration" and "social isolation" were the two key conditions fueling the growth of the underclass. By concentration, Wilson meant the increasing share of the total African-American population living in "extreme poverty" areas; by social isolation, he referred to "the lack of contact or sustained interaction with individuals and institutions that represent mainstream society." Both resulted from the movement of middle- and working-class African Americans out of poverty areas, which removed a key "social buffer," eroded institutional life, and denuded neighborhoods of mainstream role models. Unlike immigrant groups earlier in the century, the African Americans now left in inner cities inherited an economy increasingly devoid of manufacturing jobs and of unskilled and semi-skilled work.[39]

High rates of out-of-wedlock births and female-headed families also troubled Wilson greatly. They, too, he argued, resulted from structural conditions. Partly, along with crime, they reflected the age structure of the population, which was relatively young. Even more, they emerged from the lack of marriageable men. Wilson used the high proportion of young African-American men out of work, in jail, in the armed forces, or murdered to develop a "male marriageable pool index" that showed the scarcity of potential spouses for young African-American women. He predicted that increased employment for African-American men will decrease out-of-wedlock births and single-headed families.[40]

Wilson presented *The Truly Disadvantaged* as a series of hypotheses based on the best evidence available at the time, and he mounted a large research project to test his ideas. As other social scientists followed his lead, *The Truly Disadvantaged* also set the agenda for the first round of research on the urban underclass.

Even before the book's publication, a few social scientists had initiated research on the underclass. This early research attempted to identify underclass areas and to count the group. Because definitions of the underclass varied among researchers, size estimates ranged from 500,000 to 4.1 million.[41] Research intensified after 1987, when the Rockefeller Foundation asked the Social Science Research Council to consider creating a Committee on the Urban Underclass. The new committee tried to stimulate research through a program of fellowships and scholarships (undergraduate, graduate, and postdoctoral) and a set of research planning activities. The activities of the SSRC Committee on the Urban Underclass helped stimulate interest in underclass issues among social scientists and revive research on urban poverty, which had languished since the

[39] Ibid., pp. 7–8, 46–56, 60–61.
[40] Ibid., pp. 83–92.
[41] Isabel Wilkerson, "New Studies Zeroing in on Poorest of the Poor," *New York Times*, December 20, 1987; Erol R. Ricketts and Isabel V. Sawhill, "Defining and Measuring the Underclass," *Journal of Policy Analysis and Management* 7 (Winter 1988): 316–25.

mid-1970s. The key issues, largely, though not wholly, generated by Wilson's work, that dominated the committee's first deliberations echoed the great historic themes in discussions of urban poverty.[42]

One of these, the impact of environment on behavior, cropped up over and over again in nineteenth- and early twentieth-century discussions of population congestion and housing; formalized into theories of social ecology, it formed one of the major themes of early urban studies, especially in the writing of sociologists of the Chicago School. In the emerging underclass debate, it focused on the implications of concentrated urban poverty and the social composition of the inner city. What were the consequences of living in a neighborhood with a high proportion of poor residents? Did the concentration of poverty itself promote out-of-wedlock pregnancy, the high proportion of school dropouts, welfare dependence, unemployment, and crime? Wilson had identified two ecological factors, concentration and social isolation. Did they have similar effects? Which was more influential? Others asked a prior question. Was Wilson correct about the process? Had the concentration of poverty increased throughout urban America? Had poor African Americans in inner cities in fact become more isolated in recent years? Had middle- and working-class African-American families moved out of urban neighborhoods and abandoned those left behind to the extent he implied?[43]

Wilson's emphasis on male joblessness provoked research because it rested on four controversial premises: (1) the labor market offers too few unskilled and semiskilled jobs to young men in inner cities; (2) most young men who lack jobs want to work in the regular (as contrasted to the underground) economy; (3) most young jobless men have the ability to move relatively quickly into the labor force if offered jobs; and (4) young men with jobs will marry more often than those without them. For Wilson, joblessness, like other underclass behavior, signifies a condition sustained by labor markets and geography, not a culture. Others disagree. They see instead a bleak new culture of dependence as impervious to the market, responsive only to coercion by government. This is

---

[42] Martha A. Gephart and Robert W. Pearson, "Contemporary Research on the Urban Underclass," *Items* 42 (June 1988): 1–10. The committee's first major "product" is Christopher Jencks and Paul E. Peterson, eds., *The Urban Underclass* (Washington, D.C.: Brookings Institution, 1991).

[43] Paul A. Jargowsky and Mary Jo Bane, "Neighborhood Poverty: Basic Questions" (Center for Health and Human Resource Policy, John F. Kennedy School of Government, Harvard University, Discussion Paper Series #H–90–3, March 2, 1990); Christopher Jencks and Susan Mayer, "The Social Consequences of Growing Up in a Poor Neighborhood" (manuscript, Center for Urban Affairs and Policy Research, Northwestern University, April 5, 1988); Douglas S. Massey and Mitchell T. Eggers, "The Ecology of Inequality: Minorities and the Concentration of Poverty, 1970–1980" (manuscript, Population Research Center NORC, University of Chicago, January 1989); Reynolds Farley, "Changes in Racial and Class Segregation," and Jonathan Crane, "Effects of Neighborhoods on Dropping Out of School and Teenage Childbearing," in Jencks and Peterson, *Urban Underclass* pp. 299–320.

one debate that animates current research on urban poverty and the underclass.[44]

By stressing male joblessness, argue other critics, Wilson constricts the avenues out of dependence. Equally important are the opportunities available to women in inner cities and the wages they earn. There is no inherent reason why women family heads should be dependent. They are dependent because they lack decent education, wages, and child care. Wilson's neglect of occupational opportunities for women, continue critics, reflects a commitment to conventional family forms that forges an ironic link between him and conservatives. It lifts family out of the context of history by setting unchanging patriarchal standards against which to measure domestic arrangements. Like other advocates of nuclear, two-parent families, Wilson, imply his critics, misses the contingent, multiple, historically conditioned, and changing meanings of family.[45]

Wilson's argument connected the economic transformation of America's cities to the organization of families and the activities of individuals. But is it, in fact, possible to trace a path from the flight of manufacturing to the decisions of young people about fertility or to the ways in which parents raise their children? Do institutions, social networks, and kinship patterns play a mediating role? What is the causal chain? How should one draw feedback loops and patterns of interaction? Is there a testable theory linking the macro and micro dimensions of social experience that can be applied to research on the underclass?[46]

Racism was one aspect of American social experience that Wilson believed had ceased to retard African-American economic advancement. As in his earlier book, *The Declining Significance of Race*, Wilson argued that discrimination no longer prevented the movement of African Americans into better jobs and neighborhoods. As a result, stratification widened among African Americans, and the problems of African Americans left behind in inner cities reflected class rather than race. Was he correct? Has housing segregation declined significantly? Have affluent white suburbs opened to minorities? Do employers decide to hire entry-level workers without reference to race? These questions also fueled the new research on urban poverty and the underclass.[47]

[44] Richard B. Freeman, "Employment and Earnings of Disadvantaged Young Men in a Labor Shortage Economy," and Paul Osterman, "Gains from Growth? The Impact of Full Employment on Poverty in Boston," in Jencks and Peterson, *Urban Underclass*, pp. 103–21 and 122–34; Mark Testa et al., "Employment and Marriage among Inner-City Fathers," *Annals of the American Academy of Political and Social Science* 501 (January 1989): 79–91; Mead, *Beyond Entitlement,* and *The New Dependency Politics: Non-Working Poverty in the U.S.* (New York: Basic Books, 1992).

[45] An example of criticism is Adolph Reed, Jr., "The Liberal Technocrat," *Nation*, February 6, 1988, pp. 167–70.

[46] Robert W. Pearson, "Economy, Culture, Public Policy, and the Urban Underclass," *Items* 43 (June 1989): 23–29.

[47] William J. Wilson, *The Declining Significance of Race: Blacks and Changing American Institutions* (Chicago: University of Chicago Press, 1978); Massey and Eggars, "The Ecology of Inequality"; Farley, "Changes in Class Segregation"; Joleen Kirschenman and Kathryn M. Neckerman, "'We'd

Most American research on poverty and the underclass always has reinforced images of social pathology because it has focused on bad behavior: long-term welfare dependence, drugs, crime, out-of-wedlock pregnancy, low educational achievement, unwillingness to work. Areas of concentrated poverty emerge from much of the historical and contemporary underclass literature as monolithic islands of despair and degradation. By contrast, every ethnography reveals a rich array of people and associations within even the most impoverished neighborhoods. Labels such as "underclass area" impose simple and misleading stereotypes. Some families manage to guide their children successfully through extraordinary obstacles. How do they manage? What strategies do poor families adopt? Do these vary by race and ethnicity? Questions like these about family process, strategy, and the analysis of "success" represent emerging directions in poverty research. Along with the portraits painted by ethnographers, they begin to replace images of pathology with complex, nuanced understandings of how individuals and families surmount, as well as succumb to, the environment of the modern inner city.[48] (Similar questions could be asked about institutions. However, with the important exception of schools, recent underclass research has neglected institutions. It also, curiously, has neglected politics.)

Despite its title, the SSRC Committee on the Urban Underclass did not adopt an official definition of *underclass*. Rather, it defined its working focus as "persistent and concentrated urban poverty." Nor did other urban poverty researchers adopt a standard definition. Indeed, many (including members of the committee) objected to the term. In his August 1990 presidential address to the American Sociological Association, William J. Wilson, who had advocated the usefulness and objective foundation of *underclass* in *The Truly Disadvantaged*, recommended its abandonment by researchers.[49] Objections to the word *underclass* reflect various concerns. As a modern euphemism for the undeserving poor, it reinforces the tradition of blaming the victim. By stigmatizing them, it insults those it designates. It also works against their best interests, for it fosters political divisions among the working class and poor, who need each other as allies, and, through its concentration on the behavior of a relatively

Love to Hire Them, But . . .': The Meaning of Race for Employers," in Jencks and Peterson, *Urban Underclass*, pp. 203–34; Douglas S. Massey and Nancy A. Denton, *American Apartheid: Segregation and the Making of the Underclass* (Cambridge: Harvard University Press, forthcoming).

[48] Martha A. Gephart, "Neighborhoods and Communities in Concentrated Poverty," *Items* 43 (December 1989): 84–92; Terry Williams and William Kornblum, *Growing Up Poor* (Lexington, Mass.: Lexington Books, 1985); Carol Stack, *All Our Kin: Strategies for Survival in a Black Community* (New York: Harper and Row, 1974).

[49] William Julius Wilson, "Social Theory and Public Agenda Research: The Challenge of Studying Inner-City Social Dislocations" (Presidential Address, Annual Meeting of the American Sociological Association, August 12, 1990). For a sophisticated attempt to arrive at a more satisfactory definition, see Martha Van Haitsma, "A Contextual Definition of the Underclass," *Focus* 12 (Spring and Summer 1989): 27–31.

small number of people clustered in inner cities, deflects attention from the problem of poverty and minimizes its extent. The word *underclass*, its critics assert, has little intellectual substance. It lacks a consistent, defensible theoretical basis. It is not a "class" in any of the usual senses. Most definitions, in fact, substitute varieties of bad behavior for the criteria customary in stratification theories. Nor can the social scientists who use it, let alone the media, agree on a definition.[50]

However it is defined, the underclass is a metaphor of social transformation. It asserts the emergence of a new social grouping within America's inner cities. It rests on a reading of American history and requires historical evidence for its explanation. Nonetheless, unexamined historical assumptions run through most contemporary research, which ignores the rich body of recent historical scholarship on relevant issues. The purpose of this volume is to inform debate on the underclass and urban poverty with evidence from historical research. Like others who study urban poverty, the authors of the chapters that follow do not share a consensus about the definition of underclass, or, even, about the usefulness of the term. Rather, they define their work by a common concern with persistent and concentrated urban poverty and by a focus on those groups at risk of extreme poverty. The authors of this book want to signal that they do not accept the word *underclass* as an appropriate description of the conditions about which they write, and that they are approaching the word as an object of analysis as well as a subject of history. Therefore, the word *underclass* has been placed in quotation marks in chapter titles and is italicized on first use in each chapter. The authors concentrate on the history of the white working class and on the historical and current situation of African Americans; they touch only occasionally on Latinos, not because they are insensitive to their disadvantages, but because of the thinness of historical writing about them. In each instance, they frame their historical analysis with questions from the contemporary underclass debate. They take up the great historic issues surrounding urban poverty: volition, culture, family, ecology, institutions, and policy. They show the complicated, shifting relations among them, their interaction with race and gender, and their links to social and economic transformation. Through them, they trace the emergence of the cluster of social concerns captured by the metaphor of the underclass.

The chapters of this book do not divide intellectual space into the same compartments as most of the researchers who study the underclass. Their rooms are not tidy; multiple issues crowd into each. They tell complicated stories whose segments cannot easily be pulled apart. Their cumulative message

---

[50] Herbert J. Gans, "The Dangers of the Underclass: Its Harmfulness as a Planning Concept," in Herbert J. Gans, ed., *People, Plans, and Places* (New York: Columbia University Press, 1991), pp. 328–44; Martha A. Gephart and Robert W. Pearson, "Contemporary Research on the Urban Underclass," *Items* 42 (June 1988): 3.

stresses the interconnection of issues, their anchor in context, the webs of experience captured imperfectly by terms such as *poverty, underclass, homelessness, race, culture,* or *family*. They make the case against reifying these concepts as fixed entities, somehow real, sharply etched, unchanging. Instead, they present them as history, which is to say as relational, shifting in meaning and content, to be interpreted in terms of time and place.

This book, then, has a distinctive logic. Its first section focuses on the African-American experience of poverty and the creation and peopling of ghettos. The second section explicates the forces shaping the contemporary context of urban poverty and its spatial pattern in American cities. The third compares mobility and family strategies among groups differentiated by ethnicity, race, and labor-market position; accounts for the diverging histories of blacks and white ethnics; and balances an interpretation of the origins of family problems among African Americans with a theory about the source of their distinctiveness and strengths and the lessons they convey to the rest of America. The final section focuses on institutions, protest, politics, and the state in order to draw together the implications of various forms of collective action for understanding what has happened within inner cities and to the people who remain within them. My concluding essay shows how the book's chapters point toward reframing the underclass debate by moving it away from its concentration on pathology and toward the processes that are increasing inequality, harming families, and degrading public life throughout America.

This book stresses some great continuities in experience. It shows poverty anchored in patterns of inequality and discrimination reproduced repeatedly throughout America's history. It highlights the agency of ordinary poor people coping with the need for food, shelter, and medical care and taking collective action on their own behalf. It exposes the enduring poverty of America's ghettos, and the separation of classes within them, and rejects the mistaken image of a "golden ghetto" implicit in some writing about today's inner cities. Nonetheless, it emphasizes the great gulf between past and present and the creation of a new urban form in modern America. With unmistakable clarity, it limns the qualitative differences that separate today's inner cities and their poverty from conditions in cities of the past. By starting in the present with issues unresolved by current scholars and assumptions implicit in policy, each chapter underscores the centrality of history to the troubling and urgent questions that underlie the underclass debate.

PART ONE

The Roots of Ghetto Poverty

CHAPTER 1

Southern Diaspora: Origins of the Northern "Underclass"

Jacqueline Jones

IN 1942, WHEN SHE testified before a congressional committee on national defense migration, Johnnie Belle Taylor was living with her mother and five children in a Farm Security Administration labor camp in the vicinity of Belle Glade, Florida. Born in Talbot County, Georgia, Taylor had spent most of her life near the small town of Dawson in the same state. In 1937, she moved to Florida and began a seasonal pattern of migration, picking beans in the "winter garden," then moving to northern Florida to labor in the corn, lima bean, cucumber, and tobacco fields, until the late-summer cotton-picking season drew her into Georgia. By the late fall of each year she had returned to Belle Glade, ready to repeat the cycle again.[1] To some observers, the way of life followed by this black woman might seem to confirm recent studies of the Southern origins of the Northern "underclass." Taylor was living in a female-headed, extended household within a public housing project, which, along with cotton plantations and coal-mining camps, constituted one of the many Southern prototypes of Northern ghettos. She and her family led a peripatetic existence, performing backbreaking stoop labor under exploitative conditions. Perhaps Taylor might even be seen as a transitional figure of sorts, caught somewhere between the dependency of the sharecropping system in the South and the dependency of the federal welfare system in the North. In any case, in her unsettled life, she seemed to exist outside middle-class or "mainstream" American society, with its devotion to a stable homeplace and to the nuclear family.

For recent observers of the underclass, history is not, or at least not often, "the issue," to paraphrase Charles Murray. Policy implications, and not historical causes or antecedents, stand at the center of the debate over the nature, and future, of concentrated poor inner-city populations. Still, some scholars have addressed the roots of the underclass, and their views can be simply (if rather loosely) categorized according to their emphasis on either the continuity or

The author would like to acknowledge the helpful suggestions of other members of the SSRC Historical Origins of the Underclass group, and especially those of Michael Katz, Clayborne Carson, Kathryn Neckerman, and Thomas Sugrue.

[1] Testimony of Johnnie Belle Taylor, in *Hearings before the Select Committee Investigating National Defense Migration*, House of Representatives, 77th Cong., 2d Sess., pt. 33, pp. 12627–28 (hereafter *National Defense Migration Hearings*, with part no.).

discontinuity of a Southern-rooted, so-called culture of poverty. For example, in the "continuity" camp stands Nicholas Lemann, a journalist who argues that "every aspect of the underclass culture in the ghettoes is directly traceable to roots in the South—and not the South of slavery but the South of a generation ago . . . the nascent underclass of the sharecropper South." In his study of black Chicago in the 1980s, Lemann argues that in the 1950s, a specific group of Mississippi sharecroppers brought north with them "the main characteristics of the underclass—poverty, crime, poor education, dependency, and teenage out-of-wedlock childbearing"—in other words, an "ethic of dependency." He quotes an informant: "Most people on welfare here [in Chicago], they were on welfare there [in Canton, Mississippi], in a sense, because they were sharecroppers. There they were working hard for nothing, now they're not working for nothing. They have been mentally programmed that Mister Charlie's going to take care of them."[2]

In contrast to Lemann's focus on what he perceives as cultural persistence, scholars like William Julius Wilson stress structural aspects of the Northern urban economy in an effort to posit a dramatic break between the neoslave South and the big-city North. In his book *The Truly Disadvantaged: The Inner City, the Underclass, and Public Policy*, Wilson employs the term *historic discrimination* to describe those barriers to equality that black people confronted for the first time in the North (beginning, presumably, during the era of World War II). He argues that Southern migrants did not bring their poverty north with them; rather, discriminatory employment practices, combined with a changing urban economy that had less use for unskilled laborers, placed blacks at a competitive disadvantage with the Eastern European immigrants who had settled in Northeastern cities before them. Wilson draws upon the work of Herbert Gutman in arguing that the "problems of the modern black family . . . are a product of more recent social forces," rather than a legacy of either sharecropping or slavery.[3]

The theories of Lemann and Wilson are difficult to compare with one another simply because they deal with different points in time—Wilson, with the post–Great Migration period through the 1960s, when the effects of long-term unem-

[2] Charles Murray, *Losing Ground: American Social Policy, 1950–1980* (New York: Basic Books, 1984), p. 31; Nicholas Lemann, "The Origins of the Underclass, Pt. I," *Atlantic Monthly* 257 (June 1986): 35, 41, 47; and Nicholas Lemann, *The Promised Land: The Great Black Migration and How It Changed America* (New York: Random House, 1991).

[3] William Julius Wilson, *The Truly Disadvantaged: The Inner City, the Underclass, and Public Policy* (Chicago: University of Chicago Press, 1987), pp. 30, 32; Herbert Gutman, *The Black Family in Slavery and Freedom, 1750–1920* (New York: Pantheon, 1976).

For a highly idiosyncratic view stressing a degree of continuity between slavery and the modern underclass, see Orlando Patterson, "Toward a Study of Black America: Notes on the Culture of Racism," *Dissent* (Fall 1989): 476–86. Patterson makes the rather remarkable assertion that "we can trace the underclass, as a persisting social phenomenon," back to "a distinct underclass of slaves" that included "incorrigible blacks of whom the slaveholder class was forever complaining" (p. 480).

ployment on black men began to manifest themselves in high rates of female-headed households; Lemann, with the 1950s, when agricultural mechanization in the Cotton South had lessened the demand for field-workers, and when the Northern urban economy no longer depended on unskilled laborers to any great extent. Nevertheless, both perspectives are striking in their emphasis on the recent past and their lack of attention to Southern society, or African-American culture, during the nineteenth century.

In exploring the Southern origins of the Northern underclass, this essay diverges from the views of both Lemann and Wilson by stressing the historic process of marginalization that engulfed not only freedpeople but also poor whites on the Southern countryside after the Civil War, a process that continues today in the nation's largest cities. Scholars and journalists alike have been too preoccupied with the alleged "pathological" aspects of African-American history, and, together with the popular media, have promoted the idea that the black community constitutes some kind of exotic subculture quite outside the boundaries of "normal," or "mainstream," American life. The claim that, compared to black life in general, ghetto life is "a thousand times more" apart from white society, "with a different language, economy, educational system, and social ethic," not only objectifies the black poor as "others," but also misses larger issues.[4] First, stories of ordinary black people who worked hard and made do with very little in the way of material resources become lost amid generalizations about the "bizarre" quality of inner-city neighborhoods. And second, only a narrow segment of the black community—a predatory youth street culture—holds the attention of whites, who remain fascinated in their own way by sexuality, violence, and substance abuse. In any case, the grip of the black underclass on the American imagination serves to obscure the historical and economic processes that by the late twentieth century produced a multitude of underclasses, people who were neither black nor residents of Northern central cities.

In at least two striking ways, the African-American experience in the United States demonstrates a certain continuity between North and South, agricultural and industrial workers, and rural and urban areas, but not in the ways suggested by Lemann and others. First, in the post–Civil War rural South and the twentieth-century urban North, black folk of all ages and both sexes demonstrated a great deal of resourcefulness in providing for themselves; family members foraged and looked to neighborly cooperation in an effort to resist enforced dependency upon either plantation owners or welfare bureaucrats. Second, regardless of their location, blacks during this period faced overwhelming structural barriers to upward social mobility. Employer discrimination and legal statutes hindered their ability to move from place to place freely, and left them isolated in depressed communities characterized by poor housing and poor

[4] Lemann, "The Origins of the Underclass, Pt. II," *Atlantic Monthly* (July 1986): 59.

schools. Until 1916, most blacks in the rural South remained confined within the plantation economy, a function of the lack of jobs available to them in either the urban South or the North. Northern ghettos were legal creations that prevented Southern migrants from seeking out educational and employment opportunities in suburbs and other outlying areas. At the same time, the post-industrial city has introduced new, corrosive forces into black family life—long-term structural unemployment among black men, the wide availability of fire-arms and drugs, and the lure of "the street" for young people. These forces had no literal nineteenth-century rural Southern precedents.

If we return to Johnnie Belle Taylor and flesh out the facts of her life, we learn that she was committed to hard work, to preserving the integrity of her family, and to schooling her children; in other words, that her priorities were not that different from those of poor white Southerners at the time, or members of the industrial working class, or the middle class, for that matter. Taylor was divorced from her first husband, a disabled older man who now lived in a small house on a piece of land in Dawson, Georgia, a place she considered her home; though she spent little time there, she noted, "that's still home, all my things are there." Her current husband was employed on a construction project in Key West; she said that he was "trying to work down there, so he kind of hated to leave since they needed men so bad on the water line and all. He kind of hated to leave from there." Two of Taylor's children, ages six and seven, were too young to work; they stayed with their grandmother during the day. The next two oldest youngsters labored in the fields some, and attended school some, while the oldest, a daughter, worked as a wage earner along with her mother. During the recent winter months, Johnnie Belle Taylor had used her car, with its balding tires, to shuttle workers to a new construction site in Moultrie, Georgia, not far from Dawson; in this way she was able to make a little cash. Thus a wider, more expansive picture of the Taylor household reveals not a household mired in dependency, but a family that fragmented in the course of a year in an effort to make enough money to provide for itself.

Viewed within concentric circles of historical context, the Taylor household had much in common with households of other Americans, although the barriers it faced in terms of making a decent living were peculiar, and peculiarly devastating, compared to those faced by other Americans, no matter how poor. By the 1990s, the pressures that forced the Taylors to live apart had exacted a more devastating price from poor families, especially poor black families, throughout the country. Still, the snapshot of a husbandless mother with several small children and a hard lot in life—the stuff of newspaper feature stories and network television documentaries—tends to obscure the more complex histories of these households and their more complex relations between affective and economic ties. The story of the Taylors, then, constitutes not just a chapter in African-American history, but also a chapter placed squarely within the context of American labor and family history.

POLITICAL RESISTANCE AND HOUSEHOLD RESOURCEFULNESS AMONG BLACKS IN
THE RURAL SOUTH, 1865–1941

In the South, blacks were marginalized when they were barred, by law or custom, from almost all jobs that were year-round and full-time. As agricultural wage laborers, the vast majority of Southern black men and women fell prey to the annual and seasonal rhythms of the sharecropping system; under that system, the spring planting and fall harvest claimed the energies of all able-bodied blacks, and yet winter and late-summer slack times forced them to scrounge for wages, or otherwise provide for themselves, to compensate for the meager "furnishings" they received from landlord-employers. During the post–Civil War era, black urban artisans found themselves pushed out of the skilled trades; thereafter, Southern cities would systematically deny black men stable employment opportunities, and offer steady work only to black wives and mothers who toiled as ill-paid domestic servants and laundresses. Significantly, the Southern textile industry had virtually no black employees until the mid-1960s; those factory jobs went to poor whites—men, women, and children who were hardly superior to black people in terms of either formal education or "natural aptitude" for machine work. Not until 1916 did Northern industrial employers show much interest in the vast pool of untapped labor (black and white) that lay to the south of them; until that time they preferred to hire immigrant workers over native-born Americans from the South. In the 1930s, the New Deal legislation that served as the foundation of the modern welfare state quite explicitly excluded from Social Security and worker compensation programs the overwhelming number of blacks in the North as well as the South, including sharecroppers, domestics, the underemployed and chronically unemployed.[5]

The analogy between the Southern plantation and the Northern ghetto springs not from theoretical constructions or statistical models, but from the deeply felt pronouncements of men and women who had experienced both worlds. Interviewed in the late 1960s and 1970s, for example, a group of Southern-born black Northeasterners portrayed Northern society as an extension, or reflection, of the South. Conspicuous in their absence from this set of interviews are references to those themes which implied that migration had involved a radical departure from a caste-bound past—the ability of blacks to vote and participate in party politics, and the transition from sharecropping to industrial wage work. According to John Langston Gwaltney's informants, in the

[5] Roger Ransom and Richard Sutch, One Kind of Freedom: The Economic Consequences of Emancipation (New York: Cambridge University Press, 1977); Allen H. Stokes, Jr., "Black and White Labor for the Development of the Southern Textile Industry, 1800–1920" (Ph.D. diss., University of South Carolina, 1977); Raymond Wolters, Negroes and the Great Depression: The Problem of Economic Recovery (Westport, Conn.: Greenwood, 1970); Gavin Wright, Old South, New South: Revolutions in the Southern Economy Since the Civil War (New York: Basic Books, 1986).

rural South and the urban North, "the business of the white man is to rule": "During all our history here [in the United States] we have been right and they have been wrong and the only man who cannot see that is a fool or a liar." In the end, despite a change of scenery for the grandchildren of slaves, "It just has not changed all that much."[6]

No matter where or when they lived, most black folks could say, "I work. I work hard—you can ask anybody out here—but I don' seem to get nowhere." Though forced to perform the heaviest, hottest jobs—"that plantation thing"— blacks had received from whites only contempt in return: "These lazy Negroes are the ones who dig ditches and build roads and lift heavy pots and things." Ultimately, a black person's class status was irrelevant; "the one fact that we were the children of slaves and the word 'nigger' meant the same thing to [all of] us is very important." In the eyes of whites, blacks remained outside the boundaries of a consumer society that supposedly conferred materialistic aspirations on people in an equal-opportunity way: "See, they do everything to keep us down, and still we got things they think we ain' got no business with!"—the sharecropper with a Model T Ford, the welfare recipient with a color television. A rude cabin the middle of a cotton field, a tiny apartment in a concrete housing project—it is "*how* you live that's important," and "people need space and they were never meant to be jammed on top of each other." Overcrowded and underfunded schools made a mockery of the ideal of public education, whether in Jim Crow Alabama or in the South Bronx. Despite variations over time and within regions, for slaves as well as for welfare recipients, systems of enforced dependency seemed designed to maximize the humiliation of black people: "I done had all that white folks' help I can use!" And always, a code of racial etiquette rewarded deference and dissembling: "My father used to say, 'Laugh with your friends, but smile with strangers.'"[7]

These comments of Southern migrants suggest a link between the world of the nineteenth-century Southern sharecropper and the late-twentieth-century Northern urban underclass. Both times and places were marked by (to borrow a term from linguistics) "deep structural" forces of economic marginalization. Despite transformations in the national economy from postbellum South to postindustrial North, despite the passage of civil rights legislation of the 1960s, black people faced legal and institutional barriers to their political and economic advancement, barriers remarkable for their persistence and their similarity between regions. The former slaves and their descendants remained confined to temporary, seasonal, unskilled, or domestic work. Trapped within the South's plantation economy or the Northern central city, they lacked access to quality

[6] Interviews with Jackson Jordan, Jr., and Ruth Shays, in John Langston Gwaltney, *Drylongso: A Self-Portrait of Black America* (New York: Vintage Books, 1980), pp. 98, 101, 31.

[7] Interviews with Seth Bingham, Ella Turner Surry, Nancy White, Gordon Etheridge, Bernard Vanderstell, Jon Oliver, Janet McCrae, Mabel Lincoln, ibid., pp. 226, 239, 144, 235, 115, 18, 124, 234, 69.

education and to jobs that paid a living wage. As a matter of public policy, implemented by private landowners and employers as well as public institutions, blacks as a group were systematically denied the money and property that would have allowed them to achieve even the modest measure of self-determination enjoyed by the white working class. Proportionately, black women and children always worked for wages to a greater extent that even their poor-white counterparts, a fact that had far-reaching implications for age and gender relations within the black community. Nevertheless, this litany of the structural forces underpinning racial subordination obscures the historic efforts of black people to resist dependence on whites—efforts that, once again, showed striking similarities between rural South and urban North. Whether they were foragers or members of mutual aid societies, participants in an "underground economy" or "scufflers" seeking a better life for their children, black men and women struggled to provide for themselves in defiance of the dictum "The business of white men is to rule."[8]

To explore the efforts of white elites to keep Southern black people literally "in their place," and to understand the efforts of blacks to resist dependency, it is necessary to consider several issues, including the collusion between Southern employers and federal officials to preserve a large black labor force within the region's staple-crop economy; the drive for self-sufficiency in landownership and education on the part of black families and communities; black workers' efforts to earn wages off the plantation in the slack season, to compensate for the promise of payment that rarely materialized at the end of the year; and the migration imperative, which revealed a "restlessness" among Southern share-croppers determined to seek out a better way of life, and unwilling to give themselves over totally to an oppressive labor and political system.

The exploitative Southern sharecropping system was not necessarily an aberration within an industrializing society; indeed, the federal government helped to create and preserve this system as a means of producing a staple crop marketed worldwide throughout the nineteenth and twentieth centuries. Too often, scholars and modern commentators assume that employment in the private sector differs in a complete and fundamental way from reliance on government largesse in any form. In fact, historically, the private and public dimensions of black enforced dependency were not mutually exclusive categories. For the first two or three crucial years after the Civil War, the United States Bureau of Refugees, Freedmen, and Abandoned Lands enforced a labor contract system that mandated agricultural labor as the only legitimate form of employment for the newly freed slaves. Each contract covered a calendar year, an anomaly of sorts in the staple-crop South, where labor was deployed according to various crop-growing seasons, which each lasted less than twelve months. Still, bureau contracts bound individual workers (and eventually, under share-

8 "the business": Jackson Jordan, Jr., ibid., p. 98.

cropping, their families) to year-long residence on a single plantation, so that planters would not have to renegotiate for hands during the busy harvest season. In this way the Freedmen's Bureau provided a federal stamp of approval to a system that kept blacks tied to a single planter whether or not that employer had work enough to keep his workers occupied—and compensated—on a year-round basis.[9]

In the 1930s, the introduction of federal welfare programs blurred clear distinctions between local, private labor markets and patterns of public relief. On the one hand, cotton planters, like those in the Mississippi Delta, might remain "fearful of any governmental program [like a public-works project] that promises to bring independence to the sharecroppers." Labor contracts often prohibited families from keeping livestock or tending gardens, and many employers kept their workers in perpetual debt, a custom that was difficult to challenge, given the physical isolation of most plantations and the complicity of law-enforcement agents in routine employer fraud. More often than not, federal aid programs reinforced a Southern political economy that relegated almost all blacks to seasonal work on the countryside. In some cases, planters and administrators agreed among themselves (of course the two groups overlapped in many locales in any case) that needy families should qualify for aid only during the slack season; in this way the Federal Emergency Relief Administration (for example) shored up the furnishing system (whereby landlords extended credit and advanced supplies to their workers). A 1934 FERA survey, "Landlord-Tenant Relations and Relief in Alabama," found that, although the "conventional attitude" was that the landlord "is expected to 'take care of' the tenant when the latter needs aid . . . now . . . many landlords are shifting the responsibility to the relief agencies." The fact that landlords at times took the initiative to get their workers on relief rolls meant that, over the long run, federal programs enabled employers to retain a reserve army of agricultural laborers without assuming year-long responsibility for them. Moreover, in a break with tradition, some planters took advantage of relief programs and "split" households by furnishing only able-bodied workers, instead of entire household units that invariably included young, ill, and elderly members. In this way too, planters and government officials might collude to keep workers neither fully employed nor permanently on relief; the result was a system of enforced dependency that represented a linear progression from slavery through sharecropping, culminating in overtly political federal welfare policies.[10]

[9] For examples of labor contracts, see the archives of the Bureau of Refugees, Freedmen, and Abandoned Lands (Record Group 105, National Archives, Washington, D.C. [available on microfilm]). See also Gerald Jaynes, *Branches without Roots: Genesis of the Black Working Class in the American South, 1862–1882* (New York: Oxford University Press, 1986).

[10] "fearful" and "conventional": Harold C. Hoffsomer, "Landlord-Tenant Relations and Relief in Alabama," Federal Emergency Relief Administration Confidential Research Bulletin 2738 (July 10, 1934), summary, n.p., in vol. 4, Works Progress Administration Collection (Record Group 69, National Archives, Washington, D.C.); "split": A. R. Mangus, "The Rural Negro on Relief, Feb.,

The case of federal relief reveals that certain attitudes about the appropriate role of blacks in the Southern economy were not peculiar to the descendants of Southern slaveholders; rather, these views were part of a national system of white hegemony dominated by men of property. Northerners who went South after the Civil War were struck by the efforts of the newly freed slaves to establish for themselves a modest self-sufficiency, as hunters, fishers, gardeners, and foragers. Yet neither the victorious Yankees nor the vanquished Rebels considered such forms of productive labor "work" at all, since they had no place within a staple-crop economy dominated by white employers. During the 1866 slack season, Freedmen's Bureau agent Edward F. O'Brien observed that the black people near Mount Pleasant, South Carolina, were subsisting on green corn, pond lily beans, and alligator meat. He went on to describe the "idle, vicious vagrants, whose sole idea consists in loafing without working. . . . Being so close to the city of Charleston they find plenty temptation there to cause them to become idlers and they return to this parish only to plunder for the purpose of indulging their vicious practices. . . . Lead pipes taken from wells and sisterns, Harness from stables, cotton from the fields and even the iron from the cotton Gins and engines." Whatever their other shortcomings, Christ Church Parish blacks were hardly "idle." Like their slave parents who considered roast pig a delicacy, especially when pilfered from the master's hogpen, and their Northern ghetto grandchildren who earned wages "under the table," the freed-people sought to provide for themselves outside labor systems controlled exclusively by whites.[11]

Within an agricultural economy, only property conferred independence; rather than embracing a pathetic dependence upon their employers, black families throughout the postbellum period adhered to an ideal of landowner-ship, though relatively few were able to achieve it. Around 1915, the percentage of black landowners in the South peaked at 20 percent; most were concentrated in eastern Virginia, the South Carolina Sea Islands, and northeastern Texas, on poor land and small plots. First-generation owners won hard-earned reputations as "strivers." For example, W. L. Bost and his wife, Mamie, purchased "a little piece of ground" for $125 near Newton, North Carolina, in 1895. By buying lumber "a little at a time," they built a house for their family of three children. Forty-two years later, the Bosts still occupied the land, and could note with some satisfaction, "It's been a good home for us and the children."[12]

1935," FERA Research Bulletin 6950 (October 17, 1935), p. ii (Record Group 69, National Archives). On sharecropping in the Delta, see, for example, E. L. Langsford and B. H. Thibodeaux, "Plantation Organization and Operation in the Yazoo-Mississippi Delta Area," Department of Agriculture Technical Bulletin No. 682 (Washington, D.C., May 1939).

[11] Edward F. O'Brien to A. M. Crawford, Mount Pleasant, South Carolina, September 5, 1866, M869 (S.C.), Reel 34, BRFAL, RG 105, NA.

[12] W. L. Bost interview, George Rawick, ed., *The American Slave: A Composite Autobiography*, vol. 14 (N.C. Narratives), pt. 1 (Westport, Conn.: Greenwood Press, 1972–79), p. 146. See also Lewis C. Gray et al., "Farm Ownership and Tenancy," Department of Agriculture, *Agricultural Yearbook, 1923*

Even modest landowners demonstrated a self-conscious pride in their privileged status—a wife at work in the house instead of in the fields, a cotton crop piled ostentatiously in the front yard until prices began to rise in the winter and spring. Home ownership encouraged permanent improvements of cabins, outbuildings, and land, in contrast to croppers' makeshift efforts in the direction of "homelikeness." The wife of a landowner, Sara Brooks's mother could afford to lavish her time and energy on flowering perennials—"a yard *fulla* flowers"— that her family appreciated for both their beauty and medicinal qualities (the headache leaf "had big leaves and . . . pretty blooms on it"). Throughout the South, farm owners could boast a more diversified crop mix and more varied diets than those of workers dependent on a landlord. Freed from the watchful eye of a "rider," or labor supervisor, a family like the Brookses might harvest their cotton in the late fall and turn to pulling up peanuts, and then "by the time the peanuts would be put away, it'd be time then to dig the potatoes." The gathering of red and yellow plums, peaches, and pears signaled canning season for the mother of the household. Family crops also included corn, peas, and sugar cane. Descriptions of this household's bounty—the fruits and vegetables, fish, pork, beef, and chickens—present a striking contrast to the monotonous fare, high in carbohydrates and low in protein, consumed by landless people throughout the Cotton Belt.[13]

The rise of black-owned banks helps to account for at least some of the relatively few black farm owners during the early twentieth century; historians have documented the refusal of white-owned financial institutions throughout the South to grant credit to aspiring black home owners. In addition, in many areas of the South, propertied whites agreed among themselves not to sell land to blacks who desperately desired release from the plantation staple-crop economy. Nevertheless, the withholding of land and credit from blacks seemed almost moot in a place and at a time when the vast majority of workers were at the mercy of employers who paid them or not, just as they pleased, without fear of legal repercussion. Within such a society, otherwise normal forms of economic activity—accumulating and spending money—assumed ominous overtones when carried out by black people. Those black men and women who

---

(Washington, D.C.: GPO, 1924); Elizabeth Rauh Bethel, *Promiseland: A Century of Life in a Negro Community* (Philadelphia: Temple University Press, 1981); Kevern J. Verney, "Trespassers in the Land of Their Birth: Blacks and Landownership in South Carolina and Mississippi during the Civil War and Reconstruction," *Slavery and Abolition* 4 (1983): 64–78; Loren Schweninger, *Black Property Owners in the South, 1790–1915* (Urbana: University of Illinois Press, 1990).

[13] Thordis Simonsen, *You May Plow Here: The Narrative of Sara Brooks* (New York: Norton, 1986), pp. 69, 106–7, 89; W. O. Atwater and Charles D. Woods, "Dietary Studies with Reference to the Food of the Negro in Alabama in 1895 and 1896," Department of Agriculture Office of Experiment Stations Bulletin No. 38 (Washington, D.C.: GPO, 1897); Louis Ferleger, "Self-Sufficiency and Rural Life on Southern Farms," *Agricultural History* 58 (July 1984): 314–29; Mamie Garvin Fields with Karen Fields, *Lemon Swamp and Other Places: A Carolina Memoir* (New York: Free Press, 1983), p. 73.

scrimped and saved what little they had during the last decades of the nine-teenth century could hardly have been oblivious to the fact that they would be the likely victims of white resentment—lynch mobs and law enforcement agents seeking bodies for chain gangs. In the words of one woman, "You know, black folks who had money had to be kind of careful then."[14]

Just as Southern black landowners battled the odds in order to do better by themselves, so black communities all over the South invested in schools for their children, despite the violent objections of white people, rich and poor. The Northern teachers who volunteered to go into the former Confederate states left a mixed legacy to the cause of black schooling; on the one hand, they provided striking documentation of the eagerness of blacks of all ages and both sexes to learn to read and write, and of the often naive and misplaced faith these pupils had in the power of literacy to liberate them from the demands of white em-ployers. On the other hand, these teachers, together with their sponsoring organizations, often went out of their way to discourage black men and women from teaching children of their own race (on the assumption that the freedpeo-ple lacked the requisite formal training necessary for such an occupation); and in some cases Northerners, like the American Missionary Association officials stationed in postbellum Savannah, actually subverted indigenous efforts of blacks to start, staff, and sustain their own schools. Still, black people's commit-ment to formal education survived, in the smallest communities in the most out-of-the-way places. For example, in the early 1920s, the people of Bexar in Marion County, Alabama, managed to overcome their initial shock when in-formed that a new schoolhouse (to replace their "little old dingy" one) would cost seven hundred dollars. They set about building the school themselves; "Men went to the woods, cut down trees, hauled them to the saw mill and had them cut into lumber. Others cleared away the grounds, and even women worked carrying water, and feeding the men while they labored until enough material was placed on the grounds for the two-teacher building."[15]

This kind of collective effort was duplicated all over the South, despite the best efforts of whites to discourage it. Indeed, the issue of education, with all its connotations of upward mobility, provides a dramatic illustration of the way elites defined their self-interest in a rural South that was more old than new.

[14] "you know": James P. Comer, *Maggie's American Dream: The Life and Times of a Black Family* (New York: New American Library, 1988), p. 19; Ransom and Sutch, *One Kind of Freedom*; Manning Marable, "The Politics of Black Land Tenure, 1877–1915," *Agricultural History* 53 (1979): 142, 147–48.

[15] Rosenwald Building Fund agent quoted in James D. Anderson, *The Education of Blacks in the South, 1860–1935* (Chapel Hill: University of North Carolina Press, 1988), p. 165. The story of the Savannah Education Association is recounted in Jacqueline Jones, *Soldiers of Light and Love: Northern Teachers and Georgia Blacks, 1865–1873* (Chapel Hill: University of North Carolina Press, 1980), pp. 73–76. See also Robert C. Morris, *Reading, 'Riting and Reconstruction: The Education of Freedmen in the South, 1861–1870* (Chicago: University of Chicago Press, 1981); Vincent P. Franklin and James D. Anderson, eds., *New Perspectives on Black Educational History* (Boston: G. K. Hall, 1978).

Schools held out the hope that disenfranchised groups would be able to meet newly imposed literacy qualifications for voting. Although advocates of common schools in the South overestimated their potential to facilitate either social mobility or political activism, few employers seemed willing to take the chance and encourage regular school attendance, which in any case deprived them of field workers. Planters agreed that common schools "erred in educating the masses out of their proper spheres of usefulness. They all want to be teachers or preachers, lawyers or doctors; to live in towns, henceforth avoiding country life and labors. In this respect education is a distinct detriment to them."[16]

Curiously, proponents of the "culture of dependency" thesis tend to focus exclusively on individual welfare recipients, and in the process ignore the vast number and variety of black advocacy and self-help groups that touched almost every aspect of black community life, beginning in the postbellum rural South and stretching into the late-twentieth-century Northern ghetto. Indeed, the case of education is but one illustration of the way in which blacks could work together to advance the interests of their own race; after the Civil War, a flurry of institution building among the freedpeople, who started their own churches, burial societies, neighborhood and mutual-aid associations, workers' groups, and fraternal orders testified to their determination to provide for themselves. Viewed from a long-term, historic perspective, these groups in the rural South (and later the urban North)—some well funded and enduring, others makeshift and short-lived, gender- or class-based, secular or denominational—attempted to meet the same needs. They aimed to fill the gap left by the discriminatory policies of craft unions and public and private welfare agencies; to provide places of worship or study where black people could come together, apart from degrading Jim Crow policies, North and South; and to press for black civil rights in the courts, the workplace, and in the schools. Whether sponsored by the African Methodist Episcopal Church, a black college, a segregated YMCA, ad hoc neighborhood groups, the National Association for the Advancement of Colored People, the Congress of Racial Equality, or a lone, inspired individual, these groups reveal a tradition of group resourcefulness, a corporate ethos that originated in the slave quarters, persisted in the postbellum South, and found a new, if similarly harsh, home in the urban North.

This emphasis on the struggles of black families and communities to provide for themselves, and resist the debilitating dependency forced upon them by white men of property, diverges from the "conventional wisdom" that informs the current underclass debate. Whether organized in nuclear families, kin groups, or formal organizations, black women and men expressed in no uncertain terms their unwillingness to capitulate to the expectations of landlords and

---

[16] "erred": *Report of the Industrial Commission on Agriculture and Taxation in Various States*, vol. 11 of the commission's reports (Washington, D.C.: GPO, 1901), p. 81; Donald Spivey, *Schooling for the New Slavery: Black Industrial Education, 1868–1915* (Westport, Conn.: Greenwood Press, 1978).

employers. Embedded in the historical record of ordinary families, then, is a powerful refutation of the culture of poverty or culture of dependency thesis.

LABOR MOBILITY IN THE PLANTATION SOUTH AND ITS COROLLARY,
NORTHWARD MIGRATION

Black people, then, were hardly the passive victims of white hegemony. Even the poorest families often demonstrated a great deal of energy and ingenuity in piecing together a living for themselves. In households like the Holtzclaws' of Alabama, the mother found work for white folks as a cook while the youngsters gathered hog potatoes, persimmons, nuts, and muscadines; and the father and older son went off to search for temporary employment in sawmills and railroad camps. This patchwork family economy did not preclude work in the cotton fields, but since landlords routinely curtailed furnishings during the slack season, family members had to work together, and sometimes apart, to keep "body and soul together during those dark days."[17]

An extensive network of rural nonagricultural enterprises, including turpentine orchards, phosphate mines, and lumber and sawmill camps, relied on the manpower of blacks who left their sharecropper cabins once the crop had been laid by (in the early summer) and after harvest (in the winter months). The heavy work associated with the construction, extractive, and processing industries favored the employment of able-bodied men. Nevertheless, other family members found ways to add to the household income in the course of the year. When grudgingly granted the opportunity by planters, wives earned "patch" money by marketing small surpluses of vegetables and dairy products. They took in laundry and served as midwives, at times for their poor-white neighbors as well as their landlords. Children of all ages helped their fathers cut firewood and fat pine to sell, and hired themselves out as cotton pickers on nearby farms once they had fulfilled harvest-time duties at home. Local truck farms employed women and children to pick berries and vegetables during the cotton slack season.[18]

Paradoxically, as black people tried to preserve their families in an economic sense, they were often forced to depart from the family homeplace for indeterminate periods, either regularly or sporadically. The efforts of fathers, husbands, and older sons to seek out wage work stemmed from both their resourcefulness as breadwinners and from financial necessity borne of their chronic underemployment within the sharecropping system. Thus the household economy mandated the physical separation of family members, especially at certain times

---

[17] William H. Holtzclaw, *The Black Man's Burden* (New York: Neale Publishing Co., 1915), pp. 17–18, 20–25, 27, 31. See also Theodore Rosengarten, *All God's Dangers: The Life of Nate Shaw* (New York: Knopf, 1974).

[18] These points are developed more fully in chap. 5 of Jacqueline Jones, *The Dispossessed: America's Underclasses from the Civil War to the Present* (New York: Basic Books, 1992).

40 · Jacqueline Jones

of the year; it is quite possible that Herbert Gutman's data on the prevalence of late-nineteenth-century rural black two-headed households underestimates these forces of fragmentation, since federal census takers usually made their appointed rounds in April, when everyone was bound to be at home for planting time. These economic imperatives, and not some ill-defined predisposition toward a "disorganized" family life, help to account for stresses on black households in the rural South.

In myriad ways over time, and in various places, the exigencies of making a living deprived black Southern fathers and mothers, husbands and wives, parents and children, of the opportunity to live together. For example, in the 1920s, after the cotton harvest, some black men from Georgia began to venture south to Florida's winter garden (just south of Lake Okeechobee) to pick beans for wages before returning home in time for the beginning of the planting season. By World War II, thousands of black families from the Lower South were moving into the East Coast migratory labor stream on a more or less permanent basis. In the process, individual households devised survival strategies calculated to take advantage of wage-earning opportunities and the needs of family members, though as we have seen in the case of Johnnie Belle Taylor, these strategies might not always permit cohabitation. In general throughout the South, on the countryside, a mother who found herself without a husband or older sons had little choice but to move in with her kinfolk or to migrate to a nearby town or city and find work as a domestic servant. Moreover, although many of the South's rural industrial enterprises continued to rely heavily on fathers who refused to abandon their farms altogether, some sons felt compelled to take up residence in mining or phosphate camps, or in the transient sawmills or turpentine camps, and live apart from their families for months, if not years, at a time. Employees of the Armour Fertilizer Works (a phosphate mine) in Bartow, Florida, faced the trade-offs familiar to rural-industrial commuters; by renting homes in nearby villages, they might avoid the dirty, crowded company quarters, but the four- to eight-mile walk to work and back each day, plus the "long working hours[,] make their homes only a place for sleep."[19]

Pressures on the black family economy in the rural South during the Great Depression indicate that first, long-term structural underemployment was not unique to the urban North, and second, two-parent black households failed to enjoy a "golden age" of sorts between slavery and Northern migration. In the late 1930s and on into the World War II period, government construction of factories and army installations hastened the process by which agricultural workers lost their ties to the land; at the same time, these building projects spurred much interregional mobility among male wage seekers, many of whom left their

---

[19] *Employees v. Armour Fertilizer Works*, Bartow, Florida (Docket no. 689, 1918, Entry 4, File no. 0112, National War Labor Board, Record Group 2, National Archives, Washington, D.C.); Jacqueline Jones, *Labor of Love, Labor of Sorrow: Black Women, Work and the Family from Slavery to the Present* (New York: Basic Books, 1985), pp. 110–51.

families behind. Army construction projects like the Triangular Division Camp near Ozark, Alabama, could put 18,000 men on its payroll during its peak season; but half of these employees fell into the category of unskilled, and they had to move on once the work was completed—in this case in 120 days. Housing was so scarce around some of the larger projects that employees had to make do with the most primitive of conditions—about 3,000 of the 19,400 construction workers at Florida's Camp Blanding set up tents in the nearby woods southwest of Jacksonville. In Newport News, inadequate housing for black male workers led to high turnover rates among husbands and fathers who quit in order to go home and visit their families periodically, prompting white employers to denounce blacks as "irresponsible" war workers.[20]

Crop reduction programs sponsored by the Agricultural Adjustment Administration (beginning in 1933), plus large government public-works projects, pushed croppers off the plantations and forced families to regroup somehow, either as squatters nearby or as casual wage workers clustered on the fringes of major Southern cities. Family members dispersed throughout the South, their traditional way of life, based as much on foraging as on cotton culture, shattered forever. Though released in 1942, and dealing specifically with the Huntsville, Alabama, area, a study of the impact of national defense on various rural communities applied equally to households throughout the years of the Great Depression and earlier: "The family which worked at odd jobs, tilling a few acres in a haphazard manner, and augmenting earnings through scouring the woods for sassafrass roots, picking dallas green seed, trapping coons and skunks, snaring fish in baskets, and poaching on game reservations, etc., could not be dumped into another community with the expectation that the resourcefulness of the family would enable it to get by."[21]

The problem of worker mobility and migration highlights the struggle between labor-hungry rural employers on the one hand and employees resistant to exploitative conditions on the other. In particular, the phenomenon of "shifting" sharecroppers was ultimately a political issue that helped to shape labor relations on plantations throughout the Cotton South from 1865 until the large-scale replacement of agricultural wage earners with tractors in the 1940s and 1950s. Deprived of the ability to move up the agricultural tenure ladder

[20] James G. Maddox, "The Role of Low-Income Farm Families in the War Effort," *National Defense Migration Hearings*, pt. 28, p. 10786; testimony of Roberta C. Williams, Florida Travellers' Aid, *Hearings before the Select Committee to Investigate the Interstate Migration of Destitute Citizens*, House of Representatives, 77th Cong., 3d Sess. (hereinafter *Interstate Migration Hearings*), pt. 9 (1940), p. 3619; Frank S. Horne, "War Homes in Hampton Roads," *Opportunity* 20 (July 1942): 200–202.

[21] Pete Daniel, *Breaking the Land: The Transformation of Cotton, Tobacco, and Rice Cultures since 1880* (Urbana: University of Illinois Press, 1985); Jack Temple Kirby, *Rural Worlds Lost: The American South, 1920–1960* (Baton Rouge: Louisiana State University Press, 1987); "the family": E. S. Morgan, "Displacement of Farm Families Caused by National Defense Activities in Alabama, Georgia, South Carolina, and Florida," *National Defense Migration Hearings*, pt. 32, p. 12082.

(through the accumulation of land or cash), or to make a living wage in Southern cities or textile mill villages, black families engaged in an annual form of lateral geographical movement that took them down the road to a neighboring plantation every couple of years or so, without the benefit of much (apparent) gain in the way of material resources or labor contract provisions. Shifting had an urban-industrial counterpart in the high rates of job turnover among wage earners in the lowest paid jobs, a characteristic of poor white and black, immigrant and native-born workers alike. The phenomenon resulted from several factors—the impulse on the part of landlords, or employers, to evict or fire "troublesome" workers; and the desire on the part of employees to search for something better elsewhere, and to deny an exploitative boss complete control over one's labor. In the words of one Southern white man, "If he [the worker] doesn't trust you he is not going to stay long, not if he can get some place else to go."[22]

Cotton planters, federal agricultural agents, and subsequent scholars alike seemed baffled by shifting; high annual turnover rates among croppers (about 30 to 40 percent during this period) could be cited as evidence of neither a shortage of labor nor of a dynamic economy that afforded workers the opportunity to bargain for better wages and working conditions. In fact, shifting was the result of a tug-of-war between white landlords and black employees; around the turn of the century, the Georgia commissioner of agriculture described the process in deceptively neutral language: "Sometimes you have a tenant on the place, and he finds he can do a little better somewhere else, and he moves off and goes to the next place. Sometimes the landlord finds that he can get a better tenant than the one he has. He lets this fellow go and gets the other fellow. They are continually moving around from place to place."[23]

Too often Southern employers confused "shifting" with "shiftlessness" or irresponsibility on the part of croppers. In reality, households calculated their various interests, both economic and affective, on a year-to-year basis. Black families found that, over time, their needs—in terms of housing, proximity to a town or school—changed in response to household composition and size; consequently, a move to another employer might result in incremental benefits, like a better chimney or a closer spring of water, but not a noticeably higher standard of living or fairer deal at the end of the year. Too, croppers routinely fled from abusive or cheating planters, and the pervasiveness of state-sanctioned fraud practiced by rural-South employers kept many families perpetually on the move. A Georgia sharecropper, Ed Brown, likened himself to a rabbit: "Zigzag, zigzag, dodgin one hunter then the next." In the words of one contemporary observer, "[croppers'] one outstanding means of asserting freedom is mobility, although within an extremely narrow range." Together, in family groups, the

---

[22] Testimony of Luther Jones, *National Defense Migration Hearings*, pt. 33, p. 12667.

[23] Testimony of O. B. Stevens, *Report of the Industrial Commission* 10: 908–9; Charles E. Orser, *Material Basis of the Postbellum Cotton Plantation: Historical Archaeology in the South Carolina Piedmont* (Athens: University of Georgia Press, 1988).

former slaves institutionalized the practice of running away, though they could deprive only one particular white man (a current employer), but not whites in general, of their labor.[24]

On the other hand, planters as a matter of course dismissed or violently expelled workers who during the year defiantly kept a little garden spot, stole chickens, or appropriated wood for their own use, or spent too much time grubbing for wild potatoes before the crop lien was satisfied. When Southern planters complained about a "shortage" of labor between the Civil War and the Second World War, they had in mind a particular kind of laborer, one sufficiently skillful at picking time and sufficiently tractable at "reckoning" (that is, end-of-year settlement) time; according to this standard, then, most planters despaired of ever securing an "assured tenantry." In the words of one United States Department of Agriculture official, planters used a constant process of "selection and elimination." "Reliable tenants" were those who were "public-spirited and loyal to the planter and who exercise a good influence over those inclined to become dissatisfied." Still, employers could always count on hiring their neighbors' former hands, black men and women fleeing from the same kind of abuses that their new employer had committed against his previous workers.[25]

When blacks rejected the sedentary form of labor demanded of them in the rural South, they reacted in ways not unlike those of other dispossessed groups in history, the urban poor and colonized peoples who led transient lives, scavenged for a living, and participated in a "moral economy" outside the boundaries of the paid labor force. At the same time, within the context of American history, African Americans were a unique group by virtue of the political and legal restraints imposed on their mobility, restraints based on race and not on class. During the antebellum period, slave and free black alike moved around the Southern countryside, and across state lines, only at the behest of whites; after the war, the notorious "black codes" passed by Southern legislatures (and resurrected later through vagrancy statutes) made it a crime for black people to travel for reasons not directly related to the needs of a white employer. A lack of economic opportunities in other areas of the country effectively kept blacks bound to the land worked by their slave grandparents. By the late 1800s, it was clear that Northern industrial employers would continue to favor unskilled, non-English-speaking Eastern European immigrants, to the detriment of the large black population languishing in the South. In 1916, when immigration

<hr />

[24] "zigzag": Jane Maguire, *On Shares: Ed Brown's Story* (New York: Norton, 1975), p. 63; "one": John Lee Coulter, "The Rural Life Problem of the South," *South Atlantic Quarterly* 12 (1913): 64.

[25] "assured": Alfred Holt Stone, *Studies in the American Race Problem* (New York: Doubleday, Page, 1908), p. 127; "selection": C. O. Brannen, "Relation of Land Tenure to Plantation Organization," Department of Agriculture Bulletin no. 1269 (October 18, 1924), p. 50. See also W. J. Spillman and E. A. Goldenweiser, "Farm Tenantry in the United States," Department of Agriculture, *Agriculture Yearbook for 1916* (Washington, D.C.: GPO, 1917), p. 345.

slowed and the need for defense workers intensified in Northern cities, black people eagerly left the South, an impulse that one migrant to Chicago compared to shifting: "Before the North opened up with work all we could do was to move from one plantation to another in the hope of finding something better." A black man who eventually moved to Newark, New Jersey, also recalled, "After a time we moved 'round, you know, to see if we could find a better place. That's the nature of farmin'."[26]

Indeed, the very act of migration out of the South belies the theory of black "dependency." Had black people as a group embraced a hopeless and fatalistic view of the world, they probably would have avoided the considerable exertion necessary to make complicated relocation arrangements, which included keeping in touch with friends already in the North, scraping together the fare for the train ride north, selling precious belongings, and in some instances engineering an exceedingly daring late-night departure, children and chickens in tow, from a Delta plantation. Many Southern black folks felt that they were "like plants that were meant to grow upright but became bent and twisted, stunted, sometimes stretching out and running along the ground, because the conditions of our environment forbade our developing upward naturally." And so the North beckoned as a place that would fulfill their quest for "independence" defined in terms of good schools and steady work at fair wages. Summarizing a 1917 survey, Thomas J. Woofter reported that the black tenants and croppers allowed even a modicum of self-sufficiency by their landlords were the most likely to stay on plantations and resist the mass exodus northward during the war. One observer of Depression-era North Carolina suggested that black agricultural laborers were "not so ignorant that they fail to be aware of being robbed. That is why so many of them take the first opportunity to escape the eternal debt that is theirs."[27]

There is little evidence to indicate that blacks left the South for the explicit purpose of receiving higher welfare payments in the North during any period. Most migrants necessarily relinquished what little aid they might have received

[26] "before" quoted in James Grossman, *Land of Hope: Chicago, Black Southerners, and the Great Migration* (Chicago: University of Chicago Press, 1989), p. 18; "after": "The Master Called Me to Preach the Bible," in Audrey Olsen Faulkner et al., *When I Was Comin' Up: An Oral History of Aged Blacks* (Hamden, Conn.: Archon Books, 1982), p. 84. See also Eric Foner, *Reconstruction: America's Unfinished Revolution, 1863–1877* (New York: Harper and Row, 1988); Oscar Zeichner, "The Legal Status of the Agricultural Laborer in the South," *Political Science Quarterly* 55 (September 1940): 412–28; William Cohen, "Negro Involuntary Servitude in the South, 1865–1940: A Preliminary Analysis," *Journal of Southern History* 42 (February 1976): 31–60.

[27] "like plants": Mary Mebane, *Mary* (New York: Viking Press, 1981), p. 168; Thomas J. Woofter, Jr., *Negro Migration: Changes in Rural Organization and Population of the Cotton Belt* (1920; reprint, New York: AMS Press, 1971), p. 87; "not so": Newell D. Eason, "The Negro of North Carolina Forsakes the Land," *Opportunity* (April 1936): 119. See also Carole Marks, *Farewell—We're Good and Gone: The Great Migration* (Bloomington: Indiana University Press, 1989).

in the South in exchange for the chance to work in the North; in any case, Northern communities' residency requirements could prevent migrants from qualifying for assistance for any number of months or for as many as five years. Families like the Moshers of Russell County, Alabama, could confound welfare workers who assumed that blacks would automatically and unquestionably react to either the offer or the withdrawal of relief, no matter how meager. Left behind by large numbers of their kin and neighbors who moved to Chicago during World War I, in 1933 the Moshers (a family of ten) decided that they too should relocate when they found that they could not live on the small amount of public aid allotted them. After Mrs. Mosher traveled with two of the children to Chicago the following year, to attend the funeral of her brother, she remained in the city, and by September 1935 six of her other offspring had followed her there. Alarmed Chicago social workers informed the mother that she would not receive any public assistance, assuming that the threat would dissuade her husband and the two other children from coming North. Instead, the recent migrants determined "to try not only to stay in Chicago but also to bring the rest of the family North to join them." The Mosher's household strategy signaled their eagerness to move North, to preserve family ties, and to scorn local and federal efforts to confine them to one area of the country or another through the manipulation of various public-assistance programs.[28]

Too often scholars discuss the "selective" nature of black migration in terms of formal education. In fact, though easily quantifiable, an individual's grade-level attainment was less a useful indicator of intelligence and "preparation for Northern life" than the more subjective qualities we might consider "gumption." Migrants told stories of dropping out of school at an early age to "go to work and help out with the rest of the kids," all the while admiring a mother who "couldn't read or write, but you couldn't cheat her out of a penny. She could get on the ground and make marks. She could count to the last cent that anybody owed her, but she didn't know to write her name when she died." Maggie Comer, who at age seventeen left Memphis to go and live with kin in East Saint Louis, had only a few months' formal schooling but a natural facility for arithmetic: "with my fingers I could beat some people with a pencil." Her stepfather, though an abusive man, a "drifter," and a poor provider for his family, refused to curry favor with, or even labor for, a white man—"No, I don't work for nobody," he declared—and the young girl probably in some fashion imbibed his defiance of the caste system. Buried in the biographical details of many migrants, regardless

[28] John N. Webb and Malcolm Brown, "Migrant Families," Works Progress Administration Research Monograph 18 (Washington, D.C.: GPO, 1938), pp. 23–24. See also Larry H. Long, "Poverty Status and Receipt of Welfare among Migrants and Nonmigrants in Large Cities," *American Sociological Review* 39 (February 1974): 46–56. William Julius Wilson reviews the literature on the transferral of poverty and welfare dependency from South to North in *The Truly Disadvantaged*, pp. 177–80.

of whether or not they found a good job and a settled life in the North, is evidence, then, that these black people sought to rid themselves of historic forms of Southern white authority.[29]

To some observers, black migration northward represented an irrevocable break with a distinctive way of life mired in the South's regional peculiarities of slavery, and then postbellum neoslavery. But for one family that had to "scuff around" for day work in Virginia, and then "scuff around" for day work in Newark in the early 1960s, the way north seemed a less dramatic move than most "detached" observers might have imagined. To some degree, the issue turned on gender issues and on timing; for example, in the 1920s, Charlottesville domestics bound for New York City would find few other kinds of jobs open to them. On the other hand, male wartime migrants might experience a more drastic break with their past jobs, as they began to "leave off tending green growing things to tending iron monsters." Nevertheless, chronic under-employment would continue to plague black husbands and fathers in the North as well as in the South, though a modern industrial economy would present fewer alternatives for foraging and day work compared to life on the nineteenth-century countryside.[30]

THE CREATION OF THE BLACK GHETTO: THE HISTORY OF WHITE APPALACHIAN MIGRANTS AS A COUNTEREXAMPLE

In order to unravel the class and racial factors that converged to produce the black ghetto in the North, it is fruitful to examine the fate of poor-white Southerners (here the focus is on men and women from the southern Appalachian area), and the way their experiences diverged from those of black migrants to Northern cities. From World War I until the end of the Great Depression, 1.5 million black people left the South for the North. Between 1940 and 1970, about 5 million more blacks abandoned the South, and approximately 3.2 million people migrated out of the southern Appalachian region. (In the decade of the 1950s alone, Kentucky lost 35 percent of its total population through outmigration; West Virginia suffered comparable losses, of 25 percent.) Some historians and social scientists have compared Southern-born blacks with Eastern European immigrants and argued that black people found themselves at a disadvantage in the urban North as a result of transformations in the Northern economy that (beginning in the 1920s) gradually eliminated the need for large

[29] "go to": "They're Hypocritic," in Faulkner et al. *When I Was Comin' Up*, p. 103; Comer, *Maggie's American Dream*, pp. 57, 3, 15, 75, 16.

[30] "scuff": "Nine Luzianne Coffee Boxes," in Faulkner et al., *When I Was Comin' Up*, p. 60; Marjorie Felice Irwin, "The Negro in Charlottesville and Albermarle County" (Phelps-Stokes Fellowship Paper, University of Virginia, 1929), pp. 24–29; "leave off": William Attaway, *Blood on the Forge* (1941; reprint, New York: Monthly Review Press, 1987), p. 64.

numbers of unskilled workers.[31] However, if that had been the major reason for the growth of poor black inner-city communities, then Appalachian white migrants, who started their northward trek in earnest in the 1940s and had comparable (that is, comparably low) levels of schooling and job status compared to blacks, would have fared even worse in the race for good jobs and decent housing. In fact, as a group, southern Appalachians prospered early, and steadily, in their host communities, Midwestern towns and cities. These migrants were relatively successful primarily because they gained easy access to semiskilled jobs, and they had the freedom to move around within urban areas, or at least as far as their fortunes and kin ties would take them.

This comparison, which holds class factors (strictly defined) constant, and highlights the issue of race, is not without its difficulties. On the one hand, it is possible to draw some compelling, if unexpected, parallels between the two groups; blacks and poor whites adhered to a "traditional," rural way of life that valued kin connections and neighborly cooperation over an ethos of wage-based capital accumulation or individual "success." Neither black sharecroppers nor white mountain people could claim much in the way of either formal education or work experience outside the agricultural or extractive sectors. Though they came from different cultures, historically defined, members of both groups adhered to Protestant fundamentalism, and they nourished grievances (some more long-standing than others) toward planters or coal-mining companies who set in motion the forces of displacement that deprived them of homesteads and caused them to assume a seminomadic existence. When mountain folk deferred to their betters, they practiced a kind of deference ritual that blacks had perfected under slavery. Even musical forms considered the core of a "pure" Appalachian culture included elements of Southern black influence (blues and gospel music) and changed rapidly over the generations.[32]

In sum, social workers and scholars alike have spent much time and effort trying to define a distinctive Appalachian culture without realizing that many of the traits ascribed to this group were common to rural folk in general. The effort on the part of white households to combine wage work with patch farming, and to rely on kin for financial support in good times and bad, was less a "Kentucky way" than a rural way of life. Once in the North, southern Appalachians ex-

[31] See for example, Stanley Lieberson, *A Piece of the Pie: Blacks and White Immigrants since 1880* (Berkeley: University of California Press, 1980).

[32] Ronald D. Eller, *Miners, Millhands, and Mountaineers: Industrialization of the Appalachian South, 1880–1930* (Knoxville: University of Tennessee Press, 1982); Allen Batteau, "Rituals of Dependence in Appalachian Kentucky," in Allen Batteau, ed., *Appalachia and America: Autonomy and Regional Dependence* (Lexington: University Press of Kentucky, 1983), pp. 142–67; D. K. Wilgus, "Country-Western Music and the Urban Hillbilly," *Journal of American Folklore* 83 (April–June 1970): 157–79. See also Patricia D. Beaver, *Rural Community in the Appalachian South* (Lexington: University Press of Kentucky, 1986), pp. 56–78.

hibited few of the collective or associational impulses that would qualify them as an ethnic group; their extended families, rather than precisely defined cultural bonds, served as their primary reference point. And finally, the "backwardness" of Appalachian life was belied by the strenuous efforts of a considerable proportion of the population to leave it, at least temporarily. Commented Rosalie Van Houton, a Kentucky native who had moved with her husband to Detroit during World War II, "They [that is, Northerners] think we're dumb just because we come from outside. They're a whole lot dumber than we are. They've never been outside their own little community."[33]

Most Appalachian migrants headed for the Midwest, where they were soon stereotyped in terms similar to those used to describe black people. Municipal officials considered Southern whites as a group to be lazy, promiscuous, rapidly proliferating welfare seekers, a drain on the public treasury, a stain on the city's image. Educational officials tracked their children for failure in the public schools, and medical authorities decried their persistent superstitions in all manner of ailments, like rinsing out a child's mouth with urine to cure a rash called thrush. Employers expressed mixed feelings; the migrants provided cheap labor, but they were (in the eyes of some bosses and plant foremen) unreliable, inept at machine work, slow on the job, and unambitious. Landlords told them that they need not apply, citing their large families, allegedly deplorable housekeeping practices, and violent proclivities (with the knife as the weapon of choice). Their neighbors native to the North soon developed a repertoire of jokes that focused on the migrants' so-called ignorance of city ways, their primitive Southern origins, their slovenly appearance and demeanor. Condemned as shiftless, evasive, and untrustworthy, they squandered their weekly paychecks on trinkets and drink (or so it was charged). Social workers believed that in their new home, as in their old, the migrants remained willing and able to tolerate the most degraded living and working conditions, "immune to discomforts that sorely try other Americans." This last point, in particular, echoed the convictions of Southern cotton planters who justified furnishing black croppers at a bare subsistence level because of the former slaves' (reported) remarkable ability to survive on so little in the way of material resources.[34]

And yet, despite their poverty and the hostility they encountered from Northerners, Appalachian whites did not come from or adhere to a distinctive folk culture comparable (at least for analytic purposes) to Afro-American culture.

[33] Rhoda Halperin, *The Livelihood of Kin: Making Ends Meet "The Kentucky Way"* (Austin: University of Texas Press, 1990); "they": T. E. Murphy, "The Orphans of Willow Run," *Saturday Evening Post*, August 4, 1945, p. 110. See also William W. Philliber, *Appalachian Migrants in Urban America: Cultural Conflict or Ethnic Group Formation?* (New York: Praeger, 1981).

[34] "immune": E. Russell Porter, "Where Cultures Meet: Mountain and Urban," *Nursing Outlook* 2 (June 1963): 418. See also Ellen J. Stekert, "Focus for Conflict: Southern Mountain Medical Beliefs in Detroit," *Journal of American Folklore* 83 (April–June 1970): 115–47; Lewis M. Killian, "Southern

The whites hailed from a variety of local economies—subsistence farming, commercial tobacco production, coal mining, or some combination of the three—and not until they arrived in the North did (some) people from the region begin to think of themselves as a homogeneous group. Even then, any sense of cultural loyalty or identification could be fleeting. For the upwardly mobile of either sex, it was possible to leave the "ridgerunner" and "briarhopper" taunts behind forever by losing their accents, adopting Northern dress fashions, and switching the radio dial from Hank Williams to Frank Sinatra. Predictably, many of the children of migrants saw little reason to tout themselves as the kin of "hillbillies."

Southern Appalachians migrated both to the largest cities in the Midwest, where they won favor over blacks in direct competition for unskilled and semi-skilled jobs, and to the small towns of southern Ohio, where they effectively kept black people from migrating in large numbers at all, so tight was their hold over manufacturing jobs at every level. To cite an example of the process as it affected workers of both races in Detroit (known as the "capital city of Hell" for its racial and ethnic tensions and its shortage of housing during World War II and later): Waiting in line for a job in a Detroit defense plant in April 1943, a black man named Charles Denby found himself standing next to a white migrant from Tennessee. The two struck up a conversation. The white man, who had "never been North before or in a plant," mentioned that he had no idea what kinds of jobs were available. Denby, though raised on a cotton farm in Lowndes County, Alabama, had had considerable factory work experience—in a Detroit auto plant, a Pittsburgh steel mill, an Anniston, Alabama, foundry, and a Memphis machine supply company. Denby had heard from a friend that "the best job was riveting," and that it paid $1.16 an hour. When it came time for him to talk to the employment officer, Denby said he knew all about riveting ("I was lying to him but I wanted to get the job"). The officer replied that Denby's "experience wouldn't apply," and offered him the choice of attending riveting school, which paid 60 cents an hour, or taking a "laboring job" that paid 27 cents an hour more. With a family to support, Denby decided to accept the latter position. Shortly thereafter he learned that the Tennessean had also asked for the riveting job, but that no one had inquired about his work history or insisted that he undergo a period of low-paid training. Denby later recalled, "He said they had given him a job, riveting." The white man marveled, "And I just come in from the fields." In contrast, Denby was assigned to the dope room, where "the odor of glue made the average person sick," and labor turnover was high; gradually, black men took the places of white men who departed, but in the

White Laborers in Chicago's West Side," (Ph.D. diss., University of Chicago, 1949); Staff of the *Cincinnati Enquirer*, *Urban Appalachians* (Cincinnati, Ohio: *Cincinnati Enquirer*, 1981); James S. Brown and George A. Hillery, Jr., "The Great Migration, 1940–1960," in Thomas R. Ford, ed., *The Southern Appalachian Region* (Lexington: University of Kentucky Press, 1962), pp. 54–78.

course of the war, black women came to predominate in the small, suffocating space.[35]

In Detroit and Chicago (for example), racial conflicts over jobs and housing were explicit, and bloody. In contrast, southern Appalachians who migrated to Ohio's Miami Valley established an early and exclusive foothold in the heavy industries of that region, then as a group perpetuated their predominance through kin networks eagerly exploited by employment officers. In Middle-town, Ohio, in the early 1950s, one-half of all employees of the Inland Container Corporation hailed from Wolfe County, Kentucky, the home of a company superintendent who combined job recruitment with periodic visits to kin back home. In the same town, the Armco Steel Corporation as a matter of policy granted hiring preference to the children and relatives of workers; as a result, migrants from certain Kentucky counties came to predominate in individual departments. Asked about the prejudice of southern Ohioans against mountain folk, one migrant said that he had encountered "no trouble" in his entry-level job, because almost all his workers shared the same roots and "there weren't no buckeyes [that is, Ohio-born people] to get along with." Clearly, manufacturing jobs in this area of the country went to southern Appalachian whites not because they possessed superior skills or training compared to blacks (they did not), but because they were part of a chain migration that sustained itself over the generations, aided and abetted by Northern employers. Thus throughout the Midwest, Southern whites benefited from racially exclusionary hiring practices, from their kin connections, and from most businesses' policy of upgrading and providing on-the-job training for current employees who aspired to semiskilled and operative positions. The wives and daughters who migrated from Appalachia might supplement the wages of their menfolk through factory or clerical work, positions closed to most black women through the 1960s. Indeed, until that time, most black female migrants, and Northern black women in general, remained confined to domestic and institutional service.[36]

Discriminatory housing policies in the urban North—policies achieved through the red-lining practices of banks, suburban zoning restrictions and restrictive covenants, and the segregationist imperative as implemented by city councils and the Federal Housing Administration—have been described in detail elsewhere, and well. For our purposes, it is necessary to consider the

[35] "capital": "Mountain Dreams," in Robert Coles and Jane Hallowell Coles, *Women of Crisis: Lives of Struggle and Hope* (New York: Delta/Seymour Lawrence, 1978), p. 80; Charles Denby, *Indignant Heart: Testimony of a Black American Worker* (London: Pluto Press, 1978), pp. 87–89.

[36] John Leslie Thompson, "Industrialization in the Miami Valley: A Case Study of Interregional Labor Migration" (Ph.D. diss., University of Wisconsin, 1955), p. 132; "no trouble": quoted in Martin J. Crowe, "The Occupational Adaptation of a Selected Group of Eastern Kentuckians in Southern Ohio" (Ph.D. diss., University of Kentucky, 1964), p. 134. See also Gene B. Peterson, Laure M. Sharp, Thomas F. Drury, *Southern Newcomers to Northern Cities: Work and Social Adjustment to Cleveland* (New York: Praeger, 1966); Barbara Zigli, "Dream of Moving Up Becomes True for Many," in Staff of *Chicago Enquirer*, *Urban Appalachians*, pp. 16–17.

residential patterns of southern Appalachian migrants to the North, for those patterns exhibited a variety and fluidity that set them apart from the process of ghettoization that affected blacks of all classes. For example, over the generations, Appalachian migrants and their children established for themselves a number of different kinds of communities in Ohio. East Dayton, Cincinnati's Over-the-Rhine and Lower Price Hill, and Hamilton's Armondale and Peck's Addition represented classic port-of-entry communities for the first migrants and for some of those who followed. Yet these poor neighborhoods were characterized by high rates of residential turnover, as migrants and their relatively successful offspring explored other housing options—stable working-class or lower-middle-class areas like Mill Creek, near Cincinnati, or Wrightview, outside of Dayton; or small towns like South Lebanon, where families could tend some corn and fish a nearby stream; and finally, pleasant suburbs where well-to-do whites might quickly blend into the middle-American landscape. A migrant family might logically progress from Peck's Addition to a better area of the working-class Belmont district, and finally move out to Fairfield Township, where they could enjoy "at least superficially some of the isolation of the hollow . . . set up a vegetable patch and . . . find some of the [ethnic and racial] homogeneity still preserved in the Kentucky hills." On the other hand, other white migrants, depending on their own background and the location of their Northern kin, might move directly from the South to a stable suburb and stay there.[37]

Because of their physical proximity to their Southern homes, and their fondness for a "farm freedom" characteristic of the Appalachian region in the past (if not in the present or future), the poorest white migrants found it difficult to commit themselves wholeheartedly to Northern life; in accounting for the lack of associational activity among this group (in striking contrast to collective-minded ghetto residents), observers noted the ease with which poor whites might move between South and North, never fully here nor there. Unlike blacks, the poorest whites retained a fondness for the historic tradition represented by their Southern homes, and the story of their migration northward had a mournful, elegiac quality. By the 1960s, a white underclass (proportionately much smaller than the concentrated poor black population) had developed in scattered migrant communities throughout the North—families like that of Char-

[37] "at least": Stanley B. Greenberg, *Politics and Poverty: Modernization and Response in Five Poor Neighborhoods* (New York: John Wiley, 1974), p. 53; Grace G. Leybourne, "Urban Adjustments of Migrants from the Southern Appalachian Plateau," *Journal of Social Forces* 16 (December 1937): 238–46; Gary Fowler, "The Residential Distribution of Urban Appalachians," in William W. Philliber and Clyde B. McCoy, eds., *Invisible Minority: Urban Appalachians* (Lexington: University Press of Kentucky, 1981), pp. 81–94.

On housing segregation, see, for example, Arnold E. Hirsch, *Making the Second Ghetto: Race and Housing and Chicago, 1940–1960* (New York: Cambridge University Press, 1983); Dorothy Newman et al., *Protest, Politics, and Prosperity: Black Americans, White Institutions, 1940–1975* (New York: Pantheon, 1978).

lotte and Harold Gibson, who spent years in transit between their home in Logan, West Virginia, and Chicago's Uptown neighborhood, and were worn down by a series of round-trips to despair. An abusive man unable to hold a steady job, Harold would disappear for months at a time, leaving thirty-two-year-old Charlotte to rear their ten children in rat-infested apartments and to beg for help from disapproving landlords, truant officers, welfare bureaucrats, and private charity agencies. Much of the family's moving between West Virginia and Chicago reflected Charlotte's efforts to follow the whims of Harold's job quests. Bad luck seemed to dog his every step—a sudden layoff, a repossessed car. One promising stint as a coal miner in Logan came to an abrupt end soon after creditors started to garnishee his wages; he quit out of spite. The welfare officials who considered Charlotte Gibson's case saw only an irresponsible white woman unable to maintain steady contact with any agency or keep her children in school for any length of time. At least as long as the Gibson family resided in Uptown's slums, they were part of Chicago's white underclass. Though characterized by all those indexes of social pathology normally associated with blacks in big-city ghettos, poor whites in the North were more dispersed throughout metropolitan regions and so more difficult to count and study. Therefore, most experts on the underclass ignored them altogether.[38]

The case of Appalachian migrants reveals that, in Northern cities, plain white folk from the rural South were afforded advantages in jobs and housing not because of some putative superiority (to blacks) in formal education, in "factory sense," or in personal values, but because of the color of their skin. In southern Ohio, for example, when men and women from the hills and hollows of Kentucky received promotions that lifted them out of unskilled and into semiskilled work, and when they decided to move out of depressed port-of-entry communities and into stable working-class neighborhoods, they profited from the pervasive racial discrimination against Deep South black migrants. Thus the emergence of the black ghetto was not a foregone conclusion, or an unfortunate but inevitable result of migration and settlement patterns among the rural Southern poor; rather, the ghetto was a product of Jim Crow discrimination, Northern style, and Chicago offered only a variation of the forces that had beleaguered the freedpeople and their descendants in Mississippi.

By the late twentieth century, the political and economic forces that had dispossessed Southern black people of their homes and the living they wrung

---

[38] Todd Gitlin and Nanci Hollander, *Uptown: Poor Whites in Chicago* (New York: Harper and Row, 1970), pp. 239–54 (the quotation is on p. 253); Ronald Mincy, "Is There a White Underclass?" (Washington, D.C.: Urban Institute Discussion Paper, 1988); Erol R. Ricketts and Isabel V. Sawhill, "Defining and Measuring the Underclass," *Journal of Policy Analysis and Management* 7 (1988): 316–25. In her article "The Underclass: An Overview" (*Public Interest* 96 [Summer 1989]), Sawhill states, "Underclass neighborhoods are often thought of as 'inner-city areas,' or 'ghettos.' Our data indicate that they are, indeed, distinctly urban places; we find almost none in rural America" (p. 6).

from the soil, displaced them from the Southern countryside, and finally, rendered their labor superfluous within a postindustrial society, culminated in the distressed inner-city populations of the urban North. By this time the poorest black citizens lacked one of the most basic resources available to their parents and their grandparents—the hope for a better life elsewhere. And yet it would be misleading to interpret those forces of dispossession in exclusively racial terms. The United States consisted of a number of underclasses, marginalized groups that shared the same symptoms of poverty—high rates of unemployment, female-headed households, crime and substance abuse—but differed from one another in terms of culture, skin color, and regional identification. In the Midwest, the collapse of heavy industry in the 1970s left in its wake the seeming paradox of impoverished homeowners and car owners, men and women now forced to seek out menial service jobs that carried no benefits or union card. In the depressed coal regions of Appalachia, and in the backwoods of rural New England, rural folk pieced together a living by fishing and foraging, looking for odd jobs, and relying on the goodwill of more fortunate kin and neighbors. In the barrios of Los Angeles and in the decaying mill towns of Massachusetts, Hispanic youth became caught up in a violent street culture and suffered from higher school dropout rates than did black students throughout the nation. New immigrants from Southeast Asia, from the Carribbean and Latin America, desperately sought out work in the East Coast agricultural migratory labor stream and in fly-by-night sweatshops in El Paso and New York City.

Black people arrived in Northern ghettos via a path that was historically unique, a path that began in the slave South, a path pockmarked by racial prejudice and political oppression. And yet the problems that plagued their neighborhoods in the 1990s were not unique, but rather common to other poor groups scattered throughout the nation—lack of access to quality education, decent jobs, and affordable health care. America was a country not only of radical economic inequality among persons, but also of radically unequal places. Still, black ghettos seemed to attract more than their fair share of pity, or scorn, for reasons that reflected contemporary middle-class American values and priorities. More particularly, sensational stories about the underclass (a shorthand term for poor blacks in general, and a predatory youth culture in particular) brought to real life the mainstream vices of violence and mysogyny glorified by Hollywood, the popular media, and commercial advertisers. Moreover, this preoccupation with a drug and street culture seemed to confirm traditional American beliefs that poverty in the countryside was somehow cleaner, healthier, more wholesome, and less degrading than its inner-city counterpart.[39]

[39] But see, for example, United States Congress, Office of Technology Assessment, *Health Care in Rural America*, OTA–H–434 (Washington, D.C.: GPO, September 1990), and a summary of a study

In the 1860s, black people emerged from slavery, landless and confined within a plantation economy that barred them from meaningful lateral or upward mobility. In the twentieth century, black migrants arrived in the urban North, only to find themselves confined within ghettos. Throughout these transformations, from emancipation to the sharecropping plantation and then to industrial and postindustrial society, black Americans struggled to cope with the forces of dislocation, not by embracing a slavish dependence on whites, but by providing for themselves in ways that few whites could abide or even comprehend. Though the external configuration of her household failed to conform to certain middle-class notions of what that household should look like, Johnnie Belle Taylor worked to preserve the integrity of her family, and her own self-respect. And yet when present-day observers continue to scrutinize her struggles, and those of family members in Northern ghettos, through a lens of racial exclusivity, we relegate Taylor, and all African Americans, to the fringes of American social history, without appreciating the aspirations they shared with other American workers regardless of class, race, or region. Thus does a society conceived in slavery perpetuate itself; in its devotion to a politics based on race, late-twentieth-century America remains the postbellum South writ large.

---

by the Center on Budget and Policy Priorities, Washington, D.C., showing that the rural poor lack health insurance, medical coverage, and access to physicians in greater proportion than do urban residents ("Study Finds Medical Care Wanting in Rural U.S.," New York Times, March 13, 1991).

CHAPTER 2

Blacks in the Urban North: The "Underclass Question" in Historical Perspective

Joe William Trotter, Jr.

TWENTY-FIVE YEARS AGO, historian Gilbert Osofsky summarized an emerging consensus on black urban life. In his classic essay, "The Enduring Ghetto," he argued forcibly that "despite seeming transformations . . . the essential structure and nature" of black urban life had "remained remarkably durable since the demise of slavery in the North." Indeed, he concluded that there is "an unending and tragic sameness about black life in the metropolis" during the nineteenth and twentieth centuries. Over the past decade, however, a new generation of social historians advanced a different understanding of black urban history. Emphasizing shifting class and race relations, the new studies accent the African Americans' creative responses to poverty, the development of vibrant communities, and achievements despite adversity. While such studies corrected earlier emphases on the pathological and tragic dimensions of black life in cities, they have been less attentive to contemporary discussions of the "urban underclass."[1] In order to address this hiatus in our knowledge, this essay identifies key

In addition to Michael Katz and other contributors to this volume, I thank Lizabeth Cohen, Lori Cole, Matt Hawkins, Earl Lewis, John Modell, Joel Tarr, and my wife, H. LaRue Trotter, for their suggestions and comments.

[1] For insight into changing historical perspectives on black urban history, see Gilbert Osofsky, "The Enduring Ghetto," *Journal of American History* 55, no. 2 (September 1968): 243–55; Kenneth L. Kusmer, "The Black Urban Experience in American Perspective," in Darlene Clark Hine, ed., *The State of Afro-American History: Past, Present, and Future* (Baton Rouge: Louisiana State University Press, 1986); August Meier and Elliott Rudwick, *Black History and the Historical Profession, 1915–1980* (Urbana: University of Illinois Press, 1987); Joe W. Trotter, Jr., "Afro-American Urban History: A Critique of the Literature," in Joe W. Trotter, Jr., ed., *Black Milwaukee: The Making of an Industrial Proletariat, 1915–1945* (Urbana: University of Illinois Press, 1985); Joe William Trotter, Jr., *The Great Migration in Historical Perspective: New Dimensions of Race, Class, and Gender* (Bloomington: Indiana University Press, 1991). For the contemporary underclass question, see Elijah Anderson, *Streetwise: Race, Class, and Change in an Urban Community* (Chicago: University of Chicago Press, 1990); William J. Wilson, *The Truly Disadvantaged: The Inner City, the Underclass, and Public Policy* (Chicago: University of Chicago Press, 1987); Christopher Jencks and Paul E. Peterson, eds., *Urban Underclass* (Washington, D.C.: Brookings Institution, 1991); Paul A. Jargowsky and Mary Jo Bane, "Neighborhood Poverty: Basic Questions," in Michael T. McGeary and Laurence E. Lynn, Jr., eds., *Concentrated Urban Poverty in America* (Washington, D.C.: National Academy Press, forthcoming); Ronald B. Mincy, Isabel V. Sawhill, and Douglass A. Wolf, "The Underclass: Definition and Measurement," *Science* 248 (April 1990): 450–531; Martha A. Gephart and Robert W. Pearson, "Contempo-

historical assumptions in discussions of the urban underclass and evaluates them from the vantage point of recent scholarship on black urban history.

During the late 1960s and early 1970s, a variety of social scientists, policy experts, and journalists adopted the notion of *underclass* to describe and explain increases in urban poverty. According to these analysts, the urban underclass— defined as those families and individuals who existed outside the mainstream of the American occupational structure—was a new phenomenon. It signaled three overlapping transformations in black urban life.[2] First, although recognizing poverty as a recurring problem in black urban history, recent analysts emphasize a shift from relatively low levels of unemployment and social disorder before the 1960s to a new era of widespread joblessness, crime, and welfare dependency thereafter. Second, sociologists like Elijah Anderson and William J. Wilson argue that the black middle and working classes shared an increasingly segregated urban ghetto before the onset of the modern civil rights movement. Since the ghetto was the product of discrimination against all blacks, in their view it prevented the spatial isolation of the black poor.

By 1970, however, some middle- and working-class blacks gained access to multiracial institutions and moved into integrated neighborhoods. At the same time, the onslaught of deindustrialization undercut the position of black men in heavy industries, leaving behind a growing body of permanently unemployed black poor. As these processes escalated, black Americans gravitated toward single-class communities: the reversal of an earlier pattern. Accordingly, Anderson concludes his study of a Philadelphia neighborhood, "Black social life in . . . the 1940s and 1950s appears to have been highly cohesive compared with the present situation."[3]

Finally, recent studies suggest that middle- and working-class blacks not only shared the same space with the urban poor in the earlier period, they provided social stability and leadership. They spearheaded the development of a broad range of community institutions—churches, fraternal orders, and mutual benefit societies—to deal with inequality in the urban political economy. As members of these groups moved socially, economically, and geographically, however, they deprived the ghetto of its traditional leaders. Moreover, as Anderson states, "if those who are better off do remain . . . they tend to become disengaged,

---

rary Research on the Urban Underclass: A Selected Review of the Research That Underlies a New Council Program," *Items* 42, nos. 1 and 2 (June 1988): 1–10; Martha A. Gephart, "Neighborhoods and Communities in Concentrated Poverty," *Items* 43, no. 4 (December 1989): 84–92; Robert W. Pearson, "Economy, Culture, Public Policy, and the Urban Underclass," *Items* (June 1989): 23–29. See also Michael Katz's Introduction to this volume.

[2] Anderson, *Streetwise*, pp. 2–3, 56–76; Wilson, *Truly Disadvantaged*, pp. 3–19. Cf. Paul E. Peterson, "The Urban Underclass and the Poverty Paradox," and Christopher Jencks, "Is the American Underclass Growing?" both in Jencks and Peterson, *The Urban Underclass*.

[3] Anderson, *Streetwise*, p. 57.

thinking their efforts as instructive agents of social control futile and may in fact bring them trouble."[4]

To be sure, the magnitude, scope, and configuration of urban poverty changed over the past two decades.[5] Between 1965, the year of the controversial Moynihan Report, and 1980, out-of-wedlock black births increased from 25 to 57 percent; black female-headed families rose from 25 to 43 percent; and violent crimes and unemployment likewise increased.[6] Still, such urban problems were not entirely new. They characterized black life in the past. By linking the growth of the urban underclass to developments of the last two decades, social science and policy studies provide inadequate insights into the historical development of the black community, its changing class structure, and the roots of urban black poverty. A historical examination of these issues reveals more connections between the past and present than much of the current literature on the urban underclass suggests. Only by bringing systematic historical analyses to the contemporary underclass debate will we be able to fully understand the changing dimensions of urban poverty.

Focusing on black life in the urban North, this essay analyzes the interplay of class, race, and poverty in the industrial era. It links black urban life to changing patterns of racism, shifts in the larger political economy, and transformations in the class structure. More specifically, this chapter examines the spread of poverty under the impact of industrial capitalism; analyzes its uneven spatial distribution within the black community; and assesses the range of African-American responses to poverty, class, and racial inequality.[7]

[4] Ibid.

[5] Wilson, *Truly Disadvantaged*, p. 3.

[6] Ibid., p. 21.

[7] In the development of this approach, I am building upon a variety of historical studies of urban blacks, especially recent studies emphasizing the role of African Americans in shaping their own lives as migrants, members of the working class, and participants in a larger African-American community. See James R. Grossman, *Land of Hope: Chicago, Black Southerners and the Great Migration* (Chicago: University of Chicago Press, 1989); Peter Gottlieb, *Making Their Own Way: Southern Blacks' Migration to Pittsburgh, 1916–1930* (Urbana: University of Illinois Press, 1987); Dennis C. Dickerson, *Out of the Crucible: Black Steelworkers in Western Pennsylvania, 1875–1980* (Albany: State University of New York Press, 1986); Trotter, *Black Milwaukee*; Earl Lewis, *In Their Own Interests: Blacks in Twentieth-Century Norfolk* (Berkeley: University of California Press, 1990); Joe William Trotter, Jr., *Coal, Class, and Color: Blacks in Southern West Virginia, 1915–1932* (Urbana: University of Illinois Press, 1990). Also see Trotter, *The Great Migration in Historical Perspective*. For earlier ghetto formation studies, see Kenneth B. Clark, *Dark Ghetto: Dilemmas of Social Power* (New York: Harper and Row, 1967), p. xxii; Gilbert Osofsky, *Harlem: The Making of a Ghetto. Negro New York, 1890–1930* (1963; reprint, New York: Harper and Row, 1971), p. 201; Allan H. Spear, *Black Chicago: The Making of a Negro Ghetto, 1890–1920* (Chicago: University of Chicago Press, 1967); David M. Katzman, *Before the Ghetto: Black Detroit in the Nineteenth Century* (Urbana: University of Illinois Press, 1973); Kenneth L. Kusmer, *A Ghetto Takes Shape: Black Cleveland, 1870–1930* (Urbana: University of Illinois Press, 1976); Lee Rainwater and William L. Yancey, eds., *The Moynihan Report and the Politics of*

THE INDUSTRIAL ERA: RECONSTRUCTION TO WORLD WAR I

During the late nineteenth and early twentieth centuries, the onslaught of industrial capitalism changed African-American life. Under the impact of World War I, these changes gained full fruition. Black workers gradually moved out of domestic, personal-service, and common labor sectors into a variety of new skilled, semiskilled, and common laboring jobs in manufacturing, transportation, and trade. Despite its precarious economic foundation, the expansion of a black proletariat helped to stimulate the rise of a new black middle class, transform the spatial structure of the black community, and reshape the black experience with poverty. In the same years, racial segregation and concentrated poverty also increased, for residential segregation along racial lines coincided with internal segregation along class lines. Still, poor blacks managed to reveal something about volition and agency as they faced the debilitating impact of poverty on their lives.

The U.S. economy rapidly industrialized following the Civil War and Reconstruction. Between 1860 and 1920, the nation's urban population rose from 6.2 million to 54.0 million, an increase from about 20 percent of the total U.S. population to over 50 percent. At the same time, the manufacturing, construction, and mining industries supplanted agriculture as the dominant employers. Under the impact of industrialization, urbanization, and the fall of Reconstruction in the South, black migration to Northern cities gradually increased.

As the new system of Jim Crow, disfranchisement, and racial violence escalated during the late nineteenth century, Southern blacks abandoned the South for Northern cities in growing numbers. Between the Civil War and World War I,

---

Controversy (Cambridge: Cambridge University Press, 1967). Recent studies employing the ghetto approach include Darrel E. Bigham, We Ask Only a Fair Trial: A History of the Black Community of Evansville, Indiana (Bloomington: Indiana University Press, 1987); and Arnold R. Hirsch, Making the Second Ghetto: Race and Housing in Chicago, 1940–1960 (Cambridge: Cambridge University Press, 1983). For a critique of the earlier ghetto literature, including acknowledgment of important differences within it, see Trotter, "Afro-American Urban History: A Critique of the Literature," pp. 264–82; James Borchert, Alley Life in Washington: Family, Community, Religion, and Folklife in the City, 1850–1970 (Urbana: University of Illinois Press, 1980), p. xii. Borchert built upon Herbert Gutman's groundbreaking study, The Black Family in Slavery and Freedom, 1750–1925 (New York: Pantheon Books, 1976), esp. pp. 432–60; and Lawrence Levine, Black Culture and Black Consciousness: Afro-American Folk Thought from Slavery to Freedom (New York: Oxford University Press, 1977), which emphasized the cultural cohesiveness of life among slaves and postemancipation black urbanites in the North and South. Cf. Douglass H. Daniels, Pioneer Urbanites: A Social and Cultural History of Black San Francisco (Philadelphia: Temple University Press, 1980); Thomas C. Cox, Blacks in Topeka, Kansas, 1865–1915: A Social History (Baton Rouge: Louisiana State University Press, 1982); James Oliver and Louis E. Horton, Black Bostonians: Family Life and Community Struggle in the Antebellum North (New York: Holmes and Meier, 1979). Scholars who emphasized the vitality of blacks in shaping their own experience built upon the research of a number of pioneering black historians and their small coterie of white allies. See August Meier and Elliott Rudwick, Black History and the Historical Profession, 1915–1980 (Urbana: University of Illinois Press, 1986).

an estimated 400,000 blacks left the South. As historian Jacqueline Jones states in the preceding essay in this volume, the outmigration of Southern blacks highlighted the struggle between "labor-hungry" rural employers on the one hand, and black resistance to exploitative conditions on the other. The percentage of blacks living in the North and West increased from 7.8 percent in 1860 to about 11 percent in 1910. A few industrial cities like Philadelphia, Chicago, Pittsburgh, and New York absorbed the bulk of these newcomers, who came mainly from the upper South and border states of Tennessee, Kentucky, Missouri, and Virginia. Black women dominated the migration flow to the older Northeastern seaport cities of Philadelphia, Boston, and New York. Booming domestic and personal-service sectors in these cities offered relatively greater job opportunities for black women, whereas young men dominated the migration stream to the newly expanding industrial cities of the Great Lakes. In 1910, for example, there were some 85–87 men to every 100 black women in New York and Philadelphia, compared to 105–8 men to every 100 women in Chicago, Detroit, Pittsburgh, and Cleveland.[8]

Although by World War I industrial opportunities for black men had slowly expanded, they did not offset the continuing disappearance of black artisans. On the eve of the Civil War, black men had gained a modest foothold in artisan

---

[8] David M. Gordon, Richard Edwards, and Michael Reich, *Segmented Work, Divided Workers: The Historical Transformation of Labor in the United States* (Cambridge: Cambridge University Press, 1982), pp. 80, 88–89; Zane L. Miller, *The Urbanization of Modern America: A Brief History,* rev. ed. (Chapel Hill: University of North Carolina Press, 1987), p. 17; Diane Klebanow, Franklin L. Jonas, and Ira M. Leonard, *Urban Legacy: The Story of America's Cities* (New York: Mentor, 1977), p. 137; Armstead L. Robinson, "The Difference Freedom Made: The Emancipation of Afro-Americans," in Darlene Clark Hine, ed., *The State of Afro-American History: Past, Present, and Future* (Baton Rouge: Louisiana State University Press, 1986), pp. 51–74; Daniel M. Johnson and Rex R. Campbell, *Black Migration in America* (Durham, N.C.: Duke University Press, 1981), p. 71, chap. 5; Carole Marks, *Farewell—We're Good and Gone: The Great Migration* (Bloomington: Indiana University Press, 1989), pp. 2, 66–71; William J. Wilson, *The Declining Significance of Race: Blacks and Changing American Institutions* (Chicago: University of Chicago Press, 1978), pp. 66–71; Roger Lane, *Roots of Violence in Black Philadelphia, 1860–1900* (Cambridge: Harvard University Press, 1986), p. 7; Theodore Hershberg et al., "A Tale of Three Cities: Blacks, Immigrants and Opportunity in Philadelphia, 1850–1880, 1930, 1970," in Hershberg, ed., *Philadelphia: Work, Space, Family, and Group Experience in the Nineteenth Century. Essays toward an Interdisciplinary History of the City* (Oxford: Oxford University Press, 1981), p. 465; Du Bois, *The Philadelphia Negro: A Social History* (1899; reprint, New York: Schocken Books, 1967), p. 147; Spear, *Black Chicago,* pp. 12, 30–33; Dickerson, *Out of the Crucible,* pp. 7, 25; Kusmer, *A Ghetto Takes Shape,* pp. 35–52, 67–75; Gottlieb, *Making Their Own Way,* p. 91; David M. Katzman, *Seven Days a Week: Women and Domestic Service in Industrializing America* (Urbana: University of Illinois Press, 1978). In Chicago, the number of black men in manufacturing increased from 1,079, or 8.3 percent of the male Afro-American labor force, in 1900 to 3,073 or 16.6 percent of the black male labor force, in 1910. In Pittsburgh and Cleveland, a similar pattern developed, while black access to industrial jobs was less pronounced in Philadelphia, Boston, and New York, as Afro-Americans gained greater employment in transportation, trade, and domestic service in those cities than elsewhere in the urban North. Also see, above, Jacqueline Jones, "Southern Diaspora: Origins of the Northern 'Underclass.'"

jobs. Shoemakers, carpenters, tailors, barbers, painters, and ironworkers provided skilled services and crafted articles to the slowly expanding black population. Following the Civil War and Reconstruction, the artisanal class declined as
a whole, but the numbers of black artisans declined faster than those of whites.
In 1860, the U.S. census showed that over 15 percent of black males in Philadelphia worked in skilled trades. By 1890, the percentage had declined to 1.1
percent. Black barbers suffered the greatest decline. In Boston, blacks dropped
from 17 percent of all barbers in 1870 to only 5 percent in 1900. A similar
pattern characterized Cleveland, Detroit, and Philadelphia. As skilled blacks
literally died out, young men found little incentive to enter the trades. On the
contrary, as W. E. B. Du Bois noted in his classic study, *The Philadelphia Negro*,
whites took steps to bar African Americans from training as craftsmen.[9]

Throughout the pre–World War I years, most blacks gained employment as
common laborers and as domestic and personal servants. In 1900, the percentage of black men in these positions exceeded 64 percent in Chicago; nearly 58
percent in New York; 68 percent in Detroit; and 60 percent in Cleveland. Black
men worked mainly on jobs that fluctuated with the seasons, particularly as
casual laborers on the various building and construction projects, which expanded the city's physical infrastructure. Contractors employed Afro-
Americans because they believed the racial stereotype that "their superior ability
to endure heat" qualified them over (less well adapted) white workers. Thus,
wherever the work was heavy, hot, dirty, and low paying, black men could
usually be found.[10]

Black women worked almost exclusively in domestic and personal-service
occupations. Despite the relative stability of domestic jobs, they paid low wages,
required long hours, and provided little independence in work routines. Frequently on call around the clock, domestics confronted the arbitrary power of
individual employers. In New York, for example, when an employer discovered
that his servant read T. Thomas Fortune's *Freeman*, he reprimanded her: "It's an
impudent paper . . . full of slanderous publications. The whites are the freedmen's best friend, and if you want to be popular with the white employer stop
reading the paper." Moreover, promotions or advancements were impossible
except in some hotels. In prestigious hotels, however, blacks faced growing
displacement by a new wave of European immigrants.[11]

[9] Leonard P. Curry, *The Free Black in Urban America, 1800–1850* (Chicago: University of Chicago
Press, 1981), pp. 38–39, 267; Gary B. Nash, *Forging Freedom: The Formation of Philadelphia's Black
Community, 1720–1840* (Cambridge: Cambridge University Press, 1988), pp. 148, 248; Elizabeth
Pleck, *Black Migration and Poverty: Boston, 1865–1900* (New York: Academic Press, 1979), pp. 144–
47; Lane, *Roots of Violence in Black Philadelphia*, p. 37; Kusmer, *A Ghetto Takes Shape*, pp. 70–73; Du
Bois, *The Philadelphia Negro*, p. 128.

[10] Census Bureau, *Twelfth Census of U.S.: 1900, Special Reports, Occupations* (Washington, D.C.:
Government Printing Office), pp. 480–763; Trotter, *Black Milwaukee*, pp. 1–12; Pleck, *Black Migration and Poverty*, pp. 122–51; Kusmer, *A Ghetto Takes Shape*, pp. 66–74; Spear, *Black Chicago*, pp.
29–35; Du Bois, *The Philadelphia Negro*, pp. 97–146.

[11] Katzman, *Before the Ghetto*, pp. 109–10; Katzman, *Seven Days a Week*, pp. 27, 28, 204–22;

Closely intertwined with the precarious position of black workers and their families in the urban economy were the disproportionate bouts with poverty, both short and long term. In Philadelphia during the late nineteenth century, Du Bois estimated, about 9 percent of black families were very poor and another 10 percent were simply poor, earning less than five dollars income per week. "They live in one- and two-room tenements, scantily furnished and poorly lighted and heated; they get casual labor and women do washing. The children go to school irregularly or loaf on the streets." About 4 percent of the city's population in the 1890s, blacks comprised between 8 and 12 percent of those arrested for vagrancy and about 8 percent of the city's poverty statistics, including care at the city's almshouses, assistance from the county poor board, and aid for orphans. Blacks also made up 22.4 percent of all new convicts for 1890–95; 20–22 percent of children committed to the House of Refuge (a juvenile reformatory for youth under sixteen years of age) between 1860 and 1890; and a disproportionate percentage of convictions for homicide. A similar pattern developed elsewhere.[12] Although the size of the black population and the magnitude of poverty was much less than it would later become, such evidence nonetheless highlights the existence of poverty in the early development of Northern black communities. Moreover, African-American poverty unfolded within the framework of residential segregation.

It was during this period that nearly all-black residential areas emerged in major cities. Although it remained low by later standards, by as early as 1820 to 1850 the index of dissimilarity (a rough measure of segregation based on ward-level data) increased, respectively, by 29 percent, 36 percent, and 131 percent in Boston, Philadelphia, and New York. Blacks concentrated in Boston's Sixth Ward, Philadelphia's Spruce and Market wards, and New York's Fifth and Eighth wards. In New York, blacks lived in the Five Points district, the original settlement of freed slaves, referred to by contemporaries as "Stagg Town," "Negro Plantation," and, later, "Little Africa."[13]

Trotter, *Black Milwaukee*, pp. 12–13; Kusmer, *A Ghetto Takes Shape*, p. 75; Du Bois, *The Philadelphia Negro*, pp. 138–39.

[12] Du Bois, *The Philadelphia Negro*, pp. 235, 242–59, 172, 242–59, 270–75; Lane, *Roots of Violence in Black Philadelphia*, pp. 96–97, 149, 157, 166–67. Cf. Osofsky, *Harlem*, pp. 8–10; Spear, *Black Chicago*, pp. 24–26; Pleck, *Black Migration and Poverty*, pp. 36–38, 164–65; Kusmer, *A Ghetto Takes Shape*, pp. 48–50; Paul Lammermeier, "The Urban Black Family of the Nineteenth Century: A Study of Black Family Structure in the Ohio Valley, 1850–1880," *Journal of Marriage and the Family* 35, no. 3 (August 1973): 440–56; Frank Furstenberg, Jr., and John Modell, "The Origins of the Female-Headed Family: The Impact of the Urban Experience," *Journal of Interdisciplinary History* 6, no. 2 (1975): 211–13; E. Franklin Frazier, *The Negro Family in the United States* (1939; reprint, Chicago: University of Chicago Press, 1969), pp. 245–46.

[13] Curry, *The Free Black in Urban America*, chaps. 7, 8, and 9; Leon Litwack, *North of Slavery: The Negro in the Free States, 1790–1860* (Chicago: University of Chicago Press, 1961), pp. 168–70; Horton and Horton, *Black Bostonians*, pp. 2–6, 67–80; Nash, *Forging Freedom*, pp. 214, 248; Du Bois, *The Philadelphia Negro*, p. 270, Osofsky, *Harlem*, pp. 9–10.

By the turn of the twentieth century, blacks in New York City moved away from their historic concentration in Five Points. They moved to areas called the Tenderloin and San Juan Hill, both "folk designations," the latter so called because blacks and whites frequently clashed over neighborhood boundaries in the wake of the Spanish-American War. Although blacks lived near first- and second-generation Irish and German immigrants, they clustered within the area. By 1914, the New York Urban League estimated Harlem's population at nearly 50,000, but blacks lived in some 1,100 different houses within a twenty-three-block area of the city. By World War I, Harlem housed the single largest concentration of blacks "in similar limits in the world." The black ghetto was not only an area of dilapidated housing, poor health care, vice, and crime. It was also an area with real estate owned by exploitative white landlords and realtors, who used restrictive covenants and other devices to confine blacks to a circumscribed area of the city.[14]

Chicago also experienced the rise of a nearly all-black ghetto on its South Side. From the late antebellum period, most blacks had lived on the city's South Side. Yet until the turn of the century, they remained widely dispersed in small clusters, or "enclaves" (as historian Allan Spear called them). By 1910, however, the outlines of the ghetto had clearly emerged not only on the South Side, but also increasingly on the city's West Side. By 1910, over 30 percent of Afro-Americans lived in predominantly black areas, and over 60 percent lived in areas that were 20 percent black. Nonetheless, until World War I, no more than a dozen blocks in Chicago were exclusively black. As late as 1910, blacks remained less segregated from American-born whites than did Italian immigrants. In cities like Cleveland, Milwaukee, Detroit, Los Angeles, and San Francisco, where the black population remained small, segregation was even less pronounced than in Chicago, New York, and Boston.[15] Even so, in the major cities of industrial America, the interrelationship of ghettoization and poverty slowly took shape.

Although racism and ghetto formation played a powerful role in shaping the black experience during the industrial era, they remained closely intertwined with class. Blacks continued to share experiences with white workers as part of a larger multiethnic industrial proletariat. From the Civil War through the early twentieth century, black life followed closely the same rhythm as white through the swings of the urban economy. Yet African Americans suffered more than their white counterparts did during periodic downswings. The depression of

---

[14] Kusmer, *A Ghetto Takes Shape*, pp. 35–52; Osofsky, *Harlem*, pp. ix, 12, 92–93, 122–23; Charles S. Johnson (for Chicago Commission on Race Relations), *The Negro in Chicago: A Study of Race Relations and a Race Riot in 1919* (1922; reprint, New York: Arno Press, 1968), pp. 215–30; Samuel H. Preston and Michael R. Haines, *Fatal Years: Child Mortality in Late Nineteenth-Century America* (Princeton: Princeton University Press, 1991), pp. 81–85, 94–97.

[15] Spear, *Black Chicago*, pp. 11–22; Hirsch, *Making the Second Ghetto*, p. 3. Cf. Kusmer, *A Ghetto Takes Shape*, pp. 33–52; Katzman, *Before the Ghetto*, p. 69; Trotter, *Black Milwaukee*, p. 23.

1873, which began with the failure of the banking house of Jay Cook and Company, soon spread through the entire economy and lasted through the decade. By 1877, the unemployment rate rose to an estimated one-fifth of the nation's work force. Businesses failed and wages plummeted in building and construction, textile, railway, and other industries. During the 1890s, businesses again failed. Industrialists discharged thousands of workers and reduced the wages of those who remained. During economic hard times, however, employers not only let blacks go first, they frequently exploited their vulnerability by using them as strikebreakers. In the Pittsburgh district, industrialists employed blacks as strikebreakers in 1875, 1888, 1892, and 1909.[16] In the Chicago stockyards strike of 1904 and again in the teamsters strike of 1905, employers used nonunion black workers as strikebreakers. A mob of about 2,000–5,000 whites stoned about 200 black workers who entered one plant under "police protection." White workers referred to blacks in derogatory terms as a "scab race," and as "big, ignorant, vicious Negroes, picked up from the criminal elements of the black belts of the country." Moreover, unlike Poles, who had also entered the stockyards as strikebreakers in the late 1880s and remained thereafter, most black workers were discharged following the strike. An estimated 2,000 blacks entered the plant as strikebreakers, but only 365 remained by 1910.[17]

Responses to Race, Class, and Poverty, 1880s–World War I

As black migration to Northern cities escalated during the late nineteenth and early twentieth centuries, racism intensified and helped to undermine an old elite who served a largely white clientele. At the same time, a new black middle class—catering to the needs of the expanding black population—gradually emerged. While Southern blacks faced lynchings, disfranchisement, and legal segregation, Northern blacks faced increasing restrictions on their access to a variety of public accommodations (theaters, hotels, and restaurants), housing, financial institutions, and organs of public opinion. The Northern white press increasingly joined the white South in adopting a racist ideology and portraying African Americans in stereotypical terms and as inferior to whites.[18]

[16] Gordon, Edwards, and Reich, *Segmented Work, Divided Workers*, pp. 100–164; Rayback, *A History of American Labor* (1955; reprint, rev. and exp., New York: Free Press, 1966), pp. 129, 200–201; David Montgomery, *The Fall of the House of Labor: The Workplace, the State, and American Labor Activism, 1865–1925* (Cambridge: Cambridge University Press, 1987), p. 4; Dickerson, *Out of the Crucible*, pp. 2, 8–9, 85–100; Wilson, *The Declining Significance of Race*, p. 72; Trotter, *Black Milwaukee*, pp. 13–14.

[17] Spear, *Black Chicago*, pp. 37–38; Grossman, *Land of Hope*, pp. 208–45.

[18] Bart Landry, *The New Black Middle Class* (Berkeley: University of California Press, 1987); August Meier, *Negro Thought in America, 1880–1915* (Ann Arbor: University of Michigan Press, 1963); Joel Williamson, *The Crucible of Race: Black-White Relations in the American South Since Emancipation* (New York: Oxford University Press, 1984); John W. Cell, *The Highest Stage of White*

As racism gained increasing sway over the Northern political economy, the old black elite slowly gave way to the new black middle class. By 1900, black businesses—catering firms, barbershops, cleaning and repair services, and others—serving a white market had declined, while similar businesses serving an all-black clientele proliferated. By World War I, for example, the Overton Hygienic Manufacturing Company, manufacturer of "High Brown Face Powder," was the most successful black business in Chicago. Capitalized at $268,000, the Overton Company employed thirty-two people and manufactured sixty-two different products mainly serving the cosmetic needs of black people. The black millionaire Madame C. J. Walker had developed the first successful hair-straightening process in 1905, and by World War I, her factory in Indianapolis and her luxurious home in Harlem symbolized the arrival of the new black middle class in industrial America. The expansion of local chapters of the National Negro Business League, formed by Booker T. Washington in 1900, reinforced the trend toward black business as an alternative to racial restrictions in the capital and labor markets.[19]

Closely aligned with the growth of black businesses was the expansion of black churches, fraternal orders, mutual benefit societies, and social clubs. These institutions had deep roots in late eighteenth- and early nineteenth-century Northern black urban life. In the 1790s, blacks launched the African Methodist Episcopal Church in Philadelphia, followed closely by the African Methodist Episcopal Zion Church in New York, and the Baptist Church in both cities. Independent African-American Baptist and Methodist churches soon spread to Boston, Pittsburgh, and other Northern cities. By 1820, the African Methodist Episcopal Church elected a bishop and launched a major program of expansion. By then, in Philadelphia alone, some four thousand blacks claimed membership in the black churches.[20] In 1792, Boston blacks initiated the Masonic movement among African Americans. Five years later, when Philadelphia blacks established a Masonic order, the movement escalated. At the same time, in Philadelphia, the number of black mutual aid societies increased

Supremacy: The Origins of Segregation in South Africa and the American South (Cambridge: Cambridge University Press, 1982); George M. Frederickson, *White Supremacy: A Comparative Study in American and South African History* (New York: Oxford University Press, 1981); Rayford W. Logan, *The Betrayal of the Negro: From Rutherford B. Hayes to Woodrow Wilson* (New York: Collier Books, 1965), especially "National Issues in the Northern Press," chaps. 10 and 11.

[19] Spear, *Black Chicago*, pp. 111–15; Louis R. Harlan, *Booker T. Washington: The Making of a Black Leader, 1856–1901* (New York: Oxford University Press, 1972), pp. 266–71; Meier, *Negro Thought in America*, pp. 124–25; Osofsky, *Harlem*, pp. 92–123; Katzman, *Before the Ghetto*, pp. 135–206; Trotter, *Black Milwaukee*, pp. 19–33; Spear, *Black Chicago*, pp. 51–126; Du Bois, *The Philadelphia Negro*, pp. 197–234; Kusmer, *A Ghetto Takes Shape*, pp. 113–54.

[20] John Hope Franklin and Alfred A. Moss, Jr., *From Slavery to Freedom: A History of Negro Americans*, 6th ed. (1947; reprint, New York: Alfred A. Knopf, 1988), pp. 93–95; Nash, *Forging Freedom*, chaps. 6 and 8.

from eleven in 1813, to forty-four in 1831, and to nearly one hundred in 1837; they operated in virtually every neighborhood in the city, enrolled about 80 percent of all adult blacks, annually collected nearly eighteen thousand dollars in dues, and distributed about fourteen thousand dollars in benefits. "Far from living off the tax dollars of their white neighbors," historian Gary Nash concludes, "black Philadelphians appear to have been among the most provident and self-reliant of city dwellers." Moreover, according to Nash, such societies in effect operated "as a privately supported substitute for the public poor relief system."[21]

African Americans built upon these early nineteenth-century traditions and continued to fashion their own responses to poverty. In 1886, they formed the National Baptist Convention and spearheaded the formation of new churches. Black churches instituted a variety of social-welfare programs and stimulated the emergence of others.[22] They not only established unemployment bureaus and aid for orphans, widows, and the disabled, they facilitated the expansion of fraternal orders like the Masons, Odd Fellows, and Independent Order of Saint Luke, each with its own mutual aid and benefit programs. Formed in 1895, the National Association of Colored Women reinforced the social-welfare activities of black churches, fraternal orders, and mutual benefit societies. By 1913, Chicago reported forty-one clubs with a total of twelve hundred members. Organizing under its credo, "lifting as we climb," black women's clubs emphasized "service" to the community. They organized, administered, and supported homes for the aged, young women, and children; formed juvenile court visiting committees to assist dependent and neglected children; spearheaded and supported black churches in raising relief funds and feeding the unemployed; and helped the black poor secure aid from established white social-welfare agencies. Closely intertwined with their work with white organizations, public and private, black clubwomen also supported the formation of local branches of the National Urban League. Formed in 1911, the Urban League would become the premiere social service agency among blacks in the urban North.[23]

Poverty was not perceived as an issue for social-welfare, religious, and fraternal organizations alone. Black institutions linked black workers and the urban poor to the larger civil rights and political campaigns of the period. As early as 1884, the *A.M.E. Church Review*, the official organ of the African Methodist Episcopal Church, held a symposium to discuss the consequences of the Demo-

---

[21] Franklin and Moss, *From Slavery to Freedom*, pp. 93–95; Nash, *Forging Freedom*, chaps. 6 and 8, esp. pp. 272–73.

[22] C. Eric Lincoln and Lawrence H. Mamiya, *The Black Church in the African American Experience* (Durham, N.C.: Duke University Press, 1990); Franklin and Moss, *From Slavery to Freedom*, pp. 258–64, 286–90; Spear, *Black Chicago*, pp. 91–97; Philip Jackson, "Black Charity in Progressive Era Chicago," *Social Service Review* 9 (September 1978); Nancy Weiss, *The National Urban League, 1910–1940* (New York: Oxford University Press, 1974).

[23] Jackson, "Black Charity in Progressive Era Chicago"; Weiss, *The National Urban League*.

cratic victory in the election of 1884. The *Review* later opposed Jim Crow in the South and de facto discrimination in the North when it endorsed T. Thomas Fortune's Afro-American League. Formed in 1890, the Afro-American League soon spread to over forty cities, the majority in the Northeast and Midwest (Chicago, Boston, and New York). Fortune urged blacks to fight for equal rights: "It is a narrow and perverted philosophy which condemns as a nuisance agitators," he said. "Fight fire with fire. . . . Face the enemy and fight inch by inch for every right he denies us." Although the Afro-American League soon declined as a political force, it helped to link black workers and the poor to the broader civil rights struggle (until the formation of the Afro-American Council in 1898, and the NAACP in 1909).[24]

The proliferation of black institutions supports recent emphases on the development of multiclass black urban communities during the early twentieth century. As suggested above, racial solidarity among black workers and black elites underlay the growth of black institutions. Yet the bond that developed between blacks was often precarious. The rise of the new black middle class precipitated intraracial ideological conflicts within the black community. Based on service to a white clientele and political alliances with the Republican party, the old elite advocated vigorous protests against de jure and de facto racial segregation. In most Northern states, by the 1890s, their efforts led to civil rights legislation, which made it illegal to deny blacks access to a broad range of public accommodations. Conversely, as Northern whites turned toward de facto forms of racial segregation and exclusion, the new black elite advocated the development of all-black urban institutions. The new elites doubted the effectiveness of civil rights legislation. They were more impressed by the ability of whites to prevent their access to established institutions than they were by the promise of equal rights before the law. Thus they intensified their campaign for the development of a variety of African-American institutions.

Different ideological orientations—articulated respectively by W. E. B. Du Bois and Booker T. Washington at the national level—divided blacks at the local level and often hampered their efforts to fight racial discrimination. In 1889, for example, the old elite organized a protest meeting at Olivet Baptist Church in Chicago and defeated a proposal to build a black YMCA. The black weekly *Appeal* stood "unalterably opposed to any scheme that draws about it the color line." Moreover, the editor said, "there is on Madison Street one of the finest Young Men's Christian Association organizations in the country to which all young men are cordially invited regardless of race or color." Only in 1913 did the new black elite gain sufficient support to open the all-black Wabash Avenue YMCA. The new YMCA opened as "the largest and finest Association building for colored men in the United States."[25]

[24] Meier, *Negro Thought in America*, pp. 35–56, 70, 128, 129.
[25] Spear, *Black Chicago*, pp. 52, 100; Trotter, *Black Milwaukee*, pp. 29–33; Kusmer, *A Ghetto Takes Shape*, chap. 6.

Also significant was the emerging conflict between black workers and black elites, old and new. Black elites criticized the culture of the newcomers and sought to reshape their behavior. In New York City, they frequently referred to the migrants as a "hoodlum element," "rovers," "wanderers," "vagrants," and "criminals in search of the sporting life." In 1905, an editorial in the local black weekly, the *New York Age*, exclaimed, "Many of the worthless people of the race are making their way northward." In Milwaukee, one black newspaper editor delivered a scathing denunciation of black newcomers. Calling them "a floating, shiftless, and depraved element," the editor concluded on an antimigration note: "We do not . . . decry the Northern migration . . . but we would impress upon our Southern brethren and sisters to locate in the smaller towns and villages."[26]

Ordinary black workers responded to exploitation and racial discrimination in a variety of ways. While they joined black elites, their responses also recognized limitations of cross-class alliances. Throughout the period, for instance, black workers expressed their dissatisfaction by moving from job to job, in search of employers who would recognize their humanity as blacks and as workers. A Philadelphia domestic explained, "Yes, they [particularly black elites] say long service is good service but sometimes you can't *stay* at places; some of the [white] ladies and gentlemen's not very *pleasant.*" Other blacks joined white unions when they could, but most built separate all-black locals. In 1897, for example, some Milwaukee bootblacks organized a Shoe Artists Association. They protested the practices of some stores giving free shines to customers who purchased shoes from their establishments. Bootblacks, they said, had to "live as well as the shoe dealers." In addition to separate skilled unions of carpenters, barbers, and masons, black workers established semiskilled and common labor unions, including teamsters, longshoremen, and hotel, restaurant, and bar employees.

The black poor made numerous individual and collective adjustments to poverty on their own. Some sold their furniture, including beds, in order to pay medical expenses. Others accepted charity but later paid it back; and many sick, injured, or disabled workers received aid from fellow workers. These strategies overlapped with the poor of other ethnic and racial groups, but racial discrimination from without, and, to some extent, class discrimination from within, compounded the problems of the black poor, making their responses somewhat more intricate and complex than those of other groups.[27] Indeed,

[26] Osofsky, *Harlem*, p. 21; Trotter, *Black Milwaukee*, pp. 30–31.

[27] Pleck, *Black Migration and Poverty*, p. 134 (quote from Du Bois, *The Philadelphia Negro*); Trotter, *Black Milwaukee*, p. 18; John D. Finney, Jr., "A Study of Negro Labor during and after World War I" (Ph.D. diss., Georgetown University, 1967), p. 45; Katzman, *Before the Ghetto*, pp. 124–26; Du Bois, *The Philadelphia Negro*, p. 276. Cf. Olivier Zunz, *The Changing Face of Inequality: Urbanization, Industrial Development, and Immigrants in Detroit, 1880–1920* (Chicago: University of Chicago Press, 1982), pp. 259–79; Michael B. Katz, *Poverty and Policy in American History* (New York:

such evidence from the early industrial period suggests that the development of black urban communities, and the lives of the poor within them, was marked by a myriad of tensions and conflicts as well as cooperation. Under the impact of World War I, these processes would gain even greater expression.

EMERGENCE OF THE BLACK INDUSTRIAL WORKING CLASS, 1915–1945: POVERTY AND PROGRESS

The black migration of the pre–World War I era turned into a floodtide during the Great Migration. Under the impact of World War I, thousands of Southern blacks turned toward Northern cities. For the first time, black men moved into a variety of jobs in the industrial sector, giving rise to a new industrial proletariat. Conditions would improve during World War I and the 1920s, but black workers would continue to face disproportionate bouts with poverty—poverty not only concentrated within the black community as the ghetto expanded, but within certain neighborhoods. Still, black workers and the black poor developed a variety of responses to poverty, class, and racial exploitation.

Under the impact of World War I, an estimated 700,000 to 1 million blacks left the South. During the 1920s, another 800,000 to 1 million left. Whereas the prewar migrants mainly moved to a few major industrial cities (Chicago, Philadelphia, and New York), blacks now moved throughout the urban North and West. Beginning with relatively small numbers on the eve of World War I, the black urban population in the Midwest and Great Lakes region increased even more dramatically than that of the old Northeast. Detroit's black population increased by 611 percent during the war years, and by nearly 200 percent during the 1920s, rising from fewer than 6,000 to over 120,000. Cleveland's black population rose from fewer than 8,500 to nearly 72,000. In the urban West, the black population rose most dramatically in Los Angeles, increasing from 7,600 in 1910 to nearly 40,000 in 1930. Nonetheless, as in the prewar era, New York City, Chicago, and Philadelphia continued to absorb disproportionately large numbers of black newcomers. Between 1910 and 1930, Chicago's black population increased more than fivefold from 44,000 to 234,000; New York City's trebled from about 100,000 to 328,000; and Philadelphia's grew from 84,500 to an estimated 220,600.

Although upper South and border states remained important sources of black migrants during World War I and the 1920s, Deep South states increased their importance. For the first time, blacks born in the states of Mississippi, Alabama, Georgia, South Carolina, and Louisiana dominated the migration stream to Illinois and Chicago, for example (making up over 60 percent of the black

---

Academic Books, 1983), especially chap. 1; and Ewa Morawska, *For Bread with Butter: Life-Worlds of East Central Europeans in Johnstown, Pennsylvania, 1890–1940* (Cambridge: Cambridge University Press, 1985), chap. 3.

population increase between 1910 and 1920). In New York City, upper South origins remained stronger than in Chicago, but blacks from South Carolina, Georgia, and Florida came in growing numbers. Sex ratios varied with migration streams. In the relatively new but rapidly industrializing cities of Cleveland and Detroit, the percentage of black men to women escalated to between 120 and 140 men to every 100 women. In cities like Milwaukee, where the ratio of men to women was 95 men to every 100 women in 1910, the ratio reversed itself, as the number of men to women increased to 123 to 100 in 1920. Finally, in the old Northeastern cities of New York and Philadelphia, the ratio evened out to near parity as the number of men increased.[28]

A variety of forces stimulated black population movement. These included the push of sharecropping, disfranchisement, and racial violence in the South. They also included the pull of opportunities in the North: the labor demands of Northern industries, immigration restriction legislation, and greater access to the rights of citizens. In the North, blacks could vote, use most public facilities, and earn higher wages. During the Great Migration, wages in Northern industries usually ranged from $3.00 to $5.00 per eight-hour day, compared to as little as 75 cents to $1.00 per day in Southern agriculture and to no more than $2.50 for a nine-hour day in Southern industries. Although domestic wages remained at less than $15.00 weekly, between 1915 and 1925, the average wages of domestics in some Northern cities doubled. Movement to Northern cities also meant an improvement in health care. The nonwhite infant mortality rate dropped in New York City from 176 in 1917 to 105 in 1930; in Boston, from 167 to 90; and in Philadelphia, from 193 to 100. Between 1911 and 1926, according to the Metropolitan Life Insurance Company, the incidence of tuberculosis declined by 44 percent for black males and 43 percent for black females. New York, Philadelphia, and Chicago showed similar patterns of decline. With the prospect of better social conditions, higher wages, and the franchise, it is no wonder that African Americans viewed the Great Migration to Northern cities as going to "The Promised Land" and the "Flight from Egypt."[29]

Southern blacks helped to organize their own movement into the urban

[28] Bureau of the Census, *Negro Population, 1790–1915* (1918; reprint, New York: Arno Press, 1968), p. 93; *Negroes in the United States, 1920–1932* (1935; reprint, New York: Arno Press, 1966), pp. 54–55; Gottlieb, *Making Their Own Way*, pp. 12–62; Grossman, *Land of Hope*, chaps. 1, 2, and 3; Spear, *Black Chicago*, p. 141; Osofsky, *Harlem*, pp. 28–29; Kusmer, *A Ghetto Takes Shape*, p. 161; Trotter, *Black Milwaukee*, pp. 45–46; Bureau of the Census, *Negroes in the United States*, p. 85. See also essays in Trotter, *The Great Migration in Historical Perspective*.

[29] Division of Negro Economics, *The Negro at Work during the World War and during Reconstruction* (1921; reprint, New York: Negro Universities Press, 1969), pp. 32–33; Grossman, *Land of Hope*, p. 52; Trotter, *Black Milwaukee*, p. 47; Katzman, *Seven Days a Week*, pp. 310–11; Reynolds Farley, *Growth of the Black Population: A Study of Demographic Trends* (Chicago: Markham Publishing Company, 1970), chap. 2, p. 212; Charles S. Johnson, *The Negro in American Civilization: A Study of Negro Life and Race Relations in the Light of Social Research* (New York: Henry Holt and Company, 1930), pp. 158–59; Grossman, *Land of Hope*, pp. 98–119; Spear, *Black Chicago*, p. 137.

North. They developed an extensive communications network, which included railroad employees who traveled back and forth between Northern and Southern cities; Northern black weeklies like the *Chicago Defender* and the *Pittsburgh Courier*; and an expanding chain of kin and friends.[30] Using their networks of families and friends, African Americans learned about transportation, jobs, and housing beforehand. As one South Carolina migrant to Pittsburgh recalled, "I was plowin[g] in the field and it was real hot. And I stayed with some of the boys who would leave home and [come] back . . . and would have money, and they had clothes. I didn't have that. We all grew up together. And I said, 'Well, as long as I stay here I'm not going to get nowhere.' And I tied that mule to a tree and caught a train."[31] Others formed migration clubs and moved in groups.

As blacks moved into Northern cities in growing numbers, a black industrial working class emerged for the first time in the urban North. Black men gained jobs in meat-packing, auto, steel, and other mass-production industries. In cities like Cleveland, Pittsburgh, Detroit, and Milwaukee, the percentage of black men employed in industrial jobs increased from an estimated 10–20 percent of the black labor force in 1910 to about 60–70 percent in 1920 and 1930. The labor demands of wartime crisis undermined the color barrier in basic industries, as an official of Cleveland's National Malleable Casting company exclaimed: "We have [black] molders, core makers, chippers, fitters, locomotive crane operators, melting furnace operators, general foremen, foremen, assistant foremen, clerks, timekeepers[;] in fact, there is no work in our shop that they cannot do and do well, if properly supervised."[32]

In western Pennsylvania, the number of black steelworkers rose from fewer than 800 on the eve of World War I to about 7,000 in 1918. By 1923, the number of black steelworkers in the Pittsburgh district reached nearly 17,000. As early as May 1917, the Packard Company in Detroit had 1,100 blacks on the payroll. One official explained, "We have found in the Packard plant that the Negro . . . is a good worker, considerably better than the average European immigrant." But it was the Ford Company that soon outdistanced other automakers in the employment of Afro-Americans. The number of blacks at Ford rose from only 50 in 1916 to 2,500 in 1920, 5,000 in 1923, and 10,000 by

[30] Johnson and Campbell, *Black Migration in America*, chap. 5; Marks, *Farewell—We're Good and Gone*, pp. 1–18; Wilson, *Declining Significance of Race*, pp. 66–71; Gottlieb, *Making Their Own Way*, p. 4; Grossman, *Land of Hope*, p. 6; Shirley Ann Moore, "Getting There, Being There: African-American Migration to Richmond, California, 1910–19145," in Trotter, *The Great Migration in Historical Perspective*.

[31] Gottlieb, *Making Their Own Way*, p. 43.

[32] Bureau of the Census, *Fourteenth Census of the U.S.*, vol. 4, *Population, 1920, Occupations* (Washington, D.C.: Government Printing Office, 1923), pp. 1049–1257; *Fifteenth Census of U.S.*, vol. 4; *Population, 1930, Occupations*, table 12; Trotter, *Black Milwaukee*, pp. 45–56; Kusmer, *A Ghetto Takes Shape*, p. 191.

1926. Ford offered blacks a broader range of production and supervisory opportunities than did other companies.[33]

Black women also gained access to industrial jobs during the labor shortages
of World War I, although their gains were less dramatic and less permanent than
those of black men. In Chicago, the percentage of black women classified under
manufacturing trades increased from fewer than 1,000 in 1910 to over 3,000 in
1920. Industrial jobs now made up 15 percent of the black female labor force,
compared to less than 7 percent in 1910. In Buffalo, employers hired black
women in greater numbers by 1925; still, few black females entered local plants
and none entered the major factories. Pittsburgh offered neither black nor white
women substantial industrial opportunities, but the war nonetheless increased
their numbers in manufacturing. In Harlem, black women gained increasing
employment in the garment industry and in commercial laundries. Black
women gained jobs traditionally held by white women: in textiles, clothing,
food, and head- and footwear.[34]

Despite their increasing participation in new industrial sectors, most blacks
moved into jobs at the bottom rung of the industrial ladder. Racial barriers
blocked their ascent up the job ladder, leaving them more vulnerable to poverty
than were whites. In the urban North and West, employers invariably hired
blacks in a narrow range of low-paying, difficult, and disagreeable jobs. In
Milwaukee, for example, out of more than 2,000 manufacturing establishments,
only about 11 firms hired Afro-Americans in the wake of the Great Migration.
Over and over again, black men testified, as did one black steelworker, that they
"were limited, they only did the dirty work . . . jobs that even Poles didn't want."
In Chicago, blacks found semiskilled and skilled positions only in foundries. In
New York City, most black men continued to work as longshoremen, elevator
operators, porters, janitors, teamsters, chauffeurs, waiters, and "general laborers
of all kinds," while black women remained predominantly in domestic
service.[35]

Employers and white workers forced Southern blacks who entered the city as

[33] Dickerson, Out of the Crucible, pp. 35, 45; August Meier and Elliott Rudwick, Black Detroit and
the Rise of the UAW (New York: Oxford University Press, 1979), pp. 5–6, 8.

[34] Spear, Black Chicago, pp. 31, 33, 154; Lillian S. Williams, "The Development of a Black
Community: Buffalo, New York, 1900–1945" (Ph.D. diss., State University of New York at Buffalo,
1979), p. 171; Trotter, Black Milwaukee, pp. 46–47; Kusmer, A Ghetto Takes Shape, pp. 74, 195;
Gottlieb, Making Their Own Way, p. 106; Osofsky, Harlem, p. 137; E. Franklin Frazier, The Negro in
the United States (New York: Macmillan Company, 1949), p. 598; Sterling D. Spero and Abram L.
Harris, The Black Worker: The Negro and the Labor Movement (1931; reprint, New York: Atheneum,
1968), pp. 151–52, 177–78.

[35] William H. Harris, The Harder We Run: Black Workers since the Civil War (New York: Oxford
University Press, 1982), pp. 51–66; Grossman, Land of Hope, pp. 181, 182, 207; Gottlieb, Making
Their Own Way, pp. 89–145; Dickerson, Out of the Crucible, pp. 52–53; Trotter, Black Milwaukee, p.
47; Osofsky, Harlem, pp. 136–37.

skilled craftsmen (shoemakers, tailors, or blacksmiths) to start their training over again or abandon their trades completely. Northern employers imposed discriminatory standards of competence on black workers, while many crafts unions excluded them. In Pittsburgh, where blacks had acquired a significant footing in skilled jobs in the iron-and-steel industry during the prewar years, they suffered a drastic reversal because companies hired unskilled recruits in growing numbers and refused to upgrade them into skilled positions. During World War I and the 1920s, the percentage of skilled black iron-and-steel workers in Pittsburgh dropped from slightly over 20 percent to less than 4 percent. White foremen, other mill officials, and white workers relegated blacks to the undesirable, unskilled positions.[36]

As in previous economic downturns, African Americans shared the post–World War I recession and the Great Depression with members of the white working class. As in other downturns, they also faced disproportionate layoffs. In the 1920–21 recession, the number of black laborers in Allegheny County dropped by 40 percent, while the number of immigrant workers declined by 34 percent. In the steel towns of Braddock and Duquesne, the black work force dropped, respectively, by nearly 55 and 51 percent, while that of immigrants dropped by about 27 and 24 percent. When companies laid off black workers in Milwaukee, three squads of detectives entered the black community and arrested thirty-nine black men for vagrancy. In Detroit, black men made up 5 percent of the work force, but they constituted 16 percent of the 200,000 unemployed workers in 1921.[37] In 1932, when the nation's unemployment rate peaked at between 25 and 30 percent, urban unemployment was higher, and black unemployment in Northern cities was even higher: well over 40 percent in Harlem, Philadelphia, Chicago, and Detroit. Moreover, as whites returned to work in the private sector from the middle to late 1930s, blacks remained tied to work on New Deal public emergency projects. Only during the labor demands of World War II did blacks return to full employment in the private sector.[38]

The continuing use of black strikebreakers and the persistence of black women in domestic service highlight labor market discrimination during World War I and the 1920s. Meat-packing, railway, building and construction, shipping, and steel companies all employed black strikebreakers. Despite their

[36] Trotter, Black Milwaukee, p. 54; Spear, Black Chicago, p. 156; Gottlieb, Making Their Own Way, pp. 91–92; Dickerson, Out of the Crucible, p. 51.

[37] Dickerson, Out of the Crucible, pp. 93–100; Trotter, Black Milwaukee, p. 57; Frazier, The Negro in the United States, p. 599; Spear, Black Chicago, p. 158.

[38] Harvard Sitkoff, A New Deal for Blacks: The Emergence of Civil Rights as a National Issue. The Depression Decade (New York: Oxford University Press, 1978), pp. 34–57; Richard Polenberg, War and Society: The United States, 1941–1945 (Philadelphia: J. B. Lippincott, 1972); Richard Polenberg, One Nation Divisible: Class, Race, and Ethnicity in the United States since 1938 (New York: Penguin Books, 1980), pp. 69–78; Katherine D. Wood, Urban Workers on Relief, Part II (Washington, D.C.: Government Printing Office, 1937); Raymond Wolters, Negroes and the Great Depression: The Problem of Economic Recovery (Westport, Conn.: Greenwood Press, 1970).

services as strikebreakers (as in the steel strike of 1919), black steelworkers in Western Pennsylvania faced a sharp rise in unemployment after the settlement. (As we will see below, some black workers perceived strikebreaking as a strategy for combating the discriminatory practices of white workers.) Black women faced even greater restrictions on their labor force participation than did black men. Despite a brief increase in industrial jobs for black women, most remained confined to domestic service jobs, as white women gained increasing opportunities in white-collar sales, clerical, teaching, and nursing jobs. In 1920, for example, the percentage of black women in domestic service occupations exceeded 60 percent in Chicago, 70 percent in New York City, and 80 percent in Philadelphia. In the postwar years, black women lost industrial jobs as white soldiers returned from war and white women retained their former niche in the operative positions designated for women. By 1930, the percentage of black women in domestic service jobs had increased.[39]

As in the pre–World War I years, black workers continued to move around seeking higher wages and better working conditions. In Milwaukee, at one very disagreeable tannery plant, a black worker related, "I worked there one night and I quit." During the war years, the steel mills of western Pennsylvania frequently experienced a 300 percent turnover rate for black workers. In 1923, for instance, the A. M. Byers iron mill in Pittsburgh employed 1,408 Afro-Americans in order to maintain a work force of 228.[40] At the same time (as discussed above), some African Americans served as strikebreakers. They expressed bitter resentment over the discriminatory practices of white workers, who frequently referred to blacks as a "scab race" and thus justified their exclusion from labor unions. Others helped to organize independent all-black unions like the Brotherhood of Sleeping Car Porters and Maids. When whites occasionally lowered racial barriers, a few joined white unions like the Amalgamated Meat Cutters and Butcher Workmen.[41] When the Congress of Industrial Organizations emerged during the 1930s, it would build upon these traditions of collective action.

Despite efforts in their own behalf, black workers paid disproportionate costs of capitalist development in the urban North. To be sure, as discussed above, African Americans gained a foothold in the industrial sector, increased their wages, and improved their health care, cutting infant mortality and reducing deaths from diseases like tuberculosis. Still, poverty remained a central feature

[39] See n. 37, above; *Fourteenth Census of U.S.*, vol. 4, *Population, 1920, Occupations*, pp. 1049–1257; *Fifteenth Census of the U.S.*, vol. 4, *Population, 1930, Occupations*, table 12; Katzman, *Seven Days a Week*, pp. 219–22.

[40] Spero and Harris, *The Black Worker*, p. 164; Gottlieb, *Making Their Own Way*, pp. 126–27; Harris, *The Harder We Run*, pp. 77–94; Finney, "A Study of Negro Labor during and after World War I," pp. 341–84; Trotter, *Black Milwaukee*, p. 62.

[41] William H. Harris, *Keeping the Faith: A. Philip Randolph, Milton P. Webster, and the Brotherhood of Sleeping Car Porters, 1925–1937* (Urbana: University of Illinois Press, 1977); Grossman, *Land of Hope*, p. 209.

74 · Joe William Trotter, Jr.

of their lives. They continued to face lower average earnings and greater levels of poverty than did their white counterparts. In the 1920s, the average Harlem family earned $1,300, compared to $1,570 for a typical white family. According to an intensive health study of the area, the black death rate from all causes was 42 percent higher than the city's rate; infant mortality was 111 per 1,000 births, compared to 64.5 for the city; and tuberculosis deaths were two-and-a-half times the city rate. While blacks had fewer young children than the city average (17.5 percent for blacks compared to 24.5 percent for the city in 1930), their cases before the juvenile authorities rose from 2.8 percent of all cases in 1914 to 11.7 percent of all cases in 1930. By 1930, in Cleveland, Cincinnati, Chicago, New York City, and Buffalo, the percentage of black families headed by women ranged from a low of 15.4 in Buffalo to a high of 23.9 in New York City. Conversely, the percentage of American-born white families headed by women ranged from a low of 13.0 in Buffalo to a high of 17.7 in New York City. The percentage for immigrants was also lower than for African Americans. In 1916–17, although blacks made up only 5.6 percent of New York City families, they accounted for 11.2 percent of desertions recorded by the Charity Organization Society. In Chicago, desertion and nonsupport cases increased by nearly 100 percent between 1921 and 1927; blacks made up nearly 20 percent of the total but only about 5 percent of the city's population. At the same time, the city's United Charities showed an increase in the proportion of blacks receiving aid, from one-tenth to a fifth of all cases.[42] Urban black poverty was not only disproportionate to that of whites, it became more spatially concentrated within the urban environment.

RACE, SPACE, AND POVERTY: SHIFTING GEOGRAPHICAL DIMENSIONS, 1915–1945

Under the impact of World War I and the 1920s, the size (and number of) racially segregated neighborhoods increased and the relationship between ghettoization, proletarianization, and poverty intensified. Although white landowners and realtors continued to restrict blacks to certain areas, the arrival of New Deal programs heightened the process. And as blacks became more residentially segregated from whites, they also became more segregated from each other along class and status lines. Therefore, poverty not only increased within the black community, but within certain neighborhoods. These new manifestations of poverty would also stimulate the emergence of new responses to poverty within the black community. Between 1920 and 1930, residential segregation increased in all major cities. The index of dissimilarity rose from 66.8 to 85.2 percent in Chicago; 60.6 to 85.0 percent in Cleveland; 64.1 to 77.9 percent in Boston; and from 46.0 to 63.0 percent in Philadelphia. In Chicago, the number

<hr>

[42] Osofsky, *Harlem*, pp. 141–42; Kusmer, *A Ghetto Takes Shape*, pp. 225–62, includes comparative table for other cities; Frazier, *The Negro Family in the United States*, pp. 246–55.

of census tracts of over 50 percent black rose from 4 in 1910 to 16 in 1920; 35 percent of the city's blacks lived in census tracts that were over 75 percent black. By 1920, two-thirds of Manhattan's black population lived in Harlem; the area bordered by 130th Street on the south, 145th Street on the north, and west of Fifth to Eighth Avenue was predominantly black. In Cleveland, no census tract was more than 25 percent black in 1910; ten years later, two census tracts were more than 50 percent black. By 1930, 90 percent of the city's blacks lived in a restricted area: bounded by Euclid Avenue on the north, East 105th Street on the east, and Woodland Avenue on the south. Likewise, although the black population of Milwaukee remained small by comparison to other cities, four wards contained over 93 percent of the city's 7,500 blacks.[43]

The ghetto not only expanded and consolidated, it stratified internally. As the new black middle class expanded during the 1920s, it slowly moved into better housing vacated by whites, leaving the black poor concentrated in certain sections. In his studies of Chicago and New York, sociologist E. Franklin Frazier demonstrated the division of the black urban community along socioeconomic lines. In Chicago, poor and working-class blacks concentrated in the northernmost zones of the South Side black ghetto, while the higher socioeconomic groups lived on the extreme south side. In Harlem, middle- and upper-class blacks lived on the periphery, while working-class and poor blacks clustered in the center. According to Frazier, the center of Harlem was "essentially a non-family area," an area of "the emancipated from all classes and elements." In neither city were the patterns entirely unambiguous. Each city contained significant areas of interclass mixing, but poverty increasingly characterized specific sections of the ghetto.[44] In Chicago, based on the records of the city's United Charities, Frazier found "under normal conditions" between 8 and 9 percent of the families in the poorer areas "dependent upon charity." Rates of dependency declined "in the successive zones," so that only 1 percent of black families depended on charity in the highest socioeconomic zone. Spousal desertion and nonsupport, crime, lower educational and skill levels also varied from zone to zone.[45]

The development of New Deal social-welfare programs transformed responses to poverty in America. Federal relief, housing, and job programs appealed to the black and white poor. Despite declining employment opportunities, more than 400,000 blacks left the South for Northern and Western

---

[43] Osofsky, *Harlem*, pp. 122–23; Kusmer, *A Ghetto Takes Shape*, pp. 163–65; Trotter, *Black Milwaukee*, p. 67; Karl E. Taeuber and Alma F. Taeuber, *Negroes in Cities: Residential Segregation and Neighborhood Change* (Chicago: Aldine Publishing Company, 1965), p. 54; Spear, *Black Chicago*, p. 142.

[44] E. Franklin Frazier, "The Impact of Urban Civilization upon Negro Family Life," *American Sociological Review* 2, no. 5 (October 1937): 609–18; Frazier, *The Negro Family in the United States*, pp. 252–55; Frazier, *The Negro in the United States*, pp. 256–66, 325–28.

[45] Frazier, "The Impact of Urban Civilization upon Negro Family Life," pp. 614, 615, 616.

cities during the early 1930s. Although only one Northern city had a black population of more than 100,000 in 1930, by 1935 there were an estimated eleven such cities. Racial restrictions on social-welfare services in the South helped to stimulate the continuing influx of blacks to Northern cities, and with jobs declining, as Gunner Myrdal noted in his classic study, *An American Dilemma*, "a new form of livelihood arose to take the place of jobs. This was public assistance in its many forms. It was much harder for Negroes who needed it to get relief in the South than in the North. In 1935 around half of all Negro families in the North were on relief." Not only racial restrictions on social welfare, but Jim Crow, disfranchisement, and escalating racial violence fueled black population movement during the period. As Hilton Butler stated in a *New Republic* article, "Dust had been blown from the shotgun, the whip, and the noose, and Ku Klux practices were being resumed in the certainty that dead men not only tell no tales but create vacancies."[46]

Even as the state gave unprecedented assistance to the poor, it reinforced patterns of racial inequality in Northern cities. State and local officials administered programs with minimal federal interference. Thus, federal relief projects not only hired few blacks in skilled jobs, they encouraged residential segregation. In Cleveland, to take a typical example, the federal government funded three housing projects in the center of the expanding black community and two on its edges. Officials restricted blacks to the centrally located projects, allowing the others to become nearly all white. In this way, New Deal programs reinforced ghettoization, even as they relieved poverty.[47] African Americans would not take racial discrimination sitting down, however. As in earlier periods, they would act vigorously in their own interests, creating new and, in many ways, more effective responses to poverty.

The Black Poor: In Their Own Interest, 1915–1945

Calling themselves "New Negroes," an energetic new black elite helped to mobilize the black community for a new era of institution building and political empowerment during World War I and the 1920s. The expansion of prewar organizations like the National Urban League and the NAACP; the emergence of the Harlem Renaissance as a new expression of black consciousness; and the

---

[46] Sitkoff, *A New Deal for Blacks*, pp. 36, 38, 58–83; Gunnar Myrdal, *An American Dilemma: The Negro Problem and Modern Democracy* (1944; reprint, New York: Harper and Row, 1972), 1:196–97, 33–63; Wood, *Urban Workers on Relief, Part II*, p. 6.

[47] Wolters, *Negroes and the Great Depression*, pp. 83–215; Christopher Wye, "New Deal and the Negro Community: Toward a Broader Conceptualization," *Journal of American History* 59 (December 1972), 621–39; St. Clair Drake and Horace R. Cayton, *Black Metropolis: A Study of Negro Life in a Northern City*, rev. ed., vol. 1 (1945; reprint, New York: Harcourt, Brace, and World, 1962); Trotter, *Black Milwaukee*, pp. 175–80, 182–88; Frazier, "The Impact of Urban Civilization upon Negro Family Life," pp. 614–15; Hirsch, *Making the Second Ghetto*, p. xiii.

expansion of black participation in electoral politics all reflected racial solidarity across class and status lines.[48] They also reflected a growing level of interracial solidarity, as black elites cultivated an expanding core of white allies, particularly in the civil-rights and social-welfare activities of the NAACP and the Urban League. During the 1930s and 1940s, this inter- and intraracial unity gained even greater expression with the rise of the Congress of Industrial Organizations, New Deal social welfare programs, and the March on Washington movement.[49] When Franklin D. Roosevelt issued Executive Order 8802 in 1941, calling for an end to racial barriers in defense industries, African Americans achieved a major victory against racial exploitation. Their victory not only foreshadowed the rise of the modern civil rights movement, but the rise of new and more effective responses to poverty.

Despite the achievements of the interwar years, however, racial solidarity remained a precarious affair. As Southern blacks moved into Northern cities in increasing numbers, black urban communities faced growing cleavages along regional, class, and spatial lines. Established residents feared, resented, and sometimes resisted the influx of newcomers into their communities; elites feared the growth of a large lower class that might endanger their relationship with local whites; and Southern blacks for their part determined to rebuild their lives on the bedrock of Southern cultural traditions, despite Northern black and white resistance. In Milwaukee, for example, one black female newcomer complained, "Instead of the Colored Northern citizens trying to help lift up your [Southern] colored neighbor . . . you run him down." Responding to such conflicts, she also said, "We shall prove to you that we are good worthy law-abiding citizens. . . . We shall prove to be citizens in helping to make Milwaukee one of the greatest religious cities of Wisconsin."[50]

[48] For my emphasis on agency in this section, I am indebted to Earl Lewis, *In Their Own Interests: Race, Class, and Power in Twentieth-Century Norfolk, Virginia* (Berkeley: University of California Press, 1990); Katz, *In the Shadow of the Poorhouse*, p. 216; and Clark A. Chambers, "Toward a Redefinition of Welfare History," *Journal of American History* 73, no. 2 (September 1986): 407–33. Franklin and Moss, *From Slavery to Freedom*, pp. 291–338; August Meier and Elliott Rudwick, *From Plantation to Ghetto* (1966; reprint, New York: Hill and Wang, 1976), pp. 232–58; Mary Frances Berry and John Blassingame, *Long Memory: The Black Experience in America* (New York: Oxford University Press, 1982); Weiss, *The National Urban League*; William Toll, *The Resurgence of Race: Black Social Theory from Reconstruction to the Pan-African Conference* (Philadelphia: Temple University Press, 1979), pp. 136–220; Nathan I. Huggings, *Harlem Renaissance* (New York: Oxford University Press, 1971), pp. 52–83.

[49] Sitkoff, *A New Deal for Blacks*, esp. chaps. 4, 6, and 7; Harris, *The Harder We Run*, pp. 95–122; Meier and Rudwick, *Black Detroit and the Rise of the UAW*, chaps. 2, 3, and 4; Trotter, *Black Milwaukee*, pp. 148–214; Dickerson, *Out of the Crucible*, pp. 119–82; Mark Naison, *Communists in Harlem during the Depression* (Urbana: University of Illinois Press, 1983); Herbert Garfinkel, *When Negroes March: The March on Washington Movement in the Organizational Politics for FEPC* (Glencoe, Ill.: Free Press, 1959).

[50] Gottlieb, *Making Their Own Way*, pp. 187–210; Grossman, *Land of Hope*, pp. 123–60; Dickerson, *Out of the Crucible*, pp. 65–67; Trotter, *Black Milwaukee*, pp. 129–30; Kusmer, *A Ghetto Takes Shape*, pp. 252–53; Spear, *Black Chicago*, pp. 168–69.

Even middle-class black social work reflected bias against the black poor. Despite their helpful service, black clubwomen made judgments about the worthy and unworthy poor. They were particularly interested in the welfare of children, the aged, and "decent lower class girls," whom they hoped to "rescue" from vice. Operating under the motto "Not alms but opportunity," the National Urban League reflected the philosophy of white scientific philanthropy. During the 1920s, it largely supplanted women's clubs as providers of social-welfare services, but retained the prevailing distinction between the worthy and unworthy poor.[51]

Not merely passive recipients of aid from the black middle class and its white allies, the black poor took a hand in devising ways of surviving poverty. Poor and working-class blacks supported regular social-welfare efforts within the black community. They gave small sums of money and gifts of food, clothing, and time to the recurring fund-raising events for "charity." Some of these contributions supported working-class institutions like storefront churches, the Garvey Movement, and the Brotherhood of Sleeping Car Porters, each providing its own program of mutual aid and social-welfare benefits.[52] While some of these strategies had analogues among whites, others, like the use of blues songs to articulate reactions to poverty, reflected the unique culture of African Americans. One song, for example, begins, "Ain't yer heard of my po' story? / Den listen to me." The blues singer William Lee Coonley ("Big Bill") recorded many of these songs from the mid-1920s through the 1940s. In one song, titled "Looking Up at Down," he said:

> I'm just like Job's turkey
> I can't do nothing but bobble
> I'm so poor baby
> I have to lean up against the fence to gargle
> Yeah, I'm down so low baby
> . . . lord, I declare I'm looking up to down

In 1938, another bluesman, John Lee Williamson ("Sonny Boy"), recorded "Moonshine." The song captured the debilitating impact of alcohol, and efforts to overcome it:

> Now and it's moon shine
> Moon shine have harmed many men
> Now moon shine will make you shoot dice
> Make you want to fight
> Now when you go home and you can't

[51] Jackson, "Black Charity in Progressive Era Chicago"; Weiss, *The National Urban League*.

[52] See n. 40, above, and Tony Martin, *Race First: The Ideological and Organizational Struggles of Marcus Garvey and the Universal Negro Improvement Association* (Westport, Conn.: Greenwood Press, 1976). Cf. Judith Stein, *The World of Marcus Garvey: Race and Class in Modern Society* (Baton Rouge: Louisiana State University Press, 1986); Du Bois, *The Philadelphia Negro*, p. 276; Grossman, *Land of Hope*, p. 209.

Treat your wife right
You been drinking moon shine
Moon shine have harmed many men
Now that is the reason why
I believe I'll make a change

Another song captured the pain of tuberculosis, often called the "scourge of the Negro race" during the period: "T.B. is all right to have / But your friends treat you so low down; you will ask them for a favor / And they will even stop coming 'round." Describing his movement from city to city, one migrant stated, "We sing songs as we ride [on railroad boxcars] and when we stopped we sing them."[53] Songs not only enabled the black poor to articulate their reactions to poverty, they helped them to endure.

Unable to earn enough to buy food and pay rent, some blacks participated in the illegal underground economy. Numerous poor blacks played the policy game. They placed small bets amounting to as little as one cent and received relatively good returns if they "hit" the lucky number. Policy became a major business and employer of the unemployed. During the Depression, one South Side Chicago black tried to visualize the city without policy: "7,000 people would be unemployed and business in general would be crippled, especially taverns and even groceries, shoestores, and many other business enterprises who depend on the buying power of the South side." At the same time, a Harlem resident called numbers the black man's "stock market." Moreover, gambling establishments often represented a source of direct aid to the poor. As one interviewee stated, "Well, the Christians would always give me good advice but that was all, so I just got so I wouldn't bother with them and whenever I wanted anything I used to make it to the gamblers."

Others turned to prostitution. As one New York City woman stated, "I don't play the streets—I mean I don't lay every pair of pants that comes along. I look 'em over first. I'm strictly a Packard broad. I only grab a drunk if he looks like his pockets are loaded. If they get rough my man [pimp] kick 'em out. When they're drunk they shoot the works. I've gotten over two hundred dollars, and so help me, the bastard didn't even touch me. He got happy just lookin at me." Still others turned to theft and wound up in the penitentiary or jail, but even incarceration sometimes helped: "I have stole small things. I don't reckon I would care if I was turned-over to officers, because I would have a place to stay. You see I don't have any particular place to go and stay, so I could stay there. I'd just have a place to stay."[54]

[53] This analysis is based upon Frazier, *The Negro Family in the United States*, pp. 212–24; Eric Sackheim, ed., *The Blues Line: A Collection of Blues Lyrics* (New York: Grossman Publishers, A Mushinsha Book, 1969), p. 416; Robert M. W. Dixon and John Goodrich, ed., *Blues and Gospel Records, 1902–1943* (Essex, England: Storyville Publications, 1982), pp. 74–82, 846–47.

[54] Drake and Cayton, *Black Metropolis*, 1:494; *I am Harlem* (documentary); Frazier, *The Negro Family in the United States*, pp. 212–24.

In the postwar years blacks assumed a new status in American society. Building upon the gains of World War II, the civil rights movement intensified the push for full equality. The percentage of blacks living in the North and West rose from 23 percent in 1940 to 40 percent in 1960 and to 47 percent in 1970. Despite the persistence of racial discrimination, Northern blacks increased their foothold in industrial jobs, gained access to new business and professional opportunities, and took influential positions in urban politics. As they struggled to expand and consolidate their control over the political economy, setting the preconditions for reducing the poverty in their midst, new demographic and economic forces undercut their progress. The growing exodus of industrial jobs from the central cities signaled a new phase in black urban life; it cut them off from employment opportunities and facilitated the expansion of what we now call the urban underclass. One result was increasing frustration and anger. From Watts to Detroit to Harlem, the black poor torched the symbols of their oppression: rat-infested, unsanitary, and dilapidated ghetto housing. As the Kerner Commission report concluded at the time, "The frustrations of powerlessness have led some to the conviction that there is no effective alternative to violence as a means of expression and redress, as a way of 'moving the system.'"[55]

CONCLUSION

From the antebellum era through the 1960s, few African Americans escaped poverty. Within the cities, however, poverty assumed various forms with shifts in political economy, transformations of class structure, and manifestations of racism. To the burdens shared by all workers in a capitalist society, blacks added racial discrimination, as employers, white workers, and the state obstructed their access to jobs, services, and decent housing. African Americans developed

[55] Figures adapted from Richard L. Morrill and O. Fred Donaldson, "Geographical Perspectives on the History of Black America," in Robert T. Ernst and Lawrence Hugg, eds., *Black America: Geographic Perspective* (New York: Anchor Books, 1976), pp. 9–33; Gerald David Jaynes and Robin M. Williams, eds., *A Common Destiny: Blacks and American Society* (Washington, D.C.: National Academy Press, 1989), pp. 271–328; Harris, *The Harder We Run*, pp. 123–46; Sidney M. Peck, "The Economic Situation of Negro Labor," in Julius Jacobson, ed., *The Negro and the American Labor Movement* (Garden City, N.Y.: Anchor Books, 1968), pp. 209–31; Nicholas Lemann, *The Promised Land: The Great Migration and How It Changed America* (New York: Alfred A. Knopf, 1991); Ray Marshall, *The Negro Worker* (New York: Random House, 1967), pp. 92–119; Wilson, *The Declining Significance of Race*, pp. 88–121; Sidney M. Wilhelm, *Who Needs the Negro?* (Garden City, N.Y.: Anchor Books, 1971); Frances Fox Piven and Richard A. Cloward, *Regulating the Poor: The Functions of Public Welfare* (New York: Vintage Books, 1971), pp. 285–348 and appendixes; Dorothy K. Newman et al., *Protest, Politics, and Prosperity: Black Americans and White Institutions, 1940–1975* (New York: Pantheon Books, 1978), pp. 135–86; Richard Bardolph, ed., *The Civil Rights Record: Black Americans and the Law, 1849–1970* (New York: Thomas J. Crowell, 1970), pp. 280–83; Kerner Commission, *Report of the National Advisory Commission on Civil Disorders* (New York: Bantam Books, 1968), p. 205; Arthur J. Waskow, *From Race Riot to Sit-In, 1919 and the 1960s* (Garden City, N.Y.: Anchor Books, 1966), pp. 38–120, 219–24.

a variety of strategies for combating the impact of these forces on their lives. As contemporary analysts of the urban underclass suggest, they built a broad range of multiclass institutions—churches, fraternal orders, and a variety of social-welfare and civil-rights organizations.

Black urban communities of the industrial era, however, were not fully harmonious entities. Although the class divisions that they faced were not as great as they would become in recent times, they sometimes convulsed African-American communities and hampered their responses to poverty and racial subordination. As new elites displaced the old, as new industrial workers supplanted domestic service and common laborers, and as Southern blacks overwhelmed the old residents of Northern cities, intraracial cleavages intensified. Moreover, in order to combat the ravages of urban poverty, some blacks moved to the edges of the urban economy and participated in a variety of illegal pursuits, anticipating the emergence of the contemporary underground economy. A historical analysis of class, race, and poverty in the industrial era not only illuminates the impact of black migration, proletarianization, and ghettoization on black urban life. It suggests greater continuity with the present than current portraits of the urban underclass reveal. It also suggests that while we must reject the ahistoricism of the "enduring ghetto," the social concerns of its chief proponents are still relevant. As Gilbert Osofsky stated in 1970, "No perception of the American past is accurate which insists on underemphasizing the special factors of color consciousness, color caste and racism."[56] Finally, by introducing dynamic historical perspectives into the current underclass debate, we will be able to deepen our understanding of contemporary poverty and facilitate the development of promising policy initiatives.

[56] Osofsky, *Harlem*, p. xiii.

PART TWO

The Transformation of America's Cities

The Structures of Urban Poverty: The Reorganization of Space and Work in Three Periods of American History

Thomas J. Sugrue

URBAN POVERTY, PAST AND PRESENT

American cityscapes today are eerily apocalyptic. The bleak vistas and visible poverty of inner-city Detroit, the nation's seventh largest city, offer a striking example of the social and economic devastation common to the former industrial centers of the Rustbelt. Empty hulks of abandoned factories loom over acres of rubble. Whole rows of storefronts are boarded up. Abandoned houses, falling down or burnt out, are surrounded by fields overgrown with prairie grass and ragweed. Sixty thousand vacant lots lay strewn throughout the city. Although the city still has a base of manufacturing employment and a substantial middle class, a large number of the city's residents live in poverty. Over a quarter of Detroit's population is unemployed and a third receives some form of public assistance. A visit to the city's hospitals, schools, and jails makes clear the terrible toll of the impoverishment of many of the city's residents.

Is the poverty visible in Detroit and other declining industrial centers simply the most recent manifestation of a problem that has plagued cities over the last several hundred years? Are Detroit's poor the latter-day equivalent of the rag-pickers and scavengers described by nineteenth-century observers like Charles Dickens and Jacob Riis?[1] How new is the dilemma of contemporary urban poverty? Are ominous reports of a new "urban underclass" tangled in "a web of pathology" indication of a crisis of unprecedented depth and magnitude? Or have Americans simply rediscovered (as they seem to do every few decades) a persistent problem that is periodically masked by economic growth, by willful ignorance, or by political indifference? Is poverty a constant of the human condition, confirmation of the age-old biblical adage "the poor you will always have with you"? The question of the similarity or difference of poverty in the past and present is central to the underclass debate. Since the urban crisis of the 1960s, policymakers and social scientists have undergirded their work with

Acknowledgments: Thanks to Eric Arnesen, Felicia Kornbluh, James T. Patterson, Jeannie L. Sowers, Leonard Wallock, and the editor and contributors to this volume for their comments on earlier drafts of this chapter.
[1] Charles Dickens, *American Notes* (1842; reprint, New York: St. Martin's Press, 1985); Jacob Riis, *How the Other Half Lives* (New York: Charles Scribners and Sons, 1890).

assumptions about the familiarity or novelty of contemporary poverty, and have often shaped their proposals for reform on their perception of the legacy of the history of poverty. But the vision of the past that informs most recent social scientific scholarship is incomplete, based almost entirely upon data for the last twenty years, bereft of any serious historical analysis.[2]

The myopia of the current debate over poverty is in part the fault of historical scholarship. The poor remain shadowy figures in American social history, and "histories from the bottom up," in vogue since the late 1960s, have generally left the very bottom out. Even histories of poor relief and welfare have ignored the nature of urban poverty, relying on contemporary descriptive literature, rather than using the finely honed methodological tools that social historians have applied to questions of ethnicity, class, labor, and mobility.[3] That poverty has existed throughout American history is uncontested, but social scientists have generally accepted the existence of a group of economically deprived individuals in the past as a given, without systematically examining the causes and

[2] For an early version of the debate over the novelty of contemporary poverty, which focuses on the issue of the magnitude of poverty rather than on its causes, forms, and distribution, see Michael Harrington, "The Politics of Poverty," in Jeremy Larner and Irving Howe, eds., *Poverty: Views from the Left* (New York: William Morrow, 1968), 13–38; and Stephan Thernstrom, "Is There Really a New Poor?" ibid., 83–93; Thernstrom, "Poverty in Historical Perspective," in Daniel P. Moynahan, ed., *On Understanding Poverty: Perspectives from the Social Sciences* (New York: Basic Books, 1968).

[3] James T. Patterson, *America's Struggle against Poverty, 1900–1985* (Cambridge: Harvard University Press, 1986), 13, notes "the absence of longitudinal studies of poor people." For an interesting suggestion of why the history of poverty has generally been written "from the top down," see Roy Lubove, "Pittsburgh and the Uses of Social Welfare History," in Samuel P. Hays, ed., *City at the Point: Essays on the Social History of Pittsburgh* (Pittsburgh: University of Pittsburgh Press, 1989), 295. There are a number of excellent studies of poor relief and reformers' attitudes toward poverty, especially for nineteenth-century America, but there have been few efforts to write the social history of poverty. See, for example, Robert Bremner, *From the Depths: The Discovery of Poverty in the United States* (New York: New York University Press, 1956); Raymond Mohl, *Poverty in New York, 1783–1825* (New York: Oxford University Press, 1971); Susan Grigg, *The Dependent Poor of Newburyport: Studies in Social History, 1800–1830* (Ann Arbor: UMI Research Press, 1984); Priscilla F. Clement, *Welfare and Poverty in the Nineteenth-Century City: Philadelphia, 1800–1850* (Rutherford, N.J.: Fairleigh Dickinson University Press, 1985). Urban historians usually describe the poor in terms of contemporary accounts but seldom examine the question of poverty in any detail. See, for example, Edward Spann, *The New Metropolis: New York City, 1840–1857* (New York: Columbia University Press, 1981). And even works in the new urban history—for example, Stephan Thernstrom's famous *Poverty and Progress: Social Mobility in a Nineteenth-Century City* (Cambridge: Harvard University Press, 1964)—have little to say about the causes and distribution of poverty in American cities. Interestingly, some of the best histories of American poverty are for the colonial period—see note 6 below. A few important preliminary inquiries (with widely different perspectives) into the social history of American poverty in the nineteenth century include: Robert E. Cray, Jr., *Paupers and Poor Relief in New York City and Its Rural Environs, 1700–1830* (Philadelphia: Temple University Press, 1988), 168–95; Christine Stansell, *City of Women: Sex and Class in New York, 1789–1860* (New York: Knopf, 1986); Eric Monkkonen, *The Dangerous Class: Crime and Poverty in Columbus, Ohio, 1860–1885* (Cambridge: Harvard University Press, 1975); Michael B. Katz, *Poverty and Policy in American History* (New York: Academic Press, 1983).

manifestations of economic deprivation. Poverty should be viewed not as a fixed historical classification, but instead as a relationship that is shaped by its particular economic and spatial context. In that light, this essay will examine the origins of poverty in changing patterns of labor and economic opportunity and discuss the manifestation of poverty in the geography of cities. Through a comparison of poverty in Northern industrial cities in three periods of American economic history—early industrialization ca. 1840–1890, corporate industrialism ca. 1890–1950, and the postindustrial transformation ca. 1950–present—I will demonstrate that patterns of poverty today are strikingly novel, despite important continuities with the past.[4]

Since the history of poverty is still largely unwritten, any discussion about the form and distribution of poverty in the American past must be tentative. Still, three propositions emerge from a close examination of the social, labor, and economic history of the United States since the early nineteenth century.

First, with the exception of the chronically disabled, the elderly, and widows, the majority of poor people in the industrializing urban North were active in the labor market; they were an economically insecure "floating proletariat," or a mobile surplus of labor. Poverty was endemic to working-class life in early industrial American cities. Because poverty was so widespread in the early industrial city, the poor were seldom segregated residentially from the larger working-class community. The nineteenth-century "slum" was a fluid mixture of working people, some possessing a modicum of economic security, others barely surviving on the brink of subsistence.

Second, changes in the organization of capital and the nature of work at the turn of the century—brought about by the consolidation of large corporations—transformed the nature of poverty by offering greater economic security to a large number of workers, but at the same time leaving behind a segment of the working population increasingly marginal to the manufacturing economy and especially susceptible to poverty. In this period, residential segregation by class, and by poverty status, grew more pronounced.

---

[4] My periodization of American urban history relies on two important theoretical works: Sam Bass Warner, Jr., "If All the World Were Philadelphia: A Scaffolding for Urban History, 1774–1930," *American Historical Review* 74 (1968): 26–43; and David M. Gordon, Richard Edwards, and Michael Reich, *Segmented Work, Divided Workers: The Historical Transformation of Labor in the United States* (New York: Cambridge University Press, 1982). On the relationship of work and urban space, especially valuable are Theodore Hershberg, "The New Urban History: Toward an Interdisciplinary History of the City," *Journal of Urban History* 5 (1978): 3–40; and Leonard Wallock, "Work and Workplace in the City: Toward a Synthesis of the 'New' Labor and Urban History," in Howard Gillette, Jr., and Zane L. Miller, eds., *American Urbanism: A Historiographical Review* (Westport, Conn.: Greenwood Press, 1987), 73–89. There are, of course, other approaches to the question of poverty, such as that of the study of family structure and family strategies. The emphasis in this chapter on economic and spatial structures is not meant as an alternative to these approaches, but instead as a context in which they can be best understood. Economic opportunity and urban spatial patterns are the constraints to which families adapt or do not adapt successfully.

Third, shifts in the urban economy in recent decades have altered the prospects of working people in the city. Today's urban poor are increasingly marginal participants in the urban labor market, entrapped in pockets of poverty that have little precedent in the nineteenth-century city. The residential segregation of the poor in recent decades—compounded by persistent residential discrimination by race and class—replicates and solidifies unequal patterns of economic opportunity. A closer examination of these propositions offers the context for an understanding of the "urban underclass" in the contemporary United States.

Work and Poverty in Industrializing America

Patterns of poverty in the United States, from the onset of industrialization to the present, have been shaped by a number of forces, the most important of which is the structure of the economy. Industrialization brought about a fundamental transformation of the nature of work, the spatial geography of cities, and ultimately the nature of urban poverty. In the commercial city of the colonial period and the early nineteenth century, work and the household were, for the majority of city dwellers, integrally related. Most artisans were self-employed or realistically strove for economic independence. Families produced both for the market and for their own subsistence, regulated by the irregular rhythms of work seasons.[5] Impoverishment frequently accompanied work in the commercial city, despite the romantic descriptions of early modern life favored by many historians. Seasonal underemployment beset artisans and laborers throughout the early modern world. Eighteenth-century American observers expressed concern at the seemingly uncontrollable population of the "strolling poor," and few could miss the signs of poverty in the bustling port towns of colonial America. The vagaries of international trade led to the regular unemployment of seafarers; likewise, bloody colonial wars and the high urban mortality rates of colonial America created a visible class of sick and injured men and women, widows and orphans. Although colonial American towns seemed far more open and hospitable than the "infernal wen" of London, colonists expressed dismay at the poor among them.[6]

---

[5] Herbert Gutman, "Work, Culture, and Society in Industrializing America, 1815–1919," *American Historical Review* 78 (1973): 531–88; Susan Hirsch, *Roots of the American Working Class: The Industrialization of Crafts in Newark, 1800–1860* (Philadelphia: University of Pennsylvania Press, 1978), 3–13.

[6] Douglas Lamar Jones, "The Strolling Poor: Transiency in Eighteenth-Century Massachusetts," *Journal of Social History* 8 (1975): 28–54; Gary B. Nash, *The Urban Crucible: Social Change, Political Consciousness, and the Origins of the American Revolution* (Cambridge: Harvard University Press, 1979), esp. chaps. 1, 3, 5, 9, 12; Alexander Keyssar, "Widowhood in Eighteenth-Century Massachusetts: A Problem in the History of the Family," *Perspectives in American History* 8 (1974): 81–119; Billy G. Smith, *The 'Lower Sort': Philadelphia's Laboring People, 1750–1800* (Ithaca: Cornell University Press, 1990). Colonial seamen were an interesting exception to patterns of work in the eighteenth

The coming of industry to American cities changed the causes and nature of poverty enormously. The household base of the urban economy eroded as industry—whether on the scale of the workshop, the manufactory, or the factory—began to replace the home as the locus of production in the burgeoning regional and international marketplaces of the nineteenth century. Patterns and the rate of industrialization varied widely from place to place, and the social and spatial consequences of the shift to wage labor were by no means uniform.[7] Large port cities like New York experienced what Sean Wilentz called "metropolitan industrialization." Few of New York's workers in the early nineteenth century worked in the enormous factories that characterized the archetypal industrial center. But on the small scale of the shop, the independence of the traditional crafts gave way to a new methodical, disciplined form of labor, to a division of labor that precluded highly skilled craft specialization. Their skills devalued, workers were dependent on wages offered for services rendered to employers, and subject to the whims of employers and to the vicissitudes of a developing economy.[8] In nineteenth-century Philadelphia, industrialization was not uniform, and work settings ranged from the large manufactory to the sweatshop to the artisanal shop. As in New York, a large class of unskilled and semiskilled wage workers soon vastly outnumbered the self-sufficient households of the colonial and early national eras. But the patterns of work and opportunity ranged widely between the various places of employment.

Concurrent with metropolitan industrialization was the emergence of new industrial centers, peculiarly nineteenth-century cities built around a single manufacturing enterprise or a cluster of manufactories. Typical of such cities was Fall River, a somnolent farm village in 1800 that became one of the most

---

century; their work patterns and payment presaged the industrial organization of the nineteenth century. See Marcus Rediker, *Between the Devil and the Deep Blue Sea: Merchant Seamen, Pirates, and the Anglo-American Maritime World, 1700–1750* (New York: Cambridge University Press, 1987).

[7] Bruce Laurie and Mark Schmitz, "Manufacture and Productivity: The Making of an Industrial Base, Philadelphia, 1850–1880," in Theodore Hershberg, ed., *Philadelphia: Work, Space, Family, and Group Experience in the Nineteenth Century* (New York: Oxford University Press, 1981), 43–92, warn against an oversimplified model of industrialization derived from the textile industry, and point to significant local variation in industry within one city. For examples of the diversity of industrial development in nineteenth-century America, see Philip Scranton, *Proprietary Capitalism: The Textile Manufacture at Philadelphia, 1880–1885* (New York: Cambridge University Press, 1983); Christine Stansell, "The Origins of the Sweatshop: Women and Early Industrialization in New York City," in Michael Frisch and Daniel Walkowitz, eds., *Working-Class America: Essays on Labor, Community, and American Society* (Urbana: University of Illinois Press, 1983), 78–103; Jonathan Prude, *The Coming of the Industrial Order: Town and Factory Life in Rural Massachusetts, 1810–1860* (New York: Cambridge University Press, 1983); Hirsch, *Roots of the American Working Class*; Steven J. Ross, *Workers on the Edge: Work, Leisure and Politics in Industrializing Cincinnati* (New York: Columbia University Press, 1985).

[8] Sean Wilentz, *Chants Democratic: New York City and the Rise of the American Working Class, 1788–1850* (New York: Oxford University Press, 1984).

important centers of textile production in the United States by 1850. The official seal of the city depicting the belching smokestacks of the city's textile plants symbolized the new organization of labor and the new geography of mill-town industrialization, as large plants and an army of wage laborers worked in an economy once dominated by farmers, artisans, and fishermen. Other cities such as Lowell, Massachusetts, Newark, New Jersey, and Manchester, New Hampshire, followed similar patterns. These industrial towns became labor magnets, attracting temporary workers (often women) who migrated there from the countryside, small farmers displaced by nineteenth-century agricultural changes, and immigrants from Europe. The paternal organization of some mill towns occasionally protected workers from the harsher aspects of the unpredictable nineteenth-century economy, and workers who came to such cities temporarily, especially young women, simply returned to their farm homes during periodic downturns. But for most workers, mill-town work was not steady, and unemployment was common. And by the mid-nineteenth century, paternalism waned as employers faced increasing competition in the world market, and took advantage of the influx of a cheap and readily available supply of immigrant labor.[9]

As the nineteenth century progressed, few workers resembled the Jeffersonian yeomanry or free laborers of American mythology. Deskilled artisans in large cities and farmers who migrated to new industrial towns, and European and Canadian immigrants, were seldom self-sufficient, and had few alternative sources of support when out of work. As rural workers lost their tie to the land, they lost the precarious means of support that the soil could offer them. Artisans, no longer self-employed, had to subsist on the unsteady flow of wages. As regional and international economic networks expanded, workers' well-being was increasingly affected by economic decisions and market fluctuations over which they had absolutely no control. Early industrial enterprises were, moreover, notoriously volatile: a majority of nineteenth-century business ventures failed within a few years.[10] Like colonial workers, workers in the nineteenth-century industrial city suffered frequent illness and injury; but unlike their predecessors, they also lost the predictability and certainty of seasonal work and the control of self-employment.

[9] Hirsch, *Roots of the American Working Class*, 15–51; John Cumbler, *Working Class Community in Industrial America: Work, Leisure, and Struggle in Two Industrial Cities, 1880–1940* (Westport, Conn.: Greenwood Press, 1979), 99–110; Thomas Dublin, *Women at Work: The Transformation of Work and Community in Lowell, Massachusetts, 1826–1860* (New York: Columbia University Press, 1979); Tamara Hareven, *Family Time and Industrial Time: The Relationship between Family and Work in a New England Industrial Community* (Cambridge: Cambridge University Press, 1982).

[10] R. G. Hutchinson, A. R. Hutchinson, and Mabel Newcomer, "Study in Business Mortality," *American Economic Review* 28 (1938): 497–514; Clyde Griffen and Sally Griffen, *Natives and Newcomers: The Ordering of Opportunity in Mid-Nineteenth-Century Poughkeepsie* (Cambridge: Harvard University Press, 1978), 103–17.

Along with industrialization came the phenomenon of widespread and frequent unemployment. Periods of idleness were common in colonial and early nineteenth-century America, but because many workers were self-employed, few found themselves entirely lacking in work. With the coming of the factory system, by contrast, workers suffered unpredictable and prolonged periods without steady employment and wages. Poverty in industrializing urban America was largely a function of unemployment.[11] A large minority of the work force in such heavily industrialized states suffered several weeks of unemployment each year, even during the boom years of midcentury and the 1880s. In years of economic depression, unemployment rates soared. In Massachusetts, unemployment ranged from 10 percent in 1885 to 5.2 percent in 1890. In the former year, nearly 30 percent of the Massachusetts labor force was without work at some point; in the latter, over 18 percent fell into unemployment.[12] In Pittsburgh, to take another example, more than 30 percent of the population was unemployed for at least one month in 1880, 1890, and 1900.[13]

A significant feature of unemployment was its contribution to the geographical mobility of nineteenth-century urban workers. Stephan Thernstrom and Peter Knights describe nineteenth-century society as one of tremendous fluidity, filled with "men in motion." It is impossible to underestimate the effects of constant movement on the nature of the nineteenth-century city. The population of industrial America was remarkably unstable, for many cities were mere way stations; the poor and jobless moved rapidly from place to place in search of employment. From year to year in Boston between 1830 and 1860, as much as 20 percent of the population turned over; data from throughout the United States show that on average about 40 percent of the urban population remained in cities between decennial censuses from the 1830s through the early twentieth century.[14]

The phenomenon of tramping was the most visible sign of the dislocation and geographic mobility of industrial American workers. The peripatetic poor, not unfamiliar in the colonial past, became an especially common sight in the nineteenth century. According to the best available estimate, 10 to 20 percent of late-nineteenth-century Americans lived in a family with a member who

[11] Alexander Keyssar, *Out of Work: The First Century of Unemployment in Massachusetts* (New York: Cambridge University Press, 1986).

[12] Ibid., 51, 302–3, 340–41.

[13] S. J. Kleinberg, *The Shadow of the Mills: Working-Class Families in Pittsburgh, 1870–1907* (Pittsburgh: University of Pittsburgh Press, 1989), 20–22.

[14] Stephan Thernstrom and Peter Knights, "Men in Motion: Some Data and Speculations about Urban Population Mobility in Nineteenth-Century America", in Tamara Hareven, ed., *Anonymous Americans: Explorations in Nineteenth-Century Social History* (Englewood Cliffs, N.J.: Prentice-Hall, 1971), 17–47; Peter Knights, *The Plain People of Boston, 1830–1860: A Study in City Growth* (New York: Oxford University Press, 1971), 58, 63; for a summary of persistence data, see Stephan Thernstrom, *The Other Bostonians: Poverty and Progress in the American Metropolis, 1880–1960* (Cambridge: Harvard University Press, 1973), 222–23.

tramped at some point.[15] Among these wandering men (and occasionally women) were unemployed unskilled workers who formed the nineteenth-century labor surplus, and a large number of skilled craftsmen who found themselves rootless when their craft skills were superseded by technological changes.[16] The instability of the urban rental market, the whims of landlords, and the difficulty of meeting rent payments further contributed to the flow of rootless men and women in the nineteenth-century city.[17] A large part of the "floating proletariat" in nineteenth-century cities consisted of the poorest men and women, those who were compelled to move for survival.[18]

Class and Residence in the Industrializing City

Early industrial cities, whether the sprawling metropolises of New York and Philadelphia or the concentrated industrial towns of New England and the Middle Atlantic region, were relatively unsegregated by class or social status. Vestiges of the walking city were visible through midcentury in older urban areas such as New York and Philadelphia, where operatives and laborers shared residential districts with merchants and clerks, both of which could be found in proximity to the places of commerce and industry. In Boston and Newark, clerks preferred to live in row houses on the periphery of the city's business district, close to their places of employment in countinghouses, offices, and stores. The working poor of the two cities found residence near the center-city warehouse district appealing for their easy access to a number of prospective places of employment in the concentrated commercial district of the center city.[19] A similar pattern of limited class segregation held in smaller nineteenth-century commercial cities. Both white-collar and blue-collar workers had incentives to live as closely as possible to the center-city concentration of employment and business activity.[20] The reasons for lack of strict residential segregation were

---

[15] Eric Monkkonen, *Police in Urban America, 1860–1920* (New York: Cambridge University Press, 1981), 93–96. The figure is based on an estimate of men who stayed overnight in police stations. The best social histories of tramping are Eric Monkkonen, ed., *Walking to Work: Tramps in America, 1790–1935* (Lincoln: University of Nebraska Press, 1984); Michael B. Katz, *Poverty and Policy in American History* (New York: Academic Press, 1983), 157–81; and Kenneth L. Kusmer, "The Underclass in Historical Perspective: Tramps and Vagrants in Urban America, 1870–1930," in Rick Beard, ed., *On Being Homeless: Historical Perspectives* (New York: Museum of the City of New York, 1987), 21–31.

[16] Jules Tygiel, "Tramping Artisans: Carpenters in Industrial America, 1880–1890," in Monkkonen, *Walking to Work*, 87–117.

[17] Kenneth Scherzer, *The Unbounded Community: Neighborhood Life and Social Structure in New York City, 1830–1875* (Durham, N.C.: Duke University Press, 1992), chap. 2.

[18] Thernstrom, *Other Bostonians*, 231; Thernstrom and Knights, "Men in Motion," 32.

[19] Hirsch, *Roots of the American Working Class*, 92–99; David Ward, "The Emergence of Central Immigrant Ghettoes in American Cities, 1840–1920," *Annals of the American Association of Geographers* 58 (1968): 343–51.

[20] Ian Davey and Michael Doucet, "The Social Geography of a Commercial City, ca. 1853,"

sometimes ideological. The spatial order of many textile towns, for example, reflected the paternalism of evangelical industrialists. In Manchester, New Hampshire, workers and overseers of the enormous Amoskeag textile complex lived in the same neighborhoods and shared the same institutions.[21]

Early industrialization, however, carried within it the seeds of a new urban spatial order. As cities expanded, industry began to locate in areas other than the city centers. Groups of workers attracted to particular industries tended to live in neighborhoods close to their places of employment, and many large cities developed clusters of industrial communities concentrated around large workplaces or decentralized manufacturing districts. Workers found it advantageous—even necessary—to live close to prospective places of employment, for distance from the workplace in nineteenth-century America exacerbated the difficulties of obtaining work.[22] But throughout the mid- and late nineteenth century, the process of spatial divergence by class was countered to some extent by the cleavages of ethnicity. As large numbers of immigrants began to populate American cities in the nineteenth century, they often created residentially distinct subcommunities that mediated their adjustment to American urban life. In Milwaukee, immigrants settled in clusters around their churches and social clubs; in Detroit and Philadelphia, they likewise dispersed in small units throughout the city, rather than settling in large, homogeneous ethnic districts.[23]

At the same time that industrial workers were attracted to neighborhoods surrounding their places of employment, many middle-class and wealthy city dwellers found such concentrations of industry undesirable and began to build new homes in outlying areas, distant from working people, noisome factories, and congested streets. The trend toward deconcentration was visible by the 1830s in larger cities like New York, where exclusive suburban enclaves re-

---

appendix 1 to Michael B. Katz, *The People of Hamilton, Canada West* (Cambridge: Harvard University Press, 1975), 319–42.

[21] Hareven, *Family Time and Industrial Time*, 24–25.

[22] Alan Burstein, "Immigrants and Residential Mobility: The Irish and Germans in Philadelphia, 1850–1880," in Hershberg, *Philadelphia*, 174–203; Stephanie Greenberg, "Industrial Location and Ethnic Residential Patterns in an Industrializing City: Philadelphia, 1880," in Hershberg, *Philadelphia*, 204–32; Scherzer, *Unbounded Community*, 129–38.

[23] Kathleen Neils Conzen, *Immigrant Milwaukee, 1836–1860* (Cambridge: Harvard University Press, 1976); Olivier Zunz, *The Changing Face of Inequality: Urbanization, Industrial Development, and Immigrants in Detroit, 1880–1920* (Chicago: University of Chicago Press, 1983), 15–88; Greenberg, "Industrial Location," 224, is correct, I believe, in her emphasis on the primacy of industry over ethnicity in determining residence, a point with which Zunz takes issue. Her statement that "within the larger industrial cluster, small, homogeneous ethnic enclaves may have evolved" (224) points to some common ground between her findings and Zunz's for Detroit. Scherzer, *Unbounded Community*, finds that in New York, class was more important than ethnicity in determining residential patterns, and that ethnic communities were frequently "aspatial"—not bound by a particular neighborhood.

placed the undifferentiated neighborhoods of the walking city, as the well-to-do abandoned private homes in the city's former commercial district for more salubrious residences uptown or across the bay in the early commuting suburb of Brooklyn Heights, while workers continued to inhabit neighborhoods where commerce, industry, and residence crowded onto the same streets. The wealthy protected their neighborhoods from undesirable uses and unwanted residences through the use of restrictive covenants. As Elizabeth Blackmar argues, "the neutral market had carried a new class dynamic into the process of residential neighborhood formation." By the mid-nineteenth century, Manhattan's East Side was a distinctive working-class district, which had been largely abandoned by clerks, professionals, and the commercial and financial elite.[24]

Other large coastal cities took on a sharper differentiation by class as professionals, clerks, and capitalists fled the densely populated commercial districts of the center city. In the 1840s, developers began offering Boston's professionals refuge on the city's periphery. In late-nineteenth-century Philadelphia and Boston, for example, advances in streetcar transportation abetted the desires of nonindustrial workers to flee industrial and working-class districts. Manual workers by necessity inhabited areas close to their workplaces, whereas white-collar workers inhabited new neighborhoods on the edge of the city.[25] By midcentury this pattern of class differentiation in housing began to manifest itself in smaller cities as well, presaging a pattern that was to become increasingly common in the early twentieth century. Industrial cities where factories were not organized on the paternalist model, for example, Fall River, began to show a clear divergence of residence by class as early as the mid-nineteenth century. Fall River's industrialists and merchants constructed homes on the city's rocky escarpment overlooking Mount Hope Bay, while most working people lived in the lower parts of the city, close to the textile mills.[26]

[24] Elizabeth S. Blackmar, *Manhattan for Rent, 1785–1850* (Ithaca: Cornell University Press, 1990), 104. Richard Stott, *Workers in the Metropolis: Class, Ethnicity, and Youth in Antebellum New York City* (Ithaca: Cornell University Press, 1990), 191–211, discusses the increasing spatial differentiation by wealth in early nineteenth-century New York. On suburban development in New York, see Kenneth T. Jackson, *Crabgrass Frontier: The Suburbanization of the United States* (New York: Oxford University Press, 1985), 20–44. Jackson finds a similar pattern of deconcentration in nineteenth-century Philadelphia; see "Urban Deconcentration in the Nineteenth Century: A Statistical Inquiry," in Leo F. Schnore, ed., *The New Urban History: Quantitative Explorations by American Historians* (Princeton: Princeton University Press, 1975), 110–42.

[25] On suburbanization and suburb as middle-class refuge before the streetcar, see Henry Binford, *The First Suburbs: Residential Communities on the Boston Periphery, 1815–1860* (Chicago: University of Chicago Press, 1985), 169–86. On commuting and suburbanization, see Theodore Hershberg, Harold E. Cox, Dale Light, Jr., and Richard R. Greenfield, "The 'Journey-to-Work': An Empirical Investigation of Work, Residence, and Transportation, Philadelphia, 1850 and 1880," in Hershberg, *Philadelphia*, 128–73. See also Sam Bass Warner, *Streetcar Suburbs: The Process of Growth in Boston, 1870–1900* (Cambridge: Harvard University Press, 1962).

[26] On working-class residential patterns in Fall River, see Cumbler, *Working-Class Community*, 114–17; on the wealthy, see Thomas J. Sugrue, "A Generation of Leaders: Early Capitalists in Fall River, 1830–1870" (seminar paper, Harvard University, 1987).

Whether working people and the middle and upper classes lived in close proximity to each other, as in midcentury Boston or Hamilton, or in separate neighborhoods, as in Fall River or New York, few nineteenth-century American cities had a distinctive residential concentration of the poor. Nineteenth-century reformers, preoccupied with the physical conditions of the bleakest sections of the city, favored sensational descriptions of the small, highly visible districts of vice to more pedestrian descriptions of the residences of a majority of the poor and working people of the city.[27] Such descriptions, accepted un-critically by many twentieth-century scholars, overemphasized the homogeneity of urban "slums" and their residents. Seldom was there a clear distinction between the residential locations of the employed and unemployed, between the family coping with economic difficulty by sending its children to work and the household of the young family living beneath the level of subsistence on one unpredictable, hardly steady income. Most working families suffered periodic poverty, and individual workers were particularly vulnerable to life-cycle changes, injury and illness, company failures, and business cycles. In the economically precarious environment of the city, steadily employed workers and the migratory poor shared the same buildings, streets, and residential districts. Urban working-class neighborhoods were in constant flux. The most economically unfortunate were the least likely to stay in the same house or neighborhood for any period of time. Poverty was such an ordinary yet unpredictable visitor to the working-class household that it could not manifest itself in the residential segregation of the poor.[28]

URBAN POVERTY AND THE ASCENDANCY OF CORPORATE CAPITALISM

The turn of the twentieth century saw the consolidation of American industry. The large-scale accumulation and investment of capital, corporate mergers, and bureaucratic corporate organization, all of which had precedents in the nineteenth century, became the norm in the early twentieth-century city, with dra-

[27] David Ward, *Poverty, Ethnicity, and the American City, 1840–1925: Changing Conceptions of the Slum and the Ghetto* (Cambridge: Cambridge University Press, 1989), offers a trenchant critique of the perceptions of social order and control that shaped nineteenth-century observers' notions of concentrated poverty, and by implication, a critique of more recent scholarship that assumes the homogeneity of immigrant communities in American history. See also Sam Bass Warner and Colin Burke, "Cultural Change and the Ghetto," *Journal of Contemporary History* 4 (1969): 173–87; Howard Chudacoff, "A New Look at Ethnic Neighborhoods: Residential Dispersion and the Concept of Visibility in a Medium-Sized City," *Journal of American History* 60 (1973): 76–93. A useful modification of these articles is Olivier Zunz, "Residential Segregation in the American Metropolis: Concentration, Dispersion, and Dominance," in David Reeder, ed., *Urban History Yearbook* (Leicester: Leicester University Press, 1980), 23–33.

[28] Stott, *Workers in the Metropolis*, 188–90, attempts, with little evidence, to draw a distinction between workers and the poor. Studies of family budgets make clear the precariousness of working-class subsistence. See for example, Michael R. Haines, "Poverty, Economic Stress, and the Family," in Hershberg, *Philadelphia*, 240–76. Thernstrom and Knights, "Men in Motion," 38–39.

matic consequences for the organization of work and for the spatial order of the Northern industrial city. Whereas in 1870, the average workplace had fewer than one hundred employees, by 1900, an increasing number of urban workers were employed in large factories with several hundred, and often several thousand, employees.[29] Urban labor markets, of course, remained diverse. In the shadow of large conglomerates stood sweatshops, craft-based workshops, and small factories. Workers in the booming construction industry faced economic constraints not unfamiliar to their nineteenth-century predecessors: their labor market was especially sensitive to the effects of economic cycles and regional booms and busts. Likewise, a large casual work force, consisting of peddlers, day laborers, and domestics, could be found in every city. But the persistence of these forms of work was overshadowed by the growing dominance of industry by fewer and larger vertically organized corporations.[30]

Perhaps the most important consequence of the new form of corporate capitalism was the homogenization of industrial work and the stabilization of employment for a sizable number of urban workers. Across the United States, wage differentials in industry narrowed as regional labor markets replaced the bewildering local variety of the early industrial economy.[31] An emphasis on efficiency and managerial control of production, and a further intensification of the division of labor, transformed the work process in manufacturing enterprises. The new managerial bureaucracy of large corporations, unlike most of the individuals who funded and managed the small-scale family industrial enterprises of the nineteenth century, emphasized long-term corporate survival ahead of ephemeral short-term profits.[32] Large corporations—because they rested on enormous accumulations of capital—were also less susceptible to the frequent failures that plagued the smaller partnerships and small companies characteristic of early industrialization.

The stability and security of the large factory relative to earlier, small-scale production was apparent by the early twentieth century. As Theodore Hershberg has argued, the "best work settings in terms of career opportunities, security, working conditions, and wages were large factories, not small shops."[33] By the 1920s, most large corporations realized the negative consequences of a

[29] Daniel Nelson, *Managers and Workers: Origins of the New Factory System in the United States, 1880–1920* (Madison: University of Wisconsin Press, 1975), 3–10.

[30] Alfred D. Chandler, Jr., *The Visible Hand: The Managerial Revolution in American Business* (Cambridge: Harvard University Press, 1977).

[31] Gordon, Edwards, and Reich, *Segmented Work, Divided Workers*, 100–164.

[32] Chandler, *Visible Hand*, 10, argues that in large enterprises "career managers preferred policies that favored the long-term stability and growth of their enterprises to those that maximized current profits." Sanford Jacoby, *Employing Bureaucracy: Managers, Unions, and the Transformation of Work in American Industry, 1900–1945* (New York: Columbia University Press, 1985), finds the origins of corporate policy to encourage work-force stability in the turn-of-the-century period, but dates the success of these policies to the 1930s.

[33] Theodore Hershberg, "Work," in Hershberg, *Philadelphia*, 41.

high turnover of workers, especially during periods of labor shortage, and began to pursue measures to reduce unemployment. Also, in an attempt to discipline an ethnically diverse and restive work force, many companies implemented corporate welfare programs that shielded a significant minority of workers from at least some of the turbulence of the economy before the Great Depression.[34]

The well-being of a large portion of industrial workers in Northern cities was not guaranteed in the long run by corporate welfare programs, but instead by the wage, job security, and employment agreements that successful industrial unions and management hammered out in the 1930s and 1940s. Provisions in the earliest Congress of Industrial Organizations contracts established a seniority system that helped to ensure stable work for union members. Contracts negotiated by unions during the no-strike pledge of the Second World War and in the period of labor-management accord in the late 1940s guaranteed relatively high wages and secure employment for a substantial sector of the industrial work force. Wages tied to productivity increases and rises in the cost of living, pioneered by the automotive industry, became standard in a number of large industries.[35] The compromises of collective bargaining guaranteed a stratum of workers protected from the economic capriciousness that characterized the nineteenth-century factory. A large part of the urban work force, however, remained caught in the periodic downturns characteristic of the industrial economy, and vulnerable to earnings poverty. Trapped in insecure jobs with small companies increasingly marginal to a market dominated by large corporations, they shared with their nineteenth-century predecessors susceptibility to bouts of poverty. Workers in what Gordon, Edwards, and Reich call "peripheral" manufacturing jobs in "weak, poorly financed firms" had lower wages, were less likely to have the security of union membership, and suffered higher layoff and unemployment rates.[36]

---

[34] Nelson, *Managers and Workers*, 86–87, 101–39; 149–52; Jacoby, *Employing Bureaucracy*, 115–26, 195–205; Gerd Korman, *Industrialization, Immigrants, and Americanizers* (Madison: State Historical Society of Wisconsin, 1967); Stephen Mayer, "Adapting the Immigrant to the Line: Americanization in the Ford Factory, 1914–1921," *Journal of Social History* 14 (1980): 67–82; David Brody, "The Rise and Decline of Welfare Capitalism," in David Brody, ed., *Workers in Industrial America* (New York: Oxford University Press, 1980), 48–81. It is important not to exaggerate the effects of welfare capitalism. Welfare capitalism was not always successful in cushioning workers from economic disruption, even in relatively stable industries. See Lizabeth Cohen, *Making a New Deal: Industrial Workers in Chicago, 1919–1939* (Cambridge: Cambridge University Press, 1990), 183–211.

[35] Jacoby, *Employing Bureaucracy*, 243–50; Nelson Lichtenstein, "From Corporatism to Collective Bargaining: Organized Labor and the Eclipse of Social Democracy in the Postwar Era," in Steve Fraser and Gary Gerstle, eds., *The Rise and Fall of the New Deal Order, 1930–1980* (Princeton: Princeton University Press, 1989), 140–44.

[36] Gordon, Edwards, and Reich, *Segmented Work, Divided Workers*, 190–200; see also Lichtenstein, "From Corporatism to Collective Bargaining," 145, table 5.1, for a contrast between wages in the automobile industry and in miscellaneous manufacturing, apparel, and retail trade.

The Segmented Metropolis

The spatial structure of large American cities also took on a sharper differentiation by class in the early twentieth century. The trend toward suburbanization accelerated rapidly in the late nineteenth century and the first decades of the twentieth century as the rapidly expanding white-collar work force abandoned center-city places of residence to the enormous influx of immigrants. By the early twentieth century, only the rare and eccentric corporate executive chose to live near a central business district. Middle-class workers and the wealthy preferred the spacious surroundings of suburban bedroom communities. Only those with secure, well-paying jobs could afford transportation costs and the expensive amenities of these new communities. Suburban communities maintained their exclusive status through privately developed infrastructure, municipal incorporation, restrictive covenants, and, later, zoning ordinances.[37]

As cities expanded outward, blue-collar workers were increasingly concentrated in largely working-class areas. They were unable to afford the amenities of the bourgeois suburban home, and usually could not penetrate the legal and extralegal barriers of exclusivity that protected the communities of the middle class and wealthy. New residential developments designed for workers, close to new factory complexes, reinforced patterns of class separation. Neighborhoods surrounding enormous plants brought together workers from all backgrounds who found residence close to the workplace more compelling than the ties of ethnicity.[38] Working-class communities also divided by economic status, replicating in microcosm the growing division between classes in the social geography of the city. Scores of new neighborhoods for industrial workers sprung up in the vicinity of new manufacturing complexes, often tract developments built for convenient access to the workplace. Those employed in less secure and poor paying jobs, on the other hand, lived in cheaper rental housing in older sections of the city, often formerly inhabited by middle-class and working-class residents who fled to expanding residential areas on the urban periphery. Most important for the future of Northern metropolitan areas was the emergence, beginning in the 1910s and 1920s, of large black "ghettos" in the center cities, increasingly

[37] Ann Durkin Keating, *Building Chicago: Suburban Developers and the Creation of a Divided Metropolis* (Columbus: Ohio State University Press, 1988), 16–17, 77, 120–24; Patricia Burgess Stach, "Deed Restrictions and Subdivision Development in Columbus Ohio, 1900–1970," *Journal of Urban History* 15 (1988): 42–68.

[38] Olivier Zunz, *The Changing Face of Inequality*, 359. For a similar finding for Philadelphia, see Theodore Hershberg, Alan N. Burstein, Eugene P. Ericksen, Stephanie W. Greenberg, and William L. Yancey, "A Tale of Three Cities: Blacks, Immigrants, and Opportunity in Philadelphia, 1850–1880, 1930, 1970," in Hershberg, *Philadelphia*, 473–76. On the forces that generated and broke down ethnic identification, see Cohen, *Making a New Deal*; and Gary Gerstle, *Working-Class Americanism: The Politics of Labor in a Textile City, 1914–1960* (Cambridge: Cambridge University Press, 1989).

removed from the new industrial and suburban developments in the metropolis.[39]

Black Workers: A Case Apart

The exclusion of blacks from the industrial economy of the nineteenth and early twentieth centuries is well documented; the small populations of urban blacks in the North were restricted to a narrow range of jobs, and were disproportionately represented in domestic and menial work. At the turn of the century, more than two-thirds of black men in sixteen out of nineteen major American cities were employed in menial jobs.[40] Few blacks found employment in the burgeoning manufacturing sector. In Detroit, to take one example, in 1900, 139 of 36,598 men in manufacturing jobs were black; as late as 1910, only 25 of 10,000 workers in Detroit's rapidly expanding automotive industry were black.[41] Because of their exclusion from the industrial labor pool, however, black workers may have been cushioned from the chronic bouts of unemployment that affected workers in the industrial sector. In Massachusetts in the late nineteenth century, blacks were concentrated in poor paying but generally secure service jobs—the few blacks in the manufacturing sector, on the other hand, suffered high rates of unemployment.[42]

Northern industrial cities had small concentrations of blacks living in them from the antebellum period, but blacks constituted no more than 5 percent of the population in any Northern city before 1910. Northern urban blacks were often clustered in their own subcommunities, although they were seldom fully segregated from white neighborhoods.[43] Like nineteenth-century whites,

[39] Eugene P. Ericksen and William L. Yancey, "Work and Residence in Industrial Philadelphia," *Journal of Urban History* 5 (1979): 147–82, esp. 159–70.

[40] Elizabeth Hafkin Pleck, *Black Migration and Poverty: Boston, 1865–1900* (New York: Academic Press, 1979), 128.

[41] David M. Katzman, *Before the Ghetto: Black Detroit in the Nineteenth Century* (Urbana: University of Illinois Press, 1973), 105.

[42] Keyssar, *Out of Work*, 88–89. Pleck, *Black Migration and Poverty*, 134–35, offers a cautionary note that unemployment measures for the nineteenth century may not accurately reflect the underemployment of black casual and domestic workers.

[43] On black residential patterns in the nineteenth century, see Shane White, "'We Dwell in Safety and Pursue Our Honest Callings': Free Blacks in New York City, 1783–1810," *Journal of American History* 75 (1988): 445–70; David M. Katzman, *Before the Ghetto*, 26–29, 56–80; Kenneth L. Kusmer, *A Ghetto Takes Shape: Black Cleveland, 1870–1930* (Urbana: University of Illinois Press, 1976), 13, 42–52; Pleck, *Black Migration and Poverty*, 31–33; Henry M. Taylor, "Spatial Organization and the Black Residential Experience: Black Cincinnati in 1850," *Social Science History* 10 (1986): 45–69; for a static view of the black urban experience which has come under much criticism by recent scholars, see Gilbert Osofsky, "The Enduring Ghetto," *Journal of American History* 55 (1968): 243–55.

blacks lived in the vicinity of most urban workplaces, but because of discriminatory barriers in hiring, residence near factories and warehouses seldom offered
them any advantages.[44] Perhaps the only blacks to benefit from residence were
menial waterfront workers who were hired casually, domestics who inhabited
the environs of wealthy white neighborhoods, and employees of the hotels and
barber shops of commercial districts.[45]

The flood of black migrants from the South beginning during World War I
changed the landscape of Northern industrial centers. Recruited as cheap labor
during the wartime and postwar labor shortage, lured to the North by accounts
of political and social independence, and pushed out by agricultural changes
and violence, these Southern migrants entered the industrial work force in large
numbers for the first time. The process of proletarianization improved the
situation of urban blacks over their Southern counterparts: Northern cities were
a "land of hope" for blacks suffering the dislocations of life in the early twentieth-
century South. Despite the unprecedented economic opportunity of the city,
blacks found themselves economically disadvantaged relative to white workers,
often temporarily hired, squeezed into the most insecure and dangerous unskilled jobs by racial discrimination, and frequently laid off and fired.[46] The
contrast between the aspirations and opportunity of black workers and the
realities of the industrial economy persisted, even in the prosperous decades of
the mid-twentieth century.

URBAN INDUSTRIAL DECLINE AND THE NEW URBAN POVERTY

In the three decades following the outbreak of the Second World War, the high
rate of economic growth in the United States concealed important industrial and
demographic changes that had a profound impact on employment opportunity
and urban development in Northern cities. Simultaneous with the industrial
transformation of the postwar era was an acceleration of the spatial restructuring
of American cities by race and class, compounded by government policies. The

[44] Ericksen and Yancey, "Work and Residence," 170–72.

[45] On the residential patterns of waterfront workers, see Taylor, "Spatial Organization"; Katzman, Before the Ghetto, 117–20; on black service and railroad workers, see Pleck, Black Migration and
Poverty, 77–78.

[46] Dennis Dickerson, Out of the Crucible: Black Steelworkers in Western Pennsylvania, 1875–1980
(Albany: State University of New York Press, 1986), 27–53; Peter Gottlieb, Making Their Own Way:
Southern Blacks' Migration to Pittsburgh, 1916–1930 (Urbana: University of Illinois Press, 1987);
Cheryl Lynn Greenberg, "Or Does It Explode?": Black Harlem in the Great Depression (New York:
Oxford University Press, 1991), 18–28, 227–30; James Grossman, Land of Hope: Chicago, Black
Southerners, and the Great Migration (Chicago: University of Chicago Press, 1989); Richard W.
Thomas, "From Peasant to Proletarian: The Formation and Organization of the Black Industrial
Working Class in Detroit, 1915–1945" (Ph.D. diss., University of Michigan, 1976); Joe William
Trotter, Jr., Black Milwaukee: The Making of an Industrial Proletariat (Urbana: University of Illinois
Press, 1985).

new working-class migrants to the urban North, especially blacks and Hispanics, faced economic and spatial constraints that altered the forms and distribution of urban poverty. Yet the various types of poverty dominant in past periods of American history were still visible in the postwar city. The disabled, infirm, and elderly still composed a significant (but rapidly shrinking) segment of the population in poverty.[47] Unskilled day laborers and domestics, ever present in the early industrial city, made up a shrinking number of the work force in the postwar metropolis, still liable to frequent bouts of joblessness, usually uncushioned by unemployment benefits available to other workers. A sizable minority of the work force remained employed in the small, peripheral firms unusually prone to failure or instability, especially during cyclical downturns in the economy. But among them emerged a new group of poor people, those unattached or only loosely attached to the labor market, increasingly excluded from the manufacturing jobs—either core or peripheral—that had provided some opportunity to working people in the past.

The forms and distribution of recent poverty are best understood through an examination of the intersection of industry, economy, and residence in a single city.[48] Detroit, a leading industrial center, dominated by the automobile industry and, to a lesser extent, steel, chemical, metalworking, and machine-tool industries, provides a useful case study. Like other leading Northeastern and Midwestern industrial centers in the last half century, Detroit lost a large portion of its manufacturing employment, it has experienced an intensification of patterns of racial and class segregation, and its suburbs expanded rapidly, as the center city suffered an enormous population decline.[49]

[47] Mark J. Stern, "Poverty and Family Composition since 1940," chapter 7 of this volume; Christine Ross, Sheldon Danziger, and Eugene Smolensky, "The Level and Trend of Poverty in the United States, 1939–1979," *Demography* 24 (1987): 587–600.

[48] There are few models for such a study in historical scholarship. One book is especially helpful: John T. Cumbler, *A Social History of Economic Decline: Business, Politics, and Work in Trenton* (New Brunswick, N.J.: Rutgers University Press, 1989). Two important articles that link social, racial, and economic change in the postwar era are: Loïc J. D. Wacquant, "The Ghetto, the State, and the New Capitalist Economy," *Dissent* 36 (1989): 508–20; and Leonard S. Wallock, "The Myth of the Master Builder: Robert Moses, New York, and the Dynamics of Metropolitan Development since World War II," *Journal of Urban History* 17 (1991): 339–62.

[49] There are a number of sources of data for a comparison of Detroit and other Northern industrial cities. For statistics on the loss of manufacturing jobs, see John D. Kasarda, "Urban Change and Minority Opportunities," in Paul E. Peterson, ed., *The New Urban Reality* (Washington, D.C.: Brookings Institution, 1985), 44. According to Kasarda, the most marked difference between Detroit's labor market and that of other major cities was the decline in employment in Detroit's service sector, mainly after 1967 (45). On levels of segregation in 1940, 1950, and 1960, see Karl E. Taeuber and Alma F. Taeuber, *Negroes in Cities: Residential Segregation and Neighborhood Change* (Chicago: Aldine Publishing Company, 1965), 39–41. Of the twenty-four largest SMSAs in 1980, Detroit ranked fifth highest in household income and seventh highest in poverty rate. Detroit's unemployment rate in 1980 ranked twenty-fourth; Michigan was in a statewide recession by mid-1979. See Mark C. Berger and Glenn C. Blomquist, "Income, Opportunities, and the Quality of

Since the Second World War, advances in communication and transportation, the transformation of industrial technology, increasingly regional and international economic competition, and the opening of a new global market in cheap labor have reshaped the industrial geography of American industrial cities. Postwar highway construction, spurred by state and local expressway initiatives in the 1940s and federally funded highway construction after 1956, made central industrial location less necessary by facilitating the distribution of goods over longer distances. The growing preference of employers for one-story plants could not be met in heavily developed urban areas because of the lack of open land. The introduction of new automated processes, especially in the automotive and machine-tool industries, drove many small, uncompetitive firms out of business and eliminated many unskilled jobs. Other forces, especially the desire to reduce tax and wage payments, attracted firms out of the center city. Finally, employers have left industrial centers with high labor costs for regions where they can exploit cheap, nonunion labor.[50]

The process of urban industrial decline was especially visible in Detroit in the 1950s. Before the Second World War, most of Detroit's manufacturing firms were concentrated on the Detroit and Rouge rivers and on rail lines, largely within ten miles of the city's center. Over the next fifty years, Detroit's prewar industrial base dwindled, as many of the city's firms relocated production facilities in other parts of the metropolitan area, elsewhere in the United States, and abroad.[51] The automobile industry was among the earliest of the city's industries to pursue a policy of the decentralization of production. A dispersal of central-city automobile plants yielded numerous advantages to manufacturers. Auto firms constructed new single-story plants outside of the center city

Life of Urban Residents," in Michael G. H. McGeary and Laurence E. Lynn, Jr., eds., *Urban Change and Poverty* (Washington, D.C.: National Academy Press, 1988), 97. A survey of available comparative data makes clear that patterns of employment, poverty, and racial segregation in postwar Detroit are not atypical of large, Northern cities.

[50] Much scholarship on urban decline treats changes in the urban industrial base in the postwar era as the inexorable result of economic progress. It assumes that technological change and industrial location policy are neutral responses to market forces, and ignores the role of race and labor policy in corporate decisions. See for example, Paul Peterson, "Introduction: Technology, Race, and Urban Policy," in *The New Urban Reality*, 1–29. For a general discussion of regional industrial decline, see George Sternlieb and James W. Hughes, eds., *Post-Industrial America: Metropolitan Decline and Inter-Regional Job Shifts* (New Brunswick, N.J.: Rutgers University, Center for Urban Policy Research, 1975); John Kasarda, "Urban Industrial Transition and the Underclass," *Annals of the American Academy of Political and Social Science* 501 (January 1989): 26–47; Barry Bluestone and Bennett Harrison, *The Deindustrialization of America: Plant Closings, Community Abandonment, and the Dismantling of Basic Industry* (New York: Basic Books, 1982). In a 1972 survey, wages and taxes were first and second on a list of reasons why Detroit firms planned to relocate outside the city. See Lewis Mandell, *Industrial Location Decisions: Detroit Compared with Atlanta and Chicago* (New York: Praeger Publishers, 1975).

[51] For a general survey of Detroit's industrial patterns, see Robert Sinclair, *The Face of Detroit: A Spatial Synthesis* (Detroit: Wayne State University, Department of Geography, 1972), 36–41.

for numerous reasons, including parking, access to markets, and lower taxes. Labor considerations were of central importance. General Motors, the first firm to deconcentrate production, built new plants in the 1930s in rural parts of the country as a means of reducing wages and inhibiting union militance. Beginning in the late 1940s, but especially in the period following 1954, the automobile industry began to introduce automated processes to reduce labor costs and cut into union strength.[52]

Corporate planners targeted certain plants for automation and decentralization, especially those with large and militant work forces. Employment in Ford's enormous River Rouge complex fell from 85,000 in 1945 to only 30,000 fifteen years later. Rouge was home to United Auto Workers Local 600, over 30 percent black, and one of the most active locals in the UAW. A strike at the Rouge could cripple virtually all of Ford's productive capacity. Although the Rouge grounds offered more than enough room for expansion, Ford moved much of its production away from the site beginning in the late 1940s to new automated plants.[53] Automated stamping and engine production reduced the number of jobs in Detroit Ford and Chrysler plants; plant managers used the threat of layoffs to speed up production in older nonautomated plants.[54] Ford made automation and aggressive decentralization the cornerstone of its postwar corporate policy. From the end of World War II through 1957, Ford alone spent over 2.5 billion dollars nationwide on a program of plant expansion. The other automakers followed suit. Between 1947 and 1958, the three largest automobile producers, Ford, General Motors, and Chrysler, built twenty-five new plants in the metro-

[52] Douglas Reynolds, "Engines of Struggle: Technology, Skill, and Unionization at General Motors, 1930–1940," *Michigan Historical Review* 15 (1989): 79–81, 91–92; Thomas J. Sugrue, "The Origins of the Urban Crisis: Race, Industrial Decline, and Housing in Detroit, 1940–1960" (Ph.D. diss., Harvard University, 1992), 102–13; see also Stephen Meyer, "The Persistence of Fordism: Workers and Technology in the American Automobile Industry," in Nelson Lichtenstein and Stephen Meyer, eds., *On the Line: Essays in the History of Auto Work* (Urbana: University of Illinois Press, 1989), esp. 86–93. Employers and automation advocates were confident about the role of automation in weakening labor: see, for example, Floyd G. Lawrence, "Progress With Ideas," *Automation* 2 (May 1955): 22.

[53] Allan Nevins and Frank Ernest Hill, *Ford: Decline and Rebirth, 1933–1962* (New York: Charles Scribner and Sons, 1963), 340–41; *Hearings before the Committee on Unemployment and the Impact of Automation of the Committee on Education and Labor*, House of Representatives, 87th Cong. (Washington, D.C.: U.S. Government Printing Office, 1961), 512; Nelson Lichtenstein, "Life at the Rouge: A Cycle of Workers' Control," in Charles Stephenson and Robert Asher, eds., *Life and Labor: Dimensions of American Working-Class History* (Albany: State University of New York Press, 1986), 251–53; Testimony of D. J. Davis, vice president, Ford Manufacturing, in U.S. Congress, Joint Committee on the Economic Report, Subcommittee on Economic Stabilization, *Hearings on Automation and Technological Change*, 84th Cong., 1st Sess., October 1955 (Washington, D.C.: Government Printing Office, 1955), 56–57, 63.

[54] Nevins and Hill, *Ford: Decline and Rebirth*, 364–65; Steve Jefferys, *Management and Managed: Fifty Years of Crisis at Chrysler* (Cambridge: Cambridge University Press, 1986), 130–45; James C. Keebler, "Detroit Dateline: More Automatic Operation," *Automation* 6 (February 1960): 44.

politan Detroit area, all of them in suburban communities, most farther than fifteen miles from the center city. Automotive employment in Michigan increased by 116,000 in the boom years between 1947 and 1955, but 72,000 of the new jobs were in the suburbs. Even more jobs went to small Midwestern cities like Lima, Walton Hills, and Lorain, Ohio, and to the South and West, largely to California.[55] The trend toward deconcentration accelerated in the 1970s and 1980s, as the automobile industry constructed more and more of its plants in the South and abroad, replacing plants in Detroit with new production centers in places like La Rioja, Spain, and Ciudad Juarez, Mexico.[56]

Equally important was the decline of employment in independent auto-manufacturing firms and auto-parts suppliers. These plants, manufacturers of machine tools, car parts, wire, and other metal products, were subject to violent cyclical fluctuations related to automotive production. As larger, better capitalized machine-tool plants were automated, many of these small companies failed. Independent auto parts manufacturers also did not fare well in the postwar period; automobile companies, integrating their production processes, took over the manufacture of parts from many independent suppliers. Independent auto-body manufacturers, including Detroit's Murray Auto Body, Briggs Manufacturing, and Motor Products, closed between 1954 and 1957 when large manufacturers turned to automated production. After abortive automation attempts, Detroit's Packard and Hudson plants closed in the mid-1950s. Between 1953 and 1960, Detroit's East Side lost ten plants and 71,137 jobs.[57]

An example from the mid-1950s starkly reveals the impact of decentralization and plant closings. In 1947 one of Detroit's automobile manufacturers employed 13,000 workers in its stamping division and contracted parts from a nearby supplier that employed 5,000 workers. In the early 1950s, the auto company took over all stamping production. The outside supplier lost its contract and closed its plant in 1954; its 5,000 workers lost their jobs. The auto company, following the policy of decentralization, reduced employment in its Detroit plant to 6,000 workers, and opened two new stamping plants that employed 7,000 workers elsewhere in the Midwest. In the process of reorganization, Detroit lost 11,000 jobs and one manufacturer.[58]

[55] On plant deconcentration in the 1940s and 1950s, see Detroit Metropolitan Area Regional Planning Commission, "Location of Automotive Plants," Michigan P-1 (G) Project Completion Report, 1955–56, p. 18, Southeastern Michigan Council of Governments Collection, box 9, Archives of Labor and Urban Affairs, Wayne State University, Detroit (hereafter referred to as ALUA). A similar pattern occurred in Trenton: see Cumbler, A Social History of Economic Decline, 139–47.

[56] Bluestone and Harrison, The Deindustrialization of America, 166–68, 170–78.

[57] Detroit Metropolitan Area Regional Planning Commission, "The Changing Pattern of Manufacturing Plants and Employment, 1950–1960, in the Detroit Region," p. 2, SEMCOG Papers, box 9, ALUA; "When People Move" [ca. 1960], Detroit Urban League Papers, box 46, folder A10–13, Michigan Historical Collections, Bentley Library, University of Michigan, Ann Arbor; On the fate of one independent auto producer, see Stephen Amberg, "Triumph of Industrial Orthodoxy: The Collapse of Studebaker-Packard Corporation," in Lichtenstein and Meyer, On the Line, 190–218.

[58] Harold L. Sheppard and James L. Stern, "Impact of Automation on Workers in Supplier Plants:

TABLE 3.1
Decline in Manufacturing Employment in Detroit, 1947–1977

	1947	1954	1958	1963	1967	1972	1977
Manufacturing firms	3,272	3,453	3,363	3,370	2,947	2,398	1,954
Total manufacturing employment × 1000	338.4	296.5	204.4	200.6	209.7	180.4	153.3
Total production employment × 1000	281.5	232.3	145.1	141.4	149.6	125.8	107.5

Source: U.S. Bureau of the Census, City and County Data Books (Washington, D.C.: GPO, 1949, 1956, 1962, 1967, 1972, 1977, 1983).

The federal government also actively encouraged industrial deconcentration. The Warren Tank Plant, built in 1941 in an undeveloped suburban area fifteen miles north of downtown, and the enormous Willow Run aircraft complex, constructed in 1942 on over fifteen hundred acres of rural land twenty-five miles west of the city, stood as models to postwar industrial planners.[59] Government support for industrial decentralization went even further during the Korean War and afterward, when increasing amounts of federal funding went to companies engaged in military production elsewhere in the United States. Industrial centers like Detroit, New York, and Chicago, despite lobbying efforts, lost many defense contracts in the period to the booming military-industrial complex of suburban Long Island, Connecticut, and southern California.[60]

The result of industrial deconcentration was a tremendous loss of manufacturing jobs in Detroit, beginning in the mid-1950s (table 3.1). The trend of job loss in Detroit continued through the next four decades, mitigated only slightly by the temporary boom in the local economy and in automobile production from 1964 through 1969. Detroit was not alone in this loss of center-city manufacturing jobs; other Northern industrial centers also suffered marked declines in blue-collar employment.[61]

A Case Study" [1956?], typescript in vertical file, box 4, Folder: Employment-Unemployment 1950s, ALUA.

[59] "Location of Automotive Plants," 13.

[60] Detroit Area Metropolitan Regional Planning Commission, "Industrial Land Use in the Detroit Region," February 1952, p. 2, SEMCOG Collection, box 9, ALUA. See Kenneth T. Jackson, "The City Loses the Sword: The Decline of Major Military Activity in the New York Metropolitan Region," in Roger Lotchin, ed., The Martial Metropolis: United States Cities in War and Peace (New York: Praeger Publishers, 1984), 151–62; Geoffrey Rossano, "Suburbia Armed: Nassau County Development and the Rise of the Aerospace Industry," in Lotchin, Martial Metropolis, 61–87; and Martin J. Schiesl, "Airplanes to Aerospace: Defense Spending and Economic Growth in the Los Angeles Region, 1945–1960," in Lotchin, Martial Metropolis, 135–49.

[61] Kasarda, "Urban Change and Minority Opportunities," in Peterson, The New Urban Reality, table 1.

Race and Employment

The impact of Detroit's economic transformation fell heavily upon the city's black population. Discrimination in job opportunity, though gradually undermined by union activity and by antidiscrimination laws, remained a lingering problem. Beginning in 1940 and continuing through the late 1950s, a second Great Migration from the South brought thousands of black migrants to the city. Detroit's black population more than quadrupled, from 150,000 in 1940 to over 650,000 in 1970. The defense industry recruited heavily among Southern blacks, mainly to reduce the tremendous labor shortage in the urban North during the Second World War. Black Southerners, many of whom had friends and family who had migrated to the city before the Great Depression, found Detroit and other Northern cities attractive because of the expanded economic, social, and cultural opportunity there. In the 1940s and 1950s, the new urban workers experienced employment opportunities and wages unknown to them in the declining agricultural economy of the South.

The war represented a turning point in black employment prospects. Detroit's industrial unions, led by the UAW, made a tremendous push for inclusion of blacks in the workplace, against opposition both from rank-and-file workers and corporate managers.[62] The efforts of the UAW, abetted by the government's wartime nondiscrimination requirements, were largely successful: by 1945, blacks comprised 15 percent of the work force in the automobile industry, compared to only about 4 percent in 1940.[63] The commitment of the UAW to retaining black workers in the postwar decades, along with contract seniority provisions, offered blacks a foothold in automobile production. The percentage of black workers in the automobile factories in Detroit increased significantly between the end of the war and 1960, when 25.7 percent of Chrysler workers and 23 percent of General Motors workers were black.[64]

Despite the expansion of opportunity in manufacturing work, many black Detroiters faced seemingly insurmountable barriers to economic security. Because they remained concentrated in the ranks of unskilled workers, they were most susceptible to layoff and replacement when plants automated. Blacks

[62] August Meier and Elliott Rudwick, *Black Detroit and the Rise of the UAW* (New York: Oxford University Press, 1979).

[63] The increase in black wartime employment is well documented in reports on "Employment of Negroes in Detroit," UAW Research Department Collection, box 9, folder 9–24, ALUA. See also Meier and Rudwick, *Black Detroit*, 213–14; Robert C. Weaver, *Negro Labor: A National Problem* (New York: Harcourt, Brace, and World, 1946), 285. Blacks comprised 9.2 percent of Detroit's population in 1940; 16.2 percent of Detroit's population in 1950; and 28.9 percent of Detroit's population in 1960.

[64] Figures from UAW data submitted to *Hearings before the United States Commission on Civil Rights, Held in Detroit, Michigan, December 14 and 15, 1960* (Washington, D.C.: Government Printing Office, 1961), 63–65 (hereafter referred to as *Hearings*). Data for Ford plants was, unfortunately, incomplete.

found it difficult to move beyond unskilled positions in automotive plants, and were virtually absent from the ranks of craftsmen and operatives in Detroit's numerous tool-and-die and machine-tool companies. Only 24 of 7,425 skilled Chrysler workers and only 67 out of 11,125 skilled General Motors workers in 1960 were black.[65] Here union activity was of little consequence. Companies had exclusive control over hiring practices and viewed any intervention as an intrusion on managerial prerogative. With other items on its agenda in the postwar period, the UAW did not aggressively push for antidiscrimination clauses in contracts until the emergence of black trade-union militance in the 1960s.[66]

Opportunity for blacks was seriously circumscribed in other industry, even during the years of peak postwar employment. The Michigan State Employment Service reported that in December 1946, 35.1 percent of all job orders placed with it contained discriminatory clauses, rising to 44.7 percent in April 1947. Employers seeking unskilled labor also frequently refused to consider hiring black workers. In May 1948, the MSES reported that three-fourths of listings for unskilled jobs were closed to blacks. An inquiry into employment practices in 1948 reported that "discrimination in hiring is on the increase. . . . Despite a serious labor shortage in Detroit, employers refuse to employ qualified non-white workers."[67] Employers frequently turned away black workers at the factory gate. As one worker stated in a letter to the state employment agency, "I've been in those lines in which over a 1,000 people were employed. It was always the white fellow behind me that got the job. I've been in over fifteen different lines, and it's always the same thing."[68] One Detroit company that sought 4,000 workers during the labor shortage in early 1949 requested only white workers, despite the large number of available black workers in the city. The unwillingness of employers to hire nonwhite workers, despite a readily available surplus of black workers, was again clear in 1951: in one month of acute labor shortage, 508 unskilled jobs, 423 semiskilled jobs, and 719 skilled jobs listed in Detroit

---

[65] *Hearings*, 63–65.

[66] The tremendous resistance of corporations to the enactment of a state Fair Employment Practices Commission testifies to the unpopularity of measures to control hiring practice. Walter Reuther, testifying to the Civil Rights Commission, noted that implementation of fair employment policies "ha[s] been most successful in every area except hiring, where management's prerogative has been a stumbling block" (*Hearings*, 57). The Trade Union Leadership Council, composed of black UAW members, on the other hand, criticized the UAW for inaction on antidiscrimination policy.

[67] Memorandum from the Michigan Committee on Civil Rights to the Governor's Committee on Civil Rights, December 29, 1948, vertical file, box 4, folder: Fair Employment Practices, Michigan, 1940s, ALUA.

[68] "Michigan State Employment Service Experiences in the Placement of Minority Group Workers," testimony of Harry C. Markle, executive director, Michigan Unemployment Compensation Commission, before the State Affairs Committee, Michigan House of Representatives, April 18, 1951, in City of Detroit Commission on Community Relations Collection, Box 11, ALUA.

MSES offices went unfilled, although 874 unskilled, 532 semiskilled, and 148 skilled black applicants were available for immediate employment.[69]

Blacks were also unlikely to be found in manufacturing jobs in small automotive parts plants, machine-and-tool companies, and in local nonautomotive industries like brewing. Of five breweries surveyed by the Detroit Urban League in 1950, only 39 out of 3,300 employees were black. The situation had changed little by 1962, when a Detroit civil rights group complained that fewer than 120 blacks were among the brewing industry's 12,000 workers. Stroh's, Detroit's largest brewer, had 15 black employees out of a work force of 1,435, none in production jobs; Pfeiffer and Company, a smaller brewery, had 9 black employees out of about 700. Similar patterns held for Detroit's second largest manufacturing employer—machinery. Only 2.3 percent of Detroit's more than 10,000 operatives in the machinery industry in 1950 were black; only 3 percent were black in 1960.[70]

Deproletarianization

The impact of discrimination, however, tells only part of the story of the economic difficulties of Detroit's black population. Of tremendous consequence was the drying up of sources of industrial employment while the black population continued to grow dramatically by natural increase and by continued Southern migration. The decentralization of production in the 1950s had a disproportionate impact on the city's youth and recent migrants. As Detroit's black population continued to grow, the number of well-paying, entry-level manufacturing jobs steadily diminished. New employees hired during periodic booms were unprotected by the seniority that workers who came to the city in the previous decade had earned. The passage of such antidiscriminatory measures as Michigan's 1956 Fair Employment Practices law, the efforts of Detroit's Urban League and the Detroit branch of the National Association for the Advancement of Colored People to open new jobs to blacks, and even the push toward educational improvement spearheaded by the Urban League, were ironically ill timed. Coming at a time of industrial flight, these reforms improved the

---

[69] "Michigan State Employment Services Experiences in the Placement of Minority Group Workers," 6.

[70] Vocational Services Department, Detroit Urban League, "Employment of Negroes in Brewing Industry Fact Sheet," September 24, 1955, Francis Kornegay Papers, box 4, folder 4–22, Michigan Historical Collections, Bentley Historical Library, University of Michigan; letter from Frank R. Owens to Arthur S. Johnson, May 8, 1962, Detroit branch NAACP Papers, part 1, box 15, folder: Fifteenth District Democrats—1962, ALUA. "Detroit Metropolitan Area Employment and Income by Age, Sex, Color and Residence, 1960," Detroit branch NAACP Papers, part 2, box 10, folder 10–11, ALUA. For similar patterns of workplace discrimination in another industrial city, see Edward Greer, *Big Steel: Black Politics and Corporate Power in Gary, Indiana* (New York: Monthly Review Press, 1979), 100–104.

situation of some workers but had little effect on the structural loss of employment in the center city.[71]

The trend toward industrial suburbanization was especially ominous for Detroit's blacks. For the most part, firms that moved to suburban communities employed few black workers. Companies preferred to hire workers from the communities surrounding their new plants, a preference that—with the exception of a few communities with already existing black populations—excluded center-city blacks. In 1960, only 20 blacks worked among the 2,384 employees at the General Motors Fisher Body plant in Livonia, a western suburb of Detroit. The overall statistics for General Motors were only somewhat more heartening: 29.2 percent of the workers in General Motors Detroit plants were black, compared to only 12.5 percent of its work force in plants in Detroit's suburbs.[72]

The combination of persistent discrimination in hiring, technological change, decentralized manufacturing, and urban economic decline had dramatic effects on the employment prospects of black men in metropolitan Detroit. By 1980, more than half of Detroit's black males over the age of sixteen were out of work (table 3.2). Data from Chicago, also a declining industrial center, show a similar trend of joblessness.[73]

The contrast between 1950, when Detroit's postwar economy was at its peak, and 1980 makes clear the magnitude of the shift in economic opportunity. A black male in Detroit in 1950 could realistically expect factory employment, even if his opportunities were seriously limited by discrimination. Over the next three decades, with the exception of a cyclical boom in automobile employment in the mid- and late 1960s, fewer and fewer could expect steady employment. A growing segment of the city's population was unattached to the urban labor market, and underwent a process of *deproletarianization*.

[71] The increase in black youth unemployment in the late 1950s is documented but little understood. The most prominent discussion of the phenemenon is in Charles Murray, *Losing Ground: American Social Policy, 1950–1980* (New York: Basic Books, 1984), 69–82. Murray, however, does not consider the relationship of youth unemployment to the decline in entry-level manufacturing jobs in the center cities. An important scholarly examination of the problem is John Cogan, "The Decline in Black Teenage Employment, 1950–1970," *American Economic Review* 72 (1982): 621–38, but Cogan emphasizes the decline in agricultural employment, an issue not relevant to the labor-force participation of black youth in Detroit. An especially suggestive volume that addresses the issue of youth unemployment which deals with the period since 1970, but is nonetheless suggestive for the 1950s, is Richard B. Freeman and Harry J. Holzer, eds., *The Black Youth Employment Crisis* (Chicago: University of Chicago Press, 1986). Freeman and Holzer suggest that black youths are especially susceptible to unemployment during cyclical downturns, and that youth "are out of work for very long periods of time and that, once non-employed, they have great difficulty securing another job" (9).

[72] *Hearings*, 65.

[73] William Julius Wilson and Loic J. D. Wacquant, "The Cost of Racial and Class Exclusion in the Inner City," *Annals of the American Academy of Political and Social Science* 501 (January 1989): 14.

TABLE 3.2

Joblessness in Detroit, 1950–1980 (Percentages)

	1950	1960	1970	1980
All workers unemployed	7.5	7.6	6.9	11.7
Not in labor force	16.5	19.5	26.7	37.9
Not working	22.8	25.7	32.6	45.1
Blacks unemployed	11.8	18.2	9.8	22.5
Blacks not in labor force	18.7	23.3	25.4	43.9
Blacks not working	28.3	37.2	32.7	56.4

Sources: Author's calculations from *United States Census of Population* 1950, vol. 2, pt. 22, tables 35, 36; 1960, PC1-24C, tables 73, 77; 1970, PC1-C24, tables 85, 92; 1980, PC80-1-C24, tables 120, 134.

Notes: Unemployed includes all males over 14 who are in the civilian labor force and seeking work for 1950 and 1960; 16 years and older in the civilian labor force seeking work for 1970 and 1980. Not in labor force has as its denominator all males aged 14 or older for 1950 and 1960; 16 years and older for 1970 and 1980. Percentage not working includes total unemployed plus total not in labor force divided by total working-age male population.

Racial Segregation and the Divided Metropolis

The deproletarianization of a growing number of Detroit's black workers was exacerbated by the persistent racial divide between blacks and whites in the metropolitan area. Detroit's blacks lacked the geographic mobility—common to other groups in other periods of American history—to adapt to the changing labor market. Whites, on the other hand, could more readily follow the flight of jobs to the white suburbs and heavily white small towns that attracted industry. From the beginnings of the first Great Migration, Detroit's blacks had been concentrated in a few segregated sections in outlying parts of the city and in a small, densely populated, and sharply defined area in the center city that was named, somewhat bitterly, Paradise Valley.[74] Detroit's black population expanded rapidly in the postwar decades, but the city's patterns of racial separation in housing changed little. Residential segregation, as measured by the index of dissimilarity of whites and blacks, remained steady throughout the postwar period (table 3.3).

Three forces at work in the postwar period maintained patterns of racial segregation. Individual and neighborhood-based discrimination was the most

[74] Zunz, *Changing Face of Inequality*, 372–98; David Allan Levine, *Internal Combustion: The Races in Detroit, 1915–1926* (Westport, Conn.: Greenwood Press, 1976); Gloster Current, "Paradise Valley: A Famous and Colorful Part of Detroit as Seen through the Eyes of an Insider," *Detroit* (June 1946): 32–34; a superb overview of patterns of racial segregation in Detroit is Donald R. Deskins, Jr., *Residential Mobility of Negroes in Detroit, 1837–1965* (Ann Arbor: University of Michigan, Department of Geography, 1972).

TABLE 3.3
Index of Dissimilarity, Blacks and Whites,
Detroit, 1910–1980

1910	67.6
1940	89.9
1950	88.8
1960	84.5
1970	88.4
1980	86.7

Sources: 1910: Stanley Lieberson, *A Piece of the Pie: Blacks and White Immigrants since 1880* (Berkeley: University of California Press, 1980), 266; 1940–60: Karl E. Taeuber and Alma F. Taeuber, *Negroes in Cities: Residential Segregation and Neighborhood Change* (Chicago: Aldine, 1965), 39; 1970–80: Douglas S. Massey and Nancy A. Denton, "Trends in the Racial Segregation of Blacks, Hispanics, and Asians, 1970–1980," *American Sociological Review* 52 (1987): 815.
Note: Figures for 1950–80 include the entire Detroit SMSA. The index of dissimilarity is the percentage of the nonwhite population that would have to be redistributed to achieve complete racial integration.

visible obstruction to black residential choice. Real-estate practices, from restrictive covenants and agreements among agents to avoid sales that would change the racial composition of a neighborhood to speculative investments in transitional neighborhoods, limited black residential movement to a few sections of the city. Above all, government housing policies hardened the racial line within the city and extended the scope of segregation to postwar suburban developments.

The rapid expansion of Detroit's black community in the 1920s brought forth a tremendous white resistance to the residential expansion of the black population. Early skirmishes in the white struggle against neighborhood integration included the 1925 Ossian Sweet case, involving a black doctor who successfully claimed self-defense in a murder trial for firing into a white crowd that had gathered around his home in a white neighborhood, and the Sojourner Truth Riot in 1942, sparked by white resistance to the placement of a defense housing project intended for black occupation near a white residential section.[75] The most sustained period of white resistance came in the postwar years. More than two hundred violent incidents occurred in racially transitional neighborhoods

[75] Levine, *Internal Combustion*, 153–98; Dominic J. Capeci, Jr., *Race Relations in Wartime Detroit: The Sojourner Truth Controversy* (Philadelphia: Temple University Press, 1984).

between 1945 and 1965, including the gathering of angry crowds, rock throwing, cross burning, arson, and other attacks on property.[76] White Detroiters also organized nearly two hundred neighborhood "improvement" and "protective" associations, many of which dealt with such mundane matters as parking and zoning, but most of which mobilized around fears of black residential expansion.[77]

A web of interlocking real estate interests—brokers, speculators, developers, and banks—built on the base of racial animosity to preserve racial divisions in the housing market. Real estate brokers steered white buyers toward all-white neighborhoods, and black buyers toward all-black or racially transitional areas. Realtors also worked closely with white community groups to preserve neighborhood racial characteristics, and often served as officers of Detroit's protective associations.[78] The official policy of real estate agents in the Detroit area was expressed in the "Code of Ethics" of the National Association of Real Estate Boards, which explicitly banned racial mixing in neighborhoods through the 1940s, and later euphemistically prohibited members from "introducing a character of property or use which will clearly be detrimental to property values in that neighborhood." Realtors who violated the code faced expulsion from their association and the loss of business from offended white customers.[79]

Into the gap left open by more timid real estate brokers stepped speculators who employed a variety of "blockbusting" tactics in areas considered racially transitional. Taking advantage of the desperate need of black migrants for housing and of white fears of black "invasion," speculators scared whites into selling homes through tactics such as frequent solicitation, widely publicized home sales to nonwhites, and rumors. They then sold the houses they had purchased on the cheap to black buyers, usually on high-interest land contracts that yielded a hefty profit.[80]

---

[76] Author's estimate from a comprehensive survey of materials involving racial incidents in the Detroit Commission on Community Relations Collection, ALUA; Detroit Branch NAACP Collection, ALUA; the Detroit Urban League Collection, Michigan Historical Collections, Bentley Library, University of Michigan; and Detroit's black newspapers: *Michigan Chronicle* (1945–65); *Detroit Tribune* (1945–60). For an excellent discussion of similar incidents in Chicago, see Arnold Hirsch, *Making the Second Ghetto: Race and Housing in Chicago* (Cambridge: Cambridge University Press, 1983), 40–99; and for Philadelphia, see John F. Bauman, *Public Housing, Race, and Renewal: Urban Planning in Philadelphia, 1920–1974* (Philadelphia: Temple University Press, 1987), 160–64.

[77] I have found evidence of at least 192 neighborhood improvement associations in Detroit between 1943 and 1965. For evidence on the number of these associations and their role in the city, see Sugrue, "Origins of the Urban Crisis," esp. 178–207.

[78] See *Detroit Tribune*, August 10, 1940, for an early example of collaboration between real estate brokers and neighborhood associations.

[79] Rose Helper, *Racial Policies and Practices of Real Estate Brokers* (Minneapolis: University of Minnesota Press, 1969); for examples of intimidation of white real estate brokers who sold homes to blacks, see *Michigan Chronicle*, December 4, 1948; and "Protest of Negro Occupancy at 18087 Shields (September 1949)," Detroit Commission on Community Relations Collection, box 6, file 49-33, ALUA.

[80] "Scare Selling in a Bi-Racial Housing Market," DUL Papers, box 44, folder A8-1.

Developers took advantage of the booming postwar housing market and constructed new subdivisions in areas on the outskirts of the city. Few developers had any interest in the construction of new homes for blacks, and most, at least, restricted their sales to whites. The establishment of new suburban developments was made easier by the openness of the mortgage market to white home purchasers. Bank policy seldom worked to the advantage of blacks. Because banks considered loans for home purchases in black neighborhoods an actuarial risk and mortgages to blacks for new homes in all-white areas an unsound policy that would alienate white customers, only a few black home buyers could obtain credit.[81]

Federal housing policy translated private discrimination into public policy, and officially ratified the discriminatory practices of developers and banks. Federal officials used an elaborate system of neighborhood classification, developed by the Home Owners Loan Corporation in the 1930s, to determine the eligibility of an area for home loans. Sections of the city with older housing stock, a large number of working-class residents, and a racially transitional or predominantly black population seldom received federal mortgage and loan guarantees. The extreme measures to which the FHA would go to ensure the racial stability of a neighborhood were clear in a 1940 decision to offer funds to a white development adjacent to a black neighborhood on Detroit's northwest side on the condition that a wall be constructed to separate the two neighborhoods. The developer constructed a six-foot-high, foot-thick wall, which extended nearly one-half mile, and was successful in obtaining FHA-backed financing.[82]

In the wake of the Supreme Court's 1948 *Shelley v. Kraemer* decision, prohibiting restrictive covenants, the FHA excised references to the racial character of neighborhoods from its underwriting manual, but its actuarial standards continued to prevent the financing of older, rundown homes. The "iron curtain around the housing supply" constructed by the real estate industry thus prevented most Detroit blacks from purchasing homes eligible for FHA and VA loans. Although the FHA did not disaggregate its loan figures for suburban and urban development, it is clear that the net result of federal housing policy was the subsidy of newly developed suburban areas at the expense of the center city, and whites at the expense of blacks. The only black developments to receive

[81] William H. Boone, Community Services Department, Detroit Urban League, "Major Unmet Goals That Suggest Continuing Attention," March 9, 1956, DUL, box 38, folder A2-16.

[82] Burneice Avery, "The Eight Mile Road . . . Its Growth from 1920 . . . 1952," Burneice Avery Papers, box 1, Burton Historical Collections, Detroit Public Library. A photograph of the wall can be found in Burneice Avery, *Walk Quietly through the Night and Cry Softly* (Detroit, Mich.: Balamp Publishing, 1977), 190. For a general survey of the discriminatory aspects of federal housing policy, see Kenneth T. Jackson, "Race, Ethnicity, and Real Estate Appraisal: The Home Owners' Loan Corporation and the Federal Housing Administration," *Journal of Urban History* 6 (1980): 419–52, and "The Spatial Dimensions of Social Control: Race, Ethnicity, and Government Housing Policy in the United States," in Bruce M. Stave, ed., *Modern Industrial Cities: History, Policy, and Survival* (Beverly Hills, Calif.: Sage Publishers, 1981), 79–128.

FHA, VA, and HOLC support until the late 1960s were a few segregated communities constructed on open land in outlying areas and the occasional infill home, constructed on vacant land in an already black neighborhood.[83]

The combination of white resistance, the racially divided real estate market, and federal housing policy created a residentially divided metropolis, while deindustrialization drained the center city of job opportunity. In the years following World War II, the suburbs of Detroit expanded rapidly as whites fled the center city. Detroit, on the other hand, suffered a tremendous depopulation, from nearly 2 million in the early 1950s to 1.2 million in 1980. In 1980 the center city was 63.1 percent black, while its suburbs were 93.4 percent white. In the early 1980s, Detroit's average family income was $10,000 less than that of suburban communities. In 1980, 21 percent of the city of Detroit's residents lived under the official poverty line, as compared with only 5.7 percent of the residents in the remainder of the Detroit metropolitan area.[84]

Class Segregation

The effects of racial segregation did not, alone, isolate the black urban poor in the center city. Class divisions in the black community—ignored by scholars who erroneously emphasize the homogeneity of the pre-1960s "ghetto"—manifested themselves in urban housing patterns.[85] The black middle class, already sizable in Detroit in the 1920s and 1930s, began to seek housing apart from the majority of the black population as early as the 1920s. On Detroit's northeast side, nearly ten miles from Paradise Valley, stood the Conant Gardens neighborhood, settled by black middle-class families in the 1920s and 1940s. Like white neighborhoods throughout the city, Conant Gardens residents used restrictive covenants to bar multiple housing and other "undesirable" uses.

[83] Draft Letter from Legal Department, UAW, to Thomas Kavanagh, State Attorney General, July 18, 1956, DUL box 38, A2-17; for examples of homes for blacks financed by government housing programs, see *Michigan Chronicle*, May 29, 1948, and June 5, 1948.

[84] Bureau of the Census, *Census of Population Subject Reports: Poverty Areas in Large Cities* (1980), PC-80-28D (Washington, D.C.: GPO, 1985), table S-2. For detailed discussion of the contrast of city and suburban population and growth, see Joe T. Darden, Richard Child Hill, June Thomas, and Richard Thomas, *Detroit: Race and Uneven Development* (Philadelphia: Temple University Press, 1987), 67–108.

[85] The thesis that the "institutional ghetto" minimized class differences is most clearly stated in William Julius Wilson, *The Truly Disadvantaged: The Inner City, the Underclass, and Public Policy* (Chicago: University of Chicago Press, 1987), esp. 52–62; Reynolds Farley, "Changes in Race and Class Segregation," in Christopher Jencks and Paul Peterson, eds., *The Urban Underclass* (Washington, D.C.: Brookings Institution, 1991), challenges Wilson's thesis for the 1970s and 1980s, but does not consider the implications of an earlier middle-class exodus on the concentration of center-city poverty. For suggestions of class differences in the black population in other northern cities before the 1970s, see Trotter, *Black Milwaukee*, 80–144; Trotter, "Blacks in the Urban North," chap. 2 in this volume; Laurence Glasco, "Double Burden: The Black Experience in Pittsburgh," in Hays, *City at the Point*, 80–83.

Conant Gardens residents also staunchly opposed the construction of public housing at the nearby Sojourner Truth site in the early 1940s.[86] Conant Gardens established a pattern that the black middle class would repeat throughout the postwar years. Members of the black middle class were the first to leave center-city black neighborhoods after World War II. As whites vacated some of Detroit's better neighborhoods, like Arden Park and Boston-Edison, in the late 1940s and 1950s, Detroit's leading black clergy, educators, and professionals moved into spacious homes well removed from the majority of the black population.[87] The first "urban pioneers," blacks who moved into previously all-white working-class and middle-class neighborhoods, had generally high incomes and steady employment. The black bourgeoisie was particularly mobile, and was first to move into the newer housing stock in areas depopulated by whites in the 1950s and 1960s. A study of a racially transitional black neighborhood in the early 1960s noted that many high-income black residents fled parts of the neighborhood that had completed the racial transition when poorer black residents moved in. As one black respondent in the transitional Twelfth Street area stated of the influx of poor blacks, "too many folks from the eastside are here."[88]

Concentrated Poverty

The confluence of residential segregation by race and by class with lack of employment opportunity and poverty is conveyed most vividly in an analysis of poor neighborhoods in the center city. Poverty statistics by census tract for 1970 and 1980 reveal the growing concentration of poverty in certain sections of many of the largest Northern industrial cities. An increasing number of Detroiters, like their counterparts elsewhere in the urban North, lived in high-poverty areas—those with 40 percent or more of their population in poverty.[89] Between

[86] Capeci, *Race Relations*, 76–77.

[87] "Races Learn to Live Together in Area of Expensive Homes," *Detroit News*, May 13, 1956; "Boston Boulevard: Signpost of the Future," *Detroit Free Press*, May 15, 1956. See "Some of Our Distinguished Residents," Boston-Edison Protective Association Papers, box 10, folder 2, Burton Historical Collections, Detroit Public Library.

[88] Mayor's Committee on Community Action for Detroit Youth, "Report on Target Areas," (1963), chap. 1, Detroit Branch NAACP Papers, part 1, box 23, ALUA. See also Proposal for a Study of Adherence to Zoning Codes and Restrictions, Housing Department, n.d., box 53, folder A17-3.

[89] Paul Jargowsky and Mary Jo Bane, "Ghetto Poverty in the United States, 1970–1980," in Jencks and Peterson, *The Urban Underclass*, 254–57. They found that "ghetto poor [those living in census tracts with a poverty rate of more than 40 percent] in 1980 were most likely to live in the northeast and north central regions and in the largest cities" (256). Detroit ranked fifth after New York, Philadelphia, Chicago, and Newark in the increase in the number of ghetto poor between 1970 and 1980, followed by Columbus, Ohio, Atlanta, Baltimore, Buffalo, and Paterson, New Jersey (255). A recent compendium of comparative data for 1970 and 1980 is John Kasarda, *Urban Underclass Database: An Overview and Machine-Readable File Documentation* (New York: Social Science Research Council, 1992).

TABLE 3.4
High-Poverty Tracts in Detroit, 1970 and 1980

	Number	Population	Population Poor	% of Detroit Poor
1970	22	55,547	24,039	10.8
1980	44	110,111	50,670	19.6

Sources: Author's calculation from Bureau of the Census, Census of Population and Housing: Census Tracts, PHC(1)-58 (1970), tables P3 and P4; and 1980, tables P10 and P11.

1970 and 1980, the number of high-poverty tracts in Detroit doubled and the population of the city living in these areas nearly doubled as well (table 3.4). In 1970, only about one-tenth of Detroit's poor lived in high-poverty areas, a figure rising to nearly one-fifth by 1980.

Residents of high-poverty areas were twice as likely as the average Detroiter to be unemployed, and were substantially less likely to be in the labor force. Table 3.5 summarizes the economic status of residents in high-poverty tracts in both 1970 and 1980. Detroit's poor were increasingly likely to live in neighborhoods with other poor people and in neighborhoods where a growing majority of their associates were likely to be wholly unattached to the labor market.

CONCLUSION: HISTORY AND POLICY

The history of industrial decline, racial discrimination, and impoverishment in Detroit mirrors that of other major Northern industrial cities. Detroit, like Chicago, Newark, Philadelphia, Cleveland, Gary, Saint Louis, and other major industrial centers of the Snowbelt, underwent a profound economic and spatial transformation since World War II that has fundamentally constrained the economic opportunity of many of its residents, especially African Americans. The result of several decades of urban crisis is a new form of concentrated poverty, largely restricted to deteriorating center cities, which has replaced the episodic and spatially diffuse poverty of the earlier periods of American history. The large number of men and women who are excluded from the labor force in declining industrial cities can hardly be compared to the "reserve army" of the unemployed in the nineteenth century. Shifts in economic opportunity in the city have created a new spatial order in the metropolis, which bears little resemblance to the American city in the past. The implications of this historical perspective for contemporary policy debates are multifold. In light of the chang-ing economic and social context of poverty, conservative policy proposals that attempt to modify individual behavior are futile. The occupational choices of poor Americans throughout history have been shaped by shifts in the organiza-tion of work and the spatial order of the metropolis. Liberal social welfare proposals such as the expansion or standardization of welfare benefits may

TABLE 3.5
Joblessness in Detroit's High-Poverty Areas
(Percentages)

	1970	1980
Unemployed	14.0	28.4
Not in labor force	45.9	59.1
Not working	53.5	70.7

Sources: See sources for table 3.4. For citywide statistics on joblessness, see table 3.2 above.

succeed in mitigating the social costs of poverty, but they too fail to address the structural causes of urban decline that have created the new urban poverty. Liberals' continued faith in supply-side solutions to poverty, including welfare programs to encourage labor mobility and job training programs, ignores the continuing role that the economy has played in the perpetuation of poverty. The crisis of contemporary poverty calls for creative new solutions. Without an attack on the contemporary urban crisis with policy that both remedies job loss and combats persistent segregation and racial inequality, it is doubtful that many of today's urban poor will ever escape poverty.[90]

[90] There is a rapidly growing body of books and articles on poverty policy. For two compelling and important policy recommendations see, Jennifer Hochschild, "Equal Opportunity and the Estranged Poor," *Annals of the American Academy of Political and Social Science* 501 (1989): 143–55; and Theda Skocpol, "Targeting within Universalism: Politically Viable Policies to Combat Poverty in the United States," in Jencks and Peterson, *The Urban Underclass*, 411–36.

CHAPTER 4

Housing the "Underclass"

David W. Bartelt

CONSIDER THIS PARADOX: How is it that homelessness and abandoned houses coexist in many of our cities? Further, how is it that the homeless so nearly mirror the social characteristics of the "underclass," and are mainly drawn from the very neighborhoods in which abandonment dominates the landscape? Housing conditions are an integral part of the impoverishment of those we have come to call the *underclass*. Changes in the "historical ecology"[1] of the city, especially as they impact upon the housing choices available to the African-American community, are integral to a further understanding of the spatial isolation of underclass communities.

As Tom Sugrue's history of Detroit in the preceding chapter indicates, the character of neighborhoods is not just a function of their contemporary location, but of the history of their interrelationships to each other and to centers of employment, commerce, and power as well. The isolation of underclass communities forces us to examine the changes in those communities once dominated by working- and middle-class families, but now undergoing the slow neglect and decline of abandonment.

This chapter is somewhat different from others in this volume. My focus is on the recent history of urban social and spatial arrangements, and not on the particulars of a population or a community per se.[2] The works by Jones and Trotter that precede this chapter provide significant additions to our understanding of the nature of black migration to Northern cities, and of the particu-

---

[1] William Yancey and Eugene Ericksen, "The Antecedents of Community: The Economic and Institutional Structure of Urban Neighborhoods," *American Sociological Review* 44 (1979): 253–62; Eugene Ericksen and William Yancey, "Work and Residence in Industrial Philadelphia," *Journal of Urban History* 5 (1979): 147–82; Theodore Hershberg et al., "A Tale of Three Cities: Blacks and Immigrants in Philadelphia: 1850–1880, 1930 and 1970," *Annals of American Academy of Political and Social Science* 441 (1979): 55–81; David Bartelt, David Elesh, Ira Goldstein, George Leon, and William Yancey, "Islands in the Stream: Neighborhoods and the Political Economy of the City," in Irwin Altman and Abraham Wandersman, eds., *Neighborhood and Community Environments* (New York: Plenum Publishing, 1987); also Sam Bass Warner, *The Private City* (Philadelphia: University of Pennsylvania Press, 1968).

[2] I should note that I am a historical sociologist, not a historian, by trade. As such, I am interested in the history of social structures, such as markets and institutions, that serve as the stage on which individuals and communities live out their lives and create both biographies and histories. It is the history of how opportunities and barriers, advantages and disadvantages are established in the mechanisms of day-to-day urban life that forms the basis of my work.

lar community dynamics that emerged within those communities. This chapter frames the experiences of those communities by linking the character of neighborhoods to changes in the operation of housing markets, particularly in relationship to a changing economic base. The focus on housing allows us to disentangle the relative roles of race, poverty, institutional racism, public policy, and urban economic change as they have contributed to the emergence of isolated communities. Most importantly, it calls the utility of the very concept of "underclass" into question.

The underclass debate centers on the concepts of persistent poverty and a dramatically changed opportunity structure in spatially isolated urban neighborhoods. Spatial isolation is particularly vital in the concept of underclass. This notion of separation from the mainstream of urban life, from the job and housing opportunities of a metropolitan area, is central to what most commentators see as distinctive between the ghettos of the middle twentieth century and the subsequent isolation of these areas in the final years of this century. It is this isolation which is argued to be the basis for the "concentration effects" of a community "feeding on itself" with "pathological" behaviors that contribute to its social and physical reproduction.[3]

This chapter focuses on the historical dynamics of housing markets and housing policy as they have contributed to the physical and social isolation of underclass neighborhoods in our cities. It particularly focuses on the ways in which housing opportunities and urban spatial and social structures have changed in the decades since the Great Depression. This is an institutional history of the demographic, ecological, and public policy impacts on the housing of our cities, which have produced the social and spatial isolation of the modern underclass.

The housing of a community provides a distinctive lens through which the history, constraints, and opportunities facing neighborhoods can be examined. Housing, along with the workplace, is one of the major physical contexts within which people live out their day-to-day lives. In addition, housing is also a reflection of the large-scale forces that have shaped a community's place in the social structure and the historical development of a city. Housing's physical permanence provides markers of eras past and, when combined with the social, economic, and political history of a locale, provides a unique point of origin for the historical examination of communities.

Housing is a unique commodity. It is extremely durable, passing through several hands before its use value is terminated. It constitutes its own market—it does not go to market, but commands value and utility both from its location and ability to be transformed as household structures and as neighborhoods change over time (that is, as single homes convert to multifamily dwellings or to

---

[3] William Julius Wilson, *The Truly Disadvantaged: The Inner City, The Underclass, and Public Policy* (Chicago: University of Chicago Press, 1987).

commercial ventures). Finally, it is the most debt-dependent commodity consumed by the American population. Like the automobile, it must be financed to be bought or sold, and is subject to episodic major repairs. These repairs, however, often require further periodic indebtedness by homeowner or landlord, using the house itself as collateral, as housing has the ability to maintain or gain value over time.

The sensitivity of housing to its neighborhood context, plus the dependency of the housing market on long-term debt financing, places housing at the center of a web of social and institutional relationships. The intersection of the banking, appraisal, and real-estate industries in the housing market establishes a complex institutional setting for neighborhood and urban development.[4] Urban politics and planning efforts impact variably upon these markets, which come to both define and mirror the character of neighborhoods.[5]

Thus, analyses of the distribution of housing problems among subpopulations of the city go hand in hand with discussions of the changes in urban ecological and social structure. Most urban housing problems predate discussions of the underclass, especially with respect to abandonment,[6] displacement,[7] institutional patterns of segregation,[8] and differentials in white and black suburbanization.[9] These problems have their roots in the economic and demographic shifts of cities. They are seen particularly in the shifts from manufacturing to service economies, accompanying spatial transformations of cities, the abandonment of devalued property, the historical specificity of various ethnic/racial migration patterns, and recent shifts in traditional territorial constraints upon housing capital.[10]

Of all of these forces, however, none looms larger than the segregation of black communities in urban ghettos during the late nineteenth and early twentieth centuries. Without the physical separation of black and white com-

[4] John R. Logan and Harvey L. Molotch, *Urban Fortunes: The Political Economy of Place* (Berkeley: University of California Press, 1987); Mark Gottdiener, *The Social Production of Urban Space* (Austin: University of Texas Press, 1985).

[5] Daniel J. Monti, *Race, Redevelopment and the New Company Town* (Albany: State University of New York Press, 1990).

[6] George Sternlieb, *The Urban Housing Dilemma* (New Brunswick, N.J.: Rutgers University Press, 1972); David W. Bartelt and George Leon, "Differential Decline: The Neighborhood Context of Abandonment," *Housing and Society* 13, no. 2 (1986): 81–106.

[7] Chester Hartman, Dennis Keating, and Richard LeGates, *Displacement: How to Fight It* (Berkeley, Calif.: National Housing Law Project, 1982).

[8] Diana Pearce, "Gatekeepers and Homeseekers: Racial Steering and Real Estate Brokers," *Social Problems* 26 (1979): 325–42; Douglas Massey and Mitchell Eggars, "The Ecology of Inequality: Minorities and the Concentration of Poverty, 1970–1980," *American Journal of Sociology* 95 (1990): 1153–88.

[9] Reynolds Farley and Walter Allen, *The Color Line and the Quality of Life in America* (New York: Russell Sage Foundation, 1987).

[10] A particularly good unifying discussion of these interrelationships is found in David Harvey, *The Limits to Capital* (London: Blackwell, 1982).

munities, and without the limitations placed on black participation in both the job and housing markets, an underclass could not have developed in the declining urban centers of the present. The ghetto was a necessary prerequisite for the emergence of the underclass.

It is not enough to trace out the lineal descendence of underclass communities to their ghetto antecedents. The roots of the underclass lie in the marked discontinuity that exists between the manufacturing city which gave rise to the black ghetto and the contemporary decentralized, postindustrial city. Indeed, supporters and critics alike largely agree that the transformation of the urban economic base after World War II has altered the nature of community life across the entire urban landscape.

My approach to the problem of race, housing, and the isolation of the black community begins with an examination of Philadelphia but expands to a consideration of the national urban setting. It implicitly challenges the "class/mobility" framework of most analyses of the underclass, which focus on either "barriers" to the participation of underclass members in labor markets or on "disqualifying" characteristics of the underclass. The underclass perspective emphasizes strategies for change that emphasize the adjustment of underclass individuals or families to demanding but relatively benign labor and housing markets.[11] Failing these changes, the underclass is doomed to reproduce itself, socially as well as physically.

This approach is too limited in scope. American ideology to the contrary, the historical operation of the housing market suggests that markets do not, and in some instances cannot, distribute sufficient levels of basic commodities across the class structure of the city. The histories of slum housing, and of programs aimed at its improvement, of the black ghetto, urban renewal, and homelessness each suggest that the invisible hand of the market has a lower limit,[12] a "market

[11] William Julius Wilson, "Public Policy Research and the Truly Disadvantaged," in Christopher Jencks and Paul E. Peterson, eds., *The Urban Underclass* (Washington, D.C.: Brookings Institution, 1990).

[12] Jacob Riis, *How the Other Half Lives: Studies among the Tenements of New York* (New York: Charles Scribner's Sons, 1904); John F. Sutherland, "Housing the Poor in the City of Homes: Philadelphia at the Turn of the Century," in Allan F. Davis and Mark H. Haller, eds., *The Peoples of Philadelphia: A History of Ethnic Groups and Lower-Class Life, 1790–1940* (Philadelphia: Temple University Press, 1973); Thomas Lee Phillpott, *The Slum and the Ghetto* (New York: Oxford University Press, 1978); Robert Fairbanks, *Making Better Citizens: Housing Reform and the Community Development Strategy in Cincinnati, 1890–1960* (Urbana: University of Illinois Press, 1988); St. Clair Drake and Horace Cayton, *Black Metropolis: A Study of Negro Life in a Northern City* (New York: Harper and Row, 1962); Gilbert Osofsky, *Harlem: The Making of a Ghetto* (New York: Harper and Row, 1966); Allan H. Spear, *Black Chicago: The Making of a Negro Ghetto, 1890–1920* (Chicago: University of Chicago Press, 1967); David M. Katzman, *Before the Ghetto: Black Detroit in the Nineteenth Century* (Urbana: University of Illinois Press, 1975); Kenneth Kusmer, *A Ghetto Takes Shape: Black Cleveland, 1870–1930* (Urbana: University of Illinois Press, 1976); Olivier Zunz, *The Making of an Urban Working Class* (Princeton: Princeton University Press, 1982); Mark I. Gelfand, *A Nation of Cities: The Federal Government and Urban America, 1933–1965* (New York: Oxford Univer-

threshold."[13] Markets routinely fail to adequately distribute necessary commodities (jobs, food, and housing) in neighborhoods of concentrated poverty
when individuals lack the income to step over this threshold. In this view, the
defining characteristic of the underclass is not so much a "lumpenproletariat" as
what British urbanists have referred to as "redundancy" of place.

Redundancy originally referred to workers being laid off in slow economic
times; redundancy of place refers to the wholesale loss of the economic base of a
local community through national transformations.[14] Underclass formation is
an outcome of shifts in the social and spatial organization of the urban economic
base, from central city to suburb, and from industrial heartland to Sunbelt and
overseas production sites. The underclass experiences mismatches between
labor skills and new job requirements but, more to the point, is caught in the
vagaries of historical transformations of local economies.

The changing political economy of late twentieth-century cities largely excludes some communities from mobility within the class system. Discussions of
mobility barriers faced by the underclass, such as lack of education, inadequate
family structure, or behavioral deviance, may well be empirically accurate. They
shift our attention, however, from the types of social change necessary to eliminate the social and economic isolation between the underclass and the remainder of our society.

The *terms* of the debate concerning the underclass are of great moment for the
creation of public policy, particularly in the housing arena. Because the housing
market has a threshold attached to it that inhibits easy access for a significant
segment of the population, the question facing analysts is whether to focus on
the characteristics of those failing to cross the threshold or to focus on the fact
that an increasing number of markets simply exclude many people from effective participation. The current tendency of public-policy debates to target the
failure of the underclass to effectively participate in job and housing markets
begs the historical question of how the housing market in particular has
changed, and what those changes mean for the future of the underclass.

The issue of the underclass is rooted in changes in the nature of urban life and
its institutional and spatial arrangements. This chapter focuses on the shifts that
have occurred in the operation of the housing market, national and local policies toward housing, and the impacts of these forces on the creation and
continuation of the underclass. The spatial isolation central to the underclass is

---

sity Press, 1975); Nathaniel Keith, *Politics and the Housing Crisis since 1930* (New York: Universe,
1973); and Peter H. Rossi, *Down and Out in America* (Chicago: University of Chicago Press, 1989).

[13] "Markets vary in their openness. A given market is not necessarily open to all potential buyers
and sellers" (Randall Collins, "Market Dynamics as the Engine of Historical Change," *Sociological
Theory* 8, no. 2 [1990]: 111–35). I have used the concept of "market threshold" to describe the lower
boundary to effective participation in the market.

[14] James Anderson, Simon Duncan, and Ray Hudson, *Redundant Spaces in Cities and Regions*
(London: Academic, 1983).

a direct extension of the history of housing markets and housing policy, and must be confronted if the underclass is to be fully understood or addressed in either an analytic or public-policy context.

HOUSING CHANGE IN POST-DEPRESSION AMERICA

It is not enough to catalog the set of housing problems that are visited upon the urban "underclass" by virtue of their position in contemporary society. It is more important that we disentangle the historical web of housing and spatial patterns which have helped create the underclass. The history of inner-city housing is traditionally told in a narrative of squalor and overcrowding in slums.[15] The images of Depression-era foreclosures and "Hoovervilles" contend with the emergence of public housing projects for position as the dominant housing theme of the 1930s. However, during that same time the establishment of a banking agency, the Home Owners' Loan Corporation (HOLC), altered the nature of home ownership, and thus of the housing market. Housing policy emerged as a side effect of bailing out banks and savings-and-loan institutions, an adjunct of economic policy. This linkage of housing policy to the operations of financial markets is a recurring theme in the post-Depression era.

In large part, the combination of depression recovery and postwar economic shift to home ownership promised a rosy future for the American household. These forces produced a more problematic outcome for the central cities. The limited successes of urban renewal programs in the 1950s and 1960s have been replaced with a largely antiurban housing policy, while the economic disruption of the 1970s and 1980s has helped reestablish one of the central debates of the Great Depression: Can the housing market provide decent housing for the full range of American society?

The current state of housing for low- and moderate-income segments of our society is not comforting. Forty years after Congress argued that every American should have access to a decent home and a suitable living environment, the streets of our cities bear witness to the present limitations of the urban housing market. The numbers queuing up for shelter space or lying across steam vents or in the temporary protection of cardboard cartons signal a return to a harsher, almost Dickensian world. Cities now witness their self-contained tales of two cities, with the world of David Copperfield and Oliver Twist existing side by side. Gentrification and renewal, new housing starts and dramatic housing vistas appear in virtually all of the nation's cities, but usually within the shadow of deteriorated and abandoned housing. Those employed in the growing service sector brush by and step over the new homeless, unable to afford increased housing prices. We can no longer easily maintain the fiction that continued

[15] Riis, *How the Other Half Lives*; Phillpot, *The Slum and the Ghetto*; and Fairbanks, *Making Better Citizens*.

national prosperity and growth will provide the tide of change to float the ships of the poor and isolated.

A wide variety of contemporary housing issues impact upon low-income neighborhoods. At the same time that housing costs have reached new peaks during the 1980s,[16] doubling up of households was reported as a consequence,[17] as were housing abandonment, declines in quality, and depressed markets.[18] Despite new levels of black suburbanization, high levels of segregation persist, and have often increased within our cities.[19]

It is the escalating cost of housing that directly confronts the underclass. Much of the continuing crisis in housing affordability in all locations results from the inflated cost of financing both the construction and purchase of housing, complicated by the current savings-and-loan crisis.[20] At the same time, the Reagan era withdrawal of low-income housing subsidies, both to producers and consumers, contributed to the dilemma faced by many households: choosing between food and shelter, or between medical care and shelter, or between other necessities and shelter.

Both the Harvard-MIT Joint Housing Center's *State of the Nation's Housing, 1990*[21] and the Economic Policy Institute report on shelter poverty, entitled *One Third of a Nation*,[22] elaborate on this theme. The Joint Center reports that the after-tax cost of housing is beginning to increase once again, after a period of some decline. Housing costs, however, have not yet returned to the levels of the 1970s, when they were at their highest in this century, but are now moving in that direction. Further, only 20 percent of white renters and 4 percent of black renters have the income or savings to finance home ownership—even with a 10 percent down payment. The low-income housing market is particularly vulnerable, as rents paid by these households continue to rise in the face of stability in the middle-income market. Losses of housing stock due to upgrading or abandonment have exacerbated the problems of affordability for both owners and tenants. Continued increases in housing costs have substantially eroded the

[16] William C. Apgar, Jr., Denise DiPasquale, Jean Cummings, and Nancy McCardle, *The State of the Nation's Housing, 1990* (Cambridge, Mass.: Joint Center for Housing Studies, 1990).

[17] Michael E. Stone, *One Third of a Nation: A New Look at Housing Affordability in America* (Washington, D.C.: Economic Policy Institute); Rossi, *Down and Out in America*.

[18] George Leon, "Ghosttowns, Ghettoes and Goldcoasts: The Sociology of Residential Abandonment" (Ph.D. diss., Temple University, 1986); William C. Apgar, Jr., "The Leaky Boat: A Housing Problem Remains," in Peter D. Salins, ed., *Housing America's Poor* (Chapel Hill: University of North Carolina Press, 1987), pp. 67–89; Apgar et al., *State of the Nation's Housing*.

[19] Douglas Massey and Nancy Denton, "Suburbs and Segregation in United States Metropolitan Areas," *American Journal of Sociology* 94 (1988): 582–96; Douglas Massey and Mitchell Eggars, "The Ecology of Inequality: Minorities and the Concentration of Poverty, 1970–1980," *American Journal of Sociology* 95 (1990): 1153–88.

[20] Stone, *One Third of a Nation*.

[21] Apgar et al., *The State of the Nation's Housing 1990*.

[22] Stone, *One Third of a Nation*.

relatively fixed income supports provided by Aid to Families with Dependent Children (AFDC), Social Security Insurance (SSI), and other income-transfer programs.

"Shelter poverty" according to the Economic Policy Institute report, reflects the point at which housing costs effectively prevent households from spending at a minimal level for food, clothing, or other basic living expenses.[23] Shelter poverty is a function of the income, household size, and household composition relative to the cost of housing. Larger households have a greater likelihood of experiencing shelter poverty, as do African-American and Hispanic households. The analysis of the household dynamics of shelter poverty suggests the following: The number of shelter-poor households has increased from 18.7 million in 1970 to 26.5 million in 1986—an increase of 42 percent. Additionally, while the level of shelter poverty generally varies with the business cycle (as might be expected), it hovers at a persistent rate of 30 percent of households—largely centered in rental households (42 percent of rental households experience shelter poverty).[24] Together, these studies indicate that the pattern of urban housing costs is toward greater inequality, and an increased burden upon the poor.

These studies are specifically aimed at a narrow political agenda in which the housing adequacy of recent national administrations is directly challenged. They also challenge a hypothesis that is implicit in most underclass arguments, and probably shared by most Americans, namely, that the social agenda of the New Deal and New Frontier has largely succeeded. This is a problematic assumption if housing costs are indeed rising so high, and impacting disproportionately upon minority communities.

THE PHILADELPHIA STORY

Three successive epochs mark the history of Philadelphia as a colonial, an industrial, and a postindustrial city.[25] In its earliest period, it was a commercial and administrative center for foreign shipping and transshipment to the Pennsylvania interior. During the years prior to the Civil War, it began to mix some industrial development with its commercial activities, but became a major manufacturing center for tools, transportation, and textiles during the late

[23] This measure was devised by using Bureau of Labor Statistics estimates for household expenses (the "Lower Budget") combined with estimates of tax reductions, both of which varied by income and household size. Shelter poverty exists when shelter costs impact upon the ability of a household to meet the minimal budget levels for basic living costs.

[24] The growth in household formations accounts for the increase in the number that are shelter poor, while they remain a persistent fraction of total households.

[25] Warner, *Private City*; Hershberg et al., "A Tale of Three Cities"; Carolyn T. Adams et al., *Philadelphia: Neighborhoods, Division, and Conflict in a Post-Industrial City* (Philadelphia: Temple University Press, 1991).

nineteenth and early twentieth centuries. Its industrial zenith was reached during the 1920s and continued through World War II, although it had experienced dramatic declines during the Depression. The years following the Korean War saw a major suburban push from both its people and its industries, combined with a major relocation of many of its textile industries to the South and overseas.

While Philadelphia was often called a "city of homes," it was, like most other American cities, largely dominated by rental housing until the years after World War II. Its compact, row-house design has been translated into generally lower housing costs compared to those of most cities. The black community in Philadelphia has always lagged its white counterparts in home ownership and, until recently, has generally faced the contradiction of paying more for less housing than blacks have faced in other cities.[26]

Philadelphia presents a clear example of the creation of a racially isolated community fitting the criteria of underclass.[27] Its development since the Depression reflects both national economic and demographic shifts as well as the local effects of its housing market and the housing policies that have helped shape an isolated black community.

Throughout its development, its racial and ethnic divisions were largely shaped by the combination of immigration waves and differential opportunities for ethnic groups within the manufacturing sector of the economy. In particular, the development of a concentrated black ghetto from relatively scattered black settlements mirrored the experience of other cities.[28] The emerging opportunities of the city structured competition between immigrants over jobs and land. Immigrants succeeded while the economy was growing, and suffered when it did not.

Two significant waves of African-American migration from the South occurred during the twentieth century, one during the 1920s and a second beginning in the 1940s and continuing through the 1960s.[29] Both occurred as the city had reached high watermarks in its manufacturing economy, and immediately prior to significant economic declines.[30] As the accompanying maps indicate (fig. 4.1),[31] the areas inhabited by blacks dramatically increased during

[26] Osofsky, Harlem.

[27] Paul Jargowsky and Mary Jo Bane, "Neighborhood Poverty: Basic Questions" (Cambridge: Malcomb Wiener Center for Social Policy, Harvard University, 1990); Elijah Anderson, Streetwise: Race, Class and Change in an Urban Community (Chicago: University of Chicago Press, 1990).

[28] Hershberg et al., "A Tale of Three Cities," 55–81.

[29] Ibid.; John F. Bauman, Public Housing, Race and Renewal: Urban Planning in Philadelphia, 1920–1974 (Philadelphia: Temple University Press, 1987).

[30] While the first of these, the depression of the 1930s, caused most cities to lose jobs, the second, the shift away from a manufacturing economy that accelerated during the 1960s and 1970s, was more selective in its effects.

[31] This figure, as well as the subsequent figures dealing with Philadelphia, is taken from Adams et al., Philadelphia, p. 80.

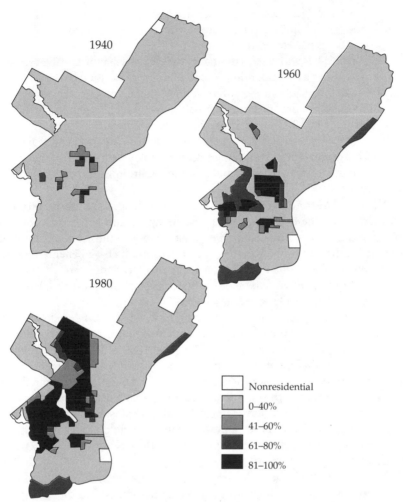

Figure 4.1. Percentage of Blacks in Philadelphia Neighborhoods, 1940, 1960, and 1980. *Source*: See note 31.

the postwar era, as did their degree of isolation from white communities. Philadelphia's segregation ratio increased from 0.68 in 1940 to 0.83 in 1980—a level that has remained constant over the past decade.

This increase in segregation was not accidental. It resulted from the timing of migration and Philadelphia's changing position within the national economy. It is a product of both the economics of transition from manufacturing to service sector, differential mobility opportunities, and the segregating forces of the housing market. The question that occurs in the context of this trend is not so much how Philadelphia came to have an underclass, but why we should be surprised that it has emerged.

Philadelphia has witnessed a dramatic decline in its manufacturing base since World War II and a corresponding increase in service-sector jobs. Nearly half of all of Philadelphia's jobs in 1947 were in the manufacturing sector; yet by 1986, this proportion had dropped to below 20 percent.[32] In the region as a whole, the ten years prior to 1987 saw a 15 percent drop in manufacturing jobs, but an increase of 37 percent in FIRE sector jobs (finance, insurance, and real estate), and a 51.1 percent increase in service-sector employment. Much of that growth was in suburban locations, and much of the loss from within the city of Philadelphia.[33]

The spatial distribution of jobs has created the image of the prosperous center surrounded by the detritus of industrial decay, in turn surrounded by more prosperous suburbs. But it would be a mistake to treat the economic transition as strictly a benefit to the suburbs. Although suburbs have benefited more so than Philadelphia in the new economy, the two locations share an important feature: employment growth seems to occur at both ends of the earning spectrum, rather than evenly across it.

If we divide the earnings of workers into those which fall below half the median, those between half and twice median earnings, and those more than twice the median, employment growth between 1980 and 1987 increased most dramatically in the upper tier of jobs for both the city (108 percent) and its suburbs (134 percent). Lower-tier jobs increased by only 15 percent in the city, but by 33 percent in the suburbs, indicating a significant limitation in the possibilities of low-wage jobs for city residents. Most striking, however, is the differential between those employed within the middle category. While the suburbs showed a small increase of 9 percent, the city witnessed a 13 percent decline.[34]

The relative shrinkage of low-earnings jobs and the absolute shrinkage of moderate-earnings jobs highlights a growing polarity within the city, if not a greater isolation of its lower-income population from the rest of its workers. The origins of this polarity lie in economic change, specifically the nature of employment in a service economy, rather than in the racial or ethnic characteristics of its population. A comparison of family income distributions of city residents with those of suburban residents emphasizes this phenomenon. As figure 4.2 indicates, the income distribution of city families in 1949 was slightly more concentrated toward the lower end of the scale than that of suburban families, while both city and suburban families showed evidence of a typical skewed distribu-

<hr>

[32] Ibid., pp. 36–39.
[33] Ibid., pp. 32–35.
[34] Ibid., pp. 45–47.

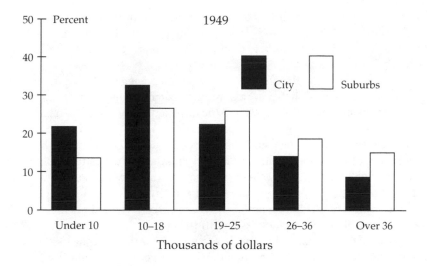

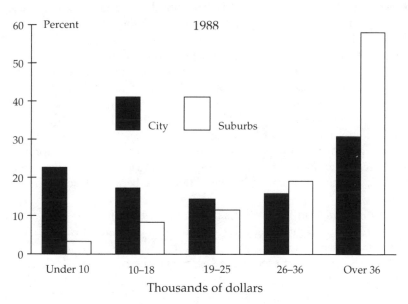

Figure 4.2. Distribution of Income Earned by Families at Different Income Levels for Philadelphia and Suburbs, 1949 and 1988. *Source*: See note 31.

tion. In 1988, not only had the suburban income distribution moved dramatically toward the upper end of the scale, but city families had begun to show a bimodal distribution, with low and high incomes tending to isolate the middle.[35]

These findings show that the effects of economic change will fall most heavily upon black households if they are disproportionately located within the city and if they remain there. In fact, while African-American households rapidly increased as a proportion of the city's population, to roughly 40 percent by 1990, they now constitute fewer than 5 percent of suburban households. The concentration of black households in Philadelphia thus increases the probability that they will be affected by these divisive economic trends. Put simply, the decline of economic opportunities within the city, and the increase of these opportunities in its suburbs, lies at the heart of the increased unemployment and poverty of black communities within the city.

Indeed, a comparison of income data from 1970 with that from 1988 underscores the twin effects of racial isolation and wage restructuring. Figure 4.3 shows the divergence of white and black income distributions for the region as a whole.[36] The proportion of black households in the $19–30,000 category diminished, while the proportions in the lower income groupings all increased. Only at the upper-income levels did the proportion of black families rise.

The immediate conclusion is that white and suburban residents of the Philadelphia region have gained more from the transition to a service economy than have black Philadelphians. Although this is undoubtedly true to some extent, the information presented here does not completely confirm this argument. In part, some of the differential may reflect differences in family structure, in particular the number of wage earners in each household. Yet the introduction of this factor into an analysis of family wage differentials showed it as only one of several significant influences on the differences between black and white incomes.

The differentials in income by race should be thought of as an overlay of historical, structural, and personal factors. There is a persistent racial differential of $8,000 in family income, which is best understood as a legacy of past differentials in job access, especially on account of discrimination. Added to this are the structural features affecting black-white income differentials, that is, the sector of the economy that produces employment. Finally, there are the family composition variables, particularly the number of wage earners present within the family.

The relationship of the housing market to income is immediately apparent. Income constraints imply housing constraints. But income constraints are not

[35] Ibid., pp. 53–55.
[36] Ibid., pp. 48–52. Sample limitations in the Current Population Survey make it impossible to isolate city residents alone, hence the need to use metropolitan area data.

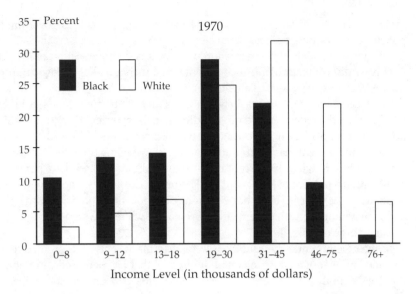

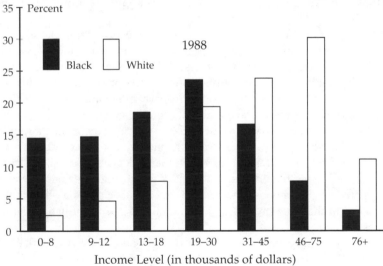

Figure 4.3. Total Family Income by Race, Philadelphia Metropolitan Area, 1970 and 1988. *Source*: See note 31.

the only constraints on the operation of the housing market, as government policy, credit restrictions, and racial steering have all played a part in the perpetuation of Philadelphia's segregation pattern. It is the intersection of institutionalized discrimination and income differentials that makes the isolation of the underclass so resistant to amelioration.

The basic income inequality between black and white households in Philadelphia directly reflects the complex differentials between black and white home ownership. Black home ownership, while increasing significantly between 1940 and the present, has been conditioned on the opening up of the suburbs to whites. While roughly 40 percent of white households owned their homes in 1940, only 10 percent of blacks did so. The rapid rise of black home ownership to about 55 percent in 1990 has occurred disproportionately within the city, and in neighborhoods that were either previously white or where black renters became home owners.

In the case of rental households, the median black renter has an income of roughly half that of a white tenant, a differential that has persisted throughout the 1980s. Fully 56 percent of black households had an income of below $10,000 in 1988; half of them paid more than 53 percent of their income in rent.[37]

In part, this information confirms a real divergence within the black community, as ownership has increased at the same time that low incomes have increased the burden of rent for others. It also highlights the barriers to home ownership for households currently renting homes present at both the national level and in Philadelphia.[38] But even a stronger employment market would not necessarily change the overall pattern of segregation.

Over the years from 1940 to the present, the city experienced a significant growth of its black population, as well as an increase in the degree of segregation within the city. This did not occur within the black ghetto as it existed in 1940, but expanded the boundaries of the black ghetto into previously white and integrated neighborhoods. The segregation of Philadelphia's black community is rooted in the same processes of migration and ghetto formation that other cities share.[39]

Once established, this city's pattern of segregation proved remarkably persistent. The perpetuation of Philadelphia's pattern of segregation has been linked to the effects of discriminatory lending practices by banks and other mortgage lenders, biases within the real-estate industry and, at times, the hostile reactions of many white communities to the "threat" of "invasion."

[37] Cushing Dolbeare, "Housing in Philadelphia" (Philadelphia: Public Interest Law Center, 1988), pp. 21–24.

[38] Apgar et al., *State of the Nation's Housing*.

[39] See Katzman, *Before the Ghetto*; Kusmer, *A Ghetto Takes Shape*; Osofsky, *Harlem*; Spear, *Black Chicago*.

As elsewhere, the Home Owners' Loan Corporation appraised Philadelphia's housing in racial and ethnic terms during the 1930s.[40] Virtually the only neighborhoods to receive positive ratings from this process were the far northern, northwestern, and northeastern sections of the city. These were largely white, and mainly inhabited by older immigrant groups and middle- to upper-income households.

Later, after World War II, the Federal Housing Administration (FHA) used these maps and lending criteria to determine its lending policies. Until the 1960s, the FHA was committed to providing mortgage insurance solely to newly constructed housing.[41] As a result, the new housing constructed in upper Northeast Philadelphia after World War II could be FHA financed; explicit restrictions against providing loans to black applicants seeking housing in white neighborhoods, on the grounds that this would disturb the social makeup of a community, ensured that the FHA subsidized segregation. The contemporary process of "redlining" neighborhoods—of attributing creditworthiness to neighborhoods on the basis of racial or ethnic characteristics—has its roots in these determinations.

Recent research focused on bank lending patterns reveals that most mortgages are provided to those seeking housing in predominately white neighborhoods (see fig. 4.4). In the years 1985 and 1986, for example, banks granted the bulk of the city's mortgages in the predominately white neighborhoods of gentrified Center City, the Northeast (which had been largely farmland until after World War II), and upper South Philadelphia. Additional research, controlling for the proportion of owner-occupied housing, concluded that there was a "persistent significance of race" in the granting of mortgages by neighborhoods.[42] Either by deliberate intent or by patterns institutionalized in the real-estate and banking industries, fewer mortgages than should have been expected were granted in black neighborhoods.

The mortgage process comes at the end of the housing search, however. The Philadelphia Human Relations Commission was originally founded to ease tensions in neighborhoods where racial change was taking place during the 1960s. One of its original targets was the behavior of real-estate brokers as they alternately "steered" black purchasers away from most white neighborhoods but used "blockbusting" tactics to cause housing turnover in others. In recent years,

[40] Another example is provided in Kenneth Jackson, *Crabgrass Frontier* (New York: Oxford University Press, 1985).

[41] Calvin P. Bradford, "Financing Home Ownership: The Federal Role in Neighborhood Decline," *Urban Affairs Quarterly* 14, no. 3 (1979): 313–35; Department of Housing and Urban Development (HUD), *Redlining and Disinvestment as Discriminatory Practices* (Washington, D.C.: Government Printing Office, 1977).

[42] Adams et al., *Philadelphia*, pp. 87–92; Ira J. Goldstein, "The Persistent Significance of Race: A City/Suburb Comparison of Mortgage Lending in the Philadelphia Metropolitan Area" (working paper, Philadelphia: Institute for Public Policy Studies, Temple University, 1987).

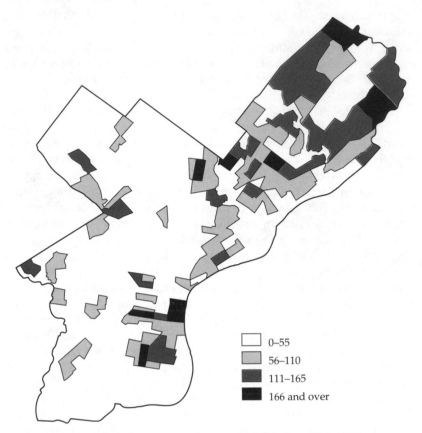

Figure 4.4. Number of Conventional Loans, Philadelphia, 1985–1986. *Source*: See note 31.

it has reported an increase in incidents of racial steering, and data from a national study suggests that this is not unexpected. In tests of racial steering, socioeconomically matched black and white couples were sent to a sample of real-estate brokers; in one city, three of four black couples reported that they were not even shown homes; most of the rest were shown homes that averaged more than $3,000 less than those shown white couples.[43]

Neighborhood reactions to racial change added to the formal institutional barriers to equal housing access. Both historically and in the present day, Philadelphians have witnessed many expressions of white outrage at efforts to break down racial barriers. These have not been restricted to the housing arena.

[43] Pearce, "Gatekeepers and Homeseekers."

Immediately after World War II, whites fought to remove blacks from public transportation jobs they obtained during the war. Several small race riots occurred when blacks moved into white working-class suburbs and into white neighborhoods during the 1960s. Racial politics came to the forefront under Mayor Rizzo's administration during the 1970s and resounded in public debates over how to best maintain segregated public schools while the city was under a court order to integrate them.[44] But public housing and urban renewal have been the most consistent triggers for racial divisions in the political arena during the postwar era.

One of the major code phrases for racial segregation during the 1970s in Philadelphia was "neighborhood control." That is, neighborhoods seeking to bar integration argued that the city and the federal government had no right to disrupt the community fabric in the name of racial integration. The Whitman Park housing protest illustrates how both urban renewal and publicly subsidized housing became the targets of a concerted antiblack political movement.

In the middle of the 1950s, the Redevelopment Authority displaced a predominately black section of Whitman Park, a small neighborhood in South Philadelphia, to allow for the development of a food distribution center and the road and bridgeworks that would create access to the center. The predominately white residents who remained in Whitman Park were provided funds for upgrading their homes once this construction was finished. Black households who were moved were promised that they could return after the construction of new housing, which would be available to them for lease/purchase at a subsidized price. This agreement was similar to promises made to other communities displaced by urban renewal.

While Whitman Park residents who remained received their housing improvements, they were also remarkably successful in forestalling the construction of new housing units for the displaced former residents. More than twenty years after the displacement of the community had occurred, the houses originally promised were finally built under court order and a full police guard for the construction crew. The federal court decision, finalized in 1977, found that the city, in collaboration with the residents of Whitman Park, had deliberately conspired to bar the black residents of the neighborhood from their promised housing relief.[45]

Whitman Park was a public symbol of the city's support of racial segregation, even in the use of federal housing dollars that ostensibly precluded such behavior. In another example of this approach to local housing policy, Philadelphia was one of the major cities cited by the Department of Housing and Urban Development (HUD) as using Section 8 to further segregate the city. HUD

[44] This order still stands, despite increased segregation at the primary-school level.
[45] "Residential Advisory Board v. Rizzo," *Federal Reporter* 2d ser., 564 (1977): 126–53.

had developed regulations requiring Section 8 certificates be applied in racially integrated neighborhoods; Philadelphia previously had been using these certificates to develop scattered-site public housing in predominately black neighborhoods.[46]

Neighborhood reactions to racial segregation extend beyond the formal political arena as well. Between 1984 and 1989, the Philadelphia Human Relations Commission reported a dramatic increase in incidents of racially motivated attacks. A major factor in the location of these incidents is their proximity to the collapse of manufacturing jobs.[47] Neighborhoods that housed the bulk of the white working class for Philadelphia's factories now wrestle with job loss and economic strain. Their residents blame "outsiders," particularly blacks and Hispanics, for job losses, either through increased competition for jobs or the flight of employers who left the city rather than employ minorities. Racial scapegoating plus the proximity of white and black neighborhoods in an era of severe economic stress reify neighborhood boundaries in expressions of racial isolation and conflict.

Philadelphia's racial division and the isolation of its underclass are thus best understood as the combined result of economic changes, the persistence of institutionalized forms of racial privilege, and the continued identification of racial boundaries by political and community processes. This process of isolation entrapped white and black communities alike. In Philadelphia, the emergence of a segregated, low-income black community has occurred side by side with the segregation of an aging, low-income white community largely concentrated in the older industrial neighborhoods of the city. Focusing on the "underclass" distorts the much more extensive effects that economic transition has had on the city. It also underestimates the concurrent effects of long-standing discriminatory patterns within the housing market, as well as those which occur in the distribution of both jobs and income.

Philadelphia has demonstrated a persistence, and even growth, of the segregation that accompanied the formation of its black ghetto in the early twentieth century. The locations of that community have changed, even while the city's overall population size has decreased since 1950. The new housing opportunities for the black community created by population losses have been tempered by the collapse of the manufacturing sector and the perseverance of institutional forms of discrimination within the housing market. The question

[46] Much of the public debate over this process assumed that public housing degraded the private market, driving down property values and encouraging white flight. In fact, a systematic review of forty years of public housing site decisions shows a converse relationship was more likely: public housing was placed in neighborhoods that had already been declining. See Ira J. Goldstein and William L. Yancey, "Public Housing Projects, Blacks and Public Policy: The Historical Ecology of Public Housing in Philadelphia," in John Goering, ed., *Housing Desegregation and Federal Policy* (Chapel Hill: University of North Carolina Press, 1986), pp. 262–89.

[47] Adams et al., *Philadelphia*, pp. 22–25.

now is whether Philadelphia's history is unique, or a part of a wider pattern shared by most cities in their housing markets.

HOUSING AND THE MODERN CITY

The housing market described for Philadelphia is hardly an isolated case. All cities have shared in the changes in housing financing brought about during the Depression, and all have had to deal with the forces of suburbanization. Still, not all cities have as extensive a pattern of segregation as Philadelphia's, nor as pronounced a division between its black and white housing opportunities.

Perhaps no single change in the American housing market has been so pervasively experienced as the transformation of the home mortgage, which occurred as a direct result of banking recovery measures during the Depression of the 1930s. The long-term, fully amortized mortgage is a relatively recent home financing instrument. It was normal practice prior to the Depression for home buyers to hold short-term, "balloon" loans. Purchasing a home usually involved a high down payment, monthly payments that were largely interest payments, and a large (inflated, or "balloon") payment at the end of the loan—typically between 50 percent and 75 percent of the sale value. It was usual for loans to mature within five years.

During the Depression, banks, building-and-loan and savings-and-loan societies alike faced a massive cash-flow crisis in their mortgage holdings. Depositor dollars depended on mortgage repayments, which often stopped when people lost their jobs. Financial institutions seeking to foreclose found no housing market enabling them to translate their foreclosed properties into cash. As a part of an attempt to free up the assets of these credit institutions, the government bought up old, short-term mortgages (often of five-year or shorter duration, under prevailing lending practices of the time) from the nation's savings-and-loan and bank institutions. These purchases were financed with the sale of bonds backed by new, twenty-year mortgages made available for properties that were regarded as safe by the Home Owners' Loan Corporation (HOLC). HOLC, which became the first federal mortgage operation, extended national appraisal norms and training to every American city with a population greater than twenty-five thousand, more than two hundred cities in all.[48]

This program, which was designed to free up frozen savings accounts in thrift institutions, created the modern mortgage system. The creation of the small-down-payment home purchase, with its long-term (originally twenty years), equal-payment amortization schedule, had significant effects beyond the period of the Depression. Its extension under the liberalized lending criteria of the Federal Housing Administration (FHA) during and immediately after World

---

[48] Jackson, *Crabgrass Frontier.*

War II was a major feature in financing the development of the new "crabgrass frontiers" of the suburbs.[49]

The long-term effect of this new mortgage policy was to transform a nation of renters (52 percent) before the Depression to a nation of home owners (65 percent in the mid-1980s).[50] The decades since the Depression have seen dramatic changes in the makeup of urban areas, largely made possible by this new financing system. For instance, since there was very little private housing construction during World War II, the economic impetus created by wartime production led to significant urban crowding. The combination of the pent-up demand within cities and the emergence of a new policy instrument after the war—the federally guaranteed, low-down-payment mortgages of the Veterans Administration and FHA—fueled the engine of suburban development. The combination of ready housing finance, a new, federally subsidized road construction program through the interstate highway system, new approaches to building housing "developments," and new manufacturing development in suburban locations provided significant "supply-side" forces facilitating suburbanization.[51]

At roughly the same time, the wartime investment in industrial production in the South and West provided a significant push toward migration out of the industrial heartland of the United States and into the Sunbelt region.[52] Between 1950 and 1980, the rapid and systematic urbanization of the late nineteenth and early twentieth centuries in the United States gave way to a combined suburbanization and exurban process. This occurred in many of the older urban areas of the Northeast and Midwest, while smaller cities in the South and West experienced significant growth patterns. However, they did not mirror the central-place development scheme of the older cities. Newer developing cities were much more likely to be dispersed in nature: polynucleated, developing around multiple centers, and thus usually less densely settled than the cities of the industrial heartland.[53]

By the 1960s, older industrial cities were facing a new era: manufacturing firms were leaving, shutting down, moving to suburbs or other regions, or moving out of the country altogether. Outmigration of the cities' populations

---

[49] Ibid.

[50] J. Paul Mitchell, ed., *Federal Housing Policy and Programs* (New Brunswick, N.J.: Center for Urban Policy Research Press, 1985), p. 37.

[51] Barry Checkoway, "Large Builders, Federal Housing Programs and Post-War Suburbanization," in William K. Tabb and Larry Sawers, eds., *Marxism and the Metropolis*, 2d ed. (New York: Oxford University Press, 1984), pp. 152–73; John Mollenkopf, "The Postwar Politics of Urban Development," in Tabb and Sawers, *Marxism and the Metropolis*, pp. 117–52.

[52] David Perry and Alfred Watkins, *The Rise of the Sunbelt Cities* (Beverly Hills, Calif.: Sage, 1978); Kirkpatrick Sale, *Power Shift: The Rise of the Southern Rim and Its Challenge to the Eastern Establishment* (New York: Random House, 1975).

[53] Rodney A. Erickson, "The Evolution of the Suburban Space Economy," *Urban Geography* 4, no. 2 (1983): 95–121.

paralleled. Neighborhoods differentially experienced the population declines and economic insecurity that accompanied this economic outmigration. The greatest burden fell upon traditional working-class communities and the black ghettos that had developed in the aftermath of the several periods of migration northward.[54] As Southern blacks moved to Northern industrial job centers in pursuit of traditional economic mobility, they found the first blush of opportunity replaced by the collapse of manufacturing and traditional entry-level jobs. This happened both during the Depression years and during the later shift away from manufacturing and toward service-sector employment during the 1960s and 1970s.[55]

From the 1970s onward, most older cities experienced the logical outcomes of these pressures. As the combined pressures of housing costs and reduced incomes of tenants took their toll, owners of low-income housing increasingly chose to abandon central-city housing stocks. The denial of credit for home sales within the city that accompanied suburban population movements in the 1950s and 1960s contributed to the development of a new generation of landlords. In addition, the housing left behind during suburbanization could not easily be sold because of these credit restrictions as well as the lower income levels of city residents. Landlords faced a constant tension between cash flow, maintenance, tax payments and the optimization of income from the property, all the while facing the absence of new migration to the city.[56] Foreclosures and tax seizures on rental properties increased, and the recession at the beginning of the 1980s drove these levels to new heights. Additionally, the significant inflationary period of the 1970s, particularly seen in the increased cost of fuel and fuel-related expenses, made the business of investing in and operating rental housing in these areas a very risky one, at best.

At the same time, the dramatic shift from city to suburb and from Frostbelt to Sunbelt had created real housing shortages in many newly developed areas. As might be expected, the cost of housing in the Sunbelt, while often more reasonable than its counterpart, was often increased dramatically by the simple inability of some housing markets to keep up with the pace of population growth.[57] Across the urban landscape, cities experienced the differential housing effects of both boom and bust economies, depending upon their position in the national economy. Downsizing was accompanied by income loss and abandonment in the housing stock; boomtowns experienced shortages and dramatic

[54] See Gregory Squires et al., *Chicago: Race, Class and the Response to Urban Decline* (Philadelphia: Temple University Press, 1987); Joseph Darden et al., *Detroit: Race and Uneven Development* (Philadelphia: Temple University Press, 1987); and Carolyn Adams et al., *Philadelphia*, for three case studies of this process.

[55] Hershberg et al., "A Tale of Three Cities."

[56] George Sternlieb, *The Tenement Landlord* (New Brunswick, N.J.: Rutgers University Press, 1965); Peter Salins, *The Ecology of Housing Destruction* (New York: New York University Press, 1980).

[57] Perry and Watkins, *Rise of the Sunbelt Cities*.

increases in housing prices, fueled by migration pressures. These diametrically opposed economic forces contributed to a shortage of affordable housing, or to the shortage of sufficient income for households to effectively participate in even a depressed housing market.[58]

The 1970s also saw an interesting reflection of the transformed central-city economies of the new service sector. Downtown centers became the source of business services to corporate headquarters, legal firms, and assorted FIRE industries.[59] These business services supported a "back-to-the-city" movement among many younger members of the professional and quasi-professional work force. Actually a throwback to the era in which workers lived near to the plant in which they worked, this movement led to the development of a "gentrification" of many neighborhoods immediately surrounding, or accessible to, the new service-sector job sites. While this movement into the city did not ever threaten to counter the underlying demographic shifts from center to suburb, or from Frostbelt to Sunbelt, many urban policy analysts treated the back-to-the-city movement as a major source of new urban resources.[60] Gentrification presented an image of what private-sector efforts could do to reshape the face of the older, often abandoned, mostly deteriorated neighborhoods of older cities. In fact, the creation of gentrified neighborhoods has generally reduced the already limited amount of viable low-income housing available in these cities.[61]

Because of the effects of both economic transition and the relocation of manufacturing across the national system of cities, divergent patterns of economic and demographic development characterize the urban centers of the United States. This uneven development of America's cities has reduced the supply of livable low-income housing, created significant problems of housing access for moderate-income households, disrupted the traditional passage from renting to ownership (particularly for black households), and hit the inner cities of the country the hardest.

The Uneven Pattern of Housing Segregation

The forces of suburbanization and economic change impacted across the range of American cities, large and small, Sunbelt and Frostbelt, manufacturing and postindustrial. Yet underclass formation is rather more selective, tending toward

[58] It was therefore not surprising to find homelessness in both Frostbelt and Sunbelt cities in the 1980s. Los Angeles, San Francisco, Seattle, Phoenix, and Portland stood alongside such Frostbelt centers as New York, Boston, Philadelphia, Chicago, and Minneapolis as major centers of homelessness. See Martha Burt and Barbara Cohen, *America's Homeless: Numbers, Characteristics and the Programs That Serve Them* (Washington, D.C.: Urban Institute, 1989); and "Differences among Homeless Single Women, Women with Children and Single Men," *Social Problems* 36 (1990): 508–24.

[59] The industries referred to here are finance, insurance, and real estate.

[60] Shirley Laska and Daphne Spain, *Back to the City* (New York: Praeger, 1980).

[61] Hartman, Keating, and LeGates, *Displacement: How to Fight It*.

cities with a strong manufacturing heritage and with a spatial isolation of residence from workplace. In particular, these tend to be cities with persistent high levels of segregation.

Residential segregation is an integral part of both the concept of isolated black communities discussed in the underclass literature and a pivotal element in the disproportionate share of housing problems experienced by African Americans in cities. Segregation, however, should not be overidentified with intentional and explicit patterns of racism; neither should it be dismissed by simply lumping it in with basic urban patterns experienced by all ethnic groups at various points in time. Although it is undoubtedly true that racism contributes to segregation, it is also a carryover, a cruel legacy, of generations of inequality inherited by the modern city.

Segregation is not a simple by-product of large-scale urban ecological and demographic forces. From the very outset of classic urban sociology, the persistent reality of the black ghetto defied the basic ecological framework of ethnic succession and assimilation, and the persistence of the black ghetto became a significant problem for generations of urban sociologists.[62] The eventual explanation by urban ecologists asserted the operation of institutional mechanisms that retarded the assimilation of black residents by disrupting normal ecological processes.[63] Problems with this interpretation persist. Segregation has persisted far longer for blacks than for other ethnic groups, and the degree of segregation they experience is higher than either the segregation of earlier immigrants or of many "newer" ethnic groups, such as Asians and Hispanics.[64] The latter finding challenges ecological arguments which predict that the newest migrants to cities should be the most isolated and ghettoized.[65]

Approaches to the persistence of segregation based on institutionalized racism argue that segregated communities are the outcome of a "rigged" market system. Various "gatekeepers," mostly institutional, maintain barriers against the integration of neighborhoods. One of those barriers is the absence of capital, especially funds for mortgages. Neighborhoods acquire their characteristics from the flow of investment capital into and away from neighborhoods and communities of the metropolis.[66] The neighborhoods of the city can be thought of as islands in the flow of investment capital, with their persistence and livelihood dependent upon industrial, commercial, and real-estate capital.[67] In this view, segregation is the outcome of a mortgage lending industry that responds to

[62] Robert E. Park, Ernest W. Burgess, and Roderick D. McKenzie, eds., The City (Chicago: University of Chicago Press, 1925); Drake and Cayton, Black Metropolis.

[63] Karl Taeuber and Alma Taeuber, Negroes in Cities (Chicago: Aldine, 1965).

[64] Farley and Allen, The Color Line and the Quality of Life in America, pp. 103–58.

[65] Massey and Denton, "Suburbs and Segregation in the United States Metropolitan Areas."

[66] Harvey Molotch, "Capital and Neighborhood in the United States" Urban Affairs Quarterly 14, no. 3 (1979): 289–312.

[67] Bartelt et al., "Islands in the Stream."

142 · David W. Bartelt

the existing economic topography of cities, perpetuating its existing sociospatial divisions.[68]

Both traditional urban-process and gatekeeper models of persistent segregation essentially beg the issue of the significant variation in levels of segregation that characterize the American system of cities.[69] Cities do not share a common level of segregation, nor a common trend line over time. Older manufacturing cities in the North and Midwest have higher indexes of segregation than do those in the South and West.[70]

These differential levels of segregation correspond to patterns of underclass formation.[71] An underclass is most developed in areas hit hardest by economic transition, especially in older, manufacturing-dependent cities. It develops in the wake of long-established patterns of segregation. In examining the large-scale economic and social forces that have shaped this historical backdrop to urban community formation, we are continually drawn to the role of capital flow.

The investment of capital—financial, technological, and human—in the built environment of the industrial city creates a relatively fixed urban environment. The buildings, roads, infrastructure, and linkages of workplace to residence hinder the ability of a city to adapt when technologies and costs of production change. When new economic forces arise, there is a tendency for open space to be converted, rather than disrupt the inertia of past factories, warehouses, roads, and housing.

As might be expected, black migrants from the South tended to settle in the larger manufacturing and commercial cities of the North and Midwest. The common thread linking ghetto formation in the early twentieth century was the combination of economic opportunity, the subsidence of European immigration, and the segregation of the rapidly growing black urban community.[72] It is ironic that the more successful a city was in attracting black migration streams to manufacturing jobs through the mid-twentieth century, the more likely these migrants were to be trapped in ghettos when the manufacturing plants left in later years.[73]

[68] David Harvey and Lata Chatterjee, "Absolute Rent and the Structuring of Space by Government and Financial Institutions," *Antipode* 6, no. 1 (1974): 22–36; Anne Shlay, "Not in That Neighborhood: The Effects of Population and Housing on the Distribution of Mortgage Finance in the Chicago SMSA," *Social Science Research* 17 (1988): 137–63.

[69] Massey and Denton, "Suburbs and Segregation in the United States Metropolitan Areas."

[70] Thomas VanValey, Wade Clark Roof, and Jerome E. Wilcox, "Trends in Residential Segregation," *American Journal of Sociology* 82 no. 4 (1977): 845–53; Massey and Denton, "Suburbs and Segregation in the United States Metropolitan Areas."

[71] Jargowsky and Bane, "Neighborhood Poverty."

[72] Osofsky, *Harlem*; Spear, *Black Chicago*; Katzman, *Before the Ghetto*; Kusmer, *A Ghetto Takes Shape*.

[73] Thierry Noyelle and Thomas Stanback, *The Economic Transition of American Cities* (Totowa, N.J.: Rowman and Allanheld, 1983); Zunz, *Making of an Urban Working Class*; Neal Fligstein, *Going North* (New York: Academic, 1982).

The shift from industrial to service-sector economies occurred against a major population shift away from older centers of manufacturing, predominately in the Northeast and Midwest, to new opportunities for growth in the West and, later, the South. This shift was fueled by the wartime expansion of rail, road, and air transportation opening up the West Coast, as well as the postwar interstate highway program.[74]

The spatial isolation central to the modern underclass is based on this combination of ghetto formation and dramatic shift in the economic centrality of cities. This isolation develops unevenly, varying from place to place as a function of manufacturing's centrality in a city's economy and the degree to which ghettoization occurred as a response to the great migration streams of the early and middle twentieth century. The process of ghetto formation familiar to most urban historians was disrupted by the new urban dynamics of suburbanization and decentralization of manufacturing production.

The investment practices of local financial institutions reinforce the process of segregation by following population flows and income constraints in the labor market from one region/metropolitan area to another. The distribution of classes and ethnic groups into more or less segregated urban residential neighborhoods thus followed from a city's development in a constantly shifting system of urban nodes in the national (and international) economy.

In the era of greatest urban industrial development, which effectively ended with World War II, ethnic and racial communities most often reflected the patterns of manufacturing development and job opportunities which developed within that national pattern.[75] Throughout the late nineteenth and early twentieth centuries these communities formed as new immigrant groups continued to expand the size and, indirectly, the spatial reach of urban areas. While significant outmigration from the older regions of the East and Midwest occurred, population losses were more than replaced by new waves of immigrants.[76]

Understanding migration is central to grasping the changing pattern of segregation in cities and its links to the economic base of cities. Unless populations are able to move within and between urban areas, they will remain locked into residential locations. Within the American economy, migration usually accompanies economic change. Persistent segregation reveals an exception to this expected result. We would expect high population mobility in a system marked by uneven development, where economic opportunity is growing in some parts of the system and simultaneously declining in others.

This has happened only in part. Although a significant migration away from older industrial cities accompanied the decline of the Frostbelt/Rustbelt/heavy

---

[74] Perry and Watkins, *Rise of the Sunbelt Cities.*

[75] Hershberg et al., "Tale of Three Cities"; Yancey and Ericksen, "Antecedents of Community"; Ericksen and Yancey, "Work and Residence in Industrial Philadelphia"; and Zunz, *Making of an Urban Working Class.*

[76] Daniel J. Elazar, *Cities of the Prairie: The Metropolitan Frontier and American Politics* (New York: Basic Books, 1970).

industry economy, many have remained trapped, unable to move to new opportunities. Thus, migration and settlement patterns in recent decades have contributed to a residual but extensive segregation in areas of economic decline.[77]

Historically, migrants have usually been either well educated (responding to attractive opportunities) or poorly educated (often responding to a relative improvement over conditions in their community of origin). By contrast, more recent migration streams across all nine census subregions of the United States have reflected education directly: the greater the education, the greater the probability of migration. This points to a relative immobility by those with less education and fewer resources. Not only do "constraints on black destination selectivity continue to exist at all socio-economic levels," but the incidence of mobility for blacks *declines* as education increases.[78] Intact families and individuals with relatively high earnings also dominate recent migration streams.[79]

Northward black migration, both in the era of World War I and after, as well as during the Second World War and the 1950s, was directed at areas of then-active economic activity, made more attractive by the opening up of housing opportunities generated by suburbanizing white populations. This pattern is discussed more fully in Joe Trotter's article in this volume. As the suburbanization and deindustrialization of economic opportunities accelerated during the 1970s, the nature of migration itself shifted. The result is a relatively immobilized black population in Northern and Midwestern cities, locked into poverty and limited opportunities in regions of economic decline.[80] Thus, the segregation patterns that developed in the aftermath of postwar migration remain, with little in the dynamics of jobs, housing, or economic change to disrupt them.

An empirical analysis of fifty-nine cities supports these arguments.[81] The analysis linked variables reflecting the economic structure of these cities over time (1929–80) to population changes and central city–suburban shifts. Additionally, it measured the changing position of cities within the banking hierarchy across these cities, using links within intercity bank correspondent relationships.[82] It used these variables to predict 1970 and 1980 levels of segregation in a multiple regression procedure.

[77] Larry Long, *Migration and Residential Mobility in the United States* (New York: Russell Sage Foundation, 1988); Fligstein, *Going North.*

[78] William Frey, "Black In-Migration, White Flight and the Changing Economic Base of the City," *American Sociological Review* 44 (1979): 425–48.

[79] Farley and Allen, *The Color Line and the Quality of Life in America.*

[80] The relative immobility of the black community in the face of tremendous economic pressure to leave is a problem beyond the scope of this chapter, and is puzzling to most observers. Given the relative lack of capital formation within the African-American community, at least compared to that of other immigrant populations, it is my hypothesis that the economic barriers that trapped blacks in the Reconstructionist and post-Reconstruction South are replicated for many communities in the postindustrial North and Midwest.

[81] David W. Bartelt, "Cities Divided: Race, Redlining and Restructuring" (Paper prepared for the Fourth International Research Conference on Housing, Paris, 1990).

[82] Banks, which were largely locally based until the deregulation efforts of the 1980s, facilitated their commercial customers' trading relationships by establishing "correspondent relationships"

The analysis showed segregation levels to be responsive to migration, economic role, job opportunities, and earlier residential patterns. Patterns of segregation in 1970 were explained by the interaction of three major factors: (1) the relative importance of a city in the banking hierarchy at the end of the industrial era; (2) job creation attractive to migration streams (job creation from 1940 to 1960); and (3) region (Northern and Midwestern locations). Continued high levels of segregation in 1980 were associated with the inertia of past segregation, particularly in larger cities, and, again, mostly in the North and Midwest.

Cities experience segregation as part of their economic and demographic histories. The segregation of black communities persists as a legacy of past opportunities denied. The very invisibility of the economy's sociospatial organization obscures the deep structural forces supporting segregation; to the contrary, it makes it much easier to account for the failures of those within underclass communities by references to their own limitations.

But the structural factors that help account for the persistence of segregation, and hence of the isolation of many black communities, do not stand alone. Their persistence over time combined with the dramatic shift in the urban economy to exert a present impact on the institutional operations of the housing market and the application of housing policy.

THE ISSUE OF POLICY

The issue of public policy is always present within discussions of the underclass, both in debates over "what to do" as well as in discussions over the potential contributions of past public policy to the formation of the underclass. Public assistance policies have taken center stage in this respect, as it is argued that they have contributed to the lack of motivation among long-term welfare recipients to seek or accept low-wage work.[83]

This chapter, however, addresses policies impacting on housing markets and institutions, which have only occasionally been raised in debates over either segregation or persistent urban poverty.[84] While the discussion has focused in particular on how financing mechanisms have changed, it is also possible to ascertain the impacts of many of the basic housing policies of the post-Depression era on the formation of the isolated communities of the underclass.

---

with other banks in cities where these customers most often traded. Examining the "sending" and "receiving" patterns of banks in each of these cities provides a useful indicator of the economic centrality of each city. See Stanley Lieberson, "The Division of Labor in Banking," *American Journal of Sociology* 69 (1964): 491–96.

[83] John D. Kasarda, "Jobs, Migration and Emerging Urban Mismatches," in Michael G. McGeary and Laurence E. Lynn, eds., *Urban Change and Poverty* (Washington, D.C.: National Academy Press, 1988), pp. 148–98; Wilson, *The Truly Disadvantaged*, pp. 93–108.

[84] Arnold R. Hirsch, *Making the Second Ghetto: Race and Housing in Chicago, 1940–1960* (New York: Cambridge, 1983); Fairbanks, *Making Better Citizens*; and Bauman, *Public Housing, Race and Renewal*.

This view of recent housing policy, combined with the economic and social changes affecting basic urban dynamics, suggests alternative ways of debating the policy alternatives for the underclass.

A commitment to home ownership, urban renewal, and the public housing program have been the three major features of federal housing policy since the Depression. While HOLC created a new mortgage system, federal housing policy concentrated on the development of public housing, which originated during the Depression, or on programs rooted in the 1949 National Housing Act. In its preface, this act established the goal of federal housing policy to be the right of a decent home for every American. The American people had experienced a decade of economic collapse, followed by a massive military expenditure that limited consumer expenditures. World War II had created such economic pressures in defense locations that federal rent control was the major housing policy of the war years.

The creation of the National Housing Act of 1949 emerged from a recognition of two facts of urban life—that the Federal Housing Administration/Veterans Administration (FHA/VA) mortgage programs, which insured mortgages on new dwellings purchased with low down payments, could be expanded significantly. This effort would spark new construction, which the cities of the United States needed if they were to both house the poor and physically upgrade existing housing stocks. Thus, the two forces set in motion in this time period were the suburbanizing force of the FHA/VA program and the urban renewal/public housing thrust of the National Housing Act.

The home-ownership component of federal policy was actually carried out, and its subsequent history, especially in the last two decades, has contributed significantly to the spatial isolation of the underclass. The saga of the suburban explosion following World War II is a part of both popular culture and academic research.[85] Although it would be a mistake to limit the discussion of suburbanization to the postwar era, the dramatic confluence of production factors with federal housing and highway policies in the postwar era fueled the movement of populations en masse from the center of cities to suburbs.[86]

In all of this movement, one additional federal policy, often not explicitly recognized as policy, effectively supported the movement of renters into home ownership. This was the income-tax deduction for taxpayers' mortgage pay-

[85] Herbert Gans, *The Levittowners: Ways of Life and Politics in a New Suburban Community* (New York: Pantheon, 1967); Peter O. Muller, *The Outer City: Geographical Consequences of the Urbanization of the Suburbs*, resource paper 75–2 (Washington, D.C.: Association of American Geographers, 1976).

[86] Jackson, *Crabgrass Frontiers*; David M. Gordon, "Capitalist Development in North American Cities," in Tabb and Sawers, *Marxism and the Metropolis*, pp. 25–63; Calvin P. Bradford et al., "Financing Home Ownership: The Federal Role in Neighborhood Decline," *Urban Affairs Quarterly* 14, no. 3: 313–35; Checkoway, "Large Builders, Federal Housing Programs and Post War Suburbanization."

ments.[87] Tax policies encouraged what the FHA facilitated: home ownership by middle- and upper-income households. In short, the home-ownership stream of federal housing policy supported the suburbanization of most metropolitan areas.

Explicit racial restrictions constrained the significant suburban growth of the immediate postwar era. Mortgage appraisal files and accompanying maps evaluating the creditworthiness of neighborhoods, which were transferred from HOLC to FHA in the early 1940s, show clearly that racial and ethnic characteristics of neighborhoods were an integral part of the decision to extend credit to some neighborhoods and deny it to others.[88]

These appraisal methods virtually guaranteed that only areas of relatively new construction, middle class or higher income, and Northern European ethnic characteristics would be eligible for the top ratings of HOLC. In Philadelphia, for instance, the files characterize one area as "excellent, but beware of Jewish encroachment." Another area was complimented for its "hard-working German stock." In a precursor of current debates, black neighborhoods were characterized differentially as either "good character" or "undesirable."[89] Both types of neighborhood were rated as hazardous for loans, however, due to their racial composition.

This use of racial composition to rate neighborhoods was a direct outgrowth of the longer-term mortgage. As the credit industry and the government, as the insurer of mortgage loans, contemplated long-term mortgages, they saw themselves taking a risk on a neighborhood, not just on a person applying for a loan. The emergence of the longer-term mortgage virtually created the concept of redlining, the drawing of boundaries around areas that were to be denied credit on the basis of arbitrary characteristics, rather than on the credit rating of the would-be borrower.

Remember the unique nature of housing. Longer-term mortgages meant that the concept of risk became dual: risk was attached both to the borrower and to the house itself. Given that housing acquires value from context, a downward trajectory indicated that a neighborhood was a bad risk should the borrower default and the creditor or insurer be forced to dispose of the property. The argument most often raised by banks was essentially economic: What would the resale possibilities be in fifteen to twenty years if the borrower were to default? Unless the bank was confident about the property maintaining value over time, it would be reluctant to mortgage the property. The system became so effective

[87] In 1985, for example, this subsidy represented a tax expenditure of some $58 billion, as that amount of taxes was not collected. See Mitchell, *Federal Housing Policy and Programs*.

[88] Jackson, *Crabgrass Frontiers*; David W. Bartelt, "Redlines and Breadlines: Depression Recovery and the Structuring of Urban Space" (working paper, Philadelphia: Institute for Public Policy Studies, Temple University, 1985).

[89] Home Owners Loan Corporation, "Neighborhood Evaluation Sheets: Philadelphia," HOLC City Survey File, record group 195 (Washington, D.C.: National Archives, 1935).

that the Department of Housing and Urban Development reported that a major appraisal manual used in real-estate practice until 1975 contained a fourteen-category rating scale of neighborhoods by ethnic and racial composition, in which black and Hispanic neighborhoods were at the bottom rung.[90]

Additionally, explicit FHA and VA policy loans offered insurance on loans only for new construction, which could not be used to disturb the basic "character" of a neighborhood.[91] In operational terms, this restricted the use of FHA and VA guaranteed loans during the 1950s to white applicants for white communities. Although President Kennedy abolished racial restrictions within the FHA/VA programs with an executive order in 1961, this act did not begin to address the twenty-five years of past practices that had become institutionalized within the real-estate and financial industries.

Given the suburbanization of private capital, it was to the urban renewal and public housing components of urban policy that central cities turned for funds aimed at improving their housing stock. Urban renewal efforts dominated federal housing policies for the inner city. Many cities saw urban renewal as a means of disposing of substandard housing and of reshaping the older downtown areas of the railroad-and-trolley-car era to the demands of the automobile.[92]

However, the relationship between urban renewal and slum clearance was seldom aimed at direct improvement of housing conditions for low-income residents of dilapidated housing.[93] Indeed, any neighborhood-level improvement as a consequence of these programs depended on two mechanisms of capital infusion. On the one hand, by reshaping a city's economic organization, a new middle class, employed in the new corporate centers, would bring their mortgage investment dollars to upgraded neighborhoods (a goal long before the term *gentrification* was used). On the other, slum areas that were cleared would "attract" new investment capital by virtue of their locations close to the center of the city, cleared status, and tax benefits which would accrue to new developers. In fact, economic transformation and gentrification did occur, but renewal efforts in low-income areas lagged as cities decentralized and investment dollars fled older neighborhoods.[94]

It is crucial to keep in mind here that most of the cities negatively affected by population losses due to suburbanization were old manufacturing cities located in the Northeast and Midwest. At first, many cities reacted to population losses with some relief, because the urban renewal efforts of the 1950s required

[90] Department of Housing and Urban Development, *Redlining and Disinvestment.*

[91] Bradford et al., "Financing Home Ownership."

[92] Edmund Bacon, *Design of Cities* (New York: Viking, 1967).

[93] Nancy Kleniewski, "From Industrial to Corporate City: The Role of Urban Renewal," in Tabb and Sawers, *Marxism and the Metropolis*, pp. 205–22.

[94] Ibid.; also, see Carolyn Adams, *The Politics of Capital Investment* (Albany: State University of New York Press, 1988).

moving large sections of the population into better-quality housing while renewed housing was being built.[95] In fact, however, in many cities another qualitative change was occurring, due to the countervailing migration of blacks to traditional manufacturing centers.

The efforts at urban renewal that characterized both the 1950s and the urban riot era of the 1960s originally targeted the very neighborhoods in which housing was the poorest and, coincidentally, where minority residents lived in greater numbers.[96] In fact, these efforts were based on two rather unrealistic assumptions about the ways in which housing markets would operate in their wake. First, urban renewal assumed that once infrastructure needs were addressed (site clearance, street repair, local institutional improvement, blight removal), housing investment dollars would flow to renewal areas.[97] When massive clearance efforts often produced vacant lots or institutional development without new housing efforts, urban renewal quickly became known as "urban removal."

Second, redevelopment efforts depended on support within the affected neighborhoods. Redevelopment efforts carried the expectation that residents would view renewal efforts as, at the least, well intentioned and, even better, as a significant improvement. In fact, neighborhoods often opposed renewal. In one of the classic analyses of community life, Gans reported on the struggle of residents to maintain a poor but tightly bonded community in the North End of Boston against urban renewal.[98] Neighborhood opposition to renewal efforts often targeted the expansion of non-neighborhood institutions, such as universities, hospitals, and firms that displaced residents while creating employment for outsiders to the neighborhood.[99]

Urban renewal efforts shifted their orientation from addressing poor housing conditions to reshaping the business communities of the city as a response to the dual pressures on neighborhood opposition and disinvestment that emerged during the late 1950s and early 1960s.[100] Revitalization efforts shifted to commercial and office centers that were centrally located, visible, and evidenced more dramatic improvements. Benefits for housing were expected to trickle down in the form of new jobs created by the new economy—a policy that continues to echo today. The creation of new, aesthetically pleasing cityscapes became the hallmark of renewal efforts, while housing efforts took on the patina of shoveling sand against the tide.[101]

[95] Bacon, *Design of Cities.*
[96] Kleniewski, "From Industrial to Corporate City."
[97] Adams, *Politics of Capital Investment.*
[98] Herbert Gans, *Urban Villagers* (New York: Free Press, 1962).
[99] Kleniewski, "From Industrial to Corporate City."
[100] Ibid.; also, Adams et al., *Philadelphia.*
[101] Gregory Squires, *Unequal Partnerships* (New Brunswick, N.J.: Rutgers University Press, 1989).

Urban renewal could not have succeeded as a housing rehabilitation strategy. It concentrated its efforts in the very neighborhoods that people were trying to leave because of the inadequate nature of the housing stock, in areas in which its efforts inspired resistance, or in areas which the private sector preferred to ignore. Moreover, limited funding always hampered its potential, particularly since the federal public housing program was regarded as a part of the renewal effort.[102]

Public housing, another instrument of federal housing policy, also had its roots in the Depression, under the auspices of the National Industrial Recovery Act. Some 21,600 units were created (in addition to some 15,000 "Greenbelt" units) to facilitate the housing of persons temporarily out of work.[103] During World War II, additional housing was built as temporary "defense" housing, some of which was maintained after the war as part of the public housing stock. During the 1950s, the FHA developed several mortgage-guarantee and subsidy programs to assist in the provision of low-rent and displaced-residents' housing, because public housing was to be used by those displaced during renewal programs.

In each of these instances, public housing was designed as a temporary way station, a short stop between migration to a city, permanent employment, and self-provided housing. However, a variety of factors transformed the role of public housing. Especially important were the growing migration from the South and the displacement of minorities by urban renewal. Public housing developed through the late 1950s had much more rigid screening of tenants, allowed for eviction procedures, and in virtually every respect was not seen as the housing "of last resort."[104] The sheer volume of low-income housing needs in the context of an urban renewal process that eliminated but did not replace existing, poor-quality housing led to dramatic pressures for the development of new housing units. These new public housing units lacked traditional linkages to either available jobs or new housing within the local community. They took on the character of a "warehouse" or, less pejoratively, a "safety net" for the poor, rather than a temporary stop on the road to independence.

Housing moved to the center of domestic public policy during the 1960s, undergirded by political debates over race and poverty. The development of a cabinet-level Department of Housing and Urban Development (HUD) in 1965 was more a response to pressures from civil rights and antipoverty advocates

---

[102] Bauman, *Public Housing, Race and Renewal*, p. 207.

[103] "Greenbelt" units refer to those built in planned communities sited on (primarily) agricultural lands, which formed a "green belt" around large cities. This was a concept borrowed directly from the British "new towns" movement. Barry Jacobs et al., *Guide to Federal Housing Programs* (Washington, D.C.: Bureau of National Affairs, 1986); see also, John Bauman, "Black Slums/Black Projects: The New Deal and Negro Housing in Philadelphia," *Pennsylvania History* 41 (1974): 311–38.

[104] Bauman, "Black Slums/Black Projects."

than to any perceived inadequacies of housing or development policy. It was a response to riots in the streets more than to institutionalized patterns of suburban development. Nonetheless, a cabinet-level department had been directly charged with the responsibility to coordinate housing subsidy programs, offer credit insurance, and provide public housing.[105]

But the 1960s had also seen the beginning of a shift away from the assumption that adequate housing would prove the key factor in alleviating or eliminating poverty. While housing remained a significant priority in the new cabinet department, many related urban programs focused on social service provision for the poor.[106]

Despite the emergence of HUD, housing policies prior to the 1970s supported a predominately white movement to the suburbs and a disproportionate allocation of home-ownership options to white families. At the same time, urban renewal and public housing policies hurt predominately black communities by displacing their residents and reinforcing de facto segregation. The urban policies of the Nixon administration did not reverse these directions.

From the moment that Spiro Agnew declaimed that, having seen one slum, he'd seen them all, it was clear that urban policy—and, in particular, urban housing policy—would not soon return to center stage of domestic policy. Nixon's domestic policy centered on welfare reform, notably his proposed Family Assistance Plan. However, three features of housing policy associated with his brief second term proved especially important. The first was a sudden moratorium in public housing construction/rehabilitation efforts, announced in January 1973. The second, closely linked to the first, was a new form of housing assistance known by its shorthand title, Section 8 (Section 8 of the Housing Act of 1974), which represented a significant shift in direct provision of public housing.

Section 8 redefined the federal role in housing provision by providing for incentives and mechanisms to lower the rents for low-income households. Instead of directly building low-income housing, the federal government would provide incentives to the private sector to keep rents at affordable levels. HUD moved from its role as a direct actor in housing provision to that of a facilitator of housing production. The agency became a financing entity rather than a production source. Of even greater impact, however, was the third leg of urban housing policy: the combination of all urban aid into a common package, or the replacement of "categorical grants" with "block grants" for all elements of community development.

Taken together, these three features of urban policy had the combined effect of limiting the inner-city agenda that had begun to take shape in the postriot years of the late 1960s and early 1970s.[107] The moratorium on housing aid

[105] Nathaniel Keith, *Politics and the Housing Crisis since 1930* (New York: Universe, 1973).
[106] Bauman, *Public Housing, Race and Renewal*.
[107] Jacobs et al., *Guide to Federal Housing Programs*.

served immediate and sudden notice that housing need would no longer be used as a guideline for housing policy.[108] The housing production goals that had been the hallmark of the still young Department of Housing and Urban Development no longer served as baselines for policy and program performance. Rather, Nixon advanced an alternative to traditional public housing: Section 8.

Consistent with conservative opposition to direct housing provision by the government, this program replaced public housing development with the lease of private-sector, low-rent housing to public housing authorities. Cities and local governments were allowed to create housing programs in which private developers created rental units for poor households, who would pay a maximum rent proportional to their income (25 percent).[109]

Section 8 started swiftly after its inception. Between 1975 and 1979, the number of units constructed approached the levels of prior programs, then rapidly declined during the 1980s. This decline was most striking in the programs focused on new construction, as opposed to those aimed at rehabilitation of existing stock.[110]

To appreciate the effects of the policy shift represented by Section 8, consider the basic problem that federal low-income policy seeks to address: the gap between the ability of low-income households to pay rent and the levels of rent which prevail within a given market. Assuming that the government takes on this responsibility, it has several options. The first of these is direct housing provision, in which the government as landlord takes a recurring loss but continues to provide basic housing. This is the traditional public housing approach. Alternatively, direct cash payments to poor households have always been problematic to legislators, as they fear the misuse of these payments on "luxury items."[111] A third role, represented by Section 8, is facilitative. The government supports the provision of low-income units with rental subsidies to the landlord, and favorable tax treatment of housing investments.

This facilitative role accepts the inevitability of a rent-income gap on the one hand, and denies responsibility for the direct provision of economic goods to disadvantaged populations on the other. Thus, Section 8 played a major ideological role in shifting responsibility for low-income housing to the private

---

[108] Public housing production peaked at 100,000 units a year in 1970; between 1972 and 1984 it averaged only 30,000 units a year. See R. Allen Hays, *The Federal Government and Urban Housing* (Albany: State University of New York Press, 1985), p. 151.

[109] Any differences between tenant rent levels and fair market rents were made up by federal subsidies to the developer. The opportunities for profitmaking came not from the subsidy program, which was designed only to provide a minimal internal rate of return, but from the favorable treatment that these units received under federal tax rules covering rental housing generally, and specifically through the provisions of accelerated depreciation. See Jacobs et al., *Guide to Federal Housing Programs*.

[110] Hays, *Federal Government and Urban Housing*.

[111] Frances Fox Piven and Richard Cloward, *Regulating the Poor: The Function of Public Welfare* (New York: Pantheon, 1971).

market. In particular, it displaced responsibility for addressing the inadequacies of housing markets from the national to the state and local levels, and to their ability to work with the private sector.

Apart from direct housing provision, changes in existing FHA and FHA-related activities reinforced a trend toward facilitation and away from housing provision. During the 1960s, the FHA expanded its scope of operations to include the underwriting of rehabilitation loans, public housing construction, senior citizen housing, and below-market loans to subsidized rental units. The government, concerned over the potential level of direct risk to the FHA, developed several mechanisms that minimized these risks, most notably the Federal National Mortgage Agency (Fannie Mae), the Government National Mortgage Agency (Ginnie Mae), and the Federal Home Loan Mortgage Loan Corporation (Freddy Mac). These mechanisms allowed high-risk loans to be packaged with low- and moderate-risk loans on a secondary mortgage market, which would attract new investment capital through the purchase and sale of these loan packages.

The major purpose of agencies such as Fannie Mae, Ginnie Mae, and Freddy Mac was to make mortgage loans more liquid, thereby generating more housing investment dollars through the reinvestment process. Long-term mortgages were and are marketed as investment vehicles, producing new housing funds through an investor's market in federally insured mortgage certificates, backed by a "bundle" of long-term notes.[112] This "secondary mortgage market" underwrote the risks of any one loan in the bundle, while federal tax laws guaranteed profitable returns for developers under Section 8. Both programs emphasized the private sector, and removed local housing authorities and the federal government from direct housing provision. As a consequence, oversight replaced landlording as the federal government's new role in the housing market.

The substitution of block grants for categorical grants further weakened the role of urban housing agencies in two significant ways. Block grants primarily forced housing agencies to compete with other categories of urban assistance for a more limited pool of aid dollars. Public housing budgets, renewal efforts, transportation subsidies, street repairs, and rehabilitation all competed for a place in funding priorities. As the state became the approving agency for city block grants, the increased role of state governments in the control of urban budget dollars further complicated the politics of housing policy. Under prior grants, cities were guaranteed direct funding under formulas developed within each category of need; however, under the block grant approach, state funds were required to be spread more "equitably" to smaller urban communities. As a

[112] Before the days of deregulation in the banking industry, mortgage loans were largely circumscribed to the regulated lending territory available to savings and loans in a given state. Thus, in Pennsylvania, a bank was restricted in its branch banking to the counties contiguous to its central branch. In Illinois, it was restricted to one branch. Achieving liquidity for mortgage investments provided a recurring pool of investment dollars.

result, suburbs actually received more Community Development Block Grant (CDBG) dollars than did central cities, and the absence of guaranteed levels of funding made central cities of one region compete with those in others, despite the clear differences in the scale and extent of their housing problems.[113]

During the tumultuous years of the 1960s and early 1970s, when riots, protests, and black political succession dominated the urban landscape, housing expenditures, welfare, and job provision formed a basic trinity of domestic policy. But the commitment to domestic expenditures flagged during the late 1970s. The rise of inflation combined with energy shortages and political weakness to severely limit urban expenditures, especially during Carter's last two years as president. Even Carter's own commission on urban issues had recommended severe limits on urban aid to cities that had ceased to be competitive due to the erosion of their economic base.[114] This "triage" approach to urban assistance, in which only viable cities were to receive significant assistance, was short-lived. Indeed, it was replaced with an even more drastic approach to scaling down federal urban assistance.

The housing policy of the Reagan years can best be summarized by reworking a Nixonian phrase: "malign neglect" instead of "benign neglect."[115] In the fiscal year 1981 budget process, Carter's proposed $30 billion budget for Section 8 and public housing was cut nearly in half, to $17.5 billion. By fiscal year 1985, HUD's housing budget had been reduced by two-thirds.[116] The systematic reduction of urban economic, welfare, and housing assistance under Reagan, and the extension of these limits under Bush, has created a hostile policy arena for urban issues generally, and low-income housing in particular. Poor communities, particularly if they are black, are now constrained in their attempts to address their housing needs by this combination of economic circumstance, hostile federal policies, and limited local revenues.[117] At the same time, the pressures sustaining the continued existence of the underclass continue.

THE UNDERCLASS REVISITED

We have discussed the process of underclass formation as a part of the historical ecology of the city, and particularly the ways in which the housing market and housing policy have combined to withdraw from older manufacturing cities.

---

[113] Hays, *Federal Government and Urban Housing*, pp. 212–15.

[114] Presidents' Commission for a National Agenda for the 1980s, *Urban America in the Eighties: Perspectives and Policies* (Washington, D.C.: Government Printing Office, 1980).

[115] A more detailed discussion is found in Helen Slessarev, "Racial Tensions and Institutional Support: Social Programs during a Period of Retrenchment," in Margaret Weir et al., *The Politics of Social Policy in the United States* (Princeton: Princeton University Press, 1988), pp. 357–79.

[116] Hays, *Federal Government and Urban Housing*, pp. 212–15.

[117] Recently enacted housing legislation, the Cranston-Gonzales Bill, suggests that this pattern may eventually shift. This legislation has renewed discussions of urban housing alternatives with its

The social and spatial isolation central to the concept of the underclass built on the ghettoization and segregation patterns of the recent past. The recent history of the institutional arrangements which constitute urban housing suggests that the underclass debate overemphasizes the disjuncture between past segregation and present underclass isolation. This places the burden for change on the least appropriate or effective persons, those individuals living in the underclass.

Put at its simplest, the analysis presented here suggests that the term *underclass* is of limited, descriptive utility as a concept organizing our responses to the deep poverty of the inner city. It presents a disjuncture between urban past and present that depends upon a problematic assumption: that the goodwill of the era of civil rights and the War on Poverty had been sufficient, either in its legislation or its attitudes, to eradicate the deep institutional patterns of discrimination and segregation. This chapter has argued that these factors were not adequately or comprehensively addressed in the urban policy of the immediate past, and that these forces maintain themselves today.

The underclass, as traditionally described, refers to a concentrated, self-perpetuating, and persistent poverty. The relative isolation of the black underclass from both mainstream society and economic opportunity is argued to facilitate destructive behavior, resulting in unstable kinship structures, lack of educational attainment, welfare dependency, joblessness, and a general mismatch with the new urban economy.

As other critics have noted, the focus of the argument upon the relative responsibility of the underclass has begged the political issue of whether the underclass should be held culpable for the combination of economic change and racial discrimination that has generated its existence.[118] It further begs an issue of social justice: Who should take on what level of financial and political burden to change the social arrangements that gave rise to the underclass?[119] The argument raised here is slightly different. It asks a prior question to that of social policy: What are the dynamics that produce and maintain a population in the economic status embodied in the summary phrase *underclass*?

The analysis presented here argues that the spatial isolation of the black ghetto in American cities can be traced back to the normal operations of the housing market and of housing policy in the context of a changing urban economic base. A set of housing dynamics have established a zone of economic irrelevance in many cities, within which residents have been cut off from struc-

---

attention to the housing needs of disadvantaged communities, and especially in its provision of local needs as a basis for housing assistance to cities. However, the pool of funds currently available is dwarfed by the size of the housing problems generated by the past two decades of neglect, and does not compare to the housing funds of even the Nixon years.

[118] See especially Herbert Gans, *People, Plans, and Policies* (New York: Columbia University Press, 1991).

[119] Charles Willie, "Rebuttal to a Conservative Strategy for Reducing Poverty," *Policy Studies Review* 7 (1988): 865–75.

tural economic change and forced to devote larger and larger proportions of a shrinking income on shelter needs. Not surprisingly, homelessness in the face of housing abandonment is one result.

Recall the paradox that lay at the outset of this paper. How is it that empty houses and homeless people should arise from the same neighborhoods? If you are a housing investor in many inner-city communities, low-cost housing is no longer a viable business proposition. Leaving aside the relatively few examples of gentrified neighborhoods, the levels of abandonment and demolition show that the housing market certainly does not extend to these communities. They are beyond the threshold of the market.

The concept of a market threshold serves to remind us that there are minimal requirements for participation in the marketplace, even in the markets which deal with the commodities of human survival, such as food and shelter. We have asserted the existence of price limits below which producers will not participate in the market. In the case of housing, we have seen that the abandonment of housing and the coexistence of homelessness are paradoxical yet understandable outcomes of this market process. Each represents a different face of the underclass community.

The allocation of housing through the market, particularly as it is affected by public policy, is also a major force in the creation of segregated communities. The intersection of housing markets with the shift in both the locus of production and the nature of work concentrates the effects of segregation in some cities and limits its effects in others. The racial isolation from employment mirrors that of housing. The question then becomes pragmatic: What are the advantages of casting the discussion of the underclass in terms of market limits and housing policy rather than class and mobility?

I would argue that there are two major advantages to this alternative perspective. First, there is the matter of conceptual consistency. In the basic theory of the underclass, structural factors are said to produce, among other things, individual behaviors that reinforce and perpetuate the underclass. This may or may not be the case. However, as a causal model it suffers from a problem of engaging the argument at two levels without specifying the nature of the links that tie day-to-day behavior to social institutions. Which behaviors of the underclass reinforce its persistence as a class? Were everyone in the underclass to establish appropriate kinship behavior, search for employment, take whatever jobs were available at whatever pay, and cease any form of addictive or illegal behavior, would the underclass disappear? Would the heritage of entrenched housing segregation and institutionalized differentials in housing market mechanisms according to race simply dissolve?

The forces of economic change, as they interact with the housing market, have created a population that finds itself increasingly limited in crossing the thresholds of both employment and housing markets. The national economy that made these communities redundant to the work force continues to feed on a regulatory and political framework which encourages the abandonment of these communities. This process of "redundancy of place" is more salient than the behavioral responses of that underclass for perpetuating concentrated poverty, segregation, and racial isolation.

The second point is an extension of the first. The development of an underclass is directly linked to the emergence of a postindustrial economy in our cities. The identity of who happens to fall into that class is a function of historical context. The migration patterns of the early and middle twentieth century and the long tradition of institutionalized racism in American society have trapped African Americans in inner cities. But to confuse responses to poverty, marginalization, and isolation with the structural features of the society that both produce and sustain the underclass shifts our attention from the difficult issues of social change which must be confronted if we are to eliminate persistent poverty in our cities.

The social and spatial isolation so central to the concept of the underclass is woven deeply into the institutional dynamics of the housing market and housing policy as they have emerged in the years since the Great Depression. This calls us to a policy debate that Michael Katz develops further in his conclusion to this volume, but that is starkly evident in confronting the housing needs of older cities and their poor communities.

In addressing the problem of the underclass as I have outlined it here, I distinguish between those programs which focus on the individuals who comprise that community and those which attack the institutional supports for its continuation. While it is almost a truism to suggest that a coordinated approach to these efforts will work best, it is rare to find such an approach among those who prescribe for the social ills of the underclass. Urging new intervention strategies targeted at the educational levels and problematic behaviors of the very poor in our cities will not, on its own, address the central dilemma of the market that refuses entry at its lowest threshold.

The debate must also take place around the great issues of social justice and redistribution that have so often disappeared from recent political discourse. This requires a persistent debate over the relative efficacy and outcomes of antidiscriminatory activity, combined with recurring efforts to break apart the institutional support of segregationist housing. Programs aimed at lowering the housing market threshold, improving the economic resources of poor households, and limiting the negative effects of the collapse of the manufacturing sector would address the roots of underclass formation and perpetuation. Taking care that welfare dependency does not contribute to the persistence of poverty is prudent only if we can assume that the isolation of the underclass is diminishing and that market thresholds are not increasing. Neither condition holds in the instance of urban housing markets

In summary, the underclass is not an alien community, an anachronistic appendage to the mainstream of urban life. It is a community perfectly consistent with the recent tides of urban history, serving as a reminder of persistent issues of inequality's face yet to be addressed.

PART THREE

Families, Networks, and Opportunities

The Ethnic Niche and the Structure of Opportunity: Immigrants and Minorities in New York City

Suzanne Model

AFTER ARRIVING in industrial America, most racial and ethnic minorities suffered privation. For some groups, such as Jews, the encounter with poverty was brief; for others, such as Italians, impoverishment persisted well into this century. These variations aside, most Europeans eventually entered the economic mainstream; in later generations, several groups attained above-average incomes.[1]

For many peoples of color, the historical record is less heartening. Despite individual success stories, the average incomes of African Americans and some Hispanic groups remain meager.[2] Recently, the purchasing power of residents in poor, minority neighborhoods has declined, while the local incidence of crime, drug abuse, joblessness, and other social ills has increased.[3] Such developments have led some observers to label these minority poor a national "underclass."[4]

---

[1] On ethnic and racial differentials in economic well-being, see Andrew Greeley, *Ethnicity, Denomination and Inequality* (Beverly Hills, Calif.: Sage, 1976), pp. 49–50; David Featherman and Robert Hauser, *Opportunity and Change* (New York: Academic Press, 1978), pp. 452–61; and Lisa Neidert and Reynolds Farley, "Assimilation in the United States: An Analysis of Ethnic and Generation Differences in Status and Achievement," *American Sociological Review* 50 (1985): 846–49.

[2] In 1980, 36 percent of persons of Puerto Rican origin, 30 percent of African Americans, 23 percent of individuals of Mexican background, and 9 percent of non-Hispanic whites had incomes below the federal poverty line. Frank Bean and Marta Tienda, *The Hispanic Population of the United States* (New York: Russell Sage Foundation, 1987), p. 371.

[3] On the increasing geographic concentration of poverty, see William Julius Wilson, *The Truly Disadvantaged* (Chicago: University of Chicago Press, 1987), pp. 46–62; Paul Jargowsky and Mary Jo Bane, "Ghetto Poverty in the United States, 1970–1980," in Christopher Jencks and Paul Peterson, eds., *The Urban Underclass* (Washington, D.C.: Brookings Institution), pp. 251–68; Douglas Massey and Mitchell Eggers, "The Ecology of Inequality: Minorities and the Concentration of Poverty, 1970–1980," *American Journal of Sociology* 95 (1990): 1174–84; and Claudia Coulton, Julian Chow, and Shanta Pandey, "An Analysis of Poverty and Related Conditions in Cleveland Area Neighborhoods" (technical report, Center for Urban Poverty and Social Change, Case Western Reserve University, January 1990), pp. 15–24.

For evidence of the relation between concentrated poverty and social problems see Wilson, *The Truly Disadvantaged*, pp. 21–29; Coulton, Chow, and Pandey, "An Analysis of Poverty and Related Conditions in Cleveland Area Neighborhoods," chap. 4; and Jonathan Crane, "Effects of Neighborhoods on Dropping Out of School and Teenage Childbearing," in Jencks and Peterson, *The Urban Underclass*, pp. 299–320. A more qualified view appears in Christopher Jencks and Susan Mayer, "The Social Consequences of Growing Up in a Poor Neighborhood" (Center for Urban Affairs and Policy Research, Northwestern University, April 1989), especially chaps. 5, 6, and 7.

[4] For a recent history of the word *underclass* see Michael B. Katz, Introduction to this volume. For

The emergence of an underclass in the late twentieth century perplexes scholars, policymakers, the media, and the public. After the civil rights movement and decades of equal opportunity initiatives, why should people of color remain stranded in the lower reaches of the American class structure?

Many different types of answers have been proposed. The more thoughtful answers have two characteristics: they are at once comparative and historical. Since all migrating groups struggled for a foothold in the American economy, only by comparing their histories can researchers make sense of the outcomes that followed. And the broad conclusion of most comparative, historical studies is that group differences in job skills and in labor market discrimination underlie the variations in economic outcome that we see today.[5]

The explanation to follow does not neglect group differences in job skills and discrimination but focuses on a particular mechanism that allowed groups to cope with modest skills and employers' prejudice. This mechanism, here called the ethnic niche, is an employment environment in which members of a particular group are overrepresented. All racial and ethnic groups established niches, but the benefits they reaped from their job concentrations were uneven. In the past, the niches of white ethnic groups more effectively offset poor job skills and labor market discrimination than did the niches of blacks and Hispanics. As a result, white ethnics moved up; peoples of color did not. After many decades, urban blacks and Hispanics eventually secured niche employment at the levels of ethnics, but the niche they established offset only discrimination, not weak job skills.

The contemporary black and Hispanic niche is, of course, government. While minority group membership is an asset in obtaining government jobs, weak educational credentials and poor test performance are liabilities. Unfortunately, these requirements exclude those most in need of niche protection, the less qualified. The consequence of this exclusion is that today's government opportunities cannot upgrade people of color in the way that white ethnic niches could. Rather, those unable to compete for rewarding employment in today's service economy are increasingly isolated and marginalized, becoming a potential underclass.

The first part of this chapter is concerned with the causes of economic inequality. The latter portion takes up a different, but related, question: Why have the rates of crime, drug addiction, and other social problems so increased

---

compelling criticism of the term, see Herbert J. Gans, "Deconstructing the Underclass: The Term's Dangers as a Planning Concept," *American Planning Association Journal* 56 (1990): 271–77.

[5] Among the studies that compare the experiences of several racial and ethnic groups across time, see especially Stephan Thernstrom, *The Other Bostonians* (Cambridge: Harvard University Press, 1973); John Bodnar, Roger Simon, and Michael Weber, *Lives of Their Own* (Urbana: University of Illinois Press, 1982); Olivier Zunz, *The Changing Face of Inequality* (Chicago: University of Chicago Press, 1982); and Joel Perlmann, *Ethnic Differences* (New York: Cambridge University Press, 1988).

in central-city minority neighborhoods? Naturally, this issue has also received enormous scholarly attention.[6] The explanation most relevant to the present undertaking is that stable, rewarding employment motivates workers to conform to mainstream behaviors.[7] But, again, this essay moves beyond this insight to explore the implications of niche employment for social control. Briefly, the claim is that the niche is an especially effective agent of social control because reaping its economic benefits requires conforming to the behavioral standards of coworkers who are also friends and neighbors. While it is true that holding any job produces a tendency toward conformity, niche jobs heighten that tendency because niche workers are enmeshed in an exceptionally broad set of mutual obligations.

When large proportions of white ethnics were weak competitors in the dominant economy, advantageous niche employment occupied a great number, effectively restraining most from engaging in antisocial behaviors. For unskilled blacks and Hispanics, fewer advantageous niches meant fewer environments offering this protection. By the 1970s, even these few niches had disappeared. Because blacks' and Hispanics' present niche, government, caters to those most able to compete in the dominant economy, the less qualified struggle on their own. In a labor market increasingly devoid of openings for the unskilled, high rates of social problems among these dispossessed workers is hardly surprising.

Thus, both the economic and the social distress of the underclass are interpreted as offshoots of the same process, a lack of adequate ethnic niches. Without niche protection, members of any economically disadvantaged racial or ethnic background would be vulnerable to similar problems. Unfortunately, the likelihood that disadvantaged groups can construct useful niches in a postindustrial society appears small. There is, therefore, a serious danger that the history of the underclass will not be a short one.

THE ECONOMIC BENEFITS OF NICHE EMPLOYMENT

This section is divided into two portions. The first develops the concept of the niche and spells out the theoretical rationale for expecting economic benefits from niche employment. It explores such questions as what is a niche? why do niches develop? and how can niches combat low job skills and discrimination? The second uses information on the economic trajectories of five New York ethnic and racial groups to illustrate the claims of the theoretical portion. Three

---

[6] For a thorough review of the literature on race and the criminal justice system, see Gerald Jaynes and Robin Williams, Jr., eds., *A Common Destiny: Blacks and American Society* (Washington, D.C.: National Academy Press, 1989), chap. 9. On the relation between concentrated ghetto poverty and social problems, see the references in note 3, above.

[7] An exemplary analysis leading to this conclusion is Emilie Allan and Darrell Steffensmeier, "Youth Underemployment and Property Crime: Differential Effects of Job Availability and Job Quality on Juvenile and Young Adult Arrest Rates," *American Journal of Sociology* 54 (1989): 107–23.

of these are white ethnic groups that profited substantially from niche involvement. Their histories are contrasted with those of blacks and Puerto Ricans, whose niche experiences have been, at best, mixed blessings. The section concludes with a brief discussion of the implications of these findings for the economic progress of disadvantaged groups.

Theory

The term *niche* refers to the overrepresentation of ethnic and racial minorities in particular jobs. The meaning of the word *niche*, therefore, rests upon the definition of both the term *overrepresentation* and the term *job*. Overrepresentation occurs when the percentage of workers in a job who are group members is greater than the percentage of the group in the work force as a whole. This definition follows from the observation that if all groups randomly entered all jobs, the proportion of workers of any background employed in any job would equal the proportion of the group in the labor force.[8] The meaning of *job* is more diffuse. In this essay, a "job" may mean an occupation, an industry, even a set of related industries. So broad a definition is necessary because, at one time or another, occupations, industries, and sets of related industries have all sustained ethnic or racial overrepresentation.

To see this variety, a few examples are helpful. In the simplest case, groups are overrepresented in particular occupations. The Italian affinity for barbering is a good example of an occupational niche. More commonly, however, members of a group cluster in a set of related occupations pursued in the same industry. Bohemians in cigar manufacture or Greeks in the restaurant business are illustrations. Less frequent but hardly unknown is the overrepresentation of group members in several occupations in related industries. The Jews, for instance, both manufactured and marketed clothing, while the Japanese grew and distributed fruits and vegetables.[9]

---

[8] It is difficult to generalize about just how overrepresented in a job a group must be before niche conditions obtain. For example, very small groups need more skewed distributions to develop niche environments than do very large groups. In this chapter, a job is considered a niche if the percentage of workers who are group members is at least one-and-a-half times greater than the group's percentage in the work force.

[9] On Italians in barbering, see Thomas Kessner, *The Golden Door* (New York: Oxford University Press, 1977), p. 57; on Bohemian cigar makers, see Gerd Korman, *Industrialization, Immigrants, and Americanization: The View from Milwaukee, 1866–1921* (Madison: State Historical Society of Wisconsin, 1967), p. 25; on Greeks as restaurateurs, see Lawrence Lovell-Troy, "Clan Structures and Economic Activity: The Case of Greeks in Small Business Enterprises," in Scott Cummings, ed., *Self-Help in Urban America* (Port Washington, N.Y.: Kennikat Press, 1980), pp. 58–85. On the pervasiveness of Jewish employ in the apparel trades see Susan Glenn, *Daughters of the Shtetl* (Ithaca: Cornell University Press, 1990), pp. 90–97. On Japanese economic organization, see Edna Bonacich and John Modell, *The Economic Basis of Ethnic Solidarity* (Berkeley: University of California Press, 1980), p. 56.

Several forces are responsible for the emergence of niches. In the case of immigrants, some groups become associated with particular occupations, industries, or sets of related industries very shortly after their arrival in this country. The usual reason is simple: many of their members arrive with previous experience in fields for which a demand exists in America. Thus, between 1899 and 1910, 31 percent of Jews with previous work experience told immigration officials that they had worked in the garment trades.[10] Early in this century, this close fit between the supply and demand for specific skills reflected similarities in the direction of economic growth among nations. More recently, this fit also reflects deliberate social policy. Beginning in 1965, the federal government secured immigration legislation that favored the admission of individuals in particular occupations. This legislation was recently strengthened. Therefore, the relationship between ethnicity and job skills will not disappear.

In other instances, no association between premigration and postmigration activity exists. For the Irish, a massive move into the public sector appeared only after the triumph of Irish political leaders in those cities where patronage was abundant. The leaders then distributed many of these opportunities to their compatriots. More commonly, a group embarks upon a new economic activity because of a lack of more attractive options. The Chinese took up the laundry business after discrimination barred them from other undertakings. Today, many Korean immigrants are grocers, not because they were food merchants in their homeland but because language barriers have impeded their entry into the mainstream economy.[11]

The most unusual of ethnic niches is the one that has emerged as a result of the antidiscrimination legislation of 1964 and the executive order for affirmative action of 1965. Eager to set a standard that private industry would emulate, government itself played a leading role in meeting the goals of these initiatives. Moreover, public-sector employment expanded considerably in the sixties and seventies, facilitating the introduction of large numbers of new workers.

Affirmative action is unique among the mechanisms producing an ethnic niche not only in its overt, public commitment to hiring particular groups but also in the stability of that commitment. Despite criticism, the policy has stood for over a quarter of a century, and government has remained its most faithful practitioner. Therefore, affirmative-action requirements not only expanded the

[10] Figures are from the United States Immigration Commission, *Reports*, vol. 3, *Statistical Review of Immigration* (Washington, D.C.: G.P.O., 1911), cited in Kessner, *The Golden Door*, pp. 33–34.

[11] For speculations about why the Irish turned to politics, see Edward M. Levine, *The Irish and Irish Politicians* (Notre Dame, Ind.: University of Notre Dame Press, 1966); and Terry Nichols Clark, "The Irish Ethic and the Spirit of Patronage," *Ethnicity* 2 (1975): 305–59. On Chinese entry into the laundry business, see Paul C. P. Siu, *The Chinese Laundryman* (New York: New York University Press, 1987), chap. 4. On reasons why Koreans, despite strong educational credentials, turn to small business pursuits, see Pyong Gap Min, "From White-Collar Occupations to Small Business: Korean Immigrants' Occupational Adjustment," *Sociological Quarterly* 25 (1984): 333–52.

concentration of minorities in government but continue to propagate that concentration today.

In most ethnic niches, however, the processes responsible for initiating the association between ethnicity and employment differ from the processes responsible for the maintenance of that association. The simplest maintenance mechanism is the emergence of a widespread belief that members of a particular group are well suited to their niche jobs and poorly suited for alternatives. Italians, for instance, were rarely employed in Buffalo's steel mills on the grounds that they performed inadequately at factory labor, while Poles were accepted enthusiastically. Blacks were widely believed well equipped to withstand the hottest, most dangerous, and dirtiest of manufacturing tasks.[12]

A more enduring hiring practice that propagates ethnic concentrations is employers' preference for applicants who come recommended by existing employees. Employers have many reasons for favoring applicants recommended by employees, not all of which have to do with ethnic and racial stereotypes. This form of recruiting costs little. In addition, workers sponsored by employees get along easily with their new coworkers and learn job tasks more readily as a result. Lastly, such recruits are under pressure to perform well, since any shortcomings would reflect poorly on their sponsors.[13]

Although employers can obtain these advantages regardless of the ethnicity of the participants, if a niche is already in place, a goodly number of existing employees are already of the same background. Accepting referrals from these workers simply reproduces existing ethnic concentrations, as an impressive number of studies have confirmed.[14] This is true especially during periods of massive migration, when coethnic recruitment operates across miles and even across oceans. Once migration declines, the segregation of newly arrived groups continues to foster intraethnic referrals. Niche proclivity diminishes only after group members begin to exploit outside sources of job information and find

[12] On employers' views about Italians, Poles, and African Americans, see Niles Carpenter, *Nationality, Color, and Economic Opportunities in the City of Buffalo* (Westport, Conn.: Negro Universities Press, 1970), chap. 3. On employers' ethnic stereotypes in general, see Korman, *Industrialization, Immigrants, and Americanization*, pp. 41–46.

[13] For economists' arguments on the benefits of hiring through employee recommendation, see George Stigler, "Information in the Labor Market," in J. Burton, L. Benham, W. Vaughn, and R. Flanagan, eds., *Readings in Labor Market Analysis* (New York: Holt, Rinehart, and Winston, 1971), pp. 233–43; and Albert Rees, "Information Networks in Labor Markets," also in Burton et al., *Readings in Labor Market Analysis*, pp. 245–52. For a more sociological view, see Roger Waldinger, *Through the Eye of the Needle* (New York: New York University Press, 1986), pp. 157–60.

[14] Examples of research documenting the relationship between hiring practices and ethnic job segregation include John MacDonald and Leatrice MacDonald, "Chain Migration, Ethnic Neighborhood Formation, and Social Networks," *Milbank Memorial Fund Quarterly* 52 (1964): 82–97; Tamara Hareven, "The Laborers of Manchester, New Hampshire: The Role of Family and Ethnicity in Adjustment to Industrial Life," *Labor History* 16 (1975): 249–65; Bodnar, Simon, and Weber, *Lives of Their Own*, chap. 3; Suzanne Model, "Mode of Entry and the Ethnic Composition of Firms: Early Twentieth-Century Migrants to New York City," *Sociological Forum* 3 (1988): 110–26.

that these in fact lead to more rewarding jobs. Such events signal the death of the niche.

During their heyday, however, niches attract group members, and not without reason. Niches have the potential to offer at least three economic advantages: a simplified job search, the benefits of unionized jobs, and opportunities for upward mobility.

With respect to the simplified job search, the previous discussion has already suggested why such a situation should obtain. At minimum, any individual seeking a position in his or her niche can expect that employers will evaluate his or her group membership in a favorable light. In addition, since group members tend to associate with one another, information about vacancies in that group's niche is more available to job seekers who are group members than to job seekers who are not. For the same reason, applicants who are group members are more likely to secure personal sponsorship into the niche than are applicants who are nonmembers.

Of course, if certain credentials are also necessary for entering a niche, admission is limited to the subset of group members with appropriate qualifications. As suggested earlier, this disturbing development is primarily associated with late-twentieth-century opportunities in government.

In addition to a simplified job search, a second, less common advantage niches may offer is unionized jobs. Occasionally, unionization precedes ethnic concentration, and group members merely partake of established benefits. The Italian move from unskilled to skilled construction jobs illustrates this trajectory. But ethnic concentrations also heighten the potential for nonunionized jobs to become unionized. This is because niches minimize one of unions' greatest obstacles, ethnic rivalry. Individuals who share the same ethnicity and employment represent a more solidary and hence more easily mobilized constituency. As already stated, their workplace bonds may be reinforced by residential and social segregation. In addition, those who obtained their jobs through the intervention of compatriots may be more willing to support worker demands than are those who secured their positions entirely by their own efforts.[15]

Early in this century, owners and managers were well aware of the relationship between ethnic homogeneity and collective action. Sometimes these gatekeepers deliberately integrated workers of different backgrounds in particular occupations and departments. But diverse groups did not always get along, and sometimes could not even communicate. Moreover, as already pointed out, skill differentials, employer stereotypes, and coethnic sponsorship promoted ethnic homogeneity on the job. This is not to say that unionization was inevi-

[15] As Charles Tilly has argued, the more characteristics that individuals share, the greater their likelihood of acting collectively. Charles Tilly, *From Mobilization to Revolution* (Reading, Mass.: Addison Wesley, 1978), pp. 84ff.

table in ethnically homogeneous jobs. Ethnic solidarity was helpful, but could not, in itself, be decisive.[16] Still, there is little doubt that such solidarity facilitated the unionization of the garment trades and the sleeping-car porters, niches valuable to some of the groups examined below.

A third way that niches can be economically rewarding is by providing avenues for upward mobility. This advantage can arise in a number of ways. If new, better occupations develop in an industry, group members already overrepresented in the industry are well placed to assume them. Or, one group may abandon an occupation, and members of other groups already employed in less desirable jobs in the same industry may appropriate the resulting vacancy. Or, a niche may originate as a hierarchy of related occupations in one industry. The most common, though hardly the only, form of hierarchically organized niche is the ethnically owned business enterprise.

Several characteristics of hierarchically organized niches facilitate advancement. Most obviously, group membership is not a barrier to promotion; indeed, it may be a prerequisite. Furthermore, the opportunity of working among coethnic superiors imparts a psychological advantage; in such environments, aspiring to better jobs is wholly appropriate. Finally, there is an instructional advantage, the ability to observe and acquire the skills necessary for advancement. The chance to obtain new skills is enhanced partly because mentoring is a natural process whenever advancement is possible and partly because the social bonds between coethnic workers frequently endure both on and off the job.[17]

In addition to nurturing occupational advancement, hierarchical niches in ethnically owned businesses support movement across class lines. Not only can employees progress across laboring, sales, and managerial occupations, but they may also move into ownership positions. Research suggests that a large percentage of small business owners were once the employees of coethnics.[18]

To summarize, racial and ethnic minorities do not flock to niches passively or irrationally. At minimum, niche employers view group membership in a positive light. At maximum, niche employees gain union protection and upward

[16] For an insightful discussion of how large employers promoted or diffused labor solidarity by manipulating workers' segregation levels at home and on the job, see Lizabeth Cohen, *Making a New Deal* (New York: Cambridge University Press, 1990), chap. 1. For an analysis of the obstacles to organizing Asian employees of small businesses against coethnic employers see Peter Kwong, *Chinatown, New York: Labor and Politics, 1930–1950* (New York: Monthly Review Press, 1979), pp. 83–91; and Bonacich and Modell, *The Economic Basis of Ethnic Solidarity*, pp. 51–58.

[17] A somewhat similar argument is offered for ethnically owned enterprises in Thomas Bailey and Roger Waldinger, "Primary, Secondary, and Enclave Labor Markets: A Training Systems Approach," *American Sociological Review* 56 (1991): 432–45.

[18] On the move from employee to employer among the Japanese, see Bonacich and Modell, *The Economic Basis of Ethnic Solidarity*, chap. 3; among Cubans see Alejandro Portes and Robert Bach, *Latin Journey* (Berkeley: University of California Press, 1985), pp. 205–16. For a small, comparative study, see Suzanne Model, "A Comparative Perspective on the Ethnic Enclave: Blacks, Italians, and Jews in New York City," *International Migration Review* 19 (1985): 75–77.

mobility. A refined analysis of the economic contribution of niche employment, however, requires not only scrutinizing the kinds of benefits offered by a niche but also examining the quality of the alternatives. And, as suggested above, the quality of the alternatives depends upon two factors: the skill levels of group members and the amount of discrimination they encounter. The weaker their educations, skills, and experience, the more restricted are their job choices. Similarly, the more discrimination they suffer, the more limited their options. Therefore, niches have greatest value when group members have few skills and/or are frequent victims of discrimination. The more these conditions obtain, the more desperately do group members need a niche, especially one that provides more than minimal benefit, say, unionized jobs or occupational mobility. The less these conditions obtain, the less the niche has to offer. Once most group members can compete effectively in the dominant economy, niche employment may do more harm than good.[19]

Strong niches combat weak skills and discrimination by providing minority workers with more rewarding jobs than they would otherwise obtain. Though niches have little influence on the discriminatory behavior of dominant-economy employers, the financial advantages they confer underwrite the educational attainment of the next generation. Armed with appropriate credentials, the children of niche workers are well positioned to take advantage of better mainstream opportunities, should these become available. If they do not, niche jobs remain an option.[20]

When strong niches are few or absent, the resulting poverty reinforces weak skills in successive generations. Even if discrimination declines, the low education of group members continues to exclude them from well-paying jobs. Personal demoralization and social disruption eventually may result. In the next section, the experiences of five New York ethnic groups are used to illustrate these trajectories.

New York Illustrations

This portion of the chapter uses data extracted from five public use samples of the United States Census Bureau to demonstrate the significance of niches for the economic performance of five New York City ethnic groups. The public use

---

[19] The danger is not only that niche rewards become less competitive but that mobility between niche and mainstream economies is blocked. For a related discussion, see Norbert Wiley, "The Ethnic Mobility Trap and Stratification Theory," *Social Problems* 15 (1967): 147–59.

[20] An enormous amount of research has confirmed the effects of social class background and educational achievement on individual success. See Peter Blau and Otis Dudley Duncan, *The American Occupational Structure* (Glencoe, Ill.: Free Press, 1967), chap. 5; William Sewell and Robert Hauser, *Education, Occupation, and Earnings* (New York: Academic Press, 1975), chap. 7; Robert Hauser and David Featherman, *The Process of Stratification* (New York: Academic Press, 1977), chap. 5.

samples cover the years 1910, 1940, 1950, 1970, and 1980. The five groups are the Irish, Italians, Russians, African Americans, and Puerto Ricans.[21] The white groups were selected because they are the only New York groups resident in large enough numbers for a long enough time to support a meaningful monitoring of their progress. African Americans, as the background at greatest risk for underclass status, constitute a mandatory inclusion. As the major other contender for representation in the underclass, Puerto Ricans offer an informative contrast to both blacks and white ethnics.[22]

Because the history of racial and ethnic mobility is primarily a tale about men and because the space for this chapter is limited, only males are included in this study. This decision is most controversial in the case of blacks, because black women, both past and present, have participated heavily in the labor force. An analysis of black women's employment in New York would show that, more than black men, black women were historically concentrated in a few jobs—all associated with domestic service. While this niche offered little in the way of economic rewards, it meant that finding a job was often easier for black women than for black men. In recent decades, however, black working women have become more dispersed. Those involved in personal service are employed more frequently in institutions than in private homes. The more educated, like their male counterparts, are attracted to civil-service posts. Were space available, an in-depth analysis of these developments would constitute a valuable addition to the discussion below.[23]

In examining the economic achievement of the included male groups, two summary measures are offered: average occupational status and average earn-

---

[21] In evaluating the economic significance of niches, computerized manipulation of information about the occupational and industrial locations of individuals in specific labor markets is necessary. Because the New York Standard Metropolitan Statistical Area (SMSA) comprises the largest labor market in the country, it was chosen as the site of study. Although a public use sample tape of the 1900 census is available, these data do not include workers' industrial location—hence, this year is excluded from the analysis. In addition, the 1960 public use sample tape does not distinguish metropolitan areas within states, so this year had to be excluded.

Group membership was assigned on the basis of questions about race, Spanish origin, and parental birthplace. Since no questions about religion are asked in the census, investigators often use Yiddish mother tongue or Russian birthplace to identify Jews. Since no inquiry about mother tongue was made in 1950, Russian parental birthplace was used as a proxy for Jews, in order to maintain consistency across years. Finally, since ethnic ancestry rather than parental birthplace was obtained in 1980, the definition of the white ethnic groups in this year is not comparable to past definitions. As a result, the white ethnics were dropped from the analysis at this point.

[22] On Puerto Ricans as candidates for the underclass, see Marta Tienda, "Puerto Ricans and the Underclass Debate," *Annals of the American Academy of Political and Social Science* 501 (1989): 105–19; Joan Moore, "Is There a Hispanic Underclass?" *Social Science Quarterly* 70 (1989): 265–84; and Douglas Massey, "American Apartheid: Segregation and the Making of the Underclass," *American Journal of Sociology* 96 (1990): 331, 354.

[23] The significance of domestic service as a niche for black women is examined in Suzanne Model, "Blacks and Immigrants from South and East Europe," in Virginia Yans-McLaughlin, ed., *Immigration Reconsidered* (New York: Oxford University Press, 1990), p. 141.

ings. Occupational status is examined both because it is an indicator of social position and because earnings data are not always available. No questions about earnings were asked in the 1910 census, while in 1940 only wage-and-salary income was obtained. The latter shortcoming is unfortunate because business and other forms of self-employment income were significant undertakings for high proportions of some of the groups under study. These omissions mean that occupational status offers the most useful basis for historical comparisons. The status measure used here is the Duncan Socioeconomic Index, or SEI. This index provides a status score for each occupational title in each census year, with the exception that the only scores available for 1910 are based on 1980 data. In creating the scores, researchers use information about the average education, income, and prestige of incumbents in each occupation. Although the range of scores varies a bit over the years, in general, scores above 65 should be considered high, while scores below 25 should be regarded as low.[24]

The average occupational statuses and, after 1910, the average earnings that groups achieved in each year are compared to those of native-born whites of native-born parents—the benchmark group in this analysis. The closer the averages of a minority group are to those of native whites of native-born parents (hereafter simply termed *native whites*), the better the minority is doing. Because occupational status varies slightly across time and because inflation changes the value of the dollar, each minority outcome is presented not only in its raw form but also as a percentage of native white in the same year. Furthermore, since the first, or foreign-born, generation rarely fares as well as the second, or native-born, generation, all comparisons are presented separately for the two generations. If a group's second generation has essentially the same outcomes as native whites, the group is assumed to have "caught up."

In the present instance, interest focuses not only on whether and when each group "catches up" but also on the contribution that niches make to the process. Recall that a niche is a job in which group members are overrepresented. In terms of the way census data characterize jobs, this means any occupation or industry or set of related industries in which group members are overconcentrated. Because, for some groups, this is a lot of occupations and industries, the discussion in this chapter focuses primarily on each group's larger niches. This makes substantive sense too, since small niches cannot have much effect on the overall achievement of group members. Thus, the primary objective in the pages to come is to uncover how niche activity affects the economic achievement of each of the five groups under study.

Because, of the groups considered here, the Irish are the first to arrive in New York, they provide an appropriate starting point. Table 5.1 compares the average occupational status and earnings of first- and second-generation Irishmen to the

---

[24] For an explanation of the technique utilized to develop the Duncan Socioeconomic Index, see Albert J. Reiss, Jr., *Occupations and Social Status* (Glencoe, Ill.: Free Press, 1961), chaps. 6 and 7.

TABLE 5.1

Occupational Status and Earnings of Irish Males in Metropolitan New York City by Generation and Year

	Occupational Status	Status as % of NWNP[a]	Annual Earnings ($)	Earnings as % of NWNP[a]
Born in Ireland				
1910	25.8	76.5	n.a.	n.a.
1940	29.6	76.5	1,356	84.6
1950	28.6	68.2	3,044	86.4
1970	32.3	71.8	8,642	88.4
Native born of Irish-born parents				
1910	29.3	86.9	n.a.	n.a.
1940	37.0	95.6	1,547	96.6
1950	40.6	97.0	3,348	95.0
1970	45.4	101.0	10,857	111.0

Source: Department of Commerce, Bureau of the Census, Public Use Microdata Samples for 1910, 1940, 1950, and 1970.

[a]Native-born white men of native-born parents.

occupational status and earnings of native whites. The table shows that, though the second generation consistently outperformed the foreign born, both groups fell considerably below native whites in occupational status in 1910. Between 1910 and 1940, however, the occupational status of the second generation jumped to within 4 percentage points of the status of native whites. Although the absence of 1910 earnings data hampers the analogous earnings comparison, the strong native-Irish earnings in 1940, 97 percent of those of native whites, suggests that occupational mobility was accompanied by gains in pay. Between 1950 and 1970, the native-born Irish advanced still further, outperforming native whites on both indicators by the later date.

From a niche perspective, the story of Irish progress is a story about government jobs. In 1910, however, the industry employing the largest percentage of Irishmen was not government but construction.[25] Fourteen percent of the Irish worked in the industry, constituting just 17 percent of its workers. Their rather high occupational status in construction—72 percent were skilled workers and

---

[25] Census data do not reveal the linkages between political power and construction jobs, but there is little doubt that Irish builders received more than their share of public works contracts. See, for example, Dennis Clark, "The Expansion of the Public Sector and Irish Economic Development," in Cummings, Self-Help in Urban America; and Steven Erie, Rainbow's End: Irish-Americans and the Dilemmas of Urban Machine Politics, 1840–1985 (Berkeley: University of California Press, 1988), p. 89.

only 20 percent were laborers—suggests that by 1910 the Irish were well established in the field. Although other niches were even more occupationally rewarding for the Irish, they were smaller. Only 7 percent of the Irish were railroad employees, but they comprised 31 percent of all railroad workers. An even smaller 5 percent worked in industries defined as "public services" in 1910, but this figure is an underestimate because census enumerators did not inquire about other forms of government employment. More appropriate, but slightly older, figures are reported by Steven Erie, who has made a systematic study of Irish activity in government. He finds that ten years earlier, 6 percent of New York Irishmen held positions supported by local government, forming just over a third of that work force.

Erie argues that in those cities in which Irish political leadership was accompanied by an abundance of patronage, most of it went to coethnics. New York was such a city, and by 1930 he finds that massive growth in the public sector brought 24 percent of the city's Irish jobs in local government, primarily in blue-collar positions.[26] The 1940 census figures confirm this growth, with nearly one in five Irishmen in "government" employ, the new census category for public workers across industries.

About a third of the posts that government offered in 1940 were in emergency work, part of the federally supported effort to alleviate the joblessness of the Depression. But Irish government workers were underrepresented in these undertakings, with over three-quarters holding nonemergency jobs. Although their percentage in nonemergency government work was not huge, the Irish constituted 13 percent of these employees, a percentage roughly twice their presence in the population. Not only did the Irish have an easier time entering nonemergency government jobs, they monopolized the more rewarding posts in that niche. As a result, native-born Irishmen, whose achievements in 1940 are so notable, averaged an occupational status of 49 and earnings of $2,270 in nonemergency government jobs versus an occupational status of 35 and earnings of $1,412 in other endeavors. Moreover, the native-born Irishmen in this niche obtained high rewards despite an average educational level roughly equal to that of other native-born Irishmen and slightly below the schooling levels of the non-Irish in the same government jobs.

Having emerged from the Depression in a relatively good position, the Irish might have been expected to move into the larger economy in greater numbers. But this prediction is only partially accurate. In 1950, 17 percent of the Irish worked for government. While still enjoying higher occupational status and income than Irish private-sector workers, by midcentury, Irish government workers began to average appreciably higher educational achievement than did their compatriots working elsewhere. By 1970 government was expanding again, and about a quarter of native-born Irishmen worked in the public sector.

[26] Erie, *Rainbow's End*, pp. 85–91.

By this time, however, Irishmen in the private sector earned slightly more than their compatriots in government did, even though the latter retained educational superiority. Nevertheless, Irish incomes were now so strong that this discrepancy hardly mattered.

In evaluating the Irish experience, it is unfortunate that more complete data on government work are unavailable for the years between 1910 and 1940, the period when Irish domination of blue-collar public employment was greatest. This gap renders it impossible to confirm that government jobs helped the Irish overcome discrimination and low skills. This interpretation seems plausible, however, in light of the strong economic performance of Irish government workers at the later date. Moreover, in 1940 the Irish had the lowest unemployment rate of any minority in this study, a reflection of the relatively greater security of public over private jobs during a time of depression. Irish job security, in turn, may have influenced the relatively strong educational performance of Irish offspring during the Depression. By 1950, the educational levels of native-born Irishmen under the age of thirty-five (the Depression generation) were essentially identical to those of native whites.[27]

In the ensuing years, there is little evidence that discrimination obstructed Irish-American progress, and their educational credentials soon surpassed those of native whites. Therefore, even though the educational requirements for government jobs expanded, Irish commitment to the public sector endured. Indeed, Irish educations were so high that, by 1970, government was merely one of several attractive Irish alternatives in an economy where not only good government jobs, but good jobs generally, demanded higher education.

Of the groups studied here, only Russian Jews have outperformed Irish Americans. Table 5.2, which depicts their economic progress, shows that already in 1910 the occupational status of second-generation Russian Jews was equivalent to that of native whites. Moreover, the failure of the Census Bureau to inquire about business income before 1950 means that the 1940 earnings figures probably underestimate the affluence of this heavily entrepreneurial group. The data can only confirm that by 1950 the earnings of both foreign- and native-born Russian Jews were slightly higher than native white earnings. By 1970, second-generation Russian-Jewish earnings exceeded those of native whites by 50 percent.

Since sizable numbers of Russian Jews entered the United States only after 1880, it is likely that the first native-born generation already attained occupational parity with native whites. Because high occupational status and high

[27] For a discussion of the relationship between Depression unemployment rates and children's educational attainment for a variety of racial and ethnic groups, see Stanley Lieberson, *A Piece of the Pie* (Berkeley: University of California Press, 1980), pp. 239–50. For a different view, see Joel Perlmann, "A Piece of the Educational Pie: Reflections and New Evidence on Black and Immigrant Schooling since 1880," *Sociology of Education* 60 (1987): 54–61.

TABLE 5.2

Occupational Status and Earnings of Russian Males in Metropolitan New York City by Generation and Year

	Occupational Status	Status as % of NWNP[a]	Annual Earnings ($)	Earnings as % of NWNP[a]
Born in Russia				
1910	27.9	82.8	n.a.	n.a.
1940	36.1	93.3	1,503	93.8
1950	39.6	94.6	3,776	107.2
1970	43.5	96.8	10,899	111.4
Native born of Russian-born parents				
1910	34.0	100.9	n.a.	n.a.
1940	45.0	116.3	1,419	88.6
1950	49.1	117.3	3,868	109.8
1970	55.4	123.1	14,717	150.5

Source: Department of Commerce, Bureau of the Census, Public Use Microdata Samples for 1910, 1940, 1950, and 1970.

[a] Native-born white men of native-born parents.

educational attainment so often go hand in hand, it would be useful to know if native-born Russians had more schooling than native whites had in 1910. Unfortunately, census enumerators did not ask about grades completed until 1940. From 1940 to 1970, however, the census data do show that native-born Russian Jews remained in school longer than did all other groups, including native whites.[28] Thus, high educational levels are doubtless part of the explanation for the achievements of native-born Russian Jews, though they also had to contend with high levels of discrimination.

Extensive niche activity likewise characterizes the Jewish experience. In 1910, just two fields, garment manufacture and retail trade, together absorbed slightly over half the foreign born and 44 percent of the native born. The association of Russian Jews with these endeavors originated in Russia, where nineteenth-century czarist edicts restricted Jews both geographically and voca-

[28] The 1910 census asked about school attendance since September 1909 but did not ascertain the quantity or quality of such attendance. Calculations based on these data suggest that native-born Russian young men were slightly more likely to be in school than were native sons of native-born parents of the same age. Similar results are reported in Perlmann, *Ethnic Differences*, pp. 139–54. For an examination of group differences in education based on the national 1910 public use sample tapes, see Jerry A. Jacobs and Margaret E. Greene, "Race and Ethnicity, Social Class and Schooling," in Susan Cotts Watkins, ed., *After Ellis Island: A 1910 Census Monograph* (New York: Russell Sage Foundation, forthcoming).

tionally. Among the few undertakings open to them were light manufacture and commerce.[29]

Premigration experience was only one reason that Jewish immigrants in America maintained their attachment to these fields, however. By the turn of the century, entering New York's garment industry required fewer skills than entering its Russian counterpart. Similarly, minimal expertise was required to sell goods in a compatriot's shop or to peddle a compatriot's wares on the streets. Personal connections, not specific skills, replenished niche labor.[30]

Still, not all niche activities were equally rewarding. Trade provided better employment opportunities than did garment manufacture. The occupational status of Russian-born garment workers in 1910 was below the group's average, while that of Russian-born traders was above the average. This lesson was not lost on the native born, who were only half as likely as the foreign born to hold jobs in garment manufacture. Yet, about a third of both generations reported employment in trade, most extensively in apparel stores.

Although native-born Russians reported higher occupational statuses outside either niche, the average in 1910 for those in trade was only two points below the group's average. If, as is likely, niche jobs tended to attract the less educated, the absence of niche protection would probably have meant a less impressive occupational achievement for native-born Russians.

This hypothesis receives some confirmation in 1940, when educational information becomes available. Compared to the averages for all native-born Russians, those in trade reported schooling levels a half year lower, nearly identical occupational status, and earnings 96 percent as great. It is thus not surprising that over a quarter worked in this niche. On the other hand, employment in garment manufacture absorbed only 8 percent of the native born by 1940, perhaps because occupational status here averaged nine points below the mean for native-born Russians. Nonetheless, the earnings of garment workers were a healthy 94 percent of the group's average, and this despite their nearly a year's less schooling. In sum, on earnings, if not on occupational status, native-born Russian niche employees fared better than their educational levels would predict. Moreover, the earnings advantage may be understated, since the 1940 census failed to inquire about entrepreneurial income.

By 1950, when both wage and entrepreneurial earnings are available, foreign-

[29] For comparisons of turn-of-the-century Jewish employment in Russia and America, see Jacob Lestchinsky, "The Position of the Jews in the Economic Life of America," in I. Graeber and S. Britt, eds., *Jews in a Gentile World* (New York: Macmillan, 1942), pp. 402–16; and Simon Kuznets, "Economic Structure and Life of the Jews," in L. Finkelstein, ed., *The Jews: Their History, Culture, and Religion*, 3d ed., vol. 2 (New York: Harper and Brothers, 1960), pp. 1597–666.

[30] A vivid account of how immigrant Jews obtained employment appears in Melech Epstein, *Jewish Labor, U.S.A.* (New York: Trade Union Sponsoring Committee, 1950), pp. 39ff. Although Jewish familiarity with needlework doubtless facilitated niche establishment, the tasks of creating a garment were so broken down that "Jewish immigrants are able to master their jobs . . . in less than a month," quotes Irving Howe in *World of Our Fathers* (New York: Simon and Schuster, 1976), p. 156.

and native-born Russians outearn native whites. Interestingly, although the 1950 earnings of native Russians in the garment trades moved to 30 percent above their compatriots' average, the percentage of native-born Russians in the industry declined to a mere 6 percent. The proportion in trade, however, held steady at a quarter, perhaps because of the more attractive occupational status of these jobs. Furthermore, earnings in trade were equivalent to the native Russian average, despite trade workers' slightly inferior educational attainment.

In 1970, 15 percent of native-born Russians worked in trade, compared to 25 percent in 1950. Declines in discrimination certainly contributed to this result. Accordingly, drops in both the relative occupational status and relative earnings of Russian trade jobs appear. Earnings, for instance, fell to about three-quarters of the native-born Russian average. Thus, the rewards of trade began more accurately to reflect the propensity of the niche to absorb the less educated. Nonetheless, the earnings of all native Russians were so high ($14,717) that the money they received in trade ($10,768) was still above the earnings averaged by all native whites ($9,781)!

The Russian experience illustrates several theoretical expectations about how niches facilitate group advancement. Already in 1910 the data indicate that Russians had access to the full range of class and occupational locations in trade and in garment manufacturing. Because few trade jobs utilize manual skills, Russians in trade averaged higher occupational status than did those in garment manufacture. But in the garment industry, ethnic solidarity soon facilitated unionization, which was well entrenched by the end of the First World War.[31] For these reasons, despite the lower educational credentials of niche workers, the earnings of Russians in both niches were soon equivalent to those of their compatriots in non-niche jobs.

Favored by niches both exceptionally strong and exceptionally large, less-educated Russian Jews were able to invest extensively in the education of their children. As discrimination declined, increasing numbers of those children moved into the expanding professional sector of the dominant economy, gleaning exceptional incomes in the process.

Despite arriving at about the same time as the Jews, Italians have made much slower economic progress. Table 5.3 presents figures on the occupational status and earnings of Italians over time. In 1910, Italian occupational status was only about 70 percent of native white, and by 1940 Italian well-being had deteriorated, especially among the foreign born. Both generations recorded substantial gains in occupational status and earnings in 1950, but native-born remunera-

---

[31] In the 1880s, German Jews were garment manufacturers and Jews from Eastern Europe their employees, but by 1900 Eastern European Jews began moving into position of authority. Meaningful union success dates to 1910, a point in time rather early relative to the formation of other industrial unions. For a discussion of labor strife in the garment trades, see Howe, *World of Our Fathers*, pp. 297–304. On the role of Jewish solidarity in union success, see Glenn, *Daughters of the Shtetl*, pp. 186–91.

TABLE 5.3

Occupational Status and Earnings of Italian Males in Metropolitan New York City by Generation and Year

	Occupational Status	Status as % of NWNP[a]	Annual Earnings ($)	Earnings as % of NWNP[a]
Born in Italy				
1910	23.8	70.6	n.a.	n.a.
1940	23.9	61.8	1,100	68.7
1950	26.1	62.2	2,856	81.0
1970	28.0	62.2	7,841	80.2
Native born of Italian-born parents				
1910	24.8	73.6	n.a.	n.a.
1940	27.5	71.7	1,004	62.7
1950	32.0	76.4	2,854	81.0
1970	38.5	85.7	10,128	103.5

Source: Department of Commerce, Bureau of the Census, Public Use Microdata Samples for 1910, 1940, 1950, and 1970.

[a]Native-born white men of native-born parents.

tion still averaged only 81 percent of native white. Not until 1970 did second-generation Italians pull away from the first in earnings, receiving pay that slightly exceeded that of native whites.

Social scientists usually attribute the relatively late economic rise of Italians to the high proportion who arrived in this country as unskilled laborers.[32] The contribution of discrimination was also substantial. Despite these handicaps, Italian immigrants quickly demonstrated an overconcentration in construction, an activity with which they were already identified in Europe. Interestingly, this proclivity both initially retarded and eventually facilitated Italian economic achievement.

In 1910, construction employed 22 percent of all Italian men, who constituted one in five construction workers. Unlike the Irish, Italians found jobs in construction that fell primarily, though not exclusively, in unskilled labor. Italians were employed most heavily in the arduous and nonunionized sectors of the industry, such as road and subway construction, while the Irish predominated in the more skilled, better organized building trades.

[32] On the skill levels of Italian immigrants, see Kessner, The Golden Door, pp. 33–34 and 120–26. Some scholars also believe that a preference for more familiar outdoor work may have retarded Italian integration into modern work organizations. See Virginia Yans-McLaughlin, Family and Community: Italian Immigrants in Buffalo, 1880–1930 (Ithaca: Cornell University Press, 1977), pp. 41–43.

Barbering constituted another field in which Italians were overrepresented soon after their arrival in this country. Although only 7 percent of Italians were barbers, Italians comprised nearly two-thirds of all New York's barbers in 1910. With 27 percent of Italian barbers reporting a position as "employer," barbering offered better chances for advancement than did construction. Yet Italian concentration in barbering is a good example of a persistent and visible niche that has had little consequence for Italians as a whole. The occupation was simply not big enough to have an impact on so large a group of immigrants.

Indeed, construction and barbering did little to underwrite Italian mobility, particularly in the face of economic depression. In 1940, despite Irish departures, Italian participation in construction had dropped from 22 percent in 1910 to 17 percent. Nearly a third of these jobs were in relief work, the great majority unskilled. Private construction offered Italians somewhat better opportunities, especially in wages for the native born, which were 20 percent above the average for this group. However, since only about 7 percent of native-born Italian men held jobs in private construction, the overall impact of these good wages was small.

Part of the problem was that a declining economy had an adverse impact on the demand for private construction. To make matters worse, Italians were one of the few New York white ethnic groups whose proportions in the labor force grew between 1910 and 1940, from 10 percent to 15 percent. Because immigration was restricted in the 1920s, growth was primarily among the native born. Thus, the opportunities in private construction, native-born Italians' most rewarding niche, could not keep up with their population growth.

Not surprisingly, other niches started appearing. One niche that can only be documented anecdotally is that of crime. Although reports going back to 1900 indicate that scattered bands of criminals preyed upon Italian immigrant communities, the Prohibition era stimulated the consolidation and expansion of Italian criminal organizations.[33] The immediate cause was the demand for bootlegged liquor. It appears that Italian Americans became engaged in producing and distributing alcohol for at least two reasons: first, these nationals had a tradition of making wine at home, and second, Mussolini's purge of the Mafia in the twenties brought many of its members to American shores. Whatever the precise antecedents, there is broad agreement that the Volstead Act created new livelihoods for uncounted Italians who worked for "crime families."[34] For most,

[33] The earliest form of criminal activity in Italian ghettos was extortion, often attributed to the notorious "Black Hand." The Black Hand, however, was not an organization but a symbol used by small bands of individuals to terrorize their neighbors. See Frederic Homer, *Guns and Garlic* (West Lafayette, Ind.: Purdue University Press, 1974), pp. 35–36; and Joseph Albini, *The American Mafia* (New York: Appleton, Century, Crofts, 1971), pp. 191–95.

[34] On the development of the bootlegging industry among Italians, see Humbert Nelli, *The Business of Crime* (New York: Oxford University Press, 1976), chap. 6; and Francis Ianni, *A Family Business: Kinship and Social Control in Organized Crime* (New York: Russell Sage Foundation, 1972), pp. 54–58.

however, the benefits of this association ended with Repeal. As Mafiosi replaced bootlegging with less acceptable undertakings such as gambling, loan-sharking, prostitution, and drugs, the number of willing Mafia collaborators declined. Still, there is little doubt that for a small but noteworthy number of Italians, organized crime offered a more protracted road out of poverty.[35]

The interwar period also witnessed a growth in Italian influence within other niches. The group increased its representation to something over a fifth of workers in both clothing manufacture and the operation of food stores. While the average occupational status in each of these endeavors stood above that in private construction, the pay did not.

By 1950, a number of new factors stimulated Italian progress. The postwar economic boom had begun. Italian proportions in the labor market had stabilized, partly a result of the lower fertility of an increasingly native-born generation. And, anti-Italian discrimination declined. The major problem facing the group was its modest educational levels.

In this context, niche employment helped a good deal. Construction occupied about 12 percent of Italians, who comprised about a quarter of that work force. Equally important, Italians began to move into the unionized, craft jobs of the industry. The mean earnings of both foreign- and native-born Italian construction workers were higher than those of each generation's average. Most importantly, they secured this wage advantage despite an average educational level of about a year less than their generational counterparts employed elsewhere.

Nearly the identical situation obtained in apparel but not in food stores. In the latter endeavor, occupational status was comparatively high, but earnings fell about $400 below the Italian average for 1950. In sum, despite their low educational requirements, construction, apparel, and food stores, which together employed nearly 30 percent of the foreign born and 20 percent of the native born, offered some of the best jobs reported by Italians.

Nor had these advantages much diminished twenty years later, by which time the earnings of native-born Italians had moved ahead of those of native whites. The average educational levels of native-born Italian construction workers remained a year below the group average, while their earnings were nearly indistinguishable from their compatriots employed elsewhere. In an economy in which educational credentials were starting to matter, this is no small contribution.

For Italians, then, the utility of niche employment changed over time. Initially, they had to share their largest niche, construction, with the better established Irish, who assumed the more desirable jobs in the industry. Then, Italian population growth and economic contraction undercut the advantages Italians

---

[35] On crime as a mechanism for upward mobility, see Daniel Bell, *The End of Ideology* (Glencoe, Ill.: Free Press, 1960), pp. 115–19.

could reap from Irish departure. By midcentury, however, these problems had abated. The occupational variety in construction as well as in other Italian niches meant that those less able to compete in the dominant economy could nonetheless advance. Consequently, Italian educational levels began to rise. By 1970, an absence of discrimination permitted the better educated to compete successfully as individuals, while the less schooled fared equally well under niche protection. As a result, Italians as a group moved ahead.

The analysis so far reveals that New York's Irish, Italians, and Jews benefited from niches in a similar fashion. At some point in time, niches offered better than average occupational status and/or earnings to group members whose educations were modest. This situation enhanced the education of their children, such that, when discrimination abated, they were in a good position to seize the new, attractive opportunities that an increasingly education-conscious economy was producing.

Blacks too have had their niches, but these niches have failed to uplift those blacks most in need of a helping hand. Early in this century, niche employment was easy to obtain but yielded little more than a job. Late in the century, just the opposite pattern prevailed; niche jobs were hard to enter but provided generous rewards. The inability of blacks to maintain niches that were simultaneously accessible and rewarding sharply distinguishes their experience from that of white ethnics.

Black economic attainment has suffered accordingly. Table 5.4 presents data on the occupational and earnings attainment of blacks by birthplace and year from 1910 to 1980. A number of trends merit comment. First, the figures show that between 1910 and 1940 the gap in occupational status between native whites and blacks widened. The source of this widening lies in the improvement in the average ranking of white occupations versus stagnation in the opportunities available to blacks.[36] Between 1940 and 1980, the racial gap in both occupational status and earnings diminished, though it did not disappear. Also noteworthy is the inconsistent advantage of the Northern born over the Southern born. While the Northern born often held higher status occupations, the wages of both groups remained about the same until 1980. Strikingly, in 1980 the Southern born earned about 15 percent more than their Northern-born counterparts. The source of this gap is ambiguous, but the more affluent Southern-born blacks still earned 20 percent less than native whites.

In seeking an explanation for the persistence of black disadvantage, the dearth of attractive black niches quickly becomes apparent. Although blacks tried to exploit their premigration skills in establishing niches, an increasingly discriminatory white populace undercut their attempts. Thus, although in the nineteenth century New York black barbers and caterers were serving a white

---

[36] Tables 5.3 and 5.4 reveal that, relative to native whites between 1910 and 1940, Italians displayed a similar but less severe drop in their occupational position.

TABLE 5.4
Occupational Status and Earnings of Black Males in Metropolitan New York City
by Generation and Year

	Occupational Status	Status as % of NWNP[a]	Annual Earnings ($)	Earnings as % of NWNP[a]
Southern born				
1910	23.7	70.3	n.a.	n.a.
1940	17.9	46.2	864	53.3
1950	19.0	45.4	2,056	58.3
1970	26.8	59.6	6,225	66.7
1980	27.3	68.5	12,330	79.4
Northern born				
1910	22.6	67.1	n.a.	n.a.
1940	22.3	57.6	877	54.7
1950	21.6	51.7	2,064	58.5
1970	30.2	67.2	6,253	63.9
1980	30.8	77.2	10,737	69.1

Source: Department of Commerce, Bureau of the Census, Public Use Microdata Samples for
1910, 1940, 1950, 1970, and 1980.
[a]Native-born white men of native-born parents.

population, already by 1910 immigrant competitors had captured most of the
white market for these services. Unable to pursue entrepreneurial activity beyond the ghetto, blacks had little choice but to seek employment under white
auspices. Here again, however, prejudicial attitudes inhibited most white bosses
from hiring very many blacks in one firm. When whites did hire blacks, it was
usually for the least attractive, most menial of jobs—with the result that some of
these posts did become occupational niches.[37] In 1910 New York, occupations
such as janitor, elevator operator, and servant all engaged larger proportions of
black men than would be predicted on the basis of their modest, 2 percent
representation in the city's labor force. But these jobs required few skills and
paid accordingly. The only bright spot was the very low unemployment rate.

This protection from unemployment, however, disappeared in the Depression, never again to return. In 1940, nearly a fifth of black men were unemployed, a fact not irrelevant to the modest educational gains of black children of
the Depression era. Further evidence of the desperation of the black condition
appears in their average earnings, only about half those of whites, as well as in
the rates at which they turned to government-supported relief work. Nearly 11

---

[37] On black displacement by immigrants and on their turn-of-the-century job distribution, see
Joe Trotter, Jr., "Blacks in the Urban North," chap. 2 of this volume.

percent of black men held such jobs in 1940, the highest percentage of any group in the city.

Nonetheless, blacks remained active in their earlier occupational niches, and the 1940 census reveals two new arenas of overconcentration: railroads and government. Six percent of blacks held positions in railroading, primarily in service occupations and in general labor. Indeed, blacks enjoyed a near monopoly in the occupations of sleeping-car porter, cook, and waiter, because of the ideas of George Pullman. When he sought a labor force to care for customers traveling in his famous Pullman cars, he decided that blacks would constitute the ideal work force. Not only were they long accustomed to serving whites, not only were they English speaking, but they would work for less than other groups. Remarkably, Pullman did not anticipate that large numbers of racially homogeneous workers might pose the threat of unionization.[38]

A. Philip Randolph, a black New York socialist, was eager to organize the black working class. His first attempt, an effort to mobilize elevator operators, failed because of Randolph's lack of experience and because these workers were spread across a multitude of firms. But Randolph ultimately met with success in his work with the more solidary sleeping-car porters. Wages and working conditions remained modest by white standards, but the 1940 earnings of the predominantly Southern-born black sleeping-car porters were 20 percent above the Southern black average.[39]

At first glance, a far larger proportion of blacks were employed by government than by railroads. In 1940, nearly one in five blacks reported public employment, nearly the same proportion as the Irish. But unlike the Irish, who predominated in regular government jobs, nearly two-thirds of black government workers were engaged in relief work, overwhelmingly construction. While relief opportunities were clearly temporary, 7 percent of black New Yorkers held regular government jobs. And two facts already stand out with respect to these black men: their educations and their salaries were well above average.

By midcentury, government no longer offered any but regular jobs, and the proportion of blacks so employed increased to nearly 12 percent. While this increase was a positive development, the competitive character of government employment had not changed. Black government workers held high-status occupations, earned exceptional wages, but also reported about a year and a half more schooling than other blacks.

Railroads continued to offer black men employment in 1950, but opportunities there could not keep pace with the expanding black population. Other industries in which black men were somewhat overrepresented included restaurants, real estate, and laundries. More striking though was the broad dispersal of

[38] For a description of the attractions black labor held for George Pullman, see Brailsford Brazeal, *The Brotherhood of Sleeping Car Porters* (New York: Harper and Brothers, 1946), chap. 1.

[39] For a superb biography of Randolph, see Jervis Anderson, *A. Philip Randolph* (New York: Harcourt, Brace, Jovanovich, 1973).

black men throughout the economy, a dispersal that contrasted strongly with the concentrations of immigrant groups earlier in the century. Unlike immigrants, blacks continued arriving in the city even though no single industry stood ready to absorb large amounts of unskilled labor.[40]

By 1970, however, the black concentration in government finally reached a level large enough to matter. Commitment to affirmative action and growth in the public sector brought one in five black men a government job. As before, these positions offered better occupational status and earnings than most blacks could expect, but demanded educational credentials that averaged over a year higher as well. Not surprisingly, research based on a national study reveals that the parents of black men prepared to take advantage of these new government opportunities were disproportionately in the upper ranks of the black occupational structure.[41]

At the same time that black opportunities in government expanded, black representation in their previous niches fell. The largest arena of black employment was construction, which occupied 6 percent, but union discrimination effectively barred blacks from the skilled building trades.[42] With no other private industry occupying as much as 4 percent of the group, a niche that could facilitate the upward mobility of less-educated blacks had still not appeared.

Ten years later, in 1980, black employment in hospital work had replaced construction in absorbing over 6 percent of black men, but some of these jobs fell under government auspices. In the private sector, the economy of the seventies brought a further increase in black dispersal. At the same time, black males extended their hold on government jobs, which occupied more than one in four by 1980. But, between 1970 and 1980, the number of government positions requiring less than a high school degree had disproportionately declined.[43] Thus, the educational credentials of black government workers, though still below white schooling levels, averaged about a year above privately employed blacks. Not unexpectedly, Northern-born black government workers

[40] In "Southern Diaspora: Origins of the Northern 'Underclass,'" chap. 1 of this volume, Jacqueline Jones contrasts Midwest employers' receptivity to newly arriving Appalachians, who congregated in particular factories, to these employers' rejection of similarly qualified black migrants, who were forced to accept positions in a greater variety of job settings.

[41] Michael Hout, "Occupational Mobility of Black Men, 1962–1973," *American Sociological Review* 49 (1984): 308–22.

[42] For a study of discrimination in the building trades, see Roger Waldinger and Thomas Bailey, "The Continuing Significance of Race: Racial Conflict and Racial Discrimination in Construction," *Politics and Society* 19 (1991): 291–323. An informative discussion of the history of union racism appears in Lieberson, *A Piece of the Pie*, pp. 339–54.

[43] Vilma Ortiz, "Latinos and Industrial Change in New York and Los Angeles" (Paper presented at the annual meeting of the American Sociological Association, Washington, D.C., 11–15 August 1990). Table 1 of her paper indicates that between 1970 and 1980, public sector jobs in New York that required less than a high school diploma declined 26 percent, while the number of similar jobs requiring a high school degree or more fell only 6 percent.

earned 79 percent of native whites incomes, while black wages in the private sector were only 65 percent of white. At the same time, this intraracial earnings difference should not be overstated; *within* federal, state, and local government, native white employees outearned blacks by substantial amounts.

Nonetheless, for blacks, the alternatives outside government were a good deal worse than the opportunities inside. Part of the reason for this situation was that by 1980, niches that had once relied upon unskilled black labor were withering. Few expanding industries or occupations still hired large numbers of modestly educated workers, and those that did rarely provided either strong unions or upward mobility.

In this context, the attractions of criminal careers again become relevant. By the 1970s, later-generation Italian Americans were displaying a declining interest in a life of crime, particularly in the drug trade. This situation, coupled with expanding Caribbean and South American sources for narcotics, opened the way for black and Hispanic entrepreneurship.[44] However, the evidence to date suggests that the organization of black and Hispanic drug trafficking is far more individualistic, and thus less "niche-like," than that of their Italian predecessors.

The Rastafarian marijuana merchants in the Caribbean and in Brooklyn provide a case in point. Initially, the religious code of Rastafarianism regulated the behavior of members, whose religious beliefs extolled the cultivation, distribution, and consumption of the drug. In 1981, just as vast amounts of Colombian cocaine came on the market, enforcement against marijuana importation intensified. Cocaine and its derivatives supplanted marijuana and Rastafarianism. In the absence of standards by which interpersonal relations could be governed, drug dealers started to rely on personal acts of violence to establish and maintain their reputations as business people of consequence. In the words of one dealer, "My support network is me, myself, and I." Other observers have noted the emergence of small bands or posses who are frequently at war, within and among themselves.[45]

This lack of cooperation among drug traders leaves them highly vulnerable to death at the hands of competitors, to say nothing of the dangers of jail or the health problems associated with their own personal addictions. In sum, few black and Hispanic drug merchants are likely to achieve the level of organization

[44] Blacks had displayed an earlier interest in criminal enterprise, especially in managing the Harlem "numbers" rackets, but by the mid-1930s, white mobsters had wrested control of this undertaking. See Nelli, *The Business of Crime*, pp. 225–29. On the reassertion of black influence in the underworld, see Francis Ianni, *Black Mafia: Ethnic Succession Organized in Crime* (New York: Simon and Schuster, 1974), and "New Mafia: Black, Hispanic and Italian Styles," in F. Ianni and E. Reuss-Ianni, eds., *The Crime Society* (New York: New American Library, 1976), pp. 127–48.

[45] Philippe Bourgois, "In Search of Horatio Alger: Culture and Ideology in the Crack Economy," *Contemporary Drug Problems* 16 (1989): 619–49; Ansley Hamid, "The Political Economy of Crack-Related Violence," *Contemporary Drug Problems* 17 (1990): 31–78; and William Finnegan, "A Street Kid in the Drug Trade," *New Yorker*, 17 September 1990.

TABLE 5.5

Occupational Status and Earnings of Puerto Rican Males in Metropolitan New York City by Generation and Year

	Occupational Status	Status as % of NWNP[a]	Annual Earnings ($)	Earnings as % of NWNP[a]
Island born				
1940	25.8	66.7	939	58.6
1950	20.7	49.5	1,838	52.2
1970	25.7	57.1	5,558	56.8
1980	25.6	64.1	10,574	68.1
Mainland born				
1970	31.9	70.9	6,328	64.7
1980	30.5	76.5	9,709	62.5

Source: Department of Commerce, Bureau of the Census, Public Use Microdata Samples for 1940, 1950, 1970, and 1980.

[a]Native-born white men of native-born parents.

and cooperation that niche environments require in order to produce long-term upward mobility for the law-abiding or the lawless.

The experiences of Puerto Ricans, one of the Hispanic groups now active in the drug business, are relatively similar to those of blacks. Indeed, they have been even less successful than blacks in establishing viable niches for their unskilled male labor force.

The data in table 5.5 summarize Puerto Rican economic outcomes. Because large numbers of Puerto Ricans did not begin arriving in New York until after World War II, this table contains fewer entries than the preceding ones do. Within generations, the occupational status figures show modest advances over the years. On income, the island born earned slightly more than half of native whites until 1980, when their incomes moved to 68 percent of those of native whites. Interestingly, Northern-born blacks and mainland-born Puerto Ricans exhibit similar earnings patterns between 1970 and 1980. Relative to native whites, both groups earned less in 1980 than in 1970. Relative to their respective migrant counterparts, both groups also earned less. In other words, by 1980 largely second-generation blacks and Puerto Ricans were both losing ground.

The history of niche employment among male Puerto Rican New Yorkers is similarly disturbing. Puerto Rican men have been least successful of all groups examined here in securing a helpful niche. The relatively small size of the group, around 1 percent of the city's 1950 labor force, diluted the potential benefits of job concentration. Moreover, Puerto Ricans were neither occupationally nor industrially very concentrated. Two service industries, hotels and restaurants, employed nearly one in five Puerto Rican men, but these workers were spread across a variety of occupations and firms. The dispersal of so small a group likely contributed to the modest earnings reported by Puerto Rican service workers.

With continuing migration and natural increase, by 1970 Puerto Ricans constituted about 4 percent of New York's male labor force. Yet, like blacks, Puerto Ricans workers were more dispersed across private industries in 1970 than in 1950. And, in a continuing parallel with blacks, government emerged as Puerto Ricans' largest employer. Eleven percent of the island born and 18 percent of the mainland born worked in government. As expected, these workers had more education, higher-status occupations, and better salaries than did their counterparts in private posts. Nevertheless, Puerto Rican government employees averaged well below native whites on all three indicators.

Ten years later, these patterns had changed only a little. Native whites earned about 20 percent more than Puerto Ricans in government, who, in turn, earned about 20 percent more than Puerto Ricans in private industry. Thus, Puerto Ricans in private industry were impoverished. Not unexpectedly, the educational level of these men was also very low. As in the case of blacks, economic trends further dampened the hope that the condition of Puerto Ricans or their offspring would soon improve.

This section has argued that niche employment had major consequences for the economic progress of minorities. At one or another point in time, each group studied here profited from one or more niches. Blacks and Puerto Ricans, however, did not profit in the way that white ethnics did. White ethnic niches, the overwhelming majority legitimate, accommodated significant proportions of modestly educated group members in well-paying jobs. In the main, blacks and Puerto Ricans were denied such attractive opportunities until public policy explicitly addressed their need. By this time, however, the economy was no longer generating rewarding positions for the less schooled. Although government accepted the primary responsibility for absorbing minority labor, government was not immune from the credentialism that characterized the private sector. As a result, the minority individuals who profit most from the new forms of favoritism have been the more educated. Moreover, while white ethnic groups ultimately secured the most desirable jobs in their respective niches, native whites still hold far more attractive government jobs than do blacks and Puerto Ricans.

In the past, white ethnics also faced skill deficits, poverty, and discrimination. But after less-educated ethnics obtained secure and rewarding niche jobs, they could expect either to pass their own jobs on to their children or to underwrite the costs of their children's higher education. In these ways was the impoverishment of the next generation averted. With neither of these options available to today's undereducated minorities, it is hard to see how the chasm between the middle class and the underclass will ever close.

THE SOCIAL BENEFITS OF NICHE EMPLOYMENT

Having shown that the quality and quantity of niche opportunities affect the economic well-being of minority groups, this essay turns to how the availability of niches impacts the behaviors recently associated with the underclass. The hypothesis is that niches provide mechanisms through which minority communities exercise a degree of self-regulation. Thus, social control will be stronger in communities where niches are well developed than in communities where niches are weak or absent.

William Wilson has recently presented a related, though not identical, argument. According to Wilson, a middle-class presence is the key to social control in the minority community. When middle-class people live and work among their poorer compatriots, they function as both role models and personal sponsors for the less fortunate. They are living proof that "playing by the rules" is worth the effort. They can provide information or even assistance in the job market. The power and prestige of these prominent citizens provides a successful challenge to disruptive alternatives.

In the past, Wilson argues, the rigid customs of housing discrimination and the relatively modest financial resources of blacks combined to restrict most of the middle class to the central city. This situation, while in many ways lamentable, enhanced the opportunity for cross-class ties. Over the past twenty years, however, declines in discrimination brought the middle class better salaries and more housing options. As a result, the black middle class has deserted the ghetto for the suburbs, leaving behind their less fortunate neighbors.[46]

Although the physical proximity of diverse classes has the potential to foster social control, the key variable in Wilson's argument is the availability of employment opportunities. Persons engaged in satisfactory employment are the most likely to conform to mainstream values.[47] Thus, the most effective way for the better off to influence the behavior of the less fortunate is to serve as brokers in the labor market. This intervention is especially welcome when the lower classes have difficulty finding suitable jobs because of either discrimination or low skills. If sponsors and protégés also share the same neighborhood, the pressures for the latter's conformity will be correspondingly greater.

[46] Wilson, The Truly Disadvantaged, pp. 7–8, 49–62. For evidence that black ghettos were class segregated as early as the twenties, see Trotter, "Blacks in the Urban North." For evidence that the geographic distance between better-off and poor African Americans has remained about the same since 1950, see Reynolds Farley, "Residential Segregation of Social and Economic Groups among Blacks, 1970–1980," in Jencks and Petersen, The Urban Underclass, pp. 274–98. Also relevant is Douglas Massey and Mitchell Eggers, "The Ecology of Inequality: Minorities and the Concentration of Poverty, 1970–1980," American Journal of Sociology 95 (1990): 1174–84.

[47] The classic statement of this position is Robert Merton, Social Theory and Social Structure (Glencoe, Ill.: Free Press, 1957), chaps. 4 and 5. See also William Julius Wilson, "Public Policy Research and The Truly Disadvantaged," in Jencks and Petersen, The Urban Underclass, pp. 471–72; and Bourgois, "In Search of Horatio Alger," pp. 619–23, passim.

What kind of job opportunities are most easily brokered in minority communities? As the previous discussion has suggested, niche jobs—legitimate and illegitimate—most closely fit this description. And just because niche jobs are brokered in minority communities, niches produce high levels of social control. Entry and advancement in niche environments depend upon good relationships with residentially and culturally proximate coethnics. Entry and advancement in non-niche jobs depend upon good relationships with residentially and culturally distant outsiders. Thus, niche employees have strong incentives to conform to the behavioral expectations of their compatriots. Non-niche employees have somewhat weaker incentives. The unemployed have the lowest incentives of all.[48]

This reasoning suggests that minorities with very high proportions in niche employment will have the fewest social problems. But the underclass debate raises at least two potential objections. First, since blacks and Puerto Ricans had few niches until recently, why did they not experience greater social problems in the past? Second, since these minorities now have a niche in government, why is their social fabric unraveling?

An initial answer to the question of why blacks and Puerto Ricans did not experience serious social problems in the past is that they did. Contemporary observers have erroneously idealized the traditional atmosphere of American ghettos and barrios. The many scholarly and personal accounts of these neighborhoods make clear that residents experienced above-average rates of criminal activity, drug addiction, and marital breakdown.[49]

At the same time, one reason that these problems were not as severe as they have now become is that some niches were available. For example, Elijah Anderson describes how "old heads," men of stable means who believed in hard work, family life, and the church, assisted young black males in obtaining work in a Northeastern city.[50] In the railroad industry, which formerly hired large numbers of blacks, a referral system is known to have flourished.

Still, comparisons between groups suggest that white ethnics enjoyed greater

---

[48] The foregoing discussion has focused on rewards as the motivation for conformity and has neglected the role of coercion. Interestingly, in those neighborhoods where organized crime functioned as a niche, criminals often provided not only economic opportunity but also coercive sanctions. In other words, unlike today's drug traffickers, the Mafia devoted some of its resources to actively enforcing the peace. See Donald Tricarico, *The Italians of Greenwich Village* (Staten Island, N.Y.: Center for Migration Studies, 1984), pp. 67–69; and Robert A. Orsi, *The Madonna of 115th Street: Family and Community in Italian Harlem, 1880–1950* (New Haven: Yale University Press, 1985), pp. 103–4.

[49] For scholarly examples, see Gilbert Osofsky, *Harlem: The Making of a Ghetto* (New York: Harper and Row, 1963); and St. Clair Drake and Horace R. Cayton, *Black Metropolis* (New York: Harcourt, Brace and World, 1962). For biographical examples, see Claude Brown, *Manchild in the Promised Land* (New York: New American Library, 1965); and Piri Thomas, *Down These Mean Streets* (New York: New American Library, 1967).

[50] Elijah Anderson, *Streetwise* (Chicago: University of Chicago Press, 1990), pp. 69–73.

leverage over the behavior of their compatriots, especially their young, than did blacks or Puerto Ricans. In his ethnography of black, Hispanic, and Italian gangs in Chicago, Gerald Suttles writes, "Among the Italians, the major share of coercive power still remains in adult hands. . . . It is the only case where the corporate power of the adolescents is tempered by that of the adults. . . . Since many of the same adults have an active role in distributing some of the benefits that are held in store by the wider community, their power is further augmented."[51]

The weaker authority of black and Puerto Rican elders stemmed not only from the paucity of niches formerly available to these groups but also from the poor quality of many niche jobs. Although quality is rarely a problem for new arrivals, who tend to be satisfied with opportunities that are good relative to those of their place of origin, more seasoned migrants and second-generation residents have higher aspirations. Those born and bred in Northern cities are the most likely to reject offers of employment in menial, poorly paid occupations.[52] Since white ethnic elders could offer the young more attractive positions than could their black and Puerto Rican counterparts, the leverage of the older generation was correspondingly greater.

Nonetheless, some mechanisms of social control did operate in poor communities of color. They have since disappeared. One reason is that, as time passed, the proportion of blacks and Puerto Ricans raised in Northern cities increased, eroding the attraction of the posts that the older generation could offer. But expanding cohorts of the locally born is not the only problem. Industrial shifts cut away at the number of brokerable positions. Thus, Anderson states, "The loss of industries has undermined the traditional leadership of the community, the 'old heads.' Some of these men and women are now retired on pensions, some are hanging on to the residual manufacturing jobs. But what they used to be able to promise 'young boys'—high-paying jobs in exchange for law-abidingness and civility and the work ethic—no longer exists. Faced with persistent racism, youths can hope only for low-paying service jobs, often in the suburbs, or jobs in fast-food restaurants."[53]

While the data on black earnings presented above indicate that, in the past, few blacks obtained high-paying jobs, opportunities for the unskilled were clearly more plentiful. Plentiful today are opportunities for the educated in the

[51] Gerald D. Suttles, *The Social Order of the Slum* (Chicago: University of Chicago Press, 1968), p. 118. For a review of studies on the difficulty of raising children in poverty, see Robin L. Jarrett, "A Comparative Examination of Socialization Patterns among Low-Income African Americans, Chicanos, Puerto Ricans, and Whites: A Review of the Ethnographic Literature" (Report to the Social Science Research Council, May 1990).

[52] For a theoretical discussion of first- and second-generation expectations, see Michael Piore, *Birds of Passage* (New York: Cambridge University Press, 1979), pp. 108–14. For evidence that Southern-born blacks have more favorable economic outcomes than their Northern-born counterparts, see Wilson, *The Truly Disadvantaged*, pp. 177–78.

[53] Anderson, *Streetwise*, p. 242.

new niche of government employ. This new niche does little to promote social control in poor minority communities because entry rests on schooling and test scores, as much as on personal ties. Neither affirmative action policies nor the intervention of parents, teachers, or community leaders can procure a stable government job for a high school dropout. Hence, it is hardly surprising that such authority figures enjoy little influence over youngsters with long-standing educational deficits.

Thus, Wilson is both correct and incorrect. He is correct that compatriots able to offer young adults employment in return for normative behavior is a major resource in minority communities. But he overstates his case when he claims that past ghetto neighborhoods were safe and tranquil locations because of the extensive assistance that the more stable classes rendered those below.[54] The sad fact is that both employed blacks and employed Puerto Ricans have had very few jobs to give, especially good jobs. In the past, this deficit was less serious because the majority of these groups were migrants, and even menial jobs were better than premigration opportunities. But contemporary youth, urban born and bred, are "high priced labor."[55] They aspire to something better at precisely the time that good jobs for the unskilled have become increasingly scarce. Today, more than ever, the success of minority youth depends on "what they know" more than "whom they know."

CONCLUSION

In a recent review of *The Truly Disadvantaged*, Christopher Jencks challenges William Wilson's belief that "historic discrimination is more important than contemporary discrimination in understanding the plight of the black under-class." Jencks goes on to write that "for this argument to be convincing, we need a detailed account of how past discrimination affects blacks' present competitive position." And, "that account must deal not just with blacks' economic resources but with their culture as well."[56]

This chapter has tried to offer such an account. It has argued that the integration of African Americans and Puerto Ricans into Northern job markets has proceeded quite differently from that of white ethnics. Contrary to theories that argue that all groups enter at the bottom of the occupational ladder and gradually work their way upward, the interpretation offered here is that immigrants concentrated in particular occupations and industries. This tendency allowed

[54] For a discussion of black class relations, see Robin Kelley, "The Black Poor and the Politics of Opposition in a New South City, 1929–1970," chap. 9 of this volume.

[55] On the wage expectations of current ghetto youth, see Harry J. Holzer, "Black Youth Non-employment: Duration and Job Search," in Richard Freeman and Harry J. Holzer, eds., *The Black Youth Employment Crisis* (Chicago: University of Chicago Press, 1986), p. 65; and Christopher Jencks, "Deadly Neighborhoods," *New Republic*, 13 June 1988, p. 26.

[56] Jencks, "Deadly Neighborhoods," p. 30.

them to develop collective mechanisms of mutual assistance that had both economic and social consequences.

For the most part, access to niches was a matter of ethnicity and personal connections, not employable skills, which were obtained on the job. Certainly, white ethnics worked hard at the jobs they obtained. But the belief, now prevalent among the descendants of white immigrants, that their grandparents did not enjoy the favoritism that public policy now accords blacks and Hispanics, is misplaced. American ethnic history is not a story about *individuals* who struggled to pull themselves up by their bootstraps in an essentially hostile world. It is a story about how *groups* established themselves in particular occupations and industries and used their collective resources either to control those industries or to upgrade the rewards associated with their occupations. In this way did white ethnics conquer an essentially hostile world.

That blacks and Puerto Ricans did not secure a niche with low barriers to entry is partly a result of their later arrival in Northern labor markets. In the post–World War II era, few such opportunities were developing. But this explanation is less than satisfying both because more recent newcomers have established niches and because blacks who were present earlier in this century were equally unsuccessful in maintaining a beachhead. The reasons that recent newcomers, such as Chinese, Korean, and Cuban immigrants, have established niches are complex, but perhaps the simplest reason is that a significant proportion of these new arrivals do not come from impoverished backgrounds. The better educated and wealthier among them play a pioneering role in establishing ethnically owned small businesses, which offer the only viable niches in a deindustrializing society.[57] Unlike immigrant entrepreneurs, black and Puerto Rican shopkeepers have lacked extensive financial resources, and have long had difficulty attracting non–co-ethnic customers. Thus barred from pursuing collective economic strategies, many New York blacks and Puerto Ricans had to negotiate employment and advancement by themselves. So, it is little wonder that they have been noted for being "individuals," for eschewing the sorts of self-help associated with other groups.[58] Certainly they helped one another when they could, but the resources at their disposal were modest.

Because blacks were overwhelmingly forced to work for whites, it was natural that they would perceive discrimination as their greatest enemy. And, they looked to government for redress. Under the pressure of the civil rights movement, government responded with affirmative action and with antidiscrimina-

[57] For an excellent discussion of the determinants of ethnic enterprise and of the obstacles that African Americans face in small business, see Ivan Light, "Immigrant and Ethnic Enterprise in North America," *Ethnic and Racial Studies* 7 (1984): 195–216.

[58] Among the writers that have remarked on black or Puerto Rican individualism are Elena Padilla, *Up from Puerto Rico* (New York: Columbia University Press, 1958), p. 29; Kenneth Clark, *Dark Ghetto* (New York: Harper and Row, 1967), pp. 189–94; Nathan Glazer and Daniel Moynihan, *Beyond the Melting Pot*, 2d ed. (Cambridge: MIT Press, 1970), p. 33.

tion legislation. Because the public sector was both highly committed to rectifying racial injustice and rapidly increasing in size, it became the major arena for black and Puerto Rican economic improvement. But access to government jobs has changed since the days of the Irish political machines and, indeed, because of those machines. Despite some preference in their favor, applicants of color still must meet civil service requirements, a barrier that effectively excludes those most in need of good jobs.[59]

The lack of niche opportunities for unskilled blacks and Puerto Ricans is one reason that they have continued so vulnerable to poverty, a major dimension of their underclass status. The lack of niche opportunities is likewise one reason these groups are most vulnerable to social problems, a second dimension of their underclass status. As this essay has shown, niches are the mechanisms responsible for the upward mobility of white ethnic groups. Faced with low skills and discrimination, white immigrants eventually found working-class security in their niches. This security, in turn, facilitated the education necessary for the next generation to enter the middle class. The historical origins of the underclass lie in the social and economic forces that enabled some groups to establish profitable niches and abandoned other groups to "catch-as-catch-can."

[59] Erie, *Rainbow's End*, p. 152. For a history of black employment in New York public service, see Edwin R. Lewinson, *Black Politics in New York City* (New York: Twayne Publishers, 1974), chap. 9.

CHAPTER 6

The Emergence of "Underclass" Family Patterns, 1900–1940

Kathryn M. Neckerman

ONE OF THE MOST OFTEN cited features of ghetto poverty is the high incidence of single-parent families. Broken homes among the poor attracted attention even before the recent increase in single motherhood. Now that most inner-city poor families are headed by women, family structure has become central to our ideas about the "underclass." Some of this concern reflects culture-bound and overly narrow conceptions of the family; social scientists tend to neglect nonresident and nonlegal kin relations that are important to the nurturing of poor children. But concern about family structure is also spurred by evidence that disadvantages associated with single motherhood contribute to chronic and even intergenerational poverty.[1]

A central question in debates over the family is the reason for the weakening of marital ties among the poor. Disagreeing about the relative importance of urbanization, economic trends, welfare policy, and race- or class-specific culture, scholars have often sought to adjudicate among these explanatory factors by correlating them with the timing of changes in family structure. The increase in single motherhood after 1940 has drawn their attention to the events and conditions of the post–World War II period, including the expansion of welfare

---

I would like to thank Kermit Daniel, Michael B. Katz, and the authors of other chapters in this volume for helpful comments on earlier versions of this paper.

[1] For conceptions of the underclass that include single mothers, or single mothers on welfare, see Ken Auletta, *The Underclass* (New York: Random House, 1982); Isabel V. Sawhill, "The Underclass: Part I, An Overview," *Public Interest* 96 (1989): 3–15. The female-headed family is a central concern for other writers about the ghetto poor; see for instance William Julius Wilson, *The Truly Disadvantaged: The Inner City, the Underclass, and Public Policy* (Chicago: University of Chicago Press, 1987); Irwin Garfinkel and Sara S. McLanahan, *Single Mothers and Their Children: A New American Dilemma* (Washington, D.C.: Urban Institute Press, 1986). Scholars reconsidering conceptions of the black family include Joyce Ladner, *Tomorrow's Tomorrow: The Black Woman* (New York: Doubleday, 1971); Walter R. Allen, "The Search for Applicable Theories of Black Family Life," *Journal of Marriage and the Family* 39 (1978): 117–29. For evidence about the role of nonresident and nonlegal kin, see Carol B. Stack, *All Our Kin: Strategies for Survival in a Black Community* (New York: Harper and Row, 1974). On the influence of single motherhood, see Sara McLanahan, "Family Structure and the Reproduction of Poverty," *American Journal of Sociology* 90 (1985): 873–901; and Frank F. Furstenberg, Jr., J. Brooks-Gunn, and S. Philip Morgan, *Adolescent Mothers in Later Life* (New York: Cambridge University Press, 1987).

programs, the decline of minority male employment, and changes in mainstream norms.[2]

This chapter takes a different approach to the question of timing. It assumes that the timing of social change is not simply a matter of demographic trends but also of changes in cultural and institutional patterns. I will argue here that early twentieth-century changes in family strategies and gender relations set the institutional "stage" for the post–World War II rise in single motherhood among the poor, and that these changes interacted with employment discrimination, causing the structure of poor black families to change most.

The early twentieth century was a time of especially rapid transition between old and new family strategies. At the turn of the century, working-class families managed the chronic risk of poverty by combining paid employment with household production and participation in the informal sector. This strategy buffered them from the instability of wage labor, and allowed young children, married women, and the elderly to contribute more to the family economy. The importance of economic exchange among family members powerfully shaped the way they saw their relationships to one another. But this family strategy, and the relationships based on it, became more precarious over time. The separation of home and work had strained gender relations by rendering women's household work both less vital and less visible, and during the late nineteenth and early twentieth centuries the increasing regimentation of industrial work caused further strain. Men were caught between family responsibilities and new and oppressive conditions of work; resentments spilled over from their working lives into their family relations, accentuating the tension between their own wants and those of their families. The mechanization of housework and the declining demand for domestic servants eroded the ways married women had traditionally contributed to the family economy. Women and children became more dependent on men, and less able to buffer the family against unemployment.

It was at this point that working-class family strategies began to be remade. Some families could live on a male breadwinner's pay, and made little or no adjustment in the family economy; for many of them, the tensions caused by women's growing economic dependence did not surface until decades later.

---

[2] Gutman's landmark work showed that in the postbellum South and in Northern cities after the turn of the century, most black families were headed by married couples; see Herbert G. Gutman, *The Black Family in Slavery and Freedom, 1750–1925* (New York: Vintage Books, 1976). His rich study is cited most often for this statistical evidence, which has led most to reject earlier interpretations such as E. Franklin Frazier's *The Negro Family in the United States* (Chicago: University of Chicago Press, 1939). The literature on the postwar rise in the proportion of female-headed families, beginning with the Moynihan report, is another example of the focus on timing of demographic trends; e.g., see Charles Murray, *Losing Ground: American Social Policy, 1950–1980* (New York: Basic Books, 1984). For other perspectives see Wilson, *The Truly Disadvantaged*; Maris A. Vinovskis, "Teenage Pregnancy and the Underclass," *Public Interest* 93 (1988): 87–96.

Other working-class wives entered the labor force, substituting wage work for the contributions that women and children used to make through household production. But the poorest white women, schooled only in domesticity and perhaps possessing limited English skills, had trouble finding work. And black women, excluded from most factory and clerical work, became even more marginalized as the demand for domestic service declined. Poor women's diminishing economic power undermined the traditional bases of working-class marital ties.

To provide for themselves and their children, poor women took advantage of expanding legal rights and welfare programs, which often discouraged work and reinforced their economic marginality. In the 1920s and 1930s, these women began to create and institutionalize what we might now call an "underclass" family pattern. A response to the weakening of marital ties, this family pattern was characterized by strong ties between mothers and children, and was sustained financially by kin networks, by women's intermittent and informal work, and by charity or public aid. Although these women and their families represented a minority of the urban poor, they established social precedents that contributed to the rise in single motherhood after 1940.

This chapter traces these changes in the family strategies of the urban poor between 1900 and 1940. It draws from the secondary literature as well as from primary documents and census data.[3] The first section discusses working-class family strategies at the turn of the century, and focuses on the role of household production in the family economy. The second describes evidence for a decline in household production between 1900 and 1940. The third section, which is the most speculative, considers the impact of men's working conditions and the mechanization of household work on gender relations.

The broad scope of this chapter imposes some costs. The urban poor were composed of many ethnic and racial groups, and the distinctive elements of their histories will not be detailed. Instead, I seek here to bring together common elements of their disparate experiences, and indeed to argue that there were many similarities in the economic strategies and family relations of diverse groups, particularly those of the white ethnic working class. The exception to this rule will be the discussion of African-American families. Although black families shared many aspects of the white working-class family economy, the distinctive economic pressures they faced led their family strategies to diverge from those of whites in ways that will receive special attention here.[4]

[3] The census data are from the public use samples of the Census of the Population for 1910 and 1940. The samples used for this chapter include only residents of non-Southern cities of 50,000 or larger. The data were provided by ICPSR at the University of Michigan.

[4] On white and black female-headed families, see Frank F. Furstenberg, Jr., Theodore Hershberg, and John Modell, "The Origins of the Female-Headed Black Family: The Impact of the Urban Experience," in *Philadelphia: Work, Space, Family, and Group Experience in the Nineteenth Century*, ed. Theodore Hershberg (New York: Oxford University Press, 1981), 441; and Andrew T. Miller, "Social Science, Social Policy, and the Heritage of African-American Families," this volume.

The Working-Class Family Economy around 1900

The family economy of the urban working class developed in the context of nineteenth-century industrialization. Working-class families lived with the chronic risk of poverty because of the instability of economic life and the prevalence of illness, injury, and death. For instance, a 1901 study of industrial workers found that half of all household heads were out of work at some time during the year; the average time out of work was more than two months. The problems of manual workers grew worse as they grew older; weakened and perhaps crippled by years of heavy work, they were often turned away by employers. With little institutional protection against unemployment, illness, or death, working-class families were vulnerable to financial disaster.[5]

But even as they were drawn into wage labor markets, both rural and urban families continued to engage in household production. The institutions of capitalism and the technology of industrial production developed slowly and unevenly. During this time, wage labor coexisted with a large, informal sector of barter and odd jobs. Even as factories took over functions that had been performed at home, they generated opportunities for informal and household work: home finishing factory-made products, boarding and lodging workers, and scavenging for cast-off items. Combined with more traditional kinds of household production, these activities supplemented wages and helped to sustain families. This combination of wage labor and household production remained a durable feature of working-class life into the twentieth century.[6]

A full accounting of the value of household production begins with the mundane tasks of cooking, marketing, cleaning, and child care. Turn-of-the-century working-class families could not afford mechanical conveniences or hired help, and housewives substituted their own labor-intensive domesticity. Most working-class families, for instance, had no icebox, let alone refrigerator;

[5] The study of industrial workers is reported in Department of Labor, Bureau of Labor Statistics, "Cost of Living and Retail Prices in the United States," *Bulletin*, no. 54 (1904): 1129–40. On seasonal work and unemployment, see Alexander Keyssar, *Out of Work: The First Century of Unemployment in Massachusetts* (New York: Cambridge University Press, 1986); on aging workers, see Roger L. Ransom and Richard Sutch, "The Labor of Older Americans: Retirement of Men on and off the Job, 1870–1937," *Journal of Economic History* 46 (1986): 1–30.

[6] Working-class family strategies were the urban analogue of the rural family strategy of "foraging," described by Jacqueline Jones, "Southern Diaspora: Origins of the Northern 'Underclass,'" this volume. For other discussion of rural wage earners and their families, see Ewa Morawska, *For Bread with Butter: Life-Worlds of East Central Europeans in Johnstown, Pennsylvania, 1890–1940* (New York: Cambridge University Press, 1985), 25–39; Virginia Yans-McLaughlin, *Family and Community: Italian Immigrants in Buffalo, 1880–1930*, 2d ed. (Chicago: University of Illinois Press, 1982), 26; James R. Grossman, *Land of Hope: Chicago, Black Southerners, and the Great Migration* (Chicago: University of Chicago Press), 30–31. For general discussion of the urban family economy, see Morawska, *For Bread with Butter*; Tamara Hareven, *Family Time and Industrial Time: The Relationship between Family and Work in a New England Industrial Community* (New York: Cambridge University Press, 1982).

working-class housewives went almost daily to the neighborhood butcher, baker, grocer, and perhaps dairy for perishable foods. Most could not afford apartments with running water; instead, women hauled water from pumps in tenement courtyards or down the street. Coal was carried from store to apartment, and garbage from apartment to alley. The weekly laundry meant a laborious process of soaking, scrubbing, wringing, rinsing, starching, drying, and ironing clothes, often spread over several days. Most cooking was fairly simple but generally involved preparation of raw ingredients: meat, potatoes, and vegetables boiled together to make the soups and stews that were the staple of the working-class diet. Supplies from poor relief also required time-consuming preparation; poor families in Chicago, for instance, received flour, lard, rice, and split peas.[7]

In addition, many married women combined housework with informal ways of earning money, such as cooking and cleaning for boarders, taking in laundry, and doing "home work." In 1910, about one of six nonworking wives took in boarders. Others did home work such as sewing, embroidering, flower making, and tag tying. Home work was not consistently counted by census takers, but evidence suggests that it was fairly common in some districts of New York and in other cities as well. Specific kinds of informal work were associated with certain ethnic groups: home sewing and flower making with Italian women; laundry work with black women; boarding and lodging with recent immigrants and migrants of any origin. Opportunity for informal economic activities was often mediated by ethnic-based networks.[8]

Housewives in small towns and cities also cultivated gardens and sometimes kept poultry or livestock. In Johnstown, Pennsylvania, for instance, the families

[7] For descriptions of housework in the nineteenth and early twentieth centuries, see, e.g., Ruth Schwartz Cowan, *More Work for Mother: The Ironies of Household Technology from the Open Hearth to the Microwave* (New York: Basic Books, 1983), 160–70; Christine Stansell, *City of Women: Sex and Class in New York, 1789–1860* (New York: Alfred A. Knopf, 1986), 46–52; Elizabeth Ewen, *Immigrant Women in the Land of Dollars: Life and Culture on the Lower East Side, 1890–1925* (New York: Monthly Review Press, 1985), 149–56; Robert A. Slayton, *Back of the Yards: The Making of a Local Democracy* (Chicago: University of Chicago Press, 1986), 67–78. On access to running water and other city services, see Susan Kleinberg, "Technology and Women's Work: The Lives of Working-Class Women in Pittsburgh, 1870–1900," *Labor History* 17 (1976): 62–63. On relief supplies in Chicago, see, e.g., Cook County, Illinois, Board of Commissioners, *Charity Service Reports* (Cook County, Illinois, 1916), 47.

[8] On boarders: author's tabulations from the 1910 census. There were about 21,000 registered home workers in New York City in 1900, and 11,500 in 1927; Thomas Kessner, *The Golden Door: Italian and Jewish Immigrant Mobility in New York City, 1880–1915* (New York: Oxford University Press, 1977), 72–75; Emily C. Brown, "Industrial Home Work," Department of Labor, Women's Bureau, *Bulletin*, no. 79 (1930): 2. Assuming one home worker per household, an average household size of five, and home workers only among the families of manual (not skilled or white-collar) workers, then about 9.2 percent of working-class households in New York included a registered home worker in 1900, and about 2.5 percent in 1927. On ethnic networks in home work, see Kessner, *The Golden Door*, 72–75.

of industrial workers rented plots of land on the edge of town, growing beets, cabbage, potatoes, and other crops and raising animals. Some even kept chickens and geese inside the city limits. A Bureau of Labor Statistics (BLS) survey conducted in 1917–19 suggests Johnstown's families were not unusual: 44 percent of urban working-class families reported earning some money during the year from their gardens or animals. Producing food was especially useful because working-class families typically spent almost half of their incomes on groceries. In large crowded cities like New York, gardens were much less common; in the 1917–19 survey, only 3 percent of New York families reported income from gardens or animals, compared to 76 percent in Johnstown.[9]

When children were still fairly young, they too began to take part in household production and the local informal economy. Children participated in a wide range of activities; contemporary sources mention children helping their mothers with home work, tending vegetable gardens, peddling flowers, newspapers, candy, or homemade items, caddying at country clubs, organ-grinding, "junking," collecting coal from railroad tracks, running errands, selling scrap metal or wood, begging, and even stealing from markets or delivery trucks. Girls minded their younger siblings, freeing their mothers for more strenuous household tasks. If there was a family business, children helped out.[10]

The activities women and children pursued at home or in the local informal economy were of considerable economic value. In 1910, when workingmen's wages averaged $10 to $15 a week, women might net more than $1 a week for each boarder. In Johnstown, Pennsylvania, it is estimated, immigrant housewives who took in boarders and produced some of their own food earned or saved almost as much income as their husbands earned in the steel mills. And housework itself must be included in the value of women's work at home. There were alternatives to this domestic work; families could eat in restaurants or taverns, employ servants, buy labor-saving devices, or live in boardinghouses. But for most working-class families, these substitutes for a married woman's labor would cost more than women could earn in the labor market.[11]

[9] Morawska, For Bread with Butter, 134–35. For other references to gardens and animals, see Slayton, Back of the Yards, 68; Hareven, Family Time and Industrial Time, 204–5. Figures on income from gardens and animals are from Department of Labor, Bureau of Labor Statistics, "Cost of Living in the United States," Bulletin, no. 357 (1924): 91, 97, 107; the survey sampled urban wage earners and low-income salaried workers.

[10] For descriptions of children's informal activities, see, e.g., Stansell, City of Women, 203–7; David Nasaw, Children of the City, at Work and at Play (Garden City, N.Y.: Anchor Press/Doubleday, 1985), 48–61, 88–113; Gertrude Howe Britton, An Intensive Study of the Causes of Truancy in Eight Public Schools (Chicago: Hollister, 1906), 7, 31; Leila Houghteling, The Income and Standard of Living of Unskilled Laborers in Chicago (Chicago: University of Chicago Press, 1927), 40.

[11] In larger cities around 1910, net earnings from boarders probably exceeded $1 per boarder per week. Morawska, For Bread with Butter, 130, 135, estimates $4–5 per month; Margaret Byington, Homestead: The Households of a Mill Town (1910; reprint, Pittsburgh: University Center for International Studies, 1974), 140, reports $3 per month for impoverished Slavic workers in a small

Relatively few married women supplemented household production with wage work. Even among working-class wives without children at home, only 18 percent worked outside the home in 1910. Having children further limited their employment; the proportion working outside the home fell to 4 percent among mothers with young children, and 8 percent among mothers with older children only (see table 6.1). Married women often held domestic- and personal-service positions. Although service work was physically exhausting, it was easier than other occupations to combine with household responsibilities: laundresses and domestics could work part-time, and charwomen often worked at night. But combining housework and regular employment came at a high cost in terms of women's well-being. It was most common among the most impoverished women, those whose husbands were out of work or ill.[12]

Ethnic differences in wives' employment were small, with one exception: although African-American women faced considerable discrimination in employment, they were much more likely than white women to be employed. Their smaller families made working more feasible for black women, and their husbands' low wages meant a greater need for income, but these family characteristics do not fully account for their higher rates of employment. Black families faced relatively high housing costs, which may have made household production less feasible and spurred wives to seek other ways of contributing to the family. Black families may also have adapted family strategies to accommodate mothers' work in the South, where poverty and sometimes pressure from local whites impelled many married black women to work. Whatever the reason, about a third of urban black wives were employed, in addition to those earning money by taking in boarders, as table 6.1 shows.[13]

---

town. Claudia Goldin, *Understanding the Gender Gap: An Economic History of American Women* (New York: Oxford University Press, 1990), 223, estimates average annual net income per boarder as $70 in 1890–91. On the value of household production, see also Joan Jensen, "Cloth, Butter and Boarders: Women's Household Production for the Market," *Review of Radical Political Economics* 12 (Summer 1980): 14–24. James R. Barrett, *Work and Community in the Jungle: Chicago's Packinghouse Workers, 1894–1922* (Chicago: University of Illinois Press, 1987), 97, argues that it was not economically advantageous for married women to work. A few simple calculations support his conclusion. In 1910, a family of five in which the mother worked would probably have paid an additional $2.50 per week to board in another household; women's wages averaged about $6.00 per week. If a similar family maintained its own household and took in three boarders (average for the stockyards district that Barrett studied), the mother would earn about $3.00 per week. The family with the working mother would come out ahead only if the housewife's other contributions to the household, including child care, were valued at less than $0.50 a week. For figures on rent and women's wages, see J. C. Kennedy et al., *Wages and Family Budgets in the Chicago Stockyards District* (Chicago: University of Chicago Press, 1914), 12, 40, 68–69.

[12] For determinants of women's work, see Christine E. Bose, "Household Resources and U.S. Women's Work: Factors Affecting Gainful Employment at the Turn of the Century," *American Sociological Review* 49 (1984): 474–90. See Houghteling, *Income and Standard of Living*, 58–59, for an assessment of the physical labor in housework compared to manufacturing.

[13] Bose, "Household Resources and Women's Work," controls for demographic and economic factors and finds that only two ethnic variables (French-Canadian and black) remain significant in

TABLE 6.1
Percentage of Working-class Wives Employed or with Boarders, by Race, Nativity, and Presence and Age of Children, 1910

	No Children	Age of Youngest Child	
		0–6	7+
Employed or with boarders	34.3	22.3	22.7
Manufacturing	6.8	2.2	3.0
Service	9.8	1.7	4.3
All other occupations	0.9	0.5	1.1
Boarders only	16.8	17.9	14.3
Employed	17.5	4.4	8.4
Native white	9.8	3.3	6.2
Black	38.8	23.2	31.1
Foreign-born white	17.2	4.1	7.7
Employed or with boarders	34.3	22.3	22.7
Native white	21.3	11.3	19.8
Black	52.8	40.6	54.1
Foreign-born white	40.7	28.1	21.6

Source: 1910 Census, public use sample. Includes women ages 18–54 married to manual workers in non-Southern cities over 50,000 population.

Note: The "boarders only" category includes women who listed hotel keeper or boardinghouse keeper as their occupation and those with no occupation who were heads or wives of heads in households containing at least one boarder. Wage earners out of work at census time were classified as not working.

Better opportunities tended to draw more married women into the labor force. The textile mill towns of New England employed many unskilled women workers, and part-time shifts and the proximity of the mills to company housing made it easier for women to combine work with housekeeping. In these towns, married women were more likely than they were elsewhere to work outside the home, and families adapted to mothers' work; children might be boarded out or sent to stay with relatives, and some husbands even helped with domestic chores. These adaptations suggest that working-class families were pragmatic, responding to opportunity rather than rigidly bound by traditional gender roles. But even in textile towns, most wives elected not to work; although jobs

an analysis of married women's labor force participation; see also Elizabeth H. Pleck, "A Mother's Wages: Income Earning Among Married Italian and Black Women, 1896–1911," in *The American Family in Social-Historical Perspective*, ed. Michael Gordon (New York: St. Martin's Press, 1978); Claudia Goldin, "Female Labor Force Participation: The Origin of Black and White Differences, 1870 and 1880," *Journal of Economic History* 37 (1977): 87–108; on the determinants of black women's work, see Claudia Goldin, "Family Strategies and the Family Economy in the Late Nineteenth Century: The Role of Secondary Workers," in Hershberg, *Philadelphia*, 303.

were abundant, the wages they could earn were not a sufficient inducement for women to substitute paid employment for household production.[14]

Instead, in textile towns as elsewhere, children were the main secondary earners. When working-class children became old enough to work legally, most left school promptly. Adolescent children generally contributed their earnings to the family fund, although they often kept or were given some spending money. The family economy mediated children's transition from school to work; first or second children left school at relatively early ages, while their younger siblings were under less financial pressure to go to work. Boys were more likely than girls to work: sons' earnings from employment clearly exceeded what they could contribute though informal activities. Daughters, on the other hand, earned lower wages and had been trained in domestic skills; more often than sons they remained at home to help with housework.[15]

But children did not begin to work until late in the family "life cycle." For the first ten to fifteen years of family life, children were too young for regular employment, and most young working-class families had only one wage earner. During this time, responses to unemployment were limited; in 1910, for example, 72 percent of working-class husbands out of work had neither wife nor child employed. Some parents sought to hasten the time when their children could work, forging or buying papers for their underage sons and daughters. But over the first few decades of the twentieth century, compulsory school and child-labor regulations were tightened, reducing the financial contribution that young adolescents could make to their families. Until children were old enough to work for wages, household production and informal work were the primary buffer against economic instability.[16]

The social and institutional context of working-class communities helped to protect families against short-term financial need. The patterns of mutual aid that existed between parents and children were also manifest between urban families and their neighbors and more distant kin. Relatives of poor families were often poor themselves and could not provide much material assistance, but it was common for them to make small loans, take in children, or help with locating jobs and housing. Friends and neighbors also lent small sums of money and passed on information about jobs. In a 1924 survey, as many as half of the working-class families had received gifts from friends, relatives, or employers during the previous year; most of these were gifts of clothing for women or children, although gifts of money were reported as well. Relations of mutual aid were formalized in the ethnic fraternal societies. Usually organized among

[14] Hareven, *Family Time and Industrial Time*, 202–7.

[15] Goldin, "Family Strategies and the Family Economy," 290–96; on older and younger children, see also David L. Angus and Jeffrey E. Mirel, "From Spellers to Spindles: Work-Force Entry by the Children of Textile Workers, 1888–1890," *Social Science History* 9 (1985): 123–43. Bose, "Household Resources and Women's Work," provides evidence on the determinants of daughters' work.

[16] Tabulations from 1910 census.

people from the same village or region, the fraternals offered life insurance and sickness benefits. Most wage earners had some form of insurance, much of which was provided through these fraternal societies. Ethnic communities also sponsored other kinds of assistance, such as charitable societies, hospitals, nurseries, and other services.[17]

Women took an active role, perhaps more than men did, in visiting and helping relatives. Their participation in these exchange relations secured for them a claim on others' resources when they themselves were in need. Gender differences in participation in kin networks continued throughout the life course. Elderly women tended to live with relatives, while elderly men were more likely to live alone, as boarders, in almshouses, or on the street.[18]

As important as both informal and formal mutual aid was to daily survival, it was limited by the resources of family and neighborhood. The residential mobility of working-class populations cut people off from many of their kin, and high mortality reduced the number of elderly dependents. In fact, nineteenth-century working-class families were less likely than middle- and upper-class families to be extended; it was not until later that family extension became associated with poverty.[19] In addition, both kin and community assistance were suited to relieve short-term problems rather than chronic poverty. Most families were unable or unwilling to assist indigent relatives over a long period of time. Likewise, merchants and landlords would eventually cut off credit, fraternal society benefits would end, and neighbors' resources or patience would be exhausted. Public relief was also inadequate to address much long-term poverty.

[17] Anecdotal evidence of kin support is widespread. For more unusual survey evidence, see Houghteling, *Income and Standard of Living*, 67. On assistance from neighbors, see Ewen, *Immigrant Women in the Land of Dollars*, 118–19; Lizabeth Cohen, *Making a New Deal: Industrial Workers in Chicago, 1919–1939* (New York: Cambridge University Press, 1990), 56–58; Jacqueline Jones, *Labor of Love, Labor of Sorrow: Black Women, Work, and the Family from Slavery to the Present* (New York: Basic Books, 1985), 228–29. On fraternal societies, Cohen, *Making a New Deal*, 58–70; Joe William Trotter, Jr., "Blacks in the Urban North: The 'Underclass Question' in Historical Perspective," this volume.

[18] Earl Lewis, "Afro-American Adaptive Strategies: The Visiting Habits of Kith and Kin among Black Norfolkians during the Great Migration," *Journal of Family History* 12 (1987): 407–20; Laura Anker, "Women, Work and Family: Polish, Italian and Eastern European Immigrants in Industrial Connecticut, 1890–1940," *Polish American Studies* 45 (1988): 23–50; Hareven, *Family Time and Industrial Time*, 105–7. For evidence that older women were more likely to live with kin (other than their husbands), see Daniel Scott Smith, "Life Course, Norms, and the Family System of Older Americans in 1900," *Journal of Family History* 4 (1979): 285–98; N. Sue Weiler, "Family Security or Social Security? The Family and the Elderly in New York State during the 1920s," *Journal of Family History* 11 (1986): 77–95. On homelessness and gender, see, e.g., Peter H. Rossi, *Down and Out in America: The Origins of Homelessness* (Chicago: University of Chicago Press, 1989), 21.

[19] On household extension, see Steven Ruggles, *Prolonged Connections: The Rise of the Extended Family in Nineteenth-Century England and America* (Madison: University of Wisconsin Press, 1987), 33–39. Likewise, there is evidence that the amount of financial aid given to relatives was positively associated with income; Department of Labor, Bureau of Labor Statistics, "Money Disbursements of Wage Earners and Clerical Workers, 1934–36, Summary Volume," *Bulletin*, no. 638 (1941): 12.

During the late nineteenth century, states began restricting able-bodied men from the use of poorhouses and outdoor relief and separating family members who entered the poorhouse together. In the interval between the restriction of poorhouse aid and the introduction of unemployment insurance beginning (at the state level) in 1932, other means of coping with unemployment became even more important.[20]

When a family exhausted these resources of kin and community, its status could spiral downward rapidly. Poorer families were less able to benefit from economies of scale. Their more affluent counterparts bought food in bulk; short of cash and unable to keep perishables cold, the poor bought their food and fuel in tiny increments, a practice that cost them 7 percent of their income, the BLS estimated in a 1906 study. Household production was limited; for instance, families in the BLS study did not bake bread because they could not afford fuel or proper ovens for cooking. Living in cheap housing increased the time families spent providing for basic needs: of the nineteen families studied, only one had running water, and six brought their water from a distance. When their last few possessions had been sold or pawned, the poor went to lenders specializing in high-risk loans; the most desperate borrowed at annual interest rates of 70 or 80 percent.[21]

At worst, the household itself might be disbanded when furniture was repossessed and the family evicted. If outdoor relief was unavailable, a destitute family had little choice but to disperse, entering the poorhouse or placing children in orphanages or with relatives. This process resembled rural proletarianization, when poor families lost their bit of land and equipment and dispersed to became transient laborers or domestic servants. In the cities as well, the very poor had only a tenuous grasp on a household of their own.[22]

This threat of losing the household gave force to the reciprocal exchange on which working-class families were based: only through cooperation could the family keep itself from the brink of destitution. Economic interdependence derived from and powerfully shaped the relations of the household members to one another. To a large extent, families functioned as economic units, with the fruits of both wage work and household production belonging not to the individual but to the family. Small deviations might be countenanced; wage-earning family members, for instance, usually kept a little money for their own

[20] For evidence of family members limiting aid, see Hareven, *Family Time and Industrial Time,* 110–12. On poorhouses and outdoor relief, see Michael B. Katz, *In the Shadow of the Poorhouse, A Social History of Welfare in America* (New York: Basic Books, 1986), 41, 92–93.

[21] For the cited study of poor families, including interest rates for loans, see Department of Labor, Bureau of Labor Statistics, "Conditions of Living among the Poor," *Bulletin,* no. 64 (1906): 598–608, 620, 622–28; on buying in bulk, see also Sadie T. Mossell, "The Condition of Living among One Hundred Negro Migrant Families in Philadelphia," *American Academy of Political and Social Science Annals* 98 (November 1921): 188–89.

[22] On the disintegration of poor households, see Michael B. Katz, *Poverty and Policy in American History* (New York: Academic Press, 1983), 18–40.

use. But larger disloyalties were deeply felt, and severely sanctioned. In the recollections of working-class children, the values of unity, loyalty, and hard work were paramount in their family lives.[23]

THE DECLINE IN HOUSEHOLD PRODUCTION, 1900–1940

Eighteenth-century New York City provided many opportunities for women to participate in economic activity. Learning their husbands' trade and perhaps even inheriting their husbands' shops, some wives and widows engaged in shipping, craft production, or other pursuits. In addition, most households had yards with vegetable gardens and fruit trees, fenced to keep out the hogs that roamed the streets; such conditions indicate a substantial role for household production, and thus for housewives, in the family economy. But women's grasp on property and economic opportunities weakened during the latter half of the eighteenth century. The growing class of laborers had neither property nor trade for their wives to assist with. The poorly equipped tenements that soon crowded the city made the production of food and the performance of other household duties more difficult.[24]

Similar transitions took place later in other American cities. Household production had been declining in importance for a century as factory production became more efficient, and as the work still done in the household was mechanized. Claudia Goldin estimates that married women's paid work declined during the nineteenth century, reaching a low point around 1910 or 1920. Then, in the 1920s and 1930s, rising wages and falling prices brought more conveniences within reach of the working class as well as the middle class; changes in the technology of housework and the production of food and other commodities began to replace the housewife's labor with commercially available products and services. Of course, these developments meant an improvement in the standard of living. But they also meant painful adjustments in women's roles: women's domestic labor and skills were less in demand both at home and in the labor market. No longer could wives make such substantial contributions to the household through their activities at home, or through domestic work in other households. The working-class family economy had to be remade.[25]

[23] The practice of pooling wages, with the housewife managing the family budget, was widespread if not universal among working-class families around the turn of the century. For discussions of parent-child relations and financial transactions, see Hareven, *Family Time and Industrial Time*, 214–16; John Bodnar, *The Transplanted: A History of Immigrants in Urban America* (Bloomington: Indiana University Press, 1985), 72–74; Nasaw, *Children of the City*, 130–37; Peter Gottlieb, *Making Their Own Way: Southern Blacks' Migration to Pittsburgh, 1916–1930* (Chicago: University of Illinois Press, 1987), 26–27.

[24] Elizabeth Blackmar, *Manhattan for Rent, 1785–1850* (Ithaca: Cornell University Press, 1989), 48, 54.

[25] Goldin, *The Gender Gap*, 42, 46–50. The phrase "decline in household production" is somewhat imprecise. It will refer here to two developments. First, increasing numbers of commodities

Changes were evident in many aspects of women's lives. The first three decades of the twentieth century brought running water and electricity and/or gas to most urban working-class families. Rising incomes paid for sinks, bathtubs, electric irons, and other appliances that began to appear in working-class homes. A survey conducted in Pittsburgh in 1934 found that even in the poorest districts of the city, 98 percent of the dwellings had running water (only half had hot water), 91 percent had electricity or gas for lighting, 75 percent had indoor water closets, and 54 percent had a shower or bathtub. This study and others indicate that working-class families of the 1930s had increasing access to utilities and appliances that made housework easier.[26]

Commercially prepared foods also became more practical on a working-class budget. The price of food fell during the 1920s and 1930s, and families diversified their diets and bought more canned and cooked foods. Women's preparation of food can be indexed by the kinds of food their families bought. Table 6.2 shows the average quantities of different types of food purchased in a year by urban families surveyed in 1901, 1917–19, and 1934–36. Consumption of flour, potatoes, and lard declined, while consumption of most canned and baked goods increased.[27]

At the same time, smaller families reduced mothers' child-care responsibilities. Continuing the long-term demographic transition of the nineteenth century, fertility fell by almost a third between 1900 and 1940; middle-class families began to limit family size first, but the working class followed in the

---

were made more cheaply in factories than in households. Second, mechanization of tasks still done in the household allowed housework to be done with less labor; thus household labor became more productive but in most cases not productive enough to compete with factory production.

[26] Philip Klein, *A Social Study of Pittsburgh: Community Problems and Social Services of Allegheny County* (New York: Columbia University Press, 1938), 206. In a 1923 survey of Chicago wage earners' homes, an estimated half had private toilets within the homes; the vast majority heated their houses with stoves; Franc Lewis McCluer, "Living Conditions among Wage Earning Families in Forty-One Blocks in Chicago (1923)" (Ph.D. diss., University of Chicago, 1928), 58, 71. The 1934–36 survey of urban wage earners and clerical workers reported household facilities for the poorest 35 percent of the families surveyed: 72.1 percent had hot running water; 96.1 percent had electric lights; 80.3 percent had gas or electricity for cooking; 55.8 percent had furnace heat; and 12.0 percent had electrical or mechanical refrigerators. See Bureau of Labor Statistics, "Money Disbursements, 1934–36," 242–43. This survey excluded families on relief and those with low earnings or long-term unemployment.

[27] The samples for the three BLS cost-of-living surveys were similar. All three were drawn from rosters of employees in urban firms throughout the United States. The 1901 survey included wage workers and salaried workers earning less than $1,200. The 1917–19 survey included wage workers and salaried workers earning less than $2,000 a year. The 1934–36 survey included wage workers and clerical workers earning less than $2,000 a year. The BLS excluded the poorest families from the survey. The 1917–19 survey excluded "slum families" and those who had lived in the community less than a year or in the United States fewer than five years; the 1934–36 survey exluded families on relief, those with incomes below $500, and those with no earners employed at least thirty-six weeks and earning at least $300.

TABLE 6.2

Annual Average Quantities of Food Purchased by Urban Families Surveyed in 1901, 1917–1919, and 1934–1936 (in Pounds)

	1901	1917–19	1934–36
Flour and meal	460.9	374.1	161.3
Bread	171.1	435.2	363.8
Lard/shortening	57.1	59.8	38.7
Potatoes	597.1	709.2	428.4
Pies	—	4.0	8.7
Canned peas	—	9.7	19.6
Canned tomatoes	—	15.2	39.0
Canned soup	—	4.8	15.6
Cooked ham	—	7.4	5.6

Sources: Bureau of Labor Statistics, "Cost of Living and Retail Prices," Bulletin, no. 54 (Washington, 1904), 1162; Bureau of Labor Statistics, "Cost of Living in the United States," Bulletin, no. 357 (Washington, 1924), 118–19; Bureau of Labor Statistics, "Money Disbursements of Wage Earners and Clerical Workers, 1934–36, Summary Volume," Bulletin, no. 638 (Washington, 1941), 236–38.

Note: For 1901, loaves of bread were converted to pounds at a ratio of 1 : 1, and bushels of potatoes were converted to pounds at a ratio of 60 : 1. The figures are adjusted for changing family size, and reflect the consumption of families with 3.32 "equivalent adult males," the average among families surveyed in 1917–19. On the survey samples, see n. 27.

early years of the twentieth century. Family limitation became more attractive as education became a more important strategy of economic advancement, and there is some evidence that the decline in fertility, which continued throughout the late nineteenth and early twentieth centuries, is related to increasing investment in schooling.[28]

As housework became less onerous, the demand for boarding and lodging services declined. With the rise of commercial services in the late nineteenth century, lodgers began to replace the more labor-intensive boarders (who paid for food as well as a place to stay). During the early twentieth century, rising incomes and the mechanization of housework made it even more feasible for

[28] On the decline in fertility, see Stanley L. Engerman, "Black Fertility and Family Structure in the U.S., 1880–1940," Journal of Family History 1–2 (1977): 117–38; on class differences in the timing of fertility decline, see Mark J. Stern, Society and Family Strategies: Erie County, New York, 1850–1920 (Albany: State University of New York Press, 1987), 52. For evidence that fertility decline is linked to education, see, e.g., Stern, Society and Family Strategies, 109–12; Avery M. Guest and Stewart Tolnay, "Urban Industrial Structure and Fertility: The Case of Large American Cities," Journal of Interdisciplinary History 13 (1983): 387–409.

single persons to maintain their own households. In addition, the cutoff of immigration in the 1920s reduced the population of young, single men who typically sought to board with other families. Increasingly during the 1920s, boardinghouse keepers advertised in vain. Between 1910 and 1940, the proportion of working-class wives taking in boarders fell from about 16 percent to 5 percent.[29]

The mechanization of housework also reduced the demand for servants. Private laundry work, traditionally a mainstay of married black women, was almost eliminated: in New York, the number of laundresses fell from 22,983 in 1910 to 1,669 in 1940. The number of "servants" rose slightly but did not keep pace with New York's growing population, and a large and probably increasing proportion worked not in private households but in hotels and other businesses. Declining demand was reflected in domestics' wages, which had formerly been competitive with the wages of factory workers; by 1940 this was no longer the case. It was also reflected in higher unemployment rates for servants, who formerly had been protected from the business cycle. This shift in the demand for servants was dramatized by the change from the much lamented shortage of servants to the appearance of the "slave markets" of the 1930s, where women gathered on street corners seeking day's work at sharply reduced wages.[30]

Children's opportunities for formal and informal work also diminished, leaving families more dependent on adult male workers. Child workers were displaced by technological and institutional innovations such as telephones, pneumatic tubes, and changes in newspaper distribution. In addition, compulsory school regulations were tightened, and many states raised school-leaving ages during the Depression. During the 1930s, the National Recovery

[29] For documentation of the late-nineteenth-century shift from boarding to lodging, see Mark Peel, "On the Margins: Lodgers and Boarders in Boston, 1860–1900," *Journal of American History* 72 (1986): 813–34. Demand for boarding and lodging services fell with the reduction in immigration during World War I and in the 1920s. Joanne J. Meyerowitz, *Women Adrift: Independent Wage Earners in Chicago, 1880–1930* (Chicago: University of Chicago Press, 1988), 75–76, describes the 1920s decline in demand for boarding, and the concurrent rise in popularity of studio apartments, furnished rooms, and "light housekeeping rooms."

[30] On the decline in demand for servants, see George J. Stigler, "Domestic Servants in the United States, 1900–1940," National Bureau of Economic Research Occasional Paper No. 24 (New York: NBER, 1946); Cowan, *More Work for Mother*, 99; Jones, *Labor of Love, Labor of Sorrow*, 206–7; Amy Hewes, "Electrical Applicances in the Home," *Social Forces* 2 (1930): 235–42. Bureau of the Census, *Thirteenth Census of the United States: 1910*, vol. 4 (Washington, D.C., 1914), 192; Bureau of the Census, *Sixteenth Census of the United States: 1940*, vol. 3, pt. 4 (Washington, D.C., 1943), 371. David M. Katzman, *Seven Days a Week: Women and Domestic Service in Industrializing America* (1978; reprint, Chicago: University of Illinois Press, 1981), 311, concludes that domestic servants' annual earnings were competitive with earnings of other unskilled workers around the turn of the century. Stigler, "Domestic Servants," 12–13, estimates that domestic servants' wages declined relative to manufacturing workers' wages between 1900 and 1940. The "slave markets" are described in Jones, *Labor of Love, Labor of Sorrow*, 205.

Administration codes and some states raised the minimum age of employment to sixteen. The relative importance of these factors is unclear, but their combined effect was dramatic: the proportion of working teenagers (ages fourteen to seventeen) declined from 42 percent in 1910 to 6 percent in 1940.[31]

The Great Depression tested these new changes in the family economy. Unemployment pressed families to economize where they could and, if possible, to substitute their own labor for money they could not obtain. Critics of married women's employment advocated a return to home production for married women, arguing that they would better serve their families by saving money at home and leaving the jobs for men. One observer wrote that immigrant women were beginning to bake their own bread again. Some urban women did try to return to home production during the Depression, doing laundry for pay or peddling home-baked goods, but most of these enterprises brought little profit and were soon abandoned. Although some women may have canned more food or sewn their own clothes, there is no evidence of a widespread return to domesticity. Instead, despite social disapproval and employer discrimination, married women continued to move into the labor market.[32]

The impact of this decline in household production on the family economy depended on both men's and women's positions in the labor market. The early twentieth century was a time of increasing segmentation of working-class men, with some gaining more employment stability while others remained in poorly paid, unskilled jobs. The situation was particularly acute for black men, who were latecomers to the industrial economy, and were impeded by racial discrimination from moving out of unskilled labor into more secure and better-paying semiskilled and skilled positions. After the war, many black men lost their jobs; recessions during the 1920s further weakened their grasp on indus-

[31] Nasaw, *Children of the City*, 187–94; Paul Osterman, "Education and Labor Markets at the Turn of the Century," *Politics and Society* 9 (1979): 103–22; David Tyack, *The One Best System: A History of American Urban Education* (Cambridge: Harvard University Press, 1974), 183–84. Author's tabulations from the 1910 and 1940 census samples.

[32] Winifred D. Wandersee, *Women's Work and Family Values, 1920–1940* (Cambridge: Harvard University Press, 1981), 98–100; Ruth Shonle Cavan and Katherine Howland Ranck, *The Family and the Depression: A Study of 100 Chicago Families* (Chicago: University of Chicago Press, 1938), 82–83; Klein, *Social Study of Pittsburgh*, 243. See also Ewan Clague and Webster Powell, *Ten Thousand out of Work* (Philadelphia: University of Pennsylvania Press, 1933), 118–19; Winona Morgan, *The Family Meets the Depression: A Study of a Group of Highly Selected Families* (Minneapolis: University of Minnesota Press, 1939), 28–29. Cecile Tipton LaFollette, *A Study of the Problems of 652 Gainfully Employed Married Women Homemakers* (New York: Teachers College, 1934), argues for increased household production but provides little evidence. John Modell, *Into One's Own: From Youth to Adulthood in the United States, 1920–1975* (Berkeley: University of California Press, 1989), 122–28, shows that youth had low rates of employment during the Depression, and that poor and working-class youth were more likely than more affluent peers to be unemployed. Informal work such as baby-sitting may have been common, however; cf. Glen H. Elder, Jr., *Children of the Great Depression: Social Change in Life Experience* (Chicago: University of Chicago Press, 1974), 66.

trial employment, and the Depression brought intensified competition with white men even for the most menial and poorly paying jobs. Black and white unemployment rates diverged; at the 1940 census, 24 percent of black men in Northern cities were out of work, compared to 15 percent of white men.[33]

For working-class women, education became more important for finding employment. Working women had been drawn disproportionately from the less-educated segments of society, but by 1940 this relationship had reversed, with educated women spearheading the increase in women's labor-force participation. Employment of black and white working-class wives began to converge, as did employment of working-class and middle-class wives (see table 6.3). Growing opportunity in the white-collar sector spurred educated women to work, despite discrimination against married women in many clerical settings. At the same time, the decline of domestic service employment eliminated jobs for the least skilled women. Some of these women were too poor to substitute conveniences for their own household labor, and remained mired in labor-intensive domesticity.[34]

The changing structure of employment opportunities for men and women led to the emergence of new patterns in the working-class family economy. In families in which male employment provided a secure income, the decline in the value of household production did not threaten the economic status of the family. These relatively advantaged working-class families were better able to sustain themselves on a male breadwinner's pay; they also had educational and social resources that helped wives and children find employment. Among disadvantaged working-class families, however, male employment became less secure, and the decline in household production left a gap in the family budget that was less easily filled. And whether these wives worked or not, the decline of household production disrupted gender relations by upsetting accustomed patterns of exchange.

GENDER, WORK, AND MARITAL RELATIONS

In the domestic exchange of the working-class family, each member justified claims with contributions to the family economy. But men's and women's contributions were different in kind—men "paid" mostly in cash, women mostly in services—and the terms of this domestic exchange were negotiated by partners of unequal power. The larger economic context impinged further on these private negotiations. Resentful of the conditions of industrial work, and of the

---

[33] Thomas Sugrue, "The Structure of Urban Poverty: The Reorganization of Space and Work in Three Periods of American History," this volume; Trotter, "Blacks in the Urban North"; author's tabulations from the 1910 and 1940 census samples.

[34] Goldin, *The Gender Gap*, 135. On domestic practices among poor women, see Laura Friedman, "A Study of One Hundred Unemployed Families" (M.A. thesis, University of Chicago, 1933), 112, 149; Jones, *Labor of Love, Labor of Sorrow*, 223.

TABLE 6.3

Percentage of Wives Employed or with Boarders, by Husband's Occupation, Race, Nativity, and Presence and Age of Children, 1910 and 1940

	1910			1940		
	No Children	Youngest Child's Age		No Children	Youngest Child's Age	
		0–6	7+		0–6	7+
Wives of manual workers						
Employed	17.5	4.4	8.4	31.3	6.9	13.9
Native white	9.8	3.3	6.2	31.8	7.2	13.2
Black	38.8	23.2	31.1	32.7	6.0	21.9
Foreign-born white	17.2	4.1	7.7	27.6	5.8	13.8
Employed or with boarders	34.3	22.3	22.7	36.3	10.3	19.4
Native white	21.3	11.3	19.8	35.2	10.3	18.2
Black	52.8	40.6	54.1	44.2	13.3	30.0
Foreign-born white	40.7	28.1	21.6	33.6	9.3	19.1
Wives of skilled or white-collar workers						
Employed	7.6	2.7	4.3	30.0	4.8	10.5
Employed or with boarders	19.8	13.5	16.1	33.8	8.1	14.4

Source: 1910 and 1940 Census public use samples. Includes married women ages 18–54 in non-Southern cities with over 50,000 population.

family needs that tied them to their jobs, some men rebelled against both work and family by drinking, deserting, or refusing to work. And with the decline in household production, women's contributions to the family economy diminished; some women responded by seeking greater financial independence, remaking the family economy and sometimes the family itself.

The asymmetry of domestic exchange was manifest in disputes over the handling of money. Many men kept a portion of their wages for carfare, drinks, and recreation, and gave their wives the rest for household expenses; others turned over their entire pay but then asked or demanded a portion back. Although legally entitled to their husband's support, women had no claim on specific sums of money; by law, even money they earned by keeping boarders belonged not to them but to their husbands. Charity records indicate it was not unusual for women to receive half or even less of their husband's wages. Men often concealed the exact amount of their pay; the fact that they did so suggests that their contribution of wages to the household was governed by some norms, if ill-enforced.[35]

[35] Stansell, City of Women, 79–80, discusses the asymmetry of marital domestic exchange. On women's right to money and disputes over the allocation of husbands' wages, see Viviana Zelizer,

Absent from the household and unschooled in the practice of domesticity, men were reluctant to give up their money partly because they did not know how much their wives worked. Their own work was indexed directly by their pay; housewives' unpaid work was less easily gauged. "Though the men show in general a frank appreciation of home comforts, they do not always realize all the work behind them," observed Byington in her study of a Pennsylvania steel town; one wife said, "The only time 'the mister' notices anything about the house is when I wash the curtains." Because men could not measure housework by wages, they relied on other simple cues. Domestic disputes often began when men found their wives drinking or late with dinner preparations. Working men had begun to articulate a right to "eight hours for what we will," but housework was less easily delimited in time. Women's leisure was interwoven with daily activities: women talked with friends and neighbors after church, during marketing, or while hanging up the wash. Evidence of women's drinking or leisure awoke men's suspicions that their wives were spendthrifts, or lazy, or worse.[36]

Domestic tensions were heightened by men's resentment of the conditions of their work. Early wage labor had shared with agriculture a flexible schedule and an orientation to task. But over the nineteenth century, craft work was mechanized and subdivided, production was rationalized, and workers lost control over the process and pace of their work. Time cards and factory whistles signaled the more regimented "industrial time." Drinking beer or whiskey on the job had once been accepted and widespread, but late-nineteenth-century employers began to prohibit it. The new factories, with their giant machinery, noxious fumes, deafening noise, and extremes of hot and cold, were increasingly alien from the rural environments and small workshops characteristic of employment in earlier times. Men's distaste for the conditions of their own work heightened their resentment of the family obligations that kept them in bondage to their jobs, and led to distinctive male and working-class patterns of resistance. At the extreme, some men found no other way to regain lost autonomy or escape oppressive working conditions than to deny or dissolve ties to their families.[37]

"The Social Meaning of Money: 'Special Monies,'" *American Journal of Sociology* 95 (1989): 354–77; see also Dorothee Schneider, "'For Whom Are All the Good Things in Life?': German-American Housewives Discuss Their Budgets," in Hartmut Keil and John B. Jentz, eds., *German Workers in Industrial Chicago, 1850–1910: A Comparative Perspective* (De Kalb: Northern Illinois University Press, 1983), 145–60; Ewen, *Immigrant Women*, 102–04.

[36] Byington, *Homestead*, 108; Stansell, *City of Women*, 80–81; also, on drinking and women's daily routines, see Perry Duis, "The Saloon and the Public City: Chicago and Boston, 1880–1920" (Ph.D. diss., University of Chicago, 1975), 557; on the right to leisure, see Roy Rosenzweig, *Eight Hours for What We Will: Workers and Leisure in an Industrial City, 1870–1920* (New York: Cambridge University Press, 1983), 39.

[37] Herbert Gutman, "Work, Culture, and Society in Industrializing America, 1815–1919," *American Historical Review* 78 (1973): 531–88. Also see Daniel T. Rodgers, *The Work Ethic in*

Drinking was one way of finding release from work. Increasingly over the nineteenth century, drinking took place away from home, as municipalities restricted the practice of selling alcohol in households and employers restricted drinking at work. Saloons were places for men to reclaim the drinking and sociability that had once been integrated into their work lives. Most catered to men only. The culture of the saloon was masculine, communal, and democratic; it represented an alternative to the values of privacy, thrift, upward mobility, and family centeredness espoused by the native middle class. Temperance advocates regarded the saloon as a home wrecker. On the other hand, the saloon may have offered a "safety valve" for working-class men, a place for them to escape the foul and congested tenements. At the very least, the saloon was a sphere into which domestic demands did not intrude, and saloon going may have signified resistance to the needs of wife and children. Heavy drinking may have been both symptom and cause of domestic tension; it diverted funds from the family budget, often leading to a deterioration of material and emotional conditions at home, making the saloon an even more inviting refuge.[38]

Some men resisted steady employment. Citing nervous ailments or a dislike of factory routine, they went from job to job or undertook only modest and poorly paying positions. Breckinridge cites an example: Mr. G "changed jobs frequently, giving as a reason that he becomes tired of working in the same place . . . . [He] bought a milk depot about three years ago but kept it for only a few months, partly because he grew dissatisfied with the business and partly because his neglect made it unprofitable." Another man, a painter and peddler by trade, sought welfare assistance for his family but repeatedly refused the jobs the agency found for him; he said "it was not possible for him to work in a factory. He has never worked indoors and he knows that he cannot stand it." In the eyes of social workers, these men were "landlady's husband" types, less ambitious or less competent than other men, or simply irresponsible. Yet failure to work steadily was more than a matter of temperament; it was patterned by historical experience and differences in opportunity. Some immigrant men, accustomed to outdoor work and to the seasonal rhythm of farming and wage labor, moved from job to job. The turnover of black men contained an element of protest against the harsh conditions and menial work to which most were confined.[39]

Industrial America, 1850–1920 (Chicago: University of Chicago Press, 1974), 160–68; David M. Gordon, Richard Edwards, and Michael Reich, Segmented Work, Divided Workers: The Historical Transformation of Labor in the United States (New York: Cambridge University Press, 1982), 113–37. On drinking at work, see Rosenzweig, Eight Hours for What We Will, 36–39. On the unfamiliarity of factory conditions to black migrants, see Grossman, Land of Hope, 188–93.

[38] See Rosenzweig, Eight Hours for What We Will, 40–45, 58–62, on the rise of the saloons and on saloon culture. Perry Duis, "Saloon and Public City," 625, notes that German saloons catered to entire families; see pp. 558–59 for his discussion of saloons and family life.

[39] Sophonisba P. Breckinridge, Family Welfare Work in a Metropolitan Community: Selected Case Records (Chicago: University of Chicago Press, 1924), 560–62, 92–119 (quotation from p. 99). On

Cases of desertion often suggest a desire to escape work as well as marriage. A New York social worker termed desertion the "poor man's vacation," citing a deserter who had recently returned. The man thanked the charity agency for supporting his family during his absence, and added that "he had always wanted to see the West, and this had been the only way he could find of accomplishing it." "Railroad Jack" wrote to his brother, "I am happy on the road and it is very fine, I feel like I never will work again onless I have seen all U.S. I am on my way to Californ but I take my time . . . . I wisht you vas not mareyt and could be with me." (His brother left home immediately.) The characteristics of more typical cases suggest that deserting men resented supporting their families and wanted to claim their wages for their own use. It was not uncommon, for example, for deserters to leave home with the family savings, or even to sell the furniture or liquidate other assets before they left. Deserting men often left when their families were most dependent upon them: right before childbirth (the "pregnancy desertion") or in the early years of marriage, when children were too young to work. Among the homeless men, researchers noted, were many who could not adapt to the pressures of industrial work. Most slept in cheap lodging houses or shelters, but they were "homeless" in the sense that they had left behind whatever family connections they had had.[40]

Not all husbands drank to excess, refused to work, or deserted. But these forms of resistance were always in the background of negotiations between husband and wife, threatening women and children with deprivation and even with dissolution of the household. Women struggled to get support for themselves and their children without pushing their husbands to the point of abuse or abdication of the family. Some resorted to elaborate subterfuges, "stealing" money from their husbands or hiding away small sums from housekeeping money. A woman interviewed by a charity worker claimed that her husband "taught her to lie, as he was always counting out every penny he gave her." In addition, they sustained their families through home production, as did Mrs. M, whose husband deserted periodically: she made dresses for friends and sewed linings for a tailoring company, making $7.50 a week when she had work.[41]

Women also sought the support of others who might exert social pressure on their husbands. In working-class neighborhoods, a man's abuse, drinking, or

social workers' attitudes, see Joanna C. Colcord, *Broken Homes* (New York: Russell Sage Foundation, 1919), 153–55. See Yans-McLaughlin, *Family and Community*, 41–42, on Italian immigrants' aversion to factory work. On black men and job turnover, see Jones, "Southern Diaspora"; Trotter, "Blacks in the Urban North"; Grossman, *Land of Hope*, 194–97.

[40] Colcord, *Broken Homes*, 8, 9; "Railroad Jack": Earle Edward Eubank, "A Study of Family Desertion" (Ph.D. diss., University of Chicago, 1916), 43. On "pregnancy desertions," see Colcord, *Broken Homes*, 34–35; on age and timing of desertion, S. Howard Patterson, "Family Desertion and Nonsupport: A Study of Court Cases in Philadelphia from 1916 to 1920" (Ph.D. diss., University of Pennsylvania, 1922), 300. On homeless men, see Rossi, *Down and Out*, 21.

[41] See n. 34, above. Breckinridge, *Family Welfare Work*, 555, 522–26.

nonsupport was seldom a secret. Kin and community members sometimes took the initiative in cases of egregious neglect of family responsibilities, providing material assistance, reporting domestic violence to the authorities, or pressuring men into supporting their wives. For instance, the employer of a drinking man was said to be "very good to Mrs. N and often sent her [Mr. N's] money and often brought him home on Saturdays when he was paid so that she might have the money." Another employer castigated Mr. N about not supporting his family, and tried to prevent him from drinking.[42]

Domestic courts were another resource for working-class women. A charity agency or court might recommend a "stay-away probation" while tempers cooled and longer-term solutions were considered. These temporary separations gave men a chance to demonstrate their willingness to reform by making contributions to their family's support, as in the case of one young husband who began drinking while unemployed. Upon advice from the social worker, his wife put their furniture in storage and went to a shelter; the man "lived in lodging houses, had an attack of stomach trouble, and was altogether thoroughly miserable. . . . Finally, when it seemed to the social worker and to the wife that his lesson had gone far enough, the home was re-established." In the Chicago Court of Domestic Relations, conferences about nonsupport cases often ended with social worker and couple agreeing upon a family budget; beyond any practical help the budget may have offered, it was a ritual affirmation of the interdependence upon which working-class marriage was based.[43]

Underlying working-class women's strategies to secure support had been the resources, both material and moral, they gained through their domestic activities. With the decline in household production, more married women sought employment to supplement family incomes and guard against the vulnerability of complete dependence. But having their own wages gave women a new kind of independence, the possibility of living apart from their husbands. Louise Walther, supervisor at the Chicago Court of Domestic Relations, observed in 1933 that "a new problem has presented itself in reference to the wife who leaves her husband to secure employment and live alone." A couple in domestic court because of the husband's nonsupport were advised to separate temporarily, and the wife, "a fine cook, started a home dining room and is rapidly improving her business. . . . She plans to make herself independent of the husband's support as quickly as possible as she fears a recurrence of trouble."[44]

[42] On neighbors' intervention in cases of domestic violence or nonsupport, see Linda Gordon, *Heroes of Their Own Lives: The Politics and History of Family Violence* (New York: Penguin Books, 1988), 277–79; Ewen, *Immigrant Women*, 103; Breckinridge, *Family Welfare Work*, 571.

[43] The description of "stay-away probation" and the case are from Colcord, *Broken Homes*, pp. 138 and 159, respectively. Ethel R. McDowell, *Report of the Municipal Court of Chicago, Social Service Department, December 1st, 1932 to December 1st, 1933* (Chicago, n.d.), 8.

[44] McDowell, *Report, 1932–1933*, 9; Ethel R. McDowell, *Report of the Municipal Court of Chicago, Social Service Department, December 1st, 1933 to December 1st, 1934* (Chicago, n.d.), 31.

The increase in women's labor force participation coincided with a modest expansion of women's rights to financial support. Penalties for nonsupport and desertion became more stringent, although they remained poorly enforced. It also became more common to grant alimony with divorce. Mothers' pensions, relief, and Aid to Dependent Children (ADC) provided a meager but independent income for some women. The establishment of domestic courts in many cities between 1910 and 1930 gave women a forum for mediation of marital problems. The court records of the 1930s suggest that in the eyes of social workers and judges, women had an unconditional right to support from their husbands. In contrast to earlier times, when charity workers visited the home in order to evaluate women's housekeeping, women's performance of domestic duties was seldom mentioned. Instead, court records detailed husbands' abuse, desertion, or failure to support; when wives were faulted at all, it was usually for mental incapacity, emotional instability, or peccadilloes such as nagging.[45]

The idea of wives' rights was new; it was not derived from the reciprocal exchange at the basis of traditional working-class family relations. What women sought, it seems, was not an entitlement to unearned income but a release from their husbands' arbitrary exercise of power. "[My husband] just wouldn't treat me right," explained a woman to a judge in Chicago. "The court in Toledo gave me these papers to carry any where I went and he couldn't do anything and couldn't take the kids but he should help support the kids." Women's new rights were limited and poorly enforced; a woman might receive $5 a week in child support, and little more from relief or ADC. But they allowed women to become more assertive in claiming support; when their husbands were abusive or incompatible, they now often sought independence rather than reconciliation. A woman who complained of a domineering husband "said that she would leave [him] and expected him to send her money"; when the court recommended a reunion, she refused, and supplemented her husband's irregular child support payments by selling baked goods.[46]

The weakening of marital ties was most evident among poor couples. Individually disadvantaged, together poor men and women faced the limitations of the traditional family economy in a changing economic setting. Women's household production could no longer buffer families against unemployment, espe-

[45] Clarence G. Shenton, *History and Functions of the Municipal Court of Philadelphia: A Report by the Bureau of Municipal Research of Philadelphia* (Philadelphia: Thomas Skelton Harrison Foundation, 1930), 69–75; Elaine Tyler May, *Great Expectations: Marriage and Divorce in Post-Victorian America* (Chicago: University of Chicago Press, 1980), 151. For examples of court cases, see McDowell, *Report, 1932–33*; McDowell, *Report, 1933–34*; City of New York, Domestic Relations Court, *Conservation: The Child and Family in Court. Seventh Annual Report of the Domestic Relations Court of the City of New York* (New York, 1939), 49–59.

[46] E. Franklin Frazier, *The Negro Family in Chicago* (Chicago: University of Chicago Press, 1932), 172, 174; McDowell, *Report, 1932–33*, 28. Gordon, *Heroes of Their Own Lives*, 259, suggests a similar change in gender relations during the 1930s.

cially the long-term unemployment that appeared during the 1930s, and poor women had limited opportunities for wage work. Newly enforceable claims on the incomes of their unemployed husbands meant little. Increasingly during the 1930s, both men and women made claims on the state instead of on each other. As relief became widespread during the Depression, it lost some of its stigma. Many in the working class viewed relief as their just due, after years as citizens and workers. In New York, for instance, a recalcitrant Mr. Z was just out of the workhouse for refusal to cooperate with the Works Progress Administration; he "manifested real interest in the welfare of his family, but felt that it was the community's responsibility to support them." The erosion of economic interdependence removed one source of marital stability, and the intrusion of social workers into family life exacerbated tensions caused by unemployment. Poor men and women became more cautious in their relations to one another, and their ties broke apart more easily.[47]

A case from the Chicago Court of Domestic Relations illustrates the instrumental tone of gender relations among the poor, as well as a calculating use of social service agencies:

> [Mrs. K's] education was limited to the fifth grade. It was necessary for her to work and support herself since her mother and father separated. She met Mr. K and they were married when she was twenty-one. Two children were born of this union and two years after they married Mr. K deserted and has not been seen since. One year later she met Mr. A, a Philipino, age 27, at a rooming house where she and her mother were living. A few months later she began living with him, as a means of getting her rent paid. About ten months later, their baby, Anita was born. Two months later, Mr. A applied for assistance at the [Unemployment Relief Service]. He registered Mrs. K as his wife and her two children by the previous marriage, as well as Anita, as his own. Mr. A left shortly afterwards to continue his course at the University of Illinois. He returned to her for visits of two or three days at a time. Shortly before Christmas of this year, Mrs. K came to the [municipal court] to ask bastardy action against Mr. A, who had not sent any money for the baby recently. She was expecting him for the Christmas holidays and asked that a warrant be issued and that the police be ready to arrest him as soon as she notified him of his return.

Mr. A was indeed arrested, and admitted paternity of Anita; he said he had planned to marry Mrs. K after he began working and could get a divorce for her. Mrs. K now refused to marry him, but finally reconsidered. Mrs. K's distrust of Mr. A is not surprising, given her past experience: she had worked since an early age because her parents separated, and her first husband had deserted, leaving

---

[47] The conflictual and calculating tone of gender and family relations in the working class during the 1930s is described by Lois Rita Helmbold, "Beyond the Family Economy: Black and White Working-Class Women during the Great Depression," *Feminist Studies* 13, no. 3 (Fall 1987): 629–55. For a discussion of relief and working-class families, see Cohen, *Making a New Deal*, 270–83; on social workers and family life, see also Jones, *Labor of Love, Labor of Sorrow*, 225–26.

her with two young children. But new legal institutions allowed her to be assertive in pursuing support when Mr. A failed to send money.[48]

The problems of poverty were accentuated among African-American couples. Black families had fewer children and more working wives, but these demographic differences were embedded in family relations similar to those of the white working class. Like their white counterparts, working-class black families were characterized by similar patterns of reliance on household production, relations of reciprocity between family members, and male resistance to industrial employment.[49] But black couples faced greater economic pressure than whites did. Concentrated in domestic service, black women were hit harder by the mechanization of household work, and most were blocked by discrimination if not lack of education from entering other occupations. Black men and women faced very high unemployment rates during the Depression, with correspondingly high rates of public aid receipt; in Harlem in 1935, 43 percent of the families were on relief. Between 1910 and 1940 the proportion of black wives earning income from employment or boarders actually declined (table 6.3).[50]

Drake and Cayton's description of a young couple in a poor section of Chicago's Black Belt is emblematic of the uneasy mixture of old and new elements of gender relations. When "Slick" and Betty Lou got together, they borrowed money and set up housekeeping in a basement room; the building's janitor let Betty Lou use his kitchen in return for a share of the food. Betty Lou "took a great deal of pride in her biscuits and occasional hot rolls. She was enjoying domesticity." When Slick got a WPA job, they moved into a first-floor kitchenette, and for a few weeks Slick brought his check home, but there was tension: "Betty Lou's conception of her role was that Slick should work and support her. Slick, however, suggested that she too should get a job, and often charged her with running around during the day, 'turning tricks.'" His jealousy and Betty Lou's aspirations for social mobility led to fights, separations, and finally a violent ending of the relationship.[51]

[48] McDowell, *Report, 1932–1933,* 29–30.

[49] Contrast Andrew T. Miller, "Social Science, Social Policy, and the Heritage of African-American Families," this volume, which emphasizes the contrasts between Euro-American and African-American families, and argues that distinctive features of the latter have African roots. But the differences between these two chapters should not be exaggerated. Miller focuses on aspects of African-American family organization such as child keeping that, whatever their origins, do seem to be quite distinctive. In gender relations or in the family economy, black and white families may have more in common with each other; the evidence I present here is consistent with this.

[50] Sharon Harley, "For the Good of Family and Race: Gender, Work, and Domestic Roles in the Black Community, 1880–1930," *Signs: Journal of Women in Culture and Society* 15 (1990): 336–49, provides evidence that black families saw domestic roles as preferable to work for married women. On unemployment and relief, see E. Franklin Frazier, "Some Effects of the Depression on the Negro in Northern Cities," *Science and Society* 2 (1938): 491. Engerman, "Black Fertility and Family Structure," 134, offers evidence that the proportion of female-headed families increased in the black population faster in the 1930s than before.

[51] St. Clair Drake and Horace R. Cayton, *Black Metropolis: A Study of Negro Life in a Northern City* (1945; reprint, New York: Harper and Row, 1962), 2: 571–75; quotations from pp. 572, 573.

This episode recapitulates familiar patterns: the woman contributing to the family economy through household production; the man suspicious and reluctant to leave his wife at home; quarrels over the disposition of the man's pay. At the same time, the woman's claim of a right to financial support, contested by the man who wants her to get a job, suggests the changes that accompanied the decline in women's economic contributions through domesticity. The couple's arrangements echo the form of the traditional working-class family economy, but it is a form stripped of nearly all function; the tiny kitchenette could not be the productive household of times past.

EPILOGUE

Contemporary ghetto family patterns emerged among a minority of the urban poor before 1940. As poor men and women sought to refashion their family economies, they developed new family patterns to replace the configuration of unpaid domestic labor, male wages, and mutual exchange now progressively rendered obsolete by transformations in work, technology, and space. In their place, even before 1940, a minority of families developed strategies that combined a redefinition of gender roles—often in female-headed families—with reliance on the state and public assistance. As Mark Stern shows in the next chapter, for decades poor families continued to try to adapt conventional family strategies to new labor market conditions and the "perversity" of public policy. The family patterns that figure so prominently in the underclass debate are one result of their failure. This chapter has shown how the adaptations of the urban poor, first to industrialization and then to economic marginalization, weakened marital ties. In the discourse and practices of poor couples today, we may discern their own attempts to reclaim the old domestic exchanges, or map out the new.

CHAPTER 7

Poverty and Family Composition since 1940

Mark J. Stern

> Stigma involves not so much a set of concrete individuals who can
> be separated into two piles, the stigmatized and the normal, as a
> pervasive two-role social process in which every individual
> participates in both roles, at least in some connections and in some
> phases of life. The normal and the stigmatized are not persons but
> rather perspectives.
>
> —Erving Goffman, *Stigma: Notes on the*
> *Management of Spoiled Identity*

EITHER IMPLICITLY or explicitly, most writers about the underclass—whether
popular or academic writers—have been forced to use contrasts to make their
point. Yet the nature of these contrasts is noteworthy. In the popular imagination, members of the underclass are outsiders. Their family life and work habits
do not conform to those of the rest of society. "They don't just tend to be poor,"
one writer has noted. "To most Americans their behavior seems aberrant."[1]

The notion of the poor as outsiders has a long pedigree, as Michael Katz has
detailed in his introduction. At least since the early nineteenth century, popular
writers and moral entrepreneurs have sought to paint the very poor in this
image. Thus, in the popular imagination, the idea of the underclass represents
the continuation of a long tradition.

Academic writers, by contrast, have focused on the novelty of the underclass.
Most writers, in explaining its emergence, have focused on the impacts of
postindustrialization, the restructuring of the city, and the new neighborhood
and family relationships spawned by these changes. For professional researchers, then, the underclass is a new social phenomenon worthy of intensive
examination.

In spite of the different contrasts they have drawn, popular images and
professional research have relied on a number of assumptions about the history
of American poverty to support their case. They agree that the work history of
the ghetto poor is distinctive both from that of past generations of urban African
Americans and the history of white Americans. In one version, the contemporary urban ghetto is contrasted with a supposed "golden age" of the ghetto

---

[1] Ken Auletta, *The Underclass* (New York: Random House, 1982), xiii.

during the 1940s and 1950s, when such neighborhoods were based on a solid middle class composed of local businessmen and blue-collar workers.

Professional and popular accounts agree as well about the role of government in the history of poverty. Earlier generations of the poor escaped from poverty thanks largely to their own efforts and economic growth. The contemporary ghetto poor have become entangled in the "spider web of dependency" woven by well-intentioned liberals and Great Society bureaucrats.

Finally, both professional and popular accounts highlight the failure of the underclass family. Again in contrast to the African-American poor of the past and to the contemporary mainstream, members of the underclass have eluded responsibility to their children, their spouses, and their kin.

The interpretations of the work experience, dependency, and family life of the underclass have run well ahead of the evidence. Although much of our interpretation of the history of the underclass must come from qualitative sources, there are key elements of the story that are best explored through quantitative methods. The occupational structure of the urban ghetto, employment rates, the prevalence of poverty among various groups, and the frequency of different family structures are all relevant to the contemporary debate. Yet, because the majority of data on the low-income population begins in the 1960s, the quantitative evidence to support the history of the underclass is largely absent.

This paper uses new evidence on the history of poverty, joblessness, and family structure since World War II to understand the origins of the underclass. The "public use samples" of the federal censuses provide researchers with individual-level records from 1940 to 1980. These data have been used sparingly in the underclass debate. Yet they allow us to gain a sorely needed degree of precision about the history of the urban poor—its work history and family life.[2] This paper uses these data to make four arguments.

The "golden age" myth of the ghetto is flawed. Because we have overestimated the economic well-being of urban blacks and Hispanics before the 1960s, the image of urban deterioration is also exaggerated.

Our understanding of the decline of poverty before 1960 has been inaccurate. In particular, we have underestimated the role of transfer payments and women's increased labor-force participation in improving the economic well-being of Americans before the War on Poverty.

Shifts in welfare policy were largely responsible for the increasing poverty gap between the urban jobless and the rest of the population during the 1970s. After thirty years of equalization, the social welfare system of the 1970s shifted toward "reverse targeting": higher benefits for those groups who needed them least.

Family, the economy, and social policy interacted more subtly than we have appreci-

---

[2] Another use of these data to discuss poverty and the family is James P. Smith, "Poverty and the Family," in Gary Sandefur and Marta Tienda, eds. *Divided Opportunities: Minorities, Poverty, and Social Policy* (New York and London: Plenum Press, 1988), 141–72.

ated. The increased number of female-headed families was not the only significant change in family structure. Traditional family strategies like child labor and
household extension lost much of their antipoverty effectiveness. The equalization of the wages of black men and women probably encouraged the increase in
female-headed families more than changes in the welfare system did.

THE GHETTO'S GOLDEN AGE?

One side effect of the underclass debate has been the growth of a certain
nostalgia for the black ghetto of the early postwar years. If we are to believe some
commentators, these communities were inhabited by a "solid" working class of
"old heads" who provided role models and job opportunities for the younger
generation.[3]

The census is silent on the perceived safety, stability, or quality of life of the
old ghetto, but it can tell us how solid the economic foundations of the black
ghetto were. Here the answer is unambiguous: the "solid working class" of the
1950s suffered from irregular work, low wages, and poverty. Although a large
share of family heads worked, discrimination and low wages assured that even
the most solid of the solid working class lived in poverty. In 1950, for example,
the poverty rate of black semiskilled operatives was 44 percent, the rate for
laborers was 56 percent, and that for domestics was 83 percent.

The economic decline of urban blacks during the postwar years forms the
foundation of the underclass debate. William J. Wilson used aggregate data to
support the idea that black joblessness and economic restructuring were the
causes of underclass formation.[4] Yet a more detailed examination of data on
individual households substantially revises his conclusions.

Joblessness and its attendant poverty are not new problems for African Americans, nor has the gap between black and white joblessness increased dramatically.[5] In 1950, the proportion of black householders who worked full-time

---

[3] Elijah Anderson, *Street Wise: Race, Class, and Change in an Urban Community* (Chicago: University of Chicago Press, 1990), is one example of employment of a "golden age" argument. "Older
black residents remember better days when life was more orderly and civilized, when crime and
drugs were almost unknown, when young people respected their elders, and when the men worked
in good jobs and took care of their families" (2).

[4] Wilson uses aggregate unemployment rates and employment-to-population ratios to measure
joblessness. His evidence on the impact of economic restructuring is John Kasarda's data on the
skills and job "mismatch" that has developed in central cities (*The Truly Disadvantaged: The Inner
City, the Underclass, and Public Policy* [Chicago: University of Chicago Press, 1987]). We examine
these two arguments using a different set of indicators. To measure joblessness I use work experience over the previous year, which indicates not only whether a person has a job at a given point, but
the number of weeks he or she worked and the number of hours worked per week. To examine the
impact of economic restructuring, I use the occupational structure and its relationship to race,
location, and work experience.

[5] This conclusion is supported as well by Phillip Moss and Chris Tilly, "Why Black Men Are
Doing Worse in the Labor Market: A Review of Supply-Side and Demand-Side Explanations" (Paper

TABLE 7.1

Poverty and Distribution of Population, by Ethnicity and Work Experience

	Whites			Blacks		
	Percentage of Population	Poverty Rate (%)	HEP Rate (%)	Percentage of Population	Poverty Rate (%)	HEP Rate (%)
1949						
Full-time, full-year	57.6	13.1	19.5	45.3	50.1	57.9
FT, 27–47 wks	10.6	26.6	36.2	14.2	61.8	70.6
FT, <27 wks	3.8	53.8	73.8	5.1	74.4	83.9
Part-time	3.6	38.7	55.4	6.6	82.2	86.5
NLF[a]	24.4	58.7	83.2	28.8	85.2	93.2
1959						
Full-time, full-year	59.2	6.7	14.5	43.4	30.9	43.2
FT, 27–47 wks	8.9	16.3	29.9	12.5	42.2	56.9
FT, <27 wks	2.2	41.6	71.1	4.0	64.4	80.9
Part-time	4.3	29.9	58.3	8.6	70.8	86.3
NLF[a]	25.5	42.4	80.7	31.6	71.0	88.5
1969						
Full-time, full-year	58.4	3.1	5.8	44.7	12.4	22.9
FT, 27–47 wks	4.4	7.3	21.4	6.0	38.5	57.1
FT, <27 wks	10.1	5.5	13.3	13.9	20.5	32.7
Part-time	6.9	31.4	71.6	9.5	45.7	74.0
NLF[a]	20.1	38.0	96.5	26.0	70.0	100.0
1979						
Full-time, full-year	53.7	2.5	5.7	40.4	7.4	16.0
FT, 27–47 wks	2.1	10.3	43.8	3.0	26.4	52.9
FT, <27 wks	11.0	6.7	15.9	12.8	14.1	28.3
Part-time	8.6	24.3	66.0	11.3	43.2	74.0
NLF[a]	24.7	24.0	98.2	32.6	57.5	99.4

[a]Not in labor force.

for the full year was 45 percent, 12 percentage points below the white rate. Blacks lost some ground during the 1950s, but after 1960, the gap narrowed slightly. Both black and white family heads experienced declines in full employment—blacks from 43 to 40 percent, whites from 59 to 54 percent (table 7.1).

The evidence on full employment is somewhat deceptive, since black full-time workers were much less likely to escape poverty. In 1949, black full-time

prepared for the Social Science Research Council Subcommittee on Joblessness and the Underclass, January 1991).

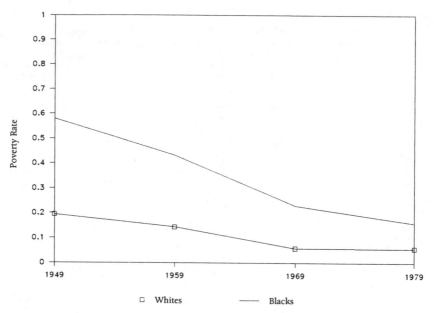

Figure 7.1. Householder Earnings Poverty Rate, by Race, 1949–1979 (full-time, full-year workers). In the 1940s, most African-American workers—even if they worked full-time—earned a living wage. This gap closed considerably by the 1970s.

workers were three times as likely not to earn a living wage than were white workers; only 13 percent of fully employed whites lived in poverty, compared to 50 percent of blacks. Thirty years later, these gaps had narrowed greatly; the poverty rates for fully employed blacks and whites were 7 and 3 percent, respectively. Although this left blacks at the same point whites had been in 1959, it represented real improvement in their economic status (fig. 7.1).

National data on work and poverty tell a somewhat different story about the 1970s from that of case studies like Thomas Sugrue's or Robin Kelley's. The rapid deproletarianization of the 1970s was in part the result of the unique conditions in Detroit and Birmingham, declines not shared by all cities or regions, as Jargowsky and Bane have shown.[6] It was a product as well of the rapid growth of opportunities in unionized, secure, well-paying jobs in these cities during the early postwar years. Nationally, African Americans fully shared neither the opening of opportunities during the 1950s nor the rapid decline of the 1970s.

As the share of whites and blacks who worked full-time fell, the proportions

[6] Paul A. Jargowsky and Mary Jo Bane, "Ghetto Poverty in the United States, 1970–1980," in Christopher Jencks and Paul E. Peterson, eds., *The Urban Underclass* (Washington, D.C.: Brookings Institution, 1991), 235–74.

Table 7.2
Work Experience, by Race and Metropolitan Location (Percentages)

		Did Not Work	Full-Time, Full-Year	Full-Time, 27–47 Weeks	Full-Time, <26 Weeks	Part-Time	Total N
Central cities							
Whites	1950	25.1	59.4	8.9	3.8	2.9	5,008
	1960	26.9	58.2	8.6	2.5	3.6	13,149
	1970	21.3	55.7	4.6	10.0	7.5	121,500
	1980	28.6	49.8	2.1	10.5	9.1	55,420
Blacks	1950	27.6	48.9	13.4	4.4	5.7	597
	1960	29.4	47.7	12.4	4.2	6.3	2,346
	1970	25.3	46.3	5.6	13.8	8.9	10,370
	1980	34.3	39.2	2.8	12.7	11.0	17,830
Suburbs							
Whites	1950	21.4	61.1	11.0	3.6	2.9	5,042
	1960	23.7	61.8	8.9	2.0	3.7	22,041
	1970	18.7	60.5	4.3	9.7	6.0	200,862
	1980	22.0	57.4	2.0	10.9	13.2	139,550
Blacks	1950	26.3	47.1	16.8	4.5	5.3	271
	1960	31.9	42.7	12.5	3.7	9.3	1,391
	1970	23.9	45.6	5.8	14.9	10.5	10,370
	1980	25.4	47.1	3.1	13.2	11.2	9,467

that were partially employed (either for part of the year or part-time) or out of the labor force increased. For example, between 1950 and 1980, the proportion of partially employed whites almost tripled (from 7 to 20 percent) and that of the black proportion doubled (from 12 to 24 percent).[7] Increases in the proportion of black and white household heads who did not work rose and fell in similar ways. Ironically, during the 1970s—when the underclass grew the quickest—the gap between blacks and whites who did not work actually narrowed.

The rise in joblessness was not confined to African Americans living in central cities. Black and white center-city residents shared the decline in full-time work, and the proportion of suburban residents—both black and white—who were partially employed or out of the labor force increased (table 7.2).

The proportion of black householders who had attended college exploded between 1939 and 1979. They made up an increasing share of fully employed workers both in the central cities and the suburbs. However, the share of chronically jobless or part-time workers among black college graduates increased even more quickly during these years. During the 1970s alone, the

---

[7] In the remainder of the paper, I will use the term *chronic joblessness* to refer to those who worked part-time or full-time for fewer than six months in the previous year.

proportion of college-educated African Americans who did not work, were chronically jobless, or worked part-time doubled. Black college graduates who lived in the suburbs experienced the same increases as those who lived in central cities (table 7.3).[8]

Wilson has emphasized the impact of economic restructuring on the deterioration of the economic status of black Americans. Blacks did suffer from the deindustrialization of America's cities during the 1970s, but they shared this decline with white workers. The percentage of blacks in craft and operative occupations fell during the 1970s (from 31 percent to 22 percent). In contrast to whites, however, African Americans moved rapidly into the expanding white-collar world during the 1970s. Before the civil rights revolution, discrimination and lack of educational background restricted black access to these jobs. In 1970, 6.5 percent of black householders were in professional and managerial jobs, and 7.7 percent were in clerical jobs. By 1980, their representation in these two categories had increased by 45 and 60 percent, respectively, while white representation in these jobs did not change. At the same time, the proportion of African Americans in the worst jobs (farm workers, laborers, and domestics) fell from 17 to 7 percent between 1970 and 1980.

These patterns reflect shifts in gender and work experience. From 1950 to 1970, black men shifted out of farming and laboring jobs and into craft, semi-skilled, and white-collar work. During the 1970s, the growth of craft and semiskilled opportunities was reversed, but the growth of white-collar opportunities continued. The weakening of discrimination and increased educational opportunity particularly benefited African-American women. In 1950, more than one-half of employed black female householders worked in domestic service. Over the next three decades this figure fell to fewer than 10 percent. In place of domestic service, employed African-American women moved into white-collar jobs and semiskilled manufacturing and service work (table 7.4).

Whites suffered as profoundly as blacks from the deindustrialization of the 1970s. Of course, the position of the solid working class was quite different on each side of the racial divide. In Detroit and Birmingham, steel and auto workers were the economic and social foundation of the black community, but only a stratum of the white middle class. Thus, even if white workers suffered as much as blacks, the impact of deindustrialization may have had a more devastating effect on black community life.

The long-standing gap between the work patterns of black and white house-holders did not widen appreciably after 1960. Both blacks and whites had

---

[8] Moss and Tilly, "Why Black Men Are Doing Worse," also conclude that the declining status of black men was not confined to the low-educated. College-educated African Americans' earnings were nearly 10 percent *higher* than those of college-educated whites in 1976 and declined to more than 10 percent *below* those of college-educated whites by the late 1980s. The wage differentials of other black men remained relatively stable, which suggests that the bulk of the deterioration of black men's relative wages was the result of trends among the college educated.

TABLE 7.3
Educational Attainment and Work Experience, by Race and Metropolitan Location, Householders, 1950–1980 (Percentages)

		Did Not Work			Full-Time, Full-Year			Full-Time, 27–47 Weeks			Full-Time, <26 Weeks			Part-Time		
		<8th Grade	High School	College	<8th Grade	High School	College	<8th Grade	High School	College	<8th Grade	High School	College	<8th Grade	High School	College
Central cities																
Whites	1950	14.5	7.2	3.5	21.3	26.2	11.9	3.9	3.9	1.1	1.5	1.7	0.6	1.3	1.0	0.5
	1960	14.4	8.8	3.7	13.5	29.1	15.6	2.7	3.9	1.9	0.9	1.1	0.5	1.5	1.4	0.7
	1970	10.2	7.2	3.9	8.6	29.1	18.0	0.8	1.9	1.9	1.6	4.6	3.9	1.7	3.1	2.7
	1980	9.1	13.2	6.3	2.5	21.0	26.3	0.2	0.9	1.1	0.9	4.5	5.2	0.8	3.2	5.0
Blacks	1950	21.0	4.9	1.7	28.9	14.9	5.1	8.1	4.5	0.8	3.3	0.9	0.2	4.6	0.8	0.3
	1960	18.4	9.4	1.6	21.5	20.3	5.9	6.0	5.1	1.3	2.2	1.6	0.4	3.7	2.3	0.4
	1970	13.8	10.3	1.2	12.7	26.5	7.1	1.8	3.4	0.4	3.2	8.4	2.2	3.0	4.6	1.3
	1980	12.7	17.7	3.9	4.3	21.6	13.3	0.6	1.5	0.8	1.5	7.1	4.1	1.6	6.2	3.2
Suburbs																
Whites	1950	12.1	6.5	2.7	19.9	27.9	13.3	4.9	4.5	1.7	1.9	1.2	0.5	1.8	0.6	0.5
	1960	11.9	8.2	3.6	13.2	30.8	17.8	2.8	4.1	2.0	0.6	0.9	0.5	1.6	1.3	0.8
	1970	8.9	6.6	3.1	7.9	31.7	20.9	0.8	2.2	1.3	2.0	4.9	2.8	2.0	2.1	2.0
	1980	7.1	10.3	4.5	2.9	26.1	28.4	0.3	0.9	0.8	0.8	5.3	4.8	6.3	3.7	3.2
Blacks	1950	22.5	3.6	0.3	32.7	11.4	3.0	14.0	2.2	0.6	4.1	0.4	0.1	3.9	0.3	1.1
	1960	23.4	6.7	1.7	24.3	14.4	4.0	7.0	4.3	1.2	2.5	0.9	0.2	6.4	2.3	0.6
	1970	15.6	6.9	1.5	15.6	22.7	7.3	2.5	2.7	0.6	4.8	7.4	2.7	5.1	4.4	1.0
	1980	12.0	10.7	2.8	5.6	24.2	17.3	1.0	1.3	0.8	2.0	6.5	4.8	2.1	5.7	3.3

TABLE 7.4
Race and Occupation, by Work Experience and Gender, Householders, 1950–1980 (Percentages)

		White-Collar	Self-Employed	Craft	Semiskilled	Domestic Service	Labor	Farm	Farm Labor	Not Reported	N
MALES											
Full-time, full-year											
Whites	1950	28.3	13.0	20.1	20.6	0.0	4.7	11.6	1.6	0.2	9,355
	1960	32.9	11.2	20.0	21.9	0.0	3.5	4.9	2.6	3.0	25,501
	1970	39.9	10.2	19.8	21.7	0.0	4.0	2.8	0.7	0.9	230,300
	1980	42.1	9.5	12.3	27.4	0.0	3.1	2.4	1.1	2.0	12,490
Blacks	1950	9.3	3.6	7.1	33.9	0.5	20.6	20.1	4.7	0.3	658
	1960	12.9	2.7	10.1	41.3	1.0	18.5	1.4	7.1	5.1	1,696
	1970	17.9	3.0	16.3	45.7	0.7	13.7	0.7	0.3	1.8	15,570
	1980	28.8	2.6	10.2	44.9	0.2	8.3	0.5	1.3	3.2	9,588
Partially employed											
Whites	1950	14.2	10.8	22.5	30.2	0.1	9.4	9.3	3.4	0.2	2,759
	1960	20.1	10.9	20.2	28.0	0.1	8.3	5.0	3.3	4.2	5,961
	1970	29.3	8.8	18.9	24.5	0.5	6.1	3.5	0.7	7.6	73,500
	1980	30.9	10.0	14.8	31.6	0.2	5.9	2.6	2.3	1.6	43,760
Blacks	1950	4.0	2.6	9.7	29.4	0.7	26.5	19.5	7.4	0.2	346
	1960	6.1	4.1	10.1	32.2	0.8	25.9	2.0	12.7	6.1	883
	1970	15.2	4.1	13.3	36.8	2.2	15.3	1.4	0.5	11.5	8,380
	1980	22.6	3.1	10.4	45.3	0.6	11.3	0.6	3.9	2.2	5,249

FEMALES

Full-time, full year

Whites	1950	57.2	7.4	2.3	29.3	1.4	0.2	1.8	0.3	0.1	577
	1960	59.3	4.6	1.7	26.0	1.9	0.3	0.8	0.1	5.3	2,134
	1970	65.4	4.0	3.6	25.9	0.0	0.9	0.0	0.0	0.0	22,400
	1980	72.0	2.1	2.0	20.5	0.7	1.6	0.3	0.1	0.7	18,310
Blacks	1950	12.4	0.4	0.4	33.8	48.4	0.7	2.6	1.5	0.0	92
	1960	17.4	1.2	0.6	39.3	30.3	2.1	0.3	0.3	8.4	333
	1970	34.1	0.6	2.6	41.4	18.5	2.9	0.0	0.0	0.0	3,140
	1980	53.4	0.5	2.0	36.8	3.6	2.9	0.1	0.2	0.5	3,674

Partially employed

Whites	1950	40.8	5.4	0.8	41.8	8.6	0.9	1.4	0.1	0.3	344
	1960	46.1	5.2	0.8	32.4	7.5	0.5	0.8	0.6	6.1	1,228
	1970	52.6	2.6	1.0	37.5	4.2	1.0	0.0	0.0	1.0	19,200
	1980	59.6	3.1	1.4	29.2	2.1	2.9	0.6	0.7	0.4	13,770
Blacks	1950	6.5	0.8	0.0	22.6	58.9	2.0	4.8	4.4	0.0	83
	1960	7.6	1.0	0.3	26.6	53.8	1.0	0.3	2.4	6.9	290
	1970	22.3	0.8	1.5	45.8	23.8	2.3	0.3	0.8	2.6	3,910
	1980	39.4	0.7	1.2	43.9	9.8	3.5	0.1	0.7	0.6	3,648

increased difficulty finding work during the 1970s. College-educated blacks shared these problems with those who were less well educated. The vision of the economic deterioration of black communities suffers from a lack of an accurate historical foundation. Poverty, joblessness, and poor opportunities characterized the ghetto in the 1950s even more than in the 1970s or 1980s.

This is not to say that black urban communities have not changed. The intense overcrowding of the 1940s and 1950s has given way to the depopulation and abandonment described by David Bartelt. Crime and fear are different in the contemporary ghetto than they were in the teeming streets of the ghetto of years past. The decline in density affected the number and accessibility of social institutions and organizations, as well. Although the urban African-American community may have experienced a unique ecological experience, their employment and poverty history was not as distinctive. Indeed, it is finely woven into the poverty story of the entire nation.

THE POVERTY STORY

The nonwhite urban jobless have become an increasing proportion of America's poor over the past half-century, not so much because their status has deteriorated but because other groups have found avenues of escape. The poverty story of postwar America includes elements that are well known—like the expansion of real wages during the 1950s and 1960s and the growth of two-earner families after 1970. Yet other aspects of it are less well understood.

The public-use samples of the U.S. census allow us to examine the postwar poverty story in greater detail than has ever been possible. The story that emerges is full of surprises. We have seriously overestimated the affluence of Americans—particularly blue-collar Americans—before the 1960s. As late as 1959, at least two in five householders did not earn a living wage. In addition, we have seriously misunderstood the ways in which families escaped from poverty, particularly before 1960. Although economic growth and wage increases were important, much of the poverty decline of the 1950s was the result of increases in the earnings of other family members and in government welfare payments.

The expansion of government programs was critical to the poverty declines of the 1950s, when a bulk of the white population escaped poverty. In contrast, the growth of social-welfare programs during and after the War on Poverty were much less likely to benefit the urban jobless than other sectors of the population. Ironically, the urban jobless "fell behind" during the 1970s not because overly generous welfare payments sapped their will to work or uphold family responsibilities, but because other groups grabbed a larger and larger share of the welfare pie.

Researchers have been divided on how to define the *underclass*. William J. Wilson, in his highly regarded work, saw the underclass as a product of the isolation of urban ghettos and the increase in the concentration of the poor and jobless in these ghettos. The influential work of Sawhill and Ricketts also used concentration, that is, living in a census tract with a high aggregate poverty rate, as the primary means of differentiating the underclass from the rest of the poor.[9]

Others have stressed the importance of employment status and behavioral measures in defining the underclass. In this paper, I will use a labor-force definition to examine a group I call the chronically jobless, or urban jobless.[10] This group is defined by four factors present in the census: work experience, school attainment, urban residence, and age. A householder's family is defined as members of the urban jobless if the householder did not work during the previous year, worked full-time for less than half the year, or worked part-time. I have also excluded those with postsecondary education, those over sixty years of age, and those who did not live in central cities.[11]

This definition is somewhat broader than that used by Wilson and others. First, it does not examine neighborhoods of extreme poverty (which is impossible with the public-use samples) or even cities with high poverty rates, but all central cities. Second, its educational standard is broader than that usually connoted by the term *underclass*. Still, within the limits of the available data and the problems of any definition imposed on data over a forty-year period, it does identify those families which are generally the object of the underclass debate.[12]

The Census Bureau's definition of poverty often muddies the discussion of economic deprivation. The poverty rate is based on the relationship of the total money income of a family in a given year and a poverty threshold defined by the age of the family head and family composition. Since it was defined for 1959, the poverty thresholds have been adjusted for inflation using the consumer price index.[13]

[9] William J. Wilson, *The Truly Disadvantaged*. See also, Wilson, "Social Theory and Public Agenda Research: The Challenge of Studying Inner-City Social Dislocations" (Presidential Address presented at the annual meeting of the American Sociological Association, August 1990); Erol Ricketts and Isabel Sawhill, "Defining and Measuring the Underclass," *Journal of Policy Analysis and Management* 7 (Winter 1988): 316–25.

[10] Because the "urban jobless" include those who worked part-time and full-time for less than half the year, they were not totally jobless. Therefore, when I am discussing the earnings of this group, I will use the phrase "marginally employed" as well. The urban jobless will be compared with the remaining householders under the age of sixty, a group I shall refer to as the "other nonaged."

[11] In 1949, 1969, and 1979, the census identified those who were unable to work. For these years, I used an alternative definition of the chronically jobless that excluded the disabled. These data do not radically change the analysis offered in the remainder of the paper. If anything, they indicate that the growth of the underclass has been overestimated. Whereas the primary definition leads to the conclusion that there was little change in the chronically jobless's proportion of the population between 1949 and 1979, the alternative definition shows a clear decline (from 4.5 to 3.5 percent). In addition, while both definitions confirm the growth in the chronically jobless's share of the poor, the alternative definition fixes this increase at 50 percent (from 6.6 to 10.0 percent), while the primary definition leads to a figure of 100 percent.

[12] Increasingly, Wilson and others have focused their attention of the social dynamics of the largest Northeastern and Midwestern cities. Wilson, "Social Theory and Public Agenda Research."

[13] The poverty rates reported for 1940 and 1950 were not "corrected" for inflation, because such

The problems with the Census Bureau definition have been discussed extensively.[14] One particular problem in examining historical trends is the impact of the increase in transfer payments since the 1950s. Danziger and Plotnick proposed the concept of "pretransfer poverty," that is, the poverty rate if we exclude income derived from government transfer payments. The comparison of official poverty and pretransfer poverty allows one to assess the effectiveness of transfers in getting individuals and families out of poverty. This was particularly important during the 1970s, when the pretransfer poverty rate rose, but the official poverty rate remained relatively stable because of the increasing effectiveness of government transfers.[15]

The method used to define pretransfer poverty can be extended to other forms of income. If we partition a family's total income by source, we can examine the role of each source in reducing the risk of poverty. For this study, I have divided family income into four parts: householder's earnings, the earnings of other family members, unearned income from sources other than public transfer payments, and income from public transfer payments. If we add these sources in turn, we can judge the role of each in reducing poverty.[16]

Take the total population in 1979 as an example (fig. 7.2). In 1979, 37.8 percent of householders did not earn enough to put their families above the poverty threshold; I will call this the householder earnings poverty rate (HEP). When we include other family members' earnings, however, the proportion of the population drops to 32.6 percent (family earnings poverty, or FEP). If we include nongovernmental transfers, like investment income, rents, gifts, and charity, the rate drops to 24.3 percent (pretransfer poverty rate). Finally, we can include transfer payments, which give the official poverty rate of 13.0 percent.[17]

---

a procedure produces unrealistically high estimates of poverty. Rather, the poverty rate for 1959 was pegged to a time-series of family budget studies for the period 1905–59. See Oscar Ornati, *Poverty amid Affluence* (New York: Twentieth Century Fund, 1966).

[14] Christopher Jencks, "The Politics of Income Measurement," in William Alonso and Paul Starr, eds., *The Politics of Numbers* (New York: Russell Sage Foundation,1987), 83–132; Patricia Ruggles, *Drawing the Line: Alternative Poverty Measures and Their Implications for Public Policy* (Washington, D.C.: Urban Institute Press, 1990).

[15] Sheldon H. Danziger, Robert H. Haveman, and Robert D. Plotnick, "Antipoverty Policy: Effects on the Poor and the Nonpoor," in Sheldon H. Danziger and Daniel H. Weinberg, eds., *Fighting Poverty: What Works and What Doesn't* (Cambridge: Harvard University Press, 1986), 50–77.

[16] For 1940, we have only income data on earnings. Therefore, I have calculated only an HEP rate and the official poverty rate. In 1950 and 1960, transfer payments were not differentiated from other income. The effectiveness rates of other income, therefore, for 1950 through 1980 have been calculated using both public and private transfers. For example, the effectiveness rate of other income in 1980 (60 percent) means that private and public transfer combined lifted 60 percent of the population that was below the earnings poverty rate above the poverty line. The effectiveness rate of public transfers alone was 47 percent.

For a more detailed discussion of the methods used in this paper, see Mark J. Stern, "Poverty and the Life-Cycle, 1939–1959," *Journal of Social History* (Spring 1991).

[17] Using the same logic, we can calculate the *effectiveness rate* of each source of income. Begin-

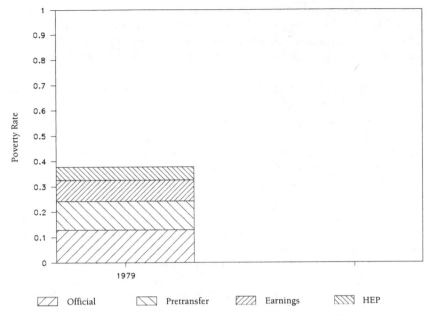

Figure 7.2. Poverty Indexes, Total Population, 1979. Although the official poverty rate in 1979 was only 13 percent, nearly 40 percent of the population would have been poor if the householder's earnings alone were considered. Other family earnings, private income, and public transfer payments allowed a quarter of the population to escape poverty.

The disaggregation of poverty allows us to examine the relative importance of each source of income. As we shall see, householders' earnings, other family earnings, and public and private transfers have played different roles in the years since 1939.

Poverty in 1939

Nineteen thirty-nine is a year out of place. It doesn't quite fit into the economic and social history of the Great Depression or that of World War II. After the ravages of the economic collapse of 1929–33 and the downturn of 1937, the

---

ning with the HEP of 37.8 percent, the effectiveness of other family members' income is equal to the difference between HEP and earnings poverty divided by HEP, or

$$\frac{37.8 - 32.6}{37.8} = 13.7\%$$

Thus, of the 37.8 percent of householders at risk, 13.7 percent were not poor when other family members earnings are considered.

economy had snapped back to the 1930s image of "normalcy." After falling from 31 to 24 million between 1928 and 1933, the number of employed workers had edged up to 30 million, still leaving the unemployment rate near 15 percent. Among those employed, average real wages had finally eclipsed their level of 1929–30.

The New Deal was in decline, but the welfare state had become part of everyday life. Even though public-works projects had been severely cut after 1937, 6 percent of employed householders worked on emergency public employment projects. The Social Security Act had brought federal dollars to public assistance for the aged, the blind, and dependent children and was on the verge of paying benefits under Old Age Insurance.

Poverty remained a pervasive phenomenon: 44 percent of householders lived in poverty in that year. Although this figure was probably 20 percentage points below that of the peak of the Depression, it shows that poverty remained a common experience. Most working-class families and a significant proportion of white-collar workers could expect to find themselves in poverty at some point in their life cycle. The aged remained the group most at risk of poverty (around two in three); but middle-aged parents often slipped into poverty because of the gap between their income and rising consumption needs. In short, in 1939, the bulk of American families lived on the edge (fig. 7.3).[18]

Moreover, most achieved this degree of security only through the concerted actions of the family. Over half of householders earned wages well below the poverty threshold. The earnings of other family members, more often children than spouses, lifted about one in ten families above the poverty line.

Even these figures may paint too rosy a picture, because some groups were much less likely to be at risk of poverty than others. Excluding white-collar and craft workers, the poverty rate for the remaining three-quarters of the population was 54 percent. For semiskilled workers, the rate stood at 29 percent, and for domestics, laborers, and farm laborers, 77 percent, 62 percent, and 87 percent, respectively.

Both blacks as a race and the South as a region remained distinctly poor. Indeed, Northern blacks with a poverty rate of 56 percent were much poorer than Northern whites (37 percent), but only a few percentage points higher than Southern whites (52 percent). The Southern black poverty rate in 1939 was 82 percent.

---

[18] Unfortunately, the only data we have on incomes for 1939 are for wages and salaries. Although this is a serious omission, we must keep in mind that most nonwage sources of income probably had little impact on poverty before 1940. The social insurances had begun to collect taxes but not to pay benefits; private pensions and insurance were rare for blue-collar workers; and benefits from public-assistance programs were too low to lift many out of poverty. The most serious implication for estimating poverty was the lack of data on earnings from self-employment. Therefore, the self-employed were omitted from all estimates of poverty. Based on the 1949 data, it is likely that the poverty rates of the self-employed in 1939 were similar to those of the rest of the population. For a more detailed discussion of this issue, see Stern, "Poverty and the Life-Cycle."

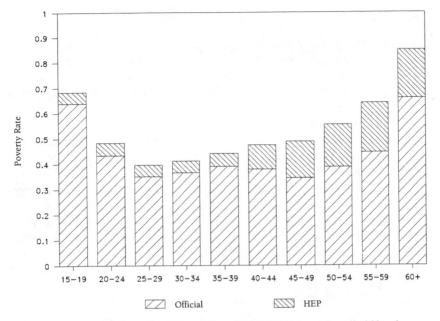

Figure 7.3. Poverty Indexes, by Woman's Age, 1939. Middle-aged household heads were less likely to earn a living wage than those who were younger. The earnings of other family members, however, pulled more families out of poverty.

The North was no crystal stair for African Americans, as Jacqueline Jones and Joe Trotter make clear. Still, there is little wonder that Northern cities attracted African-American migrants. In 1939, cities still had lower poverty rates than their suburbs or rural areas. In spite of the Depression and nascent suburbanization, the great industrial cities of the North remained the motors of economic growth and the sign of hope for those in the impoverished countryside.

In the context of widespread poverty, the urban jobless did not stand out as a unique group. Still, for the careful observer, the seeds of the underclass were present. Wedged between the Great Migrations of the 1920s and 1950s, Northern blacks, 3 percent of the population, comprised 11 percent of the urban jobless. Before World War II, the female householders, too, often found themselves among the urban jobless. At a time when female householders constituted only 14 percent of the population, they made up 34 percent of the urban jobless. In fact, the overrepresentation of female householders among the urban jobless was significantly greater in 1939 than it was forty years later.[19]

[19] Overrepresentation is defined as the difference between the representation of a group among the chronically jobless and in the population divided by its representation in the population. For example, the overrepresentation of female householders in 1939 was

$$\frac{33.7 - 14.0}{14.0} = 141\%$$

The Forties

World War II dominated the 1940s. Unemployment was virtually eliminated by the wartime command economy, and pent-up consumer demand generated economic growth through the rest of the decade. By 1949, the poverty rate had fallen to 37 percent, and the proportion of householders who did not earn a living wage dropped from 54 to 43 percent. No other decade even comes close to the magnitude of these declines.

Most occupational and ethnic groups shared the poverty declines of the 1940s. However, blue-collar workers were the greatest beneficiaries of the new economic realities. The householder earnings poverty rate of unskilled laborers fell from 71 to 48 percent. Skilled and semiskilled workers and farm laborers recorded smaller, but still substantial, declines.

Northerners of all races and Southern whites shared in the declines of these years. Poverty declined even among the urban jobless; the proportion earning a living wage rose from 13 to 29 percent. Only Southern blacks—still mired in the twin oppressions of Jim Crow and debt peonage—failed to improve. Just over one-half of Northern blacks remained below the poverty line, but more than four in five Southern blacks were.

In short, the forties' job boom brought widespread improvements to most groups in the American population. Although the economy did little to reduce inequality, the rising tide did indeed lift all boats. Southern African Americans remained the one exception. Their horrendous poverty rates of the late 1930s persisted through the 1940s.

The Fifties

The 1950s occupy a unique position in the American collective memory as an era of widespread opportunity and affluence. Yet, like the 1890s and the 1920s, two other decades that appeared prosperous, the fifties, too, had their darker side.[20] In a recent collection of essays, Paul Peterson, for example, questioned the "liberal" interpretation of the persistence of poverty by noting that substantial progress was made in fighting poverty during the 1950s, although the "welfare state hardly expanded at all." Conservative analysts have made this case even more strongly, contrasting the economic growth and strong "traditional" families of the 1950s with the stagnation and permissiveness of the sixties and seventies.[21]

However, the expansion of the welfare state and the changing work patterns

---

[20] Elaine Tyler May, *Homeward Bound: American Families in the Cold War Era* (New York: Basic Books, 1988); James Gilbert, *A Cycle of Outrage: America's Reaction to the Juvenile Delinquent in the 1950s* (New York: Oxford University Press, 1986).

[21] Paul Peterson, "The Urban Underclass and the Poverty Paradox," in Jencks and Peterson, *The Urban Underclass*, 12.

of American women accounted for the poverty decline of the decade as much as did the increased earning power of "breadwinners." Less than half of the 10 percent decline in "official" poverty during the 1950s was the result of increased householders' earnings. Nearly half of the poverty decline of the 1950s was caused by public and private welfare benefits.

Scholars are apt to ignore the quiet welfare state of the 1950s. The best-known public program during this period, of course, was Social Security. Although benefits began to be paid under Old Age and Survivors' Insurance in the early 1940s, the amendments of 1950 liberalized the benefits of lower-income workers and raised average monthly benefits by 17 percent. By 1959, the average benefit for a retired worker had reached $81.46, a real (inflation-adjusted) increase of 152 percent.[22]

In addition, the 1950 amendments added benefits for the caretakers of dependent children and for the disabled. In 1956, disabled workers were added to the social insurance program as well. Veterans qualified for the well-known educational and housing benefits and were entitled to readjustment pay for a year after their discharge. Finally, the government compensated veterans with service-related disabilities and the survivors of those killed in the service.

During the same years, Supreme Court interpretations of the Taft-Hartley Act allowed labor and management to include fringe benefits in negotiations, and the National Labor Relations Board and the tax code strongly supported the expansion of insurance, pensions, and health care. By the end of the decade, these "private" transfer payments complemented the quiet expansion of the welfare state.[23]

Wage growth alone did little to improve the economic position of workers. Only farm laborers' and farmers' family earnings poverty declined by more than 3 percentage points. Among the rest of the population, the expansion of transfer payments was the chief route for escaping poverty.

Northern blacks' poverty declined faster than that of the rest of the population, but their chance of poverty remained twice that of Northern whites. The rapid migration of Southern blacks to Northern cities fed the growth of the chronically jobless. Between 1950 and 1960, the proportion of African Americans among the urban jobless rose from 18 to 28 percent, nearly twice the increase of any other decade. Northern blacks' share of the entire population increased by over 40 percent (from 2.7 to 3.9 percent). By 1960 nearly one in five members of the urban jobless was a Northern black.

Despite the growth of the welfare state, the poverty rate of the urban jobless declined by only a few percentage points, and their share of all the poor in-

---

[22] Martha Derthick, *Policymaking for Social Security* (Washington, D.C.: Brookings Institution, 1979); *Social Security Bulletin, Annual Statistical Supplement.*

[23] Beth Stevens, "Blurring the Boundaries: How the Federal Government Has Influenced Welfare Benefits in the Private Sector," in Margaret Weir, Ann Shola Orloff, and Theda Skocpol, eds., *The Politics of Social Policy in the United States* (Princeton: Princeton University Press, 1988), 123–49.

creased for the first time from 7 to 8 percent. Indeed, the extreme concentration of the chronically jobless among people of color became marked during these years. Whereas blacks and Hispanics had been about twice as likely as the general population to be chronically jobless in 1949, by 1959, they were three times as likely, a figure that would remain relatively stable over the next twenty years.

The Sixties

The pace of the poverty decline quickened during the 1960s, stimulated by war-induced prosperity and the expansion of welfare spending. The proportion of householders whose earnings left them below the poverty threshold fell by nearly 7 percentage points, as did the official poverty rate.

The gap between the lowest occupational groups and the rest of the population closed during the 1960s. The HEP rate of laborers fell by 17 percentage points, farmers by 14 percentage points, and farm laborers by 30 percentage points (table 7.5). For the first time in American history, full-time workers almost always avoided poverty. By 1969, less than one in twelve full-time workers failed to earn a living wage (table 7.6).

At the same time, the poverty data began to reflect the new economic strength of the Sunbelt. Southerners' poverty declines exceeded even the strong reductions among Northerners. The gap between Northern and Southern whites fell from 14 to 4 percentage points between 1949 and 1959. Although Southern blacks' risk of poverty was still three times that of Southern whites and 75 percent greater than that of Northern blacks, it had fallen by more than 30 percentage points in two decades.

The War on Poverty and liberalization of welfare eligibility combined with prosperity to reduce the poverty of the urban jobless. The poverty rate of the urban jobless fell from 44 to 35 percent. The effectiveness of transfer payments (public and private) rose from 18 percent in 1959 to 28 percent in 1969, at a time when the effectiveness rate for the rest of the nonaged population increased from 24 to 28 percent. Still, during the sixties, the overrepresentation of blacks and Hispanics among the urban jobless increased from 215 percent to 275 percent.

In the spring of 1971, Lee Rainwater and his associates went around Boston, asking people to compare their well-being with that of the recent past and future. His respondents were "less than ecstatic about whether things had changed for the better in the post–World War II period," but they were nearly unanimous that "the 1960s were hell; the decade was like a bad dream come true."[24]

---

[24] Lee Rainwater, *What Money Buys: Inequality and the Social Meaning of Income* (New York: Basic Books, 1971), 65.

TABLE 7.5
Poverty Indexes, by Occupational Group (Percentages)

	White-Collar	Self-Employed	Craft	Semiskilled	Domestic Service	Labor	Farmer	Farm Labor	No Occupation
1939 HEP	16.2	59.2	28.0	40.2	88.1	70.9	92.7	90.7	96.7
Official poverty	11.9	49.7	21.6	29.4	76.8	61.9	83.3	86.8	76.6
N	2,862	1,545	1,981	3,296	212	1,623	1,332	1,436	3,057
1949 HEP	16.5	32.0	20.9	33.0	90.2	47.4	62.6	76.6	92.3
Earnings poverty	12.5	25.6	16.8	25.4	83.6	40.3	57.2	69.5	81.5
Official poverty	9.7	21.3	15.1	22.9	80.0	37.6	52.2	67.6	66.8
N	3,874	1,765	2,848	3,857	173	1,111	1,767	385	3,456
1959 HEP	18.2	47.2	18.7	34.5	90.7	46.8	64.4	73.6	76.9
Earnings poverty	14.0	37.9	13.9	26.1	81.8	36.6	52.5	65.0	66.3
Official poverty	7.6	15.7	8.8	19.6	71.5	29.2	39.4	58.3	48.2
N	838	3,532	4,817	5,471	5,915	5,566	5,051	4,371	3,768
1969 HEP	15.6	22.5	16.3	29.0	92.0	29.9	47.7	43.6	86.6
Earnings poverty	12.2	17.9	12.7	23.6	82.4	25.3	42.7	42.1	78.4
Pretransfer poverty	8.5	12.8	10.2	20.0	80.3	22.3	35.4	42.1	65.6
Official poverty	5.1	8.9	5.6	12.9	56.8	12.7	26.6	30.0	44.4
N	160,549	36,339	73,578	112,341	5,406	21,405	11,037	2,663	71,771
1979 HEP	18.3	23.0	18.4	28.8	82.2	35.1	42.8	53.2	93.3
Earnings poverty	14.6	17.1	14.8	23.0	76.2	27.5	34.8	45.9	86.5
Pretransfer poverty	9.8	11.4	10.5	18.5	71.5	23.0	24.9	38.6	64.3
Official poverty	6.3	7.1	6.2	11.7	46.7	15.5	16.1	23.3	28.6
N	107,732	20,568	28,354	79,196	1,493	11,245	5,155	3,927	63,861

TABLE 7.6
Poverty Indexes, by Work Experience, Householders, 1939–1979 (Percentages)

	Full-Time, Full-Year	Partially Employed	Did Not Work
1939 HEP	27.6	65.1	99.4
Official poverty	22.1	54.0	79.1
N	9,576	4,527	3,241
Percentage	55.2	26.1	18.7
1949 HEP	22.4	51.8	84.4
Earnings poverty	18.0	43.9	73.9
Official poverty	16.0	39.3	61.7
N	10,829	3,606	4,801
Percentage	56.3	18.7	25.0
1959 HEP	16.7	48.1	81.7
Earnings poverty	12.6	37.4	69.1
Official poverty	8.5	28.9	46.6
N	30,409	8,628	13,727
Percentage	57.6	16.4	26.0
1969 HEP	7.2	36.2	97.0
Earnings poverty	5.3	28.8	86.7
Pretransfer poverty	5.0	24.2	68.4
Official poverty	3.8	16.8	42.2
N	282,995	110,519	101,575
Percentage	57.2	22.3	20.5
1979 HEP	7.1	40.5	98.4
Earnings poverty	5.0	31.6	90.1
Pretransfer poverty	4.3	24.3	65.3
Official poverty	3.1	16.6	30.1
N	167,304	72,771	81,456
Percentage	52.0	22.6	25.3

Given the spectacular rise in wages and incomes during the 1960s, Rainwater's finding suggests either that inflation masked the real improvements in peoples' standards of living during these years or that income is a poor measure of social well-being. Of course, his respondents had no way of knowing what awaited them during the 1970s.[25]

[25] In fact, one of the interesting aspects of Rainwater's book is that his respondents *assumed* that average incomes would rise, but worried that they would be offset by social and environmental decline (ibid., 64–93).

The Seventies

Official poverty edged lower during the 1970s. The poverty rate fell to 13.0 in 1979, 1.6 percent below the 1969 figure. Yet the decline of poverty during the 1970s occurred in spite of a marked deterioration in all areas of income, except public transfer payments.

The proportion of householders with earnings below the poverty line rose from 32 to 38 percent during the 1970s, climbing to within a percentage point of the recession-level 1959 figure. Even including other family members' earnings, one in three domestic units could not earn its way out of poverty in 1979.

Family earnings poverty rose across the occupational structure. Only farmers and domestics avoided it; laborers' family earnings poverty rate increased from 30 to 35 percent. Among ethnic groups, only Southern nonwhites escaped the poverty increases.

Transfer payments—especially the expansion of social welfare payments—counterbalanced increases in earnings poverty. Yet this expansion of welfare payments did not target the problems of the urban jobless. The aged and disabled benefited the most, thanks to the rapid expansion of Social Security. The poverty rate of householders over sixty years of age fell from 26 to 17 percent during the 1970s, a decline of 34 percent. Of the aged who were at risk of poverty in 1979, nearly two-thirds escaped poverty because of transfer payments (fig. 7.4).

The urban jobless shared the economic problems of the 1970s with the rest of the population, but were not helped as much by the expansion of public programs. The contrast in public policy could hardly have been starker. During the 1970s, the federal government liberalized eligibility for disability insurance, raised Social Security benefits by over 50 percent and then protected them against inflation, and enacted Supplemental Security Income to protect the needy aged and disabled. At the same time, it did nothing to protect the programs for the urban jobless against inflation and, in fact, led efforts to restrict eligibility. The result was a 35 percent decline in the real value of Aid for Families with Dependent Children benefits and the stagnation of state general assistance programs.[26] As a result, the urban jobless increased from 4.2 to 4.5 percent of the population. By 1979, the chronically jobless included 15 percent of the poor (fig. 7.5).[27]

Imagine a waiting room shared by a number of doctors. The room is crowded with people waiting to be called out. As time passes, one person then another leaves through one door or another. But a few, for whatever reason, are never called. They sit, either resigned or impatient, hoping their time will come.

[26] June Axinn and Mark J. Stern, *Dependency and Poverty: Old Problems in a New World* (Lexington, Mass.: Lexington Books, 1988), 124–35.

[27] Although fully 54 percent of the group was nonwhite in 1979, this was about two-and-a-half times the rate for whites, a slight decline from 1969.

242 · Mark J. Stern

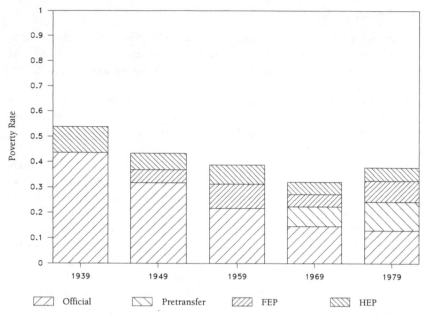

Figure 7.4. Poverty Indexes, 1939–1979. The rise in householder and family earnings poverty rates during the 1970s was hidden by the increased effectiveness of transfer payments.

In 1939, the waiting room called poverty was crowded with full-time workers, the aged, blacks and whites, Northerners and Southerners. Over time, individuals and groups slowly left. Some—blue-collar workers—benefited from the general rise in the level of wages. Others—the aged, unemployed, and disabled—were called out by the expansion of the welfare state. Others used domestic strategies—family extension, spouses' employment—to leave the room.

But one group did not get called, at least not in numbers comparable to the rest of the population. Without job opportunities or help from the government, the urban jobless relied on their families and kin to help them survive. Yet these strategies, too, were often doomed to failure.

FAMILY AND THE PERVERSITY OF POLICY

American welfare policy has been preoccupied with the female-headed family. One parent—whether father or mother—has difficulty covering the twin duties of earning a living and rearing children. The increase in the proportion of families headed by a woman—from 14 to 26 percent between 1939 and 1979—was a legitimate reason for concern.

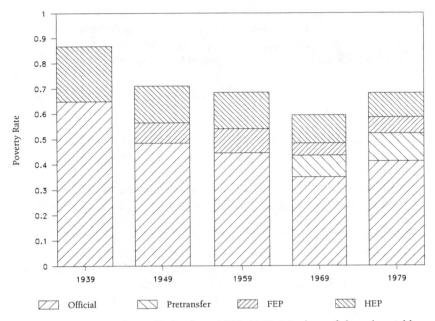

Figure 7.5. Poverty Indexes, Underclass, 1939–1979. Members of the urban jobless shared a rise in earnings poverty with the rest of the population. They did not benefit from the increased effectiveness of transfer payments, however.

Yet the preoccupation with female-headed households has obscured the breadth of strategies that the poor have used to combat poverty. For the individual, the opportunity structure and government policy are given; family strategies provide one of the few means under his or her control to address economic deprivation. An assessment of the role of family life in the poverty story must take all of these strategies—spouses' or children's employment, family extension—into account.

The preoccupation with female-headed families has also narrowed our understanding of family strategies and public policy. Charles Murray's *Losing Ground* has revived an old belief that overly generous public assistance benefits create an economic incentive for a woman not to live with her children's father. From a different perspective, Wilson and Neckerman argue that incarceration and joblessness have so reduced the number of "available" men that women have little choice but to live alone.[28]

Although Murray's argument has been largely refuted, it has been successful

28 William Julius Wilson and Kathryn M. Neckerman, "Poverty and Family Structure: The Widening Gap between Evidence and Public Policy Issues," in Danziger and Weinberg, *Fighting Poverty: What Works and What Doesn't*, 232–83.

in making the female householder the central icon in the debate over family, poverty, and public policy. Yet the variety in the poor's family strategies reflects the complexity of families' responses to public policy. Again, an account that examines female householders in isolation is bound to be flawed.

Working Children and Household Extension

Contemporary poverty studies have overlooked two family strategies with long histories: child labor and household extension. Both of these strategies remained important to urban jobless families during the postwar years. During the 1970s, each went through a precipitous decline in antipoverty effectiveness. The decline in the youth job market was responsible for the demise of child labor's effectiveness, and government policy was a major contributor to the reduced effectiveness of household extension.

Before World War II, child labor was a central means of coping with the men's low earnings, especially among immigrant and second-generation families.[29] As late as 1969, one in five urban jobless families relied on children's earnings, although these families were more often male headed and white. Still, in 1969, 16 percent of black urban jobless families had at least one working child present in the household.

The deterioration of the youth job market after 1959, however, weakened the effectiveness of this strategy. Although the percentage of urban jobless families with a working child increased from 15 to 20 percent between 1959 and 1969, the effectiveness of children's contribution in lifting these families out of poverty declined from 60 to 46 percent.

Working children declined both in frequency and effectiveness during the 1970s. The decline in youth employment opportunities reduced the proportion of urban jobless families with a working child from 20 to 13 percent. Among young people who found work, irregular employment limited its antipoverty effectiveness; only one in five of families at risk escaped poverty because of other family members' earnings. Thus, in two decades, the effectiveness of child labor had declined by two-thirds. Among blacks and Hispanics, the trend was even more profound. Between 1959 and 1979, the antipoverty effectiveness of working children declined from 47 to 14 percent among African Americans and from 55 to 15 percent among Latinos.

In contrast to working children, household extension remained a common strategy, especially during recessions. A larger proportion of households were extended in 1939, 1959, and 1979 than in the relatively prosperous years of 1949 and 1969. Even among the urban jobless and marginally employed, family extension was employed by the poorest families; the heads of extended households were less likely to earn a living wage than were the heads of nuclear

---

[29] Keep in mind that most of the children who worked were in their late teens and early twenties.

TABLE 7.7
Poverty Indexes by Household Extension, Underclass and Other Nonaged
Householders, 1939–1979 (Percentages)

	Underclass		Other Non-Aged	
	Not Extended	Extended	Not Extended	Extended
1939 HEP	85.5	93.6	42.4	48.3
Official	65.0	64.5	36.5	34.7
N	791	155	8,648	1,126
1949 HEP	69.1	80.5	32.2	44.8
Earnings	54.8	64.5	27.5	34.0
Official	46.7	57.2	24.5	29.2
N	752	152	12,302	1,212
1959 HEP	67.4	72.9	23.5	37.7
Earnings	53.3	56.9	18.5	28.9
Official	45.4	40.2	14.5	19.7
N	1,750	406	31,142	5,258
1969 HEP	57.2	70.0	14.1	24.9
Earnings	49.4	43.5	11.6	15.9
Pretransfer	43.5	43.0	10.4	14.3
Official	36.5	27.3	8.4	11.0
N	17,407	3,480	290,985	40,439
1979 HEP	65.8	76.4	17.7	31.7
Earnings	57.1	64.1	13.7	25.3
Pretransfer	50.4	59.0	10.8	21.8
Official	40.4	43.7	8.6	14.8
N	11,347	3,091	186,600	29,799

households. For example, in 1959, extended families' breadwinners were 6 percentage points *less* likely not to earn wages above the poverty line than those of nuclear families (73 to 67 percent), but their poverty rate was five percentage points lower (40 to 45 percent) (table 7.7).[30]

During the 1970s, the proportion of extended households among the urban

[30] The impact of household extension on family income is complex. If an outsider is kin and works, his or her earnings would contribute to the "other family members' earnings." If he or she pays rent, however, this income would show up as "other income." Thus, we must examine both of these sources.

Household extension helped many nonaged families escape poverty. The effectiveness rate of other family members' earnings and other income were higher for extended households in every year between 1939 and 1969 (in 1979 the effectiveness of other family earnings was slightly lower). For 1969 and 1979 (when we can differentiate between public transfers and other private income) about one extended family escaped poverty because of private income for every two who escaped through public money.

TABLE 7.8
Household Extension, by Gender and Ethnicity of Householder, Underclass Householders, 1939–1979

	Not Extended									Extended Households								
	All Races			Blacks			Hispanics			All Races			Blacks			Hispanics		
	Total	Female	Male	Total	Female	Male	Total	Female	Male	Total	Female	Male	Total	Female	Male	Total	Female	Male
1939																		
Percentage extended	—	—	—	—	—	—	—	—	—	16.4	22.5	13.1	25.9	42.9	24.0	—	—	—
Percentage of poor underclass	83.7	29.8	53.9	14.3	1.3	13.0	—	—	—	16.3	7.8	8.5	4.7	1.0	3.7	—	—	—
Percentage of underclass	83.6	27.3	56.3	10.9	0.8	10.0	—	—	—	16.4	7.9	8.5	3.8	0.6	3.2	—	—	—
1949																		
Percentage extended	—	—	—	—	—	—	—	—	—	16.8	24.3	12.8	30.4	38.5	24.3	—	—	—
Percentage of poor underclass	80.1	34.7	45.4	17.8	8.7	9.1	—	—	—	19.9	13.4	6.5	8.0	5.2	2.8	—	—	—
Percentage of underclass	83.2	26.4	56.8	12.4	4.7	7.7	—	—	—	16.8	8.5	8.3	5.4	3.0	2.5	—	—	—

1959																		
Percentage extended	—	—	—	—	—	—	—	—	—	18.8	22.6	16.7	27.4	30.5	25.1	22.2	26.1	19.7
Percentage of poor underclass	83.0	42.8	40.2	16.2	14.0	5.9	2.7	3.2		17.0	9.7	7.3	9.2	5.2	4.0	1.1	0.4	0.7
Percentage of underclass	81.2	28.3	52.9	20.5	8.3	12.2	4.2	1.6	2.6	18.8	8.3	10.6	7.7	3.7	4.1	1.2	0.6	0.6
1969																		
Percentage extended	—	—	—	—	—	—	—	—	—	16.7	24.4	11.7	18.4	19.2	17.6	19.3	21.3	17.9
Percentage of poor underclass	87.0	54.8	32.2	28.2	11.9	11.3	6.8	4.6		13.0	10.1	2.9	6.4	4.7	1.8	2.3	1.3	1.0
Percentage of underclass	83.3	29.7	53.6	27.6	13.9	13.7	8.6	3.5	5.1	16.7	9.6	7.1	6.2	3.3	2.9	2.1	0.9	1.1
1979																		
Percentage extended	—	—	—	—	—	—	—	—	—	21.4	24.0	19.4	26.1	28.4	23.0	24.9	22.6	26.5
Percentage of poor underclass	77.2	51.0	26.2	26.8	8.8	13.9	9.4	4.4		22.8	14.5	8.2	11.4	8.6	2.8	4.0	2.3	1.7
Percentage of underclass	78.6	33.0	45.6	27.6	15.6	12.1	12.5	5.5	7.1	21.4	10.4	11.0	9.8	6.2	3.6	4.1	1.6	2.5

jobless swelled from 17 to 21 percent. At the same time, the proportion of these families with a head making a living wage fell from 30 percent to 24 percent, and the effectiveness of other family earnings and private transfers fell sharply. Finally, the effectiveness of public transfers declined from 36 to 26 percent. All of these trends combined to force the poverty rate of extended urban jobless families to jump from 27 percent to 44 percent (table 7.8).

Throughout the postwar years approximately twice as many urban jobless female-headed families as male-headed families included outsiders.[31] However, after thirty years of relative stability, the proportion of extended male-headed households soared from 12 percent to 19 percent during the 1970s (table 7.8). As a result, the family structure of the urban jobless altered dramatically between 1969 and 1979. The proportion that was nuclear fell from 87 to 77 percent (with the male-headed share dropping from 32 to 26 percent), while the share that was extended rose from 13 to 23 percent (with the male-headed share rising from 3 to 8 percent). Similar trends were present among black and Hispanic urban jobless households.

The startling expansion in the numbers and poverty of extended households has no simple explanation. The most likely answer is family and social obligation, perhaps stemming from the African roots discussed by Andrew Miller. Faced with an increasing number of individuals and families unable to survive on their own resources, urban jobless householders opened their homes to friends and kin even though it did nothing to improve the economic status of their immediate family.[32]

Public policy proceeded to make a bad situation worse. The federal government used increased restrictions on earnings, assets, and family membership to reduce welfare costs during the late 1970s. These restrictions on Aid to Families with Dependent Children were effective; administrative reforms "tended to reduce the proportion of eligible individuals who participated in the program."[33]

Extended families were more at risk of finding themselves running afoul of welfare regulations and losing benefits. Extra members made it more difficult to gather information and raised the suspicion of the authorities. As administrators tightened eligibility and compliance regulations, the entrance and exit of household members provided a rationale for refusing or delaying benefits. Reduced welfare benefits compounded the economic difficulties caused by changing

[31] In 1939, for example, 22 percent of female-headed households and 13 percent of male-headed households were extended. In 1969, the proportions were 24 and 12 percent, respectively.

[32] It seems reasonable to assume that the same forces were responsible for the increase in extended families and homelessness during these years. The biographies of many of the homeless include spells of living with a friend or kin before either voluntarily or involuntarily taking to the street.

[33] Michael R. Sosin, "Legal Rights and Welfare Change," in Danziger and Weinberg, *Fighting Poverty: What Works and What Doesn't*, 276.

family circumstances.[34] The generosity that allowed the urban jobless to open their homes to others contradicts the stereotype of the anomie supposedly plaguing the underclass of the 1970s. Far from it, they were demonstrating an extraordinary degree of responsibility in the face of personal economic hardship.[35]

Family Composition and Work

Throughout the population, women's opportunities in the labor force expanded during the postwar era. African-American women, who had been virtually excluded from all but the most marginal occupations before the 1950s, were perhaps the greatest beneficiaries of the expansion of women's work and the decline in racial and gender discrimination. During the 1960s and 1970s, African-American women's average earnings and those of black men and white women converged.

Yet the expansion of African-American women's earnings had two somewhat contradictory effects. On the one hand, women's improved earning power was a major reason for the rapid decline of poverty among two-parent urban jobless families. On the other hand, improved female opportunities reduced the comparative advantage of male householders among the urban jobless. If Kathryn Neckerman is right about the emergent gender conflict in the families of the urban poor, the rapid white-collar proletarianization of black women may have increased their willingness to escape from unsatisfactory marriages or to avoid marriage altogether. Thus, the same phenomenon—women's economic emergence—may have contributed to the strengthening of two-parent families and to the proliferation of female-headed families among the urban jobless.

The proportion of dual-earner and female-headed families increased among both urban jobless and the rest of the population. Among other nonaged families, dual earners as a proportion of all families increased from 16 to 43 percent

---

[34] In 1982, Pennsylvania Governor Richard Thornburgh succeeded in severely restricting the state's general-assistance payments to able-bodied recipients. Part of the rationale for this decline was to force unmarried men and women who were living on their own and collecting general assistance to move in with their parents. Given the strain on the family economy of the urban jobless, it is hardly surprising that Thornburgh's "welfare reform" was a contributor to the increase of homelessness during the 1980s.

[35] The situation during the 1970s is quite similar to that described by Steven Ruggles in *Prolonged Connections: The Rise of the Extended Family in Nineteenth-Century England and America* (Madison: University of Wisconsin Press, 1987). Ruggles argues that the evidence suggests that families were not extended strategically (i.e., for the economic benefit of the primary family) during the nineteenth century. He concludes that a normative theory explains this pattern; the Victorian glorification of family signified a cultural value that made nineteenth-century families want to be extended whether it made economic sense or not.

The history of the 1970s raises some doubts about this explanation. While Ruggles is correct to underline the complexity of family motivations, his theory seems to gloss over the considerable gap that separates wanting to accept relatives and not being able to avoid it.

between 1950 and 1980. During the same years, the proportion of female-headed households in the other nonaged population rose from 10 to 18 percent. Thus, by 1980, male-headed, single-earner families constituted only 39 percent of other nonaged households. The direction and degree of change was similar among the urban jobless. The proportion of dual-earner households increased from 8 to 19 percent, and the proportion of female-headed households from 35 to 43 percent.

The expansion of women's job opportunities provided a new degree of flexibility to two-parent families that was particularly important to the urban jobless. Because householders did not have steady work, the earnings of spouses were crucial. Yet the restriction of women's job alternatives (and wages) meant that before the 1960s, many urban jobless families with two earners remained in poverty. In 1959, for example, the poverty rate of dual-earner urban jobless families was 28 percent. The broadening of opportunities for women (particularly African-American women) improved the odds of dual-earner urban jobless families escaping poverty. By 1979, their poverty rate had fallen to 7 percent.[36]

The proportion of both the urban jobless and other nonaged female householders who worked increased during the postwar years. Recall that the term *chronically jobless* includes both those who did not work and those who worked either part-time or for less than half the year. In 1949, about one in five chronically jobless female householders (21 percent) worked at some point during the previous year; thirty years later, this proportion had risen to 37 percent.[37]

At the same time, the jobs they held were substantially better. By 1980, 38 percent of marginally employed female householders had professional, managerial, and clerical occupational titles, compared to fewer than 15 percent of marginally employed male householders. The increased job opportunities of marginally employed female householders provided them with a strong incentive to work. In 1959, they had virtually the same poverty rate (62 percent) as those who stayed at home (65 percent). By 1979, the poverty rate of the marginally employed had fallen to 44 percent, and the rate for urban jobless female householders at home had risen to 73 percent.

Not only did working female householders do substantially better than those

[36] The increase of dual-earner urban jobless families was not shared by African Americans. While the proportion of white urban jobless families that had two earners increased from 7 to 23 percent between 1939 and 1979 (with most of the increase occurring after 1959), the black rate did not increase as rapidly. Eleven percent of black urban jobless families had two earners in 1939 (3 percent more than the white rate), and the number expanded considerably between 1959 and 1969 (from 8 to 19 percent). However, during the 1970s, while the proportion held steady for whites, the percentage of black urban jobless families with two earners fell from 19 to 13 percent.

[37] An important change occurred in the composition of the female householder population during the 1960s and 1970s. Whereas before 1960 the bulk of female householders were widowed and divorced, during the 1960s and 1970s, the proportion that was never married increased. As a result, the female householder population became younger and had fewer older children.

who stayed home, but they made strong gains relative to urban jobless men as well. In 1959, the household earnings poverty rates of chronically jobless male (without a working wife) and female householders were 57 and 81 percent, respectively. Twenty years later, the male rate had increased to 64 percent, and the female rate had fallen to 63 percent. In other words, in 1959 a women who separated from a chronically jobless man and entered the labor force would see her risk of poverty increase from 57 to 81 percent. Twenty years later, her risk would hardly have changed.[38]

The census data substantially contradict Murray's assertion that rising welfare benefits were responsible for the increased proportion of female householders. The antipoverty effectiveness of transfer payments rose for urban jobless female householders between 1949 and 1969 but stagnated during the 1970s. Compared to the powerful incentive of women's improved job opportunities and wages, welfare benefits had little demonstrable effect.

There is certainly an irony in these data. As we noted earlier, the poverty story of the 1970s was the increase in the proportion of the population with earnings below poverty. This trend was shared by dual-earner families, male-headed families with one earner, and most female-headed families. Only one group— marginally employed female householders—went against the tide. The family problems of the underclass were part and parcel of the overall decline in the economic well-being of America's families during the 1970s.

The trends in the work patterns of family members of the urban jobless and the rest of the population were substantially the same during the postwar years. For both groups, the number of dual-earner and female-headed families increased, and female householders worked more often. The key difference between the two groups was the relative improvement of the economic prospects of men and women.

Among other nonaged families, men retained a substantial economic edge over women. Although women contributed in dual-earner families, by 1969, nine in ten of these families did not need this contribution to escape poverty. The gap between the wages of male householders and female householders remained substantial throughout the period.

The improved economic status of women was much more apparent among the urban jobless. During the 1970s, more dual-earner families relied on women's wages to escape poverty. At the same time, marginally employed female householders actually improved their earnings. As a result, the earnings gap between male householders and female householders disappeared.

Women's improved economic alternatives are not pathological. Among men and women who maintained a commitment to one another—what are conven-

---

[38] Among other nonaged households, men's earnings advantage did not disappear. The householder earnings poverty rate of male householders (without an employed spouse) remained substantially below that of a female householder who worked (19 to 26 percent).

252 · Mark J. Stern

tionally called "good marriages"—women's new earning power helped urban jobless families escape poverty. For couples for which this was not the case—for "bad marriages"—the equalization of earnings removed an incentive for women to prolong the relationship. Other women may have seen the new realities as a reason to avoid "entangling alliances" and not marry. Because the equalization of wages was greater for the urban jobless than for the rest of the population, the economic incentive to stay in a bad marriage was even smaller.

Again, the changes in the urban jobless family were the same as those among the rest of the population. The divorce revolution of the 1960s established the principle that a marriage should dissolve if either partner was unwilling to maintain it. Although this revolution has had a variety of unforeseen consequences (most of which have hurt women), how could the poor be called pathological for actions consistent with dominant social norms?[39]

The family life of the urban jobless changed for the worse during the 1970s. The percentage of householders with earnings above the poverty line fell. The decline in the youth labor market eliminated the antipoverty effectiveness of working children. Household extension often backfired because it led to reduced welfare benefits. The number of female householders increased. The urban jobless shared every one of these trends with the rest of the population, with one exception: All other groups benefited from a rapid increase in transfer payments. Public policy, not family breakdown, was the source of urban jobless families' distinctiveness.

CONCLUSION

Theorists have made many assumptions, in the absence of historical evidence, about the origins of the underclass. This paper provides some support for contemporary "underclass" theory. Urban blacks did undergo a startling decline in their work experience. The proportion of blacks working in industrial employment stagnated during the 1970s. The families of the urban jobless showed signs of these economic stresses.

At the same time, the analysis contradicts or qualifies elements of the dominant portrait of the underclass. At least with respect to earnings and employment, there was never a golden age of the ghetto; it had always been dominated by joblessness and poverty. Certainly blacks suffered from the massive loss of industrial employment in American cities during the 1970s, but so did whites. Moreover, blacks, but not whites, were able to balance these losses against sizable gains in white-collar employment. Although joblessness afflicted the African-American community during the 1960s and 1970s, it had done so earlier, and it spread this time nearly as quickly among whites.

[39] Lenore J. Weitzman, *The Divorce Revolution: The Unexpected Social and Economic Consequences for Women and Children in America* (New York: Free Press, 1985).

The accepted story not only misrepresented the economic deterioration of the black community during the postwar era, it got the story wrong for the rest of American society as well. Although the rise of wages was an important contributor to the decline of poverty, social welfare spending and women's work were equally powerful forces. The expansion of private benefits—especially insurance and pensions—and welfare entitlement removed one in seven families at risk from poverty in 1949, and three in five by 1979. During the 1970s, the declining significance of men's wages was covered up by the expansion of transfer payments.

Public and private social policy worked to disadvantage the urban jobless. Employer-provided benefits, such as disability coverage, stock ownership, and pensions, more often assisted the fully employed worker than the chronically jobless. At the same time, social insurance benefits were more generous than the public assistance benefits on which the urban jobless had to rely. After 1970 the gap between social insurance and public assistance widened, which led to a system of "reverse targeting."

Although the poor used family strategies to respond to these structural realities, the results were often contradictory. At times, family strategies and social policy produced particularly perverse results. During the 1970s, as urban jobless families scrambled to use household extension to combat economic disaster, federal and state welfare regulations restricted the benefits paid to these families.

This paper shows that the crisis of the underclass has been misunderstood; it also reveals that the economic problems of the rest of the population have been minimized. The 70 percent reduction of poverty during these years covered up a much slower expansion of the earnings capacity of household heads. Particularly during the 1940s and 1950s, when the bulk of the working class escaped poverty, the "mainstream" population required other family members' earnings and transfer payments to compensate for the slower growth of wages.

In a certain sense, then, the dominant images of the underclass and the mainstream have both been drawn in extremes. The underclass worked more and relied on family more and welfare less to escape poverty. The mainstream had less secure job histories, was more at risk of poverty, and relied on government handouts more often than we have generally believed. We might go so far as to say that these stereotypes complemented one other. If economic dislocation, irregularity of employment, and urban restructuring were taking their toll on all of us, perhaps it was reassuring to imagine that there was a class at the bottom of society worse off than the rest of us; a class whose vices made us look virtuous; a class whose poverty made us seem well off; a class whose family life made ours look stable.

CHAPTER 8

Social Science, Social Policy, and the Heritage of African-American Families

Andrew T. Miller

FAMILIES ARE dangerously imperiled by isolated urban poverty and its resulting violence and despair. In African-American communities throughout the twentieth century, families have worked against such conditions, sustaining and protecting individuals as far as possible. Because these families often exhibit structures and patterns quite different from those of Euro-Americans, they have come in for criticism rather than being looked on as possible alternative models of the meaning of family. In recent times, families have undergone drastic changes in all communities in the United States, and so it may be time to seek out such alternative models and assess their effectiveness. The past lack of consideration for such variations in family practice and cultural heritage needs to be reexamined and understood in order to be moved aside.

In many ways the concerns of this chapter are quite different from, though perhaps also complementary to, the analysis provided in chapter 6 by Kathryn Neckerman. Her article examines the structural constraints on household choices and their family consequences in the rapidly changing urban contexts of the early twentieth century in the northern United States. In this chapter, I seek to examine ethnic and cultural aspects of race and family that I find also play a significant role in household choices and family definition, and may explain how different repertoires of family options may produce different strategies for families facing similar structural constraints. For this reason, I focus on the ways the 1910 household data cut across class, rural/urban, regional, and institutional lines for African Americans and for those of African descent in other parts of the world in terms of family difference. This examination takes place within the context of the changing ways in which families themselves are imagined and defined. The Darwinist or scientistic, prescriptive notion of one best or "fittest" model for families is challenged in light of different social and individual needs, desires, and constraints.

For both popular and academic purposes, the term *underclass* is a convenient shorthand, but perhaps we should be a bit more troubled by its easy and

I am grateful to Michael Katz for his editorial guidance and helpful comments and suggestions. I also benefited from the comments of Drew Faust, Susan Watkins, Antonio McDaniel, Phil Morgan, and Houston Baker. This research was supported by a grant from the National Institutes of Health (NICHD 1–RO1–HD–25856–01) and the Population Studies Center of the University of Pennsylvania.

immediate popular understanding and acceptance. The intuitive knowledge of who is meant by the term *underclass* in public perception, despite the imprecision of most academic definitions, has wider implications. The connection of the term to a large body of social and cultural thinking in the United States produced since the beginnings of social science study early in the century should not be overlooked. This thinking was centered on ideas of what was decent, modern, healthy, and respectable behavior within households and families.

The idea of an underclass implies the existence of an overclass that defines and sets ideological standards under which society in general is expected to live. In the United States, "having class" generally has not been an economic consideration in popular usage. Rather, it is seen as a matter of behavior, social skills, aesthetics, manners, and morals. This moralistic and judgmental definition of class and its implications of good breeding, background, and family play a significant role in both popular and academic views of people assigned to an underclass. They also connect to an American racial climate that has been all too willing to connect and elide race and class.

African-American families shoulder more blame for the emergence of an underclass than any other institution. Because a number of these families lack an adult male in the home, many argue that they remain incapable of rearing children to be healthy, productive adults. Such criticism then easily casts "welfare mothers," inevitably black, as responsible for a generation of drug dealers and criminals, daughters who will bear their own children too early and out of wedlock, and sons who do not know how to work. Certainly, severe concentrations of urban poverty, violence, and social isolation have devastating effects on members of families in particular African-American communities. However, the idea that families themselves produce, reinforce, or fail to halt these conditions, or that the families have "broken down," or that all those parents and children are not really families, begs historical questions of causes and effects. The changing structural environment examined in many other chapters in this volume combined with a different cultural range of strategic family options and preferences can fully account for family differences and problems that have little to do with unwise choices or an impaired sense of productive family behavior. It is also important to consider what is accomplished for current families in condemning family behavior after the fact. Alarmist arguments that call for a halt to certain practices or propose policy options that will inhibit or prevent them fail to provide viable alternatives, often ignore existing conditions and patterns in current families, and tend toward disciplinary rather than enabling environments.

I

Large differences in family and household structures have always separated Americans of African ancestry from those of European ancestry. Since the end of the Civil War, these differences have been clearly documented in the U.S. census and in local records. The significant socioeconomic differences between the groups explain large parts of the persistent disparity, but such factors have never supplied complete explanations of all differences.[1] Early on, both white and black writers attributed family differences to the degrading conditions of slavery, which included little education for African Americans. Both abolitionist and proslavery arguments held that it was not possible for African Americans to have regular family lives during slavery, and such family life could not be expected to appear immediately afterward either.[2] In this century, scholars like Franklin Frazier pointed to the distinct history of slavery which he felt had so deformed culture that certain "weak" family patterns became ingrained in African Americans.[3] This idea of deformed families persists in many popular explanations of ethnic American family differences.

The idea of "bad" families begs the question as to what a "good" family might be. By the beginning of the twentieth century, such a family model had become dominant as the middle-class ideal of a breadwinning father with a dependent wife and their children in their own household. Both Carl Degler and Mary Ryan in their key studies, supported by many others, place the origins of such families early in the nineteenth century.[4] They submit that these origins are largely middle class and urban, or at least nonrural, and thus took time to emerge authoritatively and for the model to extend its domination over other classes and groups. Chapter 6 provides a clear and compelling analysis of this extension in the early twentieth century in northern U.S. cities. The dominance of this one mainstream family model blinded many observers to people who lived in different arrangements. By 1960, a large majority of all U.S. families were structured

---

[1] In her earlier chapter, Kathryn Neckerman notes that African-American families seem to operate on a different scale when weighing the economic trade-offs of married women's employment for wages. While speculating on the possibilities of various family strategies that may have permitted higher-than-expected labor-force participation, the Neckerman article does not mention one major factor I would like to consider here. The repertoire of family strategies for African Americans may be quite different, in terms of which practices may be more or less acceptable in a cultural sense, from that of Euro-Americans. By working from this cultural/ethnic side of the social equation, I hope to flesh out, qualify, and deepen her valuable structural analyses.

[2] Scholars like Carl Degler in *At Odds* (New York: Oxford University Press, 1980) and Elmer Martin and Joanne Martin in *The Black Extended Family* (Chicago: University of Chicago Press, 1978) trace the history of these arguments. The abolitionists published numerous slave narratives about destroyed families to arouse sympathy, while those who supported slavery spoke of the need for masters in order to avoid licentious family disorganization. With both sides touting since at least the 1820s the impossibilities of black family life under slavery or in independence, it is no surprise that few people had a favorable impression of African-American family life and possibilities at the turn of the century.

[3] E. Franklin Frazier, *The Negro Family in the United States* (Chicago: University of Chicago Press, 1939), and *Black Bourgeoisie* (New York: Collier, 1957).

[4] Carl Degler in *At Odds* and Mary Ryan in *Cradle of the Middle Class* (Cambridge: Cambridge University Press, 1981).

in this private, nuclear, male-headed way, but in 1990, the figure for such "natural" families had dropped precipitously.[5] It is significant that this particular Parsonian model of "the family" reached its zenith at the same time that social science itself reached the watershed of its persuasive social and rhetorical public power.

The following period of dramatic decline is also the period in which policy-makers and social scientists have been obsessed with the differences from the family model found in African-American families. They used these differences to explain and explore many of the noted problems in African-American communities. In reaction, some scholars have sought to defend "the" black family by pointing out the extent to which it has conformed to the dominant model. Yet black families have never really conformed with the model in the first place. It is not enough, however, merely to show the differences of African-American families from the dominant model; it is important to question the model itself. In this essay, I try both to build upon and step beyond what many have done in asserting the cultural strengths of African-American families by also looking at the weaknesses of the model used to critique them. In so doing, I am not trying to assess the "worth" of different family models or practices, but rather to examine African-American families in terms of what they are, rather than what they are not. For example, given the nature of different family emphases, in terms of marriage, as shown below, African-American families will always turn up deficient when compared to Euro-Americans in the aggregate because of where compromises will be made when necessary.

Having a singular family model produces assumptions that certain race or class differentials in family structures and practices may cause or perpetuate some of the disadvantages associated with being black or poor in U.S. society. Of course, such disadvantages are very real, but their link to the structures of families and households and specifically to differences in these from Euro-American norms has never been established. These comparisons assume a certain model of the family, along with a certain agency of the family in social production, that fails to account for the enormous changes that have taken place in all U.S. families since the mid-nineteenth century. Furthermore, implicit in most of these arguments is the assumption that families produce societal condi-

[5] Estimates vary as to the percentages of American families that had a wage-earning father, a housekeeping mother, and one or more children at various points in U.S. history, but all note its dramatic decline since 1960. See James Sweet and Larry Bumpass, *American Families and Households* (New York: Russell Sage Foundation, 1987), pp. 115–71. According to researchers for the PBS documentary series "Making Sense of the Sixties," the decline was from 70 percent of all families in 1960 to 15 percent in 1990. In 1980, Barret and McIntosh note, in *The Anti-Social Family* (London: Verso, 1982), that this type of family describes only 20 percent of households. It was scholars like Talcott Parsons in the forties and fifties who described such families as ideally suited for the temperaments and natural abilities of men and women, and for the nurturing of boys and girls. If this is so, then it is remarkable how the model has been so rapidly abandoned, particularly by those who have the economic ability to follow it.

tions unidirectionally, by structuring the ways individuals will deal with society. Such attitudes lead to very limited analyses that depend upon a very specific series of psychological assumptions and do not adequately address the ways societal conditions work to shape families.

Even when environmental factors are taken into account, the social conditions of the body politic that shape families are nearly always assumed to have similar effects on all families within that society. The problems in this assumption when it comes to examining African-American families fall on both sides of the assertion. These lie in the degree to which African Americans and Euro-Americans can be assumed to share a common society, and in the degree to which family models, desires, and possibilities in the two groups are comparable. Beyond and surrounding measurable socioeconomic conditions of social structure are the contexts of cultural heritage, historical experience, and degrees of integration, isolation, and segregation, as examined in the first section of this volume. The influences of an African heritage and its amount of persisting presence, together with the ongoing consequences of historical, race-based slavery, interact with the present social structures in the lives of individuals in their families.

The amount of social and cultural experience that African Americans keep outside the view of mainstream Euro-American society, or in which Euro-Americans have not shown interest, is also significant. In addition, there is the question of a point of beginning for this separate social and cultural experience once one has acknowledged it. Many have placed this experiential baseline at emancipation, others at importation, and some in Africa, and in each case it makes a difference in both approach and the analysis of difference. The ideas of influence and inheritance do not encompass the sense of a beginning, though the analyst's narrative must.

The failures of emancipation, education, and migration to provide true equality of opportunity for the great majority of African Americans in the face of white hostility led to the racial confrontations and social crises of the post–World War II civil rights movement and its aftermath. By pinning black "juvenile delinquency" and antisocial behavior on improper family structure, the social authorities of white America both denied racial injustice and displaced its own family inadequacies. As Daniel Moynihan reported in *The Negro Family: The Case for National Action* (1965), many sociologists also purported to have identified a family "breakdown" as a recent phenomenon of urban living, without any historical or controlled regional analysis. They claimed to find a new urgent crisis in cities, then carelessly linked it to a century-old history speaking generally of all black families in the phrase "the Negro family." The persistence of this tendency to locate the crisis within such an artificial collective structure is evident in the 1984 Black Family Summit, numerous articles like Eleanor Holmes Norton's "Restoring the Traditional Black Family" in the *New York Times* in 1985, and Bill Moyers's reinscription of the Moynihan thesis in a nationally televised CBS documentary on American families in 1989.[6]

However, the types of antisocial behavior identified then, and still disturbingly present in certain urban African-American communities, of crime, drug use, vandalism, and street violence, are not directed at families. The terrible results of this antisocial behavior certainly have devastating impacts on families in these communities, but it is not families that are targets of the behavior. The same cannot be said for white communities, where huge amounts of violence are specifically directed inward toward household and family members.[7] The pathologies produced in America's racially isolated urban ghettos are very real and extremely destructive, but they are not generalized products of particular types of families. As many residents of these areas observe, they are products of "the streets," the social environments that surround families and with which they contend, and appear only after families lose members to "the streets."[8] What strikes analysts and ethnographers who examine and deal with these environments is not the way families often lose to these conditions, but the enormous resilience that many of these families exhibit by existing within them. Romanticizing the behavior and aspirations of the marginalized does them no service, and the ideas of survival and resilience are not in themselves any sort of evaluation or critique. African-American families not only cope with situations but have distinctive forms and expressions that are productive and aim toward success. These forms also have their weaknesses and disadvantages, but these exist as such not because of their differences from Euro-American forms but as

[6] The rhetoric of the Black Family Summit, sponsored by the NAACP, the Urban League, and other major organizations, and the Norton article are analyzed in Angela Davis and Fania Davis, "Slaying the Dream: The Black Family and the Crisis of Capitalism" in Angela Davis, *Women, Culture, and Politics* (New York: Vintage Books, 1990). The Norton article appeared June 2, 1985.

[7] While many associate the tremendous increase in reports of family violence to an increased awareness and more legislation (see Gerald Jaynes and Robin Williams, *A Common Destiny* [Washington D.C.: National Academy Press, 1989], p. 410; and Elizabeth Pleck, *Domestic Tyranny* [New York: Oxford University Press, 1987]), the social workers who deal with families receiving welfare aid have reported sharp differences between violence and abuse levels in white and black families. Only 8.4 percent of children in institutions for dependent and neglected and abused children are black (1960), and 63 percent of white welfare families are reported to abuse, while only 43 percent of black families are so reported (1967 study as cited in Mary Frances Berry and John W. Blassingame, *Long Memory* [New York: Oxford University Press, 1982], p. 86). Richard Gelles and Claire Cowell note a similar difference in their 1990 book, *Intimate Violence in Families* (Newbury Park, Calif.: Sage Publications), despite the propensities of medical and educational institutions to label African Americans as more likely to be abusive (pp. 53–54).

[8] For a recent example of this, see Alex Kotlowitz, *There Are No Children Here* (New York: Doubleday, 1991). The same can be observed in the autobiographical writings of James Baldwin, Malcolm X, Claude Brown, and numerous others. Conservatives might argue that "stronger" families would be able to keep children from the streets, but in the extreme absence of other institutional structures added to the level of social isolation documented in chapters 1 and 3 in this volume, this seems rather wishful thinking.

part of a full cultural system. If not from their environment or from available community role models, from where do the resilient attributes of these families come?

II

Social scientists in the twentieth century have been reluctant to consider the possibility of, let alone see, continuities and developments of African culture and patterns in African-American families. Cultural traditions and models and the consequences of historical events are not simply inherited in any direct and predictable manner. Their influence and persistence depend upon the possibilities for continuity and on renewed efforts in the lives and behavior of individuals to preserve and transmit them. Such aspects of heritage also compete with the availability of attractive and viable alternatives. There is a depth and persistence of segregation and alienation from Euro-American social assumptions of "standard," "normal," or "proper" behavior in African-American experience. Within these two groups, the shared experience of U.S. society carries vastly different meanings and interpretations.

Prior to the nineteenth century, cultural and racial variation was usually explained environmentally, but by the 1830s, theories of biological and genetic determinations of racial difference were prevalent. Typical of Southern explanations in the 1850s were George Fitzhugh's *Sociology for the South* and *Cannibals All* or Henry Hughes's *Treatise on Sociology*, which generally found black people incapable of any stable family life, and thus in need of patriarchal masters.[9] At emancipation, though many in the Freedmen's Bureau were quite struck by the family efforts of the emancipated, they did not systematically examine the matter. Debate on whether blacks were able to handle political rights and survive in freedom became the focus of study and evaluation. In *The Plantation Negro as Freeman*, Philip Bruce described the freed people as hopelessly lacking in any civil organization, and chaotic and depraved in their family life.[10]

In the twentieth century social science turned again to structural and cultural factors as predominant sources of racial differences. W. E. B. DuBois was one of the first to make use of statistical data and to argue effectively against proponents of scientific racism. Inspired by the work of Charles Booth in England and Jane Addams in Chicago, he creatively adapted their method of studying social conditions of the poor to a more comprehensive study of the social conditions of

[9] George Fitzhugh, *Cannibals All! or, Slaves without Masters* (Richmond, Va.: 1857; reprint edited by C. Vann Woodward, Cambridge: Harvard University Press, Belknap Press, 1960). George Fitzhugh, *Sociology for the South; or, the Failure of Free Society* (Richmond, Va.: 1854; reprint facsimile in Research and Work Series, no. 102, New York: Burt Franklin). Henry Hughes, *A Treatise on Sociology* (Philadelphia: 1854). Woodward asserts in his preface to the 1960 reprint of Fitzhugh that the 1854 works are the first in the United States to make use of the new term "sociology" in their titles (p. xvii).

[10] Philip Bruce, *The Plantation Negro as Freeman* (New York: G. P. Putnam, 1889).

race.[11] In *The Philadelphia Negro*, DuBois dated nearly all of his analyses from the arrival of people of African descent in the city, but in a brief section on family structure, he drew on African and slave experience. In his Atlanta Conference papers, the African and slave experiences were given a more prominent place as background and context for his social analysis. His 1908 work, *The Negro American Family*, was the first social science study of black families.[12] Carter Woodson, his contemporary, also stressed African background as an explanation for cultural differences of blacks from white society.[13] They both made extensive use of ethnographic work on Africa and used it to interpret African-American practices of their time, while recognizing the effects of the slave experience.[14]

In the 1920s, however, genetic theories of scientific racism and racial superiority held power over all other explanations of difference. Given a stereotype of abject primitivity and of humans in a savage state of nature, most respected scholars early in the century did not regard Africa itself as a possible source and location of "culture" or "civilization." There was a tendency to characterize Africa as a sort of zero on the cultural scale, and therefore not possibly a source of any organized behavior. This aspect of eugenic racial essentialism united with biological notions of race and family that obscure ethnicity, a term much more closely associated with culture and places of origin. This level of incomparability between the terms *race* and *ethnicity* is a place of slippage that has often caught social analysts in a bind, as examined by Suzanne Model in chapter 5.[15]

Developments in the field of anthropology challenged this view, even within its colonial framework, and raised the question of cultural "survivals" in the

---

[11] See E. Digby Baltzell's introduction to the 1967 Schocken edition of DuBois's *Philadelphia Negro*, pp. xvi–xviii.

[12] W. E. B. DuBois, *The Philadelphia Negro* (Philadelphia: University of Pennsylvania Press, 1899), and *The Negro American Family* (Atlanta, Ga.: Atlanta University Press, 1908).

[13] For example, see Carter Woodson, *The African Background Outlined* (Washington, D.C.: Association for the Study of Negro Life and History, 1936).

[14] It is quite interesting that they were writing very close to the time that the word *negro* replaced *African* in several contexts. In 1895, the Census Bureau substituted "negro" descent in every place that "African" descent had appeared earlier in their *Report on the Population* (Washington, D.C.: Government Printing Office). In 1904, Walter Willcox wrote on behalf of the Census Bureau; "that the dislike and avoidance of the word negro among members of the African race is disappearing seems to be implied by current usage as indicated in the title of such books as Mr. W. E. B. DuBois's 'The Philadelphia Negro' and Mr. Booker T. Washington's 'The Future of the American Negro.' As this opposition was the only known objection to the accurate term, the change of usage on the part of the census seems to be justified." (I am grateful to Anne S. Lee for pointing out these references to me through her unpublished paper "The Census and Definitions and Semantics of Race," 1988.) This change plays an important role in obscuring cultural and ethnic heritage with racial essentialism, particularly within the bipolar racial regime developing in the United States early in the twentieth century.

[15] For an examination of ethnic and racial patterns of family and household structure in 1910, see Andrew T. Miller, S. Philip Morgan, and Antonio McDaniel, "Under the Same Roof," in Susan Watkins, ed., *After Ellis Island* (New York: Russell Sage Foundation, forthcoming).

United States. Early work in folklore also established African links in language, music, religion, and folktales, so that Africa seemed to provide at least an aesthetic background, if not a social one.[16] These developments did not stimulate interest in the work of DuBois or Woodson, however. Particularly in the realm of social structures, any hint of African survivals was denied by most scholars. A prominent exception was Melville Herskovits, who stated in *The Myth of the Negro Past*, "Negroes in the United States are not Africans but they are the descendents of Africans. There is no more theoretical support for an hypothesis that they have retained nothing of the culture of their African forebears, than for supposing that they have remained completely African in their behavior."[17]

E. Franklin Frazier argued against Herskovits's assertions of African survivals, particularly in social structure and the family. Frazier felt that the violence of the Middle Passage and the mixing of people of various languages and ethnicities under the conditions of slavery wiped out African family structures and prevented the development of any coherent family system, save for that of the natural attachment of mother and child. In his books, *The Negro Family in the United States* and *Black Bourgeoisie*, as well as in a number of articles, Frazier portrayed black families as mainly disorganized and degenerating as a result of the violent and racially hostile U.S. experience of blacks. The only means he saw for African Americans to form healthy families was to emulate American middle-class norms, since all prior moral and cultural forms had been destroyed. He noted with approval that some blacks had taken the opportunity to form stable homes and families on that particular model and could thus serve as models for the masses.

Frazier's work gained extraordinary influence among those who studied the general areas of black life and race relations, and they came to rely on his findings when dealing with families. For example, in *An American Dilemma*, Myrdal found Frazier's "such an excellent description and analysis of the American Negro family that it is practically necessary only to relate its conclusions to our context and to refer to its details."[18] While Frazier was a sociologist seeking to explain social conditions, many prominent historians of slavery also supported his view of the power of the slave experience in eliminating all African forms of social organization. Writers like Kenneth Stampp overturned the generally benign view of slavery that earlier historians had portrayed, and which held until the 1950s.[19] Stampp's documentation of the extreme cruelty and harsh-

[16] One of the best recent studies of the development of this artistic appreciation of Africa in American life is Robert Farris Thompson's *Flash of the Spirit* (New York: Random House, 1983).

[17] Melville Herskovits, *The Myth of the Negro Past* (Boston: Beacon Press, 1941), p. 145.

[18] Gunnar Myrdal, *An American Dilemma: The Negro Problem and Modern Democracy* (New York: Harper and Brothers, 1944), pp. 930–31. This acceptance of Frazier's work wholesale is what ultimately led to the strong reaction against Moynihan. By 1965, times had clearly changed, and it was time to stop recycling old studies and begin the work of new interpretations. Frazier's own mixed racial heritage certainly played a role in lending authority to his work.

[19] Ulrich Phillips's *American Negro Slavery* (New York: D. Appleton, 1918) remained the standard work for over thirty years. He was a Southerner, and took the view that slavery was primarily an

ness of the slave system in the United States gave credence to Frazier's assertions about the loss of any coherent family system among those who were slaves. Stanley Elkins further strengthened such arguments, depicting slavery as a vicious psychological infantilization similar to concentration camps in its effects on its victims.[20] In response to Stampp and Elkins, a number of scholars then became very interested in probing how much control and autonomy existed under American slavery, and in the sources of African-American culture.

Some advanced the idea of many manifestations of autonomous culture within the slave communities, supporting Herskovits in many respects, but when it came to the family, they followed Frazier's argument.[21] Like Frazier, they were concerned with the lack of regulated sexual morality among slaves, which they attributed to white rape and the interference of planters with families. Others discounted the notion of any African cultural survivals on the basis of the ethnic and cultural diversity in Africa of those people who were enslaved.[22] Herskovits had specifically addressed such concerns, claiming "a sufficient degree of similarities in the cultures of the entire area so that a slave from any part of it would find little difficulty in adapting himself to whatever special forms of African behavior he might encounter in the New World."[23] This view of a general unity of African culture, specifically in family systems, is supported by the work of Niara Sudarkasa, who sees broad patterns of lineage, polygyny, and extendedness.[24] Wade Nobles took a position similar to that of Sidney Mintz by proposing a formation of what Nobles calls an African ethos, which then influ-

---

economic system of labor, and thus it was illogical for masters to mistreat their workers. Kenneth Stampp produced *The Peculiar Institution* (New York: Knopf, 1956), and while agreeing with the economic basis of slavery, cited the tremendous greed and cruelty of masters in being able to do whatever they wanted to the slaves.

[20] Stanley Elkins, *Slavery: A Problem in American Institutional and Intellectual Life* (Chicago: University of Chicago Press, 1959), portrayed slavery as a totalitarian institution of complete depersonalization. A second edition with some revision was published in 1968.

[21] John Blassingame published *The Slave Community* (New York: Oxford University Press, 1972) the same year that George Rawick produced *From Sundown to Sunup* (Westport, Conn.: Greenwood Press). Both of them emphasized that whites mainly sought to control the labor conditions of slaves, and left the slaves to themselves in the quarters on many occasions. Because of the sexual interference of white men in the quarters and their interests in reproduction as producing prosperity, in addition to the disregard masters had for slave families, both authors find that the family was not an area of autonomy for slaves. They assert that slaves could only try to cope with the ways that slavery destroyed normal family relations.

[22] Andrew Billingsley expresses this view in his *Black Families in White America* (Englewood Cliffs, N.J.: Prentice-Hall, 1968).

[23] Herskovits, *Myth*, p. 78.

[24] Sudarkasa writes about this in her essay "Interpreting the African Heritage in Afro-American Family Organization," published in 1981 (in Harriette McAdoo, ed., *Black Families* [Beverly Hills, Calif.: Sage Publications, 1981]). Many others share this opinion, and one must recognize the possibilities of different levels of generalization in culture from nation, ethnicity, lineage, family, etc., that always can be broken down further, even within individuals. In my own eleven years of experience living and working in rural Africa, I find significant local evidence for this view.

ences the shared social reality of black people outside of Africa.[25] The unity of African-American experience thus may come partly from blacks using cultural elements found in America in an African way.[26]

The Moynihan report of 1965 accepted and endorsed Frazier's assertions about black families in ways that placed blacks as helpless and pathetic victims of their own "tangle of pathology." As a government official at the time he wrote, Moynihan was deeply concerned about the increase of civil disorder in urban black communities and its revolutionary potential. He saw the connections of vast poverty and underemployment and the black consciousness movement with the independence movements of African states and openly worried about Third World ideologies and race war.[27] Attributing the problem to family life, he assumed that in order to oppose U.S. society so adamantly, the whole group must be maladjusted. Other studies took similar views, including Kenneth Clark's *Dark Ghetto* and Lee Rainwater's *Behind Ghetto Walls*, but Moynihan served as the lightning rod, perhaps because of his call for national action.[28] The media embrace of the Moynihan report, despite its wide rejection and refutation by scholars, has perpetuated its influence in popular ideology about families, and even revived it in the 1980s.[29] The sense that there is something wrong with black people, rather than with U.S. society, continues to appeal to and convince a public raised in a climate permeated by institutional racism. Revisionist history on slavery in the 1970s tried to take these issues into account, and focused on the family as a topic of consideration when examining slave society. Some

[25] Nobles does this in two of his articles, "Africanity: Its Role in Black Families," *Black Scholar* 5 (1974): 10–17, and "African American Family Life: An Instrument of Culture" (1982), in Harriet McAdoo's collection of essays, *Black Families*. The idea is further elaborated in his book *Africanity and the Black Family* (Oakland, Calif.: Black Family Institute Publications, 1985). Sidney Mintz outlines this position in his introduction to the second English edition of Alfred Metraux, *Voodoo in Haiti* (New York: Schocken Books, 1972).

[26] Blassingame in *The Slave Community* and Elmer Martin and Joanne Martin in *The Black Extended Family* also take this view. John Bodnar discusses the similar phenomenon in *The Transplanted* (Bloomington: Indiana University Press, 1985) of "emergent ethnicity," concerning the ways European immigrants constructed "national" identities after being in America for some time.

[27] As pointed out and quoted on page 1 of Lee Rainwater and William Yancey, *The Moynihan Report and the Politics of Controversy* (Cambridge: MIT Press, 1967). The Moynihan Report was an internal document of the Office of Policy Planning and Research of the U.S. Department of Labor and was originally titled "The Negro Family" in 1965.

[28] Kenneth Clark, *Dark Ghetto* (New York: Harper and Row, 1965); Lee Rainwater, *Behind Ghetto Walls* (Chicago: Aldine, 1970).

[29] Lee Rainwater and William Yancey mostly attack the "political" posturing by academics and the "civil rights crowd" in their 1967 book, *The Moynihan Report and the Politics of Controversy*. The book contains the entire report and transcripts of the public speeches surrounding it, and is a good source of information on all the characters involved and the precise timetable of its release and the public reaction. In *Race and Media: The Enduring Life of the Moynihan Report* (New York: Institute for Media Analysis, 1989), Carl Ginsburg brings up to date the influence the report continues to exert in the public sphere, particularly through its two main proponents, Bill Moyers and Moynihan himself. I have also noted above its influence on social thinking.

took a more benign view of slavery in order to allow for the existence of stable families under that regime, while others stressed the abilities of slaves to adapt even under the harshest conditions and maintain patriarchal nuclear families.[30]

Herbert Gutman took the family question head-on as a central issue of his 1976 study, *The Black Family in Slavery and Freedom*. In some ways, Gutman was so determined to refute Moynihan's portrayal of pathology that he overstated his point in making black families sound quite similar to white families.[31] However, he found certain consistencies in naming patterns, kin networks, household structures, and marriage practices in many locations and under varied conditions, and asserted there was clearly a common African-American experience. Without any particular data from Africa, he claimed the strong possibility of African influences being a source for these similarities. In this way, Gutman proposed a model similar to that of Wade Nobles's African ethos, something Nobles calls "retribalization," which African ideology created under U.S. social structures. However, this acknowledgment of African heritage did not have nearly the impact in Gutman's book as the seeming denial of difference by "refuting" matriarchy theories and emphasizing the instances of "model family" households. Gutman's work led a number of liberal scholars to make black families sound white and to seek out evidence of their conformity to a private, nuclear-family model. This exaggeration of similarity accepted the notion that deviations from this model had to be inferior or pathological. Rather than struggling to deny or explain away differences that are evident in the data, however, scholars can investigate and understand the differences in terms of an alternative model of the meaning of family.

III

Many anthropologists and some sociologists distinguish between Western and African notions of families. The Western heritage has focused on marriage as the basis of family life, while the African heritage points to children as the focal point legitimating a family.[32] In the West, a new family is formed when a couple

---

[30] Robert Fogel and Stanley Engermann pointed out, in *Time on the Cross* (Boston: Little, Brown, 1974), that it was in the interests of masters to treat slaves minimally well and not destroy families, while Eugene Genovese in *Roll, Jordan, Roll* (New York: Pantheon, 1974) saw slave resourcefulness as preserving families. All of these authors' focus was on the system of slavery, however, with only subsidiary consideration of families.

[31] Herbert Gutman, *The Black Family in Slavery and Freedom* (New York: Pantheon, 1976). In several cases Gutman makes use of identical data to that of Frazier, and both find rates of female-headedness for African Americans in a range of 15 percent to 20 percent. The difference lies in their interpretations. For Frazier these figures are remarkably high in comparison to those of whites, while for Gutman they are surprisingly low, given economic conditions and the sex ratio among blacks.

[32] Sudarkasa, "Interpreting the African Heritage," pp. 37–53. Also, Ron Lesthaeghe, *Reproduction and Social Organization in Sub-Saharan Africa* (Berkeley: University of California Press, 1989);

marries, and therefore marriage takes on great importance, while in Africa, a new family is formed by the birth of a child. Thus, in an African view, having offspring is of essential importance. The extremely formal and ritualized, and in some cases sacramental, ceremonies surrounding marriage as the beginning of families in the Western tradition stands in sharp contrast to the almost nonexistence of such wedding practices in African tradition. In their place are the elaborate birth and naming ceremonies and traditions in Africa and the high value placed on children within the family among African Americans. These views of families are not mutually exclusive, and both can be encompassed within nuclear family structures, but they do have important implications for the choices that might be made when families come under pressure.

Students of African-American families have been obsessed with marriage and household headship as the determinants of family form and stability. Euro-American and African-American families are certainly quite different in marriage patterns and female headship of households. These differences have been consistent throughout the twentieth century, so that whatever has happened to African-American families in this time period has happened to all families, with the gap maintained. DuBois attributed the difference in headship to the lack of employment for men, their high rates of incarceration, and a lesser concern with the formal legal structures of marriage among blacks. Others have reached similar conclusions, such as Cox; Furstenburg, Hershberg, and Modell; and William Julius Wilson.[33] All these theories presume, however, that the patriarchal nuclear family is the prerequisite of family stability. All available recent studies of the effects on children of experience in one-parent families show that the consequences are imperceptible except in terms of economic status.[34] This economic factor of female household headship is certainly a disadvantage, but has little to do with family choices.

The oppressive fear American society has held and continues to hold of African-American males, and which tremendously distorts these men's ability to participate in family life, is a context often left unseen. Family studies in general have long been oriented toward examining women, not only because of reproductive concerns, but because of the social construction of the household as

---

Leslie Owens, *This Species of Property* (New York: Oxford University Press, 1976); Gutman, *Black Family*; Ann Creighton Zollar, *A Member of the Family* (Chicago: Nelson Hall, 1985); and Joyce Aschenbrenner in *Lifelines* (New York: Holt, Rinehart, and Winston, 1975).

[33] Oliver Cox, "Sex Ratio and Marital Status among Negroes," *American Sociological Review* 5 (1940): 937–47. Frank Furstenberg, Theodore Hershberg, and John Modell, "The Origins of the Female-Headed Black Family," *Journal of Interdisciplinary History* 6 (1975): 211–34. William Julius Wilson, *The Truly Disadvantaged* (Chicago: University of Chicago Press, 1987).

[34] See Sweet and Bumpass, *American Families*, pp. 287–90. An ongoing study at the University of California at Los Angeles of alternative family arrangements in which the children have reached the age of sixteen as of 1992 shows similar results, as reported on National Public Radio, "Morning Edition," March 28, 1992.

a "women's sphere" that is supported by men from the outside.[35] Since this male role is restricted for African Americans, the men become invisible to household analysis. As Sweet and Bumpass point out in their analysis of the U.S. census, in 1980 black men are significantly found in the "group quarters" of the military and the prisons.[36] Herbert Gutman, in his 1976 study, looked at the unfavorable sex ratio and the high levels of male mortality, unemployment, and incarceration and stressed the level of family stability in the face of such social conditions in the late nineteenth century.[37] Yet many scholars tended to categorize Gutman's work as a "denial" or refutation of so-called matriarchy rather than a contextualization. The language of "separation" and "abandonment," along with a cynical view of the word *widow*, continue to imply a type of freedom many African Americans do not experience. Such views often lead to interpretations that criticize the "choices" blacks make, like those found about welfare dependence in Charles Murray's *Losing Ground*.[38]

There is also evidence that concern with "deviant" family structures is connected to a certain level of racial scapegoating and displacement. African Americans have always had significantly higher rates of female headship and teenage and extramarital births. Concern about these issues, however, has only come when such rates begin to rise significantly for whites. Thus, the Depression brought forth Frazier's earlier concern with matriarchy when male economic roles in the family were threatened for all Americans. The rapidly rising divorce rates in the 1960s raised Moynihan's similar concerns that a "tangle of pathology" was emerging from female headship. More recently, as teenage and unwed births have been dropping for African Americans but skyrocketing among whites, a new hysteria has arisen, which has once again been displaced onto the consistently higher, but declining, rates for African Americans.[39] These issues are certainly problems within particularly impacted urban communities, but

[35] See Sweet and Bumpass, *American Families*, p. 4. In their study of the 1980 census, they attempt to include men to a greater degree, to find them in households where they are instead of expecting them to relate to the households the investigators define.

[36] Ibid., p. 82.

[37] Herbert Gutman, *Black Family*.

[38] Charles Murray, *Losing Ground* (New York: Basic Books, 1984). This study was a favorite of the Reagan administration, since it purported to prove that it was the welfare system that caused and encouraged female-headed homes, especially in the black community. Of course, not only does Murray ignore the wider context of social experience, but he also fails to observe that this "problem" existed long before the welfare system was established. Similar arguments are advanced by George Gilder in *Wealth and Poverty* (New York: Basic Books, 1981).

[39] Again, see Sweet and Bumpass, *American Families*, pp. 397–400. These rates are tracked by the National Center for Health Statistics "Monthly Vital Statistics Report." One bit of confusion is that the overall percentage of children born to blacks in such circumstances is rising, but this is a result of the sharp decline in fertility among older African-American women. Thus, there is a higher percentage of black children in what many consider families that exhibit "underclass" behavior, but this is the result of broader social changes in fertility and not a boom in the "irresponsible" family choices of young mothers. See also Jaynes and Williams, pp. 509–68.

this is a consequence of economic effects in already isolated and desperate circumstances. Families are neither the causes of such circumstances nor the uniquely structured "traps" that perpetuate them in the rhetoric of many who examine their situation. The broad social patterns of marriage decline, teenage sexuality, and household fragmentation cannot be addressed only within the isolation of urban ghettos, nor blamed on such environments. The question becomes one of how the economic and social constraints connected to such household and family patterns can be understood and addressed.

Another measure of family structure highlights white and black differences without incurring the emotion surrounding marriage and female-headed families. It is the extent to which families are extended, and the ways in which family extension takes place. In Euro-American extended families, nonnuclear members usually live within the same household. African-American extended families, by contrast, often embrace several households. As a result, African-American families are generally more fluid and open. There also are differences in the generational focus of family extension. Extension usually takes place in the exchange of consanguineous children among African Americans, while white extended families tend to include the elderly family members of the conjugal couple. This is the conclusion of ethnographers who observe how families work, as contrasted to that of researchers who have relied on the census snapshot taken on one day.[40] All these investigators demonstrate a depth and breadth to African-American families that may not be reflected in particular living arrangements within private households. Such enlarged kin networks are families.

The extension of families through nonnuclear children, much more common among African Americans, reflects the practice of child fosterage; the informal conventions of placing dependent children in homes apart from their biological parents. Such child fosterage has been noted by several researchers in different times and places, including Robert Hill in *The Strengths of Black Families*, Charles Johnson in *Shadow of the Plantation*, and Herskovits, who referred to informal adoption as an African cultural survival but spent little time documenting the practice.[41] Several scholars, including Edith Clarke, Raymond Smith, and M. G. Smith, took note of fosterage practices in the Caribbean, but were more concerned with the debate on matriarchy than with arrangements for the care of children.[42] Carol Stack discussed "child keeping" in her book *All Our Kin*, but

[40] Such ethnographers would include Carol Stack, *All Our Kin* (New York: Harper and Row, 1974); Dimitri Shimkin, Edith Shimkin, and Douglas Frate, *The Extended Family in Black Societies* (The Hague: Mouton, 1978); Zollar, *Member of the Family*; and Martin and Martin, *The Black Extended Family*.

[41] Robert Hill, *The Strengths of Black Families* (New York: Emerson Hall, 1971); Charles Johnson, *Shadow of the Plantation* (Chicago: University of Chicago Press, 1934); Herskovits, *Myth*.

[42] Edith Clarke in *My Mother Who Fathered Me* (London: George Allen, 1957) on Jamaica; Raymond Smith in *The Negro Family in British Guiana* (London: Routledge, 1956) and M. G. Smith in *West Indian Family Structure* (Seattle: University of Washington Press, 1962) also deal with Jamaica and Carriacou.

was more concerned with households headed by women and the effects of public housing and welfare. Like Billingsley, she stressed creative adaptation to the conditions of urban poverty through the use of extended family structures rather than historical precedent. Elmer and Joanne Martin's discussion of "absorption" or "informal adoption" within extended families emphasized the importance of both economic and cultural factors. However, none of these ethnographic works drew a statistical portrait of fosterage, nor did they connect their findings to the currently developing literature on fosterage now being produced by scholars working in Africa. The use of child fosterage and the care of dependent children as a distinguishing measure along with extendedness not only shifts the terms to a model based on cultural variance sensitive to an African heritage, but also allows us to escape some of the pejorative burden carried by the long debates over female-headedness. Families can be evaluated on the ways in which they are structured to care for and nurture children, rather than on a particular model of structure deemed "moral."

Using this thread of fosterage, however, it may be possible to tie together the African-American family of today with that of the turn of the century, as well as with the ethnographic and anthropological data from Africa and the diaspora. Fosterage is evident within the standard measure of delineating the population by households, even as it operates in a community that does not define families by household. Thus, one major feature of household differences can be built upon to examine cultural arguments.

Studies of the West deal with fosterage mostly in terms of the early formation of the modern family, as in Edward Shorter's work concerning wet-nursing and apprenticeship, but not as a practice that persists. Even in these early studies it is significant how such Western fosterage takes on an economic casting. However, by constructing and using a measure of fosterage, the terms of family analysis can be shifted to a model based on cultural variance sensitive to the centrality of children to family definitions in the African heritage and not tied to the traditional social science model of a private, Western nuclear family. Fosterage does not replace nuclear families but rather reveals a concern for the consequences for children when the nuclear family is not viable, for any number of reasons.

IV

Because of its comprehensive nature, a census provides a valuable pool of information in which to look for patterns within large populations. The Public Use Sample of the 1910 U.S. Census provides a valuable tool for examining household and coresident family structure, because within the sample, children have been linked to their mothers and spouses have been linked within households.[43] In 1910, census enumerators collected information on all members of

---

[43] For a full description of the linking process, see Strong et al., "User's Guide to the Public Use Sample of the 1910 United States Census of Population" (Ann Arbor: ICPSR, University of Michigan,

the household, which included their ages and relationships to household head. After this information was used to link children to their mothers in the sample, the situations of children for whom no mother could be identified in the household were examined for signs of potential fosterage.[44]

The year 1910 comes at a strategic moment in U.S. history. It was a time of massive immigration, before the welfare state, a generation after emancipation, and also after initial large-scale American industrialization. This significant

---

1989). The meticulous care of the linking process allows one to examine the unlinked as a meaningful population, rather than as a collection of mistakes and "hard cases."

[44] For the majority of families, it was not difficult for those who made the 1-in-250 1910 sample to link mothers and children, since mothers were usually found as the wives of the household head, and the children were listed as children of the household head. Others may not have been linked so easily, but mothers and children were linked comprehensively and with extreme care, as described in the user's guide to the sample. One factor that assisted this process is that the enumerators recorded how many surviving children each married woman had. In a substantial minority of cases, there were children for whom it was not possible to find a mother in the household, and mothers who appeared not to have all of their children present. It is in these cases that there may be signs of the practice of child fosterage—cases in which dependent children are being cared for by other than their biological parents. Mothers and their biological children can be separated for a number of reasons, especially on any given census day, and so great care is needed in making conservative restrictions of the populations. The striking effect of such restrictions is that although they reduce the size of the populations under consideration as possibly practicing fosterage, at each level they sharpen the distinctions between those of African-American and those of Euro-American backgrounds.

Distinguishing between children not living with a biological mother, those that are more likely to have been fostered, and those that are just unlinked or orphaned, was done by closely examining the 161 different recorded relationships to the head of household. I worked closely with Antonio McDaniel to refine these categories. A large number of children who are not linked to biological mothers are listed as children of the household head with whom they reside, likely their biological fathers. These children appear to be linked to a parent, and so I put them with those linked to mothers in the sample and label the group "parented." Children whose relationship is missing cannot be considered fostered, and those who are listed as heads or spouses themselves are clearly not in situations of fostering, nor are those who have been institutionalized. The use of institutions to care for children seems to be a desperate measure in those communities that do not readily include fosterage as an option in the family repertoire. Most children whose mothers have died— who in 1910 are estimated by Samuel Preston, Douglas Ewbank, and Mark Hereward in "Child Mortality Differences, 1900–1910" in Watkins, *After Ellis Island*, as 9 percent of all African-American children up to age eighteen and 5 percent of white children—are likely living with a father who is head of a household, and are thus counted among the parented as described above. Those listed as children of the head may include children who are not natural children of the household head but have been "adopted" in such a way that they are called the head's children. Other children not linked to their mothers may have a father present in the home who is not the head of the household, but such children, I assume, are few. Another group of children left unlinked are those whose relationship to the head of the household is sibling and are thus generally close in age to the household head, though this category may border, in some cases, on a type of fosterage. The sibling relation, however, like that of head, child, and spouse, is one found within the nuclear family, even if there is no identifiable biological mother within the home, and so these children are not included among those considered likely to be fostered. The relationships of child and sibling include over 95 percent of children not linked to mothers in the sample in all races.

position between the two major sources of explanation in the influence of slave experiences or that of the social welfare system serves not only as a link but a control.[45] It was also the period of the initial sociological studies of society and family structure in the United States, and thus was at the beginning of the involvement of social science in questions of social policy.

The categories of children considered fostered includes grandchildren and other kin relations, in-laws, children unrelated to the household head, and of course those who are listed as fostered or adopted.[46] These then roughly constitute the population considered as dependent children fostered into homes where their biological mothers are not found. In 1910, 8 percent of all children under the age of fifteen lived in households without their mothers. Of all children under fifteen, 4.6 percent can be considered fostered. Broken down into 1910 racial categories, 3.5 percent of white children appear to be fostered, compared to nearly 10 percent of black children.[47] This analysis has important implications for the present, because the percentages living outside the maternal home show remarkable consistency, in various age groups, with figures calculated for the 1960 and 1970 censuses. In the Census Bureau's statistics for 1976, 9 percent of black children are found living apart from both parents, as are 2 percent of white children, similar to the 9.8 percent and 2.2 percent found by Sweet and Bumpass for the 1980 census, which shows very little change from

[45] The separate enumeration of the black and mulatto populations works both as a rough socioeconomic control, as well as an indicator of pre-1865 free status on a national sample level. In both cases, fosterage persists while other status measures show variation.

[46] Some of these children may be orphans, and thus not really fit the practice of fosterage on which I am focusing, but taking in children in this way rather than institutionalizing them can be a major distinction between cultural communities. Of course, one must recognize that there was a profound difference in the provision of institutional options between races. The distinction holds across regions in the United States, including those areas with minimal institutional provisions for all races. It is also evident in the kind of institutions that the groups choose to set up, for example, within religious denominations where traditionally white churches focus on children's institutions in the late nineteenth and early twentieth centuries, while traditionally black churches focus on burial, savings-and-credit societies, and educational institutions.

A close examination of children listed as boarders, servants, employees, and workers at this age led me to the conclusion that these children are not supporting themselves, and are thus in some sense under the care of the household in which they are found.

[47] For the purposes of this chapter, I am not making full use of the racial regime followed by the census enumerators, which included the designations of white, black, and mulatto. In many situations, the figures for mulattoes closely follow those for blacks, as for example, 9.81 percent of all mulatto children under 15 years are fostered and 0.58 percent are unlinked, but in some cases figures for mulattoes are found to be quite different from those for blacks. In the wider project of which this work is a part, I am probing just what distinctions constituted the mulatto racial category in 1910 (see Andrew T. Miller, "Measuring Mulattoes: The Changing U.S. Racial Regime in Census and Society," *Journal of Interdisciplinary History*, forthcoming). The peak year of mulatto measurement was 1910, when they were found to constitute 20.9 percent of all negroes, the designation of blacks and mulattoes together. The proportion declined to 15.9 percent in 1920, after which it was no longer measured, an interesting comment on the construction of American racial distinction and the current bipolar racial regime.

1910. Thus, while many investigators might regard the separation of mothers and their children as abnormal or drastic, it does take place with some regularity among certain groups in situations that seem to advantage the child and therefore suggest intentionality. Because this is not a new phenomenon, it should not be seen as a product of current social changes, nor, given the consistent proportions, can it be seen as part of a progressive "breakdown" (see fig. 8.1).

The rate of fostering rises with the age of children, but at the youngest ages the distinctions between races are sharpest. In the infant-to-five-year-old age group, African Americans in 1910 fostered at over three times the white rate. Because maternal mortality had its least effect at this age, the sharpness of this contrast demonstrates most clearly that fosterage was a much more common and acceptable practice for dependent children among African Americans than among whites. While it does not clearly establish whether such fostering of children is part of a cultural practice or simply a coping strategy to deal with social or economic hardship, it is the first of many clues. Even in Africa, where it is widely practiced in many communities, fosterage is a cultural option or alternative, not a central, normative practice. The cultural question is not only under what circumstances fosterage is practiced, but when and how it is practiced by certain groups in similar circumstances.

The means to study the extent of informal child fosterage in the African-American community on a national level have not been easily available, but it is remarkable how often the practice has been noted more or less in passing. Lucy Haskell, a teacher from the American Missionary Association who went to North Carolina to assist the freedpeople in Wilmington, wrote to Rev. George Whipple of the New York office of the association on December 30, 1865, clearly struck by fosterage practices:

> I find among them a willingness to keep others though they may be very poor themselves. A mother with seven children whose husband was dead and her only means of support the little washing she could get had taken a motherless child, no kin of hers, but she said she could not let her stay in the street, said she had been knocking about trying to get some Clothes for the children so that they might go to school and get the knowledge denied her. . . . Found Aunt Rachel in a shed, she thought "the Lord was right good to her for the woman did not charge her any rent." her only means of support was picking up rags and selling them, she too had taken in a friendless girl whom she found in the Street . . . and she had just taken in a mother and three children doing the best she could for them till she could get a room.[48]

The references and anecdotes from that time to the present in diaries, ledgers, censuses, memoirs, ethnographies, stories, studies, and other materials are numerous. They continue right up to the present day, as, for example, Sandy

---

[48] Letter 100234 from the American Missionary Association letters from North Carolina. I am grateful to Shan Holt for this reference.

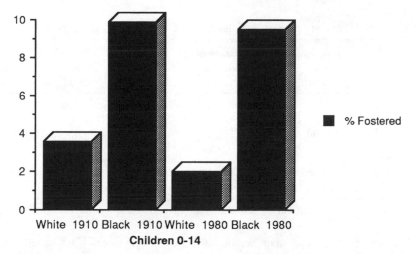

Figure 8.1. Comparative Fostering Rates in 1910 and 1980 for Children under Fifteen Years Old. *Source*: Figures for 1910 calculated by the author from the Public Use Sample of the 1910 U.S. Census. Figures for 1980 from Sweet and Bumpass, *American Families and Households*, p. 266.

Lawrence of the National Adoption Center noted on July 8, 1990: "Adoption is not new to this community. Adults have always been responsible for their children, regardless of whether they were their biological children or not. What is new to us is having to go into the system (legal) to take our children out of the system."[49] The persistence of this practice over centuries in a community that has experienced profound structural change within strong social isolation indicates a deeply rooted, culturally specific family option. Furthermore, the presence of similar practices in Africa, South America, and the Caribbean present a strong prima facie case for its cultural links.

Though all fostered children were most likely to be placed in the homes of relatives, blacks were more likely to be fostered into the homes of relatives than were whites. This is evidence of a broader sense of kin responsibility, and a possible demonstration of acceptance of the practice as normal to the family repertoire for those with an African background. It also reflects the practice as it takes place in Africa. Black children who were fostered show lower proportions of being boarders, servants, and laborers than were white children in similar situations (12.4 percent vs. 17.3 percent, as shown in table 8.1). This is a rather

[49] "A Shift in Adoption among Blacks," *The Philadelphia Inquirer*, July 8, 1990. For a less contextualized but nevertheless contemporary observation of fosterage practices, see Jane Gross, "Collapse of Inner-City Families Creates America's New Orphans," in the *New York Times*, March 29, 1992. Gross presents informal fostering as something that is not a family context, and thus takes a very alarmist view in this article.

TABLE 8.1
Household Status of Children, Ages Birth to Fourteen, in 1910 (Percentages)

	Living w/Rels	Servants, Boarders, and Household Employees	Couple as Head	Male as Head	Female as Head
Parented					
White	100.00	0.41	91.53	2.86	5.61
Black	100.00	0.77	82.56	4.48	12.95
Fostered					
White	58.06	17.27	65.52	15.35	19.13
Black	78.36	12.44	66.86	10.05	23.09

Source: Figures calculated by the author from the Public Use Sample of the 1910 U.S. Census.

dramatic finding, since many would attribute the high rate of black fosterage to an assumption that black children were being sent out as servants or laborers at younger ages than were whites. Actually, it is among the parented children that blacks show only slightly higher levels of having been servants, laborers, and boarders. The same holds true even more surprisingly for black mothers who may or may not have resided with all of their young children. Certainly the large numbers of African-American women who did work outside the home played some role in necessitating child fosterage as a form of what would now be called day care, but it was a particular option that many working white mothers did not see or use.

When a white woman headed a household, she was more likely to take in other children if she had at least one of her own present. Among African Americans, a much higher proportion of female heads with no children of their own present took in fostered children. In this way, whites do not redistribute children to make families but to add to them, whereas blacks tend to increase the number of homes caring for children. This is another characteristic, along with multigenerational families and the mixing of relatives from both sides of the family, that is similar to African practice.[50]

In linked families, whites were much more likely to have a home headed by a couple, but in homes that fostered children, black households were actually more likely to be couple-headed. Similarly for marriage, in traditionally structured homes, Euro-American children were more likely to be cared for by a married household head, but when fostered, African-American children were

[50] In communities in which fosterage is a readily accepted practice, the childless often have claims to children, as was the case in rural Quebec, where fosterage was common up to the 1930s, as well as throughout sub-Saharan Africa. This link of fosterage between French Canadians and African Americans may have important implications for the results found by Christine Bose in "Household Resources and U.S. Women's Work," American Sociological Review 49 (August 1984): 474–90, cited by Kathryn Neckerman.

more likely to experience such a household. Perhaps even more strongly than the age profile of children in a home, this indicates the likely effort of blacks who foster to practice a family strategy of care and dependence, rather than just a coping strategy of placing unclaimed, unwanted, or unsupportable children. Because these homes appear more stable and have a greater number of potential care givers, it is unlikely that African-American children merely "end up" being fostered. On these measures, in homes with no fostering, black youngsters appear worse off than whites, while in homes with fostering, they appear to be better off.

In every type of home, African Americans showed much higher percentages of female heads, a phenomenon that has long been a source of comment for those who study families, as noted above. In families where there was no fostering, African Americans also had a significantly higher rate of homes headed by a lone father, but when blacks chose to foster, children were fostered into homes where a woman was present. Thus, while African Americans seem to seek to preserve a traditional family model of adult/child relationships in a fostering home, for Euro-Americans the much rarer practice of fosterage seems to have more deeply disruptive effects on the structuring of families. This demonstrates again a black effort to care for, rather than disapprove of or neglect, children who are outside expected household structures. It also indicates the difference in the cultural acceptability of fosterage as part of a family repertoire. In constrained situations, the differences in cultural options show up in strategic decisions made at the margin.

One example of a rural African-American young couple taking in children is the Lyon family, as shown in the 1880 manuscript census. Calvin and Ellen Lyon were in their early twenties and had a fifteen-acre farm to sharecrop in North Carolina and no children of their own. Calvin's six-year-old brother, Harvey, lived with them, along with a six-year-old niece whose last name was Rogers. Calvin's sister, Isabella, was sixteen and also lived with them, perhaps to help with the farm and children, as did Calvin's brother, Jackson, who was nineteen. One might assume that in the absence of Calvin's parents, he had responsibility for his siblings, but the presence of a niece in this blended family, a child who could produce no income on a sharecropped farm, illustrates many of the points made statistically above. If the niece was also a member of Ellen's family, as the Rogers surname might indicate, it reflects even more clearly African fosterage practices, where a recently married woman may bring a relative from her own family to live among her husband's family. I do not take this individual case as evidence of such a practice, nor do I assert that it shows the probability of some sort of direct holdover, but there are many such echoes of African family practices that can be found within child fostering among African Americans.

Among African Americans in 1910, household gender roles appeared less restrictive, and again the effect was to reinforce the care of children. Many more separated men and women stayed with their own children than is the case with whites, and many more women worked to help support their households. Although these practices reflect drastic differences in the economic situation of African Americans and whites, families could cope with economic stress in a variety of ways. The choices African Americans made in such situations were different from those made by whites who found themselves in similar conditions. One case of men seeking to provide care for their children can be seen in the Howell family of Fishing Creek Township in Granville County, North Carolina, between 1879 and 1898. Jane Howell, a widow, lived with her unmarried daughter, Mazuri (or Missouri in some records—both phonetic renderings of a Bantu language variant meaning "good"), and Mazuri's two young children. When Jane's son, James, was suddenly widowed, he moved with his son to live with his mother and sister's family, having his six-year-old daughter live next door, perhaps to help with the small children of his brother, Christopher.[51] In this way, both men were able to stay with or near their children, as well as cooperatively provide for other nieces and nephews and for their mother.

In the twentieth century, with the dramatic migrations of African Americans to the urban North, efforts to care for and provide advantages for children through the use of fosterage are also apparent. Earlier in the century, it was common for parents to send children to relatives and friends in urban areas so that the children would have better educational and employment opportunities. More recently, urban children are fostered out of urban areas to the rural South, particularly in the summers, in order to escape the increasingly violent and isolating effects of many urban environments. For many, these family ties have been maintained over the course of the century precisely through such fostering practices.

In other ways, African-American families have been more flexible, particularly in the household residence "rules" for children, than have white. For blacks, the rhetoric of family and family relationships is more public, part of slang as well as of institutions like churches, and is broad and inclusive, and not given up so easily in the face of adversity. Black families seem to work to have family roles fulfilled by the people available, while white families seem to allow certain roles to be filled only by certain biological relationships. Breaking white norms of feminine employment, marriage, or residence, for instance, tends also to break white family ties and relationships. Thus, white women with children less often lived as members of extended families than did black mothers. African-American mothers remain members of families or form their own families. Similarly, white orphans are often pitied for the great tragedy that they will never have a "natural" mother, while African-American orphans are mothered by willing women. Furthermore, both formal and informal fosterage and adop-

[51] My sources are the 1880 census and Granville County tax lists, 1872–98. Christopher does not have a wife listed in these records. This example and that of the Lyon family were researched by Shan Holt.

tion among Euro-Americans is often regarded as strange or even shameful, and commonly denied, covered up, or kept secret. This is not the case among African Americans, who readily acknowledge the differences between biological parents and the relations of those others who may provide parental care.

V

What explains the differences in family organization and relationships between blacks and whites of European ancestry? Part of the answer is economic and lies in the harsh circumstances confronted by African Americans. However, a significant part of the difference also reflects an African heritage, as in fosterage, for example. The flexibility in who plays family roles, particularly in child rearing, and the use of fosterage to see that such roles are filled is a point that Esther Goody, D. K. Fiawoo, Hilary Paige, Caroline Bledsoe, Uche Isiugo-Abanihe, and Niara Sudarkasa all stress in their various studies of African families.[52] Such fostering as an alternative parenting structure is not exclusive to Africa, for it is found historically in Quebec and Japan, but within the United States, the fostering that takes place at a much higher rate among African Americans can be related to an African heritage. This shared ethnicity is a factor that crosses class divisions, regions, and communities much as fosterage does.

Several recent studies have examined the practice of child fosterage in Africa, and it has become a standard measure within the censuses conducted throughout the African continent. While nowhere is fosterage the dominant feature of child rearing, nor is it anywhere completely absent in the world, in a large number of African societies it is a prominent family strategy. In these societies, parental tasks and roles such as begetting and bearing, providing status and identity, nurturing, training, and sponsoring to adulthood are often delegated to different adults. Children, parents, and foster parents, who in African languages are not distinguished from biological parents, all exercise rights that make the propensity to foster much higher in such societies than it is in Western social systems. Current studies of fosterage have been largely confined to Africa because it is there that the practice is common and widespread, while in the Western experience of most social scientists, it may seem particularly odd or exceptional. In the United States, the study of its informal practice outside institutions and social agencies has rarely been carried out, and never before on

---

[52] Goody, in *Parenthood and Social Reproduction* (Cambridge: Cambridge University Press, 1982); Sudarkasa, "Interpreting" (1981); Bledsoe, "Strategies of Child Fosterage among Mende Grannies in Sierra Leone," in Lestaeghe, *Reproduction*; Isiugo-Abanihe, "Child Fosterage in West Africa," *Population and Development Review* 11 (1985): 53–74; Paige in "Childbearing vs. Childrearing," in Lestaeghe, *Reproduction*; D. K. Fiawoo, "Some Patterns in Foster Care in Ghana," in Christine Oppong', G. Abada, M. Bekombo-Priso, and J. Mogey, *Marriage, Fertility and Parenthood in West Africa* (Canberra: Australia National University Press, 1978).

the general national scale I describe here.[53] Those who have observed fosterage in the United States or the Caribbean within African-American families have usually attributed it to economic or social conditions, and as a sign of family stress or breakdown.[54]

There are, of course, numerous particular ethnic groups in sub-Saharan Africa, and African Americans can trace descent from a large number of these groups. But among these distinct groups are many cultural similarities that a number of scholars have observed and identified, and to which Esther Goody, Hilary Paige, and Philip Kreager have added child fosterage. Goody pulled together a great deal of ethnographic work from Ghana, Nigeria, Sierra Leone, and Liberia and compared it with both West African and West Indian practices in London. She also made use of some anthropological work in the Caribbean in order to evaluate the behavior of immigrants to London. Through this work, she built a convincing case for child fosterage as a general pattern in many of the ethnic groups of West Africa, and as a persisting practice in the immigrant communities in London. Philip Kreager produced an overview of the literature on fostering and adoption worldwide for the International Planned Parenthood Federation in 1980 and drew attention to the high rates of child circulation throughout Africa. To this work, Hilary Page has added an analysis of the household data files using the World Fertility Surveys for Ghana, Cameroon, Côte d'Ivoire, Kenya, Lesotho, Nigeria, and Sudan. The results of this work are included in the following map, and show that child fosterage is a widespread practice in several major parts of sub-Saharan Africa that served as origins for the African-American population (see fig. 8.2). While all of these sources are from the last forty years, much of the ethnographic work includes references to a continuation of past practices.

Although fosterage certainly must have changed during the Middle Passage, it was also an important feature of the Middle Passage because large numbers of children under the age of twelve were sold into slavery, especially during the late slave trade.[55] The adults with whom they traveled parented these children, much as whole shiploads of slaves often came to regard themselves as "clans" in the New World, and kept rules of obligation and exogamy, as reported by Sidney

[53] For a more complete description, see Andrew T. Miller, *Looking at African American Families: Recognition and Reaction* (Ann Arbor, Mich.: U.M.I. Dissertations, 1991).

[54] An exception to this view comes from the functionalist outlook of people like Andrew Billingsley in *Black Families in White America* (New York: Touchstone, 1978); Carol Stack, *All Our Kin*; Charles Willie in *A New Look at Black Families* (New York: General Hall, 1981); and others who point out the strengths of families that absorb other "nonrelated" members. These sociological studies are not strongly placed in a historical or African cultural context.

[55] I am grateful to Sandra Barnes for her comments and suggestions, as well as her expertise in pointing out these tracings of the fosterage thread during the sessions of the Work and Welfare seminar of the Program for Assessing and Revitalizing the Social Sciences at the University of Pennsylvania, where I presented some of these results.

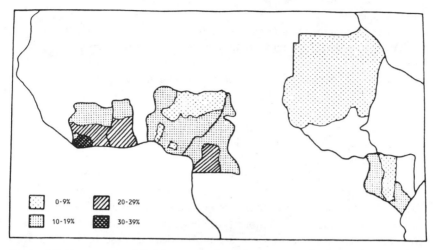

Figure 8.2. Percentages of Children under Age Fifteen Not Residing with Their Mothers, by Administrative Unit in Cameroon, Côte d'Ivoire, Ghana, Kenya, Nigeria, and Sudan. *Source*: Hilary Paige, "Childbearing vs. Childrearing," in Ron Lesthaeghe, eds., *Reproduction and Social Organization in Sub-Sahara Africa* (Berkeley: University of California Press, 1989), p. 417. Copyright © 1989 by The Regents of the University of California. Reprinted with permission.

Mintz and Richard Price.[56] The cruelties of slavery that broke immediate families apart made fosterage strategies all the more important in ensuring the survival of new generations in America. It is striking that fosterage has persisted, adapted, and developed in the United States among those with an African heritage, as it also persists in Africa and throughout the diaspora, though many of the contexts and motivations surrounding fosterage practices have changed. If anything, the oppressive structures of slavery and ensuing economic and structural disadvantages would have worked to preserve and support this practice, which allowed family survival and support for African Americans in conditions that in other communities caused the loss of family structures.

The ethnographic work from the Caribbean, done mainly in the 1950s and 1960s, emphasizes fosterage as part of family crises and matriarchy, much in the rhetoric of that era. Nonetheless, many of the descriptions found in the work of Gonzalez, Clarke, R. T. Smith, and Sanford indicate that fosterage also advantaged children. M. G. Smith, Spens, and Horowitz assert that all of the fosterage is in reaction to crises, but nearly all of these authors make no reference to Africa

[56] Sidney Mintz and Richard Price, *An Anthropological Approach to the Afro-American Past* (Philadelphia: Institute for the Study of Human Issues, 1976).

and are speaking of how Caribbean families developed "deviant" structures.[57] Goody drew together this Caribbean and the West African work, while Paige and Kreager pulled together work and measurements from across sub-Saharan Africa. These demographers and anthropologists, however, have not used the work of the sociologists who have been pursuing studies of African-American family and community practices.

Studies of extended, multihousehold African-American families over the last twenty years have all hinted at African origins for these family practices but have not been able to build historical links. They also have not emphasized the role of child fosterage in these families, though all of their work includes clear and prominent evidence of child fosterage among African Americans in both rural and urban areas. The work that I have done using the 1910 census does not definitely establish the African link, but it offers a historical link that ethnography cannot provide, and a demographic analysis that allows international comparison. Whether the African heritage in America manifests itself in survivals, reinterpretations, syncretisms, or any type of combination thereof, it is still present as a history and an influence. Racism and discrimination certainly have been the main sources of the social and economic position of blacks throughout American history. That fosterage remains a significant family choice in contemporary Africa as well as in the United States, however, even with Africa's extremely different social structures, points to reasons for fosterage that transcend the coping strategies or survival tactics of African Americans. The reasons lie in their African heritage.

VI

A comparison of black and white patterns of difference in 1910 with the differences between native-born and immigrant groups also provides some clues to the causes of racial differences. Such group differences could be rooted in demographic, economic, or cultural factors. Demographic factors, and especially mortality, account for some portion of the differences, since African-American mortality is much higher than that of other groups, but mortality differences do not provide the full story. First, African-American families are most distinctive (higher proportions of female heads and fostered children) at ages when mortality would have the least effect, that is, when both mothers and children are young. Second, some known mortality differences are not visible in family differences. For instance, Jewish immigrant mortality was substantially below Italian and Polish mortality, but among these three groups there were virtually no differences in the proportion of mothers not living with children.

[57] Clarke, *My Mother*; Gonzalez, *Black Carib Household Structure* (Seattle: University of Washington Press, 1969); R. T. Smith, *British Guiana*; M. G. Smith, *West Indian*; Michael Horowitz, *Morne-Paysan* (New York: Holt, Rhinehart, and Winston, 1967).

Some measures, like the proportion of surviving mothers who had children living elsewhere, are unaffected by mortality differences but still show substantial racial differences. And finally, calculating the proportion of children who had no mothers surviving shows that mortality can account for only some of the racial difference in children's living arrangements.[58]

Although census data do not provide clear economic measures, they do provide clues to the impact of social and economic position on family organization. The sharp racial and immigrant differences observed for household headship and family living arrangements do not fit well with most economic interpretations. At the turn of the century, African Americans and immigrant groups were together at the bottom of the socioeconomic ladder. Yet immigrants resembled native-born whites on measures of family more than both they and such whites resembled native-born African Americans.[59]

On the other hand, some differences are consistent with cultural interpretations, especially because the indicators of African-American family origin are consistent with observed patterns of family behavior in Africa, implying that there may be an adaptive non-Western heritage within African-American family patterns. Given the extreme nature of separation between the races in the United States, and the privacy accorded the family realm in American society, it is not inconceivable that there could be such cultural survival or, rather, an ongoing cultural difference.[60] These observations point toward the further investigation of such a connection for African Americans, while finding European immigrant group differences related to structural matters associated with recent immigration in 1910.[61]

The main household difference between immigrants and the native born was in the number of nonfamily members present in households. They were most common in Italian and Polish households, nearly one per household, and least common in Southern native households of all races, which averaged one per five

---

[58] A current research project of Samuel Preston and Suet Lim of the Population Studies Center of the University of Pennsylvania focuses on widowhood reports to determine if they mask a substantial amount of nonmarriage, separation, or divorce. Many suspect that taking these widowhood reports at face value would overestimate the effects of mortality on African/white family differences. Samuel Preston, Suet Lim, and S. Philip Morgan, "African-American Marriage in 1910: Beneath the Surface of Census Data," *Demography* 29, no. 1 (February 1992): 1–15.

[59] As shown in Miller, Morgan, and McDaniel in "Under the Same Roof," in Watkins, *After Ellis Island*.

[60] As mentioned above, Esther Goody, *Parenthood*, while not dealing with the United States, does some very interesting comparative studies of child-fosterage practices in various parts of sub-Saharan Africa, of African immigrants in London, and of West Indians of African heritage. DuBois, *Negro American Family*, and Herskovits, *Myth*, pointed to an African heritage present in African-American family practices, and these ideas have been developed in different ways by contemporary scholars like Gutman, *Black Family*, and Antonio McDaniel in "The Power of Culture: A Review of the Idea of Africa's Influence on Family Structure in Antebellum America," *Journal of Marriage and the Family*, forthcoming.

[61] Again, this point is further elaborated in our piece, "Under the Same Roof."

households. Among Italians and Poles, low household headship for men and large proportions of married men living apart from their wives are the two features that stand out. These features were most visible among immigrants who had very recently migrated to the United States. When time in the United States is controlled, the differences decline substantially. Therefore, with these European ethnic groups, it appears that one is not observing a gradual process of cultural assimilation so much as effects of recent migration that are relatively quickly overcome. By contrast, no statistical controls eliminate the distinctive features of African-American families.[62]

There exists a fundamental difference between the two levels of measurement, that of the household and that of the family, and differences in one area are not comparable to differences in the other. One could argue that differences on the family level are deeper and more culturally rooted than those on the household level. Unfortunately, the way in which census data are collected precludes any clearer definition of families and households, as family data are available only in terms of households. Households are primarily economic units of analysis, while families are cultural units. This investigation thus points to a larger project of including the heritage of Africa in the ongoing experience and development of African-American families in the United States. This inclusion is meant to complement the social and economic stress and prejudice that provide significant parts of explanation. What many structural arguments do not convincingly explain are the positive, nonreactive family practices that support children and create a wider "safety net" in the African-American community, and remain quite different from those used by Americans of European heritage.

VII

There have been a large number of significant critiques of the private, Western, nuclear-family ideal, including social, Freudian, Marxist, feminist, and others. The power of this family ideal creates great anxiety about families and family experiences in its public subjects and perpetuates a rhetoric that has less and less relation to the reality of people's lives, both in the past and in the future. The tremendous power granted by attribution to individual families for producing and shaping personalities and opportunities can feel overwhelmingly deterministic and oppressive. The purpose here is not to reexamine those subjectivities produced by this particular family formation but rather to question the wisdom and reality of its power as a singular ideal in American society. Approaching families through ethnicity from a child-centered, household-based position recognizes that marriage may not always be the first act in producing a

---

[62] Indeed, as Reynolds Farley has pointed out in *The Color Line and the Quality of Life in America* (New York: Russell Sage Foundation, 1987), in regression analyses race (culture) and economic factors can be demonstrated to carry equal weight, leaving the choice of emphasis up to the individual investigator.

family, and may not need to be part of the formation of successful family experiences. If families are regarded as the social units for providing care to dependents, forms can follow functions to a certain degree. Families can be assessed on how well they provide nurture and affection to members, rather than on how their members later behave in outside society. The informal fostering of children is one family practice that highlights such an approach to families.

Many people speak of modern families in the language of crisis. From the Right, as in groups like the National Family Association, this crisis is seen as a moral failure to live up to the private, Western, nuclear ideology, and from the Left, as formulated in a number of feminist and Marxist critiques, as the oppressive nature of that ideology. In the center, as in books like Richard Louv's *Childhood's Future*, it is a sense of the disappearance of "the family" as the effective, affective, and socializing center of people's lives that is seen as a tragic social failure.[63] What is difficult is in moving beyond critical positions to realistic, nonutopian alternatives. The continued force of a single-minded obsession with a private, Western, nuclear family, in which dependents are shed or made the exclusive property of those who provide care, has blinded many to the possibilities of family options. The failure of this exclusive model has left many searching for another such model, rather than being open to the many existing family options already present in society. The inability to move away from the old model has had a stultifying impact at policy levels, which reflect only one model rather than the realities of social needs and experience. This means that in health and welfare benefits, visitation and leave policies, adoption and inheritance laws, and many other areas, all of the public is not served according to the ways they may live.

It is important to realize that the dominant model represents only one kind of family among many options, and is specifically nonrural, middle class, developed in the past century, and appropriate only to adults in a certain age range, generally twenty to fifty years old.[64] It also depends on the social and economic subordination and isolation of women, and the isolation and exaggerated and prolonged dependence of children.[65] It is these last two features that

[63] Richard Louv, *Childhood's Future* (Boston: Houghton Mifflin, 1990).

[64] Here I am referring to the idea of a single family model for all, and not to the particular point or geographic origin at which that family type may have developed. This idea includes a package of attributes and not simply the concept of the conjugal nuclear family, but one that is expected to behave within a certain type of economic organization and abide by given roles. Lastly, as William Goode is careful to state in his own work, *World Revolution and Family Patterns* (Glencoe, Ill.: Free Press, 1963), this is a discussion of a family ideal by which large numbers of people have judged themselves and others, irrespective of the prevalence of its actual practice. It also, by all criteria listed above, is not racially or biologically linked, but is a product of the more fluid categories of culture and social expectations.

[65] Several authors have looked at the ways this family ideology has helped to "create" the period of adolescence in modern times, including Mary Ryan, *Cradle*; Viviana Zelizer in *Pricing the Priceless*

have led to its relatively short-lived success and its rapid demise. The psychological burden and interpersonal stresses of such families in their extreme privatized form have made them a major focus of therapy, guilt, and blame. The classical family of Western nostalgia has proven unsustainable both socially and economically, and yet the structures of the modern state have been built around it, and are dedicated to preserve it. It therefore remains as a burden and stands as the abandoned standard, a singular model in a culture of diversity.

The critique of African-American families has always used as evidence of pathology deviant social behavior outside the home rather than behavior within the home. This is a significant discrepancy. It is middle-class and upwardly mobile Euro-Americans who show high levels of living alone, have much higher levels of family violence and abuse, who abandon children and the elderly to a greater degree, who much more often support the practice of abortion, who label certain children illegitimate, will not get involved in the family problems of others, and condemn alternative living arrangements.[66] All of these features seem to indicate that it is not the families and households of blacks that cause antisocial behavior, just as it is not society that causes violent and destructive behavior within certain Euro-American families. In the ongoing crisis around family models, there are features of African-American families from which one can learn, particularly regarding the economic position of women, the isolation of families in households, and the care and raising of children. In fact, it is striking the degree to which modern critics of "the family" recommend as possible better alternatives many features already present in a number of African-American families.

This is not to assert that African-American families and communities are all simply solid and healthy. They are under tremendous pressure and attack, both social and economic, and in many places are becoming increasingly isolated from larger society. The sense of family is strong for a number of African Americans, however, and many attribute the survival and persistence of black culture in the United States to the strength of its families and community-based institutions.[67] It is families which have protected and nourished African Ameri-

---

Child (New York: Basic Books, 1985); Michael Katz in *The Social Organization of Early Industrial Capitalism* (Cambridge: Harvard University Press, 1982); and others.

[66] Figures on abuse and neglect are found in Berry and Blassingame, *Long Memory*. Living alone is examined in Sweet and Bumpass, *American Families*. Observations on abortion have long been attributed by ethnographers to religion, but the current decline in religious participation in African-American communities has not changed attitudes to abortion, as noted by Linda Burton in her research at Pennsylvania State University on single mothers and in *A Common Destiny*, p. 412. Figures on child abandonment, child welfare society records, and on elders can be seen in Sweet and Bumpass, *American Families*, for current figures and Ellen Kramerow and Gretchen Condran for 1910 in an unpublished paper presented to the 1910 U.S. Census workshop of the Population Studies Center of the University of Pennsylvania in 1989.

[67] These are generally identified as family and church as in Berry and Blassingame, *Long Memory*, pp. 70–113; Martin and Martin, *The Black Extended Family*, introduction; and Jaynes and Williams, *A Common Destiny*, pp. 526–33 and 544–48.

cans in ways that keep them in contact with home areas several generations after migration, and produce the enormous reunions of towns and counties and churches that take place in black communities every summer.[68] The terms of fondness, solidarity, and endearment in African-American communities are all family based, terms like *brother*, *sister*, *mama*, *homey*. Rather than destroying families, the harsh conditions that have been part of the American experience of African Americans have led to new coping mechanisms and configurations. Some of these structures depart from cultural ideals, but for many they have worked in ways and under conditions where private nuclear families fail miserably.

Working mothers have long been a feature of African-American households. In African-American communities, unemployed relatives and neighbors have always made it possible for those with paid jobs to work. Children move much more easily between households, tying both them and their mothers into wider social situations, and often are placed with those most skilled and interested in caring for them.[69] Siblings and partners also participate in child care to a much greater degree among African Americans than in Euro-American households.[70] The reduction in pressure on maternal time and intensity provides healthier psychological conditions for mother and child, as noted by theorists like Mark Poster and therapists like the Minuchins.[71] The shared duties also spread the economic demands as well as the nurturing responsibilities of raising children.

The sharing of maternal duties in families and communities permits the infertile and unpartnered to act as parents. It also provides a certain collective supervision of parenting practices, and an opportunity for choice and comparison for children. Discipline is clearly made a community standard rather than a frightening and ambivalent expression of the one or two significant adults

[68] Some of these have grown to sizes where they are actively recruited by hotels as convention business. Philadelphia is host to a number of these family reunions or homecomings every year, as well as to the massive general reunions of the traditionally black Greek letter organizations.

[69] As noted in Hayes, Palmer, and Zaslow's report, *Who Cares for America's Children?* (Washington, D.C.: National Academy Press, 1990), this has increasingly become a feature of care for all children, though it is more difficult for isolated suburban families, who rely on more expensive professional day-care services. In African-American extended families and communities, there are particular women who become almost professional mothers, one of the most famous of whom today is Mother Hale, of New York, because of her recent work with children with AIDS. Ann Zollar, *Member of the Family*, and Elmer and Joanne Martin, *The Black Extended Family*, document the women who take on such roles in the families they study. Similarly, there are particular teachers and youth leaders who combine their talents with actually taking young people into their homes when parental situations are difficult or when the students show particular promise. This has been the case for a number of African-American students from disadvantageous backgrounds who came to attend the University of Pennsylvania in the 1980s, for example.

[70] Documentation for this is found in Hayes, Palmer, and Zaslow, *Who Cares for America's Children?*

[71] See Mark Poster's *Critical Theory of the Family* (New York: Seabury Press, 1978); and Salvador Minuchin, Patricia Minuchin, Braulio Montalvo, Bernard Guerney, Bernice Rosman, and Florence Schumer, *Families of the Slums: An Exploration of Their Structure and Treatment* (New York: Basic Books, 1967).

in a child's life.[72] As a result, African Americans generally have much more positive attitudes toward their families as adults, and are much more likely to stay in proximity and contact with family members. Adolescence is also not as likely to be the prolonged and angst-ridden period seen in the private, suburban family, though many in black communities see other, less positive conditions force many of their children to grow up "too fast."[73]

Just as African-American mothers are rarely exclusively in charge of their children, they are also less economically dependent on a spouse. This fact is not necessarily positive or liberating, because it mainly reflects inadequate wages for both black men and women, but it does move marriage from an economic necessity to a choice. Whites will often choose to marry but not have children, while African Americans will have children but not marry. Both are likely to put such choices in terms of what they can afford, and of a desire for a companionate household.[74] This again points to rather distinct differences in what might be considered the minimum addition required to make a family in the different communities. The general demonization of black men in American popular culture may also, of course, play a role in these choices, along with the theory that producing a child is one of the few opportunities for success for unskilled black women in our society.[75] The ways in which compressed maternal generations have put considerable pressure on young grandmothers as care givers is an important current issue in many African-American communities. That grandparents are increasingly organizing to play this role more effectively, rather than moving to punish or criticize the parents, is a significant factor in the ongoing tradition of child fosterage. The reaction to young unwed childbearing in Euro-American communities is quite different, with only 34 percent of such infants remaining with family members.[76]

[72] This is noted by Minuchin et. al., *Families of the Slums*, p. 28, and also mentioned by Poster, *Critical Theory of the Family*, and by Irene Diamond in *Families, Politics and Public Policy* (New York: Longmans, 1983), p. 35.

[73] It should be noted that these observations have been made in ethnographies of community studies at many different socioeconomic levels and also vary little between urban and rural areas. Even among the suburban and professional black middle class, whom many assume seek to emulate white practices, there is notably more such family contact and sharing of familial duties. As Bart Landry, in *The New Black Middle Class* (Berkeley: University of California Press, 1987), and Ann Zollar, in *Member of the Family*, point out, ties are generally not cut when certain family members move to suburban locations. Recent cases in the Oak Park, Illinois, suburban school system show how large numbers of African-American children were fostered into the community over the fifteen years from 1975 to 1990 from the west side of Chicago to take advantage of the excellent school system (Oak Park–River Forest Board of Education, District 200, Illinois).

[74] Some of this question of affordability is involved with the qualifications for AFDC payments, but these are effects that are much stronger on the decision to marry and cohabit, rather than on the decision to bear children.

[75] Furstenberg et al., "Origins of the Female-Headed Black Family."

[76] The rate for African Americans is 73 percent, according to figures from the 1980 census, as reported in Berry and Blassingame, *Long Memory*.

One of the most destructive and pathological notions in the mainstream notion of proper families is the obsession with family privacy.[77] Elizabeth Pleck has observed that it has been precisely during periods in American history when family privacy has been stressed that domestic violence increases. Since the family is often cast as the stronghold against the state in this ideology, it becomes the place where violence is most tolerated and least likely to be reported or policed. The reluctance to intervene and a tendency until very recently to regard stories of sexual abuse as child fantasy have been features of repression and denial of abuse of those who wish to make the standard family model work. For African Americans, the family has never been as privatized, as closed to scrutiny outside the conjugal pair and their offspring, as the white family. The solution to overdetermined parenting is not to strive for some ultimate and perfect parental model, but to offer children a greater variety of models and adults from whom to learn and emulate favorable traits.[78]

Within the reality of a decline in marriage and a persistent practice of fosterage, there persists an image of the nuclear family in African-American aspiration, as shown by the types of situations into which children are fostered. It is not, however, the same as the privatized image of a nuclear family that has served as a white, middle-class norm. Parents and their children should be together, it is felt, but not exclusively together, and their various roles can be played out in a wider context of kin and community. One of the major contrasts of Euro-American thinking about families with that of African Americans is that for most blacks, the ideal does not crowd out and condemn the possible. In a social sense and in public spheres of labor and the marketplace, African Americans have been constantly insulted, overlooked, and disrespected. In the private sphere of the home and family, as well as in the church and within separate communities and institutions, African Americans have been ignored culturally, and have thus been able to continue and develop the practices and structures that were familiar and that worked.

The particular middle-class family model that operated for a century among whites in America until its recent collapse was never the one major factor in African-American family experience, and its demise has little to do with African-American life-styles or society. The failure of the private, Western, nuclear family has come from its own internal tensions and contradictions, and yet the investment in its ideology remains difficult to overcome. Policies that demand formal adoption of the dependent children residing in a household for tax

[77] This has been observed by numerous critics of contemporary families, including Michelle Barrett and Mary McIntosh in *The Anti-Social Family*; Barrie Thorne in *Rethinking the Family* (New York: Longmans, 1982); Pleck in "The Two-Parent Household," and *Domestic Tyranny*, and Poster, *Critical Theory of the Family*.

[78] As Marian Wright Edelman has stated, "It really takes a community to raise children, no matter how much money one has. Nobody can do it well alone. And it's the bedrock security of community that we and our children need" ("Kids First," *Mother Jones*, May/June 1991).

purposes, for education, or for receiving other local benefits work against informal practices like fosterage. Housing and welfare regulations are often structured to encourage the now-outmoded social and economic assumptions of the private, Western, nuclear family, as are many job-related benefits. The economic penalties faced by single mothers have become a major source of poverty and impoverishment, no longer a force to move women into the traditional role of marriage. It may be possible to look to other groups within the U.S. context, like African Americans, who have not been so imprisoned by the unified family ideology to gain insight into other family possibilities. To do so, however, will require a more open encouragement of possibilities, alternatives, and support.

Two of the most positive and needed elements in a new family regime are strategies and models for the care and nurturing of children. The crisis in child care and family stress has grown tremendously, and needs to be addressed with urgency. Much greater choice and flexibility are needed in the family equation, and caring for children and the elderly must be given a value rather than be seen only as a duty or obligation. African Americans, sometimes through force of circumstance, have always had a greater flexibility in family life and a broader range of care givers in their communities. Those recognized to be good with babies, like Mother Hale, are given babies, and those who are good with teens or can offer better environments for teenagers, like some coaches and teachers, care for teens. Dependency has been spread and shared so that it does not so often become a source of burden or resentment. While practical for a group that in many communities is often short on economic resources, these are strategies that contain a fundamental good sense in social and psychological terms as well. As white families emerge from the tangle of pathology of their own obsessions with a singular, impractical model of an oppressively private family, there may be room for more fair and reflective social comparisons. The scapegoating of African-American families has to stop in an era when all families are going through fundamental changes. In many cases, in order to open up possibilities for the future, we must be prepared to change our view of the past. The differences in African-American and Euro-American families are long-standing and in some ways can be traced to very different origins that have little to do with the contemporary "emergence" of an "underclass." Nietzsche wrote that words with histories cannot be defined, but however true that may be, coining new words is not a way to escape history.

The structural crises that currently engulf and produce the underclass are well documented in this volume, and the causes have little to do with the families who suffer the effects of their devastating pressures and constraints. It is the structuring and production of an underclass, both physically and rhetorically, that has a profound impact on families and their assessment; it is not families that produce or perpetuate an underclass. In no society or culture is fosterage the preferred family model, but it remains a valuable option to provide care when biological parents are less able. It is essential that the conditions which necessitate fosterage be addressed and changed. In the meantime, it is also essential to recognize that fosterage and other family alternatives continue to provide families effective nurturing environments for some of the most disadvantaged of U.S. children.

PART FOUR

Politics, Institutions, and the State

CHAPTER 9

The Black Poor and the Politics of Opposition in a New South City, 1929–1970

Robin D. G. Kelley

> So long as we confine our conception of *the political* to activity that is openly declared we are driven to conclude that subordinate groups essentially lack a political life or that what political life they do have is restricted to those exceptional moments of popular explosion. To do so is to miss the immense political terrain that lies between quiescence and revolt and that, for better or worse, is the political environment of subject classes. It is to focus on the visible coastline of politics and miss the continent that lies beyond.
>
> —James Scott, *Domination and the Arts of Resistance*
>
> The underclass itself is, as always, relatively quiescent politically.
>
> —Nicholas Lemann, *The Promised Land*

DESPITE GROWING national interest in the plight of the urban "underclass," social historians, unlike social scientists and urban anthropologists, have essentially ignored the black urban poor in the twentieth century, and those few scholars who have examined race and urban poverty in the United States from a historical perspective tend to focus on policy issues rather than on the lives and struggles of the poor themselves.[1] The end result has been a failure to take into account

The author would like to thank Glen T. Eskew, Michael Katz, George Lipsitz, Toni Morrison, Nell Irvin Painter, Tricia Rose, Thomas Sugrue, Cornel West, participants in the Institute for Research on Poverty small grants seminar, participants in the Works-in-Progress seminar sponsored by the Afro-American Studies Program, Princeton University, and two anonymous readers of the manuscript for criticisms, comments, and suggestions on earlier drafts of this essay. Research and writing was supported by generous grants from the Institute for Research on Poverty and the Social Science Research Council.

[1] Aside from this collection, there are a few exceptions. See, for example, James Borchert, *Alley Life in Washington: Family, Community, Religion, and Folklife in the City, 1850–1970* (Urbana: University of Illinois Press, 1980); Linda Gordon, "Black and White Visions of Welfare: Women's Welfare Activism, 1890–1945," *Journal of American History* 78, no. 2 (September 1991): 559–90, and Gordon, ed., *Women, the State, and Welfare* (Madison: University of Wisconsin Press, 1990); James Grossman, *Land of Hope: Chicago, Black Southerners, and the Great Migration* (Chicago: University of Chicago Press, 1989); Lois Rita Helmbold, "Beyond the Family Economy: Black and White Working-Class Women during the Great Depression," *Feminist Studies* 13, no. 3 (Fall 1987): 629–

opposition and human agency on the part of the poor. In particular, most social scientists overlook the role(s) of ideology and consciousness, the formation of oppositional movements among the inner-city poor, and various forms of individual and collective resistance.[2] Therefore, the purpose of this essay is to restore politics and human agency to the study of the urban poor through a

---

55, and "Downward Occupational Mobility during the Great Depression: Urban Black and White Working-Class Women," *Labor History* 29, no. 2 (Spring 1988): 135–72; Jacqueline Jones, *Labor of Love, Labor of Sorrow: Black Women, Work and the Family, from Slavery to the Present* (New York: Basic Books, 1985), and *The Dispossessed: America's Underclasses from the Civil War to the Present* (New York: Basic Books, 1992); Frances Fox Piven and Richard A. Cloward, *Regulating the Poor: The Functions of Public Welfare* (New York: Pantheon, 1971), and *Poor People's Movements: Why They Succeed, How They Fail* (New York: Pantheon, 1977); Thomas Sugrue, "The Origins of the Urban Crisis: Detroit, 1940–1960" (Ph.D. diss., Harvard University, 1992). None of these works deals exclusively with the urban poor, however. Nicolas Lemann, *The Promised Land: The Great Black Migration and How It Changed America* (New York: Alfred A. Knopf, 1991) is more historical than the work of most other journalists and social scientists writing on the subject, but his method is not very rigorous and his scope is limited mainly to a group of residents in a Chicago housing project during the period from the mid-1960s to the present. Moreover, his analysis of poverty policy is much stronger than his discussion of the poor. But this does not make Lemann's book novel, since some of the best historical work on poverty, while not primarily on blacks, has consistently focused on the history of public and private responses to the poor. See for example, James T. Patterson, *America's Struggle against Poverty, 1900–1985* (Cambridge: Harvard University Press, 1986); Michael Katz, *Poverty and Policy in American History* (New York: Academic Press, 1983), *In the Shadow of the Poorhouse: A Social History of Welfare in America* (New York: Basic Books, 1986), and *The Undeserving Poor: From the War on Poverty to the War on Welfare* (New York: Pantheon Books, 1990); Mimi Abramowitz, *Regulating the Lives of Women: Social Welfare Policy from Colonial Times to the Present* (Boston: South End Press, 1988).

[2] Jennifer L. Hochschild's stimulating essay "Equal Opportunity and the Estranged Poor," *Annals* 501 (January 1989): 144–45, criticizes social scientists for ignoring ideology and consciousness. Aside from a handful of historical studies cited above, cultural anthropologists have been more sensitive to ideology, poor people's values, and survival strategies. See, for example, Elliot Liebow, *Tally's Corner: A Study of Negro Streetcorner Men* (Boston: Little, Brown, 1967); Ulf Hannerz, *Soulside: Inquiries into Ghetto Culture and Community* (New York: Columbia University Press, 1969); Carol B. Stack, *All Our Kin: Strategies for Survival in a Black Community* (New York: Harper and Row, 1974); Betty Lou Valentine, *Hustling and Other Hard Work: Life Styles in the Ghetto* (New York: Free Press, 1978); Jay Macleod, *Ain't No Makin' It: Leveled Aspirations in a Low-Income Neighborhood* (Boulder, Colo.: Westview Press, 1987); John Hagedorn, with Perry Macon, *People and Folks: Gangs, Crime and the Underclass in a Rustbelt City* (Chicago: Lake View Press, 1988); James Diego Vigil, *Barrio Gangs: Street Life and Identity in Southern California* (Austin: University of Texas Press, 1988); Carl S. Taylor, *Dangerous Society* (East Lansing: Michigan State University Press, 1990); Martin Sanchez Jankowski, *Islands in the Street: Gangs and American Urban Society* (Berkeley and Los Angeles: University of California Press, 1991); Elijah Anderson, *Streetwise: Race, Class, and Change in an Urban Community* (Chicago: University of Chicago Press, 1990); Alex Kotlowitz, *There Are No Children Here: The Story of Two Boys Growing Up in the Other America* (New York: Doubleday, 1991). This work is extremely valuable because it captures the responses and survival strategies hidden from census data, illuminates the lived experiences of the poor, and often adopts a dynamic approach to culture that does not reduce poor people to mere reflections of economic structures. But few ethnographies pay much attention to historical and structural transformations. Rather, they describe and interpret a particu-

preliminary examination of the ways in which disadvantaged African Americans in Birmingham, Alabama, attempted to survive, mitigate, or alter their circumstances. Covering the period from the origins of the Great Depression to the post–civil rights/Black Power era, I will examine the changing socioeconomic world of the jobless and working poor; the various legal and illegal methods by which African Americans survived and resisted poverty, segregation, and racial oppression; and the relationship between poor people's oppositional practices and organized political movements that claim to speak on behalf of the black poor.

The following is much more than a historical survey of survival and resistive strategies; it is an attempt to redefine political practice in a manner that places poor people's self-activity at the center of our analysis. In other words, this study digs beneath the surface of traditional working-class politics, whose stories have captured the attention of labor historians seeking to understand the United States "from the bottom up," and attempts to uncover the hidden politics of everyday life waged by the most marginalized segments of society. My analysis is indebted to political anthropologist James Scott, who argues that, despite appearances of consent, marginalized groups challenge those in power by constructing and acting out a "hidden transcript," a dissident political culture that manifests itself in the daily conversations, jokes, songs, folklore, and other cultural forms of the oppressed, and frequently surfaces as everyday forms of resistance—theft, foot-dragging, the destruction of property, and the like—or, more rarely, in the form of an open attack against individuals, institutions, or symbols of domination. Scott labels the whole body of behind-the-scenes political discourse "infrapolitics," oppositional practices that constitute the foundational politics for all organized mass movements. I am not suggesting that infrapolitics is merely another form of political activity, or that every survival strategy should be regarded as a political act. Rather, the politics of the black poor, which even in its clearest manifestations remains elusive, cannot be understood *without* reference to the realm of infrapolitics.[3]

---

lar community during a brief moment in time. The failure to identify many of these communities only compounds the problem and presumes that region, political economy, and history have no bearing on opportunity structures, opposition, or culture (for an extended critique, see Andrew H. Maxwell, "The Anthropology of Poverty in Black Communities: A Critique and Systems Alternative," *Urban Anthropology* 17, nos. 2 and 3 [1988]: 171–92). In essence, participant observation often ignores structural forces that are not visible to the community being studied. Nevertheless, ethnographies provide valuable *primary* data regarding the way ordinary people live their lives and see the world.

[3] James C. Scott, *Domination and the Arts of Resistance: Hidden Transcripts* (New Haven: Yale University Press, 1990), 183–84 and passim. I am also indebted to C. L. R. James for the term *self-activity*, which refers broadly to the range of unorganized and organized movements that have sprung from the working class's own initiative. For an elaboration of the concept of self-activity, see C. L. R. James, Grace Lee, and Pierre Chaulieu, *Facing Reality* (Detroit: Correspondence, 1958);

In Birmingham, Alabama, where the black poor have been locked out of mainstream political institutions throughout most of the twentieth century, have been victims of legal and extralegal repression, and have had to face racial as well as economic barriers to fair wages and decent living and working conditions, it should not be surprising that much of their oppositional practice remained at the level of infrapolitics. For my own purposes, how successful these oppositional practices were is not as important as what they tell us about how the poor viewed domination and the social order, what issues were foremost in their minds, and how infrapolitics shapes more formal political institutions. By examining the realm of poor people's infrapolitics, we might begin to understand (1) why so few poor black people support or join formal political organizations that purport to speak for the poor, (2) why some organizations are more successful than others at mobilizing the black poor, and (3) the relationship between poor people's opposition and the informal economy.

Survival and Resistance in the Great Depression

We begin our story with the onset of the Great Depression. Although poor African Americans have been part of Birmingham's landscape since the city was founded a half-century earlier, the economic crisis of the 1930s propelled thousands of stable working-class blacks into the growing ranks of the jobless and underemployed. Less than a decade after the collapse of biracial trade unionism in Birmingham and three decades after Alabama blacks were stripped of the right to vote, the increasingly impoverished African-American working class had few organizational weapons to which they could turn to improve conditions. Yet, despite what appeared to be a hopeless situation, the Depression had a tremendous impact on poor people's politics in Birmingham. Most residents developed individual and collective self-help initiatives to survive, in addition to depending on public and private relief, and a small but significant segment of Birmingham's black population turned to the Communist party for help. The latter had important political implications for racial politics because the presence of a radical movement in Birmingham dominated by poor and working-class blacks exposed the underlying class conflicts that had long existed within the black community.

Like most Southern cities, Birmingham began to feel the effects of the Great Depression much earlier than most Northern cities. The Birmingham Trades Council reported an unemployment rate of 18 percent in February 1928, and between 1926 and 1929 the Jefferson County Red Cross's relief rolls more than doubled. In 1931, mines and mills owned by the Tennessee Coal, Iron, and

---

George Rawick, "Working-Class Self-Activity," *Radical America* 3, no. 2 (March–April 1969): 23–31; Martin Glaberman, *Wartime Strikes* (Detroit, Mich.: Beckwick/Ed, 1980); George Lipsitz, *Class and Culture in Cold War America: A Rainbow at Midnight* (New York: Praeger, 1981).

Railroad Company (TCI) cut wages by 25 percent, followed by a 15 percent reduction in May 1932. More devastating for workers, however, were drastic cutbacks in operations that effectively forced some steelworkers and miners to accept a two-day-per-month work schedule.[4] Black working women, most of whom labored as domestics, earned as little as thirty cents and whatever they could "tote" from their employers' kitchens for a full day's work. With few job opportunities, the responsibility of child rearing, and spouses who frequently had to accept long-distance employment, women were more dependent on private and public relief than men were.[5]

As the effects of the Depression began to take their toll, Birmingham's poor had few avenues to which they could turn for assistance. The families of miners and steelworkers residing in company-owned suburbs received some support from their employers, but company-sponsored welfare programs were extremely limited. Municipal and county resources also proved inadequate, thus leaving the Red Cross to bear the brunt of Birmingham's relief needs. By 1933, at least 27 percent of Birmingham's total black population was receiving some form of welfare.[6] As former sharecroppers or descendants of rural folk who lived

[4] Edward S. LaMonte, "Politics and Welfare in Birmingham, Alabama, 1900–1975" (Ph.D. diss., University of Chicago, 1976), 160; Barbara Bailey, "Ten Trying Years: A History of Bessemer, Alabama, 1929–1939" (M.A. thesis, Samford University, 1977), 49; Wendell M. Adamson, "Coal Production in Alabama," *University of Alabama Business News*, February 15 and June 15, 1931; E. M. Henderson, Sr., "Relief in Jefferson County: A Brief Survey" (typescript, Birmingham Public Library), 9; Douglas L. Smith, *New Deal in the Urban South* (Baton Rouge: Louisiana State University Press, 1988), 17–18; Morris Benson interview, conducted by Peggy Hamrick, June 8, 1984, Oral History, Working Lives Collection, University of Alabama (hereafter cited WLC), p. 15; Samuel Andrews interview, conducted by Peggy Hamrick, July 18, 1984 (WLC), 20–21; King Chandler, Jr., interview, conducted by Brenda McCallum, May 23, 1983 (WLC), 3–4; Willie Johnson interview, conducted by Brenda McCallum, June 26, 1984 (WLC), 10; Cleatus and Louise Burns interview, conducted by Cliff Kuhn, June 12, 1984 (WLC), 1.

[5] Lizzie May Lopp interview, conducted by Brenda McCallum, June 26, 1983 (WLC), 5–11; Essie Davis interview, conducted by Peggy Hamrick, August 20, 1984 (WLC), 2; Evelena McClindon, oral testimony, May 5, 1981, Birmingham Papers and Related Materials (BPRM), 1. In 1930, 34.5 percent of the black female population was gainfully employed, compared to 17.4 percent of the white females in Birmingham. Bureau of the Census, *Fifteenth Census of the United States: 1930*, vol. 1, *Population* (Washington, D.C.: Government Printing Office, 1932), 93. In 1935 at least 8,000 black female domestic workers, or one-half of the total number of black female domestics, had registered with the Alabama Employment Service; see U.S. Employment Service, *A Report on the Availability of the Services of the National Reemployment Service, Affiliated with the U.S. Employment Service, to Negro Applicants, Particularly Birmingham* (typescript, December 16, 1936), in L. A. Oxley's Files, Records of the Department of Labor, RG 183. For a discussion of how the Depression affected women's work and the response of some male wage earners to the crisis, see Helmbold, "Beyond the Family Economy," 629–55, and "Downward Occupational Mobility," 169–71; Jacqueline Jones, *Labor of Love*, 221–30; and Jacqueline Jones's essay in this volume.

[6] Marlene Hunt Rikard, "An Experiment in Welfare Capitalism: The Health Care Services of the Tennessee Coal, Iron and Railroad Company" (Ph.D. diss., University of Alabama, 1983), 270–79; Virginia Foster Durr, *Outside the Magic Circle: The Autobiography of Virginia Foster Durr* (University, Ala.: University of Alabama Press, 1985), 79; *Birmingham Post*, February 23, 1931; LaMonte,

through many harsh winters, most poor blacks, like the immigrant poor described by Kathryn Neckerman in chapter 6, adopted dozens of creative methods of survival. In addition to performing odd jobs in exchange for food, obtaining grocery store throwaways, selling roasted peanuts, and hauling and selling firewood, the poor turned to urban cultivation—both as a source of additional food as well as cash income. The unemployed and working poor invested in various forms of livestock, from milk cows to pigs, and cultivated small vegetable gardens on vacant city lots and in the back alleys of industrial suburbs. According to a 1934 Health Department report, 7,595 pigs and 1,996 cows were discovered within the city limits, the vast majority belonging to black families.[7]

The poor took pride in their ability to get through difficult times, but they also insisted on receiving some government or private assistance. Despite their public demeanor of humility and gratitude toward social workers and other agency representatives, welfare recipients frequently contested caseworkers' decisions and insisted on more relief. When welfare agencies were not responsive enough, frustration and fear of starvation could turn the most humble, mild-mannered poor person into a militant. Birmingham resident Curtis Maggard, an unemployed steelworker during most of the Depression who took pride in his ability to "make it . . . without stealing or robbing," was pushed to a point of desperation by the city welfare agency's reluctance to provide relief. He and his wife had not eaten in four days, and his daughter was crying for something to eat. Angry and desperate, Maggard marched down to the welfare office armed with a "croker sack" and insisted on some material aid. When he was told that a relief check was in the mail, he delivered a powerful monologue, a public declaration of the hidden transcript: "I said, 'You been telling me that for four weeks. . . . You got a grocery store up there, and here is a croker sack. When I get home, I'm going to have that croker sack full of food. Ya'll got a grocery store down there, and I'm going to send somebody to hell to get me

---

"Politics and Welfare," 204–6; Henderson, "Relief in Jefferson County," 9; "Minutes of the City Commission, City of Birmingham," November 18, 1930, 139; Mark Cowett, *Birmingham's Rabbi: Morris Newfield and Alabama, 1895–1940* (University, Ala.: University of Alabama Press, 1986), 105–6; Douglas L. Smith, *New Deal in the Urban South*, 36–37, 41; U.S. Employment Service, *A Report on the Availability of the Services.*

[7] Constance Price interview, conducted by Cliff Kuhn, July 18, 1984 (WLC), 7. Several WLC interviews describe urban farming as a Depression survival strategy. See especially, Mitchell Jerald interview, by Peggy Hamrick, August 9, 1984, 9; Andrews interview, 21; Morris Benson interview, by Peggy Hamrick, June 8, 1984, 15; George J. Brown interview, by Cliff Kuhn and Brenda McCallum, April 25, 1983, 3; Alex Bryant interview, by Brenda McCallum, June 26, 1984, 6; Chandler interview, 3; Clarence Darden interview, by Steve McCallum, May 24, 1983, 12–13; Mack Gibson interview, by Cliff Kuhn, July 14, 1984, 6. The data on livestock and gardening are from Bailey, "Ten Trying Years," 51; and J. D. Dowling et al., "Consolidated Report and Analysis of Surveys and Studies of the Blighted Areas of Birmingham and Bessemer, Alabama" (typescript, Jefferson County Board of Health, 1936), 5.

something to eat.' And that's the only thing that stirred them up." Although Maggard did not leave with a full croker sack, he was issued a check immediately.[8]

How relief was administered and *how* individuals were treated in welfare offices or on public-works projects was just as important as *what* one received. On public-relief projects, black workers frequently complained that the easier jobs were reserved for whites, and occasionally resisted work they thought to be demeaning or too tiring. A black woman on a Work Progress Administration beautification project near Bessemer who, along with other black women, had to dig trenches, remove rocks, and repair roads irrespective of the weather, probably summed up the feelings of her fellow workers when she wrote, "We are colored women [are] treat [sic] worse than stock."[9] Birmingham's relief applicants especially resented the condescending attitudes of caseworkers, many of whom established reputations for being verbally abusive to poor blacks. According to one former welfare recipient, black caseworkers were no better than whites. "They was rough folks. See they was getting [theirs], but they have to treat us mean. . . . So they do like the whites tell them to do against their color."[10] Occasionally, an applicant would reach a breaking point and curse out a social worker or demand to be accorded at least of modicum of dignity and respect, but such action might lead to a total withdrawal of assistance—a consequence few could afford. Nevertheless, in the context of a welfare office crowded with hungry and frustrated applicants, a lone voice of protest often brought collective shouts of approval from other relief applicants who shared the same feelings of frustration. An anecdote told by Birmingham resident Hosea Hudson, is very revealing on this score:

> I said, "Everytime I come out here, 'Get back side the wall,' and when I get in the office, they tell me 'your coal's on the way.' When I get home, I ain't got no coal to make a fire." I said, "I'm getting tired of getting back side the wall!"
>
> I was talking loud. That was just loud-mouthing. Let the people know somebody had some courage to speak. And several guys in the line there knew me, had worked in Stockham foundry with me, they said, "Tell them about it, Big Red!" "I hear you, Big Red!" cause I was always raising the devil in the shop anyhow. There was about 75–100 people, it was a lot of people there.

---

[8] Curtis Maggard interview, by Peggy Hamrick, July 13, 1984 (WLC), 22–23.

[9] Unsigned letter to Labor Policies Board, November 5, 1936, box 784, Works Progress Administration Records, National Archives, Washington, D.C. There are numerous examples of black relief workers complaining about the work they had to perform. See, for example, Beulah Banks to Mrs. Eleanor Roosevelt, February 23, 1938, box 786, WPA Records; Thomas Gadson interview (interviewer not identified), October 7, 1981 (BPRM), 2; Curtis Maggard interview (WLC), 16–17; *Daily Worker*, December 5, 1932; and examples of opposition to relief foremen in Robin D. G. Kelley, *Hammer and Hoe: Alabama Communists During the Great Depression* (Chapel Hill: University of North Carolina Press, 1990).

[10] Curtis Maggard interview, 4.

In some cases, disdain for condescending and insensitive caseworkers manifested itself in more collective, even violent, confrontations. According to one observer, during the early 1930s a group of angry black women who simply had enough of one particularly notorious black caseworker "called her out and almost whooped her naked. The way she treat them."[11]

Welfare recipients contested the agencies' practice of forcing applicants to sell personal belongings thought to be superfluous, such as radios, watches, clothes, or new furniture, and canceling assistance to people possessing *too much food* or a large garden. The poverty threshold was so low that most people on relief had to hide things and lie about extra income in order to make ends meet.[12] Of course, nobody went to jail for lying to a social worker, but those who hid food and personal items, moonlighted, or maintained gardens were clearly breaking the rules and regulations governing the activities of welfare recipients. Some of these same individuals went further, however, adopting strategies for which many wound up behind bars. Shoplifting, fencing, "numbers" running, prostitution, and making and selling liquor were just a few of the variety of crimes committed by the poor. Most common were forms of theft that rarely lead to prosecution, and therefore were not reflected in crime statistics. Domestic workers were adept at "pan toting" or stealing from their employers; coal miners and people residing near the railroad appropriated chunks of coal and coke for their home ovens; and vacant homes were torn apart by the poor desperately in need of fuel.[13] The appropriation of coal from the railroad is an especially

[11] Nell Irvin Painter, *The Narrative of Hosea Hudson, His Life as a Negro Communist in the South* (Cambridge: Harvard University Press, 1979), 161; Curtis Maggard interview, 4. Hosea Hudson, who refers to her as "Hallie Moses" in his narrative, had similar run-ins with Shepherd (161–62). The fact that these women chose to assault an African-American social worker suggests a clear knowledge of power relations. If they had attacked a white woman, we can be quite certain that the consequences for their actions would have been more severe.

[12] Curtis Maggard interview, 1–3; also Rosa Jackson interview, July 23, 1984 (WLC), 10; George J. Brown interview, 3; Painter, *Narrative*, 162. Of course, within the complicated matrix of "welfare politics" we find survival strategies that entailed collaboration with the powerful. Some residents offered welfare agents and social workers their services as neighborhood spies in exchange for a larger grocery order or extra coal. They informed on neighbors who hid food, earned unreported wages, or maintained gardens. However, serving as a "neighborhood stool pigeon" was a rare strategy. No matter how beneficial such practices might have seemed, they led to ostracism, character assassination, and even verbal and physical harassment. Jackson interview, 10; George J. Brown interview, 3; Painter, *Narrative*, 162–63. As James Scott argues, the powerless also have sanctioning power within their own world; the hidden transcript enforces certain forms of conduct among subordinates, and thus social pressure is, in and of itself, a powerful weapon of the poor. "This means that any subordinate who seeks privilege by ingratiating himself to his superior will have to answer for that conduct once he returns to the world of his peers" (*Domination*, 191).

[13] Essie Davis interview, 3–5; Benson interview, 15; Curtis Maggard interview, 6, 13–15; Painter, *Narrative*, 100, 157–59; Kelley, *Hammer and Hoe*, 19; and for a broader discussion of "pan toting" and other survival and resistance strategies practiced by domestic workers in the urban South, see Tera W. Hunter's brilliant study, "Household Workers in the Making: Afro-American Women in Atlanta and the New South, 1861–1920" (Ph.D. diss., Yale University, 1990), 82–96.

interesting survival strategy precisely because of its collective character. Before sunup or in the late evening, as trains passed through certain sections of Birmingham, black firemen would "accidentally" shovel or kick pieces of coal off the train to black *and* white residents waiting in the darkness with empty sacks and carts by their sides. The trains that carried coal and coke from the mines were also prime targets: residents would jump on slow-moving trains and roll the coal off for everyone bold enough to show up. According to Hosea Hudson, "Nobody fighting over 'this is my coal' or nothing, but everybody trying to get what they can get. It wasn't any jim crow line around that coal, and there wasn't any fights among the Negroes and whites."[14]

The appropriation of coal, then, had enormous implications for collective action, as did other forms of working-class theft. Birmingham's jobless, irrespective of race, showed increasingly less respect for the boundaries of private property and, in the process, disrupted the political economy. While theft in and of itself can hardly be considered a "political" act, in the context of opposition to wage labor it might be viewed as a form of infrapolitics. Indeed, several criminologists have cautioned against viewing property crimes committed by the poor as little more than deviant behavior; theft, especially at the workplace, should be regarded as a strategy to recuperate unpaid wages, compensate for low pay and mistreatment, and obtain precious resources necessary to survive or improve one's living standard.[15] Moreover, participation in the illicit economy can potentially lead to a more direct challenge to the sanctity or "naturalness" of private property as well as enable workers to resist industrial discipline.[16]

---

[14] Painter, *Narrative*, 157–59.

[15] For examples see, Alvin Ward Gouldner, *Wildcat Strike* (Yellow Springs, Ohio: Antioch Press, 1954); Steven Box, *Recession, Crime, and Punishment* (Totowa, N.J.: Barnes and Noble Books, 1987), 34; J. Ditton, *Part-Time Crime* (London: Macmillan, 1977); Richard C. Hollinger, *Theft by Employees* (Lexington, Mass.: Lexington Books, 1983). For a general discussion of the informal economy and working-class opposition, see Cyril Robinson, "Exploring the Informal Economy," *Crime and Social Justice* 15, nos. 3 and 4 (1988): 3–16.

[16] Although most scholars are willing to accept this argument when discussing antebellum slavery, no one has thought to explore the oppositional potential of theft in the postbellum experiences of the African-American working class. Part of the reason, I think, lies in Southern labor historians' noble quest to redeem the black working class from racist stereotypes. The company personnel records, police reports, mainstream white newspaper accounts, and correspondence have left us with a somewhat serene portrait of folks who, only occasionally, deviate from what I like to call the "Cult of True Sambohood." The safety and ideological security of the South required that pilfering (not to mention slowdowns, absenteeism, tool breaking, and other acts of black working-class resistance) be turned into shiftlessness and immorality. (For an extended discussion, see my "'We Are Not What We Seem': Rethinking Black Working-Class Opposition in the Jim Crow South," *Journal of American History* [forthcoming].) Another reason has to do with the problems of trying to make fine distinctions between "social bandits" and "crimes of resistance" on the one hand, and "predatory" crimes on the other. But as historian Peter Linebaugh points out, it is the immiseration of the working class that gives rise to various forms of property crimes among the poor, which means

Birmingham's black poor did not depend solely on incipient strategies of survival and resistance. As many as three thousand to four thousand unemployed and working poor affiliated themselves with the Communist party and/or its various auxiliary organizations in an effort to improve conditions. Although blacks who joined or supported the Communists comprised a small minority—about 10–15 percent of the total black relief recipients—their influence was far greater than their numbers would suggest. Besides, in a city where the consequences of open resistance compelled the black poor to adopt evasive forms of opposition, party work was dangerous business. Hundreds of black radical activists were harassed, arrested, kidnapped, and beaten severely for their participation in Communist politics. Yet, despite a clear knowledge of the dangers involved, a substantial segment of the poor black community continued to support Communist organizations in Birmingham because party leaders spoke directly and unambiguously to the jobless and working poor. In 1931, for example, the Communists demanded that the unemployed receive a weekly minimum of ten dollars cash relief, free coal and carfare, a minimum of twenty dollars per week for city relief jobs, and a moratorium on evictions and utilities shutoffs.[17]

More significantly, because the party and its auxiliaries were composed of poor black people, community activists simply brought local oppositional practices into the movement—in short, they enveloped organized radicalism with their own infrapolitics. Everyday forms of resistance and survival were far more common than dramatic marches and demonstrations. For example, when a family's electricity was shut off for nonpayment, Communist organizers surreptitiously appropriated electricity from public outlets or other homes by using heavy-gauge copper wire, or "jumpers." They also found ways to reactivate water mains after they had been turned off.[18] In short, the Communist-led neighbor-

---

that the distinctions between "crimes of resistance" and crimes limited to poor communities are always blurred. As Linebaugh advises, "If we categorize them too quickly as social criminals taking from the rich, or criminal-criminals stealing from the poor, in the process of making these judgements we cloud our attentiveness to theirs" (Peter Linebaugh, *The London Hanged: Crime and Civil Society in the Eighteenth Century* [London: Allen Lane, Penguin Press, 1991], xxiii); and for an example of a Marxist historian who attempts to make clear distinctions between "predatory" or "lumpen" crimes and "crimes of resistance," see Richard Quinney, *Class, State, and Crime: On the Theory and Practice of Criminal Justice* (New York and London: D. McKay Co., 1977), 55–57.

[17] See Kelley, *Hammer and Hoe*, chap. 1.

[18] Ibid.; Painter, *Narrative*, 162–63. For a discussion of Unemployed Councils' tactics in other major urban areas, especially Chicago and New York, see Robert Fisher, *Let the People Decide: Neighborhood Organizing in America* (Boston: Twayne Publishers, 1984), 35–42; Franklin Folsom, *Impatient Armies of the Poor: The Story of Collective Action of the Unemployed, 1808–1942* (Niwot: University Press of Colorado, 1991); Daniel J. Leab, "'United We Eat': The Creation and Organization of the Unemployed Councils in 1930," *Labor History* 7 (Fall 1967): 300–315; Mark Naison, *Communists in Harlem during the Depression* (Urbana: University of Illinois Press, 1983), 41; Albert Prago, "The Organization of the Unemployed and the Role of Radicals, 1929–1935" (Ph.D. diss.,

hood committees worked from an understanding of power relations that developed out of the everyday oppositional practices and specific social locations of the poor.

Birmingham's Communists were more successful than the traditional black elite in their efforts to garner support from economically disadvantaged blacks. Part of the reason is linked to the black elite's refusal to regard the activities of the black poor as politically significant. During the early 1930s, for example, the Birmingham branch of the National Association for the Advancement of Colored People never made an effort to recruit poor blacks, and looked askance at individuals who showed up to NAACP meetings in overalls. Hence, in January 1931, while the Communist-led International Labor Defense claimed two hundred black members, the Birmingham branch of the NAACP reported only six dues-paying members.[19] The inability of traditional black leadership to mobilize support from the poor cannot be attributed entirely to their insensitivity or inability to understand poor people's lives. A handful of individuals, like newspaper editor Robert Durr, chose to side with the status quo. A preacher from Mississippi who moved to Birmingham in 1931, Durr received financial backing from TCI to launch an antiunion newspaper, the *Weekly Review*, whose columns he used to exhort the black masses to accept their plight and utilize only the "proper channels" to improve conditions. In an interview granted five years later, Durr offered an epigrammatic explanation of his politics: "By all means keep in with the man who hires and pays you."[20]

Most traditional black leaders, however, straddled the line between their class interests and what they perceived to be the "collective" interests of the race. This was especially evident among black clergy, whose vocation often depended on the accumulation of pennies, nickels, and dimes poor churchgoers could contribute to the collection plate. Some churches served as centers of charity, providing food, clothes, and other basic necessities to their most destitute members. A few modest preachers who had no pastoral obligations went so far as to devote time and energy to building the labor movement, and some even became active in Communist organizations. Nevertheless, most pastors opposed black involvement in radical or protest politics, and some preached sermons blaming the poor for their plight and condemning to hell those whose survival depended on illicit activities. Indeed, Birmingham's black clergy were notorious for using the pulpit to preach a politics of accommodation and dissuade poor blacks from joining radical organizations, and some received healthy subsidies from companies to do so. The Tennessee Coal, Iron, and Railroad Company and other companies built and maintained segregated

---

Union Graduate School, 1976); Roy Rosenzweig, "Organizing the Unemployed: The Early Years of the Great Depression, 1929–1933," *Radical America* 10 (1976): 37–60.

[19] Kelley, *Hammer and Hoe*, 109.

[20] Ibid., 110.

churches for their employees and hired only pastors willing to disparage organized labor from the pulpit.[21]

The party's influence among the black unemployed and working poor waned during the mid- to late 1930s. When the Communist party shifted its political stance in 1935 and concentrated on building a Popular Front with white liberals, establishing the Congress of Industrial Organizations, and working with New Deal politicians, it lost much of its mass base among the black poor—the one possible exception being the Communist-influenced Workers Alliance.[22] On the eve of the Second World War, the poor had few viable political organizations to which to turn, and those that purported to speak for them simply did not speak their language.

During the Depression, then, the black poor chose to either struggle on their own or turn to political organizations that openly articulated the grievances and aspirations they tended to keep to themselves. The evidence suggests at least a partial disjunction between the infrapolitics of the black poor and the political practices of "traditional" black leadership. Indeed, given the lack of mass support for mainstream black organizations during the 1930s, historians might begin to reevaluate the notion that black middle-class organizations could be used as barometers for determining the political attitudes of the black poor or working class.

WARTIME MOBILIZATION AND THE POLITICS OF OPPOSITION

With the onset of World War II, the emphasis on survival issues that had characterized poor people's opposition during the Depression shifted toward a more race-conscious politics of resistance that, in some cases, cut across class lines. Part of the shift can be attributed to the nature of the war itself, since wartime rhetoric unintentionally undermined the legitimacy of white supremacy. Black Americans were expected to support a war against Hitler—whose plan for Aryan supremacy was treated as a threat to Western democracy—while white supremacy and segregation continued to be a way of life in the Deep South. The black poor, especially the youth, knew racism could no longer be justified on home soil, and those who were unwilling to tolerate it any longer

---

[21] Ibid., 111–16; on clergy supportive of the labor movement, see Benson interview, 2, 5; Maggard interview, 2; Earl Brown interview, by Cliff Kuhn, June 29, 1984 (WLC), 7; Paul Worthman, "Black Workers and the Labor Unions in Birmingham, Alabama, 1897–1904," in Milton Cantor, ed., Black Labor in America (Westport, Conn.: Negro Universities Press, 1969), 64–65. On clergy who opposed the labor movement, see Jesse Grace interview, by Cliff Kuhn, July 16, 1984 (WLC), 4–5; William Mitch, Jr., interview by Cliff Kuhn, June 27, 1984 (WLC), 7. According to a Department of Labor Report in 1919, "all the Negro preachers had been subsidized by the companies and were without exception preaching against the negroes joining unions" (H. B. Vaughn to George E. Haynes, March 5, 1919, file no. 8/102–D, "Special Problems—Birmingham," Records of the Department of Labor, RG 174).

[22] Kelley, Hammer and Hoe, chaps. 6–10. The Workers' Alliance, however, collapsed in 1940.

exhibited greater militancy in public spaces such as buses, and streetcars or on city streets.[23]

The perpetuation of racist employment practices in the midst of a booming economy also frustrated Birmingham's already embittered black poor and working class. Although a rather large percentage of jobless black males found employment, either in the armed services or in the lower echelons of industry, and thousands left Alabama to take advantage of Northern employment opportunities, racism limited the extent to which African-American working people could benefit from Birmingham's booming economy. The majority of blacks were denied access to employment training programs, and white-controlled industrial unions actively limited black occupational mobility. The Fair Employment Practices Commission, which held hearings in Birmingham in 1943, was apparently powerless to bring about changes. In fact, during the war the percentage of blacks employed in the steel industry actually declined from 41 percent in 1940 to 38 percent in 1945, and black steelworkers on average earned 80 percent of what their white coworkers earned. Conditions for black women were certainly no better; many tried desperately to escape domestic work and take advantage of industrial jobs, but in Birmingham virtually all "female positions" were reserved for white women. Those who successfully moved out of domestic work merely filled other kinds of service jobs—as dishwashers, cooks, bus girls, mechanical laundry workers, and the like—positions white women had vacated.[24]

It is no accident that public transportation became one of the most important sites of resistance during the war. First, as more rural residents moved into the city to take advantage of wartime employment, the sheer number of people moving to and from work overtaxed an already limited fleet of streetcars and buses. Battles over space, as well as the manner in which space was allocated, resulted in intense racial conflict. Second, public transportation, unlike a waiting room or a water fountain, was "commodified" space. When one pays for a service that one depends on for her/his livelihood, there seems to be less willingness to accept certain forms of domination—particularly forms that affect one's ability to get to his/her destination on time. Finally, Birmingham's buses and streetcars might be regarded as "moving theaters." Here I am using

[23] On the political and ideological changes caused by the war, see Pete Daniel, "Going among Strangers: Southern Reactions to World War II," *Journal of American History* 77 (December 1990): 893, 906–8; Robert Korstad and Nelson Lichtenstein, "Opportunities Found and Lost: Labor, Radicals, and the Early Civil Rights Movement," *Journal of American History* 75 (December 1988): 786–811; Bernice Reagon, "World War II Reflected in Black Music: Uncle Sam Called Me," *Southern Exposure* 2 (Winter 1974); Lipsitz, *Class and Culture*; Harvard Sitkoff, "Racial Militancy and Interracial Violence in the Second World War," *Journal of American History* 58 (December 1971): 661–81.

[24] Robert J. Norrell, "Caste in Steel: Jim Crow Careers in Birmingham, Alabama," *Journal of American History* 73, no. 3 (December 1986): 687; Mary Martha Thomas, "Alabama Women on the Home Front, World War II," *Alabama Heritage* 19 (Winter 1991): 9; Geraldine Moore, *Behind the Ebony Mask* (Birmingham, Ala.: Southern University Press, 1961), 28.

theater in two ways: as a site of performance and a site of military conflict. First, plays of conflict, repression, and resistance are performed in which passengers witness, or participate in, a wide variety of "skirmishes" that shape the collective memory of the passengers, illustrate the limitations as well as possibilities of resistance to domination, and draw more passengers into the "performance." Second, theater as a military metaphor is particularly appropriate in light of the fact that all bus drivers and streetcar conductors carried guns and blackjacks, and used them pretty regularly to maintain (the social) order. In August 1943, when a black woman riding the South East Lake–Ensley line complained to the conductor that he had passed her stop, he followed her out of the streetcar and, in the words of the official report, "knocked her down with handle of gun. No further trouble."[25]

Despite the repressive atmosphere on public transportation, black passengers, especially youth, still resisted. Over the course of twelve months beginning September 1941, fifty-five incidents were reported of African-American passengers either refusing to give up their seats or sitting in the white section. More importantly, in most incidents the racial compartmentalization of existing space was not the primary issue. Rather, most poor blacks who had no alternate means of transportation focused their complaints on the manner in which they were treated by operators and other passengers; drivers giving incorrect change, allocating or limiting space for black passengers, or forcing blacks to pay at the front door and enter through the center doors. It was not uncommon, for instance, for half-empty buses or streetcars to pass up African Americans on the pretext of preserving space for potential white riders. Nor was it unusual for a black passenger to pay at the front of the bus and be left standing while s/he attempted to board at the center door. Black female domestics complained regularly of having been passed up by bus drivers, resulting in their being late to work or left stranded at night in hostile white communities.[26]

While not every black passenger was willing to breach the public transcript of accepted behavior, some black male riders seemed to thrive on "testing the limits" of Jim Crow. Between 1941 and 1944, there were over a dozen incidents that could have been candidates for a place in the "Stagolee" folklore of urban African Americans. These "baaad niggers" put on public displays of resistance that embarrassed some black passengers and left others in awe, though they did not lead to improvements in conditions—nor were they intended to. Some boldly sat down next to white female passengers and challenged operators to

---

[25] James Armstrong interview, by Cliff Kuhn, July 16, 1984, (WLC), p. 9; "Report Involving Race Question," August 1943, p. 1, box 10, Cooper Green Papers, Birmingham Public Library.

[26] Report by N. H. Hawkins, Jr., Birmingham Electric Company Transportation Department, n.d., box 10, Cooper Green Papers; "Analysis of Complaints and Incidents Covering Race Problems on Birmingham Electric Company's Transportation System, Twelve Months Ending August 31, 1942"; and see numerous examples from "Reports Involving Race Question" (1942–44), box 10, Cooper Green Papers.

move them, often with knife in hand. Others refused to pay their fare or simply picked fights with bus drivers or white passengers.[27]

Yet, despite what we might think about "male assertiveness" and—more precisely—the role of black servicemen as the vanguard of resistance, black women slightly outnumbered black men in the number of incidents of resistance on buses and streetcars. This should not be surprising, since more black working women rode public transportation. Those who did resist rarely fit the prim and proper Rosa Parks stereotype; dozens of black women were arrested for fighting or cursing out the operator. One of those cases involved nineteen-year-old Pauline Carth. When told there was no more room for "colored" passengers on the College Hills bus, she forced her way into the bus anyway, threw her money at the driver, cursed and spit on him. The driver responded by knocking her out of the bus, throwing her to the ground, and holding her down until police arrived.[28]

African-American passengers adopted a score of other oppositional practices, many directed at the symbols of inequality and segregation. The most common forms include hiding or moving the color dividers, insisting on paying only part of the fare, holding the center door open while dozens of unpaid passengers forced their way into the bus, and vandalism. Perhaps the most fascinating and often overlooked form of resistance was the use of sound to invade space designated for whites. Black passengers were ejected frequently for making too much noise, which in many cases turned out to be harsh words directed at a conductor or passenger, or a monologue about racism in general. One passenger on the East Lake–West End line was eventually arrested after he "started talking in a loud voice to negroes about white people." Black youth were particularly bold, especially when traveling in groups. On the Central Park–Vinesville line, the operator reported "a bunch of negro draftees who were 90% drunk . . . made improper remarks to everyone they passed."[29]

Because African-American passengers shared a collective memory of how they were treated on a daily basis, both within and without the "moving theaters," an act of resistance or repression sometimes drew other passengers into the fray, thus escalating into collective action. A very interesting report from an Avenue F. line bus driver illustrates just such a moment of collective resistance: "Operator went to adjust the color boards, and negro woman sat down quickly

[27] "Report Involving Race Question," September 1943, p. 1; see also numerous incidents from "Reports" (1942–44). For a general discussion of "Stagolee" folklore and the political implications of "baaad niggers" in African-American working-class consciousness, see John W. Roberts, *From Trickster to Badman: The Black Folk Hero in Slavery and Freedom* (Philadelphia: University of Pennsylvania Press, 1989), 171–215; Lawrence Levine, *Black Culture and Black Consciousness: Afro-American Folk Thought from Slavery to Freedom* (New York: Oxford University Press, 1977), 407–19.

[28] "Reports Involving Race Question," June, August, September, October, December 1943.

[29] "Report Involving Race Question," May 1944, pp. 2–3; "Report Involving Race Question," February, 1943, p. 3; also see "Reports" for June, August, September, October, November, December 1943, January, February, and March 1944.

just in front of board that operator was putting in place. She objected to moving and was not exactly disorderly but all the negroes took it up and none of [the] whites would sit in seat because they were afraid to, and negroes would not sit in vacant seats in rear of bus." In some instances, black riders invented ways to protest that protected their anonymity. On the College Hills line in August 1943, black riders grew impatient with a particularly racist bus driver who, in the course of a few minutes, twice drew his gun on black passengers, intentionally passed one black woman's stop, and ejected a man who complained on the woman's behalf. According to the report, "the negroes then started ringing bell for the entire block and no one would alight when he stopped."[30]

Some passengers attempted to take the idea of collective action to still another level. Following the arrest of Pauline Carth in 1943, a group of witnesses brought the case to the attention of the Birmingham branch of the NAACP, but aside from a perfunctory investigation and an article in the black-owned *Birmingham World*, no action was taken. The Southern Negro Youth Congress, a left-wing youth organization based in Birmingham, took up the case of Mildred Addleman, a black woman who was beaten and arrested by Fairfield police for moving the color boards on a bus. The incident prompted the SNYC to form a short-lived organization called the Citizens Committee for Equal Accommodations on Common Carriers. Unfortunately, the treatment of African Americans on public transportation was not a high-priority issue for either organization, and thus the working poor, whose livelihood depended on city transit, had to literally fend for themselves.[31]

The critical point here is that self-activity on the part of black passengers, most of whom were poor or working class, forced mainstream black political organizations to at least consider conditions on Jim Crow buses and streetcars. More importantly, *what* they resisted tells us a great deal about how poor blacks viewed segregation. Sitting with whites, for most black riders, was never the issue; rather, African Americans wanted more space for themselves, they wanted to receive equitable treatment, they wanted to be personally treated with respect and dignity, they wanted to get to work on time, and above all, they wanted to exercise power over institutions that controlled them or on which they were dependent.

The fact that most regular black riders were not primarily concerned with challenging the idea of allotting separate (but equal) space for blacks and whites did not diminish or mitigate repression on Birmingham's public-transit systems. Their very acts of insubordination challenged the system of segregation, whether they were intended to or not, and their defiance in most cases elicited a swift and decisive response. By the end of the war, everyday acts of resistance on

[30] "Report Involving Race Question," October 1943, p. 3; "Report Involving Race Question," August, 1942, p. 2.
[31] FBI Report, "Southern Negro Youth Congress, Birmingham," June 14, 1943, p. 2, file 100–82; *Birmingham World*, October 29, 1943.

buses and streetcars actually declined, according to transit officials, because of increased police intervention, harsher punitive measures, and more vigorous enforcement of the segregation laws, although a decrease in passengers due to postwar layoffs and declining job opportunities undoubtedly played a role.[32]

Increased police repression against the black poor was not limited to public transportation. Beginning in 1941, a wave of homicides and beatings by police reignited resistance to police brutality, and nearly all of these incidents were sparked by an act of insubordination—in most cases, a young black man arguing with a white person.[33] These and other incidents attracted the attention of civil rights organizations because they were dramatic, clear-cut cases of injustice resulting in injury or death. But poor people's attitudes toward the police were informed by an accumulation of daily indignities, whether or not they were experienced or witnessed. What must be understood is the semi-public discourse between the police and the black poor that rarely appears in the evidence scholars must rely on. The case of Bessie Ammons, a fifty-year-old janitor employed by Smithfield Court Housing Project, is instructive in this respect. On January 20, 1951, at about 5:45 A.M., Mrs. Ammons was on her way to work when two police officers pulled up, and one asked, "Gal, where are you going? Come here!" She not only refused to walk over to the car, but would not get in the car when ordered to do so, despite the fact that one of the officers had drawn his gun. Taken aback by her open defiance of the law, the two officers continued to harass her. "I ought to put your black a—— in jail for vagrancy," one of the officers declared. "Whenever any policeman tells you to get in the car, you had better do it. I mean what I say. I'm the law. Get on down the street." These incidents took place in public spaces on a daily basis, and were witnessed by many, although there is very little public record of such exchanges.[34]

Of course, not all African Americans arrested or harassed by police were consciously engaged in acts of public insubordination. The fact remains that more African Americans, especially poor black male youth, were arrested and prosecuted than any other group in relation to their percentage to the total population. Numerous criminological studies suggest that the high arrest rate of marginalized black male youth can be attributed to at least three factors. First, poverty and relative deprivation, exacerbated by a lack of employment oppor-

[32] N. H. Hawkins, Jr., Birmingham Electric Company Transportation Department, n.d.

[33] The best-known incidents resulted in the deaths of O'Dee Henderson and John Jackson, both of whom were killed by police in Fairfield, an industrial suburb of Birmingham. Henderson, who was arrested and jailed for merely arguing with a white man, was found the next morning in his jail cell handcuffed and fatally shot. A few weeks later, John Jackson, a black metalworker in his early twenties, was shot to death as he lay in the backseat of a police car. Jackson made the fatal mistake of arguing with the arresting officers in front of a crowd of blacks lined up outside a movie theater (Kelley, *Hammer and Hoe*, 217).

[34] "Statement by Bessie B. Ammons, Janitress, Smithfield Court Project," January 24, 1951, N. C. Ward, Manager, Smithfield Court to Eugene Connor, Commissioner of Public Safety, January 24, 1951, box 14, James Morgan Papers, Birmingham Public Library.

tunities due to race, leads to greater incidents of criminality. Because African Americans made up the majority of Birmingham's poor, it is likely that blacks would commit a higher percentage of crimes than would whites. A report submitted by a Birmingham police official in charge of the vice squad concluded that most juvenile arrestees come from families dependent on welfare or some form of charity or where the parents earned extremely low wages.[35] Second, gender differences help explain the higher incidence of male criminality, a pattern that is consistent across regional and national boundaries. Although the matter is far too complicated to discuss in detail here, several scholars attribute these patterns to higher rates of male unemployment, greater freedom from the restraints of the household compared to females (i.e., more opportunities to engage in criminal activity), and a patriarchal culture that socializes men to be more aggressive and makes earning power a measure of manhood.[36]

The third reason for the higher black arrest rates—the fact that the criminal justice system tends to cast all marginalized black male youth as criminals—ironically mitigates the importance of the first two factors. In addition to reflecting the relative poverty of African Americans, the disproportionate rate of black arrests is also indicative of the racist assumptions and practices of police officers, judges, and juries that African Americans are criminal by nature.[37] During the

[35] Report from Earl Heaton to M. S. Davis, City Detectives in Charge Vice Squad to C. F. Eddins, Assistant Chief of Police, May 24, 1943, box 8, Cooper Green Papers. The literature demonstrating a relationship between poverty and crime is voluminous. See Box, *Recession, Crime and Punishment*; D. Glaser and K. Rice, "Crime, Age, and Employment," *American Sociological Review* 24 (1959): 679–86; A. J. Reiss and A. L. Rhodes, "The Distribution of Juvenile Delinquency in the Social Class Structure," *American Sociological Review* 26 (1961): 720–43; Elliot Currie, *Confronting Crime* (New York: Pantheon Books, 1985), 146; E. Green, "Race, Social Status, and Criminal Arrest," *American Sociological Review* 35 (1970): 476–90; R. W. Beasley and G. Antunes, "The Etiology of Urban Crime: An Ecological Analysis," *Criminology* 11 (1974): 439–61; J. R. Blau and P. M. Blau, "The Cost of Inequality: Metropolitan Structure and Violent Crime," *American Sociological Review* 47 (1982): 114–29; James W. Messerschmidt, *Capitalism, Patriarchy and Crime* (Totowa, N.J.: Rowman and Littlefield, 1986), 54–58; I. Jankovic, "Labor Market and Imprisonment," *Crime and Social Justice* 8 (1977): 17–31; D. Humphries and D. Wallace, "Capitalist Accumulation and Urban Crime, 1950–1971," *Social Problems* 28 (1980): 179–93; A. D. Calvin, "Unemployment among Black Youths, Demographics, and Crime," *Crime and Delinquency* 27 (1981): 9–41; Richard B. Freeman, "The Relation of Criminal Activity to Black Youth Employment," in Margaret C. Simms and Samuel L. Myers, Jr., eds., *The Economics of Race and Crime* (New Brunswick, N.J.: Transaction Books, 1988), 99–107; Llad Phillips and Harold Votey, Jr., "Rational Choice Models of Crimes by Youth," ibid., pp. 129–87; Llad Phillips, H. L. Votey, Jr., and D. Maxwell, "Crime, Youth, and the Labor Market" *Journal of Political Economy* 80 (1972): 491–504.

[36] Messerschmidt, *Capitalism, Patriarchy and Crime*, 58–60; Anne Campbell, *The Girls in the Gang* (New York and Oxford: Basil Blackwell, 1984), and *Girl Delinquents* (New York: St. Martin's Press, 1981); Pat Carlen, *Women, Crime and Poverty* (Philadelphia: Open University Press, 1988).

[37] Birmingham is not unique in this respect. See Messerschmidt, *Capitalism, Patriarchy and Crime*, 52–53; Jefferey Reiman, *The Rich Get Richer and the Poor Get Prison* (New York: Wiley, 1984); Lee P. Brown, "Bridges over Troubled Waters: A Perspective on Policing in the Black Community," in Robert L. Woodson, ed., *Black Perspectives on Crime and the Criminal Justice System* (Boston: G. K. Hall, 1977), 87–88.

war, for example, although the number of black juvenile delinquency cases in Birmingham actually decreased, crime among black youth was viewed by government officials, social workers, police officers, and mainstream black leaders as a growing and alarming problem. In 1943, a Committee for the Prevention of Delinquency was created, and the Jefferson County Youth Protective Association decided to invite black leaders to a special "Negro meeting." Out of this meeting emerged in 1945 a Birmingham Negro Youth Council, whose stated agenda was to offer religious guidance, provide recreational and educational opportunities, and improve employment and health conditions for poor black youth. City Commissioner Cooper Green even invited FBI director J. Edgar Hoover to Birmingham to speak on the subject. "In this large industrial area," Green reported to Hoover, "of which 38 percent of the residents are Negro, we have an immediate and growing problem."[38]

Many middle-class blacks unwittingly reinforced stereotypes by accepting the image of poor blacks, especially young people, as lazy, self-destructive, and prone to criminal behavior. Geraldine Moore, a black middle-class resident of Birmingham and author of *Behind the Ebony Mask*, wrote the following description of the Magic City's "truly disadvantaged": "For some Negroes in Birmingham, life is a care-free existence of wallowing in the filth and squalor typical of the slums with just enough money to eke out a living. Some of these know nothing but waiting for a handout of some kind, drinking, cursing, fighting and prostitution. But many who live in this manner seem to be happy and satisfied. They apparently know and desire nothing better." The demand for black police officers in Birmingham advocated by a score of mainstream black political organizations during the 1940s and 1950s was motivated as much by their desire to reduce black crime as by their interest in ending police brutality. *Birmingham World* editor Emory O. Jackson waged a campaign during and after the war to clean up black crime. In 1946 he called on Birmingham police to step up their work in the predominantly black Fourth Avenue district and get rid of the "profaners, number racketeers, bootleggers, and foul-mouthers" once and for all.[39] In Jackson's view, he was merely fighting a situation he found embarrassing for the race. Although most residents probably shared Jackson's concern for cleaning up the district, it is doubtful that all shared his sentiments. Aside from the fact that some local residents depended on illicit activities as a source of income, many of Birmingham's poor understood that a greater concentration of police in the area without reforms in law enforcement practices opened the doors for greater police repression.

[38] W. Cooper Green to James E. Chappell, August 9, 1943; Florence Adams to Green, September 7, 1943; Adams to Celia Williams, September 7, 1943; "Minutes of the Executive Committee of the Youth Protective Association," January 31, 1945; and W. Cooper Green to J. Edgar Hoover, August 3, 1943, box 15, Cooper Green Papers; "Youth Protective Association of Jefferson County," *Alabama Social Welfare* 10, no. 5 (May 1945): 12–13.

[39] Moore, *Behind the Ebony Mask*, 15; *Birmingham World*, November 5, 1946.

The Birmingham police department might not have shut down operations on Fourth Avenue, but it did crack down on the black poor in general. Although the police responded to wartime black opposition with violence and intimidation, a substantial segment of the black poor, youth in particular, grew increasingly militant as well as optimistic that Birmingham would become a little less racist and more democratic. By the war's end, however, the poor did not have a whole lot to be optimistic about. Not only had police-civilian conflict and incidents of police brutality increased in poor black communities, but the material conditions of the poor had gone from bad to worse. In Birmingham, signs of postindustrial decline began to appear as early as the 1950s, and in the racial and class hierarchy that characterizes the urban South, these signs spelled disaster for African-American working people. To make matters worse, the black middle class—which had become increasingly militant during war and to whom segments of the poor turned for leadership—offered no viable solutions to mitigate poverty and joblessness.

CIVIL RIGHTS, INDUSTRIAL DECLINE, AND THE FAILURE OF BLACK MIDDLE-CLASS POLITICS

Much like the Detroit described by Thomas Sugrue in chapter 3, Birmingham also experienced industrial decline and an expansion of black poverty and unemployment after the war. During the 1950s, seven out of every ten black miners in Birmingham lost their jobs, in part because Birmingham steel companies began importing higher grade ore from South America and the coal industry introduced a machine called the "continuous miner," which replaced scores of black underground workers. Furthermore, the transition to "strip mining" led to greater mechanization overall, thus reducing the need for unskilled (i.e., black) labor. However, there are significant differences between Detroit and Birmingham that underscore the specificity of race and region in the urban South. First, whereas the auto industry in Detroit experienced growth in the 1950s and 1960s, Birmingham's steel industry did not significantly increase production and its mining industry actually declined once TCI began importing iron ore. The corporate leaders of TCI, which remained linked to its parent company, U.S. Steel, contributed to Birmingham's no-growth economy by blocking nearly all efforts to diversify. In 1945, for example, TCI executives successfully opposed efforts by Ford and General Motors to open plants in Birmingham.[40]

[40] Norrell, "Caste in Steel," 675, 686–87; George W. Blanks to Cooper Green, September 21, 1945; Louis Pizitz to Cooper Green, August 24, 1945; J. B. Roberts, Jr., to Cooper Green, September 5, 1945, box 8, Cooper Green Papers. Indeed, the Birmingham Chamber of Commerce was apparently so dominated by TCI that several businessmen supportive of diversification formed the Birmingham District Industrial Development Corporation for the purpose of attracting new industries. Jack Yauger to Cooper Green, May 19, 1945, box 8, Cooper Green Papers.

Second, although Sugrue has found that trade-union activity was of little consequence in altering racist practices in hiring and promotion, he adds that the United Auto Workers in Detroit at least made some motions on behalf of black workers, especially during the late 1960s. In Birmingham, however, the white-dominated locals of United Steel Workers of America (USWA) put pressure on companies *not* to promote blacks to skilled positions. The union, therefore, became a tool to maintain white supremacy, which had the effect of undermining any vestiges of job security for black steelworkers. The only major industrial union that consistently fought against discrimination, the International Union of Mine, Mill, and Smelter Workers of America, not only operated in Birmingham's fastest-declining industry but had been weakened considerably by racist and anticommunist attacks from the state CIO council and USWA locals.[41] Thus industrial opportunities for black workers begin to diminish much earlier and more rapidly in Birmingham than in other industrial cities, including Detroit: the percentage of blacks employed in heavy industry declined from 54 percent in 1930, to 41 percent in 1950, to 33 percent in 1960.[42]

Third, whereas Detroit's industries expanded and moved out of the central city to the suburbs, most of Birmingham's heavy industry, as well as a large number of black working-class residences, were already located in suburban areas. Some workers who lost their jobs were forced out of company housing, and many returning black veterans unable to secure work in the mines and mills had to turn to public housing concentrated in the inner city or multifamily housing located near the already overcrowded black business district. Black communities in the industrial suburbs had already become crowded, and racist zoning practices made expansion impossible. Moreover, at least 88 percent of the city's black dwellings were deemed substandard by the Birmingham Housing Authority, and the Jefferson County Board of Health found a direct correlation between poverty, housing conditions, and the high rates of infant mortality

[41] "Report of the President of the Alabama State Industrial Union Council, Period from March 1, 1949 to March 1, 1950" (typescript, March 1, 1950), 1, 5, box 2, Philip Taft Papers, Birmingham Public Library; *Birmingham Age-Herald*, May 29, 1949; *Birmingham Post-Herald*, September 4, 1950; *Birmingham World*, May 12, 1949; *Proceedings of the Alabama State Industrial Union Council, Ninth Constitutional Convention, CIO, 1948* (typescript, n.d.), 271–74, box 2, Philip Taft Papers; *Alabama (CIO) News Digest*, May 4, 1949; Horace Huntley, "The Rise and Fall of Mine Mill in Alabama: The Status Quo Against Interracial Unionism, 1933–1949," *Journal of the Birmingham Historical Society* 6, no. 1 (January 1979); 7–13, and "Iron Ore Miners and Mine Mill in Alabama, 1933–1952" (Ph.D. diss., University of Pittsburgh, 1976), 110–69; *Alabama (CIO) News Digest*, April 27, May 18, 25, 1949; Vernon H. Jensen, *Nonferrous Metals Industry Unionism, 1932–1952: The Story of Leadership Controversy* (Ithaca: Cornell University Press, 1954), 233–38; Hosea Hudson, "Struggle against Philip Murray's Racist Policies in Birmingham," *Political Affairs* 53, no. 9 (September 1974): 55–57.

[42] Charles L. Joiner, "An Analysis of the Employment Patterns of Minority Groups in the Alabama Economy, 1940–1960" (Ph.D. diss., University of Alabama, 1968), 51–55; John Franklin Pearce, "Human Resources in Transition: Rural Alabama since World War II" (Ph.D. diss., University of Alabama, 1966); Norrell, "Caste in Steel," 675, 686–87.

and tuberculosis in black communities. Although the city instituted a massive slum-clearance program that left thousands of African Americans homeless, its public housing projects fell far short of fulfilling the housing needs of poor blacks. By 1959, Birmingham's seven housing projects, consisting of 4,862 units, designated only 1,492 units for black residents.[43] Thus, during the 1950s Birmingham's displaced jobless or underemployed black workers were forced to reside in the housing projects, two-family shotgun houses, and dilapidated apartments, most of which were concentrated within a two-mile radius extending out from the center core of the city. By 1960 the census tracts located in this area had both the highest percentage of African Americans as well as the highest percentage of families below the poverty line. What occurred in Birmingham, therefore, was not a case of corporations fleeing the central city for the suburbs, leaving the unemployed behind. Rather, Birmingham's coal-and-steel industry discarded a large segment of its black labor force, and the city's racist zoning laws, uneven and overcrowded housing market, and public-housing policies propelled some former industrial workers and other poor people deeper into the inner city and left pockets of unemployed black workers in the industrial suburbs.

If there had not been a significant northern migration of Alabama blacks after World War II, the material conditions of the poor might have been much worse.

---

[43] Bobby Wilson, "Black Housing Opportunities in Birmingham, Alabama," *Southeastern Geographer* 17, no. 1 (May 1977); 49–57; George A. Denison, M.D., "Health as an Indication of Housing Needs in Birmingham, Alabama, and Recommendations for Slum Clearance, Redevelopment and Public Housing" (report by Jefferson County Board of Health, April 12, 1950), 1 and 9; Birmingham Housing Authority, *Ninth Annual Report of the Housing Authority of the Birmingham District* (June 30, 1948); "Statement of J. C. De Holl, Manager of the Birmingham Housing Authority, Birmingham, Ala.," U.S. Congress, Joint Committee on Housing, *Study and Investigation of Housing: Hearings Before the Joint Committee on Housing*, pt. 2 (Washington, D.C.: Government Printing Office, 1948), 1280, 1286–92; George Denison, M.D., to Birmingham City Commission, November 10, 1949, box 8, Cooper Green Papers; Robert A. Thompson, Hylan Lewis, and Davis McEntire, "Atlanta and Birmingham: A Comparative Study in Negro Housing," in Nathan Glazer and Davis McEntire, eds., *Studies in Housing and Minority Groups* (Berkeley and Los Angeles: University of California Press, 1960), 58, 61, 65. The city also severely restricted potential housing sites by limiting the number of areas zoned for black residence. Indeed, in 1948 Birmingham had only one residential area in the city zoned for blacks; most black dwellings were located in areas zoned for industrial or commercial use. This had an adverse affect on attracting potential home owners, since those who purchased homes in areas zoned industrial/commercial were not eligible for FHA loans. In the eyes of most African Americans, the poor as well as the middle and working classes, racist whites conspired to limit black housing opportunities: federally supported and private lending institutions regularly turned down black home-loan applicants; Birmingham Water Works refused to extend piping to potential black subdivisions; and several blacks who purchased homes in or near white neighborhoods during the late 1940s were victims of bombings. "Statement of Molton H. Gray, Chairman, National Council of Negro Veterans," U.S. Congress, Joint Committee on Housing, *Study and Investigation of Housing*, 1368–71; "Statement of Emory O. Jackson, Representing the Alabama Conference of the NAACP Branches," ibid., 1373; Thompson et al., "Atlanta and Birmingham," 59–73.

Although the mechanization of agriculture in the countryside drove thousands of rural African Americans into the city during and after the war, Birmingham did not receive the mass influx of black migrants that most Northern industrial cities had to absorb. Instead, Birmingham experienced a net loss of over twenty-one-thousand residents between 1950 and 1960. When we compare changes in black population in Birmingham with other urban centers, especially after World War II, we find that the *percentage* of African Americans in Birmingham remained virtually the same throughout the twentieth century, hovering between 39 percent and 43 percent. And yet, because of the combination of racist hiring practices and Birmingham's slow-growth industrial economy, conditions for poor black families had hardly changed since the 1930s. By 1955, 42.1 percent of black families, compared to 8.4% of white families, earned less than $2,000 annually. Public assistance remained woefully inadequate; the city could barely afford to maintain its welfare program, which mainly consisted of distributing surplus food. Altogether, some thirty-five-thousand residents took advantage of the program, many of whom stood in lines that stretched at least four blocks.[44]

Ironically, as war contracts reinvigorated Birmingham's economy, it seemed as though both mainstream black political leaders and white liberals were taking a greater interest in the plight of the black poor. As early as 1943, traditional black leaders and a handful of white liberals attempted to establish a chapter of the National Urban League in Birmingham, but the project was eventually aborted in the face of virulent white opposition. The idea of an interracial organization with national, specifically Northern, links was not very popular among Southern white liberal or conservative politicians. Despite the fact that the short-lived chapter counted a few major Birmingham corporate executives among its executive board, it did not have sufficient support and was subsequently abandoned in 1950.[45] After the war, the Jefferson County Coordinating Council of Social Forces, founded in 1939, took on most of the responsibility for assisting the city's poor. In 1951, an interracial organization was created within the council consisting primarily of businesspeople, social workers, liberal politicians, educators, and ministers. The Interracial Committee (IC) was created to administer to the needs of black residents, and served as an acceptable substitute for the Urban League.[46]

[44] Department of Commerce. Bureau of the Census, *County and City Data Book, 1962* (Washington, D.C.: Government Printing Office, 1962), 433. For a comparison of changes in the percentage of black population, see table 3; Robert Gaines Corely, "The Quest for Racial Harmony: Race Relations in Birmingham, Alabama, 1947–1963" (Ph.D. diss., University of Virginia, 1979), 36; LaMonte, "Politics and Welfare," 245, 251; Thompson et al., "Atlanta and Birmingham," 54.

[45] Corely, "The Quest for Racial Harmony," 44–46, 54; Florence S. Adams to Mrs. E. D. Wood, Controller's Office, September 28, 1950, box 1, Jefferson County Coordinating Committee on Social Forces Papers, Birmingham Public Library.

[46] "Organization and Rules of Procedure of the Interracial Committee of Jefferson County Coordinating Council" are "Minutes of Interracial Committee Meeting, Friday June 15, 1951,"

Not surprisingly, committee members never talked directly to, or requested input from, the poor. Indeed, its policies ostensibly on behalf of the poor reflect the class interests and ideologies of its black leadership. In the area of recreation, for instance, black IC leadership placed at the top of its agenda the construction of a nine-hole Negro golf course. Also placed under the rubric of recreation was the "distressing number of young unmarried parents." Mrs. H. C. Bryant, long-time black clubwoman and YWCA leader, believed that the growing number of unwed mothers in poor black communities stemmed from a lack of guidance and recreational facilities for young black women. Perhaps most revealing was black IC leaders' emphasis on the "development of a real estate subdivision for high class Negro homes" rather than of low-income rental units.[47]

Although poor working women were in dire need of day-care facilities, the IC never made it a top-priority issue. There had not been any public-service day-care facilities since the war, and the three day-care centers run by the Community Chest were exclusively for mothers too sick to care for their children. Moreover, the primary day-care center for black children in Birmingham was comprised mainly of children whose parents were "not disadvantaged." When the committee, with the support of the Community Chest, finally succeeded in establishing an extra day-care facility, the cost to parents was set at $6.50 per week, a relatively high figure in relation to the earnings of single working mothers, or even of two-parent working-class families, who had to survive on as little as $20 to $30 per week.[48]

Likewise, IC's subcommittee on employment was not always cognizant of the specific needs of the black poor, as well as of the disastrous effects that technological change and racist hiring practices were having on black industrial labor. First, committee members did not attempt to use their influence to improve wages and working conditions for existing black industrial workers, in part because its members clearly sided with employers. Second, the committee put more emphasis on hiring college-educated blacks in civil-service and public-relations positions.[49]

By the time the Interracial Committee was disbanded in 1956, it had accom-

---

Jefferson County Coordinating Committee on Social Forces Papers, Birmingham Public Library (microfilm).

[47] "Minutes, Interracial Committee Meeting," September 18, 1951, January 10, 1952, December 18, 1952, November 4, 1953, May 17, 1955; "Minutes, Interracial Committee, Subcommittee on Housing," July 31, 1951, September 15, 1955, Jefferson County Coordinating Committee on Social Forces Papers, Birmingham Public Library (microfilm).

[48] "Minutes, Interracial Committee, Subcommittee on Daycare," September 17, 1951, August 17, 1954, Jefferson County Coordinating Committee on Social Forces Papers, Birmingham Public Library (microfilm).

[49] "Minutes, Interracial Committee, Subcommittee on Employment Relations," May 31, 1955, Jefferson County Coordinating Committee on Social Forces Papers, Birmingham Public Library (microfilm).

plished very little, especially with respect to the needs of the poor. Yet racist white residents and politicians viewed the committee as a radical threat to the status quo. White members of the committee decided to disband because "of the violent attacks upon it by proponents of the White Citizens Councils." The decision was made unilaterally, without input from black members. Moreover, the Jefferson County Coordinating Council of Social Forces decided that, while it would continue to work toward improving social services for black residents, it "would not engage, directly or indirectly, in any activity toward desegregation."[50]

Birmingham civil rights organizations that were devoted to desegregation, however, were only slightly more sensitive to the needs and problems of the black poor in the 1950s and early 1960s, in part because most leading civil rights activists were middle-class African Americans who tended to misunderstand or overlook the plight of the poor. The Alabama Christian Movement for Human Rights (ACMHR), under the leadership of the Reverend Fred Shuttlesworth, had the largest working-poor membership of any of the city's civil rights organizations. Yet when we examine the ACMHR's makeup, we find that in 1959 only one-third of its membership earned less than $2,000, 55 percent of its members were home owners, and 40 percent earned more than $4,000 annually (in the city as a whole, only 20 percent of black residents earned that much or more). What is most significant is that practically all of its members were employed.[51]

Although Shuttlesworth was far more sympathetic to working people than Birmingham's traditional black bourgeoisie had been, the strategies and long-term goals of the ACMHR were not directed at improving the material impoverishment of the poor or the horrible conditions in the black slums. Of course, issues such as school and bus desegregation and the hiring of black police officers affected, and even drew support from, the black poor, but ACMHR leadership defined racial equality in employment in terms of opportunities in civil-service and professional jobs for qualified blacks and viewed conditions in the slums as essentially a moral dilemma rather than a product of poverty. Meanwhile, according to a report produced by the Jefferson County Coordinating Council, in 1960 at least seventy thousand people of Jefferson County were malnourished, most of whom were black Birmingham residents. In this same year, when the city experienced a recession in steel and related industries, the median income for black wage earners was a paltry $1,287,

[50] "Minutes of Joint Community Chest—Red Cross Meeting, Executive Committee, April 2, 1956," box 1, Jefferson County Coordinating Committee on Social Forces Papers, Birmingham Public Library.

[51] Clarke, "Goals and Techniques," appendix B, 134–49; Glenn T. Eskew, "The Alabama Christian Movement for Human Rights and the Birmingham Struggle for Civil Rights, 1956–1963," in David Garrow, ed., Birmingham, Alabama, 1956–1963: The Black Struggle for Civil Rights (Brooklyn, N.Y.: Carlson Publishers, 1989), 45–46.

compared to $3,456 for whites; 28.6 percent of black adults earned less than $1,000 annually.[52]

The contradictions between the goals of the civil rights movement to de-segregate public space and the daily struggles of the black poor—most no-tably declining employment opportunities, inadequate housing, and police repression—came to a head during the Southern Christian Leadership Con-ference's nonviolent mass demonstrations in May 1963. One need only examine film footage of the Birmingham confrontation to know that the hundreds of schoolchildren who crowded into the Sixteenth Street Baptist Church, recruits of the direct-action campaign who marched peacefully into the hands of Eugene "Bull" Connor's waiting police officers, were *not* products of Birmingham's worst slums. Rather, the vast majority of neat, well-dressed, and orderly children were the sons and daughters of activists or movement supporters. The slum dwellers, teenagers, and young adults alike did show up at Ingram Park to participate *on their own terms* in the May demonstrations. Historians and activists have labeled them "onlookers," "spectators," or "bystanders" merely because they were not directed by any civil rights organization. But when Bull Connor ordered the use of police dogs and clubs on the demonstrators, the crowd of so-called onlookers taunted police, retaliated with fists, profanity, rocks, and bottles, and, if possi-ble, escaped into their own neighborhoods. On the very next day, a group of "spectators were seen brandishing knives and pistols along the fringes of the demonstrations." Shocked by the show of armed force, SCLC leadership decided to call off the demonstration that day. While these "fringe dwellers" had no intention of filling the jails, they were clearly demonstrating their utter contempt for the police in particular and for racist oppression in general.[53]

A more dramatic example of collective opposition on the part of the poor occurred late Saturday night, May 11, after Reverend A. D. King's home and A. G. Gaston's motel were bombed by racists. An angry crowd gathered in front of the Gaston Motel and began throwing bottles and bricks at police officers on the scene. The fighting escalated into a full-scale riot, as hundreds of black residents destroyed glass storefront windows, overturned cars, set buildings on fire, and seized all the commodities they could get their hands on. Police officers themselves were prime targets. One patrolman chased a group of rioters down a

[52] Petition from Alabama Christian Movement for Human Rights to City Commissioners, July 25, 1965, box 12, Boutwell Papers; Eskew, "The ACMHR"; *Birmingham News*, September 27, 1960; U.S. Bureau of the Census, *Eighteenth Census of the U.S.: 1960*, vol. I, pt. 2, *Characteristics of the Population: Alabama* (Washington, D.C.: Government Printing Office, 1961), 461.

[53] David J. Garrow, *Bearing the Cross: Martin Luther King, Jr., and the Southern Christian Leadership Conference* (New York: Morrow, 1986), 254–55; Eskew, "The ACMHR," 82, 85; Taylor Branch, *Parting the Waters: America in the King Years, 1954–1963* (New York: Simon and Schuster, 1988), 759–60; Lee E. Bains, Jr., "Birmingham, 1963: Confrontation over Civil Rights," in Garrow, *Birmingham, Alabama, 1956–1963*, 181. All of the accounts cited above describing the Birmingham demonstrations refer to those who engage in acts of violence as "onlookers," "spectators," people "along the fringes," or "bystanders."

dark alley and emerged with three stab wounds in his back. A police inspector was found soaked in blood, having been "brained by a rock." Armed with megaphones, SCLC leaders A. D. King and Wyatt T. Walker implored the rioters to stop the violence and go home, but their efforts were to no avail. Walker himself was struck in the leg by a brick tossed by a rioter. The uprising finally came to an end after state troopers intervened with unbridled violence.[54]

Civil rights leaders treated the uprising as an impediment to the progress of the "real" movement and variously described the rioters as "wineheads" or "riff-raff." While the epithets were uncalled for, this was not an unreasonable posture for mainstream black leaders to assume. On the eve of the uprising, white liberals and the chamber of commerce, with the silent support of moderate black political figures, barely won a battle to scrap Birmingham's city commission system for a mayor–city council structure. Whereas the old system concentrated municipal power in the hands of three men and enabled segregationists like Bull Connor to entrench themselves in office, the new system would expand representation to districts and, presumably, entice the outlying suburbs to join the Birmingham municipality. Most important, however, was the presumption that the more democratic mayor-council structure could incorporate the demands of moderate blacks and facilitate the transition to a more equitable system of segregation without disrupting business. By the time the crisis occurred, white liberal David Vann, who had been elected mayor just days before the Birmingham confrontation, was locked in battle against segregationists for control over city government, as the old city commission under Bull Connor initially refused to disband. Black leaders who actually supported SCLC's civil-disobedience campaign feared that the rioters would jeopardize both the movement's gains as well as the new administration's stability. But the rioters felt their own lives had been in jeopardy far too long. Despite the protestations of black leaders, the people of Birmingham's slums and segregated pool halls resisted injustice and oppression on their own terms, which included attacking police officers and taking advantage of the crisis to appropriate much needed or desired commodities. The irony is that the very movement that sought to control or channel the aggressive, violent behavior of the poor was the catalyst for their participation.[55]

In spite of the movement's failure to deal with the specific problems of the poor, the 1963 peaceful demonstration was itself a powerful declaration of aspects of the usually veiled dissident political culture.[56] However, from the

---

[54] Garrow, *Bearing the Cross*, 261; Branch, *Parting the Waters*, 793–802; Bains, "Birmingham, 1963," 182–83.

[55] Eskew, "The ACMHR," 75–77; Bains, "Birmingham, 1963," 228–29; Howell Raines, *My Soul is Rested* (New York: Putnam, 1978), 190; LaMonte, "Politics and Welfare," 285–91

[56] Glenn T. Eskew, a doctoral candidate working on the civil rights movement in Birmingham, is one of the few historians who has commented on this strained relationship between Birmingham's black poor and the civil rights movement. As he points out, "While the demands of the Birmingham

perspective of the poor, the accumulation of indignities and level of anger was so great that it precluded, for younger people in particular, the possibility of nonviolent resistance. Their unmitigated rage directed at the police reflected years of brutalities, illegal searches and seizures, and incidents of everyday harassment. As James Scott surmises about subordinate groups in general, "if the politics they engender is tumultuous, frenetic, delirious, and occasionally violent, that is perhaps because the powerless are so rarely on the public stage and have so much to say and do when they finally arrive." The black poor, I would argue, had more to be angry about and much more to say about their plight—grievances over which even their "leaders" were unaware. When the opportunity came in the series of crises of 1963, they seized it.[57]

The change in the public posturings of black poor youth and young adults caught much of white Birmingham off guard. Throughout the mid-1960s, complaints by white residents of the growing impudence and discourteousness of Birmingham blacks flooded the police department and mayor's office. In 1964, a white woman whose residence bordered a black community observed to her utter horror, "Negro boys . . . step out in front of the car driven by a white woman—wanting to ride. Hitch-hiking." In her view, the attitudes and actions of black passengers after desegregation rendered public transportation unbearable: "Can't get on the bus and ride to town because the colored have taken the buses."[58] But the same circumstances that unleashed such fervent opposition to the powerful and emboldened the powerless to assert a public oppositional presence also unleashed a more sustained effort on the part of the state to put things back in order. The public posturings on the part of African Americans actually led to an increase in confrontations with the police, whose reputation for racial tolerance left much to be desired. Police repression reached an all-time high between 1963 and the early 1970s, and, of course, black male youth from poor communities were the victims of the majority of incidents.

During the tumultuous year of 1963, a large proportion of confrontations between black youth and police were more explicitly political than the run-of-

---

movement failed to address the needs of the underclass, the campaign itself led to the involvement of these poor and powerless blacks in the struggle" ("The ACMHR," 94).

[57] Scott, *Domination*, 277. In some ways this argument resembles Frantz Fanon's interpretation of violence by the oppressed as a transformative process that ultimately alters the personalities of subordinate groups (see esp. Fanon, *The Wretched of the Earth* [New York: Grove Press, 1966], 29–74; Luther P. Gerlach and Virginia H. Hine, *People, Power, Change: Movements of Social Transformation* [Indianapolis and New York: Bobbs-Merrill, 1970], 148–49). However, what I am suggesting is that collective violence served to lay bare the hidden transcript. The feeling of frustration and hatred existed long before the uprising but only occasionally found a public platform. What appeared to be a transformation in personality was really a change in the public posturings of segments of the black poor.

[58] Memo from George Seibels to Albert Boutwell, October 15, 1964, Re: "Probable Dope Consumption by Teenagers in the Elyton Housing Project Area"; "Telephone Conversation between Mrs. Virginia Davis and Birmingham Police," May 11, 1964 (transcript), box 30, Boutwell Papers.

the mill criminal cases.[59] For example, although the number of black juvenile delinquency cases increased 40 percent between 1962 and 1963, 550 of those cases, or 23.4 percent of all cases brought to juvenile court in 1963 (irrespective of race or sex), were placed under a new category called "demonstrating." Property offenses, which usually account for the majority of juvenile cases, comprised only 34.1 percent of the total cases. Altogether, although African Americans comprised about 39 percent of Birmingham's total population, in 1963 black males made up 1,012, and black females 626, of the total cases, whereas white males and females constituted 556 and 255 of the total cases, respectively.[60] Moreover, police frequently used excessive force in politically volatile situations. On September 15, 1963, hours after the bombing of the Sixteenth Street Baptist Church killed four black girls, sixteen-year-old Johnny Robinson was fatally wounded by police after he and an unidentified black youth were seen throwing rocks at a passing car full of white teenagers. "Negroes Go Back to Africa" was scrawled on one side of the car in shoe polish, and a Confederate flag was draped over the other side. The white youth, who were apparently celebrating the murder of the four black children, yelled racial epithets to the two black teenagers. As soon as police in the vicinity observed Robinson and his companion throwing rocks at the passing car, they gave chase. According to the police version, they told Robinson several times to halt, but he kept running away. When the smoke cleared from a volley of police gunfire, Robinson lay dead.[61]

Nevertheless, two years after the mass demonstrations of 1963, arrests of black youths were still proportionately higher than arrests of white youths, and blacks fared worse at the hands of police. By 1966 the number of white juveniles convicted of crimes nearly equaled that of blacks; white males and white females accounted for 662 and 282 of total cases, respectively, whereas black males and females accounted for 712 and 263 cases, respectively. And yet, as in most other cities during the 1960s, poor black male youth were disproportionately affected by the use of excessive force by Birmingham police officers. In the fourteen

[59] In 1965, four sociologists and criminologists completed a study which concluded that crimes of violence against other blacks decline when there is a well-organized, direct-action campaign, because race pride replaces self-hatred. The movement allowed "lower-class" blacks to channel their aggression in more positive directions. See Frederick Solomon, Walter Walker, Garrett J. O'Connor, and Jacob R. Fishman, "Civil Rights Activity and Reduction in Crime among Negroes," *Crime and Social Justice* 14 (Winter 1980): 27–35 (originally published in *Archives of Psychiatry* 12 [1965]: 227–36).

[60] Juvenile and Domestic Relations Court of Jefferson County, *Annual Report* (1963), 15, 25.

[61] Memo from Det. C. L. Pierce to Chief Jamie Moore, September 15, 1963, Re: Shooting of Johnny Robinson, Birmingham Police Department, statement of Officer J. E. Chadwick, September 16, 1963; statement of Marvin Kent, September 16, 1963; statement of Jimmy Sparks, September 16, 1963; Statement of Officer P. C. Cheek, September 16, 1963; statement of Sidney Howell, September 16, 1963, box 31, Boutwell Papers. Statements were taken from the whites in the car, though no black people were asked to submit statements or serve as witnesses.

months between January 1966 and March 1967, ten black men, the majority of whom were teenagers or young adults, were killed by Birmingham police. During this same period there were no white victims or black female victims of police homicides.[62]

Besides black youth, other segments of the poor fell victim to police brutality. An arrest or beating prompted by a mistaken identity or a particularly racist attitude of a patrolman could prove to be a substantial setback for poor working residents whose families depended on meager wages to stay afloat. A case in point is the arrest of North Birmingham resident Catherine McGann, a single mother of seven children who worked as a domestic. On the night of September 4, 1964, she and two black men whom she did not know were standing in front of a store in her neighborhood when several police officers drove up and forcibly shoved the two men into a police car. When she tried to walk away, two of the officers "rushed up and grabbed me and were hollering, 'Get in this car nigger.'" She struggled desperately to break free, but they hit her several times, dragged her into the vehicle, and slammed her ankle in the door. McGann was subsequently taken to jail and was refused medical attention, though she was not charged with anything until her son appeared to post bail. The court found her guilty of resisting arrest and loitering after a warning, for which she was fined $125. The beating and arrest turned out to be much more than "a very terrible and humiliating experience." It nearly devastated Catherine McGann financially. "All my children are in school and I do not have the money to get books for them or to pay their fees. I don't earn much and then to have what little I earn to be taken away from me for no reason at all is very hard."[63]

By 1967, local civil rights organizations, spearheaded by the ACMHR, placed the rising tide of police brutality at the top of their agenda. This marked a significant change since the late 1940s and early 1950s, when black middle-class spokespersons were more concerned about reducing black crime than about police use of excessive force. Although the movement's tactics had not

[62] Juvenile and Domestic Relations Court of Jefferson County, *Annual Report* (1966), 18; "Negroes Are Calling a 60-Day Period of Mourning for the Dead!" (ACMHR flyer, ca. March 1967), unsigned; "Racial Notes [Birmingham Police Department]," March 6, 1967, box 15, Boutwell Papers. There is a large body of research that suggests that black males are more likely to be victims of police homicides than whites are. See, for example, G. D. Robin, "Justifiable Homicide by Police Officers," *Journal of Criminal Law, Criminology and Police Science* 54 (1963): 225–31; S. Harring, T. Platt, R. Speiglman, and P. Takagi, "The Management of Police Killings," *Crime and Social Justice* 8 (1977): 34–43; P. Takagi, "A Garrison State in 'Democratic Society,'" *Crime and Social Justice* (Spring–Summer, 1978): 2–25; A. L. Kobler, "Figures (and Perhaps Some Facts) on Police Killing of Civilians in the United States, 1965–1969," *Journal of Social Issues* 31 (1975)a; 163–91; M. W. Meyer, "Police Shootings at Minorities: The Case of Los Angeles," *Annals* 452 (1980): 98–110; J. J. Fyfe, "Blind Justice: Police Shootings in Memphis," *Journal of Criminal Law and Criminology* 73 (1982): 707–22.

[63] Statement by Mrs. Catherine McGann (typescript), n.d.; Lawrence E. McGinty to Mayor Albert Boutwell, September 15, 1964; Interoffice communication from Jamie Moore, Chief of Police, to Mayor Boutwell, September 17, 1964, box 30, Boutwell Papers.

changed (the ACMHR organized a sixty-day boycott of downtown stores to protest recent killings by the police), its rhetoric reveals a heightened level of militancy. Shuttlesworth not only threatened to build alliances with black militant organizations, but his group distributed a flyer proclaiming in no uncertain terms that "Negroes are TIRED of Police Brutality and Killing Our People. Negroes are tired of 'One Man Ruling' of 'Justifiable Homicide' every time a NEGRO IS KILLED!" More significantly, the ACMHR was less willing to negotiate; instead, Shuttlesworth attempted to file suit against the city in order to obtain police department and coroner's records so they might investigate past cases of homicides by police.[64]

The ACMHR's efforts failed to bring about any major improvements in police practices with respect to African Americans. Both Mayor Boutwell and his successor, Mayor George Seibels, refused to form civilian review boards. Indeed, no significant progress was made on the issue of police brutality until the fatal shooting of Bonita Carter by Birmingham police in 1979. During the early 1970s, a number of poor and working-class African Americans joined grass-roots organizations that investigated and fought police misconduct, such as the Committee Against Police Brutality and the Alabama Economic Action Committee (which investigated at least twenty-seven separate incidents in 1972), but these movements received very little support from the black elite. Thus, the utter refusal of "old guard" leadership to deal with the problem of police brutality led Richard Arrington, Jr., Birmingham's first black mayor, to the following conclusion: "The failure of the so-called black leaders in this community to speak out about police brutality simply confirms my belief that there is really no such thing as black leaders in this community—they are people who are used by the white power structure in this community who take an ego trip because they are called upon by some powerful white citizens to fit black folk into an agenda that has been set up by the white community, particularly the business structure here."[65]

While police brutality remained an important issue in the public political discourse of and about the black poor, long-term structural changes were forcing more and more African Americans into an increasingly marginalized existence. Deindustrialization, in particular, dealt a devastating blow to young black workers entering the work force and to existing black industrial laborers. Although antidiscrimination laws and successful litigation on the part of the NAACP removed racially based ceilings to occupational mobility, by the late 1960s and throughout the 1970s it no longer mattered. TCI laid off thousands of workers in the 1970s and ceased operating altogether by 1982. The Sloss-

[64] "Negroes Are Calling a 60-Day Period of Mourning for the Dead!"; Unsigned, "Racial Notes [Birmingham Police Department]," March 8, 1967, box 15, Boutwell Papers.

[65] Jimmie Lewis Franklin, *Back to Birmingham: Richard Arrington, Jr., and His Times* (Tuscaloosa: University of Alabama Press, 1989), 92–133, quote from p. 104. In fact, Franklin argues that Arrington's successful bid for mayor can partly be attributed to his stand against police brutality.

Sheffield furnace shut down in 1971, and Pullman-Standard closed shop in the early 1980s. The shift from industrial to service-sector jobs, combined with years of racial discrimination in terms of occupational status and wages, meant that the ratio of black-male income to white-male income had actually decreased since World War II. In 1949, black men in Birmingham earned an average of 53 percent of what white men earned; the ratio dropped to 48.8 percent in 1959, and rose slightly to 51.5 percent in 1969, thus representing a decrease of 1.5 percent since the immediate postwar period.[66]

In addition to structural changes in employment, demographic shifts contributed to the concentration of poverty in core-city and North Birmingham census tracts. But unlike Northern cities that experienced a rapid influx of African-American migrants, Birmingham's population declined by 11.7 percent between 1960 and 1970. During this decade, then, urban renewal—particularly slum-clearance programs and the expansion of the University of Alabama Medical Center—played a more significant role than black inmigration in shaping the city's demographic shifts and formation of concentrated poverty neighborhoods. The Medical Center, which is located in the heart of the inner city, displaced a thousand black families, and the subsequent demand for black housing infringed on white neighborhoods. As a result, the percentage of African Americans in census tract 44 decreased from 76 percent in 1950, to 48 percent in 1960, to 28 percent in 1970, whereas tract 15 increased its percentage of black residents from 17 percent in 1950, to 30 percent in 1960, to 94 percent in 1970. Tract 44's substantial decrease in black residents is especially significant, since it had the fifth largest percentage of poor families in 1960 out of ninety-two tracts, suggesting that the poor were disproportionately affected by urban renewal programs.[67] Moreover, although it was one of the nine inner-city tracts, the percentage of African Americans and families below the poverty line still increased significantly between 1960 and 1970, which suggests that the remaining eight tracts underwent an even greater concentration of poor black families.[68] Nevertheless, dramatic shifts in the racial composition of Bir-

[66] Norrell, "Caste in Steel," 690–91.

[67] Bobby Wilson, "Racial Segregation Trends in Birmingham, Alabama," *Southeastern Geographer* 25, no. 1 (May 1985): 32–33; Marilynn Kindell, "A Descriptive Analysis of the Impact of Urban Renewal on a Relocated Family: A Case Study of the Medical Center Expansion Project" (M.A. thesis, University of Alabama, Birmingham, 1982); U.S. Bureau of the Census, *Seventeenth Census of the U.S.: 1950*, vol. 3, *Census Tract Statistics* (Washington, D.C.: Government Printing Office, 1952), 7–10; Richard Fussell, *A Demographic Atlas of Birmingham, 1960–1970* (University, Ala.: University of Alabama Press, 1975), 65–66; and for a general description of urban renewal policies in the urban South, see David R. Goldfield, *Black, White, and Southern: Race Relations and Southern Culture, 1940 to the Present* (Baton Rouge and London: Louisiana State University Press, 1990), 205.

[68] Indeed, if we were to exclude tract 44 from our definition of inner city, then the percentage of blacks would have increased by 5 percent between 1960 and 1970 rather than decrease by 1 percent, and the percentage of families below the poverty line would rise slightly from 45.5 percent to 49 percent.

mingham's inner city did not occur until the mid- to late 1970s. As a result of white flight to the suburbs and the city's successful annexation of low- and middle-income black communities on the fringe of the city limits, African Americans had become the majority by 1980.[69]

Ironically, it was in the midst of massive deindustrialization and demographic shifts that President Lyndon Johnson's Great Society was established in Birmingham. From the outset, Mayor Albert Boutwell welcomed the adoption of the Economic Opportunity Act (EOA), which he regarded as a much-needed infusion of federal aid into Birmingham's economy. Following a somewhat rocky start,[70] the Jefferson County Committee for Economic Opportunity (JCCEO) was established in June 1965 to administer a total of twenty-four different service programs in the ten years after its founding. Broadly speaking, the black poor, who on average constituted about 95 percent of the participants in JCCEO agencies, took advantage of employment opportunities in human services, job training programs, early childhood education, free legal services, and emergency food and medical aid. The committee also provided a source of jobs for black Birmingham residents, establishing administrative posts for working-class African Americans in a variety of social-welfare agencies. But overall, neither the city nor the state contributed the necessary financial support to render JCCEO agencies effective tools to fight poverty. Largely because the state legislature refused to appropriate sufficient funds to match available federal funds, all recipients of benefits received payments below the poverty level throughout the 1960s, and Aid to Dependent Children, whose caseload in 1965 consisted of 80 percent black children, allocated only 35 percent of the minimum survival budget to each family. Furthermore, by 1970 the state still had no basic assistance program, and the food-stamp program reached only 10 percent of the families eligible because of an especially complicated application process and the lack of information available to the poor. In that same year, over one-third of all black families in Birmingham fell under the poverty line, compared to 14.7 percent of white families.[71]

[69] Wilson, "Racial Segregation Trends in Birmingham," 32–33; Fussell, *A Demographic Atlas of Birmingham*, 20–21; U.S. Bureau of the Census, *Twentieth Census of Population and Housing, 1980: Census Tracts* (Washington, D.C.: Government Printing Office, 1983), 235–40.

[70] Originally called the Birmingham Area Committee for the Development of Economic Opportunity, this precursor to the JCCEO was established in January 1965 to oversee at least forty EOA programs, but its director, Erskine Smith, was forced to resign and the organization had to be restructured following attacks by Governor George Wallace for their establishment of ties with the Urban League and, later, by the federal government for not complying with its charge of encouraging "maximum feasible participation of the residents." Six months later, however, the organization reemerged as the JCCEO, after it was deemed acceptable in both Montgomery and Washington, D.C. LaMonte, "Politics and Welfare," 349–58; *Birmingham Post Herald*, May 15, 1965.

[71] LaMonte, "Politics and Welfare," 281–82, 352–60; Community Service Council, *Family and Children Study of Jefferson County: Priorities and Recommendations* (Birmingham: Community Service Council, 1970), 11, 19; Fussell, *A Demographic Atlas of Birmingham*, 20–21. For background on the

While the War on Poverty might have failed to reverse the deteriorating conditions for the black poor, it ultimately played an important role in mobilizing an already politicized segment of the poor, strengthening ties between white liberals and mainstream black leadership, and providing poor residents a greater voice in the affairs of certain social agencies—especially Head Start. As a result of pressure from both the federal government and the black poor themselves, the JCCEO evolved after two years from a twenty-one-member board of directors consisting entirely of mayoral appointments to a forty-eight-member board comprised of sixteen public officials or representatives of public agencies, sixteen representatives from private community groups, and sixteen representatives from poor "target" communities, each elected by their respective neighborhood advisory councils. Thus the new structure, established in 1967, not only allowed the black poor direct representation for the first time in the history of Birmingham's welfare agencies, it also substantially reduced the power of the mayor within the committee. In the end, however, the neighborhood councils exercised very little power to shape the long-term agenda of the JCCEO. The committee not only allocated insufficient funds for projects initiated by the neighborhood councils, but the bureaucratic independence of various agencies made long-term planning virtually impossible. Moreover, the employment of African Americans in responsible positions within JCCEO agencies initially prompted a backlash from white social workers who argued that these newly appointed men and women "lacked qualifications."[72]

Yet even if the neighborhood councils turned out to be relatively ineffective in terms of determining the long-range agenda of the JCCEO, its constituents exhibited a sense of a militant entitlement reminiscent of the Communist-led movements of the 1930s, the public-transportation battles of the 1940s, and the uprisings surrounding the SCLC's direct-action campaigns. And in nearly all of the conflicts between the black poor and JCCEO, protesters found themselves fighting black as well as white bureaucrats. One particularly memorable confrontation occurred in 1969, when a predominantly black women's organization called the Poor People's Action Committee (PPAC) protested what it felt were discriminatory practices within the JCCEO's Concentrated Employment Program. The program, which coordinated the work of several public and private agencies into a comprehensive training program for the poor, had placed the majority of black women who had completed the program in a chicken packing plant rather than in human relations positions, as promised. The PPAC also complained of being threatened and intimidated by two staff members— the director, who was white, and the black assistant director—for participating in the protest. Ironically, with the assistance of another OEO-funded agency, the

EOA and its federal administrative arm, the Office of Economic Opportunity, see Katz, *The Undeserving Poor*, 79–101, 112–23; Patterson, *America's Struggle against Poverty*, 142–54.

[72] LaMonte, "Politics and Welfare," 358, 364–66.

Legal Services Program, the PPAC won their case, exposed the deficiencies in the Concentrated Employment Program, and ultimately forced the director to resign and the JCCEO to take disciplinary action against the assistant director. A second major struggle erupted in 1971, when the United Neighborhood Improvement Association (UNIA) picketed JCCEO headquarters to protest the dismissal of two black employees. Despite several stormy meetings, the JCCEO board of directors did not accede to the UNIA's demands, which included the removal of two black project directors and the white executive director. The UNIA came away from the battle quite bitter, accusing the JCCEO of not doing an effective job assisting the poor, since "these hard-core people are not being reached."[73]

The rise of militant opposition to the JCCEO, combined with deteriorating conditions of the poor caused by deindustrialization, urban renewal, concentrated poverty, police repression, the limitations of the civil rights agenda, and a general mistrust of traditional black leadership, compelled some poor folks to turn to more radical alternatives. In 1970 several community-based interracial organizations created specifically to concentrate on poor people's needs came into being, including the Jefferson County Welfare Rights Organization—a local chapter of the National Welfare Rights Organization—the Southside Action Committee, the Alabama Economic Action Committee, the Committee for Equal Job Opportunity, and the Southern Organizing Committee for Economic Justice (formerly the Southern Conference Educational Fund).[74] The black poor also turned to black nationalist organizations influenced by Malcolm X, the Black Power philosophies of the late 1960s, and/or the Nation of Islam. These movements—much like the Communist party three decades earlier—showed more sensitivity to the specific problems of poor residents and sought change through alternative means of opposition. However, they were ultimately crushed by police repression, which served as a powerful deterrent to the participation of the vast majority of poor people. The most important example is the Alabama Black Liberation Front, a short-lived organization that attracted considerable attention from both the black poor and city officials. Like the Black Panther Party, the ABLF went beyond demonstrating against police brutality to advocating armed self-defense groups. Its primary agenda, however, was to help the poor resist evictions, obtain relief, and establish collective self-help programs to provide food, clothes, and other necessities to community folks. Its long-term goal was to educate black residents and prepare the groundwork for revolution.[75]

Most of its leaders were poor, young residents who had at one time or another

---

[73] *Birmingham News*, July 29, 1969; LaMonte, "Politics and Welfare," 368–70.

[74] Carl Braden, "Birmingham Movement Grows," *Southern Patriot* 30, no. 7 (September 1972).

[75] Anne Braden, "Law and Order in Birmingham: Two Black Liberation Front Leaders Jailed," *Southern Patriot* 29, no. 3 (March 1971): 5.

been arrested or engaged in petty crimes. One of its founding members in 1970 was twenty-three-year-old Ronald Williams: "I guess I used to be what you'd call an illegitimate capitalist. I acted for myself alone—whatever I could take, I took it. I did time. I'm not ashamed of all that. I learned to survive the way people had to survive in this society. Until I got hip—and I learned how we have to organize and help each other and change the system." Another founding member, forty-three-year-old Wayland Bryant, was radicalized by his utter disappointment with the "so-called civil rights movements," in which he had participated for over twenty years. He came to realize that integration was not the panacea he believed it would be, since it did not attack the fundamental problems of poor people under capitalism.

From the outset, the police and FBI made it virtually impossible for the ABLF to operate in Birmingham. Literally within weeks of their founding, its members were rounded up en masse and arrested in a preemptive strike by police to stop a "planned ABLF ambush." The incident centered around Bernice Turner, a fifty-five-year-old domestic who was being forced out of her home by land developers. Before the ABLF had an opportunity to investigate the case, Turner was served an eviction notice on September 14, 1970. Five Liberation Front activists, including Bryant, Williams, Harold Robertson, and another man and a woman—both unidentified—decided to stay with Mrs. Turner that night and leaflet the community the next morning. The next day, after Mrs. Turner had left for work, nearly two dozen police officers surround her home to arrest the ABLF activists. "A Malcolm X record was playing," recalled Wayland Bryant, "when I heard the door crash open—I never heard any knock." The officers tossed tear gas through the doors and windows, shot Ronald Williams, and beat the remaining members occupying the house. Five ABLF members were jailed, and Bryant and Williams were charged with assaulting a police officer with a deadly weapon and intent to murder. Over the next few weeks, practically the whole membership of the ABLF was arrested for distributing literature and on other assorted charges, thus breaking the backbone of the organization before it had an opportunity to mobilize mass support.[76]

The rapidity with which the Birmingham police crushed the ABLF served as an important reminder that no matter how many reforms the civil rights movement secured in terms of extending participatory democracy to African Americans, the poor still remained powerless to alter conditions and relationships that affected them the most. Although some segments of the black poor did not totally abandon organized politics, especially since newly formed community-based organizations were more concerned with issues of poverty, joblessness, survival, and police brutality than earlier civil rights organizations had been, they were reminded of the consequences of militant action. Some, like Mrs.

[76] Ibid., 5–6.

Turner, viewed the collapse of the ABLF with anger and remorse. As she expressed soon after the arrests, "those men are in jail and it's just not right. . . . All they wanted to do was help."[77]

The efforts of the 1970s were not a complete loss. The political stirrings of poor and working-class residents prompted city government to form the Citizen Participation Program (CPP) in 1974, a well-structured "grass-roots bureaucracy" of neighborhood associations with a limited voice in issues affecting their communities (i.e., city services, zoning, development, etc.). As Steven Haeberle's recent study of the CPP argues, residents from low-income black neighborhoods had the highest participation rate in the program throughout the 1970s and 1980s. When these government-sponsored institutions were not responsive enough, black poor and working-class residents often formed their own voluntary associations to tackle specific problems. More significantly, the dramatic shift in the city's racial makeup during the 1970s contributed to black political empowerment. Richard Arrington's successful bid for the office of mayor in 1979 heightened the entire black community's sense of power. Although class distinctions and tensions within the African-American community by no means disappeared, the black poor generally believed that a black administration was a marked improvement over the past century of white, largely racist city governments. (In many cases they were right: incidents of police brutality, for example, decreased dramatically after Arrington implemented reforms in police operations.) Coming out of a decade in which Black Power slogans shaped much of African-American political discourse, Birmingham's black poor showed greater interest in mainstream politics and were much more willing in the 1980s to support municipal government and to participate in political institutions, including those originating in city hall, intended to improve the quality of life. More importantly, the black poor not only expressed a sense of enfranchisement through relatively high rates of participation, but their protests also suggest a failure on the part of Arrington's administration to provide essential city services for the poorest neighborhoods. This dual sense of empowerment and dissatisfaction is revealed in Philip Coulter's recent study of residents who take advantage of the Mayor's Office of Citizens Assistance (MOCA), established soon after Arrington's election. Coulter demonstrated that in 1983 African Americans with incomes of less than $5,000 (along with the wealthiest whites) were most likely to file complaints with MOCA. Because the majority of complaints center on city services, the persistent protest of the poorest communities suggests that the administration has been unable to solve most of their problems. Not only do these studies challenge William Wilson's hypothesis that the underclass is socially isolated from and indifferent toward political institutions, but, as I have suggested throughout this essay, their high

77 Ibid., 6.

participation rate also reflects a tradition of activism that now has found expression in greater access to legitimate political avenues.[78]

The two decades after 1963, therefore, turned out to be a mixed bag of victories and defeats. During the 1960s, the black poor exhibited greater militancy and political participation, on the one hand, but faced an intensification of police repression, poverty, and joblessness, on the other. Although the civil rights movement succeeded in desegregating public space, winning the franchise, securing federal job antidiscrimination legislation, and eventually paved the way for black empowerment, neither the vote nor legislative initiatives were effective weapons against poverty, joblessness, and plant shutdowns. As more Birmingham steel and iron mills are turned into museums and fewer high-wage industrial jobs are made available, increasing numbers of unskilled African Americans are forced to turn to public assistance, low-wage service-sector positions, or, in some cases, crime.

Although the black poor continue to resist and survive the best way they know how, the complex set of issues they must face, the self-active nature of oppositional politics, and the contradictory, hidden world of the poor make predicting what future struggles might look like a difficult task indeed. To understand the often quotidian politics of the poor, as I have argued throughout this essay, requires both a redefinition of politics, a long-term historical perspective, and an ability to read the actions of the so-called inarticulate.

THE HIDDEN TRANSCRIPT WRIT LARGE: READING THE INFRAPOLITICS OF THE POOR

By shifting our focus from an emphasis on structural factors to the self-activity of the poor, we have been able to at least glimpse the multiple ways in which disadvantaged African Americans in a Southern industrial city experienced, interpreted, and resisted poverty, racism, and economic exploitation. Poor blacks did not sit passively as structural changes acted upon them; rather, the poor developed strategies of survival and resistance that grew out of their specific social and historical locations, and those strategies changed as conditions changed. Cognizant of the racial and class dimensions of power in the

[78] Steven H. Haeberle, *Planting the Grassroots: Structuring Citizen Participation* (New York: Praeger, 1989), 123; Philip B. Coulter, *Political Voice: Citizen Demand for Urban Public Services* (Tuscaloosa and London: University of Alabama Press, 1988), 46–55, 92; and on black politics in Birmingham during the 1970s and 1980s, see Franklin's thorough biography of Arrington, *Back to Birmingham*. Similarly, Jeffrey Berry, Kent Portnoy, and Ken Thomson's study of the political behavior of the poor in four cities, including Birmingham, concludes that the political behavior of the black poor differs little from that of other groups, though African Americans across class lines have a slightly higher participation rate than do whites ("The Political Behavior of Poor People," in Christopher Jencks and Paul E. Peterson, eds., *The Urban Underclass* [Washington, D.C.: Brookings Institution, 1991], esp. 369–70).

Deep South, the black poor tended to adopt evasive strategies—from stealing to vandalizing buses—to resist material and symbolic domination. Occasionally, a few individuals openly challenged authority in isolated acts of resistance. Birmingham's poor black communities constituted multiple, even contradictory, voices; they were not a monolithic group concerned only with material well-being and day-to-day survival. In some cases, issues of personal dignity and/or state-sanctioned violence outweighed those of material needs. During the Depression, men and women gambled with their relief checks by insisting that welfare authorities treat them more courteously. In the midst of war, hundreds of unemployed and working-poor black residents risked arrest or beatings to resist racist practices on public transportation. And for many black Birmingham residents living on the edge, police harassment constituted a greater threat than hunger.

The historical and structural relationship between the hidden transcript and organized political movements during these four decades suggest that even when poor people adopted more public, direct forms of resistance, few joined organized political movements, and those who did were drawn to certain kinds of organizations. Those rare political movements able to mobilize segments of the black poor were successful because they articulated the grievances, aspirations, and dreams that remain hidden from public view. But when those same political organizations openly challenged the status quo, they faced an inordinate amount of repression from the state in the form of law enforcement agencies, which in turn had the effect of deterring poor people's participation. On the other hand, the black poor generally avoided most black middle-class or liberal interracial organizations, which would have been far less dangerous than radical movements such as the ABLF or the CPP. The disinterest, and even disdain, segments of Birmingham's black poor exhibited toward traditional black political institutions that claimed to speak for them is tied to the character of class relations within the black community. A small class of black businessmen and religious leaders, whose livelihood often depended on a consumer base of poor and working-class blacks, ensured peaceful relations by creating alliances with white industrialists, and a handful secured enough "respectability" to retain the franchise. Although black middle-class leaders generally espoused a political outlook that they felt reflected the collective interests of the "race," as we have pointed out several times, they were not always knowledgeable or sensitive to the specific problems, needs, and desires of the poor, nor did they encourage poor blacks to participate in decision-making or leadership capacities within their organizations.

The character of intraracial class relations in Birmingham has important implications for William Wilson's argument that the deepening of class divisions within the black community is largely a post–civil rights phenomenon—the result of the collapse of segregation and the migration of the black middle class out of the ghetto. The portrait he paints of intraracial class harmony and the importance of black middle-class role models in the inner city before the 1970s is not entirely true for Birmingham. Sharp class divisions within the black community existed throughout the period of our study. Racism certainly lessened class divisions, but the black poor and the middle and upper classes did not experience racism in exactly the same way. Besides, traditional black leaders did not always earn the respect or trust of poor and working-class African Americans, and the black poor resented the rude and condescending treatment they sometimes received from the "better class Negroes." While these findings do not completely refute Wilson's hypothesis that the removal of the black middle class and stable working class from the inner city led to a greater concentration of poverty, they do challenge his presumptions regarding the importance of black middle-class institutions for the poor during the age of segregation. Furthermore, in Birmingham the concentration of poverty resulted not only from demographic shifts but also from government housing policy and urban renewal.[79]

In closing, the Birmingham example offers important lessons for developing an approach to the problems of the black urban poor. First, the ways in which the black poor have historically experienced, interpreted, and resisted poverty and racism on a daily basis provide insights that cannot be found in computer-generated data bases. Indeed, few, if any, mainstream black political institutions that claim to speak for the poor have succeeded in understanding the complexity of everyday life from the perspective of poor people themselves, or the multiplicity of voices and experiences within inner-city communities. In short, the poor need to play a more direct role in creating policies that affect them, particularly since they clearly understand the inner workings and contradictions of their world better than do middle-class politicians and academics. A case in point—which in and of itself carries important policy implications—is the black poor's sustained opposition to police brutality in Birmingham. Indeed, that police repression remains one of the most salient political issues in poor black communities today was powerfully demonstrated in Los Angeles on April 29, 1992. The city exploded after four officers were acquitted for the brutal beating of black motorist Rodney King. Unlike most police brutality cases, this was captured on videotape; most of the nation watched King writhe in pain as he absorbed fifty-six blows in eighty-one seconds. Although the riots were multi-cultural, involving African Americans, Latinos, whites, and Asians, the center of the uprising was the black communities of South Central Los Angeles. Aside from the actual riots, one might even refer to the mass popularity of rap songs criticizing police treatment of African Americans. Despite the staggering in-

[79] William J. Wilson, *The Declining Significance of Race: Blacks and Changing American Institutions* (Chicago: University of Chicago Press, 1978); Wilson, *The Truly Disadvantaged: The Inner City, the Underclass, and Public Policy* (Chicago: University of Chicago Press, 1987), 56–57; Wilson and Loic J. D. Wacquant, "The Cost of Racial and Class Exclusion in the Inner City," *Annals* 501 (January 1989): 26–47.

crease in violent crimes, inner-city residents—youth in particular—continue to return to the issue of police repression.[80] If the actual complaints of the poor were part of the policymaking process, then perhaps the problem of policing the poor would take center stage as a "poverty" issue.

Finally, those who operate outside of government agencies and organize grass-roots, community-based movements need to be able to read the infrapolitics of the poor, the hidden transcripts that are continually being revised and reiterated in the tenements and projects, laundromats, and liquor stores, barber shops and beauty salons, sidewalks and basketball courts of the inner city. This offstage political discourse, from the language and culture of Hip Hop to the reconstructed memories of the elderly, express the often contradictory thoughts and dreams of the poor. The success of any effort to mobilize poor people depends on a movement's ability to articulate and comprehend that hidden transcript, no matter how incongruous it might seem in relation to what policymakers and grass-roots organizers believe are the "real" needs of their constituency.

[80] On the Rodney King beating and subsequent Los Angeles riots, see *Los Angeles Times*, April 30, May 1, 2, 3, 1992; *L.A. Weekly* 14, no. 23 (May 8–14, 1992); Independent Commission on the Los Angeles Police Department, *Report of the Independent Commission on the Los Angeles Police Department* (Los Angeles, 1991); and Robin D. G. Kelley, "Straight from Underground," *Nation*, June 8, 1992. One scholar has argued persuasively that inner-city blacks are more likely to be victims of police repression than of "black on black" violence. See Bernard D. Headley, "'Black on Black' Crime: The Myth and the Reality," *Crime and Social Justice* 20 (1983): 52–53.

CHAPTER 10

Nineteenth-Century Institutions: Dealing with the Urban "Underclass"

Eric H. Monkkonen

> Forty thousand vagrant children . . . in the dens and stews of the city . . . are driven from their vile homes to pick rags and cinders, collect bones, and steal. As they grow up they swell the ranks of the dangerous classes. To rescue them . . . they are made clean, are clad comfortably, and learn to sing the sweet songs about the Savior and the better land. They owe their deliverance from disgrace and shame to the outstretched arms of these Missions.[1]

We have lost many of the nineteenth century's institutions that dealt with the urban poor. It was a world at once cruel and ineffective, rich and complex. It locked blind children in the same room with deranged criminals. It tolerated starvation.[2] Yet it could be simple, direct, and unbound by rules. It located nonbureaucratic custodial child care right where parents needed it, gave out overnight lodging to the homeless in each police precinct station house, offered the poor free baths.

This world differed most dramatically from ours in the face it presented: a very visible face of large, well-made buildings, buildings of which the most prominent city dwellers were proud. On the one hand, the faith that social reformers placed in these buildings and their programs to us seems astonishingly naive, on occasion cruel. Their physical layouts deliberately forced the poor into inappropriate molds, splitting up families, mixing the criminal with the abandoned, and somehow expecting the internal lockstep discipline to translate to social change. Almost as soon as they were built, almshouses and reform institutions became targets of crusading reformers, who exposed their internal cruelties and inadequacies.

Yet on the other, these efforts challenge us, for our predecessors took pride in

I wish to thank Robert Fogelson, Joan Waugh, Bruce Schulman, Sanford Jacoby, Julie Szende, Robin Einhorn, Daniel Scott Smith, and Thomas C. Clark for their comments and suggestions. Also, I wish to thank Michael Katz and the members of the SSRC staff and study group on the history of the underclass for their comments and suggestions. And in particular, I wish to thank Bruce C. Bellingham for his extensive remarks.

[1] Elizabeth Oakes Smith, *The Newsboy* (New York: Derby, 1854), 208.

[2] For instance, police found Isabella Grant dead of apparent starvation in a rear room at 312 West 28th Street. Lying on a pile of straw, she had no furniture or material resources. Her daughter Kate, nine, had been out all day begging ("Subterranean Civilization," *National Police Gazette*, November 21, 1863).

their ways of dealing with social inequality. And few Americans today would point to their welfare system with pride. In addition, there may have been an unplanned advantage to this system of aid and control, for it emanated from easily identified buildings scattered across the landscape. Their visibility and location made them an accessible part of a community in a way that we have lost.[3]

Historians have overlooked the most striking difference between the nineteenth and twentieth centuries' worlds of urban poverty. That we have done so is itself testimony to the nature of the transformation: in looking back at a very different world, we are able only to look for what we can understand, for the familiar. We have not looked at the physical manifestation of that world, at the literally thousands of poorhouses, dispensaries, orphanages, police stations, jails, settlement houses, Magdalene houses, lodging houses, wayfarers' homes, and kindred institutions, all showing their imposing facades to city dwellers.

These facades—"handsome buildings," as their builders termed them—formed an integral part of nineteenth-century cities, cities whose architectural features could be absorbed at a much slower and more intimate pace than can most of today's cities. In contrast with today, the social-welfare and social-control apparatus of the nineteenth century was visible, comprehensible, and physically accessible in a way that we can no longer imagine; it is no wonder that historians have themselves neglected this.

Although we have forgotten the complex and varied nineteenth-century institutions that dealt with the urban underclass, their heritage is still invisibly with us.[4] We have built our current systems either directly from them or in

---

[3] I wish not to exaggerate: some poor farms were actually farms, hence on the outskirts of any town or city, two or three miles away.

[4] Like most contributors to this volume, I am uncomfortable with any one term to designate the various groups of people and behaviors we indicate with the word *underclass*. Our nineteenth-century predecessors called them the "dangerous class," the "perishing class," or, much more usefully, the "defective, delinquent, and dependent classes." The terminology poses practical problems in its inexactitude, which becomes apparent when grouping various specialized institutions. Those which took in prostitutes or juvenile delinquents clearly dealt with the kind of people of interest here, but the all-purpose poorhouse (or poor farm, or almshouse, or infirmary) literally took in the whole range of defective, delinquent, and dependent people. It is very difficult to refer to the group found in a poorhouse—a foundling, a tramp with frozen feet, a pregnant destitute women, a dying old man, and a delinquent "half-orphan"—all as the dangerous class or the underclass.

The phrase *dangerous class*, which appeared in the United States in the 1840s and in England slightly earlier, preceded the word *underclass*, although one could argue that the nineteenth-century concepts of the "deserving" and the "undeserving" poor also divide the poor into two groups, the latter corresponding to the underclass. The "dangerous" or "under" class corresponds as a concept to what Marx called the *lumpenproletariat*, a group he was careful to identify as a class enemy of the proletariat. The transliteration of *underclass* also appears in a similar usage in the eighteenth century in Germany; see Norbert Finzsch, *Obrigkeit und Unterschichten: Zur Geschichte der Rheinischen Unterschicten Gegen Ende des. 18 und zu Beginn des 19. Jahrhunderts* (Stuttgart: Franz Steiner Verlag, 1990).

In all varieties of the term, the fundamental notion is that this class is an enemy or at least a threat to society.

direct rejection of them: in either case, history governs our policies with a heavy hand. The nineteenth-century beginnings and subsequent transformations of these institutions have been of significant importance in shaping the way in which we deal with the urban underclass today. Institutions that deal with the urban underclass can be grasped only by locating them in the context of their historical transformations.

If there is a pattern to this institutional tangle of branches and stems, it is that of a shift from a few kinds of organizations dealing with many kinds of people to many kinds of organizations dealing with narrower ranges of people. This long shift has resulted in the confusing welter of organizations today, but the underlying logic has been to narrow the kinds of problem people any one organization treats. The consequence, from the individual's viewpoint, is a complex bureaucratic world: from the bureaucratic viewpoint, the outcome has been a narrowing of particular function and a more specific kind of treatment or aid regime.

More to the point, this institutional world of the nineteenth century differed from ours in a way somewhat difficult to comprehend: it was much more physically visible. Today cultural historians talk about "reading" buildings, by which they mean that the visual and spatial and material aspects of buildings can supply a communicative discourse to the properly accelerated "reader." That was precisely what happened in the nineteenth century, when the poor and needy could easily "read" the buildings about them. What they read led them directly to help. The difference with our day is dramatic: then a tramp on the brink of starvation could ask, "Where is the police station?" or "Where is the poorhouse?" and expect to walk or be carried there. Today, as Joel Handler and others have amply documented, even the simplest emergency aid requires that the needy person find a General Relief office of the county welfare system, which in turn will give the person vouchers for meals and housing. The difference now is that the physical location is a low-visibility office building that gives only pieces of paper. Nineteenth-century places of aid were highly visible, in fact, were often architectural high points, and directly gave aid, then and there (see fig. 10.1). It takes an able person to be needy today.[5]

An abbreviated description of police functions can give a sense of this transition from the nineteenth century to the twentieth. At the time of the Civil War, a police department consisted of uniformed police officers but had no detectives. In addition to accommodating patrol and arrest activities, the station house had separate rooms to house the homeless overnight, and the patrol officers also reported dangerous boilers and overflowing sewers, rounded up stray animals and lost children. By the 1890s, police matrons tended the children and also oversaw the women lodgers. Separate divisions of the city's bureaucracy treated the roving animals, the sewers and boilers. Policing of crime had grown more complex, with detectives now in charge of investigating serious offenses, bicycle

---

[5] For a poignant example, see Joel Handler, "The Transformation of Aid to Families with Dependent Children: The Family Support Act in Historical Context," *New York University Review of Law and Social Change* 16 (1987): 457–533, esp. 529–33.

Figure 10.1. Tramps Being Booked for Lodging or Vagrancy, Hartford, 1895. This photo, from the rich collection of tramp scholar John J. McCook, shows men whose names are being entered on the police "blotter." McCook's interest was in what caused tramping: he was one of the first to proclaim that it had its roots in unemployment. The men pictured here were laborers, cooks, and former saloon keepers. They wear many layers of clothing. By April, when this picture was taken, most tramps no longer stayed in police stations but slept in other, less restrictive shelters, in this case, a local barn. *Source:* J. J. McCook. Photographer, Mr. Wadsworth. (Courtesy Butler-McCook Homestead Corporation, Antiquarian and Landmark Society, Inc.)

patrols aggressively chasing down offenders, and a telegraph system allowing officers to contact the station houses. In another twenty years, the lodgers were gone from the station houses, and police chiefs had a professional organization. While the police organization was more complex, it covered far fewer functions, and each of the discarded activities now had a separate bureaucracy.

Paying for the Poor

"But," says the objector, "this would cost something." So do our houses of correction, police courts, and jails. . . . Is it not more humane and wise to *prevent* crime than to *punish* it?[6]

[6] G. W. Quinby, *The Gallows, the Prison, and the Poor-House* (Cincinnati, Ohio: G. W. Quinby, 1856), 252–53.

From the colonial period, the welfare structure of U.S. cities inherited a tradition of blending the public and the private. There had always been a willingness to allow private groups or individuals to accomplish public responsibilities. Thus budgets show monies or in-kind payments to individuals for taking care of the sick poor or the invalid, or to large institutions for that part of the program taking care of a public obligation. Although local taxes, mainly on property, provided the funding for the operating costs of local institutions, circumstances varied considerably from place to place. The cash outlays can be relatively well documented, for they were the most visible form of public tax accounting and were usually required by law. But variation and ambiguity occurred with other important forms of local support. The picture is least ambiguous for schools, which, by the early decades of the nineteenth century, had become "public" in our contemporary sense of blending both "ownership" and "control." The Northwest Ordinance (1795) set aside public lands for schools, county buildings, and welfare-related institutions, thus establishing a template for the future.[7]

Most states, either through legislation or their constitutions, enabled local governments to care for the poor and to catch and punish criminals by using land as an asset, with construction and operating costs coming from taxation. Cities often followed the same model, introducing even more variety and freely mixing private and public funding and land subsidies. For instance, by 1841, New York City spent 3 percent of its teaching budget for instruction in private orphan asylums and granted them buildings and grounds.[8] Until 1935, a viable

---

[7] "Local governmental responsibility, family responsibility, and legal settlement—the three principles expressed in the English Poor Law—were transplanted some 250 years later to a new Midwestern American territory" (Ethel McClure, *More Than a Roof: The Development of Minnesota Poor Farms and Homes for the Aged* [St. Paul: Minnesota Historical Society, 1968], p. 7). Sophonisba P. Breckenridge, *The Illinois Poor Law and Its Administration* (Chicago: University of Chicago Press, 1939), 9–13, discusses the Northwest Territory's welfare provision of 1795.

[8] For example, the city had granted twenty lots to the Association for the Benefit of Colored Orphans by 1843 (later burned by a mob in the Draft Riot of 1863). Report of New York City Commissioners of School Money, in *Documents of the Board of Aldermen*, vol. 9. document no. 8 (New York: Charles King, 1843), 70–71. Across the country, such "free" lands, real property confiscated or purchased from Native American people, when turned to local public uses, should have been calculated into the revenues and expenditures in several ways. First, the land's value should have been calculated as its "opportunity cost," or the income it would have generated had it been rented. Second, the lost property tax was important, because property tax was the major source of local revenues. The latter was never calculated, and the former only when a locale actually purchased property and paid a mortgage (which was usually only for the buildings). This aspect of nineteenth-century institutions confounds measurement efforts, for nowhere in city budgets do we find an estimate of the annual opportunity costs these structures represent, and as a result, recent econometric analyses are downwardly biased. Nor do more recent studies or accounts of welfare or criminal-justice expenditures calculate these opportunity costs. Many locales opted to convert their set-aside lands into cash, thus lowering their opportunity costs except for that land upon which the untaxed structures actually sat. As the years passed, these structures and their lands appreciated

alternative to the model of local public support for local public and private institutions did not really exist. In an ironic twist of enduring significance, the United States, under its very modern Constitution, continued to operate a local welfare system based on the Elizabethan Poor Law, rather than on the much less localist New Poor Law of 1832, simply because the Revolution had come prior to parliamentary modernization.[9]

Urban Institutions

Uniformity in the states relative to public charity does not exist. Each state has evolved its system, or rather a lack of a system, by a slow process.[10]

Nineteenth-century cities inherited from the colonial era two institutional forms dealing with those who would soon be called the "dangerous class"—the criminal justice system of constables and jails, and the relief system, including the almshouse in bigger cities or straightforward outdoor relief in smaller ones.[11] This limited array of institutions reflected in part the more intimate scale of colonial society but also the more attenuated colonial state.

The period from 1830 to 1890 saw vigorous institution building on the local level by private and public groups. Chronologically, these included orphanages, various institutions for women, police departments, newsboys' lodging houses, armories, settlement houses, and an early social-work system. Structurally, the shift was to move the institutions and institutional funding away from the local to the state and federal: this was an uneven and incomplete shift, so that traces of the local remain in the federal.

After 1890, the urban locus of reform activity began to shift to the county and, more especially, to the states. Urban variety and inconsistency frustrated reformers who wished to use higher levels of governments to ensure more rational bureaucracies and more consistent institutional forms. Thus the period from 1890 to 1930 was one of increased rationalization and coordination as the multiple organizations were gathered into state and county governments.[12]

Almost all local revenues came from property taxes, and home owners defaulted on tax payments in the Depression. Shortages of cash and credit

considerably, so that by 1890, the real property infrastructure represented a large but as yet unmeasured opportunity cost for local governments.

[9] For a summary of the New Poor Law, see Derek Fraser, *The Evolution of the British Welfare State: A History of Social Policy since the Industrial Revolution* (London: Macmillan, 1984).

[10] C. L. Stonaker, "Report of Committee on County and Municipal Institutions," in *Proceedings of the National Conference of Charities and Corrections* (Boston: Press of Fred. J. Heer), 375.

[11] See Carl Bridenbaugh, *Cities in the Wilderness: Urban Life in America, 1625–1742* (New York: Ronald Press, 1938), for extensive colonial detail.

[12] See Peter C. Seixas, "'Shifting Sands Beneath the State': Unemployment, the Labor Market, and the Local Community, 1893–1922" (Ph.D. diss., University of California at Los Angeles, 1988), for a discussion of local, state, and federal government welfare structures.

exacerbated this revenue problem for cities, over three thousand of which went into default after the banks temporarily closed in the Bank Holiday of 1933. Compounding the stress already felt by relief organizations, the Depression's tax crisis caused the near fiscal collapse of most state and local organizations. By the third decade of the twentieth century, the previous century's heavy programmatic emphasis on infrastructure already had begun to shift toward experts, bureaucracies, and intensive treatments involving "outdoor relief." Thus the fiscal crisis precipitously capped a longer underlying transition away from local welfare, moving the United States permanently into the era of the nation-state. Although police remained tied to local government through this crisis, they were affected too: the FBI actually created the Uniform Crime Reports in 1930, possibly the single most centralizing action on local police to date.[13]

This dense web of buildings and land dedicated to helping or reforming the poor, from the poor farms on the outskirts of nearly every county seat to the rooms set aside for lodgers in police stations, gave a physical and symbolic presence to the local state that we have a hard time imagining now. Their monumental quality has been interpreted by many historians as representing the intimidating force of the state. My interpretation differs for several reasons. First, as illustrated by Rothman, who wished to contrast the cottagelike earlier buildings with the post-1830 buildings, any actual scaling of figures in the foreground to the pictured buildings in the background demonstrates that in all cases the artists dramatically exaggerated building sizes, giving them fifteen-foot doors and preposterous external dimensions.[14] This exaggeration suggests that both the early buildings as well as later ones were often pictured as grand achievements of local government.

We know about the appearance of mid-nineteenth-century institutions because they appeared so often in the promotional/descriptive/historical local literary genre so popular in the late nineteenth century. The boosters who wrote this literature about a city or region tried to give positive assessments in order to attract people and business. Odd as it may sound now, a handsome new poorhouse qualified as one of a city's positive features. For example, Jacob H. Studer's *Columbus, Ohio: Its History, Resources, and Progress* (1873), a typical boosterish history and promotional book, includes with the engravings of the city's markets, parks, commercial blocks, churches, schools, and banks the architect's rendering of the new poorhouse (Franklin County Infirmary—today, the Alum Creek Manor). Studer narrates a brief history of the institution, details the purchase of a new tract by the county commissioners just outside the Columbus city limits for seventeen thousand dollars, and elaborates on the plans for this impressive structure. He represents the building to impress the outside world with Columbus's achievements, not to terrify the poorhouse's inmates. These

[13] Samuel Walker, *Popular Justice: A History of American Criminal Justice* (New York: Oxford University Press, 1980), 186.

[14] David Rothman, *The Discovery of the Asylum* (Boston: Little, Brown, 1971), 37.

buildings are still with us, usually transformed by additions, facelifts, and new, friendlier names (see fig. 10.2).

OUTDOOR RELIEF AND ALMSHOUSES

> Needless burdens are imposed on the public by indiscriminate giving to the poor, or a possible perversion of the fund to other purposes than those contemplated by the law.[15]

Smaller cities and towns often relied upon outdoor relief in the colonial period. One must be careful in drawing too precisely the distinction between indoor and outdoor relief, for poor farms and almshouses sometimes, counter to their rules, gave outdoor relief. Moreover, city size or degree of urbanization did not prove determinative of relief forms, for by the end of the nineteenth century, many Southern rural counties had their poor farms. Outdoor relief was more fiscally visible than relief administered through fixed real property: city and village accounting called for the listing of cash and in-kind payments. In addition, corrupt municipal politicians could funnel outdoor relief to party supporters (of course, they could funnel jobs in the institutions to party supporters, too).

This inherent visibility helps account for a turn away from the principle of outdoor relief, for it appeared every month, quarter, and year as a drain on the cash resources of local government: Why not change the people taking these payments rather than continually fund them? The underlying notion became one of malleable individuals passing on to their children their inadequacies; once cured, their social defects would be eliminated and the problem eradicated for ever. The response became poorhouses. Starting in the 1830s, state governments began to rewrite (or write for the first time) laws covering the poor, mandating that every county have a poor farm.[16] States just writing their constitutions at the time included such features in their new governments.[17] Thus

---

[15] *Seventh Annual Report of the Board of [Ohio] State Charities* (Columbus, 1883), 43.

[16] A late entry, Texas legislated poorhouses in 1869, requiring inmates to take a pauper's oath, which took the paupers' citizens' rights, similar to the restrictions placed on felons. Most were in rural counties. See Debbie M. Cottrell, "The County Poor Farm System in Texas," *Southwestern Historical Quarterly* 93 (1989): 169–90.

[17] When not in the state constitutions, this local obligation appeared in city charters. For instance, in "an Act to Incorporate the City of Alton," sec. 9. "The common council shall provide for, and take care of all paupers within the limits of said city; and to accomplish this object, they shall have the exclusive right, power and authority to license and tax all ferries, taverns, merchants, auctioneers, parlayers, grocers, vendors of spirituous liquors and wines, . . . public houses of entertainment, theatrical and other shows" (*Laws of the State of Illinois* [Vandalia: William Walters, 1837], 21). When revised twenty-two years later, the charter incorporated children of the "dangerous class": "To authorize and direct the taking up and providing for the safe keeping and education, for such periods of time as may be deemed expedient, all children who are destitute of parental care and left to wander about, and growing up in mendicancy, ignorance, idleness and vice" (*Laws of the State of Illinois* [Springfield: Bailhache and Baker, 1859], chap. 5, sec. 46, p. 51). One might call this the Huck Finn Law.

Figure 10.2. *View of Columbus Poor House, about Two Miles from the State Capitol.* By this time, the poorhouses in Ohio had been officially renamed infirmaries, capturing the reality that so many inmates were ill as well as poor. This institution's replacement, Alum Creek Manor, is now the county nursing home. This view of the new building is included in local publisher Jacob Studer's promotional *Columbus Ohio: Its History, Resources, and Progress* (1873). The end papers of the book included advertisements for local businesses—including insurance, coal, and railroad companies—suggesting the pride the city elite took in its institutions, including those of the poor.

the responsibility shifted from the town to the county. For approximately one hundred years, then, the county poorhouse was the single broadest and most inclusive institution for the poor.

The poorhouse, as ubiquitous in local government's political landscape as the courthouse, stood at once as a dread symbol of the life of the unsupported and unattached and, simultaneously, as a place for reform. Outdoor relief was suspect throughout the nineteenth century, whether because it could be subverted for corrupt partisan political purposes or because it could be imagined as an income supplement going unearned. In an era and nation with a firm political commitment to education, such an analysis could make ground: the control possible in the poorhouse offered a location for such mechanisms of change. Thus the factory model of the poorhouse, which tried to reap a profit from the labor of the inmates, and the individual reform or educational approach of the early nineteenth century provided a positive alternative to constant local budget drains. And the principal urban institution dealing with the poor—straightforward relief—suffered continual ideological and fiscal attack throughout the nineteenth century. When charity reformer groups such as the Charity Organization Societies argued for a reform of the whole diverse welfare system, so that a thorough scrubbing of society of its inadequate could be accomplished, they usually identified outdoor relief as a problem, leaving some form of indoor relief as a solution.[18]

Whether called poor farms, infirmaries, or almshouses, these institutions sheltered a variety of dependent people for long periods of time, while often dispensing outdoor relief or temporary overnight shelter.[19] Although these institutions were not intended for the "undeserving poor," for instance, prostitutes and thieves, they often ended up aiding such people. They took in those without personal resources or family members able or willing to help. And on occasion, from the eighteenth to the nineteenth centuries, judges sentenced criminal offenders to the poorhouse, an action reformers often complained about.[20]

[18] Michael Katz, In the Shadow of the Poorhouse: The Social History of Welfare in America (New York: Basic Books, 1986); Joan Waugh, "Unsentimental Reformer: Josephine Shaw Lowell and the Rise and Fall of the Scientific Charity Movement" (Ph.D. diss., University of California at Los Angeles, 1992).

[19] Dorothea L. Dix campaigned against keeping the insane in poorhouses and jails. In her Memorial: To the Legislature of Massachusetts (Boston: Monroe and Francis, 1843), she describes visiting lunatics in jails and almshouses throughout Massachusetts. These people were from very poor families and were chained or locked up in pens or cages like wild animals; typically, only a slightly more able pauper cared for them. On Concord, better known to us for its transcendentalists, she noted: "A woman from the hospital in a cage in the almshouse. In the jail several, decently cared for in general, but not properly placed in a prison. Violent, noisy, unmanageable most of the time" (5). She also notes how the insane were often auctioned by towns, the bidding for the lowest cost to the town (23).

[20] Arthur E. Peterson and George W. Edwards, New York as an Eighteenth Century Municipality (1917; reprint, Port Washington, N.Y.: Friedman, 1967), 298–99. For instance, New York City built

In essence, the apparently specialized institutions actually served multiple functions, in part because there were so few structures of any kind to which governments had access. (This is why city market houses sometimes contained a jail cell.) Thus their functional capacity was partially related to their buildings, their infrastructure, but also to their mechanism for funneling aid or punishment on an ad hoc basis.

On occasion, cities tried to reform as well as to warehouse, which in practice usually meant setting the inmates to work. Boston began as early as 1702 "'To sett and keep the poor people and Ill persons at work'" in the almshouse.[21] Later, the Boston Workhouse (1739), followed by a "Manufactory" (1750), kept the poor spinning and weaving. New York City inaugurated its workhouse in 1736; Philadelphia, its "bettering house" in 1766.[22] They were all modeled on the much earlier workhouses in Amsterdam, where the women spun and the men rasped wood into ship caulking material.[23] These factories for the poor dated back to the sixteenth century in Europe, and their introduction to North America represented no uniquely American spirit of reform or repression.

By 1827, the Boston poorhouse was formally known as the House of Industry: its genuine industriousness may be sensed by what the residents actually did. Of its 408 inmates, 28 percent were children and 29 percent were too sick to work: nearly 60 percent, in other words, could not be asked to work. Twenty-five percent of the able men picked oakum (that is, picked apart tarred rope to create a sticky, fibrous mass which could be used for caulking ships) or did unskilled labor, and 30 percent of the women spun or worked in the kitchen. The remainder worked at various other tasks. The oakum pickers produced forty dollars a year apiece in oakum, not nearly so much as the nearly one hundred dollars per year of farm products generated per worker.[24]

The end to the poorhouse can be dated with some precision to 1935, the

---

a municipal poorhouse in 1736, which functioned as an almshouse, a place for "Beggars, Servants running away or otherwise misbehaving themselves, Trespassers, Rogues, Vagabonds, poor persons refusing to work" and, in addition, employed a public whipper and served as a site of corporal punishment for criminal offenders. This building actually preceded the first separate city jail, which the city built twenty-three years later, in 1759, and which attracted travelers' attention as a fine prison. Its replacement, built in 1775, was considered the "most imposing public building erected on Manhattan Island during the colonial period" (303).

21 Bridenbaugh, Cities in the Wilderness, 234.

22 Gary B. Nash, "The Failure of Female Factory Labor in Colonial Boston," Labor History 20 (1979): 165–88; "Poverty and Poor Relief in Pre-Revolutionary Philadelphia," William and Mary Quarterly 33 (1976): 3–30; Peterson and Edwards, New York Eighteenth Century Municipality, 98, 99.

23 Peter Speirenburg, "From Amsterdam to Auburn: An Explanation for the Rise of the Prison in Seventeenth-Century Holland and Nineteenth-Century America," Journal of Social History 20 (1987): 439–61.

24 Calculated from David Rothman, ed., Poverty U.S.A.: The Historical Record. The Almshouse Experience, Collected Reports (New York: Arno, 1973), 34–36.

middle of the Depression, a time when one might expect the poorhouses to have been bulging.[25] By 1935, many of the children, the insane, and the retarded were no longer in poorhouses, which contained principally the poor aged. The federal Old Age Assistance Program of 1935, part of the Social Security Act, began to give direct monthly grants to needy persons over sixty-five who did not live in public institutions. Counties acted quickly to establish welfare boards to administer the funds. In some states, as the old moved out of poorhouses, other destitutes moved in. "'Governors may tell the world that they have "abolished" the "poorhouse" when they sign old age assistance bills, but a small cash pension, which cannot buy medical and nursing care, does not answer the need of hundreds of aged persons today.'"[26] In Minnesota, for example, some counties sold their poorhouses, while others leased theirs to private individuals. In this way, the county retained control. The change in ownership patterns then brought about new names: the Dodge County poor farm became the Fairview Rest Home.[27]

Many of the issues, patterns, and problems associated with the almshouse paradigm have persisted until today, and it is very difficult to study them without a sense that nothing has changed. But, indeed, there have been significant alterations. The perception of outdoor relief, the granting of assistance to people in their own homes, slowly shifted from that of a vice which nineteenth-century policy tried to eliminate to that of a virtue in the Progressive Era. In other words, in the mid-nineteenth century, reformers thought that aid to the poor had to be given in an institutional setting where the poor, as captains of their own fates, could be taught new ways of living. As the analysis of poverty changed, reformers challenged the institutional reform mission: by the early twentieth century, preservation of the nuclear family became the reform goal. The sad practice of lumping together all sorts of people in need has diminished with the provision of broader aid to the elderly and the ill. On the other hand, the sense in the nineteenth century that the very poor and dependent somehow trapped their children into repeating their lives has come back as a major social belief. In the nineteenth century, this outcome was understood as a result of

[25] The marginal location of these institutions and the marginal social status of their inmates has made what was once a network of structures and reams of internal records vulnerable to neglect and destruction. Cottrell, "The County Poor Farm System," discusses the results of a systematic identification and preservation effort in Texas. She concludes that in the next decade "most remaining physical evidence of poor farms will vanish," and that with the disappearance of the written records, poor farms will become "a completely invisible part of the state's past" (189). For a similar story of erasure, see Steven R. Hoffbeck, "'Remember the Poor' (*Galatians* 2:10): Poor Farms in Vermont," *Vermont History* 57 (1989): 226–40.

[26] Quoted in McClure, *More Than a Roof*, 165, from Helen G. Tyson, "The Poorhouse Persists," *Survey Monthly* 74 (March 1938): 76.

[27] McClure, *More Than a Roof*, 166–67.

346 · Eric H. Monkkonen

mixing different kinds of people in the almshouses. Later in the nineteenth and well into the twentieth century, the notion that genetic patterns propagated the poor and criminal gave seemingly scientific grounds for separating different kinds of needy people: promiscuous "mixing" could lead to more genetically defective children.[28] Thus, from the visible evidence confronting almshouse managers—that is, people of inappropriate kinds and conditions grouped in forced social arrangements—a simple explanation for a range of human ills began. The almshouse and its mutations functioned then to provide an explanation as well as accommodation.

An important exception to the mixing of people in the poorhouse was race: fragmentary evidence suggest that early in the nineteenth century, poorhouse officials racially segregated occupants, occasionally defining Irish as a race.[29] In the post–Civil War South, blacks appear to have been excluded from state institutions except in the most desperate situations. Jails were segregated, and cities in which police did take black lodgers kept separate facilities.[30] From the point of view of African Americans, racial segregation might have been preferable to what appears to have been simple exclusion in many locations. In the postbellum South, for instance, poorhouse occupants appear to have been mainly white, which clearly indicates that poor, disabled, or very sick black people were simply excluded from even the minimal aid of the poorhouse.[31] This exclusion raises several as yet unresearched questions about social structure and institutional intervention: What was the regional pattern of black exclusion from state institutions? What were the differential impacts of this exclusion, comparing, for instance, blacks and the Irish or, later in the nineteenth century, other very poor white groups? Did the "indiscriminate" mixing of children with derelicts in poorhouses harm them more than the black children's exclusion from all aid?

---

[28] Richard Louis Dugdale, The Jukes: A Study in Crime, Pauperism, Disease, and Heredity (New York: Putnam's, 1877).

[29] Rothman, Discovery of the Asylum, 8, 14.

[30] Gilles Vandal, "The Nineteenth Century Municipal Response to the Problem of Poverty: New Orleans Free Lodgers, 1850–1890, as a Case Study," Journal of Urban History (forthcoming 1992), citing the Picayune, December 19, 1866, December 17, 1867, March 13, 1875.

[31] Booker T. Washington used this example of obvious discrimination to argue that rural blacks relied on families for aid rather than on the state, and that "in our ordinary southern communities we look upon it as a disgrace for an individual to be permitted to be taken from that community to any kind of an institution for dependents" ("Destitute Colored Children of the South," Proceedings of the Conference on the Care of Dependent Children Held at Washington, D.C., January 25, 26, 1909 [Washington, D.C.: 1909), 114–17, cited in Robert H. Bremner, ed., Children and Youth in America: A Documentary History, vol. 2 [Cambridge: Harvard University Press, 1971], 301). Exclusion of blacks from welfare continued well into the twentieth century. Police intimidated Houston blacks in relief lines; see Randy J. Sparks, "'Heavenly Houston' or 'Hellish Houston'? Black Unemployment and Relief Efforts, 1929–1936," Southern Studies 25 (1986): 358–59.

HOSPITALS AND DISPENSARIES

> In our best communities, the almshouse today is recognized as an infirmary and hospital.[32]

If the poorhouse is no longer a visible part of the urban scene, the hospital, in particular the hospital for the urban poor, still is. It may in fact be the one exception to the greater trend away from large institutional settings. Illness has always been a constant and dangerous companion of the poor. For families paying rent by the week and buying food daily, illness and disease were more instantly threatening than unemployment. Narratives of the lives of the poor are always punctuated by episodes of illness.[33]

While the big-city hospital did very often provide the place of last resort for the nineteenth-century urban poor, they were far more likely to seek treatment at the poorhouse (or infirmary) or dispensaries.[34] Intended to be the major form of medical care for the "industrious poor," dispensaries treated a vast range of ailments.[35] An institution originating in England and Europe, the dispensary spread across the United States from the late eighteenth century onward, declining in favor of the hospital outpatient clinic only in the early twentieth century. Again, these institutions were highly visible urban establishments, dispersed throughout larger cities in prominent if smaller buildings. Unlike the publicly funded hospitals, early dispensaries were formed with a combination of private and public monies. In 1830, for example, the New York City Dispensary had 40 percent city funding.[36] They were quite dispersed throughout the city by the late nineteenth century; New York City had 29 (1874) and Philadelphia 33 (1877), but an exact account has been elusive thus far (see fig. 10.3).[37]

From our point of view, the dispensary, in particular one that emphasized preventative medicine, seems like a logical and reasonable way to get health care to the poor at a point prior to the person's need for hospitalization.[38] The demise

---

[32] Stonaker, "Report of Committee on County and Municipal Institutions," 376.

[33] Michael Katz, *Poverty and Policy in American History* (New York: Academic Press, 1983); Ruth Rosen and Sue Davidson, eds., *The Maimie Papers* (Old Westbury, N.Y.: Feminist Press, 1977).

[34] Charles E. Rosenberg, "Social Class and Medical Care in America: The Rise and Fall of the Dispensary," *Journal of the History of Medicine* 29 (1974): 32–54; and *The Care of Strangers: The Rise of America's Hospital System* (New York: Basic Books, 1987), 5, 419.

[35] Charles E. Rosenberg, *Caring for the Working Man: The Rise and Fall of the Dispensary. An Anthology of Sources* (New York: Garland Publishing, 1989), 58.

[36] Ibid., 51.

[37] Ibid. has an excellent short introduction; see also David Rosner, *A Once Charitable Enterprise: Hospitals and Health Care in Brooklyn and New York, 1885–1915* (New York: Cambridge University Press, 1982), 217, n. 1.

[38] See on this point, George Rosen, "The First Neighborhood Health Center Movement: Its Rise and Fall," *American Journal of Public Health* 61 (1971): 1620–27.

Figure 10.3. View of New York City's Central Dispensary. Appearing in the *Manual of the Corporation of the City of New York* for 1870, the descriptive paragraph which followed explained that "a large portion of the Dispensary district is thickly covered with a shanty population, and these unfortunate people are, as a rule, extremely poor and improvident; so that should the head of the family be taken sick, the entire household at once suffer for the very necessaries of life. . . . It is undoubtedly not only a matter of charity to the unfortunate, but also wise political economy, to restore such people to health as soon as possible" (371). The numerous views in the *Manual* suggest that those institutions designed for "fallen" women were more modest in their facades and lacked signage.

of the dispensary and its replacement by the large central hospital with an emergency room providing almost all treatment for the urban poor came about in the first decades of the twentieth century. The shift had very little to do with the medical needs of the poor. Instead, the nature of the medical profession allocated prestige and research principally to doctors practicing in large hospitals. Medical training, too, spliced its need for students' patients (the poor) with the location of research in the central hospital: the outcome—medical care for the poor at one place in most cities, the emergency room of the central training hospital.

BATHS

Three years ago the Amelia Street School introduced a bath tub.[39]

The poor in cities had neither bathtubs nor hot water, and the New York Association for Improving the Condition of the Poor had as early as 1852 built the People's Bathing and Washing Establishment. It closed nine years later, no doubt because the Lower East Side residents could not afford to use it. Bathing, that is, in swimming pools, came to American cities between 1865 and 1885, with public baths for the purpose of cleanliness not arriving until the 1890s. Public baths, another imported idea, spread across U.S. cities in the early twentieth century. As cleanliness became a virtue in the mid-nineteenth century, access came to be seen as an access to virtue. Like other reform institutions, the baths were in elegant-looking buildings, buildings that belied their rather humble purposes. New York State in 1895 required all cities with a population of over 50,000 to provide free public baths.[40] Of course, they disappeared as rising real incomes turned into plumbing and bathtubs in the mid-twentieth century. More than providing cleanliness, however, public baths may have actually accomplished a significant life-saving purpose by making it unnecessary for poor city residents to bath in rivers and harbors.[41]

JAILS

It is universally agreed by students of penology that the county jail system of the United States is bad.[42]

Probably the most famous jail of the nineteenth century was New York City's Tombs Prison, so named because of its Egyptian revival architecture. Its popular name—"The Tombs"—says all that need be said about the U.S. jail, for people put there were and are less likely to be targeted for programmatic attention than are people in almost any other institutional setting. We must keep in mind that prior to the creation of separate institutions, jails held the insane (as they do once again), that police handled a range of welfare activities, and that prostitute

[39] Dana W. Bartlett, *The Better City: A Sociological Study of a Modern City* (Los Angeles: Neuner, 1907), 90.

[40] Marilyn T. Williams, *Washing "The Great Unwashed": Public Baths in Urban America, 1840–1920* (Columbus: Ohio State University Press, 1991), 16; Frank D. Watson, "Public Baths," in Andrew C. McLaughlin and Albert B. Hart, eds., *Cyclopedia of American Government* (1942; reprint, Gloucester, Mass.: Peter Smith, 1963), 122–23.

[41] The high rate of nineteenth-century drownings has puzzled many historians, and rather than seeking an explanation in swimming skills, we might instead turn to the rise of the bathtub and public bath. Roger Lane, *Violent Death in the City: Suicide, Accident and Murder in Philadelphia* (Cambridge: Harvard University Press, 1979), 36, 48–51, has shown that for Philadelphia, the rate of drowning peaked between 1850 and 1885, then slowly began to decline by the 1890s.

[42] Hastings H. Hart, "County Jails," 497, in McLaughlin and Hart, *Cyclopedia of American Government.*

reform involved family counseling and child care. Just as the scope of the orphanage included juvenile offenders, so jails took in orphans.

Jails have never aroused the same ideological contestation that poorhouses did, for they had been purposely built to punish and detain, not to shelter and reform. Local governments designed city and county jails to house those accused of crimes, offenders serving short sentences for non-felony crimes, witnesses who might bolt, persons lacking sufficient self-control to be put in the poorhouse (the insane), and, after the creation of the uniformed police, occasional tramps. Even today, jails still serve no ostensible punishment, reform, or treatment goal. As long as the inmates do not die and do appear at the correct place at the correct time, jails are considered functional. Always and still administered by local governments, jails continue to have a deservedly terrible reputation. This derives from their purpose: custody and mild punishment.

For as long as outside observers have visited them, jails have been overcrowded and have mixed the seriously deviant with nondeviant people. (Empty jails do not get reported or commented on, as they are never newsworthy.) In essence, jails cannot work well: they hold people against their will, including those who may not deserve to be there. In administering the jail, local government has a thankless task, and its response has never been satisfactory. Jails have slowly narrowed their inmate mix by removing children, the insane, the sick, the homeless, witnesses to crimes, and otherwise dependent, noncriminal populations. Yet even this may be changing: recent reports of jails holding more mentally ill than other institutions do have appeared in the media.[43]

It is of interest and importance that of all local institutions dealing with the underclass, jails were least affected by the Depression and New Deal programs. Only more recently have the combined efforts of the federal government and inmate lawsuits begun to seriously challenge these known jail deficiencies. Regular federal surveys of jail suicides, for instance, have highlighted inadequate prisoner protection, especially for juveniles. Even this way of measuring jail treatment—by its lack of violence—highlights the peculiarly custodial and neutral role of jails.

Although jails organizationally belong more often to the county than to the city, physically and functionally they are tied to the police, a city organization. For about a fifty-year period, 1870–1920, there was an intermediary functional and physical institution between the two, the police station lodging house. Now gone and forgotten, this institution filled an important service gap, taking in the destitute for overnight shelter. But the proper context for understanding lodging is that of the police.

---

[43] E. Fuller Torrey, "The Madness of Deinstitutionalization," asserts that 15 percent of the Los Angeles County Jail population is mentally ill, more people than are in state institutions for the mentally ill (*Los Angeles Times Book Review*, September 9, 1990).

THE POLICE

Why not create an efficient police?[44]

Of course, the major institution interacting with the poor and criminal offenders was and still is the police. The nature and quality of the police and the structure of their public interaction has changed dramatically over the past two centuries. The United States is unique in its form of independent yet highly dependent local government, and the police are a key part of this political organization. City governments are creatures of state government: they are a privilege created by state constitutions and laws, with no status beyond that. The police organizations of the United States were copied from the London Metropolitan Police (1829), itself modeled on the Royal Irish Constabulary. The police were created for multiple reasons, but the principal resistance to their initial creation came from stingy city councils, for the system that they replaced took no tax dollars, but ran on fees. This system, referred to as the *constable watch system*, echoed directly early medieval police. The night watch was essentially a guard service: the constables arrested people, served warrants, and performed other tasks for courts, civil and criminal.

Lack of systematic patrol and policing led many urban dwellers to use lower criminal courts and justices of the peace to prosecute criminal offenders.[45] In these ward-based courts, crimes and misdemeanors were prosecuted on the initiative of the victims. Evidence suggests that the volume of prosecutions was considerably greater than in the subsequent police system. Of particular significance is evidence that the police were introduced, among other reasons, to reduce the numbers of privately originated criminal prosecutions, in part because some of the cases were frivolous and corrupt, and in part because there were just too many of them.

Originators of the new police specifically designed them to be preventative, to stop crime before it happened. Uniforms made them more visible to the public and to their supervising officers. Introduced with some fits and starts (New York City's police did not stay a consistent organization until after 1853), police departments spread to most major cities by the 1880s. They were not expected to do the other non-crime related activities that they immediately took on, however. Almost instantly they were taking lost children to the station houses, checking for open sewers and roving livestock, and putting up homeless wanderers and tramps overnight. While women did not appear on patrol until the very end of the nineteenth century, they were quickly hired to be matrons in the

[44] James Bryce, *The American Commonwealth* (New York: Macmillan, 1895), 2:568.
[45] Allen Steinberg, *The Transformation of Criminal Justice: Philadelphia, 1800–1880* (Chapel Hill: University of North Carolina Press, 1989), has unearthed the most detailed evidence of the activity in these lower criminal courts in his study of Philadelphia's aldermen's courts.

rooms for lost children and in the dormitory rooms for women "lodgers," and even to help reform "vicious" women and girls.[46] Patently unrelated to crime control, police station-house lodging became a massive activity in every city with a police department.

The police deserve special attention in order to highlight their role in housing the homeless, referred to in the nineteenth and early twentieth centuries as "lodgers." Lodging came under external criticism at the end of the nineteenth century because of its very nature: short term, with no questions asked. Like outdoor relief, lodging seemed to many Progressive Era reformers to accomplish the antithesis of quality aid: it made no demands on those lodged, taught them no moral or fiscal lessons, and made it possible for the lazy to survive. As a substitute, urban reformers created municipal lodging houses, which provided overnight beds but for a price—delousing and chemical disinfectant baths and usually a "work test," which involved chopping wood or breaking up rocks. Because the wood-lot tasks took place in the early morning, the tramps who depended on getting to early morning hiring points for day laborers avoided the municipal lodging houses, preferring to sleep outdoors or to try to get in at police stations. As police slowly went out of the lodging business after 1900, this service essentially disappeared, unless it was picked up by other private organizations like the Salvation Army. By the crisis of the Great Depression, most cities, when faced with thousands of homeless people, were at a loss, typically turning to armories for housing. New York even used its armories for daytime shelter in 1934. Robert Fogelson points out the irony of using for shelter a "structure designed to intimidate the 'dangerous classes,' not to accommodate them."[47]

Any analysis of the police must locate them in their city-government context. The police chief reports to the mayor; the city council determines their budget; property taxes provide the revenue. Police deal with offenders more than any other criminal justice organization does. But unlike most other organizations dealing with poor people or offenders, police do not have a long-term responsibility toward individuals; they deal with them only prior to and including their arrest, but not afterward. In addition, potentially violent force underlies police actions. Consequently, police/individual relationships are asymmetric and tense. The communities that need and want the police the most are usually at the same time the most hostile. The police are visible and accessible symbols of bad news. They represent the state in an inevitably distasteful and conflicted way.

[46] A movement "mothered" and paid for by the Women's Christian Temperance Union since 1876, in Portland, Maine. See Sarah W. Devoll, "The Results of the Employment of a Police Matron in the City of Portland, Maine," *Proceedings of the National Conference of Charities and Corrections* (1881), 309–17.

[47] Robert M. Fogelson, *America's Armories: Architecture, Society, and Public Order* (Cambridge: Harvard University Press, 1989), 231.

As an additional constraint, policing remains labor intensive, with few technological substitutes to increase productivity, and stressful. Police are primarily present at the actual point of crisis, of failure, of victimization. But in any policy considerations, we must continue to include the police, to comprehend the particular constraints upon their role, to reconsider their historic role and presence in poor communities, and to think creatively about using them as a positive social force.

OTHER DEPENDENCY-DRIVEN INSTITUTIONS

At a Place called "Long Island Farms," not far from the city of New-York, there are 1200 once abandoned children, who were picked up in the vilest portions of that great metropolis, and are now supported and educated at the public expense. . . . Ohio takes criminal parents and locks them in jail, while the children wander about the streets, sleep under carts, in door yards and haylofts, and furnish themselves the means of sustenance by theft.[48]

The process of separating the dissimilar groups of people in poorhouses began to accelerate in the early nineteenth century with orphanages leading the way.[49] As in the case of the poorhouse and other forms of care and control, the orphanage had a long tradition in Europe, where the institution accomplished a broad range of functions, everything from providing the church with young recruits to supporting children of the urban bourgeoisie, as in the Amsterdam Burgerweeshuis.[50] Folks identifies the first public orphanage in the United States as that established by the city of Charleston in 1794.[51] Private orphanages predated this considerably; one was established in New Orleans in 1729, followed by one in Savannah in 1738.

From their beginning, orphanages tended to specialize, by religion, race, and ethnic origins. This specialization reflected the wishes of parents as much as it reflected social fissures. We have a sense of parents' wishes through the "half-orphanages," institutions that took in the children of poor one-parent families, and that often specialized by religion and ethnicity.[52] Parents often employed

---

[48] Quinby, The Gallows, the Prison, and the Poor-House, 246, 256.

[49] See for the best recent analysis, Bruce Bellingham, "Waifs and Strays: History of Childhood, Abandonment and the Circulation of Children between Households in the Mid-Nineteenth Century," in Peter Mandler, ed., The Uses of Charity: The Poor on Relief in the Nineteenth-Century Metropolis (Philadelphia: University of Pennsylvania Press, 1990).

[50] John Boswell, The Kindness of Strangers: The Abandonment of Children in Western Europe from Late Antiquity to the Renaissance (New York: Pantheon, 1988); Ann McCants, "The Burgerweeshuis" (Ph.D. diss., University of California, Berkeley, 1991).

[51] Homer Folks, The Care of Destitute, Neglected, and Delinquent Children (New York: Macmillan, 1902), 7–11.

[52] Note how the terminological focus has changed from "half-orphans" in the nineteenth century to "single-parent families" in the twentieth. This shift suggests the nineteenth-century concern with

orphanages as strategic resources, leaving their children during times of economic stress, sometimes returning to reclaim the whole family.[53] Other times, they might leave one or two of their children in institutions in times of family need, removing them when they could.[54] Valentine's Manual for New York City (1864) lists the following orphanages, which indicates the institutional range of orphanage client populations: the Female Roman Catholic Orphan Asylum, the Roman Catholic Orphan Asylum for Boys, the Orphan Asylum, Orphan's Home Asylum, Protestant Half-Orphan Asylum, Leake and Watt's Orphan House and School, the House of Refuge, the New York Infirmary for Indigent Women and Children. (The Colored Orphan Asylum had been burned by this time, but it also had received some city subsidies, including its land.)

The outdoor relief equivalent of the orphanage was indenture, and in all probability, more children were indentured than housed in orphanages until perhaps the post–Civil War era. Related to indenture were the "orphan trains," which rounded up street children from the 1850s until the early twentieth century, sending them to rural areas in the West, where families shopped for them.[55] Cities also saw this marketing of children: in Boston until 1940, orphanage workers took children from parish to parish for church services, afterward lining them up for inspection by potential adopting families.[56]

The reform of almshouses contributed to the pressure on orphanages and foster homes; New York passed the first law forbidding the housing of children in almshouses in 1875, and other states followed suit. By 1910, when the data become most reliable, there were 1,151 orphanages in the United States, about 90 percent of which were private but that typically had considerable support from public sources.[57]

---

the child as individual, the twentieth century with the family unit. None of the following discussion of the orphanage should be taken to imply that orphanages dealt only with children of the underclass. But what should be kept in mind is that these institutions were available to all children, so by definition represent a resource and institutional intervention in the lives of dependent children, including those of the underclass.

[53] See Peter C. Holloran, *Boston's Wayward Children: Social Services for Homeless Children, 1830–1930* (Rutherford, N.J.: Fairleigh Dickinson University Press, 1989), who details the interactions between parents and orphanages in a way that shows a variety of family interactions with the orphanage. See also Judith Ann Dulberger, "Refuge or Repressor: The Role of the Orphan Asylum in the Lives of Poor Children and Their Families in Late-Nineteenth-Century America" (Ph.D. diss., Carnegie Mellon University, 1988), who argues that "poor families used nineteenth-century institutions to meet their needs and advance their interests" (ii).

[54] In a curious confirmation of these tendencies, for example, Louis Armstrong went into the New Orleans Colored Waifs Home (1913) after being caught for shooting a revolver on New Year's Eve when he was thirteen. Both of his parents were alive but separated. He spent a year and half there, where he learned the bugle and coronet and joined their band.

[55] Charles L. Brace, *The Dangerous Classes of New York and Twenty Years' Work among Them* (New York: Wynkoop and Hallenbeck, 1872).

[56] Holloran, *Boston's Wayward Children*, 1989, 103–4.

[57] Bremner, et al., eds., *Children and Youth in America* 2:1523, 284.

The disappearance of the orphanage followed state legislation creating "mothers' pensions" and New Deal legislation augmenting the state efforts. Illinois created the first such program to aid mothers in 1911, and by 1921 forty states had similar programs.[58] These programs supported poor mothers and sometimes fathers, and in turn kept them from being forced to give up their children as half-orphans. An additional factor in the decline came from a parallel decrease in family size and the number of children at risk: a parent's death in a large family put children at risk of entering an orphanage.[59] This decline in children at risk for the orphanage preceded the baby boom, which theoretically should have produced a similar orphan boom. But with declining institutional support, these orphans of the baby boom must have gone to adoptive and foster parents. The scenario is not well documented. For instance, the usual source for such information, *The Historical Statistics of the United States*, has no data on orphans or orphanages, and there is only one scholarly book on the subject, Holloran's *Boston's Wayward Children*, which for all its unique detail does not supply a time series. Figure 10.4 reproduces the best historical data.[60] These data make clear the trajectory of the orphanage as an institution, expanding until the New Deal, then virtually disappearing. Only very recently has there been the hint of a reversal, as forms of the orphanage return, one oriented toward children too old and independent to be placed in foster homes but too young to live on their own, and the other more of a group home.[61]

In the second half of the twentieth century, the foster home has replaced the orphanage. Foster homes represent, first, the rejection of the large institution as

[58] Grace Abbott, *The Child and the State* (Chicago: University of Chicago Press, 1938), 2:229–34, cited in Bremner et al., *Children and Youth in America* 2:384–85.

[59] Marshall B. Jones, "Crisis of the American Orphanage, 1931–1940," *Social Service Review* 63 (1989): 613–29, argues that the financial crisis of the Depression, rather than the dynamics I have described, triggered the demise of the orphanage. In essence, the New Deal welfare legislation substituted other forms of cash support for orphanages in a structural shift parallel to that ending the poorhouse.

[60] Data sources: for 1960–85, *Statistical Abstract of the United States* (Washington, D.C.: G.P.O., 1986), 366, taken from Social Security Administration's unpublished data; for 1910–60, Martin Wolins and Irving Piliavin, *Institution or Foster Family: A Century of Debate* (New York: Child Welfare League, 1964), 37; for 1880–1900, Folks, *Care of Destitute Children*, 195–96, from Frederick H. Wines, *Tenth U.S. Census: The Defective, Dependent, and Delinquent Classes* (Washington, D.C.: Government Printing Office, 1888); *Eleventh U.S. Census: Crime, Pauperism, and Benevolence* (Washington, D.C.: Government Printing Office, 1895); population, *Historical Statistics of the United States: From Colonial Times to the Present* (Washington, D.C.: G.P.O., 1977), 10; Seth Low, "Foster Care of Children: Major National Trends and Prospects" (Washington, D.C.: Dept. of Health, Education and Welfare, Welfare Administration, Children's Bureau, 1966).

[61] For an argument in favor of the orphanage, see Lois G. Forer, *Unequal Protection: Women, Children, and the Elderly in Court* (New York: Norton, 1991). See also Penelope Lemov, "Return of the Orphanage," *Governing* (May 1991): 31–35, cited in Liz Westerfield, "Children by Order and System: The Making of a Separate Children's Institution in Philadelphia, 1820" (Unpublished paper, University of California at Los Angeles, 1991).

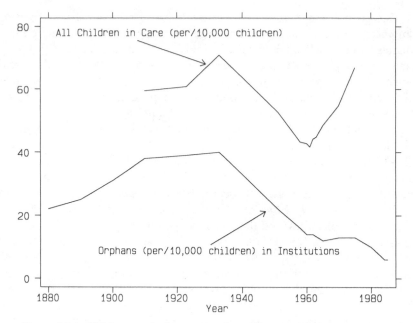

Figure 10.4. Children in Orphanages and in All Forms of Care, 1880–1985. *Source:* See note 60.

a preferred setting for child rearing.[62] Second, they substitute private care largely invisible to outside public scrutiny for the more visible treatment afforded by publicly funded institutions. The current crisis in foster care points to the dilemmas resulting from this transition. The foster-care system depends on a coordinating bureaucracy and a financial arrangement that in some ways resembles an older tradition of a private/public mix. The orphanage's near disappearance reflects the transition from a visible and accessible urban institution to an invisible bureaucracy. Did the presence of orphanages across the urban landscape make a meaningful, positive difference to urban life that we have not yet discovered?

NEWSBOYS' LODGING HOUSES

The attention of the poor boys [to speeches by Judge Kirtland and Mssrs. Roosevelt and Howe at the Boys' Lodging House] who find a temporary home here is marked, evidencing that those gentlemen who take so kindly an interest in them are not laboring in vain.[63]

---

[62] Jack Patten, *The Children's Institution* (Berkeley, Calif.: McCutchan, 1968).
[63] *New York Times*, January 9, 1871.

The newsboys' lodging houses were dormitories with plain furniture, open bunks, lockers, a clerk, and rounds of speech-making visitors. Their residents: young boys who supported themselves by the "street trades."[64] For us in the late twentieth century, it is difficult to imagine the newsboys' lodging house, which starkly symbolizes the harshness of nineteenth-century urban life. The first, started in New York City in 1853, was, in fact, located in the third story of the *Sun* newspaper building. These institutions were charitable but not free dorms for boys who supported themselves. Their label, *newsboys* (or, alternatively, *street arabs*), indicates that they became common and visible with the introduction of the penny press in the 1830s. This new media depended on constant street sales; thus the boys and the press needed one another. The term *newsboy* was generic for children who slept in doorways and supported themselves by shining shoes, doing odd jobs, and selling the many daily newspapers.[65] What has been written about them is all cheerful and bright: plucky lads socializing around the warm stove in the evening and leading adventurous lives on the streets. But one fact should give us pause: Horatio Alger, Jr., who gave us the quintessential and brilliant portrait of a newsboy in *Ragged Dick* (1868), had been evicted from his pastorate for sexually abusing young boys.[66] We have no idea about what went on in these or in other institutions that never showed a rent in their Victorian screen of sentimentality, and it may well be that Alger was an exception and no longer a child abuser when he worked in an institutional setting.[67]

We might use the newsboys' lodging house as a reminder: the second half of the nineteenth century permitted large numbers of children to live as self-supporting individuals, representing them as boy heroes through literary and journalistic portrayals.[68] Newsboys and their lodging houses served as transitional institutions between the orphanage and the streets; they were viable in an age that offered jobs to children. But they should serve to remind us of the shocking lack of social responsibility that obtained in our cities less than a century ago.

[64] See David Nasaw, *Children of the City: At Work and at Play* (New York: Oxford University. Press, 1985), appendix, 207–8, for an excellent list of primary sources on "newsboy studies." Bruce Bellingham, "The 'Unspeakable Blessing': Street Children, Reform Rhetoric and Misery in Early Industrial Capitalism," *Politics and Society* 12 (1983): 303–30.

[65] John Morrow, *The Newsboy: A Voice from the Newsboys* (New York: Published for the benefit of the author by John Morrow, 1860), xii.

[66] Gary Scharnhorst with Jack Bales, *The Lost Life of Horatio Alger, Jr.* (Bloomington: Indiana University Press, 1985), dismisses the claim that Alger lived at the Newsboys' Lodging House, but documents that through his life he spent much time with young boys, as a tutor (including E. R. A. Seligman), foster parent, and benefactor.

[67] Albert Wilson, *These Were the Children* (Menlo Park, Calif.: Wilson, 1963), visited his former (and hostile) orphanage supervisor and reports his shock at discovering that her room was filled with pictures of nude girls.

[68] See, for an early example of the boy hero genre, Morrow, *The Newsboy*.

WAYFARERS' HOMES

All vagabondage has its origin in neglected childhood.[69]

Religious and charitable organizations created a range of institutions to deal with "little wanderers," which I cluster in this section. Like the newsboys' lodging houses, they took in children who were not in their families. Their creators had mixed humanitarian and social motives: rescuing children and preventing future criminality and poverty. Gender segregated, these included several organizations designed to prevent girls from becoming prostitutes or to reform the still-malleable young prostitute, and yet others to deal with young boys, either the homeless or the young criminal offender. These homes were often local and usually specialized by race and religion. State governments also created a few such institutions, for instance, the Minnesota State Public School for Dependent and Neglected Children (1886), and the federal government funded state-level agencies for children of war veterans. The "Michigan system" removed all neglected children from poorhouses, providing a widely copied model for the centralized, nonlocal state care (including indenturing and foster-home placement) of children.[70] These institutions differed somewhat from the prototypical New York House of Refuge (1825), the first U.S. reform school for child offenders. The intent was the same, however: on the one hand rescuing children and on the other preventing their future criminality.[71]

All these institutions aimed at children administered heavy doses of moral teaching (and denominational preaching). The newsboys' lodging house taught the ethic of hard work and saving, encouraging the boys to build up individual bank accounts held by the superintendent. Thrift, usually aimed at keeping the boys out of the thriving street culture described by Stansell (1987), would bring them security; the lodging houses deliberately served dinner when popular

[69] LeRoy Ashby, *Saving the Waifs: Reformers and Dependent Children, 1890–1917* (Philadelphia: Temple University Press, 1984), 48, quoting the words of Victor Hugo favored by child reformers.

[70] Homer Folks, "Municipal Charities in the United States," *Proceedings of the National Conference of Charities and Corrections* (Boston: National Conference of Charities and Corrections, 1898), 113–84; and Folks, *Care of Destitute Children.* The New York State Senate committee of 1857 discussed twenty-six state-funded orphanages, containing 2,816 children in 1857: arguing that children in poorhouses were "much more pitiable" than those in orphanages, it recommended their removal to orphanages (Gerald Grob, *The State and Public Welfare in Nineteenth-Century America: Five Investigations* [New York: Arno, 1976], 10).

[71] Holloran, *Boston's Wayward Children,* has an astonishingly complete survey of these institutions for Boston; Linda Gordon, *Heroes of Their Own Lives: The Politics and History of Family Violence. Boston, 1880–1960* (New York: Viking, 1988), follows the interventions of one Society for the Prevention of Cruelty to Children for several decades, also in Boston; while Barbara M. Hobson, *Uneasy Virtue: The Politics of Prostitution and the American Reform Tradition* (New York: Basic Books, 1987), works out from Boston, tracing a longer history of those organizations dealing with prostitutes. This recent research carries on a tradition of concern about abandoned or abused children that began in the 1830s and has not diminished since, in spite of the recent "discovery" of child abuse in its varied forms.

theaters opened to keep the boys away from this costly entertainment. The theme of thrift echoed into the twentieth century as settlement houses (and schools) created similar banks. Their innovative significance has been overlooked, but working people had no access to savings banks, so the various "Penny Provident" funds actually were a new resource for the poor.

A related emphasis on order, both in daily routine and visual presentation, permeated this class of institutions. Photographs usually showed before-and-after pictures: the contrast the viewer was supposed to notice was in the disheveled, dark, and dirty clothes versus the white, starched, and somehow angelic clothes. Often the same institutional reports containing these images also printed the daily institutional schedule: again, in it, reformers made their message clear—order in presentation and daily activity. The contrast with what seemed to be the urban poor's daily life—a physically disordered environment and unpredictable, apparently impulsive, daily (and nightly) activities—was deliberate and dramatic. Since the early Middle Ages, the spread of the state has socialized people to become more orderly, less impulsive, and more predictable in social interactions. Some theorize that this emphasis on order, especially in the public schools, had a "civilizing" effect on urban immigrants, training them for the factory and indirectly suppressing opportunistic and random crime.[72] This broad similarity in internal organization and goals across varied child-saving institutions mirrored schooling, both public schools and Sunday schools, and we may conclude that for all the institutional variety, there was remarkable internal consistency in the institutional experiences of "at-risk" children in the nineteenth and early twentieth centuries.

Perhaps the most innovative of the child-saving institutions were the "junior republics," begun in the 1890s. They modeled themselves on republican virtues and on republican social and political organization in order to shelter and shape children. These institutions deliberately rejected the distinctions between delinquency and dependency: "any difference between the youthful criminal and the homeless youth was deceptive."[73] Yet in their very goals and organizations, the best of these raised a new problem: Did they really want to reproduce the larger society that had victimized the children? Ashby concludes that this question troubled them deeply, leading one reformer in 1926 to question "'whether society, as it is, is worth reproducing.'"[74]

These histories reveal that while we have a long distance to go on care for children, it is quite easy to forget just how bad things were until very recently. For instance, a glance at Minehan's Depression classic, *Boy and Girl Tramps of America*, can serve to remind us that thousands of ten-year-old children in the

[72] This is the now-classic argument of Norbert Elias, *The Civilizing Process*, trans. Edmund Jephcott (New York: Urizen Books, 1978–82). Lane, *Violent Death in the City*, uses this notion to account for the decline in late-nineteenth-century urban crime.

[73] Ashby, *Saving the Waifs*, 133.

[74] Ibid., 212.

Depression roamed the country looking for food. Some estimates run as high as 1.25 million homeless children.[75] There must be many seventy-year-olds today who spent a childhood of insecurity and desperation in their daily struggle to survive.

MAGDALENE HOUSES

> We have satisfactorily ascertained the fact that the numbers of females in this city, who abandon themselves to prostitution is not less that TEN THOUSAND!!!!! [which works out to about one woman in five][76]

Magdalene Houses deserve special attention for their role in actively dealing with prostitutes.[77] American Magdalene homes originated in mid-eighteenth-century England, where philanthropic homes at once protected and imprisoned fallen women.[78] In Boston, the City Missionary Society in 1822 founded the Penitent Females' Refuge, theoretically taking women who wished to escape prostitution. Hobson found evidence that no more than one inmate in six applied voluntarily and that most were informally sentenced or forced into the institution. In addition, she found that most ran away rather than formally asked for permission to leave. In any case, the institution was intended to shelter and reform its inmates in a more homelike setting than a jail or poorhouse—and the women got white bread instead of brown, as in the poorhouse.[79] Only slightly later, a similar Catholic institution came to American cities. Administered by the Sisters of the Good Shepherd, a French order, and called the House of the Good Shepherd, it occupied a similar niche in many American cities. The earliest included Louisville (1842), Philadelphia (1856), New York (1857), Chicago (1858), and Boston and six other cities by the end of the Civil War.[80] In the second half of the nineteenth century, Protestant homes grew with the urban West, where women activists "rescued" Chinese prostitutes, women running from polygamous marriages, and Indian women.[81]

These homes could accommodate a relatively small number of long-term

---

[75] Jones, "Crisis of the American Orphanage," 625.

[76] Christine Stansell, *City of Women: Sex and Class in New York, 1789–1860* (Urbana: University of Illinois Press, 1986), 172, quoting John McDowall, *Magdalene Facts* [first annual report of the Magdalene Society] (New York, 1832).

[77] These institutions designed to reform women should be distinguished from those which appeared a bit later in the century, and which simply provided a place to stay. For instance, in 1873 "'The Fraternals, a band of young men connected with the Church of the Strangers,'" created the "Free dormitory for Women" a "stone's throw from Washington Square" in New York City. In December 1873, it lodged 124 women (*New York Times*, February 1, 1874).

[78] For the details, see Hobson, *Uneasy Virtue*.

[79] Ibid., 120.

[80] Holloran, *Boston's Wayward Children*, 127.

[81] See Peggy Pascoe, *Relations of Rescue: The Search for Female Moral Authority in the American West, 1874–1939* (New York: Oxford, 1990).

occupants; there were also those designed for more short-term stays, such as the Temporary Home for Fallen Women in Boston, founded in 1844. Hobson found that while the Penitent Females' Refuge had an inmate population of about twenty, the Temporary Home took in one hundred to four hundred women per year and also ran a boardinghouse.[82] In both, the women were young, between fifteen and twenty-five, and in "various stages of delinquency." While in the short-term institution, women were not trained for domestic service as they were in the long-term institution, but only sewed themselves nice, new clothes for their departure. The designers of these institutions consciously intended them to prevent participation in crime and vice, both by the inmates and their children, born and unborn. The *Prisoner's Friend* in 1850 cited a New York City police chief: "'What fearful fruit will the seeds of sin, thus early sown, bring forth in womanhood?'"[83] By targeting mothers, reformers hoped to stop the production of potential criminals. The same question ultimately was to trouble many leaders in the quintessential and most visible urban reform movement: the settlement house.

Settlement Houses and the "Institutional Church"

The typical settlement is one which provides neutral territory traversing all the lines of racial and religious freedom.[84]

In the last decade of the nineteenth century, as reformers philosophically opposed institutional, or indoor, relief, urban social reform took on several new aspects. The reformers themselves moved into institutions, while those they aided stayed outside. This resulted in part from simple city geographical growth; middle-class and wealthy people no longer lived near or came into daily contact with the very poor. The rowdy boys of the nineteenth century who threw snowballs at gentlemen's tall hats or sold pencils door to door moved out of the middle-class vision.[85] But the social and structurally significant churches remained in the central city, so that by 1880, churches whose name began with "First" had their elite congregations travel in from afar; the neighbors were usually poor and often Catholic. Sometime ministers and parishioners cared: from them came the "Social Gospel" movement, which used the large church structures as a base for social programs. A parallel movement came with an English innovation that captured the imagination of a larger body of American

[82] Hobson, *Uneasy Virtue*, 118–30.

[83] Ibid., 125.

[84] Ruth Hutchinson Crocker, *Social Work and Social Order: The Settlement Movement in Two Industrial Cities, 1889–1930* (Chicago and Urbana: University of Illinois Press, 1992), 66, quoting Robert Woods and Albert Kennedy, *The Handbook of Settlements* (New York: Charities Publication Committee, 1911), v.

[85] Elizabeth Oakes Smith met the boy she wrote about as he sold her newspapers at her window (*The Newsboy* [New York: Derby, 1854]), 5.

social activists: the settlement house. Almost like colonial outposts of the middle class in the slums, these institutions housed mainly nonresidential activities that broadly constituted what we now call social work.[86] Programs in these buildings took features of the preexisting children's institutions, such as the banks, the moral entertainments, and music, and added to them an extensive variety of educational, social-activist, and counseling types of activity.[87]

Though not nearly so well off as the white churches, black churches also launched programs dealing with the plight of the urban poor. Rather than build programs within one church, they often cooperated with other churches to create programs. In late-nineteenth-century Philadelphia, for instance, the Women's Union Christian Association (founded in 1873) aided the destitute with "job placement, guidance, day care and groceries."[88] Lane argues that such reform efforts helped unite black Philadelphians across church and social class lines.

It is important to note that the settlement house, like other urban institutions, had a solid physical presence. Hull House, the best known, started in a large house of relatively recent construction and expanded its infrastructural base to a much larger building complex over the years. Across most U.S. cities, settlement houses either purchased or built their presence in the slum or in working-class districts of cities.[89] Many of the approximately four hundred still stand. Their architectural history is yet to be written, for these structures were examples of sophisticated programmatic design.

From their settlement-house base camps, reformers launched programs for social and individual reform and change. While historians have detailed settlement-house histories, calling them, in Davis's memorable phrase, "spearheads of reform," they have yet to evaluate their many and varied programs.[90] This may never be possible, because the settlements had a physical as well as programmatic presence. As noted in the Introduction to this book, William J. Wilson has made a two-part argument concerning the lack of role models in very poor neighborhoods today: his argument about the exit of working-class

---

[86] See Allan F. Davis, *Spearheads for Reform: The Social Settlements and the Progressive Movement, 1890–1914* (New Brunswick, N.J.: Rutgers University Press, 1984); Clarke A. Chambers, *Seedtime of Reform: American Social Service and Social Action, 1918–1933* (Minneapolis: University of Minnesota Press, 1963).

[87] See for the classic description, Jane Addams, *Twenty Years at Hull House* (New York: Macmillan, 1910).

[88] Roger Lane, *William Dorsey's Philadelphia and Ours* (New York: Oxford University Press, 1991), 296. See also Ralph E. Luker, "Missions, Institutional Churches, and Settlement Houses: The Black Experience, 1885–1910," *Journal of Negro History* 69 (1984 [published 1989]): 101–13.

[89] Ruth H. Crocker, *Social Work and Social Order*, discusses location of settlement houses in the context of race, detailing at least one occasion when a house moved away from an African-American neighborhood. This study explicitly compares white and African-American settlement houses in Gary and Indianapolis.

[90] Davis, *Spearheads for Reform*.

people is most widely noted, but the second part may be more relevant, the exit of institutions. This is because after the 1950s, most social programs became purely bureaucratic: outdoor relief, in nineteenth-century parlance. Settlement houses, orphanages, and various houses of refuge have all disappeared from the landscape of the slum. Dealing with modern institutions of criminal justice or welfare often takes on a Kafkaesque quality, even for the mentally and physically able, because they are complex bureaucracies that require organizational skills and a high degree of literacy to navigate.[91]

Even the large, original churches with their institutional programs have now left. Like settlement houses, the large churches had exerted a physical and programmatic presence in the slum. Settlement houses were almost exclusively Protestant, which enabled them to dovetail ideologically and culturally with programs of the reform-oriented Protestant churches. But after the 1920s, the large, old Protestant churches became less of a reform presence in their neighborhoods, as did settlement houses. Catholic churches proved the exception, and through them some exceptionally important programs of reform and intervention were enacted.[92]

CONCLUSION

For some urban poor, institutional presence made a tremendous difference, and for others, it made none whatsoever. For the tramp Bill Aspinwall, life in the 1890s was a daily struggle to survive, literally on the very margins of the more stable world. Paying train passengers cheered his efforts to hang on to their car's smokestack; he reflected on the tramping worker's marginality as "somewhat exciting, but not pleasant, ennobling nor remunerative."[93] But he proudly avoided the kinds of institutions I have discussed above, carefully distinguishing himself from that class of tramps which would use such institutions. Aspinwall argued that only a small portion of tramping workers corresponded to what we call the underclass, a group for which most tramps had "no use": "They are composed of ex-convicts, Jail Birds, and Regular Dead Beats. . . . It is [this] Class that . . . patronizes the Poor Houses, Jails, &c."[94]

In the remarkable letters of Maimie Pinzer, we do have a chance to see the impact of a reform institution. In 1899, when she was fourteen, her mother and

[91] See Joel Handler, "The Transformation of Aid to Families with Dependent Children: The Family Support Act in Historical Context," *New York University Review of Law and Social Change* 16 (1987): 457–533, app. 2, 529–33. Dulberger, "Refuge or Repressor?" working with letters children wrote back to the superintendent of the Albany Orphan Asylum, cites at least two instances where they ask for or comment on views of the asylum buildings. Rather than finding it oppressing, one boy seemed proud of its size—"'almost as big as a City, well not quite'" (291–92).

[92] See the appendix on research needs for an example of research on such a church-based effort.

[93] From a letter to reformer John J. McCook. Quoted in Roger A. Bruns, *Knights of the Road: A Hobo History* (New York: Methuen, 1980), 66.

[94] Quoted in Bruns, *Knights of the Road*, 64–65.

uncle, working with a city magistrate, had her put in a Magdalene Home, which she described as "a mild sort of reform school for girls who had gone astray," for one year.[95] In her hundreds of pages of letters, this experience merited only one short paragraph, allowing us little more than the assessment that as an institutional experience, she found it neither terrible nor scary.

The specific forms of institutions described here have not always survived— the police lodging rooms, the newsboys' lodging houses—most often because other, less-specific forms of aid have alleviated the original symptoms. Young children, for instance, can live at home and not need to be self-supporting because of Aid to Families with Dependent Children. And for most children, the result is a vastly better and more humane life.

But is it possible that we have also lost some valuable features of institutional life? We know that on occasion these institutions actually seemed to accomplish their ends: perhaps when they helped people achieve regularity and follow rules, they really helped some people to gain an ability to order their daily lives. In our efforts to help the nuclear family be the center of caring, we have perhaps turned too far away from one alternative form and in so doing stigmatized it and the people it has helped. In a sense, we continue today with a radical individualism, which tries to be sensitive to individual differences then rejects institutional variety. Thus we have built a welfare state that is more comprehensive than its nineteenth-century predecessor but that is in its own way so bureaucratic as to lose all flexibility and responsiveness.

We have something to learn from our predecessors about our welfare and crime-control systems. They were proud of what they did, perhaps out of naïveté. If we were to value our own public commitments, we might also regain some of that pride, and we might be able to see our difficult social responsibilities in another light. If we were to value our professional, social, and political expenditures the way that our predecessors did, we might work at improving the public sector. We may no longer need the imposing public buildings that we once had, but we do need to value the public sector in order to make it work better. Such pride need not preclude serious criticism and evaluation. Indeed, a part of responsibility would be to seek out criticism and work to make a better civic response. Such pride would help us conceptualize the organizational and bureaucratic responses to need as a part of our civic obligation, an obligation which we should accept openly and positively as that of a mature society.

Appendix: Research Tasks

The increasing number of historians working on histories related to the welfare, social-control institutions, and the people with which they deal suggests that

---

[95] Rosen and Davidson, *The Maimie Papers*, 196.

there is little need to urge more of all kinds of research. But there are a few key areas that may be overlooked, and in which serious work is very much needed so that we may continue to augment our understanding of both the past and present.

First, serious efforts at constructing data series are essential. These include data on the number of and people in or served by various institutions, including the number and kinds of institutions themselves.

Second, we need an accounting of social expenditures that includes local, state, and federal governments plus private organizations, infrastructural costs, opportunity costs (in addition to lost taxes; this includes the opportunity costs represented by women and members of religious orders who worked for dramatically lower salaries because of a restricted labor market). Both of these efforts must be at a standard that would result in new data series for the *Historical Statistics of the United States*.

Third, we need imitations of Schlossman and Sedlak's evaluation of a Catholic-church-based program, Clifford Shaw's Chicago Area Project, which operated from the 1930s until 1959, and was a long crime-reduction project that embodied many of the most popular early twentieth-century reform theories.[96] A neighborhood-based project launched out of a church, it incorporated active interventions into the lives of children and families. In their work, Schlossman and Sedlak conclude that the project had important and, at the time, ignored successes. Now, twenty-five years after Shaw's own self-critical evaluation of his project, the question for social programs has become, What works? Reevaluating previous histories becomes a significant way to evaluate policy.

Finally, there is a significant theoretical problem: the transition from yesterday's local systems to today's national/local mix, once adequately measured, then needs to be recast in the context of the Peterson thesis, which shows how transfer payments migrate to levels of government that deter bidding while promotional expenditures remain local and market oriented.[97] This thesis, which makes complete sense of the current scene, appears to contradict the actual trajectory of the institution-building period of the American state. Only careful research and reanalysis will resolve this contradiction: so doing will lead to new analyses of proper governmental roles in policy for the underclass. And along the way, we may find a great deal to learn from our predecessors' successes and failures.

[96] Steven Schlossman and Michael Sedlak, "The Chicago Area Project Revisited" (Santa Monica, Calif.: Rand, 1983).

[97] Paul Peterson, *City Limits* (Chicago: University of Chicago Press, 1981).

CHAPTER 11

Urban Education and the "Truly Disadvantaged": The Historical Roots of the Contemporary Crisis, 1945–1990

Harvey Kantor and Barbara Brenzel

THIRTY YEARS AGO James Bryant Conant alarmed the nation by calling attention to the inadequacies of urban education. Concerned about the growing disparity between inner-city schools and schools in the suburbs, Conant pointed out that while suburban schools prospered, urban schools were in a state of crisis, plagued by insufficient funding and outdated facilities, low academic achievement, and exceedingly high drop-out rates. Indeed, Conant warned the nation that the deterioration of urban schooling coupled with high levels of youth unemployment and the persistence of racial segregation was a recipe for social disaster that threatened the health of the nation's large cities and which could be avoided only by improving urban schools and broadening the employment prospects of inner-city youth.[1]

Beginning in the 1960s, the federal government launched an unprecedented series of programs to address the urban problems Conant had documented. Together with other initiatives begun by states and local school districts, these programs provided much-needed funding for urban schools and contributed to some measurable gains in achievement as well as an increase in educational attainment among economically disadvantaged and minority children. But despite these programs and the improvements they produced, urban schools today remain in a state of crisis. After two-and-a-half decades of federal, state, and local efforts to improve urban education for low-income children, achievement in inner-city schools continues to lag behind national norms, and drop-out rates in inner-city high schools (especially among African-American and Hispanic youth) remain distressingly high, while many of those who do graduate are often so poorly prepared they cannot compete successfully in the labor market. One recent report on urban education concluded that because of their continued failure to educate city children, many people now dismiss urban

We would like to express our appreciation to the Spencer Foundation for supporting this research and to Sharon LaSalle for her research assistance. We would also like to thank Andrew Gitlin, Ellen Lagemann, Robert Lowe, and Frank Margonis for their helpful comments.

[1] James Bryant Conant, *Slums and Suburbs* (New York: McGraw Hill, 1961).

schools "as little more than human storehouses to keep young people off the streets."[2]

Liberals and conservatives offer different explanations for the persistence of this crisis in urban education. The standard liberal view generally attributes the contemporary crisis in urban education to the inadequacies of the reforms instituted in the 1960s. According to this view, even though the Great Society stimulated a considerable effort at both the national and local levels to address the problems of urban education, the escalation of the war in Vietnam, the growth of inflation, and the urban riots of the 1960s eroded the country's financial and political commitment to equal opportunity and racial justice before the new school reforms could be funded sufficiently or implemented adequately. The end result has been a patchwork of new programs too marginal and too fragmented to have much impact on urban schooling and the education of poor and minority children. Many liberal observers contend that because of the constraints imposed on the social policies of the 1960s, the changes in schooling were actually much less substantial than some critics have subsequently claimed.[3]

Conservative critics also blame the crisis in urban education on the failure of the policies initiated in the 1960s. But in contrast to the liberal view, the conservative perspective maintains that the current failure of urban schooling is due to the very nature of the reforms themselves. According to this view, efforts to end school segregation, provide compensatory educational services for the poor, and expand participation in school governance, however well intentioned, undermined academic requirements and trapped school leaders in a web of regulations that made it impossible for the schools to perform their essential educational and social functions. Conservative critics contend that schools today should return to a conventional, discipline-based approach to subject matter and a structured approach to the mastery of skills in order to restore standards of excellence undermined by the educational policies of the 1960s and 1970s.[4]

---

[2] The Carnegie Foundation for the Advancement of Teaching, *An Imperiled Generation: Saving Urban Schools* (Princeton: Princeton University Press, 1988), p. xi. On the condition of urban schools and their failure to serve economically disadvantaged students and students of color, also see Henry M. Levin, "The Educationally Disadvantaged: A National Crisis" (Institute for Research on Educational Finance and Governance, Stanford University, program report no. 85-B1, July 1985). For a review of recent reports on the condition of urban education, see James H. Lytle, "Reforming Urban Education: A Review of Recent Reports and Legislation," *Urban Review* 22 (1990): 199–220.

[3] For a statement of this position, see Carl Kaestle and Marshall Smith, "The Federal Role in Elementary and Secondary Education," *Harvard Educational Review* 52 (November 1982): 384–408.

[4] For example, see Diane Ravitch, *The Troubled Crusade: American Education, 1945–1980* (New York: Basic Books, 1983). This is also a common theme of many of the major commission reports that sparked the interest in educational excellence in the early 1980s. For instance, the report of the Twentieth Century Fund Task Force, *Making the Grade*, stated that "[government] emphasis on

These disagreements are hardly minor. But because they tend to focus on matters of educational policy per se at the expense of long-term trends in the social and economic context in which schools operate, both of these perspectives on the recent history of urban education generally fail to acknowledge how fundamental changes in the society and economy—particularly changes in the social ecology of cities and the structure of urban labor markets—have shaped the development of urban education since World War II. Consequently, neither liberal nor conservative analyses of the contemporary crisis in urban education explain adequately why the educational initiatives begun in the 1960s have failed so frequently to live up to the expectations of their proponents or why conditions in urban schools have not substantially improved over the last two decades.

A few exceptional books have been written on poverty and the urban crisis that shed light on these issues, most notably William Julius Wilson's *Truly Disadvantaged* and David T. Ellwood's *Poor Support*. Both of these books analyze the limitations of antipoverty policies that fail to take into account the deterioration of employment opportunities for the inner-city poor. They point out how the reorganization of the American economy since World War II has created a bifurcated labor market, locking poorly educated inner-city youth into low-wage jobs, despite the implementation of social policies designed to improve their life chances. Neither book discusses educational policy, though they both suggest that the contemporary crisis in urban education cannot be understood apart from recent changes in the nature of the urban labor market.[5]

Equally important is Ira Katznelson and Margaret Weir's recent book, *Schooling for All*. Whereas Wilson and Ellwood focus chiefly on the lack of employment opportunities for inner-city youth, Katznelson and Weir examine changes in geography, society, and politics that over the past four decades have altered fundamentally the sociology of public education. Their analysis points out how changes in the geographic distribution of the American population between cities and suburbs and the spatial patterning of race and class that accompanied these changes have undermined public education's capacity to redistribute resources and opportunity in American society. In contrast to both liberal and conservative analyses, their argument suggests that the inequities and difficulties in urban education have become so inextricably bound up with basic features of social geography that they pose a fundamental challenge to the nation's commitment to equal schooling for all.[6]

---

promoting equality of opportunity has meant a slighting of its commitment to educational equality." See *Making the Grade: Report of the Twentieth Century Fund Task Force on Federal Elementary and Secondary Education Policy* (New York: Twentieth Century Fund, 1983), p. 6.

[5] William Julius Wilson, *The Truly Disadvantaged: The Inner City, the Underclass, and Public Policy* (Chicago: University of Chicago Press, 1987); David Ellwood, *Poor Support: Poverty and the American Family* (New York: Basic Books, 1988).

[6] Ira Katznelson and Margaret Weir, *Schooling for All: Race, Class, and the Democratic Ideal* (New York: Basic Books, 1985).

The current condition of urban education is not of course solely a product of these changes in social geography and labor markets. Nor is it entirely new. There has never been a "golden age" when urban schools provided equal educational opportunity for the mass of students.[7] But the postwar transformation of social space and urban labor markets reshaped the urban landscape and changed the social and economic contours of urban education in ways that have made equal opportunity and popular control particularly difficult to secure. Without reference to these developments, it is impossible to make sense of the recent history of urban schooling or to understand the constraints on the capacity of public policy to shape the development of urban education.

This chapter addresses these issues. It argues that the postwar transformation of American cities gave new form to long-standing racial divisions and economic inequities in American education and intensified the barriers to educational success facing low-income and minority students. At the same time, changes in the structure of urban economies pushed undereducated minority workers out of the labor market and increasingly dimmed the economic prospects for many better-educated workers as well. As a result, urban schools have been unable to expand educational and economic opportunities for inner-city children. But neither have urban schools and school systems done much to address the new problems they have faced or to counteract the inequities on which they have been based. On the contrary, largely because of the persistence of bureaucratic structures of decision making and organization, they have responded grudgingly and inadequately to their changed social and economic setting and remain nearly as unresponsive to the voices of low-income and minority students and parents as they were when Conant wrote *Slums and Suburbs*, three decades ago.

THE SOCIAL ECOLOGY OF AMERICAN CITIES

The most basic factor in the development of urban school systems since the end of the Second World War has been the spatial redistribution of the population from cities to suburbs. Though urban outmigration was hardly a new phenomenon in American life, the pace and dimensions of this postwar shift in the territorial distribution of the population and its effects on the organization of social space were unprecedented. Facilitated by public policies that encouraged home ownership in the suburbs, city dwellers in the postwar years left for the urban fringes more rapidly and in greater numbers than ever before. In the process, as the chapters by Thomas Sugrue and David Bartelt show, the nation's metropolitan areas were remade, and the social and economic context of urban education was substantially transformed.

---

[7] Ann Bastian, Norm Fruchter, Marilyn Gittell, Colin Greer, and Kenneth Haskins, *Choosing Equality: The Case for Democratic Schooling* (Philadelphia: Temple University Press, 1986), p. 8.

This shift in the territorial distribution of the population dwarfed prewar migration patterns and reversed long-term trends in city growth, particularly in the Northeast and Midwest. What made this reorganization of space after World War II so significant to the history of urban education, however, is not just its magnitude but the spatial patterning of race and class that accompanied it. For what changed most dramatically with the suburbanization of the American population was not just the relative proportion of the population living in cities and suburbs, but the racial and economic distribution of the population within metropolitan areas.

Two processes were at work here: the migration of African Americans and Hispanics to Northern cities, as described in Joe Trotter's chapter, and the flight of white Americans to the suburbs. Though black migration to Northern cities first began during World War I, as late as 1940, nearly 80 percent of the nation's black population still lived in the South and 63 percent lived in rural areas. But the mechanization of Southern agriculture and the wartime demand for labor in Northern factories pushed black Southerners off the land and pulled them into urban centers in the North. During the 1940s, 1.6 million African Americans migrated from the South to Northern and Western cities and another 1.5 million followed in the 1950s. By 1970, 47 percent of all African Americans lived outside the South and three-quarters lived in metropolitan areas.[8]

African-American migration from the South slowed in the 1970s. At the same time, however, Hispanic immigrants from Mexico, Central America, and the Caribbean (especially from Puerto Rico) began moving to major American cities in growing numbers. Mexicans and especially Puerto Ricans had of course been present in American cities earlier, but their numbers increased especially rapidly after 1970. By 1980, the Hispanic population numbered 581,000 in Chicago, 118,000 in Philadelphia, 90,000 in Boston, and over 1.5 million in New York, where nearly one-fifth of the population was Spanish speaking. In 1985, Hispanics accounted for nearly 16 percent of the population of central cities in the Northeast, compared to 11.5 percent ten years earlier.[9]

---

[8] Mark I. Gelfand, *A Nation of Cities: The Federal Government and Urban America, 1933–1965* (New York: Oxford University Press, 1975), p. 196; Raymond C. Hummel and John M. Nagle, *Urban Education in America: Problems and Prospects* (New York: Oxford University Press, 1973), pp. 75–78; William Issel, *Social Change in the United States, 1945–1980* (New York: Schocken Books, 1985), pp. 162–63. For a social history of the black migration to Northern cities after World War II, see Nicholas Lemann, *The Promised Land: The Great Black Migration and How It Changed America* (New York: Alfred A. Knopf, 1991).

[9] William H. Frey and Alden Speare, Jr., *Regional and Metropolitan Growth and Decline in the United States* (New York: Russell Sage, 1988), p. 273; John D. Kasarda, "Jobs, Migration, and Emerging Urban Mismatches," in Michael G. H. McGeary and Laurence Lynn, Jr., eds., *Urban Change and Poverty* (Washington, D.C.: National Academy Press, 1988), p. 57; Gary Orfield, *The Chicago Study of Access and Choice in Higher Education: A Report to the Illinois Senate Committee on Higher Education* (Chicago: University of Chicago, Committee on Public Policy Studies Research Project, 1984), pp. 38–39.

While African Americans and then Hispanics moved into Northern cities in steadily increasing numbers, first middle-class and later working-class whites moved out. As the pace of suburbanization accelerated during the 1950s, New York, Chicago, Philadelphia, Detroit, Boston, and Saint Louis all suffered a net loss of white population, a trend that persisted in the 1960s and 1970s. By 1980, only 28 percent of the white population in metropolitan areas in the Northeast and Midwest lived in central cities, compared to 77 percent of blacks.[10]

This racial division between city and suburb was not just the result of consumer preference or the chance workings of the market. In the 1940s and 1950s, as Bartelt's chapter demonstrates, white hostility toward minorities together with the use of restrictive covenants that prohibited white homeowners from selling to minorities, Federal Housing Authority policies that discouraged loans to racially mixed neighborhoods in favor of those to all-white residential developments in the suburbs, and suburban zoning practices designed to preserve residential class segregation all effectively closed the suburbs to minority families. This began to change in the 1960s and 1970s, when the passage of antidiscrimination legislation coupled with rising income among the black middle class helped open segments of the suburban housing market formerly off-limits to African Americans and other people of color. But even then, the persistence of discrimination continued to keep the majority of African-American families in the city, while the process of ghettoization in the suburbs confined most black suburbanites to areas already housing blacks or abandoned by whites.[11] Although the pace of black suburbanization accelerated in the 1970s, the result of the reorganization of social space after the war was the racial and economic polarization of the nation's large metropolitan areas.[12]

The economic distinction between center and periphery that accompanied this shift in the racial distribution of the population was equally striking. Though median family income rose in cities as well as suburbs between 1950 and 1980, the income gap between city and suburban families grew wider each decade. After 1950, the suburb-to-city ratio of median family income increased in every major metropolitan area of the country. By 1980, median household income in all central cities had fallen to 74 percent of that in the suburbs,

[10] Paul Peterson, "Economic and Political Trends Affecting Education," in Ron Haskins and Duncan MacRae, eds., *Policies for America's Schools: Teachers, Equity, and Indicators* (Norwood, N.J.: Ablex Publishing, 1988), pp. 44–46; Frey and Speare, *Regional and Metropolitan Growth*, p. 522.

[11] Kenneth T. Jackson, *Crabgrass Frontier: The Suburbanization of the United States* (Oxford: Oxford University Press, 1985), p. 241; U.S. Commission on Civil Rights, *Racial Isolation in the Schools* (Washington, D.C.: Government Printing Office, 1967), 1:21–25; Issel, *Social Change*, p. 100; Gelfand, *Nation of Cities*, pp. 219–20.

[12] Frey and Speare, *Regional and Metropolitan Growth*, p. 524; John D. Kasarda, "Emerging Urban Mismatches," p. 157. On this point, also see U.S. Commission on Civil Rights, *Racial Isolation in the Schools*, pp. 11–12, 18; Jackson, *Crabgrass Frontier*, pp. 150, 241, 274; Issel, *Social Change*, pp. 99–101.

compared to 80 percent in 1970, and just three years later had declined again to 72 percent.[13]

This connection between income and location was tightened after 1970 largely because poverty was increasingly concentrated in central cities. Though poverty rates declined everywhere during the 1960s, the number of poor people living in the nation's central cities nearly doubled during the 1970s and early 1980s, and the urban poverty rate climbed while it continued to fall in the suburbs and nonmetropolitan areas. This hardly made poverty unique to the city. But as poverty rates rose in central cities and fell outside them, the proportion of all poor people in the United States living in cities increased from 27 percent in 1959 to 43 percent in 1985, and poverty came to be seen more and more as an urban phenomenon.[14]

Urban poverty was not limited exclusively to African Americans and other people of color. But the concentration of the poverty population in central cities was strongly linked to the changing racial composition of urban areas and rising poverty rates among African Americans and Hispanics.[15] Moreover, poor African Americans and Hispanics were also more likely than poor whites to live in low-income neighborhoods. For this reason, as the racial composition of the city shifted and as urban poverty rates rose, poverty also became concentrated in particular "poverty areas" within cities. Kathryn Neckerman and William Julius Wilson have calculated that in the nation's fifty largest cities, the number of people living in poverty areas (i.e., census tracts with a poverty rate of at least 20 percent) rose by more than 20 percent between 1970 and 1980, though the total population in these cities fell 5 percent. In the nation's ten largest cities in 1970, the concentration of the poor in poverty areas was even more pronounced, especially among African Americans.[16]

[13] Frey and Speare, *Regional and Metropolitan Growth*, p. 528; Jackson, *Crabgrass Frontier*, p. 8. Also see U.S. Commission on Civil Rights, *Racial Isolation in the Schools* 1:19–20; Robert Havighurst, *Education in Metropolitan Areas* (Boston: Allyn and Bacon, 1966), p. 61; Hummel and Nagle, *Urban Education*, p. 80; and specifically on poverty in New York City, Emmanuel Tobier, *The Changing Face of Poverty: Trends in New York City's Population in Poverty, 1960–1990* (New York: Community Service Society, 1984), p. 40.

[14] Paul Peterson, "The Urban Underclass and the Poverty Paradox," in Paul Peterson and Christopher Jencks, eds., *The Urban Underclass* (Washington, D.C.: Brookings Institution, 1991), p. 7; William Julius Wilson, Robert Aponte, Joleen Kirschenman, and Loic J. D. Wacquant, "The Ghetto Underclass and the Changing Structure of Urban Poverty," in Fred Harris and Roger Wilkins, eds., *Quiet Riots: Race and Poverty in the United States* (New York: Pantheon Books, 1988), pp. 125–28; Martha A. Gephart and Robert W. Pearson, "Contemporary Research on the Urban Underclass," *Items* 42 (June 1988): 1.

[15] Wilson et al., "Ghetto Underclass," pp. 125–28.

[16] Kathryn Neckerman and William Julius Wilson, "Schools and Poor Communities," in Council of Chief State School Officers, ed., *School Success for Students at Risk* (Orlando, Fla.: Harcourt Brace Jovanovich, 1988). Nationally, in 1980, approximately 9 percent of the poor lived in extreme poverty areas. The proportion of the poor living in these areas varied by race, however. Only 2 percent of the non-Hispanic white poor, compared to 16 percent of the Hispanic poor and 21 percent of the African-American poor, lived in extreme poverty areas. As a result, in 1980, 65 per-

This connection between race, class, and location was of course hardly an entirely new feature of urban life in America. From the moment of the first great black migration to Northern cities during World War I, the combination of discriminatory local real estate practices (later reinforced by federal housing policies) and white violence segregated blacks from whites and forced African Americans to live in the least desirable city neighborhoods, while discrimination in the labor market kept many black and other minority families locked in poverty.[17] But together with the fragmentation of local political jurisdictions, the new social ecology of American cities institutionalized prewar patterns of class and racial separation, creating geographically distinct communities with different social and economic opportunities and problems, and different capacities to meet them.[18]

THE SOCIAL TRANSFORMATION OF URBAN EDUCATION

Nowhere were the effects of these changes in the social organization of space more evident than in the public schools. As the pace of suburbanization accelerated after 1950, distancing the white middle class from the city, the class and racial composition of city schools was altered, and the connection between race, income, and school location was tightened. In the process, city schools became more and more associated with low educational achievement, and the inequities between city and suburban schools became more clearly marked. As Peter Schrag observed over twenty years ago, just as the Supreme Court was mandating the dismantling of the old dual system of schooling, the transformation of space was creating two new separate and unequal systems of schooling in many metropolitan areas: one mainly for low-income children of color in the cities, the other largely for middle-class children in the suburbs.[19]

---

cent of the 2.4 million poor people living in extreme poverty neighborhoods were African American, 22 percent Hispanic, and 13 percent non-Hispanic white. On the concentration of urban poverty, see Paul A. Jargowsky and Mary Jo Bane, "Ghetto Poverty in the United States," in Jencks and Peterson, *Urban Underclass*, pp. 251–52; Wilson et al., "Ghetto Underclass," pp. 129–31; Wilson, *Truly Disadvantaged*, chap. 2.

[17] On the development of racial segregation in northern American cities, see Allan H. Spear, *Black Chicago: The Making of a Negro Ghetto, 1890–1920* (Chicago: University of Chicago Press, 1967); Gilbert Osofsky, *Harlem: The Making of a Ghetto*, 2d. ed. (New York: Harper Torchbooks, 1971); Kenneth L. Kusmer, *A Ghetto Takes Shape: Black Cleveland, 1870–1930* (Urbana: University of Illinois Press, 1976); Gary Orfield, "Ghettoization and Its Alternatives," in Paul Peterson, ed., *The New Urban Reality* (Washington, D.C.: Brookings Institution, 1985), pp. 161–93.

[18] Katznelson and Weir, *Schooling for All*, p. 219. Also see Orfield, "Ghettoization," p. 163; Jackson, *Crabgrass Frontier*, p. 241; Douglas S. Massey, Gretchen A. Condran, and Nancy A. Denton, "The Effect of Residential Segregation on Black Social and Economic Well-Being," *Social Forces* 66 (September 1987): 29–56.

[19] Peter Schrag, *Village School Downtown: Boston Schools, Boston Politics* (Boston: Beacon Press, 1967), pp. 154–56. Also see John L. Rury, "The Changing Social Context of Urban Education: A National Perspective" (Milwaukee Public Schools History Project, March 1990), p. 13.

As white families moved out of the city and African Americans and Hispanics moved in, the racial and economic composition of the urban school population changed dramatically. In nearly every major urban school system in the country, the number of white students declined while the number of minority students increased. And even in those cities where whites increased absolutely, the proportion of whites in the school population declined because African-American and Hispanic enrollment rose more rapidly. Whereas whites had been a majority in all of the nation's largest school systems except Washington, D.C., in 1950, by 1968, six of the ten largest school systems in the country were more than half minority, and by 1980 all were two-thirds and most were at least three-fourths minority.[20]

Indeed, because African-American and Hispanic city dwellers were younger, had more children, and were less likely to send their children to private schools than were whites, city school systems enrolled a greater proportion of minority students than the proportion of minorities in the city population as a whole. In 1970, for example, people of color made up 31 percent of New York's entire population but 54 percent of those enrolled in school. The pattern was the same in Chicago, Philadelphia, Detroit, and Los Angeles, and nothing altered it in the 1970s. By 1980 the proportion of minority children enrolled in city schools was at least one-and-a-half times as great as the proportion of minorities in the entire city population in all of the fifteen largest city school systems.[21]

Segregated housing combined with local school-attendance policies intended to separate blacks and whites by sending them to different schools meant that as the proportion of minority students increased, most found themselves in segregated schools in the North and Midwest as well as in the South. The U.S. Commission on Civil Rights reported that in seventy-five cities in 1965–66, 75 percent of African-American elementary children were in 90-percent-black schools (while 83 percent of white students were in nearly all-white schools) and nearly nine of ten African-American elementary students attended majority black schools. In Los Angeles, Detroit, Philadelphia, Chicago, Dallas, Houston, and Milwaukee, the proportion of African-American elementary students in majority black schools ranged from 87 to 97 percent. According to the commission, between 1950 and 1965 (and twelve years after the *Brown* decision), segregation actually increased in many inner-city schools, especially in the

[20] U.S. Commission on Civil Rights, *Racial Isolation in the Schools* 1:12–19; Gary Orfield, *Public School Desegregation in the United States, 1968–1980* (Washington, D.C.: Joint Center for Policy Studies, 1983), p. 23; Gary Orfield, "Separate Societies: Have the Kerner Warnings Come True?" in Harris and Wilkins, *Quiet Riots*, p. 113; Reynolds Farley, *Blacks and Whites: Narrowing the Gap* (Cambridge: Harvard University Press, 1984), p. 32.

[21] Joel S. Berke and Michael Kirst, *Federal Aid to Education* (Lexington, Mass.: D. C. Heath, 1972), p. 17; National Advisory Commission on Civil Disorders, *Report of the National Advisory Commission on Civil Disorders* (New York: Bantam Books, 1968; reprint, New York: Pantheon Books, 1988), p. 431; Orfield, *Public School Desegregation*, pp. 27–28.

North and Midwest. In fifteen Northern cities studied by the commission, 84 percent of the increase in African-American enrollment was absorbed in nearly all-black schools and 97 percent in majority-black schools.[22]

After 1968, school segregation of African Americans decreased nationwide. Largely because of increased pressure from the federal courts, the proportion of African Americans in nearly all-black schools declined from 64 to 33 percent between 1968 and 1980, and the proportion in majority-black schools decreased from 76 to 63 percent. But changes in segregation varied by region. Although the proportion of African-American students in all-black and majority-black schools dropped substantially in the South, segregation remained above the national average in the Midwest and West and increased in the Northeast, especially in Northern cities. In New York, Chicago, Philadelphia, and Detroit, African-American students actually became more isolated from white students during the 1970s, while in Chicago, Cleveland, and many other large cities, the level of school segregation in 1980 was similar to what it had been in many Southern cities in the early 1960s.[23]

This increase in racial isolation in Northern and Midwestern cities was partly attributable to tensions over court-ordered school integration. Though pressure from the courts succeeded in reducing segregation in some cities (especially small and middle-size ones), it also threatened many middle-class whites. Fearful that school integration would undermine the quality of urban education, they began sending their children to private schools or moving to the suburbs, where they thought schools were superior, leaving city schools to African Americans, Hispanics, and those whites too poor to leave or to opt out of the public system.[24] But the growth of racial isolation was not due only to the escalation of

[22] U.S. Commission on Civil Rights, *Racial Isolation in the Schools*, 1:3–9; also see Kenneth Clark, *Dark Ghetto: Dilemmas of Social Power* (New York: Harper Torchbooks, 1965), p. 112.

[23] Farley, *Blacks and Whites*, pp. 25–29; Orfield, *Public School Desegregation*, pp. 12, 15–19. Hispanic students also became more racially isolated in the 1970s, even though the Supreme Court ruled in 1973, in *Keyes v. Denver School District No. 1*, that Hispanics as well as African Americans should be included in any desegregation plan. Indeed, in contrast to the desegregation picture for African Americans, which varied by region, Hispanics became more segregated in every region of the country between 1968 and 1980. In the West, which had 44 percent of the nation's Hispanic students and where Hispanics made up one-fifth of the school population, the percentage of Hispanic students in predominantly minority schools increased from 42.4 to 63.5 percent, though Hispanic students remained most segregated in the Northeast, where 76.3 percent were in predominantly minority schools in 1980.

[24] African-American parents also made use of private schools, including Catholic schools, in greater numbers during the 1970s. Black enrollment in Catholic schools increased 20 percent and the total number of black elementary- and secondary-school students attending private schools increased 30 percent between 1970 and 1979. After 1979, however, the number of black private-school students declined by 25 percent, chiefly because of a decline in the number enrolled in church-related schools. As a result, in 1985 the proportion of African-American students enrolled in private schools was a little under 4 percent, approximately what it was in 1970. Largely because Hispanics and non-Hispanic whites had higher enrollment rates in church-related schools, the

white fears about the consequences of court-ordered integration. Although integration plans accelerated the movement of whites to the suburbs, especially during the first year in which a city's schools were desegregated, the decline in white enrollment due to "white flight" was relatively small compared to long-run trends such as the movement of whites away from central cities. Because suburbanization left so few whites in city schools, African-American and Hispanic students became more isolated from white students whether or not a city was under a court-ordered plan to desegregate.[25]

In the early 1970s, civil rights groups challenged the legality of this pattern of city-suburban school segregation. But in contrast to its earlier decisions in Southern and urban school desegregation cases, the Supreme Court in 1974 ruled out for all intents and purposes legal action to remedy the effects of city-suburban segregation on the racial composition of city schools, at least in the Northeast and Midwest. In *Milliken v. Bradley*, the court reversed the decision of the lower federal court, which had found that metropolitan school segregation in Detroit was the product of unconstitutional state and local actions and that metropolitan desegregation was required to alleviate the situation. Instead, the court stressed the importance of "local control over the operation of schools" and held that concern for "local autonomy" must take precedence over the effort to desegregate the children of Detroit and its surrounding suburbs. In order to secure a broader remedy, the court concluded, it must be proven that violations had occurred in suburban districts, most of which had few minority students, or that suburban district lines had been drawn with racial intent. Otherwise, desegregation must proceed only within the city limits, even though, as Justice Thurgood Marshall pointed out in his dissenting opinion, this meant that because of the social ecology of American cities, racial and economic segregation would only get worse.[26]

---

private-school enrollment rate of Hispanic and non-Hispanic white students was considerably higher. In 1985, 11.9 percent of non-Hispanic white students and 6.7 percent of Hispanic students were enrolled in private schools. This represented a decline from sightly more than 8 percent in 1970 among Hispanic students and only a slight increase among non-Hispanic whites. For all racial groups, the proportion attending private school increased with family income. Overall, the proportion of elementary- and secondary-school students enrolled in private schools was about the same in 1985 as in 1970 and actually decreased in central cities between 1980 and 1985, perhaps because the 1982–83 recession made private schools too expensive for many families. On private school enrollments, see Center for Education Statistics, *Private School Enrollment and Tuition Trends* (Washington, D.C.: Office of Educational Research and Improvement, 1986).

[25] Farley, *Blacks and Whites*, pp. 25–29; Orfield, *Public School Desegregation*, pp. 12, 15–19; David R. James, "City Limits on Racial Equality: The Effects of City-Suburb Boundaries on Public-School Desegregation, 1968–1976," *American Sociological Review* 54 (December 1989): 963–85. On the effects of court-ordered school desegregation on white flight, see Diane Ravitch, "The 'White Flight' Controversy," *Public Interest* 51 (Spring 1978): 135–49, and the responses by Christine Rossell and David Armor in the same issue.

[26] J. Harvie Wilkinson III, *From Brown to Bakke: The Supreme Court and School Integration, 1954–1978* (Oxford: Oxford University Press, 1979), pp. 216–26; Gary Orfield, *Must We Bus? Segregated*

Indeed, absent court action, the changing racial composition of the urban school population increasingly concentrated minority students in the city and intensified the racial and economic distinctions between urban and suburban schools. As whites fled city schools and the proportion of minority students grew, central-city schools enrolled the vast proportion of minority students in metropolitan areas, especially in the Northeast and Midwest, and had a much greater number of schools with a majority of minority students. At the same time, because African-American, Hispanic, and other students of color were more likely to come from poor families than were their white (or minority) counterparts in the suburbs, the number of economically disadvantaged students in city schools also increased, and city schools accounted for a growing proportion of all poor students in metropolitan areas.[27]

Nowhere did these connections between race, poverty, and location become more apparent than in Chicago, as Gary Orfield's 1984 study of the metropolitan Chicago public schools illustrated. By 1980, 60 percent of the students enrolled in Chicago's schools were African American, 18 percent were Hispanic, and 22 percent were white; 58 percent also came from low-income families. Of these low-income students, 57 percent attended all-minority schools, while 22 percent of the city's minority students attended schools that were composed completely of children from low-income families. By contrast, 85 percent of the students in the suburbs were white, and 9 percent came from low-income families. Only ten out of eighty-five of these suburban districts had a minority enrollment over 20 percent and a low-income enrollment above the suburban average of 9 percent; sixty-six had minority enrollments of less than 10 percent, half had less than 5 percent low income, and only six of the eighty-five districts had low-income enrollments over 20 percent.[28]

The connections between race, poverty, and urban education are especially

---

Schools and National Policy (Washington, D.C.: Brookings Institution, 1978), pp. 31–36; Gary Orfield, "Federal Policy, Local Power, and Metropolitan Segregation," *Political Science Quarterly* 89 (Winter 1974–75): 793–95.

[27] One U.S. Office of Education study, which examined poverty rates in the nation's schools, reported that in the late 1970s 49 percent of the schools in big cities (over 500,000) but only 4 percent of suburban schools had more than 50 percent low-income students. Cited in Alison Wolfe, "The State of Urban Schools," *Urban Education* 13 (July 1978): 190–91. On poverty rates and urban education, also see Mary M. Kennedy, Richard K. Jung, and Martin E. Orland, *Poverty, Achievement and the Distribution of Compensatory Education Services: An Interim Report from the National Assessment of Chapter 1* (Washington, D.C.: Office of Educational Research and Improvement, 1986), pp. 54–56; Orfield et al., *Chicago Study*, pp. 100–114; Christopher Jaeger, "Minority and Low Income High Schools: Educational Inequality in Metropolitan Los Angeles" (University of Chicago, Metropolitan Opportunity Project, October 1987); Marc V. Levine and John F. Zipp, "City at Risk: The Changing Social and Economic Context of Milwaukee Public Schooling, 1920–1988" (Milwaukee Public Schools History Project, University of Wisconsin at Milwaukee, March 1990); Havighurst, *Education in Metropolitan Areas*, chap. 3.

[28] Orfield et al., *Chicago Study*, pp. 100–114.

well documented for Chicago. But evidence from other cities makes clear that the situation in Chicago was not unique. In Milwaukee, for instance, over half of those enrolled in the city's schools in 1985 were African American, 11 percent were Hispanic and other students of color, and 35 percent were white; approximately one-third of the students were also low income, and in some city schools, over 60 percent of the students came from poor families. In the typical Milwaukee suburban high school, on the other hand, most of the students were white, and only 8 percent were low income. Overall, 58 of 102 schools in Milwaukee but only one school in its surrounding suburbs had more than 25 percent low-income students. In Los Angeles, in contrast to Milwaukee, Hispanics were the largest group in the city schools in 1986. They made up 44 percent of the city's students (up from 15 percent in 1967), while African Americans were 15 percent (a 2 percent increase since 1967). But, as in Milwaukee, a strong connection existed between the percentage of minority students and the concentration of low-income students in city schools. Of the ten lowest-income schools in metropolitan Los Angeles in 1976, six were in the city in 1976 and seven were in the city in 1986, and all ten were in Los Angeles County.[29]

The concentration of poor and minority students in city schools thus tightened the connection between the class and racial composition of the school and its location. But this was not the only consequence of the changes in the composition of school enrollment that occurred after the war. As middle-class whites left urban schools and the proportion of poor and minority students grew, urban education also became more and more associated with educational failure. Although nationwide, African-American and Hispanic students succeeded in school in greater numbers than in the past, in inner-city schools in the nation's largest metropolitan areas educational outcomes consistently lagged behind outcomes in the suburbs, especially in those urban schools with the greatest concentrations of minority and economically disadvantaged students.

This was evident both in school achievement and school completion rates. In large Northern cities in 1973, 42 percent of the children fell below the 25th percentile in reading, compared to 15 percent in the suburbs; in 1977, 41 percent of big-city schools reported that half their students were reading one year or more below grade level, while suburbs had only 3.5 percent of their schools in this category. In Chicago five years later, only two out of seventy high schools scored above the national average in reading, whereas all of the suburban high schools had average achievement scores at or above the national norm, while in Los Angeles in 1985 the ten top-scoring high schools in the metro-

[29] On Milwaukee, see Levine and Zipp, "City at Risk," pp. 13, 18; Daniel J. Walsh, "SES, Academic Achievement, and Reorganization of Metropolitan Area Schools: Preliminary Implications of the Milwaukee Area Study," *Metropolitan Education* 1 (Spring 1986): 86. On Los Angeles, see Jaeger, "Educational Inequality in Metro Los Angeles," pp. 13, 17.

politan area were predominantly suburban and the bottom ten were all in the central city.[30]

Achievement varied not only between cities and suburbs but by race and income within the city and by the proportion of low-income and minority students in different schools. Those city schools with the largest proportion of low-income and minority students generally scored the poorest on achievement tests. In Chicago in the early 1960s, for example, average sixth-grade achievement in reading and arithmetic in those districts with the most African-American students was more than a year and a half below those schools with the fewest, while average sixth-grade achievement in the "lowest socioeconomic districts" was two years below achievement in the "highest socioeconomic districts." The situation was the same in Detroit, New York, Boston, and in Pittsburgh, where in June 1964, average sixth-grade achievement in the ten lowest schools (located in "deprived neighborhoods") was three years below the ten highest schools in arithmetic, four years below in reading, and one year below the national average in verbal ability, reading, and arithmetic.[31]

Some recent evidence suggests that these patterns may have changed since the late 1960s and that achievement scores for poor and minority students in urban schools may actually have risen. According to the results of the National Assessment of Educational Progress (NAEP), for example, nationwide reading and math achievement among African-American and Hispanic students rose substantially in the late 1970s and 1980s, though both groups were still considerably behind non-Hispanic whites.[32] But other evidence suggests that these gains were not uniform and that poor and minority students in the inner city continued to lag behind their peers nationwide. According to NAEP data ana-

---

[30] Wolfe, "State of Urban Schools," pp. 181, 186; Orfield et al., *Chicago Study*, pp. 134–37, 141; Jaeger, "Metro Los Angeles," pp. 5–10; Harvey Pressman "The Failure of the Public Schools," *Urban Education* 2 (1966): 65; Ruben Espinosa and Alberto Ochoa, "Concentration of California Hispanic Students in Schools with Low Achievement: A Research Note," *American Journal of Education* 95 (November 1986): 80.

[31] Pressman, "The Failure of the Public Schools," pp. 64–66. On elementary school achievement in Chicago in the early 1960s, also see Havighurst, *Education in Metropolitan Areas*, pp. 59–60. Some evidence also suggests that achievement actually declined as students progressed through school. In Central Harlem in New York, for instance, 21.6 percent of third-grade students read above grade level and 30 percent read below grade level. By the sixth grade, however, only 11.7 percent of the students read above grade level and 80.9 percent read below grade level. In arithmetic, Central Harlem students were one-and-a-half years below the city norm in the sixth grade, and two years below by the eighth grade. See Harlem Youth Opportunities Unlimited, *Youth in the Ghetto: A Study of the Consequences of Powerlessness and a Blueprint for Change* (New York: Harlem Youth Opportunities Unlimited, 1964), pp. 166–72, 190–93.

[32] Office of Educational Research and Improvement, *Youth Indicators, 1988* (Washington, D.C.: Government Printing Office, 1988), pp. 58–59, 62–63; Marshall S. Smith and Jennifer O'Day, "Educational Equity: 1966 and Now," in Deborah A. Verstegen and James G. Ward, eds., *Spheres of Justice in Education* (New York: Harper, 1991), esp. pp. 72–79; Christopher Jencks, "Is the American Underclass Growing?" in Jencks and Peterson, *Urban Underclass*, p. 70.

lyzed by Lyle Jones, for example, while reading achievement among African-American children in the elementary grades rose as fast in central cities as in the rest of the nation between 1970 and 1984, reading achievement among central-city African-American students at the high school level improved at only one-fourth to one-half the black rate nationally. And within central cities, according to Jones, except for gains among nine-year-olds, African-American students made no progress in closing the black-white achievement gap.[33]

Evidence from individual cities confirms that low-income and minority high school students in central cities have continued to do much worse than other students on achievement tests and that especially in high schools with a large proportion of minority and low-income students, achievement has improved little, if at all, over the last two decades. In Chicago in 1964, for example, eight of the top ten high schools in reading achievement were in the highest socioeconomic districts of the city, and only two had any minority students. By contrast, all ten of the poorest-scoring schools were in the lowest socioeconomic districts, eight were more than 80 percent minority, and in five of these schools, over 40 percent of ninth graders were reading below sixth-grade level. Two decades later, only one of Chicago's top ten high schools in reading achievement had a minority enrollment above the city average and only one had more than 50 percent low-income students, while the ten lowest scoring schools were 98 percent minority and 92 percent low income. The same was the case in Los Angeles, where in 1986 the typical minority high school had 20 percent more low-income students than the typical white high school had and scored ten to twelve points lower on citywide reading tests, which was actually worse than ten years earlier.[34]

The recent history of school completion and drop-out rates for low-income and minority students also presents a contrasting picture of nationwide progress and inner-city decline. From the end of World War II until the 1960s, for example, high school completion rates rose and drop-out rates declined for African Americans, Hispanics, and other minorities. After the 1960s, minority drop-out rates continued to decline in the nation as a whole, and completion rates continued to rise. But, despite these gains, racial differences in drop-out rates persisted, and in central cities increasingly large numbers of poor and minority students dropped out of school. Consequently, even though the overall gap between white and minority educational attainment narrowed after World War II, drop-out rates remained much higher in cities than in the suburbs or in

[33] Cited in Paul E. Peterson, "Are Big City Schools Holding Their Own?" (Milwaukee Public Schools History Project, University of Wisconsin at Milwaukee, January 1991).

[34] Robert J. Havighurst, *The Public Schools of Chicago* (Chicago: Board of Education, 1964), pp. 208–9; Orfield et al., *Chicago Study*, pp. 134–37; Jaeger, "Metro Los Angeles," p. 22; Gary Orfield, "Race, Income and Educational Inequality: Students and Schools at Risk in the 1980s," in Council of Chief State School Officers, *School Success for Students at Risk*, p. 53. On school achievement in Milwaukee, see Walsh, "Milwaukee Area Study," p. 79.

rural areas and even worsened in many inner-city high schools, especially in the Northeast and Midwest.

These trends are evident in the statistics on school completion, attainment, and drop-out rates in the nation as a whole and in individual cities. Nationwide, the percentage of African Americans ages twenty-five to thirty-four who did not finish high school began to decline after World War II, and between 1974 and 1986 fell even further, from 32 to 19 percent, while the percentage of Hispanics without a high school diploma dropped from 51 percent in 1974 to 40 percent twelve years later. Partly as a result, average educational attainment among African Americans ages twenty-five to thirty-four increased from eight years to eleven years between 1960 and 1970 and to slightly over twelve years by the early 1980s; average attainment among Hispanics was lower for Puerto Ricans than for Mexicans, but overall it too rose, though it was about one year less than for African Americans in 1980.[35]

This substantially reduced the racial gap in educational attainment. By the early 1980s, for example, average black attainment was less than a year behind white attainment. Yet, despite these gains in attainment, drop-out rates in the 1980s, as in the 1960s and 1970s, continued to differ by race as well as by gender. Nationwide, in 1968 Hispanics were twice as likely to drop out as non-Hispanic whites and one-and-a-half times as likely to drop out as African Americans. By 1984, drop-out rates had declined for all racial groups, and the gap between whites and African Americans and Hispanics had been reduced. But Hispanics still dropped out nearly twice as often as African Americans, who continued to leave school much more frequently than whites, except for African-American females, who dropped out at about the same rate as white females and slightly less often than white males.[36]

---

[35] National Center for Educational Statistics, *The Condition of Education, 1989*, vol. 1, *Elementary and Secondary Education* (Washington, D.C.: Office of Educational Research and Improvement, 1989), p. 92; Robert D. Mare and Christopher Winship, "Ethnic and Racial Patterns of Educational Attainment and School Enrollment," in Gary Sandefur and Marta Tienda, eds., *Divided Opportunities: Minorities, Poverty, and Public Policy* (New York: Pantheon, 1988), p. 182; James P. Smith and Finis Welch, *Closing the Gap: Forty Years of Economic Progress for Blacks* (Santa Monica, Calif.: Rand, 1986), p. 27.

[36] More specifically, the Census Bureau estimated that nationwide drop-out rates for eighteen- and nineteen-year-olds declined from 23.8 percent in 1968 to 19.7 percent for African-American males and from 24.7 to 14.5 percent for African-American females, while drop-out rates for Hispanics the same age declined from 36.6 percent to 26.2 percent for males and from 39.6 to 26 percent for females. Over the same period, drop-out rates also declined for eighteen- and nineteen-year-old white females from 14.6 to 14 percent but increased for white males from 14.3 to 15.8 percent. For an overview of national trends, see Russell Rumberger, "High School Dropouts: A Review of Issues and Evidence," *Review of Educational Research* 57 (Summer 1987): 101–21; Russell Rumberger, "Dropping Out of High School: The Influence of Race, Sex, and Family Background," *American Educational Research Journal* 20 (Summer 1983): 199–220. On drop-out rates, also see Michelle Fine, "Bein' Wrapped Too Tight: When Low-Income Women Drop Out of High School," in Lois Weis, Eleanor Farrar, and Hugh G. Petrie, eds., *Dropouts from School: Issues, Dilemmas, and*

In individual cities, too, drop-out rates declined and graduation rates climbed steadily after World War II, at least until the early 1960s. In New York City, for instance, the drop-out rate declined from 55 percent in 1941 to 35 percent in 1960. But since poor and minority children were more concentrated in inner cities, drop-out rates remained substantially higher in big cities than in the rest of the nation from the late 1950s on. In the early 1960s, the drop-out rate in the nation's five biggest cities (New York, Chicago, Los Angeles, Philadelphia, and Detroit) ranged anywhere from 10 to 21 percentage points above their respective statewide rates, and the difference persisted in the 1960s and 1970s. Of these five cities, only Philadelphia reduced its drop-out rate between 1963 and 1980. Even then, 40 percent of the city's high school students still left school without graduating, and the city's graduation rate continued to lag far behind the statewide graduation rate, as it did in cities in other states. Nationwide in 1980 the drop-out rate in urban communities was 19 percent, compared to 12 percent in the suburbs and 13 percent in rural areas.[37]

That urban drop-out rates have remained so high at the same time that African-American and Hispanic school completion rates rose and their average educational attainment increased is rather puzzling. But there are two reasons why this has been the case. One is that part of the overall gain in minority high school completion rates, at least for African Americans, reflects changes in the South. This gain was due partly to the postwar mechanization of Southern agriculture, which reduced the demand for young black workers in rural labor markets, and partly to pressure from the civil rights movement, which improved black access to secondary education throughout the South. These changes did not entirely eliminate racial differences in attainment between blacks and whites in the region. But together they raised substantially the number of blacks who finished high school in the area of the country where black high school completion had historically been the lowest, and, in doing so, pushed up African-American completion rates in the nation as a whole even as minority drop-out rates remained high or increased in central cities in the Northeast and Midwest.[38]

Solutions (Albany: State University of New York Press, 1989) p. 26; Roberto Fernandez and Ronnelle Paulsen, "Dropping Out among Hispanic Youth," Social Science Research 18 (1989): 21–52; Tobier, Face of Poverty, pp. 194–98.

[37] On city and state drop-out rates in the 1960s, see David Schreiber, The Holding Power of Large City School Systems (Washington, D.C.: National Education Association, 1964), pp. 28, 35; National Education Association, School Dropouts: Research Summary, 1967 (Washington, D.C.: National Education Association, 1967), p. 8. On urban drop-out rates in 1980, see U.S. News and World Report, June 2, 1980, p. 64. On the overall difference between urban, suburban, and rural rates, see Pallas, School Dropouts, p. 6. For more on urban drop-out rates in the 1980s, see Floyd Morgan Hammack, "Large School Systems' Dropout Reports: An Analysis of Definitions, Procedures and Findings," in Gary Natriello, ed., School Dropouts: Patterns and Policies (New York: Teachers College Press, 1987), pp. 25–29.

[38] Between 1973 and 1988 the percentage of African Americans in the South who had not completed high school declined from 38 to 21.4 percent, whereas the percentage of African

The second reason for the apparently paradoxical trend in minority drop-out and school-completion rates is that in the 1970s and 1980s many students who dropped out of high school subsequently returned or obtained a general equivalency diploma (GED). Between 1961 and 1985, for example, the number of people taking the GED examination increased tenfold, peaking in the early 1980s at just over 800,000 per year. Of these, only about 450,000 passed the exam. But together with those dropouts who returned to high school and graduated, this meant that about 30 to 40 percent of those who dropped out of high school in the 1970s and early 1980s eventually received a high school diploma or an alternative credential. The result has been the coexistence of high minority drop-out rates and increased school completion.[39]

These trends in drop-out rates, school completion, and educational attainment were not, of course, characteristic of every big-city high school. Nor was the pattern of low achievement. In some central-city schools in the 1960s and 1970s, achievement scores improved, drop-out rates declined, and graduation rates rose.[40] By and large, however, the nationwide rise in minority achievement and school completion has not been due to gains made by students in urban schools. Rather, by concentrating poor and minority students in the city, the postwar transformation of social space tightened the link between urban education and educational failure and intensified the educational barriers facing inner-city children. For many poor and minority students in the inner city, particularly those in schools with high poverty rates and a large proportion of minority students, the educational disaster Conant warned about thirty years ago has become a reality.

Some conservatives have argued that the reason for this connection between urban education and educational failure is that children from poor and minority families are simply less academically capable than their more advantaged peers. To support their position, they point to more than two decades of research documenting the connection between poverty, race, and educational failure. Other observers argue, however, that there is little evidence in this research that

---

Americans in the Northeast who had not completed high school declined from 30.5 to 25.1 percent, and in the Midwest from 28.6 to 22.6 percent. See John Bound and Richard B. Freeman, "What Went Wrong? The Erosion of the Relative Earnings and Employment of Young Black Men in the 1980s" (unpublished paper, August 1990): Table A2. On changes in teenage employment by race and region since World War II, also see Dave M. O'Neil, "Racial Differential in Teenage Unemployment: A Note on Trends," *Journal of Human Resources* 17 (Spring 1983): 295–306.

[39] One consequence of the rising proportion of dropouts who return to high school or take the GED is that the proportion of individuals who have not finished high school has declined with age. In 1985, for instance, only 67.6 percent of eighteen-year-olds but 81.5 percent of nineteen-year-olds and 87.4 percent of thirty-one- to thirty-four-year-olds had completed high school. On the increase in the number of people taking the GED exam and the rise in high school completion by age, see Aaron Pallas, *School Dropouts in the United States* (Washington, D.C.: Center for Educational Statistics, 1986), pp. 1, 9–10.

[40] For a description of two successful urban high schools, see Sara Lawrence Lightfoot, *The Good High School: Portraits of Character and Culture* (New York: Basic Books, 1983), chaps. 1 and 2.

socioeconomic status itself makes poor and minority children incapable of learning. A more reasonable explanation for the connection between income, race, and school achievement, they say, is that children from low-income and minority families lack the economic and social resources that support and encourage success in school. As a result, they bring to the classroom fewer of the tools that have traditionally been required for academic learning and that the majority of middle-class students acquire more or less routinely because they come from economically privileged families.[41]

As important as the social and economic conditions of students lives may be, however, they do not fully account for the connection between poverty and low school achievement. On the contrary, though growing up in a poor family increases the likelihood that a student will experience academic difficulties, increases in the proportion of low-income students in a school are associated with decreases in achievement even after individual and family characteristics have been taken into account. In fact, according to the report on poverty and school achievement from the national assessment of Chapter 1, nonpoor students attending a school with a high proportion of low-income students are more likely to have low achievement scores than are students from impoverished families attending a school with a small proportion of low-income students.[42]

One possible explanation for this is that schools with high poverty rates frequently lack peer norms supporting academic success and the value of additional schooling. But the problem is not just the negative influences of friends and classmates. As Michelle Fine, Jeannie Oakes, and others have documented, schools with large numbers of low-income and minority students are also those most likely to have institutional features—including an irrelevant, fragmented curriculum, rigid retention policies and disciplinary practices, and, most important, low teacher expectations for student success—that adversely affect performance in the classroom and that make it difficult for students to stay in school. Indeed, what these studies, as well as the Chapter 1 assessment, suggest is that the reason for the postwar deterioration of urban education is not only that city schools have had to serve a more economically disadvantaged clientele. It is also that the transformation of the social ecology of American cities has compounded the educational obstacles confronting poor and inner-city minority students by concentrating them in schools that discourage learning and achievement and that precipitate dropping out.[43]

[41] For a review of the research on race, income, and achievement, see Diana T. Slaughter and Edgar G. Epps, "The Home Environment and Academic Achievement of Black American Children and Youth: An Overview," *Journal of Negro Education* 56 (Winter 1987): 3–20.

[42] Kennedy, Jung, and Orland, *Poverty, Achievement and the Distribution of Compensatory Education Services*, pp. 20–25, 51–52, 61–63.

[43] Michelle Fine, *Framing Dropouts: Notes on the Politics of an Urban Public High School* (Albany: State University of New York Press, 1991); Jeannie Oakes, *Keeping Track: How Schools Structure*

RACE, BUREAUCRACY, AND EDUCATIONAL REFORM

Urban schools cannot do much about the changes in the social ecology of metropolitan America, though some have tried. In the early 1970s, for instance, several Southern metropolitan areas implemented city-suburban desegregation plans. The largest were in Wilmington, Delaware, and Louisville, Kentucky, where court-ordered mergers combined once-independent city and suburban districts. But following the *Milliken* decision, no city-suburban desegregation plans have been implemented in any of the largest metropolitan areas in the Northeast or Midwest. In the 1980s, both Saint Louis and Milwaukee sued the schools in their surrounding suburbs for discrimination. Eventually, however, school officials in both cities agreed to settlements that permitted voluntary transfers between city and suburban schools but left many segregated schools in each city and only marginally affected overall rates of metropolitan segregation.[44]

Faced with these constraints, several cities have also tried to keep their remaining middle-class students and reduce class and racial segregation within urban school districts by implementing selective academic and/or magnet schools. For the most part, however, the creation of these schools has produced ambiguous results. Although some of them have been able to provide "islands" of quality education, in many cities they have also functioned to increase class distinctions within city school systems. In New York, Chicago, and Milwaukee, for instance, academic and magnet schools generally have attracted students from the most advantaged families, while those from the poorest families, who lack transportation and access to information about the choices available to them, or who are filtered out by selective screening procedures, generally attend neighborhood elementary schools or comprehensive-zoned high schools.[45]

Urban schools thus face obstacles to reform that have proven exceedingly

---

Inequality (New Haven: Yale University Press, 1985); Kennedy, Jung, and Orland, *Poverty, Achievement, and the Distribution of Compensatory Education Services*, chaps. 2–3. Also see Smith and O'Day, "Educational Equality," pp. 70–71; Ruth Ekstrom et al., "Who Drops Out of High School and Why? Findings from a National Study," *Teachers College Record* 87 (Spring 1986): 356–73; Gary Whelage and Robert Rutter, "Dropping Out: How Much Do Schools Contribute to the Problem?" in Natriello, *School Dropouts*, pp. 71–87; Carnegie Foundation for the Advancement of Teaching, *An Imperiled Generation*, esp. chaps. 1–3.

[44] On Saint Louis, see Daniel J. Monti, "*Brown's* Velvet Cushion: Metropolitan Desegregation and the Politics of Illusion," *Metropolitan Education* 1 (Spring 1986): 52–64; on Milwaukee, see Michael J. Stolee, "Racial Desegregation in the Milwaukee Public Schools" (paper prepared for the Milwaukee Public Schools History Project, University of Wisconsin at Milwaukee, 1990). Also see Daniel U. Levine and Eugene E. Eubanks, "The Promise and Limits of Regional Desegregation Plans for Central City School Districts," *Metropolitan Education* 1 (Spring 1986): 36–51.

[45] Fine, *Framing Dropouts*, p. 15; Walsh, "Milwaukee Area Study," pp. 87–88; and, especially, Jonathan Kozol, *Savage Inequalities: Children in America's Schools* (New York: Crown Publishers, 1991), pp. 107–9, 185–86.

difficult to surmount. While the reorganization of social space has tightened the connection between race and income, urban education, and low educational achievement, the nature of American federalism, which divides political and legal power between local units of government, has ruled out metropolitan solutions to the educational problems stemming from class and racial isolation in inner-city schools. Yet without metropolitan involvement, urban systems have not only been unable to alter the class and racial composition of city schools, but in order not to become entirely poor and minority, they have also fostered the development of two types of schools within one system, one for the highest achieving students, the other for the "poorest of the poor." So it is, Jonathan Kozol has recently observed, that the existence of one dual system (city vs. suburb) has almost inevitably led to the creation of another (the city poor vs. the city not-so-poor).[46]

It is impossible to overestimate how much these features of the social ecology of cities and suburbs and the organization of political authority in the American federal system have limited the possibilities for reform in urban education. But they have not been the only barriers to change. Urban schools and school systems have also been slow to respond to their altered social context. Indeed, though the popular literature on urban education is filled with accounts of talented teachers who are sensitive to the needs of their students and help them succeed in spite of the adverse conditions of their lives,[47] city schools and school systems appear for the most part to have been indifferent—sometimes even hostile—to the needs of their new clientele.

One reason for this is that after World War II the fiscal capacity of urban school systems began to decline, especially relative to the fiscal capacity of their suburban neighbors. This is partly because suburbanization eroded urban tax bases and partly because cities had a greater demand for other public services and could not devote as much of their budgets to education. Consequently, even though cities taxed themselves harder and increased their absolute expenditures on education, not only did they raise less per capita for schools than their suburban counterparts, but because they were operating on tight budgets, they also found it increasingly difficult to purchase the additional resources and services they needed or to alter their practices to provide a more appropriate education for low-income and minority students.[48]

[46] Kozol, *Savage Inequalities*, pp. 59–60, 107–9, 186.

[47] For one such account of a dedicated teacher in a predominantly low-income, minority school in New York City, see Samuel Freedman, *Small Victories* (New York: Harper and Row, 1990).

[48] On the fiscal crisis in urban education, see Hummel and Nagle, *Urban Education*, pp. 171–78; U.S. Commission on Civil Rights, *Racial Isolation in the Schools* 1:25–30; Berke and Kirst, *Federal Aid to Education*, pp. 9–13, 11–14; Allan C. Ornstein, "Redefining the Urban Problem," *Phi Delta Kappan* 63 (April 1982): 516–19; Allan C. Ornstein, "The Urban Setting: Frostbelt/Sunbelt Differences" *Phi Delta Kappan* 64 (October 1982): 102–7; Daniel Duke, Jon S. Cohen, and Rosyln Herman, "Running Faster to Stay in Place: Retrenchment in the New York City Schools," *Phi Delta Kappan* 63 (September 1981): 16–17.

In the early 1970s, these fiscal problems sparked a movement to reduce the funding disparities between urban and suburban school systems and provide more funding for city schools. Though in 1973 the Supreme Court, in *San Antonio Independent School District v. Rodriguez*, reversed the federal district court's decision that differences in spending levels violated the equal-protection clause of the Constitution, legislatures in several states passed laws to equalize spending between school districts. But these efforts had only a short-term effect. Although they initially raised the level of resources available to inner-city schools, by the late 1970s, the combination of high inflation, budgetary constraints, and changes in funding formulas eroded many of the early gains. And, though interest in equalizing funding has recently resurfaced in New Jersey, Texas, and some other states, in the late 1980s, in many states the fiscal inequities between cities and suburbs remained pronounced. Even in California, where reformers organized the first and one of the most successful efforts to equalize school spending, in 1986–87 the highest district per-pupil expenditure was eight thousand dollars, the lowest three thousand dollars.[49]

But, despite these inequities, the history of the last three decades suggests that the failure of urban schools to respond adequately to their new social context has not been due only to their insufficient resources. Other characteristics of urban schools have presented equally fundamental obstacles to change. Of these, the most important has been the persistence of bureaucratic structures that have separated urban schools from the communities they are supposed to serve and made them resistant to reform.

The history of urban school bureaucracy is a long one. Urban educators began constructing bureaucratic organizations in the mid-nineteenth century, though it was not until the early twentieth century that urban school bureaucracies took on their modern form.[50] Following organizational models and ideas pioneered in the business community, early twentieth-century educators and their university and business allies sought, in David Tyack and Elisabeth

[49] Smith and O'Day, "Educational Equality," pp. 65–66, 92; Kozol, *Savage Inequalities*, chaps. 2 and 6; Milbrey McLaughlin and James Catterall, "Notes on the New Politics of Education," *Education and Urban Society* 16 (May 1984): 375–81.

[50] On the bureaucratization of schools in the nineteenth century, see Michael B. Katz, *The Irony of Early School Reform: Educational Innovation in Mid-Nineteenth Century Massachusetts* (Boston: Beacon Press, 1968); Michael B. Katz, *Class, Bureaucracy, and Schools, The Illusion of Educational Change in America* (New York: Praeger, 1971), pts. 1 and 2; Carl Kaestle, *The Evolution of an Urban School System: New York City, 1750–1850* (Cambridge: Harvard University Press, 1974); Carl Kaestle, *Pillars of the Republic: Common Schools and American Society, 1780–1860* (New York: Hill and Wang, 1983); Stanley Schultz, *The Culture Factory: Boston Public Schools, 1789–1860* (New York: Oxford University Press, 1973). On the centralization of school decision making and the bureaucratization of school administration in the twentieth century, the best book is still David B. Tyack, *The One Best System: A History of American Urban Education* (Cambridge: Harvard University Press, 1974). On the twentieth century, also see Raymond E. Callahan, *Education and the Cult of Efficiency* (Chicago: University of Chicago Press, 1962).

Hansot's words, to shift school decision making "upward and inward in school bureaucracies" and "to vest it increasingly in the superintendent and his specialized staff." To accomplish this, they proposed to eliminate the old ward-based city boards, elect school board members at large rather than by ward, and reduce the size of the school board. They hoped in doing so to end the influence of urban political machines on school politics and to transform controversial political decisions into matters of administration to be decided by professionally trained experts who, they maintained, had the best interests of the entire community in mind.[51]

Early twentieth-century reformers were never able to eliminate completely the influence of big-city political machines on the schools. Mayors found it as easy to manipulate small school boards as large ones, and in many cities, political considerations continued to dictate appointments to the school board. In other ways, however, reformers at the turn of the century were remarkably successful. Not only did they abolish the ward-based system of governance and reduce the size of city school boards, they also succeeded in institutionalizing new forms of educational decision making based on the ideals of bureaucratic efficiency and professional expertise. Because of their efforts, power shifted more and more to the superintendent, the size of the professional staff grew rapidly, and school administration became more hierarchical, specialized, and differentiated. In the process, these leaders fulfilled their professional aspirations. At the same time, however, they also built what Tyack and Hansot have called a "closed system of school governance" that was responsive to higher administrative authority and to input from organized professional associations but was insulated from lay influence and from community involvement.[52]

In retrospect, the contradictions in this system seem readily apparent. Early twentieth-century school reformers argued that their innovations would take the schools out of politics and put educational decision making in the hands of disinterested experts free from the influence of city politics. In reality, of course, they merely exchanged one form of decision making for another and enhanced the power and authority of middle-class professionals and civic elites at the expense of the cities' white working-class and ethnic communities. Yet, since reformers also sought to reach out and include children from immigrant and white working-class families, this system was seldom contested. Not until the late 1950s and 1960s, when black school movements and their supporters challenged the history of racial exclusion and the unequal character of black incorporation into the public schools, was it called seriously into question. It is,

[51] David Tyack and Elisabeth Hansot, "Conflict and Consensus in American Public Education," *Daedalus* 110 (Summer 1981): 9–11; also see Tyack, *One Best System*, pt. 4.

[52] Tyack and Hansot, "Conflict and Consensus," p. 16. On the professionalization of school administration and the professional aspirations of educational leaders, also see David Tyack and Elisabeth Hansot, *Managers of Virtue: Public School Leadership in America, 1820–1980* (New York: Basic Books, 1982), esp. pt. 2.

in fact, precisely because the black demand for inclusion and equal treatment threatened this system of school organization that it proved so difficult to accommodate.[53]

This became evident when school reformers and civil rights groups began to document the failure of urban education to respond to the educational needs of minority children, who were making up an increasingly greater proportion of the city school population. In several popular exposés, writers such as Jonathan Kozol, Herbert Kohl, Peter Schrag, and David Rogers described how established bureaucratic structures and procedures isolated urban school officials from the communities they were supposed to serve and frustrated any attempt to respond to the demands of their new clientele. Mostly white, wedded to the norms of bureaucratic and professional authority, urban school officials appeared, according to these writers, more concerned with protecting their personal political ties, diverting challenges to their authority, and preserving established channels of decision making than in fostering educational innovation to deal with the difficulties low-income and minority students had in the classroom or in opening up the insular system of school governance to encourage community input and involvement.[54]

Stimulated by the civil rights movement, local black school movements in the 1960s and 1970s launched a major challenge to alter this set of institutional arrangements and make urban schools more responsive to the educational needs of minority children. In many cities—including Chicago, Boston, San Francisco, and Milwaukee—this challenge focused on desegregation, as it had since the 1950s. In some other cities, most notably New York, black activists tired of white intransigence on integration and began to attack the traditional model of school governance. Believing that schools would respond to African-American interests only if blacks gained greater control over the educational process, they shifted the focus of black protest to community control.[55] Both

[53] On this point, see Katznelson and Weir, *Schooling for All*, chap. 7.

[54] Jonathan Kozol, *Death at an Early Age* (New York: Bantam Books, 1967); Herbert Kohl, *36 Children* (New York: New American Library, 1967); Peter Schrag, *Village School Downtown: Boston Schools, Boston Politics* (Boston: Beacon Press, 1967); David Rogers, *110 Livingston Street: Politics and Bureaucracy in the New York City Schools* (New York: Random House, 1968). Also see, Charles Silberman, *Crisis in the Classroom: The Remaking of American Education* (New York: Vintage, 1970).

[55] On the dispute over community control in New York City, see Maurice R. Berube and Marilyn Gittell, eds., *Confrontation at Ocean-Hill Brownsville* (New York: Praeger, 1969); Mario Fantini, Marilyn Gittell, and Richard Magat, *Community Control and the Urban School* (New York: Praeger, 1970); Martin Mayer, *The Teachers Strike: New York, 1968* (New York: Harper and Row, 1968); Diane Ravitch, *The Great School Wars: New York City, 1805–1973* (New York: Basic Books, 1974), pp. 251–399. On community control of schools and other urban institutions more generally, see Alan A. Altschuler, *Community Control: The Black Demand for Participation in Large American Cities* (New York: Pegasus, 1970); Leonard J. Fein, *The Ecology of the Public Schools: An Inquiry into Community Control* (New York: Pegasus, 1971); Henry M. Levin, ed., *Community Control of Schools* (New York: Simon and Schuster, 1970).

strategies, however, sought to end the history of black exclusion and unequal treatment in the public schools, and both encountered stiff opposition.

This opposition came initially from local school officials who wanted to preserve their decision-making prerogatives and from working-class whites who feared black encroachment on their neighborhood schools. Increasingly, however, it also came from teachers in the National Education Association (NEA) and the American Federation of Teachers (AFT). Newly militant, the NEA and AFT had struggled in the late 1950s and 1960s against the school bureaucracy in several cities for union recognition and the right to bargain collectively. But in the late 1960s and 1970s, leaders of both groups began to worry that black protest threatened teachers' rights to job security and better working conditions, and to protect these rights, they joined with their former adversaries on local school boards and in the school bureaucracy to oppose black demands for integration and community control and to defend established ideas and practices about school organization and governance.[56]

In the late 1960s and early 1970s, these divisions often erupted in open conflict. In many cities, this ultimately produced some concessions beneficial to urban blacks. In the 1970s, African-American representation on city school boards increased, more cities made provisions for parent councils, and city schools hired more black and other minority administrators and teachers.[57] But despite these changes, the centralized structure of control and administration first institutionalized early in the twentieth century remained largely intact. One recent study by Allan Ornstein found that after a flurry of interest in decentralization in the mid-1970s, in 1980 more than one-half of the largest cities claimed they had decentralized the administration of their schools, but only one-quarter even claimed they were decentralized in 1988. And when Ornstein looked more closely at the number of administrators inside central district offices compared to the number in offices outside it, only New York and Saint Louis had more administrators outside than inside the central office; some districts reported as many as ten to twenty times more administrators inside than outside the central office.[58]

---

[56] On the conflict between the black community and teachers' unions, see especially Marjorie Murphy, *Blackboard Unions: The AFT and the NEA, 1900–1980* (Ithaca: Cornell University Press, 1990), esp. chap. 12. This conflict was of course most evident in New York, where the local chapter of the American Federation of Teachers engaged in a long and bitter strike in 1968 to protest the city's experiment in community control. But conflict between educators and the black community was not limited to New York. In other cities, too, teacher unions and school officials found themselves at odds with black activists, especially when union representatives and local supervisors refused to acknowledge that poor teaching was related to educational failure or when contract stipulations regarding transfers and working conditions conflicted with plans for desegregation and educational reorganization.

[57] Norman Drachler, "Education and Politics in Large Cities, 1950–1970," in National Society for the Study of Education, *76th Yearbook* (Chicago: 1977), pp. 188–217.

[58] Allan C. Ornstein, "Centralization and Decentralization of Large Public School Districts," *Urban Education* 24 (July 1989): 233–35. On the persistence of bureaucracy and centralization, also

This does not mean that centralization and bureaucratization have finally rid the schools of outside influences. Urban school politics today is considerably more contentious and more pluralistic than it was in the 1950s. What Ornstein's study suggests, however, is that even though urban school officials talked a good deal about making their schools more responsive to the needs of inner-city residents, the long-term response to the urban upheavals of the 1960s and 1970s has been toward more bureaucracy and greater centralization, not less. Although African Americans and Hispanics gained more access to positions of authority in large urban school systems, for the most part black protest was accommodated within the existing system of school organization and governance rather than by changing it.[59]

The bureaucratic structure of urban schools can of course be changed. As Michael Katz has shown, bureaucracy was not the only form of organization that educational reformers in the past could have chosen; alternative forms of governance and organization existed, just as they do today.[60] Bureaucracy prevailed, however, partly because it served the interests of educators (especially male administrators) and partly because it promised equal opportunity for the majority of white Americans while discriminating against the poor and excluding most people of color. That, as we noted above, is why the African-American demand for inclusion in the 1960s and 1970s was so difficult for urban schools to deal with and why, despite the gains African Americans, Hispanics, and other minorities have made during the past thirty years, it remains so difficult to realize today.

Largely for these reasons, the idea of decentralizing the control of schools—now labeled school restructuring—has recently resurfaced as the cutting edge of reform. Disillusioned by the intransigence of urban school bureaucracies and particularly by their response to the state-initiated reforms of the early 1980s, which emphasized academic content and sought to legislate higher standards for students and teachers, the current advocates of restructuring argue that meaningful reform must come from within schools themselves and from the communities they serve. To accomplish this, they propose to decentralize decision-making authority so that teachers, principals, and parents have the opportunity to fashion new models of teaching and learning based on their own experience, knowledge, and expertise.[61]

---

see David Tyack, "Public School Reform: Policy Talk and Institutional Practice," *American Journal of Education* 100 (November 1991): 1–19.

[59] On this point in relation to black protest and other social and political institutions, see Robert C. Smith, "Black Power and the Transformation from Protest to Politics," *Political Science Quarterly* 96 (Fall 1981): 431–33.

[60] Michael B. Katz, *Reconstructing American Education* (Cambridge: Harvard University Press, 1987), chap. 2.

[61] For a discussion of various proposals for school restructuring, see Richard F. Elmore and Associates, *Restructuring Schools: The Next Generation of Educational Reform* (San Francisco: Jossey-Bass, 1990).

If the advocates of restructuring can overcome educators' opposition to meaningful parent involvement and the hostility and suspicion that many poor parents have for the schools, decentralizing authority to the school level has the potential to free schools from bureaucratic control and make them more responsive to the needs of local communities. But however promising the idea of restructured schools might be, decentralizing decision making and giving local schools more autonomy to control their own practices will by itself hardly be sufficient to make well what ails urban education. To be effective, urban school reform must be linked to programs and policies that attack the social and economic effects of inner-city isolation and that expand educational and economic opportunities for poor and minority youth once they finish high school. For the problems that afflict urban schools today extend well beyond the classroom not only to the new ecology of American cities but also to labor market changes that have eroded the rewards for work and altered the relationship between education and income.[62]

EDUCATION AND THE NEW URBAN LABOR MARKET

Discrimination has always mediated the relationship between education and work for African Americans, Hispanics, and other urban minorities. Today, as in the past, minority workers suffer higher unemployment and receive lower wages than do white workers with similar levels of education. But despite the persistence of racial discrimination, from the end of World War II to the early 1970s, economic opportunities for urban minority workers, including those with little education, improved substantially. Drawn to Northern cities by the wartime demand for factory labor, increasing numbers of unskilled minority men found jobs in the manufacturing industries that constituted the backbone of the urban economy. In addition, minority women began to escape domestic service for jobs in government offices and the white-collar service sector of the economy, and college-educated minorities found their way in greater numbers than before into professional and managerial occupations. Some studies estimated that by the mid-1970s, recent African-American male college graduates received nearly the same return to their investment in education as did college educated white men.[63]

The 1970s and 1980s witnessed a striking break with this postwar pattern, especially, though not only, for African-American men. Whereas those who dropped out of high school after the war had been able to find jobs in manufac-

[62] On the tension that exists between schools and poor parents and the limits of restructuring proposals that ignore the need for changes in the economic and social structures of society, see Kenneth M. Zeichner, "Contradictions and Tensions in the Professionalization of Teaching and the Democratization of Schools," *Teachers College Record* 92 (Spring 1991): 363–79.

[63] On black economic progress, see especially Smith and Welch, *Closing the Gap*; Farley, *Blacks and Whites*.

turing, it has become harder and harder for poorly educated urban minorities to secure employment since the mid-1970s. At the same time, however, education no longer seems able to guarantee an escape from poverty. Although education became more necessary than ever to secure employment in the most desirable sectors of the urban labor market, even many better-educated minority workers have found themselves during the last decade confined to jobs at the bottom of the occupational hierarchy and faced with falling real earnings and declining opportunities for advancement.[64]

It is not entirely clear what accounts for the diminished economic prospects of minority workers since the mid-1970s or what has eroded the power of schooling to provide them with an exit from poverty. Researchers have pointed to several explanations, including the slowdown in the growth of government employment, changes in public policy that have made it harder to prove discrimination in the workplace and that have weakened affirmative action, the decline of unions, and shifts in the size and nature of the supply of labor that has allowed employers to be more selective in their hiring, especially for entry-level jobs in central cities.[65] But most important has been the deindustrialization and postindustrial transformation of the urban economy and its effects on the relationship between education and urban labor markets.[66]

The deindustrialization of the urban economy did not begin all of sudden in the 1970s and 1980s. Cities had been losing industrial jobs to the suburbs at least since the early twentieth century and especially since the 1950s, when the relative decline in transportation costs, attributable partly to the Interstate Highway Act, freed manufacturers to locate some distance from older industrial centers. As Thomas Sugrue observes in his chapter, however, beginning in the late 1960s and continuing into the 1970s and 1980s, the decline of manufacturing activity in central cities, especially in the older cities of the Northeast and Midwest, proceeded at an accelerated pace, as the stagnation of the American

[64] Bound and Freeman, "What Went Wrong?"; McKinley L. Blackburn, David E. Bloom, and Richard B. Freeman, "The Declining Economic Position of Less Skilled American Men," in Gary Burtless, ed., *A Future of Lousy Jobs: The Changing Structure of U.S. Wages* (Washington, D.C.: Brookings Institution, 1990), pp. 31–67; Phillip Moss and Chris Tilly, "Why Black Men Are Doing Worse in the Labor Market: A Review of Supply-Side and Demand-Side Explanations" (paper prepared for the Social Science Research Council Subcommittee on Joblessness and the Underclass, January 1991); Bennett Harrison and Lucy Gorham, "What Happened to Black Wages in the 1980s?" (unpublished paper, June 1990).

[65] For a review of the various explanations for the decline in African-American economic progress since the mid-1970s, see Moss and Tilly, "Why Black Men Are Doing Worse in the Labor Market."

[66] On deindustrialization, see especially Barry Bluestone and Bennett Harrison, *The Deindustrialization of America* (New York: Basic Books, 1982); Bennett Harrison and Barry Bluestone, *The Great U-Turn* (New York: Basic Books, 1988), esp. chap. 3; Saskia Sassen-Koob, "The New Labor Demand in Global Cities," in Michael P. Smith, ed., *Cities in Transition: Class, Capital, and the State* (Beverly Hills, Calif.: Sage, 1984), pp. 139–71; Thierry J. Noyelle, *Beyond Industrial Dualism: Market and Job Segmentation in the New Economy* (Boulder, Colo.: Westview Press, 1987).

economy and the growth of international competition forced many factories to close, move to less expensive, larger spaces in the suburbs, or to relocate in the South and West or overseas, where labor and production costs were lower. Whereas cities had once been centers of goods processing and basic industry, by the 1980s the combination of plant closings and corporate flight had reduced manufacturing to a secondary role in the urban economy.[67]

This decline in manufacturing severed the historical link between the city and the factory. But it was not the only change in the organization of urban economies. At the same time that deindustrialization decreased the importance of manufacturing in central-city economies, the globalization of economic activity thrust other institutions into positions of economic dominance in the city. Among these newly dominant central-city institutions were corporate headquarters, banks, and management consulting firms, nonprofit organizations, including universities and hospitals, and federal and local government agencies. Based on an expanding demand for advanced corporate services, higher education, research, and health care, the growth of these institutions transformed central-city economies, orienting them away from industrial production toward the provision of financial, administrative, and social services and the processing of information.[68]

The outcome of this transformation in the economy of cities was a dramatic shift in the employment base of older industrial centers. Between 1953 and 1985, for example, New York City lost over 600,000 jobs in traditional manufacturing industries, and lost another 168,000 jobs in retail and wholesale trade since 1970. At the same time, white-collar service industries, those in which executives, managers, professionals, and clerical employees constituted more than half the industry labor force, increased by 800,000 jobs. The trends were the same in Philadelphia, Baltimore, Boston, and Saint Louis, all of which experienced substantial employment declines in manufacturing and wholesale and retail trade while employment in white-collar service industries increased.[69]

As manufacturing declined in central cities, many factories relocated in the suburbs. During the 1960s and 1970s, the suburbs surrounding Boston, Chicago, and Philadelphia all added jobs in the goods-producing sector; suburban employment in trade and producer services also expanded substantially. But the growth of manufacturing in the suburbs did not fully make up for the

---

[67] John H. Mollenkopf, *The Contested City* (Princeton: Princeton University Press, 1983), chap. 1; Bluestone and Harrison, *The Deindustrialization of America*; Sassen-Koob, "The New Labor Demand in Global Cities"; John Kasarda, "Caught in the Web of Change," *Society* 21 (1983): 41–47.

[68] Mollenkopf, *Contested City*, pp. 23–27; Harrison and Bluestone, *Great U-Turn*; Noyelle, *Beyond Industrial Dualism*, chap. 2; John D. Kasarda, "Urban Industrial Transition and the Urban Underclass," *Annals of the American Academy of Political and Social Science* 501 (January 1989): 28.

[69] Kasarda, "Emerging Urban Mismatches," pp. 169–70. Also see Kasarda, "Urban Industrial Transition," pp. 28–29; Wilson et al., "Ghetto Underclass," p. 141; Mollenkopf, *Contested City*, pp. 21–22.

loss of manufacturing in the city. Nor did manufacturing employment in the suburbs expand as rapidly as employment in the suburban white-collar sector. The result was a reduction in the proportion of jobs in the manufacturing sector of the nation's economy as a whole. Whereas manufacturing accounted for 27 percent of domestic employment in 1970, it accounted for only 19 percent in 1986.[70]

Because African Americans were concentrated in cities and because in many cities (especially in the Midwest) they were overly dependent on jobs in the manufacturing sector for employment, this shift to white-collar service industries displaced disproportionately large numbers of minority workers.[71] Especially hard hit were those with little education. Since jobs in white-collar services on average required more education for entry than did jobs in the declining manufacturing sector, they found it more difficult to secure employment, and many simply stopped looking for work. Yet the economic distress produced by economic restructuring was not restricted to the poorly educated. Although the growth of white-collar services raised the average educational level of the urban labor force, it also expanded the number of low-wage jobs and widened the wage differential between the best-paying and worst-paying jobs. Consequently, not only poorly educated workers but also those with a high school diploma began to encounter greater economic problems, especially people of color who were restricted to the low levels of the job hierarchy in the service sector of the economy.

The employment problems faced by undereducated city workers are evident in the increased educational attainment of central-city job holders, many of whom were suburban commuters. In Boston, for instance, the number of jobs held by those who did not graduate from high school decreased by 80,260 between 1970 and 1980, while the number of Boston's jobs held by college graduates increased by 58,280. In Chicago, Cleveland, Detroit, New York, and Philadelphia, jobs held by those with less than a high school education declined over 40 percent, while jobs held by college graduates increased anywhere from 31 percent in Cleveland to 57 percent in Chicago and Philadelphia.[72]

That the educational attainment of central-city job holders may have risen does not of course necessarily mean that central-city jobs actually required more educational training; it may simply reflect an overall rise in the educational

[70] Kasarda, "Urban Industrial Transition," p. 30; Harrison and Bluestone, *Great U-Turn*, p. 28; Noyelle, *Beyond Industrial Dualism*, pp. 9, 104.

[71] In 1970 in the nation's ten largest cities, 42 percent of African-American male workers and 37 percent of Hispanic male workers, compared to 22 percent of white male workers, were employed in blue-collar occupations in manufacturing. See Wilson et al., "Ghetto Underclass," p. 141. On the role of space and the way those concentrated in the urban core are spatially disadvantaged in the metropolitan labor market, see Kasarda, "Urban Industrial Transition," pp. 36–42; John Kasarda, "Structural Factors Affecting the Location and Timing of Underclass Growth," *Urban Geography* 11 (May/June 1990): 234–64.

[72] Kasarda, "Urban Industrial Transition," p. 31.

attainment of the metropolitan labor force, or employers' preference for better-educated employees even in occupations where higher education is not necessary to job performance.[73] But if employers tend to favor those with higher education, thus increasing the number of jobs held by better-educated employees, educational requirements will rise and the consequences for those without a diploma will be the same whether or not more education is connected to performance on the job. Indeed, whatever the reason, this shift in the educational attainment of the urban labor force led to a widening gap between the educational requirements of the leading sectors of the labor market and the educational level of a substantial number of inner-city youth.[74]

This shift in the connection between education and the urban labor market led to a decline in the economic fortunes for poorly educated male workers, as indicated by the rising unemployment rate and decreasing rate of labor-force participation among undereducated African-American men in the central city. All central-city men have experienced a long-term rise in unemployment since the late 1960s. But the absolute rise in unemployment has been much greater for the poorly educated of both races, and has been much larger for African-American men than for white men at all levels of education. For example, the unemployment rate for white male dropouts in central cities rose from 4.3 to 15.5 percent (11.2 percentage points) between 1969 and 1985, while it increased from 1.6 to 3.6 percent (2 percentage points) for those with more than one year of higher education. For black male high school dropouts in central cities, the unemployment rate increased 20.7 percentage points, from 6.6 to 27.3 percent, during the same period, while the rate for those with more than one year of college increased from 3.7 to 13.1 percent, or 9.4 percentage points. That so many African-American men with at least some college also remained unemployed even two years after the 1982–83 recession suggests that the dislocations caused by the restructuring of the urban economy were not restricted to poorly educated minority workers, but they clearly suffered the most.[75]

[73] On the overall rise in the educational attainment of the American population and its impact on equal educational opportunity, see David K. Cohen and Barbara Neufeld, "The Failure of High Schools and the Progress of Education," *Daedalus* 11 (Summer 1981): 69–90. On the mismatch between educational attainment, educational requirements for jobs, and job performance, see Ivar Berg, *Education and Jobs: The Great Training Robbery* (Boston: Beacon Press, 1971); Richard B. Freeman, *The Over-Educated American* (New York: Academic Press, 1976). For a review of the research on the skill requirements of occupations in the 1980s, see Kenneth I. Spenner, "The Upgrading and Downgrading of Occupations: Issues, Evidence, and Implications for Education," *Review of Educational Research* 55 (Summer 1985): 125–54; Kevin Murphy and Finis Welch, "Wage Premiums for College Graduates: Recent Growth and Possible Explanations," *Educational Researcher* 18 (May 1989): 17–26.

[74] William Julius Wilson, "Social Policy and Minority Groups: What Might Have Been and What Might We See in the Future," in Sandfeur and Tienda, *Divided Opportunities*, p. 244.

[75] Kasarda, "Emerging Urban Mismatches," pp. 184–86. Also see John D. Kasarda, "Urban Change and Minority Opportunities," in Peterson, *New Urban Reality*, p. 57; Charles Hirschman,

The magnitude of the employment difficulties experienced by undereducated African-American men became strikingly apparent in several central cities in the Midwest and Northeast by the beginning of the 1980s. In 1980 in Chicago, for example, 58 percent of those black males out of school and jobless had fewer than twelve years of schooling; in Cleveland 56.7 percent had fewer than twelve years of school; in Detroit, 56.1 percent; in New York, 52.1 percent; and in Saint Louis and Philadelphia, over 60 percent of those African-American men out of school and jobless had less than a high school education. Black male high school graduates in these cities were much more likely to be working, though even a high school degree did not guarantee them employment. In Boston, nearly 35 percent of jobless African-American men had a high school degree in 1980, as did 26.6 percent in Chicago, 28.9 percent in Detroit, 28.3 percent in New York, and 28.8 percent in Philadelphia.[76]

Even more striking has been the decline in labor-force participation among black male workers and the corresponding rise in chronic black joblessness described in Mark Stern's chapter. As manufacturing declined and those without skills and credentials were excluded from the expanding sectors of the urban economy, many African-American men simply stopped looking for work. Among those eighteen to twenty-four years old not enrolled in school, upwards of 90 percent of white males were in the labor force, and the rates remained stable, between 1964 and 1983. For African-American men, however, the rates drifted downward in the 1960s and plummeted in the recessions of 1975 and 1982. In 1983, only 72 percent of African-American men ages eighteen to nineteen not enrolled in school were in the labor force, compared to 89 percent for whites. In the early 1980s, upwards of one-quarter of all black men ages eighteen to nineteen not enrolled in school were not even looking for work.[77]

"Minorities in the Labor Market," in Sandfeur and Tienda, Divided Opportunities, p. 57; Farley, Blacks and Whites, pp. 50–55; Smith and Welch, Closing the Gap, p. 108.

[76] Kasarda, "Urban Industrial Transition," p. 34.

[77] Hirschman, "Minorities in the Labor Market," pp. 76–77; Farley, Blacks and Whites, pp. 43–46; Smith and Welch, Closing the Gap, pp. xvii–xviii; Tobier, Face of Poverty, pp. 91–93. The unemployment and labor-force participation rates of Hispanic men were less affected by the trends in employment and education. Like blacks and whites, Hispanic unemployment rates drifted upward in the 1960s and 1970s and inched downward after 1983. But Hispanic unemployment rates at all age levels remained lower than black unemployment rates—about midway between black and white men—and male Hispanic workers stayed in the labor force in much greater numbers. Throughout the 1960s and 1970s, while young black men withdrew from the labor market in greater and greater numbers, participation rates for Hispanics ages eighteen to twenty-four equaled rates for white male workers. Indeed, even though Hispanic educational attainment lagged slightly behind African-American educational attainment nationwide (except for Cubans, whose educational attainment equaled educational attainment among whites), Hispanics were less likely to be unemployed and more likely to be in the labor force than were African Americans.

What accounts for this difference in employment rates between Hispanics (especially Mexican Americans) and African Americans is not entirely clear. Part of the explanation, according to some researchers, may be that because Mexican culture stresses the importance of marriage and the

The restructuring of the urban economy thus made it more difficult for many poorly educated workers, especially African-American men, to find employment. As a result, long-term unemployment rates rose, and many minority workers without a high school degree dropped out of the labor market altogether. For many others, however, the problem was not unemployment or even insufficient education. On the contrary, the problem for these workers was the low wages paid by the jobs they did find and, even for those with some college, their declining earnings relative to their white peers.[78]

One indication of the worsening economic position of minority workers, particularly relative to that of whites, is the increase in low-wage employment among African-American workers. According to a recent study by Bennett Harrison and Lucy Gorham, the incidence of poverty-level employment among whites rose from 24.3 to 29.3 percent of all white full-time equivalent workers between 1979 and 1987, while the proportion of black workers earning less than poverty level wages grew from 33.9 to 40.6 percent during the same period. Black women fared better than black men, increasing their incidence in high-wage jobs by 33 percent, to 5 percent of all black women workers. At the same time, the proportion of black men earning three times above poverty level declined from 10.8 to 5.8 percent, and the percentage earning below the poverty line doubled from 18 to 36 percent. Although black women prospered more than black men, they too experienced a 37 percent increase in those earning poverty-level wages between 1979 and 1987.[79]

---

husband's role as the breadwinner, Mexicans take a dimmer view of welfare than do African Americans. Some researchers have also found that employers prefer to hire Mexicans over African Americans because they believe Mexicans work harder. Equally important, however, African Americans are more likely than Mexicans to live in the poorest urban neighborhoods, where there are few employment opportunities or other employed people. As a result, they are isolated from the informal job networks that are decisive for obtaining employment, especially for undereducated workers who must rely more on friends and acquaintances than on educational credentials to find jobs and gain entry to the labor market. On the connection between the concentration of poverty and the isolation of poorly educated minority workers, see Loic J. D. Wacquant and William Julius Wilson, "Poverty, Joblessness, and the Social Transformation of the Inner City," in Phoebe H. Cottingham and David T. Ellwood, eds., *Welfare Policy for the 1990s* (Cambridge: Harvard University Press, 1989), p. 96; Chris Raymond, "Results from a Chicago Project Lead Social Scientists to a Rethinking of the Urban Underclass," *Chronicle of Higher Education* 38 (October 31, 1991): A11–13; Mercer Sullivan, *"Getting Paid": Youth Crime and Work in the Inner City* (Ithaca: Cornell University Press, 1989), chaps. 3 and 4.

[78] Nationwide, the percentage of African-American workers employed in service industries grew from 6.2 to 13.7 percent between 1973 and 1987, while the percentage of white workers in service industries grew from 6.5 to 10.4 percent during the same period. At the same time, the percentage of African-American workers in service occupations grew from 13.6 to 21.3 percent and in sales from 3.2 to 6.6 percent. For white workers, the increases were from 6.9 to 9.6 percent in service and from 6.9 to 11.2 percent in sales. See Moss and Tilly, "Why Black Men Are Doing Worse in the Labor Market," p. 28.

[79] Harrison and Gorham, "What Happened to Black Wages in the 1980s?" On the decline in black wages, also see Moss and Tilly, "Why Black Men Are Doing Worse in the Labor Market"; and Bound and Freeman, "What Went Wrong?"

This increase in low-wage work was especially pronounced for poorly edu-cated workers. Between 1979 and 1987, those African Americans without any college experienced a 34 percent increase in the number working below the poverty line (compared to a 24 percent increase for whites with the same amount of education).[80] But the rise in low-wage work was not limited to the poorly educated. In 1987, 20 percent of African Americans with a college education (compared to 17 percent of whites with the same level of schooling) earned less than poverty-level wages, whereas 16 percent earned poverty-level wages in 1979 (compared to 14.8 percent of whites with similar education). Indeed, according to Harrison and Gorham, between 1979 and 1987, the number of college-educated black men and women who earned less than poverty-level wages grew faster than those who earned high-level wages, so that the proportion of all black college graduates who earned three or more times the poverty level actually fell.

Not all of this decline in earnings and increase in low-wage employment among African Americans was attributable to the deindustrialization of the economy. The contraction of the public sector in the mid-1970s, where African Americans had made significant employment gains in the 1960s and early 1970s, also retarded black economic progress and eroded black earnings, as did the weakening of affirmative action and government antibias efforts and the elimination of public employment programs.[81] But the shift from manufactur-ing to white-collar services especially hurt the economic fortunes of many inner-city minority workers, both high school dropouts as well as those with greater amounts of education.

[80] This meant that the proportion of African-American high school drop-outs earning less than poverty wages increased from 48.9 to 58.5 percent between 1979 and 1987, and the proportion of high school graduates earning poverty wages rose from 30 to 43 percent. Sheldon Danziger and Gregory Acs have also documented an increase in the incidence of low-wage employment among African-American workers. According to their study, the proportion of African-American high school graduates with low earnings (defined as anyone making less than twelve thousand dollars in 1987 dollars) rose from 16 to 38 percent between 1973 and 1987 (*New York Times*, June 9, 1991, p. 14).

[81] In 1980, African Americans were much more dependent on government jobs than whites were and much more dependent than whites were on government employment for professional and managerial jobs. Overall in 1980, 22.5 percent of African-Americans compared to 15.3 percent of whites, had government jobs, while 53.3 percent of African Americans in managerial and profes-sional jobs, compared to 27.5 percent of whites in these jobs, were employed by the government (Thomas Byrne Edsall and Mary D. Edsall, *Chain Reaction: The Impact of Race, Rights, and Taxes on American Politics* [New York: Norton, 1991], p. 162). On the importance of government employment for African-American workers, also see Michael K. Brown and Steven P. Erie, "Blacks and the Legacy of the Great Society: The Economic and Political Impact of Federal Social Policy," *Public Policy* 29 (Summer 1981): 299–330; Roger Waldinger, "Changing Ladders and Musical Chairs: Ethnicity and Opportunity in Post-Industrial New York," *Politics and Society* 15 (1986/87): 369–401. On the con-tribution of affirmative action and antidiscrimination policies to African-American employment, see John Bound and Richard B. Freeman, "Black Economic Progress: Erosion of the Post-1965 Gains in the 1980s?" in Steven Shulman and William Darity, Jr., eds., *The Question of Discrimination: Racial In-equality in the U.S. Labor Market* (Middletown, Conn.: Wesleyan University Press, 1989), pp. 32–49.

There are two related reasons for this. The first is the post-1970s wage polarization within service industries compared to the more uniform distribution of wages in manufacturing. This reflects both the feminization of service jobs, which reduced their status and wages, and the widening wage differential by educational level within service work. These processes confined most women workers, including many with a high school degree, to relatively low-paying work in pink-collar ghettos, while male workers of all educational levels increasingly found themselves in jobs that paid less than they could once expect to earn in manufacturing.[82]

The second reason the shift to services hurt minority workers is that they were often confined to the lower levels of the job hierarchy in the service sector. In New York, for instance, African-American employment in financial, business, and professional services grew by 90,000 jobs during the 1970s. In fact, by the end of the decade, African Americans were actually overrepresented in professional services in the city. But in professional services, the chief source of jobs for African Americans was in hospitals, which usually employed blacks as nurse's aides or in other low-paying jobs in housekeeping and food services. Similarly, in business services, African Americans were concentrated in jobs in security and "services to buildings" as well as in marginal personal services. In short, for many African-American workers the problem has not been their inability to gain access to the service sector but their restriction to poor jobs within it.[83]

Although researchers disagree with one another about why minority workers have been restricted to the lower levels of the job hierarchy in services, a good part of the reason is the persistence of racial discrimination. Sometimes this is explicit. Many white employers and workers, for instance, resist hiring people of color—especially black men—to supervise whites. In other cases, employers equate race with characteristics that disqualify minorities from higher level positions. As Joleen Kirschenman and Kathryn Neckerman discovered in their interviews with employers in Chicago, many employers associate race with inner-city schools, which in turn signifies poor education, inadequate work skills, and insufficient commitment to the work ethic. Either way, however, race militates against the hiring of African-American and other minority workers for better paying, higher status jobs.[84]

---

[82] Sassen-Koob, "The New Labor Demand," p. 153; Barbara F. Reskin and Patricia A. Roos, *Job Queues, Gender Queues: Explaining Women's Inroads into Male Occupations* (Philadelphia: Temple University Press, 1990); Harrison and Bluestone, *U-Turn*, p. xxi.

[83] Thomas Bailey and Roger Waldinger, "A Skills Mismatch in New York's Labor Market?" *New York Affairs* 8 (1984): 3–18. On this point, also see Norman Fainstein, "The Underclass/Mismatch Hypothesis as an Explanation for Black Economic Deprivation," *Politics and Society* 15 (1986/87): 403–51; Thomas Bailey, "Black Employment Opportunities," in Charles Brecher and Raymond D. Horton, eds., *Setting Municipal Priorities, 1990* (New York: New York University Press, 1989), pp. 80–111.

[84] Joleen Kirschenman and Kathryn M. Neckerman, "'We'd Love to Hire Them, But . . .' : The Meaning of Race for Employers," in Jencks and Peterson, *Urban Underclass*, pp. 203–24. On the

None of this means that education no longer provides minority workers with an advantage in the labor market. But it suggests that the returns on education for minorities have begun to shift in an unprecedented direction. Although high school graduates continue to earn higher wages and experience less unemployment than do high school dropouts, since the late 1970s the real wages of minorities and women stuck in low-level white-collar work, and even the wages of many with some college, have been declining, reversing the upward trend that characterized minority wages from 1959 to 1973.

Urban schools are not of course responsible for these structural changes in the urban labor market. But the deindustrialization and postindustrial transformation of the economy coupled with changes in government policy and the persistence of discrimination in the workplace have intensified the difficulties of urban schools and magnified the consequences of unequal education. Without the skills or credentials required by the new employing institutions, poor inner-city youth have found themselves excluded from the new growth sectors of the urban economy. Yet faced with a future of low-wage work and with little opportunity for advancement in the service sector, many have little incentive to come to class or stay in school. As one young black high school student summed up the situation he faced: "I stay in school cause every morning I get off the subway and I see this man, he's a drunk, sleeping by the side of the station. I think 'not me' and then I think 'I bet he has a high school degree.' "[85]

CONCLUSION

As urban schools enter the 1990s, they face a situation of compounded disadvantage. By concentrating poor and minority children in inner-city schools, the reorganization of social space has intensified the educational problems of urban schoolchildren, while the persistence of bureaucratic structures of control and administration has made it difficult for urban schools to respond effectively to their altered social context. At the same time, the deindustrialization and post-industrial transformation of urban economies coupled with the continuation of discrimination in the labor market has raised doubts about the power of schooling to lift low-income and minority children out of poverty and into prosperity.

The result of this situation is apparent in the current conditions in central-city schools. More than thirty years after Conant called attention to the deterioration of urban education, academic failure has become commonplace in the nation's inner cities. Though racial differences in school attainment have decreased in the nation as a whole and the overall racial gap in achievement has been re-

persistence of racial discrimination in the labor market, also see Fainstein, "The Underclass/Mismatch Hypothesis," esp. pp. 446–47; Bailey, "Black Employment Opportunities," esp. pp. 88–92.

[85] Fine, "Urban Adolescents," p. 399.

duced, for many poor and minority students in central cities, the new social ecology of urban life, the resistance of urban school bureaucracies to change, and the transformation of the urban labor market have combined to inhibit achievement, increase drop-out rates, and stifle reform.

The current movement for school restructuring has raised many important questions about the bureaucratic structure of urban schools and school systems. But the changes in social ecology and urban labor markets pose other questions that have been asked much less frequently, though they are equally crucial to the education and future of poor urban children. Why, for instance, has a high school degree become so worthless? Could more effective schools turn out graduates who command good wages and have a chance for rewarding employment? Or has the labor market changed so much that a large proportion of young people will necessarily be confined to a future of low wages and dismal work no matter how much urban schooling is improved? And, if so, what should the posture of schools be in these circumstances? In the recent flurry of interest in school restructuring, these questions have too often been overlooked. But the recent history of urban education suggests that unless they are addressed, restructuring city schools will leave the urban poor with control over their own poverty but with little real opportunity to escape the sobering realities of inner-city life. And school reform will once again serve as a substitute for more fundamental changes in the structure of American society, just as it has so often in the past.

CHAPTER 12

The State, the Movement, and the Urban Poor: The War on Poverty and Political Mobilization in the 1960s

Thomas F. Jackson

To HISTORIANS, recent social scientific work on the urban "underclass" exhibits certain serious limitations, especially a neglect of history and politics. In their analyses of concentrated and persistent urban poverty, social scientists generally work within foreshortened time frames, rarely drawing evidence from earlier than about 1970. They also typically ask precise questions framed in narrowly quantitative terms, detailing, for example, how living in a poor neighborhood affects measurable underclass behavior, such as the rates with which teenage girls get pregnant or blacks drop out of high school.[1] In so doing they often neglect more synthetic questions about the basic sources and potential remedies of urban poverty in America. Most seriously, in its approach to policy, recent social science has assumed without much question a managerial model of social change that has defined American liberalism since the Progressive Era.[2] According to this model, reformist experts and policymakers debate and design programs that can be sold to the overwhelmingly middle-class electorate, without seeking to redress the class bias in the electorate itself, and without more directly involving the poor in transforming the conditions of their own lives.[3]

[1] The example is from Jonathan Crane, "Effects of Neighborhoods on Dropping Out of School and Teenage Childbearing," in Christopher Jencks and Paul E. Peterson, eds., *The Urban Underclass* (Washington, D.C.: Brookings Institution, 1991), pp. 299–320. Crane concludes that neighborhood effects matter, but that his findings "do not indicate how to go about improving neighborhoods," other than to suggest that "desegregation by class . . . should be actively encouraged" (p. 318). Crane makes no reference to the political and historical roots of community decline or the history of various political strategies around race, community, and class in U.S. cities.

[2] On the continuity of the Great Society with Progressivism, see Norman I. Fainstein and Susan S. Fainstein, *Urban Political Movements: The Search for Power by Minority Groups in American Cities* (Englewood Cliffs, N.J.: Prentice-Hall, 1974), pp. 26–27. On the history of the Progressive model of social change, see Clayborne Carson and Rebecca Lowen, "A Short History of American Attitudes toward Poverty," in Clayborne Carson and Mark McLeod, eds., *Poverty with a Human Face: Poverty, Justice, and Equality in the Contemporary United States* (San Francisco: Public Media Center, 1985). James T. Patterson, *America's Struggle against Poverty, 1900–1985* (1981; reprint, Cambridge: Harvard University Press, 1986) is the best introduction to the Progressive poverty reformers, although he pays insufficient attention to what he calls their "paternalism" and to poor people's own struggles. See also Michael B. Katz, *In the Shadow of the Poorhouse: A Social History of Welfare in America* (New York: Basic Books, 1986).

[3] Few analysts of the emergence of the underclass make connections between the social and economic trends they describe and what Thomas Byrne Edsall has identified as a coincidental

Their concern is with how to frame policies benefiting the poor in the context of the current political structure, which favors the middle class and the wealthy, local elites, and powerful economic interests. They are less concerned with the possibilities for policy innovation and political mobilization of the poor to move in tandem. Much of this work assumes that politics and ideology are less important determinants of social divisions than measurable attributes such as income, neighborhood residence, high school drop-out rates, crime rates, or other behavioral indexes. Recently, the *Annals of the American Academy of Political and Social Science* devoted an entire issue to the underclass debate. The authors wholly neglected questions of national and local political structures as they may have contributed to urban poverty. Only one author, Jennifer Hochschild, mentioned the possibility of political empowerment of the poor, a point she relegated to a footnote.[4]

More than anyone else, recent conservative critics of welfare policy have argued that the state contributed to the current underclass problem. They have seized on a contemporary paradox quite distinct from the poverty paradox of the 1960s, in which poverty was seen to persist despite unprecedented economic growth. The updated conservative version of the poverty paradox downplays the performance of the economy and blames the state. Despite the legislative victories of the civil rights movement and the antipoverty measures of the Great Society, poverty has not been eliminated; indeed, urban poverty has become both *more* concentrated and *more* persistent since the late 1960s. In the view of conservative scholars such as Charles Murray and Lawrence Mead, poverty increased not in spite but *because* of the expansion of social policy expenditures in the 1960s and 1970s, which eroded poor people's work ethic, family values, and sense of social obligations.[5] By implication, the demoralization of urban poor communities thus seemed to flow powerfully from the actions of the welfare state.

"intensification of the class bias of voting patterns" and elite domination of American politics in the 1970s and 1980s. See *The New Politics of Inequality* (New York: Norton, 1984), p. 183.

[4] William J. Wilson edited the collection in *Annals, of the American Academy of Political and Social Science* 501 (January 1989). Other useful surveys of recent research on poverty, policy, and the underclass include Jencks and Peterson, *The Urban Underclass*; Sheldon H. Danziger and Daniel H. Weinberg, eds., *Fighting Poverty: What Works and What Doesn't* (Cambridge: Harvard University Press, 1986); Fred R. Harris and Roger W. Wilkins, eds., *Quiet Riots: Race and Poverty in the United States* (New York: Pantheon Books, 1988); Gary D. Sandefur and Marta Tienda, eds., *Divided Opportunities: Minorities, Poverty and Social Policy* (New York: Plenum, 1988); National Research Council, *Urban Change and Poverty* (Washington, D.C.: National Academy Press, 1988); National Research Council, *Inner-City Poverty in the United States* (Washington, D.C.: National Academy Press, 1990).

[5] Charles Murray, *Losing Ground: American Social Policy, 1950–1980* (New York: Basic Books, 1984); Lawrence Mead, *Beyond Entitlement* (New York: Free Press, 1986); a useful review of conservative arguments is Michael B. Katz, *The Undeserving Poor: From the War on Poverty to the War on Welfare* (New York: Pantheon Books, 1990), pp. 151–65.

Liberals responded by defending social policy, detailing the achievements of the welfare state in reducing income poverty, especially among the aged poor, and in alleviating hunger, educational disadvantage, and medical neglect. Other liberal social scientists concerned themselves with narrower empirical questions, such as refuting the direct causal connection that Murray drew between expanding social-welfare spending and the rising poverty of female-headed families. By the end of the 1980s, it was no longer intellectually defensible to blame welfare for the alarming rise of female-headed families in poverty.[6]

Among major social scientists, only William Julius Wilson offered a synthetic counterexplanation for the increasing concentration and persistence of poverty in America's cities, one that placed changing values and behaviors in the context of urban social and economic change. Wilson focused on economic and demographic factors related principally to shrinking urban labor markets, black middle- and working-class outmigration from the cities, and increasing numbers of female-headed families in poverty, which he linked to the joblessness of young black men. In short, Wilson offered a compelling economic structural argument to replace the conservative argument linking the expansion of the welfare state to the cultural and behavioral problems that allegedly kept the poor in poverty.[7]

Yet in rejecting the conservative thesis, Wilson and others neglected the importance of political structures and the effects of a broader range of government policies than simply social welfare policy on the changing shape of twentieth-century urban poverty. They did not address the relationship between political and economic power in the postindustrial city, in which the electoral successes of minority officials coincided with a trend in many cities toward increasingly concentrated poor and minority urban populations. And they neglected the history and possibilities of political action broadly defined as a vehicle for mobilizing the poor themselves on their own behalf. Like others who continue to advocate a "universal" approach to poverty policy, Wilson recognized the need for policy-making elites to fashion policies that will not alienate the broad middle-class American electorate. Yet he left unaddressed questions of how a constituency could be mobilized to support these policies and of what role the inner-city poor themselves could play in the political process. Wilson's forthright attempt to recapture from conservative critics discussions of the values and behavioral problems of the urban poor, and place them in the context

---

[6] The literature on families is ably summarized in David T. Ellwood, *Poor Support: Poverty in the American Family* (New York: Basic Books, 1988), pp. 57–62. The best liberal defense of the positive effects of some Great Society programs is John E. Schwarz, *America's Hidden Success: A Reassessment of Public Policy from Kennedy to Reagan* (1983; reprint, New York: Norton, 1988). See also Sar A. Levitan and Robert Taggart, *The Promise of Greatness* (Cambridge: Harvard University Press, 1975); and Danziger and Weinberg, *Fighting Poverty*, for positive program assessments.

[7] William Julius Wilson, *The Truly Disadvantaged: The Inner City, the Underclass and Public Policy* (Chicago: University of Chicago Press, 1987).

of the changing economy and social ecology of cities, was laudable. But at the same time he failed to revive the 1960s liberal rhetoric of community action and empowerment, continuing, as have other liberals, to allow the term *empowerment* to be appropriated and deprived of its political and collective meanings by conservatives and identified with narrower issues such as tenant ownership, enterprise zones, school decentralization, and individual mobility through hard work.[8] Few heeded the continuing voices of local black empowerment activists, who, according to James Jennings, continue to seek collective means "to strengthen the black community institutionally, rather than focus on public policies the effects of which may primarily benefit black individuals or improve individual black mobility within the American economic system."[9]

Few critics in the 1980s used history at all in discussing black urban poverty, other than to lament the passing of more stable communities supposedly integrated by class, the so-called golden ghettos ably critiqued by Joe Trotter in this volume.[10] Much less did anyone elaborate a historical interpretation implicit in much of the black political thought and activism of the 1960s: that concentrated urban black poverty was a legacy of centuries of Southern racism and economic deprivation, transplanted to the North at a time when urban unskilled labor markets were beginning to shrink, and when powerful racial codes excluded blacks from better neighborhoods and job opportunities. In this context, the Great Society failed because it did too little, not too much, to overcome racial segregation, economic subordination, and the obstacles to self-determination in urban black communities.

[8] See Wilson, *Truly Disadvantaged*, chap. 2. If, as Wilson claimed, frank discussions of the behavioral problems of the ghetto poor ended as a result of the acrimony over the 1965 Moynihan Report on the black family, it is no less true that among liberals, another of Daniel P. Moynihan's writings, *Maximum Feasible Misunderstanding* (New York: Free Press, 1969), was much more persuasive in arguing that social action by the poor themselves held no promise and grave dangers for social policymakers brave enough to toy with it. For other advocates of "universal" policies, see Hugh Heclo, "The Political Foundations of Antipoverty Policy," in Danziger and Weinberg, *Fighting Poverty*, and Theda Skocpol, "Targeting with Universalism: Politically Viable Policies to Combat Poverty in the United States," in Jencks and Peterson, *Urban Underclass*.

[9] Jennings's article is a valuable description of a local black politics of empowerment that "focuses on the control of land in black urban communities," a politics that transcends the mere substitution of black elected officials for white and addresses the need for structural changes in both class inequality and community institutional weakness. See "The Politics of Black Empowerment in Urban America: Reflections on Race, Class and Community," in Joseph M. Kling and Prudence S. Posner, eds., *Dilemmas of Activism: Class, Community and the Politics of Local Mobilization* (Philadelphia: Temple University Press, 1990), pp. 113–33. For a more comprehensive national plea for black empowerment, see Theodore Cross, *The Black Power Imperative: Racial Inequality and the Politics of Nonviolence* (New York: Faulkner Books, 1987).

[10] Theodore Cross's impressive and overlooked work is an exception to the rule, yet despite his powerful arguments of historical oppression's impact on current black poverty, even he joins conservative critics in arguing "that the full powers of the state undermined the human powers and work ethic of a body of people already weakened by decades of repression." See Cross, *The Black Power Imperative*, p. 420.

Still, we historians have yet to offer our own interpretations of post–New Deal urban poverty that synthesize the elements of racial subordination, economic relations, political power, and cultural change. Historians breaking ground in the new historiographical frontier of the 1960s, especially, find the terrain heavily traveled by social scientists and journalists, and this poses challenges of method and theoretical approach. Despite our own eclecticism, historians share guiding concerns that are as yet peripheral to the underclass debate, but that are potentially very productive in illuminating the historical factors underlying the facts of contemporary concentrated and persistent urban poverty: the long-range economic and political processes affecting the social ecology of cities; the contingent decisions and events that have shaped the economic and social policy landscape; the historical agency of disadvantaged groups and the possibilities for social action among the poor; the roles of politics and ideology, not just economic forces and social structures, in shaping contemporary urban poverty and social policy; and, finally, what Barrington Moore has called the "suppressed historical alternatives" that exist at various junctures of historical change.[11]

My own vision of this historical synthesis follows several lines of argument: (1) explanations of contemporary urban poverty must take into account not only the large economic changes in postindustrial cities, but also the impact of the state, which has acted in many ways outside of the arena of social policy to disadvantage the urban poor; (2) the War on Poverty, long on rhetoric and short on results, basically continued a tradition of top-down hierarchical reform that benefited mainly the middle class, leaving control of social policy in the hands of local elites and perpetuating the exclusion of minorities and the poor from decisions affecting their lives. Powerlessness, both in relation to the electoral system and to the basic institutions touching the lives of the urban poor, has consistently remained a central feature of urban poverty; (3) the central elements of a varied and developing African-American economic agenda were basically ignored in the 1960s and have been since. These included calls for jobs programs and income support as well as the widespread call for political em-

[11] The most significant recent historical work has focused on general poverty and social policy developments, and includes Margaret Weir, Ann Orloff, and Theda Skocpol, *The Politics of Social Policy in the United States* (Princeton: Princeton University Press, 1988); Allen J. Matusow, *The Unraveling of America: A History of Liberalism in the 1960s* (New York: Harper and Row 1984); Katz, *The Undeserving Poor*; Carl M. Brauer, "Kennedy, Johnson, and the War on Poverty," *Journal of American History* 69 (June 1982): 98–119; and Patterson, *America's Struggle against Poverty, 1900–1985*. In narrative frameworks, this work has sought to synthesize social and economic trends with political and ideological analysis, and to explain the course of policy and social change with an appreciation of the sheer contingency of past events. Nicholas Lemann's *The Promised Land* (New York: Knopf, 1991) is an important work, but is flawed by an overreliance on narrative and interview sources, and an inattention to institutions of the inner-city. The concept of "suppressed historical alternatives" is discussed in Barrington Moore, *Injustice: The Social Bases of Obedience and Revolt* (New York: Sharpe, 1987).

powerment. The original meaning of empowerment essentially took shape in the context of a challenge from below to local power, to racism, and especially to the large urban bureaucracies that touched the lives of the poor at so many points. Much of the mobilization of the decade, despite the hopes of social democrats who sought class-based solutions, was conducted on ethnic and community grounds, independent of federal sponsorship. Yet several organizations and individuals attempted to broaden the struggle beyond the boundaries of race and community, ultimately failing to create broad interracial alliances of disadvantaged groups, but learning valuable lessons in the process.

THE STATE AND THE URBAN POOR

The general history of social policy and the particular history of the Great Society both form pieces of the broader story of the expansion of state power in the twentieth-century United States. Their effects need to be placed in the context of the aggregate effects of a broad array of state policies on urban poverty.[12] Recent scholarship reveals the degree to which federal mortgage-guarantee programs, public housing programs, urban redevelopment and renewal programs, transportation, taxation, military, macroeconomic, employment and income-support policies have all contributed to the general problem of poverty and the specific concentration of a more intensely marginalized and racially segregated poor population in impoverished inner-city neighborhoods.[13] Social policy has in certain instances achieved redistribution, especially among the aged, but when we consider a fuller range of governmental activities, the main beneficiaries have not been the poor, even in the liberal heyday of the 1960s, but the wealthy and the middle class. After the New Deal especially, the federal government became a key protagonist in the drama of urban racial and economic polarization.[14] The state has indeed been a powerful

[12] See especially the chapters by David Bartelt and Thomas Sugrue in this volume, and summaries of the range of policies by myself in this article and Michael Katz, in *The Undeserving Poor*.

[13] A body of evidence and argument is accumulating to confirm the insights of the National Committee against Discrimination in Housing, which in a 1967 report argued, "Thanks to Federal largess, white Americans have separated themselves from Negro Americans" (National Committee against Discrimination in Housing, *How the Federal Government Builds Ghettos* [New York: NCDH, 1967], reprinted in Helen Ginsburg, ed., *Poverty, Economics and Society* [Boston: Little, Brown, 1972], p. 251).

[14] There is a nascent and as yet undeveloped historical debate about the degree to which the state merely followed trends and market forces evident before it intervened, or the degree to which it entered the arena as a key player. Mark Gelfand has asserted, in all dimensions of urban policy, that the federal government was a "supporting player, not a protagonist." More recently, however, scholars have uncovered and emphasized the degree to which state policy has acted in new ways to reconfigure the urban distribution of race and class through space. According to Kenneth Jackson, the FHA did not merely follow the preferences of bankers and home owners in their prejudicial attitudes. "For perhaps the first time, the federal government embraced the discriminatory attitudes of the marketplace. Previously, prejudices were personalized and individualized; FHA exhorted

engine of redistribution, but on the whole has not acted in the interests of the poor or minorities.

The historical and social-scientific scholarship ranges over a wide territory of issues and disciplines, but a basic pattern of unequal state economic benefits emerges in various arenas. First, the turn-of-the-century movement toward suburban political independence from core cities created an alliance of class privilege and local power in the suburbs that endures to this day. The middle class created safe havens isolated from the social costs and social problems of the cities, and as a result, the cities were cut off from suburban resources and tax bases.[15] Second, New Deal agricultural and minimum-wage policies accelerated the outmigration of blacks from the South in the 1940s and 1950s by hastening the collapse of the low-wage Southern labor market and the mechanization of agriculture.[16] Third, federal mortgage-guarantee programs disproportionately benefited middle-class homeowners in the suburbs (and large builders), and accelerated middle-class flight from inner-city neighborhoods. The tax code has also subsidized suburban development through mortgage interest and property tax deductions, while rental payments have not been deductible.[17] Fourth, federal urban-renewal and public-housing legislation, as locally implemented, benefited private developers and bondholders, but not the poor who were displaced from their homes and either not relocated at all or relocated in crowded, racially segregated public housing.[18] Fifth, new urban highway con-

---

segregation and enshrined it as public policy." Arnold Hirsch has also emphasized the "deep involvement of government" in a host of fresh decisions that remade the urban ghetto. Redevelopment, urban renewal, and public housing not only reinforced previous patterns but lent "them a permanence never seen before." It "virtually constituted a new form of de jure segregation," according to Hirsch. See Mark I. Gelfand, "Cities, Suburbs, and Government Policy," in Robert H. Bremner and Gary W. Reichard, eds., *Reshaping American Society and Institutions, 1945–1960* (Columbus: Ohio State University Press, 1982), p. 268; Mark I. Gelfand, *A Nation of Cities: The Federal Government and Urban America, 1933–1965* (New York: Oxford University Press, 1975); Kenneth Jackson, *Crabgrass Frontier: The Suburbanization of the United States* (New York: Oxford University Press, 1985), pp. 213–15; Arnold R. Hirsch, *Making the Second Ghetto: Race and Housing in Chicago, 1940–1960* (New York: Cambridge University Press, 1983), pp. 253–58.

[15] David M. Gordon, "Capitalist Development and the History of American Cities," in William K. Tabb and Larry Sawers, eds., *Marxism and the Metropolis* (New York: Oxford University Press, 1978), pp. 52–53; Jackson, *Crabgrass Frontier*, pp. 146–56.

[16] Gavin Wright, *Old South, New South* (New York: Basic Books, 1986), chaps. 7–8.

[17] Jackson, *Crabgrass Frontier*, pp. 195–209, 293–96; Barry Checkoway, "Large Builders, Federal Housing Programs, and Postwar Suburbanization," in William K. Tabb and Larry Sawyers, eds., *Marxism and the Metropolis*, 2d ed. (New York: Oxford University Press, 1984), pp. 152–73. See also the chapters by David Bartelt and Thomas Sugrue in this volume.

[18] For information on the control of urban redevelopment by corporate interests, see Hirsch, *Making the Second Ghetto*, pp. 268–74: "The charges so often leveled at the federal effort—that it neglected the poor; that it was actually anti-poor because of its demolition of low-rent housing and inadequate relocation procedures; that it simply subsidized those who needed aid least; and that it was transformed into a program of 'Negro clearance'—were hardly evidence of a plan gone awry. These were not 'perversions' of the enabling legislation, they were the direct consequences of it."

struction further displaced poor people, hastened middle-class flight to the suburbs, and promoted the relocation of industries and jobs to the suburbs.[19] Sixth, military spending policies tended to diminish other, more labor-intensive and productive public economic investments, and accelerated new city growth in the Sunbelt at the expense of the older industrial cities of the Midwest and Northeast.[20] Seventh, proposed national full-employment policies have repeatedly failed to win presidential or congressional support. The consistent use of unemployment to fight inflation has always had a disproportionate impact, according to one economist, on "the poor, the black and the underprivileged."[21] Recent historical work has focused on the political failure of the Truman presidency to institute national labor market policies tied to public spending, the crucial failures being the abolition of the National Resources Planning Board and the defeat of the Full Employment Bill of 1945. These defeats resulted in a restriction of the full-employment policy options available later on, when urban unskilled labor markets experienced decline.[22]

Lastly, the Great Society extended but did not substantially reform the unequal two-tier system of income support inherited from the New Deal, in which

---

Displacement of the poor and the use of vacated land for "commercial, high-rent residential and institutional purposes" is the dominant pattern of urban redevelopment identified by Susan S. Fainstein and Norman I. Fainstein, "Economic Change, National Policy and the System of Cities," in Susan S. Fainstein et al., *Restructuring the City: The Political Economy of Urban Redevelopment*, rev. ed. (New York: Longman, 1987), pp. 16–18. See also Katz, *Undeserving Poor*, p. 134. On public housing, see Jackson, *Crabgrass Frontier*, pp. 222–27; Gelfand, "Cities, Suburbs, and Government Policy," pp. 268–71. Hirsch has detailed how the Chicago Housing Authority's brief experiment with scattered site selection and integration was ended in 1948, after white ethnics rioted at a public housing project, and after the Chicago City Council obtained authority from the state legislature over site selection. Federal funds for public housing under the 1949 housing act did not curtail the Chicago City Council's power. Strict segregation was maintained throughout the 1950s: of thirty-three projects approved from 1950 to the mid-sixties, twenty-five were located in census tracts containing over 75 percent blacks. The result was a solid corridor of high-rise public housing along State Street. See Hirsch, *Making the Second Ghetto*, pp. 212–45.

[19] Fainstein and Fainstein, "Economic Change, National Policy and the System of Cities," pp. 13–14; Gelfand, "Cities, Suburbs, and Government Policy," pp. 273–75.

[20] Jackson, *Crabgrass Frontier*, pp. 190–91; Seymour Melman, *The Permanent War Economy* (1974; reprint, New York: Simon and Schuster, 1985), pp. 122–25; Kenneth T. Jackson, "The City Loses the Sword: The Decline of Major Military Activity in the New York Metropolitan Region," in Roger Lotchin, ed., *The Martial Metropolis: U.S. Cities in War and Peace* (New York: Praeger, 1984), pp. 155–58.

[21] Alan S. Blinder, *Hard Heads, Soft Hearts* (New York: Addison-Wesley, 1987), p. 55. See also Rebecca M. Blank and Alan S. Blinder, "Macroeconomics, Income Distribution, and Poverty," in Danziger and Weinberg, *Fighting Poverty*, pp. 180–97.

[22] Ira Katznelson, "Was the Great Society a Lost Opportunity?" in Steve Fraser and Gary Gerstle, eds., *The Rise and Fall of the New Deal Order* (Princeton: Princeton University Press, 1989), pp. 185–211; Margaret Weir, "The Federal Government and Unemployment: The Frustration of Policy Innovation from the New Deal to the Great Society," in Weir et al., *The Politics of Social Policy in the United States*, pp. 149–90.

social insurance rested on firm political and ideological grounds, and welfare suffered from lack of funding and legitimacy. As James Patterson has shown, the movement of planners in the National Resources Planning Board toward merging Social Security and welfare stalled after World War II. Some reforms in the calculation of Social Security benefits occurred, but the stigmatizing distinction remained.[23] Social Security has since had the single largest effect in reducing poverty, cutting the poverty rate of the aged in half over the period from 1966 to 1983, but these beneficial redistributive effects came at some cost, a cost rarely mentioned by advocates of universal antipoverty policies. Economists have estimated that since 1960, around 80 percent of social-welfare expenditures have been in programs not focused exclusively on the poor. Although Social Security and Medicare have been effective at improving the incomes of poor or near-poor aged, and although generous payments to the nonpoor aged are usually regarded as the political guarantee of a viable redistributive program, nonaged nonwhites and members of female-headed households, especially among the poor, have benefited far less from the system of income provision. Poor people have increasingly received "in-kind" assistance, such as Medicaid and food stamps, reflecting the middle-class mistrust and stigma of cash relief.[24] A continuing measure of the two-tier nature of the income support system lies in the fact that Social Security was indexed for inflation in 1972, while Aid to Families with Dependent Children was not. The rising value of Social Security benefits since then, and the relative decline in the real values of AFDC and other targeted antipoverty programs, means that despite the effect that the universal Social Security program had on the aged poor, in a sense the fundamental division in social provision has been exacerbated. And the method of financing Social Security, through increased payroll taxes, has left Social Security more regressive and placed greater burdens on the working poor.[25]

WAR ON POVERTY: THE PERSISTENCE OF CLASS BIAS IN THE WELFARE STATE

Ambiguous standards of success and failure complicate contemporary understanding of the War on Poverty, which is further muddled by ambiguity about just what social policy developments of the 1960s should be included under its umbrella. I understand the War on Poverty programs to include those provided

---

[23] For discussion of the historical development of the bifurcated system of social provision, see Patterson, *America's Struggle against Poverty, 1900–1985*, pp. 76, 92–94; Katz, *In the Shadow of the Poorhouse*, p. 251; Theda Skocpol, "The Limits of the New Deal System and the Roots of Contemporary Welfare Dilemmas," in Weir et al., *The Politics of Social Policy in the United States*, pp. 295–98.

[24] Gary Burtless, "Public Spending for the Poor: Trends, Prospects, and Economic Limits," and Sheldon Danziger, et al., "Antipoverty Policy: Effects on the Poor and the Nonpoor," in Danziger and Weinberg, *Fighting Poverty*, pp. 19–33, 56–57; Henry J. Aaron, *Politics and the Professors: The Great Society in Perspective* (Washington, D.C.: Brookings Institution, 1978), tables, pp. 11–15.

[25] Blank and Blinder, "Microeconomics, Income Distribution, and Poverty," p. 200.

412 · Thomas F. Jackson

for under the Economic Opportunity Act of 1964, whether operated by the newly created Office of Economic Opportunity (OEO), such as the Community Action Program (CAP), Legal Services, Head Start, Volunteers in Service to America (VISTA), or those administered by other agencies, such as the Job Corps, administered by the Department of Labor. The Demonstration Cities (Model Cities) legislation of 1966 could also be included under this rubric. That said, it is evident that expenditures under the War on Poverty were a small percentage of the social-welfare budget of the 1960s. More general Great Society legislation included expansions in Social Security, public assistance, veterans' benefits, pubic housing, urban renewal, Medicare and Medicaid, and Title I of the Elementary and Secondary Education Act of 1965, all of whose expenditures expanded dramatically after 1965. Taken as a whole, then, only a small part of total expenditures represented programs targeted exclusively on the poor. "In dollar terms," Henry Aaron has argued, "most of the War on Poverty was a by-product of programs intended primarily for the middle class."[26]

Success and failure are equally slippery categories of analysis. To oversimplify, conservatives have argued either that the federal government tried to wage war on poverty and that it failed, or (more commonly in the early 1980s) that the government was so successful that poverty need no longer be considered a state responsibility. Liberals responded with the contention that the War on Poverty was never fully tried, even in the scope envisioned by its architects, or that a variety of particular programs were modestly successful and should be continued. Indeed, there are notable and well-documented achievements of the Job Corps, Head Start, and Legal Services, as well as other related Great Society programs, such as the food stamp program's success in reducing hunger and the effects of Medicaid on poor people's access to medical care.[27] Moreover, measured against the historical reversals that followed, the War on Poverty seems worth defending as a modest example of what the state can accomplish given the political will.

But overcoming poverty is not simply a matter of political will; it is and has become even more one of political structure. Placed in the historical and political context of the welfare state as a whole, and measured against its own rhetorical promises and the expectations these aroused, the Great Society's shortcomings outweigh its strengths. It was hardly the egalitarian revolution some liberals celebrate from the vantage point of the conservative 1990s.[28] Both

[26] Aaron, *Politics and the Professors*, pp. 26–27.

[27] For program assessments, see Robert Haveman, ed., *A Decade of Federal Antipoverty Programs: Achievements, Failures and Lessons* (New York: Academic Press, 1977); Danziger and Weinberg, *Fighting Poverty*; Levitan and Taggart, *The Promise of Greatness*; Schwarz, *America's Hidden Success*; Allen J. Matusow, *The Unraveling of America: A History of Liberalism in the 1960s* (New York, 1984), chap. 8.

[28] See Thomas Byrne and Mary D. Edsall, *Chain Reaction: The Impact of Race, Rights and Taxes on American Politics* (New York: Norton, 1991), chap. 3, for this benign view.

Left critics and black activists at the time recognized its limits, a view supported in many respects by recent historical scholarship. Both the War on Poverty and the Great Society did little to overcome the two main limitations of federal social and urban policy of the forties and fifties, as discussed in the chapters by Thomas Sugrue and David Bartelt and summarized earlier: its middle-class bias and its appeasement of local economic interests and bureaucratic elites. They did not benefit the poor because they centrally rested on a middle-class constituency and a political structure that denied power and participation to the poor. As was widely recognized at the time among those active in the black movement and the Left generally, social policy failed in three crucial dimensions, to provide jobs, income, and power for the poor. The human capital, services, and community action programs of the War on Poverty failed to eliminate income poverty or reduce income inequality; to increase the aggregate supply of jobs in urban and other labor markets; or to mobilize an adequate constituency, either poor, working class, or middle class, to support effective antipoverty policy on a sustained basis.[29] Most of the progress against income poverty in the sixties and early seventies resulted from economic growth or the growth in New Deal entitlement programs, or measures like Medicare, Medicaid, and food stamps, which were not at the center of the War on Poverty as embodied in the Economic Opportunity Act of 1964 and related measures. The War on Poverty did little to democratize urban politics over the long run; the enfranchisement of the black middle class accompanied a further demobilization of the black poor.

In the 1960s, civil rights activists and white leftists commonly argued that the black movement, either in the South or the urban North, had been necessary to the origins of the War on Poverty. As such, the black movement served as an example of what democratic social mobilization and strategies of protest can achieve. For example, Martin Luther King, Jr., declared in August 1965 that when "Negroes took to the streets to demand job opportunities for themselves they helped to stimulate a broad 'war on poverty' concept which ultimately will benefit more whites than Negroes." Or as Michael Harrington later wrote, the "civil rights struggle forced the country to see the shacks and tenements and rotting houses in which Negroes lived. It simultaneously opened the eyes of the nation to a poverty that, though it is unconscionably and discriminatorily black, is, in reality, chiefly white."[30] In 1971, Frances Fox Piven and Richard Cloward

[29] See especially S. M. Miller and Pamela Roby, "The War on Poverty Reconsidered," in Jeremy Larner and Irving Howe, eds., *Poverty: Views from the Left* (New York: Morrow, 1968), pp. 68–82. This is largely the view of Matusow, *Unraveling of America*, chaps. 8–9. For an eloquent plea from within the black freedom struggle for jobs, income, and power, see Martin Luther King, Jr., "Statement," in U.S. Senate, Subcommittee on Executive Reorganization, Committee on Government Operations, *Federal Role in Urban Affairs*, pp. 2966–99.

[30] Martin Luther King, Jr., "Annual Report to the Southern Christian Leadership Conference," August 11, 1965, Papers of Martin Luther King, Jr., King Library and Archives, Martin Luther King, Jr., Center, Atlanta, Ga., Series 3, Speech files; Michael Harrington, *Fragments of the Century* (New York: Saturday Review Press, 1973), p. 94.

offered a more pessimistic but plausible interpretation that the main impetus to the War on Poverty and related urban programs had been political calculation within the Johnson administration to co-opt the nascent Northern urban black movement and to neutralize its energies.[31] Yet Piven and Cloward overestimated both the importance of the cities in the overall political calculations of the poverty planners and the degree and strength of official commitment to political mobilization of the poor against the big-city political machines. Other factors were equally important in the declaration of a War on Poverty: Johnson's need for an issue to distinguish his liberalism from Kennedy's, his search in the South for an issue that would transcend the nettlesome racial issue that was splitting the Democratic party, the dramatization of Appalachian poverty, the need to appeal, in the words of Robert Lampman, to "the suburban, churchgoing house-wife," and not least, the initiatives of professional reformers themselves.[32] In the absense of any in-depth historical study of the issue, Lawrence Friedman's judgment probably comes closest to the truth: although the civil rights move-ment did exert some influence on the legislation, the reason the War on Poverty was so limited, and ultimately so compromised by existing power groups and the middle class, was that there was weak constituent support for the program from the beginning.[33]

Still, despite the fact that blacks were conspicuous by their absence from the planning of the War on Poverty, administration strategists did appropriate central themes of the black movement that had entered into liberal social thought: equal opportunity and community action.[34] And as we shall see, after

[31] Frances Fox Piven and Richard A. Cloward, *Regulating the Poor: The Functions of Public Welfare* (New York: Random House, 1971), p. 249.

[32] Those arguing the importance of black protest, but not in the way Piven and Cloward do, include Matusow, *Unraveling of America*, pp. 119–20; Nick Kotz, "Comments," in Haveman, *A Decade of Federal Antipoverty Programs*, pp. 48–51. Those pointing to other factors include Brauer, "Kennedy, Johnson, and the War on Poverty," pp. 98–119, who discusses Johnson's Southern strategy; and Lawrence Friedman, "The Social and Political Context of the War on Poverty: An Overview," in Haveman, *A Decade of Federal Antipoverty Programs*, pp. 21–54. Daniel P. Moynihan, "The Professors and the Poor," in Daniel P. Moynihan, ed., *On Understanding Poverty* (New York: Basic Books, 1968), pp. 3–35, argues the importance of professional reformers, but Brauer has issued the necessary corrective that it was mainly economists, rather than sociologists, who planned the War on Poverty. Michael Katz's analysis of the divisions that emerged at a 1973 conference of antipoverty planners is useful: generally, "insiders" in policy-making circles denied the importance of mobilization, while "outsiders" allied with the movement, like Piven and Cloward, stressed its importance. See Katz, *Undeserving Poor*, pp. 81–88.

[33] Freidman, "Social and Political Context," p. 37. The most compelling case for the position that the War on Poverty would not have been possible without a civil rights movement adopting economic issues is Nick Kotz's, in his critique of Freidman: "Even if the social scientist drafters did not sense the pressures that gave them their opportunity to start writing brave new pro-grams . . . there was real political pressure for change that came from a rapidly evolving civil rights movement that already was engaged in the struggle against poverty as well as against segregation and discrimination" (Kotz, "Comments," p. 49).

[34] See Matusow, *Unraveling of America*, pp. 119–20, on the importance of political culture and ideology. There is clearly need for more research on this question, but note the continuity discerned

the initiation of the War on Poverty, black activism was responsible for directing the energies of the Community Action Program in certain locales toward community organizing, political empowerment, and welfare-rights mobilization. Left-liberal advocates of community mobilization within the Office of Economic Opportunity shared this purpose, but their influence, and their tenure, was limited.[35] Within government, the dominant constituency for all but the OEO radicals was not the poor themselves but the middle class. Yet in the end, the federal poverty warriors largely failed to mobilize even this constituency or to answer the more fundamental question, how was *any* constituency to be formed that could sustain the programs over a long enough term both to understand poverty and effectively end it? Their failure was not centrally due to the backlash effects of black militancy on the legitimacy of the programs, but to the limitations of any strategy that relies on the goodwill and benevolence of the middle class rather than on the political expression of the interests of those in whose benefits social policy is formulated. The Johnson administration sought to rhetorically mobilize the large middle class through the highly publicized metaphor of war,[36] but the constraints on policy innovation placed by middle-class political culture limited the program from its inception, in at least three ways.

First, this media-focused, middle-class politics limited the resources the federal government could devote to eliminating income poverty. The tax cut of 1964 had been a major legislative goal of the Kennedy administration; in conversations between Kennedy and Walter Heller, the idea of a poverty program came up almost as an afterthought, as a concession to poor and working people after a generous handout to the middle class. Johnson therefore felt constrained not to raise taxes, so the War on Poverty never incorporated proposals for job creation and expansion of income support. Labor Department economists and academics such as John Kenneth Galbraith and black leaders such as A. Philip Randolph throughout the decade proposed to undertake Keynesian spending to create jobs, but Lyndon Johnson vetoed this approach at an early stage of War on Poverty planning. So the administration's labor market strategy focused on job training, which had no effect on the inadequate supply of good jobs in urban labor markets.[37] Moreover, throughout the sixties, academics and policymakers

by Earl Raab in 1966: "The ostensible aim of the Economic Opportunity Act is highly traditional: a more perfect equality of opportunity for the individual, regardless of race, creed, or previous condition of destitution" ("What War and Which Poverty?" *Public Interest* 3 [Spring 1966]: pp. 46–47).

[35] For the limited influence of "Hackett's guerrillas," see Matusow, *Unraveling of America*, pp. 244–54.

[36] David Zarefsky, *President Johnson's War on Poverty: Rhetoric and History* (University: University of Alabama Press, 1986).

[37] On Kennedy's tax cut and its effect on the impetus for a War on Poverty, see Matusow, *Unraveling of America*, pp. 56–59; and Brauer, "Kennedy, Johnson, and the War on Poverty," pp. 102–4; On Johnson's veto of jobs spending, see Weir, "Federal Government and Unemployment," pp. 168–71.

proposed major reform of the system of income maintenance, yet Johnson shelved proposals for a negative income tax or an overhaul of the two-tier system of social provision because of his reluctance to raise or reform taxes to re-distribute income. This reluctance was also present in Johnson's financing of the Vietnam War, with disastrous consequences in terms of inflation.[38]

Second, middle-class politics and the modest resources the administration committed to the War on Poverty dictated a definition of the poverty population restricted to those whose family income fell below a low and fixed poverty line. Poverty defined in such absolute terms, rather than in terms of relative inequal-ity (as with a definition based on a percentage of median income), virtually guaranteed the "success" of Johnson's program, on its own terms. With eco-nomic growth, whole categories of the poor would move across the poverty line with no significant redistribution of income, no significant infringement of the interests of the middle class, and no tax increases. Because the 1964 tax cut had set the outer limits of permissible commitments, Johnson chose to fight poverty on the cheap, largely through an expansion of services, such as education and job training, rather than through more sweeping measures that would more substantially benefit both the working poor and the unemployed.[39]

Third, politics dictated not only a restricted poverty population, but assured that the poverty planners would define the nature and causes of poverty in cultural and behavioral rather than structural economic and political terms. Governing rationales of improving "human capital," correcting "community pathology," breaking the "culture of poverty," healing the "broken family" all tended to restrict the problem to a "disadvantaged" population outside what was considered a basically sound "mainstream." Structural issues of low wages, low demand for labor in depressed labor markets, systemic racism in employment and union practices, and inadequate income support for those outside the labor market were all widely discussed as causes of poverty but did not shape the characteristics or justifications of programs. Instead, poor people remained in both official policy and popular conception "a culpable rather than a victimized group."[40]

Whatever hope the War on Poverty aroused was ultimately dashed by the

[38] Mark I. Gelfand, "The War on Poverty," in Robert Divine, ed., *The Johnson Years* (Lawrence: University Press of Kansas, 1987), p. 143. Brauer, "Kennedy, Johnson, and the War on Poverty," pp. 118–19. See Godfrey Hodgson, *America in Our Time* (New York: Vintage, 1976), pp. 253–60, for the effects of Johnson's choice not to raise taxes to pay for Vietnam on the 1970s inflation.

[39] Matusow, *Unraveling of America*, pp. 217–21. Katz, *Undeserving Poor*, pp. 167–69. See also Patterson, *America's Struggle Against Poverty*, p. 160, on the exclusion of many working poor from the official poverty population.

[40] The role of culture of poverty and human capital assumptions in informing the programs of the War on Poverty has been widely noted. See Brauer, "Kennedy, Johnson, and the War on Poverty," pp. 105–9; Friedman, "Social and Political Context," pp. 36–37; Katz, *Undeserving Poor*, pp. 91–94; Zarefsky, *President Johnson's War on Poverty*, pp. 106–9; and Patterson, *America's Struggle Against Poverty*, chap. 7.

logical outcome of America's cold war global containment policy: the war in Vietnam.[41] Little more than a year after the passage of the Economic Opportunity Act, as Michael Harrington remembered, "the political and emotional priorities of the Government changed. Domestic reconstruction was no longer central; Southeast Asia was."[42] In the summer of 1965, OEO's Office of Plans, Progress, and Evaluations produced a long-range plan for ending poverty; it called for a jobs program, more social services, and a negative income tax, with a recommended outlay of $10 billion a year, a serious proposal ten times the then-current OEO appropriation. By December 1965, the Vietnam escalation had induced a "reign of austerity," and thereafter OEO had to defend even its current low level of appropriations.[43] In the eyes of its many critics, the War on Poverty appeared to be scarcely more than a skirmish.

Despite the limitations on sustainable programs that would truly benefit the poor, two phenomena intersected to dramatically reduce the official poverty rate in the sixties and early seventies: the economic growth resulting from Vietnam-related deficit spending and the "unsung revolution" in the expenditures of New Deal transfer programs. Neither was an intended consequence of the War on Poverty as originally conceived. The effects of this expansion were very uneven. The poor who benefited most from the expansion of these existing programs and economic growth were the aged, disabled, or the working white-male heads of household, not the nonaged, minority, and poor in female-headed households.[44] Substantial segments of the middle class benefited, from both the expansion of cash transfers and subsidies, and from new employment in the social service sector.

Furthermore, the most direct beneficiaries of even the targeted antipoverty programs, according to one historian, were "the middle-class doctors, teachers, social workers, builders, and bankers who provided federally subsidized goods and services of sometimes suspect value." Middle-class service providers benefited so thoroughly because most of the programs targeted on the poor provided services and not cash. As importantly, the federal programs left a great deal of discretion to local politicians and administrators. The fact that local school superintendents controlled money allocated under Title I of the Elementary and Secondary Education Act meant that most of it was diverted to the nonpoor; the

[41] George Herring, *America's Longest War: The United States and Vietnam, 1950–1975* (New York: Wiley, 1979), portrays Vietnam as the inevitable outcome of the postwar policy of containment, rather than a bureaucratic blunder or specific liberal failure, in much the same way as I interpret domestic policy as constrained by longer term choices and misplaced policy priorities.

[42] Michael Harrington, *Fragments of the Century* (New York: Saturday Review Press, 1973), pp. 204–5.

[43] Matusow, *Unraveling of America*, pp. 250–51.

[44] See ibid., p. 240, on the antipoverty effect of war spending; see Sheldon H. Danziger and Daniel H. Weinberg, "Introduction," and Danziger, Haveman, and Plotnick, "Antipoverty Policy," in Danziger and Weinberg, *Fighting Poverty*, pp. 9, 56–57, on the effect of New Deal transfer programs. The phrase "unsung revolution" is Patterson's, in *America's Struggle against Poverty*.

fact that hospitals and doctors could charge customary fees under Medicare and Medicaid meant that physicians' salaries expanded dramatically along with medical price inflation. In 1968, by one estimate, doctors gained an average of $3,900 as a result of these programs. As Kenneth B. Clark and Jeannette Hopkins concluded at the time, with thinly veiled scorn, "Politicians, social workers, social scientists, community actionists, and some indigenous workers have all benefitted to one degree or another from anti-poverty programs. The poor seem to have benefitted less."[45]

COMMUNITY ACTION: THE FAILURE OF POLITICAL MOBILIZATION

Many commentators identify the War on Poverty most closely with the Community Action Program (CAP), the diverse collection of over a thousand federally funded, local, neighborhood-based antipoverty agencies whose mission was to coordinate existing social services and bring new services closer to the poor. Together with Head Start, Legal Services, and the Job Corps, CAP formed the centerpiece of the new War on Poverty. Although it absorbed a relatively small portion of the social-welfare budget, CAP attracted ceaseless controversy and media attention in the midsixties. The image of radical sociologists "stirring up the poor" at the center of Daniel Patrick Moynihan's *Maximum Feasible Misunderstanding* came to dominate images of CAP and the War on Poverty far in excess of reality, however. In fact, local political elites controlled most of the local Community Action Agencies from the start; in most local agencies, social workers administered traditional services with minimal heed to the original legislative intent, that the programs be developed with "maximum feasible participation" of the poor residents themselves.[46] Yet community action *was* different from other social policy efforts, at least in its use of the neighborhood and the community as the unit of rehabilitation rather than the individual or the family, or a fictional community of people who happened to fall below an arbitrary income line.

From the beginning, community action incorporated conflicting purposes. Initially it was supposed to incorporate social scientific study, but the idea of scientifically controlled demonstration projects collapsed when Johnson decided to give a Community Action Agency to any city that wanted one,

---

[45] Matusow, *Unraveling of America*, pp. 240–42, 221–32. On localism, see Friedman, "Social and Political Context," pp. 38–41. Kenneth B. Clark and Jeannette Hopkins, *A Relevant War against Poverty: A Study of Community Action Programs and Observable Social Change* (New York: Harper and Row, 1969), p. 252.

[46] Daniel P. Moynihan, *Maximum Feasible Misunderstanding: Community Action in the War on Poverty* (New York: Free Press, 1969). On elite domination of most of the programs, see Matusow, *Unraveling of America*, pp. 245–46, 251–52. On the overwhelming service orientation of most CAAs, see Peter Eisinger, "Comments," in Haveman, *Decade of Federal Antipoverty Programs*, pp. 279–81.

spreading CAP's already meager resources even thinner. Another goal was to encourage the coordination of local social service agencies at the neighborhood level, but this was also unsuccessful, because established city institutions were reluctant to give up sovereignty over social-welfare resources. The goal of citizen participation, enshrined in the "maximum feasible participation" clause of the federal legislation, was never adequately defined, yet it became the principal focus of controversy as local militants challenged the control of the programs by mayors and social service agencies. Some of the more radical antipoverty planners such as Richard Boone and Lloyd Ohlin, who had participated in President Kennedy's Committee on Juvenile Delinquency, envisioned various forms of political organization and direct pressure by the poor themselves to challenge urban institutions to change. They had wanted to develop community competence and indigenous leadership among the poor, and help them to confront bureaucratic rigidity and unresponsiveness. Yet despite the controversy and scholarly attention they attracted, their tenure and influence was limited.[47]

In a small number of the over one thousand cities that received Community Action Agencies, civil-rights and poverty-rights activists did win control over neighborhood programs and pressured local institutions to change. But in most cities, the mayors who initiated Community Action Agencies minimized the participation of the poor by centralizing control and stacking the poverty boards with political appointees. Local community action faced many political pitfalls, from hostile traditional agencies withholding support and cooperation, to established political machines, black and white, wanting to use the resources for building political strength, to ethnic militants more concerned with tactics of disruption and building personal political bases than with community organizing.[48] For the most part, local Community Action Agencies provided services to the poor without their political involvement and with little support for political mobilization.

Nonetheless, in some cases, local CAAs did produce dramatic results. This happened when strong, independent black rights organizations pressured CAAs to support institutional change, political mobilization, and community organization in poor neighborhoods. Without an independent and nonviolent

---

[47] For the genesis of the conflicting community action ideas in the President's Committee on Juvenile Delinquency, the Ford Foundation, and in New York's Mobilization for Youth, see Peter Marris and Martin Rein, *Dilemmas of Social Reform: Poverty and Community Action in the United States*, rev. ed. (Chicago: Aldine, 1977); and Matusow, *Unraveling of America*, pp. 107–12. For the transformation of Community Action's organizational mission to include citizen participation, though their case is overstated and not generalizable to all CAAs, see Paul E. Peterson and J. David Greenstone, "Racial Change and Citizen Participation: The Mobilization of Low-Income Communities through Community Action," in Haveman, *Decade of Federal Antipoverty Programs*, pp. 242–56. For a range of purposes, see Katz, *Undeserving Poor*, pp. 97–101.

[48] Matusow, *Unraveling of America*, pp. 248–64, surveys a range of cities, and arrives at dim conclusions of the efficacy of community action, mainly due to its vulnerability to local elites.

black community movement, local political elites went unchallenged in the control and shaping of Community Action Agencies and programs. The existence of an independent black movement was not a sufficient condition for this innovation; a case in point was Chicago, where the mayor's office managed to maintain control of the poverty program despite vigorous opposition. And even where black militants were able to capture control of the local CAA, as in San Francisco, the resources available through that control were often not sufficient to create a broad community movement. Yet, as a number of studies of local agencies have shown, those few communities that stressed nonviolent mobilization and community organizing got more results in terms of institutional reform and better services than those who focused just on services. Cities with strong, independent black movements to back up these efforts went farthest down the road of empowerment and institutional change.[49] In some cases, then, federal sponsorship did provide needed resources and legitimacy, but the driving force of social change in these instances was independent and strong black leadership and organization, not community action. Michael Katz has stated that "community action, for all its problems, nourished and intensified a growing citizen's movement, reshaped local politics, and launched a new generation of minority leaders, many of them women, into public life." More local studies of the War on Poverty dealing with the question of long-range impact need to be written before a final judgment can be made, but it seems that the statement is much more appropriate applied to the black movement itself, rather than to the Community Action Program.[50]

By 1966, the scope of CAP's activities had been sharply curtailed by a coalition of big-city mayors and members of Congress unsympathetic to political mobilization in any form, even voter registration. The outlines of a trend are evident by the end of 1965. In early 1965, the U.S. Conference of Mayors, threatened by experiments in voter registration and political organizing in cities like Syracuse, New York, interceded with administration officials to pressure them to stop these activities. By the fall of 1965, the administration had forced radicals such as Richard Boone out of OEO. Congress thereafter explicitly prohibited voter registration activities in federal antipoverty programs. The administration's rejection of James Farmer's grant application for his proposed Center for Community Action Education in early 1966 signaled to African Americans the waning commitment of the federal government to anything that

[49] On the importance of strong, independent black movements on a successful CAP, see J. David Greenstone and Paul E. Peterson, *Race and Authority in Urban Politics* (Chicago: University of Chicago Press, 1976); Paul E. Peterson and J. David Greenstone, "Racial Change and Citizen Participation: The Mobilization of Low-Income Communities through Community Action," in Haveman, *A Decade of Federal Antipoverty Programs*, pp. 242–47, 266–67; James J. Vanecko, "Community Mobilization and Institutional Change: The Influence of the Community Action Program in Large Cities," *Social Science Quarterly* 50 (December 1969): 610–11; and Matusow, *Unraveling of America*, p. 268.

[50] Katz, *Undeserving Poor*, p. 114.

smacked of political organizing or voter registration. Thereafter, Congress increasingly mandated the kinds of programs local CAAs could run, limiting local options to the so-called national emphasis programs such as Head Start that showed little taint of political mobilizing. Never a great threat to local power, Community Action in the War on Poverty settled back into traditional client-bureaucrat forms of service provision and accommodation to political and bureaucratic elites.[51]

OEO's purpose was gradually recast. As urban rioting became a central concern of the agency, OEO directed its resources even further away from mobilizing the poor toward employing local activists in social service agencies. A number of assessments claim that federal money was sent in to placate the ghettos and to incorporate black elites into the political system by expanding employment in urban agencies.[52] Whether the movement of civil-rights activists from community politics to bureaucratic politics represented the co-optation of movement energies, or indeed, whether the black movement had much energy to co-opt after 1966, is a matter of some disagreement. In different contexts, government may have served to co-opt, in others to stimulate, local community mobilization.[53] Nonetheless, the dominant legacy of the Great Society expansion of social services for the black community was the incorporation of middle-class blacks into urban politics and the creation of a new class structure of middle-class public-sector employees and lower-class service recipients. In Saint Louis, for example, a recent case study found that the Community Action Agency hired local activists and subjected them to local and federal guidelines, creating a segregated "arena" of poverty politics insulated from the main levers of power in the city.[54]

Far more destructive of the more radical grass-roots community organizations were the federal and local-law enforcement policies of repression, harassment, and infiltration discussed in the chapter by Robin Kelley and in various other studies.[55] These studies stress the aggressive and disruptive effect on black

[51] Frances Fox Piven and Richard A. Cloward, *Why Americans Don't Vote* (New York: Pantheon, 1988), p. 177, on congressional restrictions on voter registration in antipoverty programs. For incidents in the curtailment of OEO political mobilization, see Matusow, *Unraveling of America*, pp. 245–50.

[52] Zarefsky, *President Johnson's War*, p. 104; Michael K. Brown and Steven P. Erie, "Blacks and the Legacy of the Great Society: The Economic and Political Impact of Federal Social Policy," *Public Policy* 29 (Summer 1981): 317.

[53] Brown and Erie, "Blacks and the Legacy of the Great Society," pp. 317–19; Piven and Cloward, *Regulating the Poor*, pp. 272–76; Raab, "What War and Which Poverty?" pp. 54–55; Fainstein and Fainstein, *Urban Political Movements*, pp. 231–32.

[54] Brown and Erie, "Blacks and the Legacy of the Great Society," pp. 317–28; on Saint Louis, see Robert J. Kerstein and Dennis R. Judd, "Achieving Less Influence with More Democracy: The Permanent Legacy of the War on Poverty," *Social Science Quarterly* 61 (September 1980): 208–20.

[55] In addition to Robin D. G. Kelley's work, see, on the local level, William Chafe, *Civilities and Civil Rights: Greensboro, North Carolina, and the Black Struggle for Freedom* (New York: Oxford University Press, 1980). On the FBI, see David J. Garrow, *From "Solo" to Memphis* (New York: Norton,

rights groups of law enforcement officials, who often purposefully tried to exacerbate the tensions between rival groups or, less covertly, resorted to out-right violence against black organizations in pursuit of "law and order." What-ever the motivations, and whatever the effects of the widespread civil violence in the inner cities of the 1960s, most often the precipitating event involved police in community tensions over issues of police brutality. And as William Ryan pointed out at the time, although rioters destroyed millions of dollars in prop-erty, it was the police who killed the most people by far in the riots of the 1960s.[56]

LOCAL POLITICAL MOBILIZATION: ACHIEVEMENTS AND LIMITATIONS

At root, the problem of poverty as envisioned by a broad range of black activists was one of power. In terms that were widely employed and debated within the black freedom movement, George Wiley offered in 1968 a theory of poverty and power voiced in pragmatic terms:

> I am not at all convinced that comfortable, affluent, middle-class Americans are going to move over and share their wealth and resources with the people who have none. But I do have faith that if the poor people who have the problems can organize, can exert their political muscle, they can have a chance to have their voices and their weight felt in the political processes of this country—and there is hope.[57]

Similarly, Martin Luther King, Jr., wrote in 1967 of black people's confinement to lives of "voicelessness and powerlessness," where they are "subject to the authoritarian and sometimes whimsical decisions of the white power structure." King noted an essential continuity in the life experiences of the black poor: "The plantation and the ghetto were created by those who had power both to confine those who had no power and to perpetuate their powerlessness. The problem of transforming the ghetto is, therefore, a problem of power."[58] Other, more stri-dent voices at the time were employing the rhetoric of revolutionary violence and ideological nationalism in response to the challenges posed by urban riot-

---

1981); Kenneth O'Reilly, "Racial Matters": The FBI's Secret File on Black America, 1960–1972 (New York: Free Press, 1989); Ward Churchill and Jim Vander Wall, Agents of Repression: The FBI's Secret War against the Black Panther Party and the American Indian Movement (Boston: South End Press, 1988).

[56] For the riots as a form of protest against grievances in the ghetto, chiefly police practices, and that involved a broad cross-section of black communities, not simply the underclass, see Robert M. Fogelson, Violence as Protest: A Study of Riots and Ghettos (Garden City, N.Y.: Doubleday and Co., 1971). On the "black body count," see William Ryan, Blaming the Victim, 2nd ed. (New York: Vintage, 1976).

[57] Quoted in Nick Kotz and Mary Lynn Kotz, A Passion for Equality (New York: Norton, 1977), p. 231.

[58] Martin Luther King, Jr., Where Do We Go from Here? (New York: Harper and Row, 1967) p. 36.

ing and a national government apparently reneging on its commitment to full equality for blacks and opportunity for the poor. Still, Wiley's and King's quieter viewpoints were testimony to the enduring hope as well as the anger and disillusionment in black activist circles.

To many black leaders, collective empowerment always had a dual meaning: as Wiley and many of the exponents of black reparations understood it, in the sense of the potential impact that political power could have on the resources available from outside of black communities; and as Kenneth Clark articulated in *Dark Ghetto*, in the sense of the effect of community organization and social action on the transformation of black communities from within, its effect on the morale of the poor, their sense of purpose and hope. Martin Luther King, Jr., in his later social thought and public rhetoric exhibited both themes, synthesizing them into a coherent plea for federal resources and internal community transformation through social mobilization.[59]

Yet the urban challenge to local and national power in the sixties did not begin in political theory, but in the specific tensions and social relations of the inner cities. The social history of the urban North after World War II represents one of the most challenging frontiers for twentieth-century historiography. The methodologies required to analyze the dynamics and achievements of local political movements differ profoundly from analyses of the origins and effects of federal policymaking. Narrative community histories of the urban North do not yet approach the quality of Southern studies such as William Chafe's substantial study of the Greensboro, North Carolina, black movement.[60] Case studies, participant observation, and memoirs are of mixed usefulness in answering the questions posed by historians concerned with gauging the potential for grassroots political mobilization to change the political and economic context of urban poverty.[61] Research is complicated by the absence of the detailed records kept by more formal organizations and agencies, by the transience and sheer numerical profusion of many local organizations, and by their localist orientation, which makes generalization hazardous. Data on the composition of urban movements is not as extensive as the arrest and survey data on rioting in the

---

[59] Kenneth Clark, *Dark Ghetto: Dilemmas of Social Power* (New York: Harper and Row, 1965); Kenneth Clark and Harlem Youth Opportunities Unlimited, Inc., *Youth in the Ghetto: A Study of the Consequences of Powerlessness and a Blueprint for Change* (New York: Harnov, 1964); see also my dissertation, "'Beyond Civil Rights': African-American Political Thought and Urban Poverty, 1960–1973," for a discussion of King's synthesis of self-help and reparations themes.

[60] Chafe, *Civilities and Civil Rights*.

[61] To take only Chicago movements as an example, the following are all studies by participants or leaders who approach their subjects from religious and moral standpoints: Arthur M. Brazier, *Black Self-Determination: The Story of the Woodlawn Organization* (Grand Rapids, Mich.: Eerdmans, 1969); Alan B. Anderson and George W. Pickering, *Confronting the Color Line: The Broken Promise of the Civil Rights Movement in Chicago* (Athens: University of Georgia Press, 1986); and John Hall Fish, *Black Power/White Control: The Struggle of the Woodlawn Organization in Chicago* (Princeton: Princeton University Press, 1973).

1960s, or as extensive as the data on the composition of Community Action poverty boards. A survey of available data from case studies by Norman and Susan Fainstein revealed that complex quantitative socioeconomic variables could not predict whether people would or would not be likely to become involved in local movements. Blacks predominated in urban protest, and movement leaders were not exceptionally higher or lower in economic status than were typical members of their communities. Leadership ranks included more women and lower-class blacks than in the Southern black movement. Explanations of why blacks protested therefore would have to take into account the political consciousness and life histories of activists in all of their particularity.[62] Assessments of "success" and "failure" will occur in the absence of quantifiable "outcomes," and will be influenced by the perceptions of general decline in inner-city neighborhoods that attention to the underclass has created.

What is most notable about the Northern urban insurgency that gathered strength in the sixties is its diversity of tactics and goals. In contrast to the civil rights movement in the South, Northern movements lacked an overarching goal, such as the elimination of legalized segregation and restrictions on black voting. Indeed, these movements faced perennial problems of identifying clear enemies and objectives. They targeted issues of housing, educational quality and segregation, jobs, political representation, and bureaucratic abuses in institutions from hospitals to police departments to welfare offices. The structure of urban politics made it inevitable that these movements would occur outside of conventional electoral politics and favor tactics of protest and disruption. The logic of mobilization made it inevitable that they would be local and interest-specific, focusing frequently on specific community issues like the installation of stoplights, school curriculum and hiring practices, or the provision of winter clothing allowances by welfare departments. Local public service bureaucracies became the targets of most urban political mobilization in these years. Focusing on issues of racism, exclusion, and bureaucratic abuse, local movements brought large numbers of poor people into direct confrontation with the local face of the welfare state.[63]

Relatively little scholarship has focused explicitly on what I call the "social relations of clientage" in the inner cities after World War II, and this scholarly neglect has tended to obscure the sources of resentment that poor people turned upon the dominant public bureaucracies of their communities. Poor people were not oblivious to the fact that the state was increasingly the arbiter of distributionist decisions, or that political elites worked closely with economic elites, that the "power structure" had stacked the cards against them. Janet Mcrae, one of the women interviewed by John Langston Gwaltney in the early

[62] Fainstein and Fainstein, *Urban Political Movements*, pp. xiv–xv, 172–78.
[63] Ibid., pp. 53–57, 206–8.

1970s for his book *Drylongso*, gave rich testimony to some of poor people's attitudes toward a range of institutions, including the welfare system:

> Look, the idea of welfare is good, but what happens to this idea when they actually start doing something with it? The same thing that happens with every good idea that you leave to bad white men to carry out! I have worked and paid taxes since I was seventeen, so I think that the country should help me if I can't get work or if I can't work. That's what a decent country should do for everybody in the country! But I don't have to tell you what really happens. It's just like everything here. Poor people get the leftovers and that's how it is with the welfare program too. It's just poisoning black people, men and women. We need to get *up*, not just get *over*, John! We'll never do that on this welfare system. If they thought there was any chance, they would cancel welfare yesterday. It's just more reconstruction![64]

In the urban North, the earliest battles were waged in the 1950s and early 1960s against the highway and redevelopment authorities. By 1970, four hundred community fights against various highway plans were in progress, largely "negative" campaigns aimed at stopping the residential demolition connected with urban redevelopment. They were relatively effective, but their ability to address the economic sources of neighborhood decline was limited. Nonetheless, it was in these fights that many urban activists obtained essential skills for later battles. And some movements, such as the Cooper Square Development Committee in New York, functioned for over ten years, generated their own renewal plans, and supported various subsequent community mobilizations around tenants' rights, education, welfare rights, and medical eligibility issues. The Cooper Square Development Committee exemplified another tendency, that once they gained momentum, organizations would broaden the range of issues they addressed.[65]

School systems were the most frequent targets of protest, with battles over segregation, educational quality, curriculums, and administrative control raging in many cities. The battle in Chicago between Superintendent Benjamin Willis and the Chicago Freedom Movement, and the New York City fights over community control were only the more notable of many bitter and intense educational battles. Confrontations with the police over brutality were the occasions for some of the most militant protests; the Black Panthers made self-defense against the police the central issue of a mass movement in Oakland. Neither schools nor police were the most powerful institutions that created or sustained poverty, but the daily interaction of these officials with the poor on terms often

[64] John Langston Gwaltney, *Drylongso: A Self-Portrait of Black America* (New York: Vintage, 1980), p. 123.

[65] Harry C. Boyte, *The Backyard Revolution: Understanding the New Citizen Movement* (Philadelphia: Temple University Press, 1980), p. 11; Fainstein and Fainstein, *Urban Political Movements*, pp. 43–46.

degrading and humilitating and their proximity in poor neighborhoods made them logical targets of protest.[66]

Client-centered political mobilization reached its zenith with the formation of welfare rights groups in scores of cities: their center of gravity was Boston and New York. Although they involved a small proportion of the welfare caseload, they were able though tactics of protest and disruption to win important benefits for all people on welfare and to remove some of the stigma attached to welfare that kept eligible people from applying. Frances Fox Piven and Richard Cloward have pointed to the roots of welfare rights mobilization in federal programs: the new services that offered the poor information, legal assistance, and skills in community organizing, as in the cases of Mobilization for Youth in New York or the VISTA volunteers who acted as welfare rights organizers. But community organizing around welfare rights had sources independent of federal initiative, which can hardly be said to have been the main spur to welfare rights activism, except perhaps in New York, where Piven and Cloward conducted most of their research. The civil rights movement was a far greater example and impetus to welfare rights mobilization.[67] Welfare rights organizers came from civil rights groups, such as the Congress of Racial Equality, who supplied George Wiley, the energetic executive secretary of the National Welfare Rights Organization; from white leftists such as the students who staffed the Students for a Democratic Society's Economic Research and Action Projects; and, not least, from the ranks of welfare recipients themselves, women such as Johnnie Tillman and Beulah Sanders, who achieved positions of national leadership on the basis of their success in winning local victories around campaigns for special grants and winter clothing allowances to which they were entitled but which welfare caseworkers arbitrarily withheld.[68] Together with the legal and administrative reforms of the late sixties and early seventies, broadly based welfare rights activism shares the credit for the expansion of the AFDC rolls and other programs such as food stamps, and the consequent alleviation of some of the deepest income poverty in the cities. Winter clothing allowances and greater

[66] On community control, see Alan A. Altshuler, *Community Control: The Black Demand for Participation in Large American Cities* (New York: Pegasus, 1969); and Fainstein and Fainstein, *Urban Political Movements*, chaps. 4, 6, and pp. 206–8. On the Chicago school fight, see Matusow, *Unraveling of America*, pp. 200–202; and Anderson and Pickering, *Confronting the Color Line*, chaps. 4–5.

[67] See Frances Fox Piven and Richard Cloward, *Poor People's Movements* (New York: Vintage Books, 1979), chap. 5, and Piven and Cloward, *Why the Poor Don't Vote*, p. 176, for the claim that federal programs were the crucial stimulant to welfare rights activity. On the importance of the civil rights movement, see George T. Martin, "The Emergence and Development of a Social Movement Organization among the Underclass: A Case Study of the National Welfare Rights Organization" (Ph.D. diss., University of Chicago, 1972), p. 223.

[68] Kotz and Kotz, *A Passion for Equality*. On the ERAP projects, see James Miller, *"Democracy Is in the Streets"* (New York: Simon and Schuster, 1987), pp. 201–5; Sarah Evans, *Personal Politics* (New York: Knopf, 1979), pp. 126–45; and Wini Breines, *Community and Organization in the New Left* (New York: Praeger, 1982), pp. 125–26, 136–39.

cash and in-kind welfare payments did not eliminate poverty—indeed, welfare has never lifted families above the poverty line—but these things did matter to poor women trying to raise families. And as did no other mobilization of poor people in the twentieth century, welfare rights activism demonstrated the capacity of poor people to overcome the political "passivity" so often associated with their poverty and engage in purposeful and organized political action on their own behalf.[69]

Not all movements were directed against public bureaucracies, to be sure. A substantial number of community protests targeted private interests: corporations, retail establishments, and landlords with economic power over the job opportunities and consumer options of the black community. Rent strikes and squatters' movements were common throughout the decade—Jesse Gray's leadership of the Harlem rent strike of 1963–64 was only the most well known. Although victories over particular landlords were frequent, rent strikes failed to halt the larger processes of neighborhood deterioration, for landlords were as often the victims of the same processes creating depressed job and housing markets.[70] Operation Breadbasket, an effort of the Southern Christian Leadership Conference (SCLC) based in Chicago under Reverend Jesse Jackson, achieved modest success in winning employment from corporations through the boycott tactic, which was used earlier by FIGHT in Rochester, New York, with dramatic success in its contest with Kodak.[71] Campaigns against retail practices and pricing policies in the ghetto were common: the Square Deal campaign in Chicago's Woodlawn neighborhood brought community pressure on establishments selling inferior merchandise or dispensing short-weighted goods. Campaigns against credit discrimination and the prevalent practice of "redlining" neighborhoods by local banks often combined in the late sixties and early seventies with community-based movements for housing rehabilitation and community development corporations devoted to indigenous economic development.[72]

[69] See Patterson, *America's Struggle against Poverty*, pp. 167–84, for the many sources in the expansion of social welfare, although he downplays the impact of the small number of welfare rights members; Piven and Cloward, *Poor People's Movements*, chap. 5; Kotz and Kotz, *A Passion for Equality*. The most thorough and thoughtful assessment of welfare rights, one that stresses the positive achievements of the movement despite its many setbacks, is Guida West, *The National Welfare Rights Movement: The Social Protest of Poor Women* (New York: Praeger, 1981), esp. pp. 384–87.

[70] Michael Lipsky, *Protest in City Politics* (Chicago: Rand-McNally, 1970), stresses the limitations of rent strikes in city politics, the importance of publicity and alliances with more powerful actors.

[71] For an account of the limited successes of Operation Breadbasket, see Adam Fairclough, *To Redeem the Soul of America: The Southern Christian Leadership Conference and Martin Luther King, Jr.* (Athens: University of Georgia Press, 1987). For an account of the contest between FIGHT (Freedom, Integration, Honor God Today) and Kodak in Rochester, see Sanford D. Horwitt, *Let Them Call Me Rebel: Saul Alinsky: His Life and Legacy* (New York: Knopf, 1989), pp. 461–500.

[72] Horwitt, *Let Them Call Me Rebel*, p. 299; Harry C. Boyte, *The Backyard Revolution: Understanding the New Citizen Movement* (Philadelphia: Temple University Press, 1980), pp. 132–33. On CDCs, see Charles Hampden-Turner, *From Poverty to Dignity* (New York: Anchor Press, 1974); and Harry

Another example on the local level, the Woodlawn Organization (TWO) in Chicago, demonstrates both the potential and limits of independent community organizing as an important antipoverty strategy. Founded under the auspices of Saul Alinsky's Industrial Areas Foundation, TWO was the most sustained and successful community organization of the inner-city poor in the 1960s. Over the course of the decade, TWO emerged and sustained itself largely independent of federal funds, and in the face of indifference or hostility from Mayor Daley's machine and the Daley-controlled antipoverty establishment. TWO was a model of indigenous community organization, with a varied range of protest targets, mobilizing techniques, and service programs, recognized and even overpraised at the time by commentators. Created in 1961 in protest against the University of Chicago's South Campus Plan for slum clearance and redevelopment, TWO quickly initiated a Square Deal campaign against consumer exploitation, as well as a campaign against school segregation and overcrowding. In 1962, two thousand residents of Woodlawn under the auspices of TWO rode to city hall on a Northern Freedom Ride and inaugurated a campaign against slum landlords. Although TWO received several job-training grants from the Department of Labor, OEO usually neglected its proposals because they competed with the city's poverty bureaucracy, controlled by Mayor Daley. After a long struggle, TWO won financing for the development of low-income housing. Finally, TWO formed a multimillion-dollar Woodlawn Community Development Corporation, credited with developing low-income housing and sponsoring local businesses.[73] It is true, as Nicholas Lemann has recently argued, that the Woodlawn Organization failed in the long run to stop urban neighborhood decline in Woodlawn, whose origins lay in economic change and the migration of middle-class blacks out of the inner city. Yet recognition of the overwhelming forces contributing to community decline in inner cities should not drown out appreciation of the achievements and possibilities in this grass-roots organizing approach. In the eyes of its most thoughtful analyst, John Fish, TWO's positive contributions outweigh its limitations, notably the retarding of physical decay and redevelopment that might have occurred, and TWO's role in developing hope and competence and leadership among the poor.[74]

Edward Berndt, *New Rulers in the Ghetto: The Community Development Corporation and Urban Poverty* (Westport, Conn.: Greenwood Press, 1977).

[73] Joan E. Lancourt, *Confront or Concede: The Alinsky Citizen Action Organizations* (Lexington, Mass.: D. C. Heath, 1979), pp. 8–11; Boyte, *Backyard Revolution*, p. 56; Horwitt, *Let Them Call Me Rebel*, chap. 23 and passim; Fish, *Black Power/White Control*; and Brazier, *Black Self-Determination*. TWO was praised exhuberantly by journalist Charles Silberman in *Crisis in Black and White* (New York: Random House, 1964), chap. 10.

[74] Nicholas Lemann, *The Promised Land: The Great Black Migration and How it Changed America* (New York: Knopf, 1991), p. 122. Lemann characterizes TWO as "a perfect demonstration of the shortcomings of the empowerment theory in the real world of a late-twentieth-century American city: no matter how well organized a community was, it could not become stable and not-poor so

For all of their limitations, these local movements did involve poor people in considerable numbers in neighborhood-based community mobilizations that cut across class lines, strengthening community institutions, developing local leadership, and transforming the lives of those who became involved. These movements produced tangible benefits for poor people as well: the rehabilitation and construction of new housing, the expansion of welfare benefits and rights, and for some, new forms of social service employment. Yet for all their strength, vitality, and creativity, local political movements encountered obstacles that caused leaders and activists to search for broad, national coalitions and political solutions. Localism was at once the great strength and the great weakness of these movements, for however effective neighborhood groups might have been in stopping renewal and highway plans or in obtaining special grants from the local welfare office, they had no control over state and national policies, economic trends, and the historically fragmented structures of local metropolitan governance. The fundamental causes of black poverty lay in the political economy of cities and, indeed, of the nation, and not merely in the network of social service agencies and institutions such as the police and the schools that more directly touched the lives of the poor. In many protests, the problems of mobilizing people with few resources made reliance on third parties essential, but support from the press and foundations, not to mention the federal government, was sporadic and unreliable at best. Even more, this support could lead to adoption of social service strategies that did little to mobilize and maintain a constituency for social change, and instead lead to the co-optation of leadership into bureaucratic politics. As one assessment put it, "Even movements which began entirely in conflict with local governments were, when they incorporated positive goals, susceptible to the same temptations as movements which arose directly out of an official mandate."[75]

What became apparent to black leaders such as Martin Luther King, Jr., and George Wiley was that a politics of race and community was necessary but insufficient to transform the political economy of cities, that a real war on poverty had to be waged on behalf of all poor people. Fissures remained in the black movement between those who primarily saw emancipation through racial consciousness and struggle in local contexts and those who saw the importance of alliances with the white Left, labor, and liberals. Vietnam widened the fissures, limiting the Great Society, discrediting the black liberals who supported labor's pro-war position, feeding frustration and the rhetoric of revolutionary violence. As the energies of the white Left became absorbed in the acrimony

---

long as the people with good jobs kept moving out and the people left behind had very little income." This view is as partial as Silberman's utopian hopes almost thirty years previous. For a positive assessment, see Fish, *Black Power/White Control*, pp. 314–18.

[75] Fainstein and Fainstein, *Urban Political Movements*, pp. 46, 49, 57, 192, 227; Boyte, *Backyard Revolution*, pp. 11–12, 45–46; Lancourt, *Confront or Concede*, pp. 172–75.

between liberals and radicals on the war issue, the options on either side of the central dilemma of black politics became less viable: racial appeals were often the most effective ways to mobilize the black poor, but they were increasingly tainted with the specter of violence and militant separatism; fulfillment of the broader agenda of providing jobs and income and eliminating poverty involved alliances with whites and a class perspective, but the possibilities of class politics were fading as the white ethnic working class began its divorce with liberalism. Racial politics were a mixed blessing to antipoverty efforts, but were not all negative in their effects, as recent authors have argued: on one level, they did make class-based coalitions more difficult, especially with labor in the industrial Northeast; on another level, they mobilized many poor (though not always to stay in the ghetto) and developed leadership and possibilities for the future. Militancy and violence captured the headlines, but quieter forms of community organization continued in the inner cities.[76]

NATIONAL LOBBYING AND POOR PEOPLE'S MOBILIZATIONS

National civil rights organizations were limited in their ability to mobilize the black poor, both by scarce resources and by traditional civil rights approaches that failed to appeal to poor blacks. For the most part, national civil rights leaders and organizations hoped to guide the multifaceted grass-roots political activism of the decade, but they did not initiate it. Much of their effort after 1965 involved defending the civil rights gains that were made, monitoring the enforcement of new legislation, and lobbying on behalf of the "maximum feasible participation" provisions of the Community Action Program.[77] They also offered telling criticisms of the War on Poverty and alternatives to the limited programs designed by the liberals in power. After the legislative civil- and voting-rights victories of mid-decade, black leaders increasingly spoke to a broad range of social and economic policy issues, acknowledging the importance of class as well as race and community in their proposals and strategies for social change. They did so both in terms of making alliances with the working class and poor of other ethnic groups, and in terms of incorporating the black poor more fully in what had been generally regarded as a middle-class black movement. Formal proposals included Whitney Young's "Marshall Plan for the Negro" in 1963, Martin Luther King, Jr.'s "Bill of Rights for the Disadvantaged"

---

[76] The historiography of the black freedom struggle in the North after 1965 is very thin. See Manning Marable, *Race, Reform, and Rebellion: The Second Reconstruction in Black America, 1945–1990*, 2d ed. (Jackson: University Press of Mississippi, 1991); and Jack M. Bloom, *Class, Race and the Civil Rights Movement* (Bloomington: Indiana University Press, 1987); as well as forthcoming work by James Ralph and Komozi Woodard. For those arguing that racial politics were mainly destructive of the antipoverty commitment, see Hugh Heclo, "The Political Foundations of Antipoverty Policy," in Danziger and Weinberg, *Fighting Poverty*, pp. 312–40, and Edsall and Edsall, *Chain Reaction*.

[77] Charles V. Hamilton and Dona C. Hamilton, "Social Policies, Civil Rights and Poverty," in Danziger and Weinberg, *Fighting Poverty*, pp. 286–311.

in 1963, the "Statement of Demands for Rights of the Poor" by the Poor People's Campaign in 1968, and A. Philip Randolph's "Freedom Budget for All Americans" in 1965, all of which called for expenditures and programs for the poor and for blacks far exceeding what the administration implemented, important as standards against which to measure the disappointing appropriations of the War on Poverty. Targeting in an eclectic way both the racial and economic dimensions of black urban poverty, these proposals called for measures targeted at the racial ghettos as well as larger programmatic objectives that would benefit all Americans. They sought both internal community regeneration through self-help and community organization, and external redress through federal aid to blacks and poor people generally. Black organizations reached other pragmatic accommodations: between local political organization and national lobbying for legislation, and between race-based advocacy to address the economic sources of black underdevelopment, and class-based income and jobs policies that would benefit all Americans. Even the platform of the Black Panther party, like the later pronouncements of Martin Luther King, Jr., called for an eclectic program of urban revitalization and full employment that would appeal to both black and white, working and nonworking poor.[78]

The National Urban League was the one national organization with a traditional base in the cities. Until the 1960s, the league had been a conservative ally of business, influenced by social work philosophy, with its stress on individual rehabilitation and employment. When Whitney M. Young, Jr., took over as executive director in 1961, he worked, under the pressure of broadening militancy, to invigorate the league's programs. Examples of programs started under his administration include the National Skills Bank, to find positions for blacks; On-the-Job Training, funded by the Department of Labor, which apprenticed blacks to private firms; tutoring and fellowship programs; and services such as family counseling. In the process, Young garnered a greater share of federal and foundation resources for his programs than had any other contemporary black organization. Yet these programs shared the limitations of the more service-oriented poverty programs and did not substantially contribute to political and economic empowerment. They reached only a small percentage of the poor, and according to one historian, "tended to help those closest to the poverty line,

---

[78] On the Domestic Marshall Plan, see Nancy J. Weiss, *Whitney M. Young, Jr., and the Struggle for Civil Rights* (Princeton: Princeton University Press, 1989), pp. 151–54. King's "Bill of Rights for the Disadvantaged" is contained in Martin Luther King, Jr., *Why We Can't Wait* (New York: Harper and Row, 1963, 1964), pp. 136–40. "A Freedom Budget for All Americans," and supporting testimony by Bayard Rustin and A. Philip Randolph, can be found in U.S. Senate Committee on Government Operations, *Federal Role in Urban Affairs*, pp. 1853–2013. For the platform of the Black Panther party, see Robert L. Allen, *Black Awakening in Capitalist America: An Analytic History* (New York: Doubleday and Co., 1969), pp. 84–86. See also "Statements of Demands for Rights of the Poor Presented to Agencies of the U.S. Government by the Poor People's Campaign and Its Committee of 100, April 29–30, May 1, 1968," Southern Christian Leadership Conference Papers, King Library and Archives, Atlanta, Ga.

those with relative confidence, ambition and the knowledge to take advantage of a social agency."[79]

The Congress of Racial Equality's (CORE) efforts in the urban North centered around equal employment opportunity and school desegregation. CORE achieved some notable successes in winning jobs for blacks: in Saint Louis banks in August 1963, and in Newark's General Electric plant in November 1963, for example. These were at best piecemeal victories, however. More typically, the CORE chapters "suffered unmitigated defeats" because of their inability to win allies and national publicity (as had the Southern protests), because of divisive disputes with other organizations, and because of the failure of middle-class blacks and white volunteers who dominated the chapters to frame issues that would involve ghetto blacks.[80]

By 1965, the Student Nonviolent Coordinating Committee's (SNCC) Southern community organizing and political campaigns among the Mississippi poor had borne fruit in several independent organizations such as the Poor People's Corporation and the Mississippi Freedom Labor Union. The SNCC model of local, indigenous community organization also inspired OEO radicals such as Richard Boone to push for similar approaches in the urban North. Yet SNCC, which failed largely to build a base in Northern communities, even eventually lost its Southern base as it became absorbed in a militant politics more concerned with ideology and media exposure than with the work of community organizing.[81]

In the 1960s, the National Association for the Advancement of Colored People (NAACP) confined its antipoverty activities to lobbying for civil rights legislation and to the legal fight against job discrimination. The NAACP Labor Department, under Herbert Hill, actively filed complaints with the Equal Employment Opportunity Commission, charging violations of Title VII of the Civil Rights Act of 1964 by private contractors and labor unions. It also conducted local protests at federal construction sites in a number of cities and fought discrimination in the steel industries of Pittsburgh and Birmingham, Alabama.[82]

[79] Robert Weisbrot, *Freedom Bound: A History of America's Civil Rights Movement* (New York: Norton, 1990), pp. 166–67; Nancy J. Weiss, "Whitney M. Young, Jr.: Committing the Power Structure to the Cause of Civil Rights," in John Hope Franklin and August Meier, eds., *Black Leaders of the Twentieth Century* (Chicago: University of Illinois Press, 1982), pp. 335–36; Weiss, *Whitney M. Young, Jr.*

[80] August Meier and Elliot Rudwick, *CORE: A Study in the Civil Rights Movement, 1942–1968* (New York: Oxford University Press, 1973); Weisbrot, *Freedom Bound*, pp. 167–70.

[81] Clayborne Carson, *In Struggle: SNCC and the Black Awakening of the 1960s* (Cambridge: Harvard University Press, 1981). For the effect of SNCC on Boone's thinking, see the unpublished transcript of a conference held at Brandeis University, June 16–17, 1973, "The Federal Government and Urban Poverty," John F. Kennedy Library, pp. 351–55.

[82] Gloster B. Current, "The Significance of the NAACP and Its Impact on the 1960s," *Black Scholar* 19 (January/February 1988): 17–18.

As a militantly nonviolent alternative to spreading urban violence, the Southern Christian Leadership Conference (SCLC), under the leadership of Martin Luther King, Jr., initiated its first Northern organizing drive in Chicago in 1966. King had absorbed criticisms of his dramatic and media-focused Southern campaigns; as a result, in Chicago he tried initially to build a sustained grass-roots union of slum dwellers who would exercise political power on an ongoing basis. When the initial results of these drives seemed disappointing by the summer of 1966, SCLC turned from grass-roots organizing of slum-dwellers' unions to pursue an open-housing agreement with the city administration, a single issue that could be dramatized with protest marches like Birmingham and Selma, but that had limited appeal to the ghetto poor. The result cannot be called a success, although it did radicalize the movement and King, teaching him the limitations of confrontations with local power. In part, the success of Birmingham and Selma depended on a sympathetic press and Congress, as well as on broad support from unions and church groups, none of which could be counted on to support the Chicago protests.[83]

Three separate centers of national black political activity tried to overcome the limitations of localism and to forge broader national antipoverty constituencies: Martin Luther King's Poor People's March on Washington, George Wiley's National Welfare Rights Organization, and Bayard Rustin's and A. Philip Randolph's activities at the A. Philip Randolph Institute on behalf of a black-labor alliance. All three efforts tried to forge broad interracial constituencies around the expansion of jobs, income, and power for poor people. Although the conservative trend in national politics evident by 1966 undermined them all, they hold valuable lessons for those who continue to seek political and economic empowerment of the black poor and other disfranchised groups.

After the ambiguous achievements of Chicago, King and the SCLC sought to extend the tactics of earlier confrontations into an interracial protest movement of the poor that would directly challenge the federal government to provide both jobs and income. King's Poor People's March on Washington occurred after his death in 1968. Rallying under the "jobs or income" slogan, the Poor People's Campaign advanced proposals for jobs programs, income support, access to land and to capital, and the empowerment of the poor in the antipoverty program. Unfortunately, the specter of violence haunted the whole effort, discrediting both the Memphis marches and the national march in the eyes of the

[83] On the Chicago Freedom Movement and SCLC, see David J. Garrow, *Bearing the Cross: Martin Luther King, Jr., and the Southern Christian Leadership Conference* (New York: Morrow, 1986), chaps. 8–9; Adam Fairclough, *To Redeem the Soul of America: The Southern Christian Leadership Conference and Martin Luther King, Jr.* (Athens: University of Georgia Press, 1987), chap. 11; David L. Lewis, *King: A Biography*, 2d ed. (Urbana: University of Illinois Press, 1978), chap. 11. For the preconditions for success in Birmingham and Selma, see David J. Garrow, *Protest at Selma: Martin Luther King, Jr., and the Voting Rights Act of 1965* (New Haven, Conn.: Yale University Press, 1978). James Ralph is publishing a full-length account of the Chicago campaign, based on his dissertation.

media and Congress. The disorganization, the lack of strategic or programmatic focus, the interethnic divisions, especially between blacks and Mexican Americans, and the hostility organizers showed to the press did little to advance the cause. Although the march did dramatize the limits of federal policy and the need for a broad interracial movement for economic justice, it also uncovered the limits of dramatic confrontational protest in a conservative climate and on less focused issues than legal segregation in the South.[84]

Bayard Rustin and A. Philip Randolph's strategy of linking the black movement with a revitalized labor movement behind full-employment legislation represented one of the best hopes for the social-democratic Left in the sixties. Like William J. Wilson twenty years later, Rustin and Randolph argued for the economic advancement of blacks under the protective umbrella of full employment and minimum-wage legislation that would appeal to all Americans. At the A. Philip Randolph Institute, Rustin and Randolph devoted their energies to labor organization among blacks, voter education, and registration in the cities. But the "Negro-labor alliance" foundered on the shoals of Vietnam and the racial polarization of the later sixties, as exemplified in the Ocean Hill–Brownsville conflict in the late 1960s. Even earlier, the Johnson administration had weakened possibilities for coalition, by ruling out a large jobs program, despite the lobbying efforts of the AFL-CIO.[85] A portent of the deepening fissures in the urban working class could be seen during the violence-marred march on Cicero, Illinois, in the summer of 1966, when the angry white mob included many rank-and-file union members, not only from the traditionally conservative construction unions but also from unions whose leadership had supported the Chicago Freedom Movement.[86]

The National Welfare Rights Organization (NWRO) was the decade's most successful attempt to join local client-based movements in an organization that could lobby and protest at the national level. Although George Wiley played a crucial role in facilitating the coalition of local welfare-rights groups, raising money, and staffing the organization, the achievement was really that of the poor women who built the local organizations and the national movement. Even after the local militancy that produced concessions from local welfare agencies peaked in 1968, NWRO was able to sustain its lobbying and protest activities throughout the long fight over the Nixon administration's Family Assistance

[84] The best accounts of the Poor People's March are Fairclough, *To Redeem the Soul of America*, and Charles Fager, *Uncertain Resurrection: The Poor People's Washington Campaign* (Grand Rapids, Mich.: William B. Eerdmans Publishing Co., 1969). For details of the Poor People's March program, see "Statement of Demands for Rights of the Poor," SCLC Papers.

[85] For the social democratic alternatives advanced by Rustin and Randolph, see n. 77 above, and Bayard Rustin, *Down the Line* (New York: Quadrangle, 1971). See also Paula F. Pfeffer, *A. Philip Randolph: Pioneer of the Civil Rights Movement* (Baton Rouge: Louisiana State University Press, 1990), chap. 8. On Johnson's veto of jobs programs, see n. 37 above.

[86] Philip S. Foner, *Organized Labor and the Black Worker, 1619–1981* (1974; reprint, New York, International Publishers, 1981), p. 364.

Plan (FAP) in the early 1970s. Though NWRO's uncompromising demand for "$5500 or fight" contributed to the failure of FAP, and NWRO was accused by others on the Left of dampening local militancy by diverting political energies into a national bureaucracy, there were larger forces moving to discredit and undermine the movement. And the fundamental failure of FAP was Nixon's, who at an early stage abandoned his own legislation. The defeat of FAP led Wiley to consider the importance of broader alliances with the middle class and of policy goals that included jobs as well as welfare.[87]

Not all activists learned the same lessons from these three efforts. The March on Washington highlighted to many the importance of strengthening local organizations, to others the importance of sustained national lobbying in contrast to dramatic national protest. The NWRO held promise for organizing poor people but highlighted the pitfalls of formal organization and the importance of coalitions, of reaching out to new constituencies of poor, working and middle classes. The failure of all of these efforts to achieve their goals reflected broader trends in national politics that narrowed the options of the black movement in the North after 1966, even as African Americans were moving increasingly into public sector employment and beginning to win the mayor's office in cities such as Cleveland and Newark. The decline of labor as a crucial constituent force on the Left helped undermine the possibilities for class politics that many blacks realized were crucial to black economic liberation. The conservative resurgence in Congress and in state governments, exemplified by Ronald Reagan's gubernatorial victory in California in 1966, foreshadowed a conservative era where the rationale of economic policy turned toward redistribution of income to the richest citizens. The disaffection of the white working class in the Northern cities from the Democratic party proceeded from a complex mixture of economic stagnation and the identification of an increasingly elite-dominated national Democratic party with racial policies such as busing and affirmative action in employment. The fragmentation of the Left became evident most glaringly perhaps in the Ocean Hill–Brownsville controversy, which pitted a white teachers' union against a black community united behind community control of its schools, and accelerated the disintegration of the Black-Jewish civil rights alliance of the 1960s.

The economic and political context of ghetto poverty only worsened in the 1970s and 1980s. Economic and political power shifted to the Sunbelt and the suburbs, and the cities declined in national political power and economic resources. Real wages and productivity fell for workers generally, and urban labor markets experienced structural changes that disadvantaged young, unskilled minority males especially. The middle class developed strong resistance

[87] Kotz and Kotz, A Passion for Equality; West, The National Welfare Rights Movement; Vincent J. Burke and Lee Burke, Nixon's Good Deed: Welfare Reform (New York: Columbia University Press, 1974); Daniel P. Moynihan, The Politics of a Guaranteed Income: The Nixon Administration and the Family Assistance Plan (New York: Vintage, 1973).

to growing tax burdens, on which conservative politicians gathered support for retrenchment of welfare and social service programs. Elite control of both parties grew as the power of unions declined and the class bias in the electorate and the welfare state was exacerbated. The Reagan era witnessed the inauguration of economic policies intended to redistribute income from working- and middle-class people to the wealthy.[88]

CONCLUSION

A recurrent theme of this volume and some recent work on the underclass is that the ghetto poor cannot be understood in isolation, that general social and economic trends evident to some degree in the whole society have more adversely affected the most disadvantaged members of the society, the inner-city minority poor. A complementary insight of much recent historical research is that policies other than antipoverty, urban, and social policies have profoundly affected the shape of urban poverty. The implication of both insights is that political forces necessary to transform urban poverty must extend beyond cities to include broader social mobilization of lower-income people and minorities.

The history of social policy demonstrates a capacity to alleviate income poverty, and in rare instances, a willingness to support grass-roots social change. Yet larger policy decisions will continue to work in ways disadvantageous to the poor, unless there is more basic political mobilization of low-income people and minorities. The twentieth-century state has shown itself to be a powerful engine of social change, but the structure of politics as usual just as clearly favors elites and the enfranchised middle class. And the elite domination of American politics has gotten worse since the 1960s, not better. State support for political and electoral empowerment of poor communities has been extremely rare, for Democratic mayors in the 1960s were no more willing than Republicans to endorse grass-roots community organization and voter registration, which might upset their control of local politics. Little wonder that self-help themes have remained strong in the black community. In 1986, Marion Wright Edelman, president of the Children's Defense Fund and the woman credited with suggesting the idea of a Poor People's March on Washington to Martin Luther King, Jr., argued that "for most of the history of black America, the government has been our opponent, not our ally. The black community knows in its bones that without its strong leadership now, as in the past, little help can be expected from government or other institutions."[89]

Some contemporary analysts see hope for the Democratic party in the growing disaffection of middle-income Americans from elite domination of political

---

[88] Edsall, *The New Politics of Inequality*; Frank Levy, *Dollars and Dreams: The Changing American Income Distribution* (New York: Norton, 1988); Kevin Phillips, *The Politics of Rich and Poor* (New York: Random House, 1990).

[89] Quoted in Manning Marable, *Race, Reform and Rebellion*, p. 212.

and economic life. Their hope is that a "new populism" will take hold and inaugurate a new liberal cycle of reform, through which the urban underclass will benefit from a renewed commitment to domestic economic renewal. Others concerned with poverty policy advocate "universal" policies that will appeal to working and middle-income Americans while benefiting the poor disproportionately.

Yet history offers a cautionary note. In the past, universal policies such as Social Security or veterans' benefits have enjoyed great legitimacy, but their effectiveness as antipoverty programs has been diluted by the fact that their overwhelming beneficiaries have not been poor. Certain categories of poor people did benefit from the sheer volume of expenditures under these programs, but never in a scope adequate to the needs of all the poor. Even programs exclusively targeted on the poor have seen their resources diverted to nonpoor groups or to the operating budgets of social service bureaucracies. Clearly, policies need to sell, but just as clearly, the poor will not be politically enfranchised and economically advanced on the terms of middle-class politics, but on terms that appeal to them as aggrieved minorities, as members of depressed communities, and as marginalized workers.

Among the inner-city minority poor, the institutions that in the past supported political mobilization have weakened as the communities themselves have become more impoverished and as grass-roots political activism has waned. Middle-class activists who in the past might have contributed to community politics have either left the cities or are attracted into public bureaucracies just as unresponsive and even more economically strapped than in the 1960s. The social history of this process of institutional decline, of which the process of weakening social and family structures forms only a part, is yet to be written.

Yet grass-roots politics has not died in inner-city communities. To a certain extent, a politics of race and community will continue to be dominant on the local level. Indeed, for all of the qualifications on the statement, the War on Poverty was profoundly conditioned, for better or worse, by this politics. The claim that racial politics was uniquely and wholly destructive of the antipoverty commitment ignores the positive achievements of grass-roots mobilization, and the other forces undermining that commitment: the restricted constituent basis of the programs themselves; the intrusion of Vietnam into the calculus; the importance of economic resentments as well as racial tensions in the defection of the white working class from the Democratic party.

In the broader society, if not in social science, the intellectual dynamism of the 1960s black freedom struggle and its dialectic with white America provided some of the essential terms in which the problems of race and poverty in the cities will be addressed into the next century. The recency of the decade and its profound impact on contemporary politics, the fact that the central challenge of the decade, the integration and provision of opportunity of the urban minority poor, is still central to the domestic agenda—all these factors make balanced assessment of the decade difficult. Yet the complex and sometimes contradictory vision of the black movement is worth recapturing in all its fullness. The primacy of jobs, and the related notion that income support is a right of all Americans, was central to this vision. So was the insistence that poor people need to be mobilized politically as well as helped economically, both to further their own capacity for social competence and for the very practical purpose that antipoverty policy needs an effective constituency to support it. Finally, the specifically racial imperative in black antipoverty politics needs to be taken more seriously, that black solidarity across class lines is essential to advancement of black people economically, though not necessarily on the traditional terms of middle-class black politics, and that it is in this context as much as in the context of broader class appeals that the black poor will advance.

In August of 1967, Martin Luther King, Jr., at a Louisville voter registration rally, voiced the compelling need to deal creatively with the concentration and entrapment of poor blacks in inner cities, by using majority electoral power there to win the mayor's office and, King suggested, to "begin taxing everybody who works in the city who lives in the suburbs."[90] At the time he was groping beyond the politics of local empowerment to embrace metropolitan solutions that directly challenged the historic alliance of class privilege, racial exclusion, and independent political power in the suburbs. Yet over the past two decades, as national electoral power has shifted to the suburbs, toward upper-income voters, and toward political elites dependent to an unprecedented extent on money, the inner-city minority poor have lost power, despite the trend toward increased African-American and other minority representation in city governments. By the 1990s, the chasm separating city and suburb was widening. The development of metropolitanwide solutions to separate and unequal education, city services, housing, employment, and transportation, solutions that have made Toronto, Canada, a model city compared to Detroit and most other large U.S. cities, is still largely missing from the political agenda.[91]

Whether America's Simi Valleys can emerge from behind their curtains of historical innocence and their walls of political independence and contribute in a lasting way to metropolitan integration and economic justice remains to be seen. Whites still cling to notions of their own racial innocence, to a belief in the sufficiency of the market in achieving social justice, to the fiction that truly egalitarian social programs cannot work (they can) because they were tried and proven failures in the sixties (they were not), and, finally, to the fiction that urban poverty is principally a problem of eroding family values, welfare dependency, or deviant behavior among the poor themselves. Black America faces the challenge of bridging its own long-standing and growing class divisions while

[90] Martin Luther King, Jr., "Which Way Its Soul Shall Go," Voter Registration Rally, Louisville, Kentucky, August, 2, 1967, King Papers, series 3, Speech Files, King Center.
[91] See *Economist*, May 19, 1990, pp. 17–20.

continuing to challenge these larger social myths, making the case for social justice for all. African Americans have always offered more than "the fire next time," in the form of a variety of articulate and critical leaders making proposals for integration, jobs, income, empowerment, and social justice. Yet more than merely sounding rhetorical notes of hope and healing, and more than merely offering concrete policy prescriptions for new programs and better services, African Americans must work to reinvigorate their own and the Left's traditions of social analysis and social action.

Reframing the "Underclass" Debate

Michael B. Katz

As a metaphor of social transformation, *underclass* signifies novelty, complexity, and danger, and it conveys urgency. Unprecedented circumstances in America's cities demand action. Only, the old formulas will not work because the problems are so multifaceted and intense that they resist the usual stock of remedies on the social-policy shelf. Despite this presumption of novelty, discourse on the underclass reflects very old preoccupations about poverty and social welfare and equally ancient ways of framing the problem of the urban poor. This disjunction between the emergent metaphor and the language of analysis poses two immediate historical problems. One is tracing the origins and role of the language of poverty; I sketched this history in the Introduction. The other is empirical: assessing the claims for novelty by tracing the configurations of urban poverty, social problems, and urban form in America's past. Several of the authors of this book's chapters have addressed this issue directly.

Although journalists rather than scholars popularized the idea of an underclass, the task the authors in this book faced was less unmasking the rhetoric of the mass media than deconstructing the ideas of the social scientists who have tried to rescue the idea of the underclass by giving it a precise and scientific content. This volume's authors have showed how many of the major questions about the underclass cannot be answered without reference to history and how an inaccurate or incomplete historical understanding often undercuts the work of social scientists.

One way of organizing this concluding chapter would be to take the issues in the underclass debate one by one and comment on them from the vantage point of recent historical research. This does not seem to me either the most interesting or productive tack or the one that follows most consistently from the analyses in this book. For I take one message of the authors to be this: social scientists have framed the underclass debate in ways that limit the usefulness of their work for both understanding the phenomenon and guiding policy.

For the most part, the underclass debate concentrates on individual or family pathology among African Americans and, to a lesser extent, Latinos. Both popular commentators and social scientists try to explain the interconnections between out-of-wedlock pregnancy, joblessness, prolonged welfare dependency, low educational achievement, drugs, and criminal behavior and to chart their collective relation to the concentrated, persistent poverty in America's inner cities. However, the sources of the concentration and persistence of poverty receive much less attention than do their alleged results. This is one reason why institutions and politics have played so small a role in the debates and research. A few issues have received most of the attention by scholars directly concerned with the underclass: among institutions, only schools; and among social processes, only the presumed outmigration of middle-class African Americans from inner cities, the emergence of a spatial mismatch between people and jobs, and, to a lesser extent, deindustrialization. Even these function primarily as backdrops that set the scene for the individual and family behavior of primary concern.

Historians take a longer view. The point is not that they take one side in the debate between the relative importance of social structure and culture. Most of the authors of this book would consider the dichotomy silly, not simply because most human actions reflect a little of both but because of its implicit assumptions. Indeed, the dichotomy between culture and structure is a social construction more reflective of the institutional organization of knowledge than of social experience; social science research often translates culture as the unexplained variance in regression equations that measure structural influences and frames culture and structure as fixed, opposing entities rather than as contingent and interactive. The search for the relative influence of each reveals more about the methodological preferences within academic disciplines than the phenomena signified by "family," "race," or "class."[1] Even more, the dichotomy between culture and structure constricts the options for interpretation, for it leaves individuals only as either victims or atoms, as helpless before the tides of history or detached from the larger world around them, acting out of compliance with the norms that govern narrow subpopulations or from a corrupted free will. This view gives no scope to politics, to the social constraints on individual choice, or to the role of institutions in structuring available alternatives. It leaves no room to develop interpretations that blend constraint and agency.

Agency, however, is one of the most important themes in contemporary historical writing. As it is used by historians, *agency* has three meanings. One refers to action directed toward "private" goals, such as the maintenance of home and family or the pursuit of rewarding work. In its second sense, agency means collective action directed toward "public" goals, including politics, protest, and war, among many others. A third form of agency also involves collective action, only on a much larger scale, "the collective pursuit of global social transformation," as in revolution.[2] Agency, in its first and second meanings, flows through the chapters of this book as the authors show how throughout

---

[1] On the dichotomy between culture and structure, see Andrew Thompson Miller, "Looking at African American Families: Recognition and Reaction" (Ph.D. diss., University of Pennsylvania, 1991).

[2] Alex Callinicos, *Making History: Agency, Structure and Change in Social Theory* (Ithaca, N.Y.: Cornell University Press, 1988), pp. 9–10.

American history, urban poor people individually and collectively pursued their own survival and how politics, institutions, and ideologies shaped and constrained their struggles.

As with culture, the authors reject any rigid dichotomy or opposition between agency and structure. For structures do not simply limit action; as explanations, they are not alternatives to agency. Rather, structures create a framework for the exercise of action. They present agents with possible paths to follow in the pursuit of their goals, and they provide them with resources to use along the way.[3] As they move through them, agents do not leave structures unscathed. They use, change, and rebuild them. Structures and actions, therefore, remain inseparable, bound in a dynamic mutuality constantly reshaping itself over time and understood best as history.

This book is about the interplay of structure, culture, and action. It tells a story of processes, politics, and ideas. It reframes the underclass debate by shifting the focus away from individual and family pathology to a set of processes at work over a very long span of time and to the ideas and politics that generated and sustained them. Those processes were various: structural transformations of the economy; the working out of racism in time and space; the consequences of institutional development; the reshaping of urban space; and the activities of the state. Understanding the underclass in this way also reframes the issues for policy, because it casts doubt on the ability of policies that attempt to micro-manage individual and family behavior to redirect the processes that have resulted in concentrated and persistent poverty and their correlates.

There is another reason for reframing the debate. The historical processes described in this book transformed more than the circumstances of the urban poor. They have transformed all of urban America and most American families as well. Social science scholarship on the underclass generally ignores these connections. It hives off the underclass, which it places alone under a very high-powered microscope. It offers a class analysis based almost entirely on the examination of one class; it uses the language of class but misses or ignores its relational dimension. Indeed, it defines the underclass as outside of, beyond, not part of the class structure. Social science thereby misses a very important point: the processes creating an underclass degrade all our lives. The degradation of civic experience, democracy, and the public sphere in contemporary urban America result from the same forces that produced the underclass. Neither, therefore, can be understood without reference to the other. The message for policy is very clear: We will flourish or sink together.

The four sections of this concluding chapter reframe the underclass debate. They shift the focus of attention away from individual and family behavior and toward *places*. They suggest policies that concentrate on regenerating inner cities rather than on reforming their residents. The first section shows why the

[3] Ibid., pp. 235–37.

current situation in inner cities is unprecedented. The second examines four great processes—migration, marginalization, exclusion, and isolation—that shaped the transformation of America's cities. The third outlines the role of government policy and social reform in shaping responses to social transformation and contributing to the decline of once-vital cities and the increase of poverty within them. The final section reintegrates the underclass with the rest of America by highlighting the individual and collective agency of the urban poor, the social and economic trends that affect all classes, and the institutional failure that degrades the lives of all Americans and their cities.

NOVELTY

Consider, first, the question of novelty. Is there an unprecedented configuration of poverty and related problems within today's cities? Or, as Nicholas Lemann asserts, do contemporary inner cities embody "really an old problem that has become more isolated and concentrated and, as a result, gotten worse and more obvious"?[4] The chapters of this book very clearly demonstrate the qualitative differences between past and present. Certainly, poverty pervaded American cities throughout their history, even in periods commonly remembered as prosperous; racism disfigured the lives of African Americans; even sympathetic observers reported high levels of out-of-wedlock pregnancy and social disorganization within turn-of-the-century ghettos. But poverty, racism, and social disorganization are not fixed, objective categories. In part, they express relations between individuals, groups, institutions, and their settings.[5] Always they have taken their shape and meaning from their context, and in recent decades, that context changed dramatically with the emergence of the postindustrial city.

I use *postindustrial city* as shorthand for the new urban form that emerged in the decades following World War II. Its defining features include the production of services instead of goods, more flexibly structured workplaces, computerized work, and the dispersal of central-city functions to new mini-cities adjacent to the freeways that surround it.[6] Three transformations have shaped postindustrial cities: the transformation of their economy, demography, and space. The economic transformation consists of the replacement of manufacturing with services, especially in formerly industrial cities now characterized more by

[4] Nicholas Lemann, *The Promised Land: The Great Black Migration and How It Changed America* (New York: Alfred A. Knopf, 1991), p. 344.

[5] On race as a relational concept, see Barbara Jean Fields, "Ideology and Race in American History," in J. Morgan Kousser and James M. McPherson, eds., *Region, Race, and Reconstruction: Essays in Honor of C. Vann Woodward* (New York: Oxford University Press, 1982), pp. 143–77.

[6] On postindustrialism as a concept, see Fred Block, *Revising State Theory: Essays in Politics and Postindustrialism* (Philadelphia: Temple University Press, 1987), p. 27. I have developed the ideas in this paragraph at greater length in *The Undeserving Poor: From the War on Poverty to the War on Welfare* (New York: Pantheon, 1991), chap. 4.

the production of information than of goods, and to the new, increasingly bifurcated occupational structure that supports this emergent urban role. Demographic transformation refers to various processes: depopulation; the replacement of whites primarily of European ancestry with African Americans and Latino immigrants; the increased proportion of residents who are poor; and much larger numbers of both young adults living apart from their families and female-headed families. Spatial transformation includes suburbanization; heightened segregation; increased concentrations of poverty; the revitalization of downtowns and the decay of neighborhoods; the balkanization of districts through the location of freeways and public housing; and gentrification. All these changes, which are intricately connected, have combined to create an urban form unlike any other in history.

The transformations of economy, demography, and space constitute a national story because postindustrial cities have emerged throughout America. Nonetheless, urban patterns vary within as well as among regions. High concentrations of poverty (census tracts in which 20 to 40 percent of the residents are poor, in most definitions) cluster in older Northeastern and Midwestern cities.[7] Although Detroit and Birmingham, for example, both have a declining industrial base and a high rate of poverty, they differ in a number of ways: the growth trajectory of poverty after World War II; the timing of industrial decline; changes in the racial composition of the population; the location of industry; and the history of urban renewal.[8] In Buffalo, New York, a medium-sized city, to take another example, spatial patterns of minority poverty differ from those in the largest Northeastern cities.[9] Therefore, the generalizations that follow build a case whose details, on close inspection, vary in significant ways from city to city.

Both variations among cities and the redefinition of space within them result from late-twentieth-century patterns of uneven development. The deindustrialization of America's once-great manufacturing cities reflects a shift in the location of manufacturing rather than a decline in its importance, and links the rising industrial prosperity of some regions of the world to American urban decline. The flow of manufacturing capital out of older cities to other regions and nations precipitated their economic transformation. Within them, uneven development resulted, as well, from the flow of capital away from older minority neighborhoods into revitalized downtowns and gentrified areas. Thus, concentrated and persistent urban poverty embodies chains of disinvestment and reinvestment linking individual cities to regional, national, and global economies.

---

[7] Paul A. Jargowsky and Mary Jo Bane, "Neighborhood Poverty: Basic Questions" (Discussion Paper #H–90–3, Malcolm Wiener Center for Social Policy, John F. Kennedy School of Government, Harvard University, March 2, 1990); see also the chapter by David Bartelt.

[8] See the chapters by Thomas Sugrue and Robin D. G. Kelley.

[9] Henry Louis Taylor, Jr., "Social Transformation Theory, African Americans and the Rise of Buffalo's Post-Industrial City," *Buffalo Law Review* 39, no. 2 (Spring 1991): 569–606.

For some underclass theorists, the persistence and concentration of poverty defines the "new" problem in America's postindustrial cities. For others, poverty remains secondary to behavior, particularly the combination of out-of-wedlock childbirth, welfare dependence, poor school achievement, and crime, which, they believe, coexist in dangerous conjunction within certain neighborhoods of America's inner cities. In this section, I focus on the former—concentrated and persistent poverty—because its defining contemporary features, hopelessness, labor force detachment, and concentration, lie at the root of the behaviors that alarm other observers.

One could, however, establish a case for qualitatve difference using some of the other measures as well. Out-of-wedlock childbirth has never stood as high and marriage rates fallen as low as among African-American women in today's inner cities.[10] Crime is harder to measure over time, especially the street crime that so terrorizes inner-city residents. Official crime statistics do not help very much. Whether they capture street crime remains open to question, and they do not extend back into the nineteenth and early twentieth centuries. Nonetheless, many indicators point to a lower incidence of crime then. Recollections of those who grew up in earlier periods imply the relative safety of city streets and transportation, which young people roamed and used with a freedom impossible now. Certainly homes, apartment buildings, and offices constructed in earlier eras lacked the elaborate security precautions with which their current occupants have retrofitted them as minifortresses. Urban schools did not require armed guards. Police reports concerned themselves with different sorts of problems. Newspapers did not reflect a preoccupation among their readers with personal safety. Nor is there evidence that illegal drugs played anything like their contemporary role, that they devastated huge numbers of individuals and families, that they bred random violence and death as they do on modern city streets.

Other measures are less clear and the direction of change less certain. Welfare use is a poor indicator of behavior over time because it is partly a product of policy. It soared in the 1960s, when pressure from welfare-rights organizations and court decisions forced reluctant municipalities to accept more eligible applicants onto the rolls.[11] As for education, although dropout rates worry many today, far more minority children attend school during their adolescence and graduate from high school than in times past. Between 1939 and 1979, black college attendance soared. Whether the education minorities (or anyone else) receive is better or worse remains unclear.[12]

[10] On family trends, see David T. Ellwood and Jonathan Crane, "Family Change among Black Americans: What Do We Know?" *Journal of Economic Perspectives* 4, no. 1 (Fall 1990): 1–20.

[11] Some of this story is told in Frances Fox Piven and Richard A. Cloward, *Regulating the Poor: The Functions of Public Welfare* (New York: Pantheon Books, 1971), and *Poor People's Movements: Why They Succeed, How They Fail* (New York: Pantheon Books, 1977).

[12] On education, see the chapter by Harvey Kantor and Barbara Brenzel. See also Ira Katznelson and Margaret Weir, *Schooling for All: Class, Race, and the Decline of the Democratic Ideal* (New York: Basic Books, 1985).

America's cities always have housed large numbers of poor people. In the nineteenth century the proportion living in absolute poverty—unable to feed, clothe, and house themselves adequately—appears huge by today's standards. No strictly comparable measures exist, but at any point in the nineteenth century, an estimate that half the population of any city were poor would not exaggerate the extent of poverty. Poverty, of course, was not an exclusively urban problem. As late as 1939 more poor people lived in rural than in urban areas. I do not discuss them here because the focus of this book is on the urban situation. Nor was widespread urban poverty only a product of the old days or of the years before the Second World War. Indeed, the vaunted near-universal prosperity of the 1950s turns out to rest largely on nostalgia. In 1949, 20 percent of white and nearly 60 percent of black fully employed householders earned too little to escape poverty. As late as 1959, two of five householders in America's cities did not earn a wage large enough, by itself, to keep their families out of poverty. Without doubt, the amount of poverty in America decreased sharply after 1960.[13]

The prevalence of poverty among urban African Americans in the post–World War II years highlights a situation that bears directly on the contemporary underclass debate. There is no era in the history of urban racial ghettos to which one can look with nostalgia or for inspiration and models applicable to today. However the situation of African Americans in today's cities has changed, they never experienced prosperous, class-integrated neighborhoods. (I use integration here to signify social interaction rather than residential proximity.) Most urban African Americans, including those who worked, always were poor, and the small middle class that did exist distanced itself from its less-fortunate neighbors. Early black civil rights organizations, with their middle-class leadership, for instance, concerned themselves with access to institutions and public places and voting, not with the poverty of their communities. Black politicians cut deals with big-city machines that brought jobs and patronage to some of their supporters, but they remained by and large unwilling to shake the system that guaranteed the continued poverty of most African Americans.[14]

Nonetheless, despite the long history of urban poverty, the experience, meaning, and implications of poverty in today's cities differ from poverty of the past on three dimensions: context, relation to the labor market, and spatial distribution. The poverty of earlier periods coexisted with expanding opportunity and urban growth as unskilled and semiskilled work in cities increased throughout America's industrialization. Large industries, in fact, provided steadier work, better wages, and limited hierarchies that working people could climb. As a result, expanding opportunities opened modest avenues for social mobility. The wages of employed family members might be combined to buy property; steady

[13] See the chapters by Thomas J. Sugrue and Mark J. Stern.
[14] See the chapters by Joe W. Trotter and Robin D. G. Kelley.

employment might lead to higher pay within a factory; with the help of schooling, children could improve upon the status of their parents. These processes worked imperfectly; dramatic mobility remained rare; simply getting by continued to be difficult for most working people. Still, over time, real wages rose, most ethnic groups improved their living conditions, and their rate of poverty decreased. Poverty existed within a context of hope.[15]

All this has changed for the mostly minority populations who remain in inner cities. Deindustrialization and depopulation, not growth, shape the new context. Very few opportunities exist for industrial work; government jobs, one avenue for economic security and mobility among African Americans, have shrunk; for the most part, new jobs in the service sector either pay well but demand more education than most minorities acquire or offer part-time, non-union work that pays badly; the value of public benefits directed exclusively to poor people has eroded, many programs have been scaled back or cut, and the construction of public housing almost ceased during the 1980s. Although more muted, racism continues as well to limit the opportunities of African Americans, especially men who confront employers unwilling to hire them. Poverty now increasingly exists within a context of hopelessness.[16]

Of course, African Americans always fared worse than whites have in the labor market. Forced out of trades, excluded from many jobs, they never shared the opportunities open to white workers. In late-nineteenth-century Philadelphia, African Americans lived closer to industrial jobs than did any other group, but they held fewer of them. Still, early in the twentieth century significant numbers of black migrants to Northern cities found industrial work. In Northern cities these former sharecroppers and agricultural workers became proletarians earning their living from wages in a primarily industrial labor market that offered higher rewards and a better standard of living than did the South, the most impoverished region of the country. With the disappearance of industrial work, all this has changed. African Americans no longer live close to jobs frequently denied them. In contrast to that of the early twentieth century, the contemporary African-American experience is one of *deproletarianization*.[17]

Deproletarianization signifies both the new relationship of African Americans

---

[15] See the chapter by Thomas J. Sugrue.

[16] On job trends, see Emma Rothschild, "The Reagan Economic Legacy [part II]," *New York Review*, July 21, 1988, p. 37; and David C. Perry and Beverly McLean, "The Aftermath of Deindustrialization: The Meaning of 'Economic Restructuring' in Buffalo, New York," *Buffalo Law Review* 39, no. 2 (Spring 1991): 345–83; see also the chapter by Thomas J. Sugrue; and Joleen Kirschenman and Kathryn M. Neckerman, "'We'd Love to Hire Them, But . . .': The Meaning of Race for Employers," in Christopher Jencks and Paul E. Peterson, eds. *The Urban Underclass* (Washington, D.C.: Brookings Institution, 1991), pp. 203–32.

[17] See the chapter by Thomas J. Sugrue; Theodore Hershberg et al., "A Tale of Three Cities: Blacks, Immigrants, and Opportunity in Philadelphia, 1850–1880, 1930, 1970," in Theodore Hershberg, ed., *Philadelphia: Work, Space, Family, and Group Experience in the 19th Century* (New York: Oxford University Press, 1981).

to the labor market and the defining characteristic of the new poverty. Excluding those who could not work on account of infirmity or age, dependence (which I use in contrast to poverty because low wages kept so many workers poor) in earlier periods resulted when people lost work, usually temporarily, often in slack seasons or economic downturns. Now, especially among minorities in inner cities (and despite the growing number of working poor), poverty and dependence denote detachment from the labor force. They are the statuses associated with a very large number of people who do not work (at least in the regular economy), who have not worked for a long time, who may, in fact, never have worked, and whose prospects for employment grow increasingly dim. Although the proportion of African Americans who are poor has declined steeply since the 1960s, the number who are chronically without jobs has risen sharply. As a result, the chronically jobless compose an ever larger share of the poor, and African Americans constitute a greater share of those chronically without jobs than they did in earlier periods. This connection between race, urban poverty, and dissociation from the labor market is new in American history.[18]

The problem extends beyond joblessness. Mounting evidence points to declining wages among African Americans in recent years, even for those with more advanced educations. Should the trend hold, it will represent a consequential break with historic patterns, for it will reverse the long-term trend toward higher real wages and diminish the growing returns on schooling, evident as education became an increasingly important form of human capital in the twentieth century. It will mean that education and work do not guarantee an escape from poverty, as in post–World War II America they at long last began to do.[19]

The spatial distribution of poverty in postindustrial American cities also is new. Nineteenth-century commentators who reported growing concentrations of poverty in American cities worried about an increasing lack of contact between rich and poor, and their images prefigured the rhetoric of the underclass literature today. In fact, spatial differentiation remained far muddier than in contemporary cities, and districts like New York's notorious Five Points were exceptions. In the era before inexpensive and convenient mass transportation, rich and poor lived for the most part in close proximity as poor people clustered into pockets and alleyways near the homes of the affluent. This is the clear conclusion of social historians who have reconstructed urban neighborhoods. (It reinforces the dangers of relying on literary sources without checking out

---

[18] See the chapters by Thomas J. Sugrue and Mark J. Stern.

[19] John Bound and Richard B. Freeman, "What Went Wrong? The Erosion of the Relative Earnings and Employment of Young Black Men in the 1980s" (unpublished manuscript, August 1990); Bennett Harrison and Lucy Gorham, "What Happened to Black Wages in the 1980s? Family Incomes, Individual Earnings, and the Growth of the African-American Middle Class" (unpublished paper, June 1990).

their empirical foundation.) Indeed, even in New York City in the late nineteenth and early twentieth centuries, the geographic distance between rich and poor was usually not great. This is why the city's leading philanthropic agency, the Charity Organization Society, could develop a strategy that divided the city into districts, each with a resident committee of professionals to devise a plan for every local applicant for aid and friendly visitors who lived and ministered within the same district. Only the tip of Manhattan lacked enough well-to-do residents to put the strategy into action. A similar strategy would be impossible today.[20]

Racial ghettos began to develop even before the Great Migration of the post–World War I era. They were the seeds from which contemporary patterns of racial isolation grew. But, with African Americans comprising a relatively low proportion of urban populations until the decades following World War II, ghettos remained generally small pockets within diverse cities, and indexes of segregation stood far lower than they do now. Early in the twentieth century, European immigrants lived in more segregated neighborhoods than African Americans did. Indeed, the spreading concentration of districts both poor and black within today's cities, the ecological foundation of the underclass, is without precedent in America's history.[21]

MIGRATION, MARGINALIZATION, EXCLUSION, AND ISOLATION

Throughout modern American history four great processes shaped the experience of poverty. With the urban transformations that gave rise to the postindustrial city, each of them intensified. One result was the configuration some observers have labeled the underclass. Those processes are migration, marginalization, exclusion, and isolation. This book's chapters document them in detail. These processes interconnect so tightly that pulling them apart for discussion threatens to reify them as separable and self-contained. In truth, together they form a great force, for which no adequate label exists, driving urban transformation. The separate presentation of each, which follows, is, then, only a convenience, a way of trying to understand the same developments by looking at them from slightly different directions.

Migration, or the movement of people in space, always has constituted one of the great themes of American history. For the story of this book, it is useful to consider three sorts of population movement: the inmigration of peoples to America; the short-distance, often seasonal migration of workers within the same regions of the country; and major interregional movements, especially from the rural South to the urban North.

---

[20] For references on spatial distribution, see the chapters by Joe Trotter and Thomas J. Sugrue. On the Charity Organization Society, see Michael B. Katz, *In the Shadow of the Poorhouse: A Social History of Welfare in America* (New York: Basic Books, 1986), pp. 58–84.

[21] On the origins of ghettos, see the chapter by Joe W. Trotter.

There are two ways to think about the relation of immigration to the under-class story. One is the comparison of group experience, which centers on the familiar but still critical question: Why did the descendants of European immigrants move out of both inner cities and poverty more successfully than African Americans have? I will return to this issue. The other question is this: What impact have immigrants had on the rewards, opportunities, and life chances of the poorest Americans? For most of American history the question translates into the impact of European immigrants on African Americans, although, especially in recent years, Latino and Asian immigrants to major cities have made the issue immensely more complicated.

Racism gave European immigrants advantages over African Americans already living in Northern and Midwestern cities. In the antebellum era, Irish and other immigrants displaced African Americans from trades, such as barbering, in which they had been well represented. At the same time, employers hired white European immigrants for the new jobs in the emergent industrial economy. The same pattern repeated itself in the late nineteenth and early twentieth centuries. In Philadelphia between 1860 and 1890, the proportion of artisans among black males declined from 15 to 1.1 percent. Despite a pool of inexpensive labor among blacks in the South, Northern employers recruited huge numbers of semiskilled industrial workers from southern and eastern Europe. Only when World War I and then immigration restriction created a labor shortage and dried up their transatlantic sources did industrial employers seriously begin to recruit Southern blacks. The use of African Americans as strikebreakers constitutes the major exception to the pattern. This practice, of course, only heightened hostility between blacks and immigrants.[22]

Within America, frequent, short-distance migration defined the experience of a very high proportion of workers. As one recent social historian after another has shown, the nineteenth- and early twentieth-century American working class was transient. In most cities studied by historians only a minority of workers could be located at intervals a decade apart, and rates of labor-force turnover within industry remained staggeringly high at least through the 1920s. This population churning, far from random, had structural sources and an identifiable social structure. Through their labor-market practices, industrial employers fostered high turnover, and the irregularity of employment sent workers on the road in search of jobs. With workplaces small and no mass transportation available, workers needed to live within walking distance of their jobs, and finding employment often meant moving to a new town or city. Older workers, especially home owners, remained the least likely to move. The ability to stay in one place for a long time was in fact a privilege that only a minority of workers enjoyed.[23]

[22] Ibid.

[23] For a discussion of the literature of transiency, see Michael B. Katz, Michael J. Doucet, and Mark J. Stern, *The Social Organization of Early Industrial Capitalism* (Cambridge: Harvard University Press, 1982), chap. 3.

Only in part did the experiences of blacks in the rural South in the latter nineteenth century reflect the transience of the American working class. For in one important way the intraregional movement of Southern African Americans differed sharply from that of any other group in American history: It was proscribed by the state. After the Civil War, Southern legislatures enacted "black codes" prohibiting blacks from traveling for reasons unrelated to the needs of white employers. These laws were enforced unevenly. Although some planters tried desperately to hold on to their labor force, others, equally desperate for workers, encouraged blacks to move, and some federal officials took seriously their obligation to prevent peonage and involuntary servitude. Later in the century, vagrancy statutes also constrained black mobility. Far more than other workers, blacks often remained unable to use migration to search for better work and to escape poverty. Nonetheless, some blacks managed short-distance or seasonal moves. Regularly cheated and exploited by landlords, sharecroppers often moved every year or so in search of more favorable terms and more equitable treatment. Unable to eke out a living on their own farms, large numbers of men took seasonal work elsewhere in the South (referred to as "shifting"), leaving behind their families. This need to fragment families in order to survive underlay much of what observers saw as marital instability and wrongly attributed to cultural preference.[24]

American history is also a story of great interregional migrations. The westward migration is one of them; another is the forced migration of Native Americans; a third is the movement of African Americans from the South to the urban North. Between World War I and the 1920s, 700,000 to 1 million moved North; 800,000 migrated during the 1920s. From 1940 to 1970, another 5 million followed. They moved for various reasons: to escape sharecropping; as a result of the mechanization of Southern agriculture; to answer labor demands in Northern industries after immigration restrictions closed the supply of European workers; to move out from under the shadow of Southern racial violence; to be able to use public facilities; and to find relatively greater access to the ordinary rights of citizens. In the first wave, more men moved to the industrial cities of the Midwest and more women to the older cities of the East, where the demand for domestics was high; later, gender ratios evened out. The result changed America profoundly. In 1940, who would have thought that the majority of African Americans would soon live not in the agricultural South but in the urban North? Some Southern states experienced significant population losses while the composition of Northern cities changed rapidly and irrevocably. In Chicago, for instance, blacks were only 8.4 percent of the population in 1940 and 14.1 percent in 1950. By 1960 their share had increased to 23.6 percent,

[24] See the chapter by Jacqueline Jones; the most thorough and definitive study of black mobility in the South after the Civil War is William Cohen, *At Freedom's Edge: Black Mobility and the Southern White Quest for Racial Control, 1861–1915* (Baton Rouge and London: Louisiana State University Press, 1991).

and by 1970 to more than a third, 34.4 percent. Here was the demographic origin of the modern ghetto.[25]

At the same time Southern blacks moved into Northern cities, whites increasingly left in search of new opportunities in either the suburbs or Sunbelt. Despite the inmigration of African Americans, the populations of older Northern and Midwestern cities began to decline, and their population densities decreased. Abandoned housing joined abandoned factories as symbols of formerly industrial cities. Unable to move because they lacked the skills and education required by the new postindustrial economy and because of discrimination, blacks remained locked into increasingly segregated neighborhoods. As a consequence, contemporary inner-city poverty and segregation reflect a partial reversal of the historic relation between migration and income or education. In the past, economic opportunity stimulated migration by both the most and the least educated, by the affluent and the poor. Now, the relation has turned linear because the least educated and poorest city residents have become the least likely to migrate.[26]

The links between migration and marginalization always have been close. By marginalization, I mean the process whereby some combination of factors—for instance, technological change, racial competition, or government action—pushes groups to the edges of the labor force, leaving them redundant, unwanted, or confined to the worst jobs. The great changes in Europe unleashed by capitalism in the eighteenth and nineteenth centuries resulted in mass migrations throughout the Continent and across oceans as landless workers, newly displaced artisans, and others pessimistic about their futures at home sought to relocate where better opportunities seemed to beckon. Among the variety of factors that brought European immigrants to American shores, marginalization, thus, ranked very high.[27]

The arrival of European immigrants helped marginalize African Americans in cities. Displaced from skilled trades, denied industrial employment, they clustered in the hardest, most unrewarding work, taking jobs no one else wanted. Men found jobs in hard, unskilled labor and forms of personal service; women found them almost exclusively in the various branches of domestic work. Because employers paid black men so badly, so much less than whites, their wives worked outside their homes far more often than the wives in any other group. When they did work in heavy industry, such as steel or coal mining, employers relegated them to the most difficult and dangerous jobs. In moments of acute labor shortage, during the two World Wars, industrial employers called on black labor and began to move African Americans away from the margins and

[25] See the chapters by Jacqueline Jones and Joe W. Trotter.

[26] See the chapter by David Bartelt.

[27] A good overview of the relations between the spread of capitalism and transatlantic migration is John Bodnar, *The Transplanted: A History of Immigrants in Urban America* (Bloomington: Indiana University Press, 1985).

toward the center of the blue-collar world of work.[28] Otherwise, until the results of affirmative action registered their impact, African Americans remained in the stagnant eddies at the edges of America's industrial economy.

After the 1940s and 1950s, within America as earlier in Europe, marginalization also ranked high among the factors encouraging Southern blacks to move northward. Until then, planters needed them for cheap labor. Although paid wretchedly, cheated, exploited, terrorized, and killed, blacks remained at the very center of the Southern economy until mechanical cotton pickers began to displace them in the post–World War II era. Then their movement northward swelled into a mighty tide.[29]

Marginalized European immigrants by and large had entered American cities at the zenith of America's industrial power during the peak demand for labor. For this reason, they found jobs waiting and real wages growing. Although the Great Depression derailed their progress, the Wagner Act of 1935 and the subsequent development of unions combined with the economic growth of the immediate postwar period to bring them a degree of unprecedented comfort and to open almost undreamed of opportunities for their children. By contrast, African Americans finally entered the industrial North and Midwest at the start of their decline. As they moved from marginal positions in the Southern labor force to the margins of the Northern economy as well, they inherited deindustrializing cities. In the 1960s a new black middle class of government workers emerged primarily through the combined expansion of government jobs and affirmative action, but they did not represent a majority of African Americans, who could see no very bright future for themselves or their children in the dying industrial economies of old cities. Stuck within spreading ghettos that they were too poor to escape, their children trapped in failing schools that they were too poor to leave, a large share of African Americans lacked the skills and cultural capital to grasp the new opportunities in information processing and related fields available in the upper reaches of the dual economies of postindustrial cities.

The marginalization of African Americans in the North and Midwest resulted from their race as well as their lack of applicable skills, as the case of Appalachian immigrants to the same cities shows clearly. In the decades between 1940 and 1970, when 5 million blacks migrated from the South to the North, 3.2 million whites left the southern Appalachian region and followed the same route. The two groups shared similar levels of education, skills, and work experience. Indeed, the whites were leaving subsistence farming, commercial tobacco plantations, coal mining or some combination of these. Yet, with easy access to semiskilled work and greater freedom of movement and residence, many more of these Southern whites than African Americans prospered. In the largest

---

[28] See the chapter by Joe W. Trotter.
[29] Lemann, *Promised Land*; see the chapter by Jacqueline Jones.

Midwestern cities, employers favored them over blacks for unskilled and semiskilled work; in some areas, they banded together to exclude blacks altogether. The upwardly mobile among the first generation, and many of their children, dropped their accents, dressed in Northern fashions, and moved into neighborhoods where no one knew or could identify their geographic origins. The experience of African Americans moved in precisely the opposite directions.[30]

Deindustrialization, of course, has marginalized great numbers of white as well as black workers. Formerly highly paid automobile or steel workers pump gas, if they are lucky. Not only unemployment but the structure of the postindustrial economy, its bifurcation into "symbolic analysts" (to use Robert Reich's phrase) and poorly paid, often part-time routine service workers, permanently relegates huge numbers to the labor market's unrewarding margins. Unhampered by racial stereotypes, racial antagonism, or statistical discrimination, whites fare better than blacks, especially black males, in the competition for even these jobs. Still, the experience of white males illustrates how the forces sustaining black poverty are early, particularly intense, examples of trends that are reshaping America's social structure.[31]

A process, which I call exclusion, combined with technological change to repeatedly push African Americans to the margins of the labor market. Its basis is a combination of racial beliefs, antagonisms, and competition. The story of exclusion is in part a familiar one: employer preference, the concerted actions of white workers, and the policies of unions excluded African Americans from trades, industrial employment, white-collar work, and other economic opportunities. Voter registration procedures excluded them from the normal prerogatives of citizenship. Legal segregation, social customs, and private arrangements excluded them from public facilities and white neighborhoods. However, there is an additional story about this process: the exclusion of African Americans (and now, it appears, Latinos) from the processes that facilitated the economic and social mobility of white ethnics. It shows why neither African Americans nor Latinos in postindustrial cities will recapitulate the experience of white European immigrants of an earlier era.

Because African Americans lacked an ethnic employment niche, they remained excluded from the dominant process of immigrant economic mobility. An ethnic niche refers to the overrepresentation of a group in an occupation or industry. That is, the proportion of the ethnic group employed in it exceeds the

---

[30] See the chapter by Jacqueline Jones.

[31] Robert B. Reich, *The Work of Nations* (New York: Alfred A. Knopf, 1991), pp. 177–80; on the "convergence" thesis, see June Axinn and Mark Stern, *Dependency and Poverty: Old Problems in a New World* (Lexington, Mass.: Lexington Books, 1988); for an excellent review of the literature on the labor-force disadvantages of young black men, see Philip Moss and Chris Tilly, *Why Black Men Are Doing Worse in the Labor Market: A Review of Supply-Side and Demand-Side Explanations* (New York: Social Science Research Council, 1991).

group's share of the population. Ethnic niches developed for different reasons: some groups arrived with special skills; in other instances, early arriving members established a beachhead in an occupation and then recruited their compatriots. The Irish built a niche in politics and government, the Jews in the garment industry, and the Italians in construction. Even post–World War II Southern Appalachian migrants built niches in Midwestern cities. These niches were important for three reasons: they provided relatively stable work to unskilled and semiskilled immigrants; they facilitated economic mobility; and they exerted social controls by requiring members to conform to standards of behavior set by coworkers, friends, and neighbors.[32]

Neither African Americans nor Latinos were able to create the same sort of ethnic niches that earlier immigrant groups did. Every time African Americans gained a modest presence in a promising trade, discrimination undercut their efforts, and whites replaced them. In New York City, by 1910, immigrants had displaced the black barbers and caterers who had served whites in the nineteenth century. Locked out of entrepreneurial activities, most blacks worked for whites, and then only in the worst jobs. Affirmative action finally provided African Americans with an occupational niche in the 1960s: government employment. Unlike the niches that facilitated the economic progress of immigrants, government employment required at least modest educational skills. Therefore, it did not facilitate the upward mobility of unskilled African Americans in the way that nineteenth-century public employment, the garment industry, or construction had assisted the Irish, Jews, and Italians. With good blue-collar manufacturing work disappearing, unskilled or poorly educated African Americans and Latinos could hold little hope of building a niche of their own, and cutbacks in government employment narrowed even their new route into the middle class.[33]

Statistics demonstrate the exclusion of African Americans and Latinos from the processes that fostered white immigrants' economic progress. The social consequences remain more speculative, but they may have been similar for most of those who remained on the outside, including the many whites not employed within an economic niche. Exclusion from niche employment, that is, may have translated into an absence of important forces that promoted social order and stability in the presence of poverty. This is one way to think about the reasons for differences in crime or indicators of social disorganization among and within groups.[34]

Patterns of migration, marginalization, and exclusion fostered the isolation of the poorest African Americans in inner cities. This isolation has four dimensions: economic, spatial, social, and cultural. I refer to isolation as a process

---

[32] See the chapter by Suzanne Model.
[33] Ibid.
[34] Ibid.

because it is ongoing: inner-city African Americans have become more isolated now than at any other point in American history.[35]

Economic isolation refers, first, to the increased detachment from the labor force and, within the labor force, from the rewarding sectors of the new postindustrial economy, which I already have discussed. It also refers to the exclusion of ghetto neighborhoods from the real-estate market. Because the federal government and banks began to "redline" them in the 1930s, inner-city neighborhoods remained starved for capital for housing and business. As the manufacturing base of cities began to erode in the 1960s, financial institutions and private investors not only failed to pump in the capital needed to reverse their deterioration, they began to disinvest in them. Banks and businesses moved or closed; landlords, unwilling to pay taxes and maintenance costs on unprofitable property, simply abandoned housing. Rents nonetheless rose faster than the incomes of the inner-city poor, many of whom found themselves homeless in a sea of abandoned houses. With no prospect of profit, no rational investor would put money into inner cities, where property values often declined. As a consequence, these "redundant" areas moved beyond the boundaries of the market or the reach of market-based policy, and remained dependent, instead, on infusions of capital from the government or private philanthropy or on devising their own community-based approaches to economic development.[36]

Spatial isolation is another way of thinking about the expansion of ghettos. Although the homes of African Americans always clustered together in cities, in the nineteenth century they formed pockets, not districts, often filling in behind other housing or in alleyways. The first identifiable ghettos emerged in major cities in the late nineteenth and early twentieth centuries and expanded during the Great Migration of the 1920s. Even these remained relatively small because African Americans did not yet constitute a large share of Northern urban populations.

The great era of ghetto expansion began after World War II as a coincidence of two population movements: the migration of African Americans and later Latinos into Northern cities and the outmigration of whites to suburbs. Together, these movements reconfigured urban populations. As the areas encompassed by ghettos expanded, measures of segregation within cities rose dramatically, signifying the isolation of their populations.

Especially in the 1970s, ghettos also grew poorer. The proportion of their residents living in poverty rose as geographic boundaries expanded. How much of this impoverishment, this concentration of poverty, reflects the outmigration of middle-class African Americans and how much is the result of greater poverty among existing residents remains unclear. What is clear, though, is that

---

[35] Isolation is a major theme of William J. Wilson in *The Truly Disadvantaged: The Inner City, the Underclass, and Public Policy* (Chicago: University of Chicago Press, 1987).

[36] See the chapter by David Bartelt.

social isolation, the separation of income classes, has accompanied the growing spatial isolation of African Americans in inner cities.[37]

Historians and social scientists disagree about the amount of social interaction between middle-class and poor African Americans when they lived closer to one another in earlier decades. In fact, the authors in this book remain skeptical about the extent and quality of relations between income classes within ghettos. They stress the poverty of earlier ghettos, the friction between their classes, and the attempt of the black middle class to distance itself from the poor; they doubt the extensive influence of "old heads" that other writers see in the recent past.[38] Whatever the past and present status of class relations within the ghetto seems to be, social isolation has influenced culture unmistakably. Linguists find a growing divergence between the speech patterns and language of inner-city African Americans and other versions of American English. Language itself, thereby, has become another factor contributing to the isolation of African Americans in inner cities.[39]

The State, Politics, and Reform

Explanations that rely solely on great processes of social transformation often minimize the importance of agency by substituting inexorable, impersonal forces for actions and decisions. However, as several chapters of this book show, the situation of contemporary inner cities and the people who live in them cannot be understood without reference to the state, politics, and reform.

The mix of novelty, complexity, and danger within inner cities signified by underclass did not just happen; its emergence was not inevitable; like the postindustrial city of which it is a part, it is the product of actions and decisions over a very long span of time. Nonetheless, concentrated and persistent poverty was not, as Charles Murray and other conservatives would argue, the unintended result of well-meaning but misguided social programs.[40] To the contrary, beginning in the 1930s, programs that offered direct aid to poor people often succeeded.

[37] Wilson, *Truly Disadvantaged*; Jargowsky and Bane, "Neighborhood Poverty"; Douglas S. Massey and Mitchell L. Eggers, "The Ecology of Inequality: Minorities and the Concentration of Poverty, 1970–1980" (Population Research Center, University of Chicago, January 1989); Reynolds Farley, "Residential Segregation of Social and Economic Groups among Blacks, 1970–1980," in Jencks and Peterson, *Urban Underclass*, pp. 274–98; Douglas S. Massey and Nancy A. Denton, *American Apartheid: Segregation and the Making of the Underclass* (Cambridge: Harvard University Press, forthcoming).

[38] William J. Wilson stresses the interaction of middle-class and poor ghetto residents in *The Truly Disadvantaged*; "old heads" is the phrase reported by Elijah Anderson in *Streetwise: Race, Class, and Change in an Urban Community* (Chicago: University of Chicago Press, 1990).

[39] William Labov, *Language in the Inner City: Studies in the Black English Vernacular* (Philadelphia: University of Pennsylvania Press, 1972).

[40] Charles Murray, *Losing Ground: American Social Policy, 1950–1980* (New York: Basic Books, 1984).

Until the mid-1960s, city, state, and federal governments did little to slow or reverse the processes that resulted in the emergence of concentrated and persistent poverty, especially among African Americans in America's inner cities. Instead, many government policies contributed to their marginalization, exclusion, and isolation. One chapter cannot even list, let alone explicate, the myriad ways governments served these ends. What follows is a very abbreviated listing of some of them, enough to demonstrate that the condition of today's inner cities and their populations result partly from the actions of governments, that they are the product of deliberate decisions as well as of the great impersonal forces of social transformation.

The modern American state's role in the exploitation and poverty of African Americans began, of course, with the Constitution's acceptance of slavery and its subsequent protection at every level of government and by the Supreme Court. It is not only a story of the South, however. In the antebellum North, local governments and the courts permitted the segregation of schools and did little to protect blacks from other forms of discrimination or from racist violence.[41]

After the Civil War, the federal government not only failed to redistribute land or otherwise compensate former slaves, the Freedmen's Bureau helped tie freed slaves to plantations in a neoslave relation. Despite constitutional amendments, the federal government did not consistently nor for any duration promote either voting or civil rights, and it even refused repeatedly to pass a law outlawing lynching. State and local governments in the South tried to preserve a cheap labor force by limiting the mobility of blacks through "black codes" and vagrancy statutes. They also legalized segregation, disenfranchised African Americans, and maintained separate and unequal public facilities. Schools for black children suffered especially from the pitiful funding they received.[42]

Southern states attempted to control blacks through violence as well as law. Juries did not convict whites who lynched and murdered blacks. Police treated them brutally; they lacked access to courts or found in them unequal justice (if "justice" can be used at all); later in the twentieth century, state and local governments not only used police to prevent demonstrations and mobilization, the FBI infiltrated and sometimes destroyed groups working for civil rights and related causes.[43] Police brutality, unequal justice, and the infiltration of civil rights movements, of course, all happened in the North as well.

Southern agricultural interests contributed to the impoverishment of African

[41] Leon Litwak, *North of Slavery: The Negro in the Free States, 1790–1860* (Chicago: University of Chicago Press, 1961).

[42] See the chapter by Jacqueline Jones. There is a large literature on the origins of segregation and on the underfunding of education for blacks. See, for instance, John W. Cell, *The Highest Stage of White Supremacy: The Origins of Segregation in South Africa and the American South* (New York: Cambridge University Press, 1982); and Louis Harlan, *Separate and Unequal: Public School Campaigns and Racism in the Southern Seabord States, 1901–1915* (Chapel Hill: University of North Carolina Press, 1958).

[43] See the chapter by Robin D. G. Kelley.

Americans through their influence in Congress, even in President Franklin Delano Roosevelt's New Deal. Federal agricultural policies forced lands out of production, thereby shrinking employment opportunities for blacks, and few farmers adhered to the law requiring them to share their crop subsidies with former black tenants. As a result, blacks began to migrate to cities, where they confronted massive unemployment.[44]

Although the Economic Security Act of 1935, the charter of America's federal welfare state, eventually helped African Americans, it initially excluded, at the insistence of Southern congressmen, agricultural and domestic workers, the two occupations that employed most black Americans.[45] Despite Social Security and unemployment insurance, most black workers remained for a long time unprotected in times of unemployment and in old age.

One other legacy of the New Deal was America's dual welfare state. The New Deal cemented into the foundation of the welfare state a distinction between social insurance and public assistance. Social insurance is an entitlement for everyone based on fixed criteria such as age, disability, or unemployment. Because its benefits cross class lines, its political support is powerful. The great current example, of course, is Social Security as conceived in the 1930s. By contrast, public assistance is means-tested aid. It is what used to be called relief or what, now, we usually think of as welfare. Major contemporary examples are AFDC (Aid to Families with Dependent Children) and, at the state level, General Assistance.[46]

What we have come to call "welfare" originated as Aid to Dependent Children (later Aid to Families with Dependent Children), also a component of the Economic Security Act of 1935. Its subsequent history differs in every way from Social Security's. Aid to Dependent Children did not start as a program for unmarried or separated women with children. Rather, it grew out of state programs of mothers' pensions designed to assist widows. Its transmutation, which took place unexpectedly in the post–World War II period, resulted from changing patterns of work, residence, and family. As a program of public assistance directed only toward poor (and increasingly minority) women, AFDC has been able to muster only limited political support. Its benefits, set by state governments, vary dramatically, but in no state do they lift families out of poverty, and they remain much lower than Social Security's. In fact, the gap between the two programs widened as hostility to AFDC provoked both a reaction against "welfare" and punitive policies intended to control the behavior of its clients. In the 1940s and 1950s, some states introduced "suitable home" clauses into their ADC regulations to control the sexual behavior of black

---

[44] See the chapter by Jacqueline Jones.

[45] On the influence of Southern members of Congress on the Social Security legislation, see especially Jill S. Quadagno, *The Transformation of Old Age Security: Class and Politics in the American Welfare State* (Chicago: University of Chicago Press, 1988).

[46] I have written about this distinction in *In the Shadow of the Poorhouse.*

women and to assure a supply of cheap domestic labor in the South. The result only worsened the poverty of black women and children, as did welfare policies that contributed to family breakup by even denying aid to needy families with a man present. In the 1980s, the punitive, moralistic component of welfare policy continued in its "perverse" way by increasing the isolation of poor women with children through "deeming," in effect cutting off aid when women with children lived with working relatives or friends. In this instance, policies failed to recognize that increasing numbers of families responded to hard times and rising rates of poverty by forming extended households.[47]

The architects who designed the welfare state during the New Deal deliberately excluded relief from the responsibilities of the federal government. Indeed, in 1935, President Roosevelt turned relief back to the states, where he thought it belonged.[48] As a program that applies only to the poorest people, public assistance inherits the stigma always attached to relief, and its funding has remained much lower than Social Security's and more variable across the states. Social Security is but one welfare program that delivers disproportionate benefits to the middle class. Other subsidies add to this inequality of benefits. The largest of these is the income-tax deduction for home mortgage interest. In all, one authority estimated that in 1990 combined direct and tax expenditures for federal welfare for the poor were $124.6 billion, or 16 percent of the total, and for the nonpoor $651.0 billion, or 84 percent.[49]

The New Deal's relief and employment programs, especially the WPA (Works Projects Administration) literally kept many African Americans from starving, even though they received less than their fair share of benefits. With a federal administration providing relief for the first time and First Lady Eleanor Roosevelt campaigning for civil rights, blacks switched their electoral support from the Republicans to the Democrats.[50]

Nonetheless, the Democrats did little to promote the welfare of African Americans or to facilitate their civil rights. Not until 1950 did President Harry Truman abolish segregation in the armed forces. John F. Kennedy promised to end discrimination in public housing, but only in 1963 did he sign the necessary order, which applied only to new construction and excluded existing housing. The only federal action came from the judiciary, most notably the *Brown v. Board of Education* decision of 1954, which declared segregation uncon-

[47] Winifred Bell, *Aid to Dependent Children* (New York: Columbia University Press, 1965); Katz, *Shadow*, chap. 5; James T. Patterson, *America's Struggle against Poverty* (Cambridge: Harvard University Press, 1981); Roy Lubove, *The Struggle for Social Security, 1900–1935* (Cambridge: Harvard University Press, 1968), pp. 91–112; also see the chapter by Mark J. Stern.

[48] On this episode see, Piven and Cloward, *Regulating the Poor*; and Katz, *Shadow*.

[49] Michael Sherraden, *Assets and the Poor: A New American Welfare Policy* (Armonk, N.Y.: M. E. Sharpe, 1991), p. 65.

[50] See the chapter by Jacqueline Jones. On blacks' shift to the Democratic party, see Nancy J. Weiss, *Farewell to the Party of Lincoln: Black Politics in the Age of FDR* (Princeton: Princeton University Press, 1983).

stitutional. Kennedy's administration also proved slow to assist the civil rights movement, even when prodded by black leaders and their allies and shocked by the violence directed at civil rights workers in the South.[51] Only in the administration of President Lyndon Johnson, with the Civil Rights and Voting Rights Acts of 1964 and 1965, did the legislative and executive branch of the federal government take a major step toward reducing discrimination and the practices that sustained it.

Until the mid-1960s, then, the welfare and civil rights policies of the federal government did little to slow the marginalization, exclusion, and isolation of African Americans and sometimes even facilitated it. The story of federal housing and urban policies in the same years is depressingly similar. In effect, the federal government manipulated market incentives in ways that lured middle-class whites to the suburbs and trapped blacks in inner cities.[52]

In the wake of massive mortgage foreclosures during the Great Depression of the 1930s, the federal government for the first time began to underwrite mortgages. It saved tens of thousands of homes and, by changing the terms of mortgages, helped a great many people to become home owners. Nonetheless, the Federal Housing Administration, which administered the mortgage program, "redlined" areas of cities considered poor risks (that is, it identified areas in which it would not underwrite or recommend mortgages). Redlined areas included virtually all neighborhoods with black residents and many with a sizable proportion of European immigrants as well. In this way, the federal government simultaneously hastened the decay of inner cities by denying them capital and by encouraging those residents able to purchase homes to leave. The FHA placed racial restrictions on its mortgages until the 1960s.[53]

Other factors—widespread automobile ownership, highway policy, tax exemption for mortgage interest payments, mortgages for veterans, and the development of techniques for producing massive amounts of tract housing quickly and cheaply—also promoted the growth of suburbs. Because suburbs are minigovernments, they exercise a great deal of autonomy in land use, zoning, and related policies, and they used these, along with deed restrictions and covenants, to exclude blacks. As cities filled with poor newcomers requiring expensive services and paying little in taxes, the historic relations between cities and suburbs changed. Whereas in the nineteenth and early twentieth centuries, cities had annexed their suburbs, offering municipal services as a lever, later suburban governments successfully began to resist incorporation, and annexation largely ended, allowing suburbs to draw their boundaries tighter against blacks, who remained trapped in inner cities. As pressures for integration mounted in the 1960s, suburbs chose to diversify by race rather than class. They

[51] The foot-dragging of the Kennedy administration emerges vividly in Taylor Branch, *Parting the Waters: America in the King Years, 1954–1963* (New York: Simon and Schuster, 1988).

[52] See the chapter by David Bartelt.

[53] See the chapters by David Bartelt, Thomas Sugrue, and Robin D. G. Kelley.

retained zoning and other restrictions that allowed only affluent blacks (and in some instances Jews) to enter, thereby intensifying the concentration and isolation of the urban poor.[54]

Urban renewal and highway policies also intensified the concentration of poverty and the isolation of poor minorities in inner cities. Urban renewal (chartered by the ironically named Housing Act of 1949) often ripped down viable neighborhoods, displaced their residents, and failed to rehouse them. Between 1950 and 1960, according to one estimate, urban renewal tore down 128,000 units, which rented for an average of $50 or $60 a month, and replaced them with only 28,000 units with an average rental of $195. In place of homes, urban renewal and subsequent policy encouraged the redevelopment of central cities with office towers, hospitals, universities, and the facilities that service them. The 1956 Highway Act, which created the interstate highway system, funneled immense sums into cities because it reimbursed them for 90 percent of construction costs. The new highways and expressways not only encouraged more movement away from cities to the suburbs; they also created barriers between the sections of cities, walling off poor and minority neighborhoods from central business districts. Like urban renewal, highway and expressway construction also displaced many poor people from their homes.[55]

Public housing reinforced the impact of mortgage policy, urban renewal, and highway construction. Housing is a very old problem in America's cities. New York City suffered the first of its successive housing crises in the early years of the nineteenth century; other cities followed later. Everywhere, urban politicians and elites described housing crises as the unavoidable consequence of market processes. In truth, they resulted at least as much from the transformation of housing and urban land into speculative commodities. In various ways, nineteenth-century city governments facilitated rising real estate prices; the separation of cities into districts based on function, wealth, and race; and the progressive displacement of the poor into crowded, inferior housing. Early housing reformers, unwilling to intervene in the market by building municipal housing, stressed model housing and regulations to control the sanitary conditions and safety of tenements. The latter resulted in marginal improvements in tenement construction, but the larger problem of housing the poor remained unsolved.[56]

The federal government built its first public housing in the 1930s, but only after World War II did the government begin to sponsor the construction of a

[54] On the history of suburbs in America, see Kenneth T. Jackson, *Crabgrass Frontier: The Suburbanization of the United States* (New York: Oxford University Press, 1985).

[55] See the chapters by David Bartelt and Thomas Sugrue; Martin Anderson, *The Federal Bulldozer: A Critical Analysis of Urban Renewal, 1949–1962* (Cambridge: MIT Press, 1964).

[56] Elizabeth Blackmar, *Manhattan for Rent* (Ithaca: Cornell University Press, 1989); Roy Lubove, *The Progressives and the Slums: Tenement House Reform in New York City, 1890–1917* (Pittsburgh: University of Pittsburgh Press, 1962).

large number of units. Originally designed for "respectable" working families, public housing turned into shelter for the poor. Resistance to public housing perceived as only for minorities by white neighborhoods and the politicians they supported forced the federal government to agree to build only in areas dominated by minorities and poverty. Influenced by considerations of cost, the need to cram as many units as possible onto a small space, and the ideas of architects inspired by visions of high-rise living, authorities designed public housing in the form of large apartment towers, with disastrous results. Because of its location and size, public housing fostered the isolation of African Americans in areas of increasingly concentrated poverty.[57]

In the mid-1960s, federal urban policy began to tilt toward cities in more constructive ways, but it lacked the time for major accomplishments before Richard Nixon, in his second administration, began to disengage the federal government from urban programs. Among other actions, Nixon placed a moratorium on the construction of public housing. In the 1980s, President Ronald Reagan accelerated the withdrawal of the federal government from assistance to the cities. The result was a decade disastrous for cities and their poor. As city governments confronted increased poverty, homelessness, crumbling infrastructures, rising drug use, crime, and AIDS, the federal government virtually stopped building housing, shrank its aid to cities, reduced benefits to individuals, and raised the taxes of the poor at the same time it lowered them for the rich.[58] These are some of the ways that the actions of government fostered the concentration of persistent poverty in inner cities and the isolation of the minority poor.

Organized campaigns to reform the family life of the poor, reduce crime, and ameliorate the worst effects of urban poverty did not begin in the 1960s, or even the 1930s. They date from the late eighteenth and early nineteenth centuries, when the consequences of city growth first seriously alarmed leading citizens. Voluntary associations, often affiliated with Protestant denominations, formed to relieve poverty, suppress vice, and reform morals; public authorities created poorhouses, schools, and penitentiaries; and public funding blended with private sponsorship in the support of hospitals and orphaned children.[59]

The pre–welfare state history of these activities can be characterized, first, by what they did not try to do. They did not intervene in market relations. They did

[57] See the chapters by Thomas Sugrue, David Bartelt, and Robin D.G. Kelley. Arnold Hirsch, *Making the Second Ghetto: Race and Housing in Chicago, 1940–1960* (Cambridge and New York: Cambridge University Press, 1983); John F. Bauman, Norman P. Hummon, and Edward K. Muller, "Public Housing, Isolation, and the Urban Underclass," *Journal of Urban History* 17, no. 3 (May 1991): 264–92.

[58] See, for instance, David R. Goldfield and Blaine A. Brownell, *Urban America: A History*, 2d ed. (Boston: Houghton Mifflin, 1990), pp. 433–35.

[59] For an overview of these activities in the nineteenth century see Paul Boyer, *Urban Masses and Moral Order in America, 1820–1920* (Cambridge: Harvard University Press, 1978), esp. pp. 3–190; and Katz, *Shadow*, chap. 4.

not attempt to relieve poverty by redistributing power or resources, by modifying working conditions or raising wages, or by using public authority to control the cost of housing or the price and use of land. Instead, they translated the conditions and activities that alarmed or disturbed them into questions of behavior, character, and personality, which they approached through educational reform, the regulation of drinking and sexuality, evangelical religion, reinvigorated personal contacts between rich and poor, and institutionally based programs directed at personal transformation. None of these strategies accomplished their goals.[60]

In the early twentieth century, state programs of workmen's compensation, widows' pensions, and, in a few instances, unemployment and old-age insurance began a cautious modification of earlier traditions.[61] In the same period, however, Prohibition represented a massive victory for the older reform pattern on a national level. The great break with past approaches happened in the 1930s. The New Deal not only sponsored the constitutional amendment that repealed Prohibition; more important for the long run, it set precedents by intervening in economic relations in unprecedented ways, affirming labor's right to organize, federalizing (if only temporarily) relief, utilizing massive public-works programs to create employment, and initiating guaranteed economic support to dependent children, the unemployed, and the elderly.

The older tradition lingered, shaping, even, one of the two main strategies of the 1960s War on Poverty. The War on Poverty (I refer here to the programs developed by the Office of Economic Opportunity) defined its target as blocked opportunities. For this reason, it stressed education, job training, the accessibility of legal assistance, and the reform of other services. Despite the pleas of the Department of Labor, it rejected a strategy based on job creation and employment. Its major programmatic legacies are Operation Headstart, the Job Corps, and the Legal Services Corporation. Important and successful as each of these have proven, they represent oblique assaults on urban poverty and the conditions that sustain it.[62]

Community action, the War on Poverty's other strategy, broke more decisively with reform traditions. The Economic Opportunity Act (1964), charter of the War on Poverty, required "maximum feasible participation" in the design and administration of programs. In practice, this meant the creation of community action agencies to apply for and receive federal funds. Community action threat-

[60] An excellent discussion of how reluctance to intervene in market relations handicapped reform is in W. Norton Grubb and Marvin Lazerson, *Broken Promises: How Americans Fail Their Children* (New York: Basic Books, 1982).

[61] This story is told in Patterson, *Struggle against Poverty*, and Lubove, *Struggle for Social Security*, among others.

[62] Katz, *Undeserving Poor*; Margaret Weir, "The Federal Government and Unemployment: The Frustration of Policy Innovation from the New Deal to the Great Society," in Margaret Weir, Ann Shola Orloff, and Theda Skocpol, eds., *The Politics of Social Policy in the United States* (Princeton: Princeton University Press, 1988), pp. 169, 171; see also the chapter by Thomas Jackson.

ened established political arrangements by channeling funds directly to new agencies, bypassing city and state governments, and putting large amounts of money in the hands of people outside of, and often hostile to, politicians and social agencies. State and city politicians, not surprisingly, attacked community action from the start and quickly won modifications that seriously compromised its initial intent. Nonetheless, aside from its programmatic accomplishments, community action stimulated and legitimated grass-roots activism, helping to nurture what Harry Boyte has called the "new citizen's movement," which continues to exert a profound influence on American politics and public life. Community action also recruited new leaders, predominantly minority, often women, into politics. Many of them began careers that have led to leadership positions in city governments and social agencies.[63]

The War on Poverty fell victim to the war in Vietnam, which siphoned off the funds it had been promised by President Lyndon Johnson; President Richard Nixon, who despised it, began to wind it down. The War on Poverty therefore lacked a design, the time, and the money necessary for a frontal attack on poverty.[64]

Given its small budget, the political hostility it confronted, and its short life, the War on Poverty's legacy emerges as much more impressive than in most assessments based on conventional wisdom, or even those of historians and social scientists. However, in the same years it was programs outside the War on Poverty that did the most to reduce poverty and promote the health of disadvantaged Americans. By increasing and indexing Social Security benefits, the federal government reduced poverty among the elderly by about two-thirds. In fact, improvements in the Social Security system had started in the 1950s under the quiet sponsorship of the program's administration. Those improvements accounted for most of the reduction in poverty during the decade, which, wrongly, is usually attributed to economic growth. In 1972, Supplemental Social Security extended the benefits provided the blind, disabled, and elderly. Expansion of the food-stamp program measurably decreased hunger; nutritional programs improved the health of pregnant women and infants. Medicare and Medicaid (1965) extended health care to people who previously could not afford it. Visits to physicians by poor people increased and infant mortality declined. Other programs increased public housing and improved its quality and design. Affirmative action opened educational opportunities and careers to women and minorities, with dramatic results, especially in higher education and government. The common quip that "government fought a war on poverty and poverty won" is ideological slander, not history. To the contrary, the record

---

[63] See the chapter by Thomas Jackson; and Harry Boyte, *The Backyard Revolution: Understanding the New Citizen Movement* (Philadelphia: Temple University Press, 1980).

[64] A useful account of the War on Poverty, whose interpretation differs in some way from mine, is in Allen J. Matusow, *The Unraveling of America: A History of Liberalism in the 1960s* (New York: Harper and Row, 1984).

shows that government has the capacity to reduce poverty; extend health care, access to legal counsel, and housing; improve education and job training; and counter discrimination. The problem is not a lack of precedents or of good program ideas. It is politics and will.[65]

The "Underclass" and the Rest of America

America is a rich, inventive country full of energy and imagination. But its debates on poverty replay old, stale themes, and its public policies on poverty or the underclass lack initiative. Its resources for innovation more often flow into technology than to social programs. America leads the world in space exploration but lags behind several other industrial nations in reducing infant mortality; it pioneered in electronic computing but, alone among industrial democracies, has been unable to introduce universal health insurance. It always can find the money for war but claims to be too poor to rebuild its cities. It can afford to bail out the savings-and-loan industry but not to move children out of poverty, build housing, or train the unemployed for work. One reason American poverty discourse and policy have remained so dull and backward is a perception that the poor are different from the rest of us. Sometimes the point is explicit; at other times it remains unstated. But the assumption of two Americas lurks almost always not far from the surface of discussion. Because one of them, the America of the poor, is not as worthy as the other, its claims deserve less of our attention, energy, and resources. The second America remains cut off largely because of its own failings; for this reason it needs discipline more than encouragement, restraint more than resources.[66]

The assumption of two Americas errs in some very important ways. First are the ethical issues raised by its denial of community and its implications for citizenship in a democracy. Second is a narrow, partial reading of history. For the great transformations concentrating poverty in cities and contributing to the phenomenon labeled underclass are reshaping the lives of all Americans by changing their experience of work and family, eroding their once-vital cities, undermining their institutions, and degrading their public life. Third is a class-based human psychology in which incentives motivate everyone except the demoralized poor, who respond best to punishment.[67]

[65] See the chapter by Mark J. Stern; Patterson, *America's Struggle*; John E. Schwarz, *America's Hidden Successes: A Reassessment of Twenty Years of Public Policy* (New York: Norton, 1983).

[66] On the idea of two Americas, the classic statement, of course, is Michael Harrington, *The Other America* (New York: Macmillan, 1962; reprint, New York: Penguin Books, 1963); on the tendency to see and talk about the poor as "other," see Michael Harrington, *The New American Poverty* (New York: Holt, Rinehart and Winston, 1984; reprint, New York: Viking Penguin, 1985), pp. 8–11, 13; and National Conference of Catholic Bishops, *Economic Justice for All: Pastoral Letter on Catholic Social Teaching and the U.S. Economy* (Washington, D.C.: United States Catholic Conference, 1986), p. 144.

[67] The idea of a class-based psychology is developed by Frances Fox Piven and Richard Cloward in "The Contemporary Relief Debate," in Fred Block et al., eds., *The Mean Season: The Attack on the Welfare State* (New York: Pantheon, 1987), pp. 45–108.

A long intellectual tradition views the poor (except for clever paupers who play the system) as demoralized and denuded of the will and capacity for constructive self-help. This is one major theme that runs through commentary on the inner-city poor from the early nineteenth century to the contemporary underclass. One of the great services of social historians and ethnographers in recent decades has been to redraw the portrait of ordinary city people. In place of demoralization and passivity, they have written histories of political action and the strategies poor people have developed for their survival.[68]

Strategies assumed many forms, and examples are legion. One place to observe them is within families devising ways of coping with hunger and poor housing, illness and accident, periodic unemployment and bereavement. Supplying daily necessities—food, shelter, clothing, and medical care—required intelligence, effort, and planning. Among members of ethnic groups, fraternal associations and mutual benefit societies provided limited, though important, forms of insurance, of which the most common was for burial. However, in this ongoing struggle for survival, networks of mutual exchange were an even more vital resource. Traditions of reciprocity linked relatives; other networks joined neighbors, workmates, and, sometimes, even casual acquaintances. These patterns of reciprocity often reflected impressive generosity because none of their members usually had much, if anything, to spare. Nor did they assume an immediate, or even direct, return. Rather, it was as if most people contributed as they could to a revolving fund on which they could draw in times of need. Still, family members expected help from kin who could afford it, and negotiations over these expectations very often injected ambivalence, anger, and guilt into family relations.[69]

Even the families of employed unskilled workers found survival on one income difficult. For widows, or women who had been deserted, it was impossible, and poor families often pooled multiple incomes. Married white women, who rarely worked for wages outside their homes, contributed to family incomes by taking in sewing, laundry, or outwork; keeping boarders; and tending gardens that supplied their families with vegetables. In many families, children's wages proved the margin of survival. In the early twentieth century, children from both poor and working-class families customarily left school to begin work as soon as the law allowed (generally around fourteen) and usually lived at home for several years before they married. Many poor families, especially the families of widows, escaped from charity on the backs of their children.[70] In fact, even in

[68] The first contemporary major work in this vein was Carol Stack, *All Our Kin: Strategies for Survival in a Black Community* (New York: Harper and Row, 1974).

[69] See the chapter by Kathryn Neckerman. I have given an example of networks in "The History of an Impudent Poor Woman in New York City from 1918 to 1923," in Peter Mandler, ed., *The Uses of Charity: The Poor on Relief in the Nineteenth-Century Metropolis* (Philadelphia: University of Pennsylvania Press, 1991), pp. 227–46.

[70] See the chapter by Kathryn Neckerman. Also, for examples of family strategies see Ewa Morawska, *For Bread with Butter: The Life-Worlds of East Central Europeans in Johnstown, Pennsylvania,*

the early post–World War II era, children's earnings helped lift a sizable share of families out of poverty. In subsequent years, as children remained in school longer and left home earlier, married women compensated for their lost income by entering the regular labor force in great numbers. Although more nonfamily members have crowded into poor households in recent decades, these new additions have not offered much economic help. Most of them have been relatives unable to support themselves rather than paying lodgers. This increase in family extension during an era of rising poverty testifies to the persistence of mutual assistance among the poor.[71]

One very important and understudied question is whether the situation within areas of persistent and concentrated poverty in postindustrial cities has undermined the intricate networks that helped sustain families. A number of factors point in the direction of attenuated networks. Welfare reduces the dependency of family members on each other; lack of work leaves black men, especially, unable to fulfill the expectations on which their role in networks of reciprocity rested;[72] widespread and sometimes indiscriminate crime and violence substitute fear for trust in relations within neighborhoods; and the withdrawal of institutions removes public settings that facilitate the formation of networks. If these suppositions should prove accurate, they highlight the depletion of one key resource on which poor people within inner cities have drawn for centuries.

The attenuation of networks represented only one change in family strategies among the poor. Others, which began before 1940, set the stage for the post–World War II rise in single motherhood among all the urban poor. Their intersection with racial discrimination resulted in the most sudden change among African-American families. A number of factors (already described) drove men to the margins of the labor force, leaving them unable to support families and straining gender relations by increasing tensions between men and women and disrupting marriages. Other factors eroded the value of the household production with which women and children had buffered themselves against unemployment, forcing women into the work force. As the demand for the domestic and unskilled work to which they had been confined by lack of education and experience declined, poor women, increasingly marginal to the labor force, turned for support to expanding welfare programs. Unfortunately, those programs reinforced their marginality and discouraged both family work and family formation. In the end, a new family pattern and survival strategy, represented by single motherhood and welfare dependence, emerged among a minority of poor women.[73]

1890–1940 (New York: Cambridge University Press, 1985); and Lizabeth Cohen, *Making a New Deal: Industrial Workers in Chicago, 1919–1939* (New York: Cambridge University Press, 1990).

[71] See the chapter by Mark J. Stern.

[72] See the chapter by Kathryn Neckerman.

[73] Ibid.

Because poor people often have voted less than others, or because they participate less in formal political activity, historians, among other observers, have labeled them apolitical and apathetic. The label applies only under the narrowest definition of politics as participation in the electoral process and its related activities. (Even then, it confuses lack of participation with lack of awareness and concern; a telling example is the turnout of about 90 percent of Philadelphia's eligible black voters for the election of the city's first African-American mayoral candidate in 1984 or the huge black turnout to support the mayoral election of Harold Washington in Chicago.) A more inclusive definition of politics shows intense, continuous activity, a politics of everyday life manifest in personal and collective resistance, protest, and in interactions with institutions and authorities.[74] Disparities in power and resources have limited the achievements of poor people, but within those constraints a history of action on their own behalf stretches from enslaved people's acts of resistance on plantations to protests in welfare offices in the 1960s. It is manifest, too, in the creation of institutions, especially the black church, which, starting in the nineteenth century, played a prominent role in the struggles against slavery and for civil rights.[75]

Resistance takes place outside as well as within institutions and organizations. Consider the example of African Americans. Throughout African-American history a dissident political culture manifested itself in the activities of daily life (jokes, folklore, conversation, music); resistance to authority (foot-dragging at work; petty theft; the destruction of property); and, occasionally, in open rebellion. For black women living under slavery or in its aftermath, building a family of husband, wife, and children was itself an act of political defiance. This dissident political culture surfaced, for example, in Birmingham, Alabama, when individuals defied the petty tyranny of a local welfare office, formed a Communist-led movement in the 1930s, resisted segregation on city buses in the 1940s, or confronted police in the 1960s.[76] What joins these examples is not only resistance to oppression but the participation of poor people in all of them. Their example not only undermines the automatic equation of poverty with passivity and demoralization; it substitutes a new story based on action, commitment, and intelligence.

By its concentration on family pathology, the underclass debate resonates with another very old theme in writing about the urban poor. Its concern with casual sex, unwed mothers, and incompetent parenting echo complaints about the urban poor that have influenced American social policy since early in the nineteenth century. In the early 1800s, reformers promoted public schools for children of the urban poor to counteract the influence of their parents and train them in the moral values they would not learn at home; they blamed families for

[74] See the chapter by Robin D. G. Kelley.
[75] See the chapters by Joe W. Trotter and Robin D. G. Kelley.
[76] See the chapter by Robin D. G. Kelley; Jacqueline Jones, *Labor of Love, Labor of Sorrow: Black Women, Work, and the Family from Slavery to the Present* (New York: Basic Books, 1985).

the juvenile delinquency and crime that forced them to build reform schools and new prisons; over and over again, they feared the influence of immigrant families with non-American values and customs. Those families subjected to the most withering attacks always have been African American. In the third decade of the century, reformers and officials even advocated forcibly separating parents and children as their preferred strategy for breaking the chains that transmitted immoral behavior and dependence from one generation to another. When family preservation replaced family breakup as social policy in the 1890s, reformers, who still distrusted the capacity of poor parents, invented ways for government to supervise the relations between parents and children. They shared the old and persistent assumption that in family relations as well as in work, leisure, and politics, the poorest city people formed a nation apart from the rest of America.[77]

Historians familiar with this heritage of discourse about poor families find the current panic about African-American families depressingly similar. By probing the reality instead of the rhetoric of family life, contemporary historians have tried to relegate these long-standing views about the relations between families and poverty, especially among African Americans, to the dustbin of historical mythology; other liberal social scientists have generally applauded and joined their efforts. When in his notorious (and usually misunderstood) 1964 report, Daniel Patrick Moynihan attacked the black family as matriarchal and linked its current features to slavery, historians and other social scientists reacted with outrage. They tried to show that African-American family values did not differ from those of mainstream America. In the process, they unwittingly accepted one premise of their opponents: to be different was to be worse. They wanted to measure black families against an idealized 1950s standard of mainstream America and to find them the same.[78]

But are African-American families essentially the same as those of most other Americans, and, if they differ, how are the variations to be explained and evaluated? Should difference be shunned as automatically inferior? These questions can be answered in various ways. First is the evidence from the recent past that trends within African-American and white families run in the same directions. (The same point holds for a comparison between trends among the "chronically jobless" and those who are steadily employed.) Divorce has increased among both groups; so have out-of-wedlock births; teenage fertility among black young women actually has declined; it has risen among whites. Single-parent families have been increasing among all groups, though fastest among Hispanics. One reason for the rise in single-parent families is the decline in the proportion of women who marry. Among black women ages fifteen to forty-four, the proportion ever married dropped from 71.7 percent in 1960 to

---

[77] See the chapter by Eric Monkkonen; Katz, Shadow; and Michael B. Katz, Reconstructing American Education (Cambridge: Harvard University Press, 1987), chap. 1.

[78] See the chapter by Andrew T. Miller.

47.8 percent in 1988; in the same years the proportion for white women of the same age declined from 76.0 percent to 67.0 percent. As a result of these developments, nearly 30 of every 100 black children lived with an unmarried parent in 1988, compared to slightly more than 3 of whites.[79]

We can interpret these numbers in two ways. One is to point to the very large differences that still separate whites from blacks on measures of family structure. The other is to draw out the implications of trends that run in the same direction. Because the same pressures have reshaped all families, black, Hispanic, and white, the story of underclass families is not unique; it cannot be told without reference to the rest of America. The issue is not what has happened to the black, Hispanic, or underclass family. Rather, the questions are: What are the forces that underlie massive family change in late-twentieth-century America? Why do they buffet some groups more strongly than others? How do the same pressures translate into rates of family change that vary in different settings?

Another perspective has remained outside the mainstream of recent history and social science, which has concentrated on denying, or explaining away, differences among African-American and other families. Despite their efforts, evidence of those differences persist, and those historians who have stressed the prevalence of two-parent families among blacks in the Reconstruction South and early twentieth century cities have overemphasized their case; they have believed that any differences not explained by poverty or exploitation would mark black families as inferior. By accepting conventional templates of family patterns, they have overlooked the origins and meaning of distinct traditions, and they have failed to deconstruct "family," which is a relative, culture-bound concept, not one fixed and unchanging across time and space.[80]

African definitions, which often equate the origins of families with the birth of children rather than the marriage of a man and woman, have influenced African-American practices. African traditions, of course, were by no means the only influences on the formation of black American families, and they assumed different forms in Africa and America. However, they remain one important and persisting influence neglected by most writers on African-American families. In the African tradition, families extended across households; they concentrated their energies and resources on the care of children; and they often fostered children to childless relatives. At the turn of the century, critics of African-American families neglected to point out that they shunted a much smaller proportion of their children to institutions than did whites. Nor do current critics of African-American families notice that the rate of child abuse among them is lower than among comparably poor white families or that exceptionally strong family ties persist among adults. Although evidence for child fostering and other aspects of African family patterns abounds in the history and current

[79] Ellwood and Crane, "Family Change among Black Americans," tables 1 and 2; see the chapters by Mark J. Stern and Andrew T. Miller.
[80] See the chapter by Andrew T. Miller.

practices of African Americans, research and commentary framed in conventional categories, failing to observe it, misses the reciprocity among households and misinterprets what it sees. In their concern with children, mutuality, and flexibility, African-American families hold important lessons for others. None of this is to deny the forces tearing apart inner cities and placing often intolerable strains on the families trapped within them. Nor is it to deny that family patterns among African Americans represent adaptations to the effects of poverty and racial discrimination. It is to say only that the problems that afflict inner cities did not originate within African-American families. To scapegoat the black family is to do something more than blame the victim; it is to miss the point. For policy, the consequences are very serious.[81]

The concentration of debate on the family life of the poor obscures another link between them and the rest of America. Poverty signifies a position at the far end of a spectrum of inequality. It is defined in part by its relation to other positions, and its increase indicates a widening of economic distances. The rise in ghetto poverty, therefore, is not an isolated event. Rather, it is the most visible instance of growing income inequality in America, a trend that many researchers have documented for the 1980s. The growth of the working poor is another, less outwardly noticeable, example. For this reason, a focus that lingers solely on ghetto poverty distracts attention from its sources in transformations of social structure that threaten the well-being of a very large share of Americans.[82]

Underclass behavior did not incubate within the historic properties of black families, and ghetto poverty is an extreme example of a more general trend toward inequality. Nonetheless, African-American families always have lived within settings that have impeded the realization of their ideals and goals. Among the obstacles they have confronted, the failure of public institutions in recent years ranks high, for institutional failure relates directly to every aspect of underclass life. Schools do not educate most of their students; the police have not prevented the escalation of crime, violence, and the use of illegal drugs; the health-care system has not reduced the differences in infant mortality between inner cities and suburbs; public welfare rarely helps its clients escape poverty or even survive with minimal comfort and dignity.

This failure of public institutions spreads beyond the underclass or very poor. Because it touches all Americans, institutional failure represents one more link between the underclass and the rest of America. It impacts poor people with greater force because they lack alternatives. They cannot purchase private schooling, security systems, and health care or, as the well-off have done in central Philadelphia, create their own special service districts to assure clean and

[81] Ibid.

[82] On the rise of income inequality in recent years see Frank Levy, *Dollars and Dreams: The Changing American Income Distribution* (New York: Russell Sage Foundation, 1987).

safe streets. This cumulative failure of institutions degrades public life and raises the question of whether any common collective life remains possible in American cities. If privatization proves the only viable response, what will prevent the distribution of institutional resources from becoming more unequal? What happens to the definition of citizenship and the possibility of community?

Discussions of inner-city institutions focus on three dimensions: access, adequacy, and responsiveness. Access to institutions refers to a cluster of issues: who may use them (as in struggles around segregation); how persons may tap their resources (as in health care); how institutional resources are distributed (as in differences in per-pupil spending among schools); and even whether institutions are present (in Camden, New Jersey, for instance, there are currently no supermarkets, and many individuals lack automobiles). Once access is settled, the question of adequacy remains: Do institutions accomplish official purposes? Do the schools educate, the police protect? The question of purposes, however, remains far from transparent. To whose purposes do institutions answer? Do they respond to the needs and aspirations of the communities and people they serve? Do they facilitate the professional goals and convenience of their staffs by distancing themselves from their clients? Do they reflect an attempt by other classes to assure order, control, conformity, and a reliable labor supply? In inner cities, assertions of institutional failure imply related and consistent answers to these questions. Poor people lack access to some institutions; those to which they do have access remain underfunded; and institutions not only generally do not meet their official goals, they remain unresponsive, cut off from the communities they serve, linked more closely to the needs of their staffs and the projects of other classes.

Many writers have documented the failures of contemporary inner-city institutions, but few have offered coherent or comprehensive explanations for the conditions they describe or a very precise, detailed, and convincing argument about how and when institutions changed. Institutional criticisms usually imply declension. At some point in the past, urban schools taught children well, the cop on the beat stopped crime before it happened, and voluntary associations and families looked after those who could not help themselves. The problem with this implicit account is threefold: it is usually offered with almost no evidence; it probably is not true; and it misses the qualitative differences between past and present situations.

The method that compares past and present, documents the process of change, and explains the source of current institutional failure is, of course, historical. Nonetheless, it remains the method most neglected by researchers on the underclass and contemporary inner-city institutions.[83] Although recent writing in social history is full of clues for understanding the puzzles posed by

---

[83] The recent overview of research on the urban underclass, Jencks and Peterson, *Urban Underclass*, contains no chapters that focus on institutions.

inner-city institutions, most of it necessarily has focused on single categories of institutions and on their origins and early histories. Few historians have joined their institutional histories to the current situation in more than a cursory way; even fewer have tried to relate institutions to each other and to write about their changing configurations; and virtually no one has traced the pattern of institutional change within a city or neighborhood during the years of the great urban transformations since World War II. Still, as some of the chapters in this book show, historians can offer useful observations about inner-city institutions.[84]

Modern public institutions date from the early and middle decades of the nineteenth century. Public school systems, mental hospitals, police departments, penitentiaries, poorhouses, reform schools, and teaching hospitals all emerged in the same era. Although each addressed a specific set of problems, all were in one sense or another responses to urban transformation during the transition to commercial capitalism. Together they formed a new strategy for dealing with crime, poverty, ignorance, and disease. Their sponsors shared a widespread belief that the growth of cities, the increase in immigration, and new forms of work eroded family stability, loosened morals, and undermined existing mechanisms for maintaining social order. They shared an unprecedented faith in the potential of institutions as social policy to reform society through their impact on individual personality and behavior. Although they worried most about the inner-city poor, their inventions irrevocably rechanneled the lives of everyone, for they created the institutional state that became one hallmark of modernity.[85]

Early architects of the institutional state needed to give a new meaning to "public." Colonial practice did not differentiate very sharply between public and private; to take one important instance, in education public referred not to schools administered and paid for by government but to free education provided the poor. Common school reformers set out to break this equation between public and pauper because their educational and social goals necessitated the incorporation of all classes into the same schools. With remarkable skill, they created a new, immensely popular, inclusive public institution. Schools reflected the optimism and pride that underpinned the creation of a public sphere in antebellum America. The monumental architecture of other new public buildings, even poorhouses, expressed the same point. A vibrant local politics and high voter turnout also reflected widespread involvement in and commitment to public life.[86]

It would be a mistake to overstress either the inclusiveness of public life or the quality of public institutions. Only white male citizens could vote, and public

[84] See the chapters by Eric Monkkonen and by Harvey Kantor and Barbara Brenzel.

[85] I have written about this in detail in various places: *Reconstructing American Education*; *In the Shadow of the Poorhouse*; and Katz, Doucet, and Stern, *Social Organization*, chap. 9.

[86] See the chapter by Eric Monkkonen; Katz, *Reconstructing American Education*, chap. 1 and 2; Katznelson and Weir, *Schooling for All*.

institutions embodied contradictions from their inception. Many institutions reflected the attempt of one class to reshape another more than an effort to embrace them all in an inclusive public community. Penal and welfare institutions mixed goals of reform, deterrence, punishment, and compassion. Voters and legislators asked public institutions to perform vast and difficult tasks with insufficient funds and political interference. These contradictions crippled new public institutions from the start. The glowing early accounts of many of them soon gave way to gloomy assessments either by their staffs or outside critics. Reform schools, penitentiaries, and mental hospitals, for instance, all saw their early emphasis on reform give way to custody. The stigma of pauperism tarnished poorhouses from their inception, and they always were terrible places. By the 1870s, critics charged that urban public schools had become rigid, self-serving bureaucracies which failed to educate students as well as had the little country schools they thought they remembered from their youths.[87]

Although nostalgia colored their memories, critics accurately represented the organizational history of urban public-school systems in the third and fourth quarters of the nineteenth century. The administrative structures of other institutions also grew not only larger but more formal, hierarchical, and specialized. Nonetheless, bureaucracies did not emerge suddenly or in one piece. In education, administrators and school boards in older cities, such as Boston, responded to one new problem after another by building structures with all the classic features of bureaucracies. Newer cities, such as Portland, Oregon, adopted bureaucratic structures from early in their history because they copied older cities. Bureaucracy, however, was only one organizational model contending for dominance in the nineteenth century. Each rested on a distinct cluster of priorities and social values. For the advocates of what we have come to think of as bureaucracy, efficiency, order, the division of labor, uniformity, and professionalism ranked very high and guided their responses to specific problems.[88]

The triumph of bureaucracy should be thought of as the result of choice; there were, for instance, a variety of ways that cities could (and still might, as they are learning) have arranged for the education of their children. Bureaucracy succeeded, in part, because it served professional aspirations. In education, it offered male teachers a career hierarchy through which they could advance, greater job security, more authority, and a buffer against outside interference. New positions within school bureaucracies created a new profession: school administrator (the first of these new positions was superintendent). In a parallel way, other new professions grew out of administrative practice within

---

[87] A large literature on individual institutions supports these generalizations. Many of the most important works are listed in the chapter by Eric Monkkonen.

[88] Katz, *Reconstructing American Education*, chap. 2 and 3; David B. Tyack, *The One Best System: A History of American Urban Education* (Cambridge: Harvard University Press, 1974); Selwyn Troen, *The Public and the Schools: Shaping the St. Louis System, 1838–1920* (Columbia: University of Missouri Press, 1975).

nineteenth-century institutions: psychiatry (superintendents of mental hospitals); penology (superintendents of penitentiaries); and public welfare (superintendents of poorhouses), to name three.[89]

Three observations about this institutional history have special relevance for understanding and reforming the institutions that service contemporary inner cities. First, the twin processes—the emergence of bureaucracies and professions—drove a wedge between institutions and the families and communities they served. Administrative structures and professionalism buffered them from community or client influence. This is why they became, and stayed, so unresponsive. It also bears on the reasons for their inadequacy, for bureaucracy and professionalism have protected large urban institutions from demands for accountability and change. Second, it is the intersection of bureaucratic structures and professional interests that leaves urban institutions so resistant to reform. Reformers often have failed to bring about major change because they usually have attacked one or the other. They have tried to alter the behavior of professionals without doing very much about the structures in which they work; or they have concentrated on structural reforms with little attention to the interests of the professionals who work within the system. Third, the current structure of public schooling, or any urban institution, is a historical product. It represents decisions and choices; it is not the only way. There is no "one best system"; alternatives always exist.

Attacked for inaccessibility, inadequacy, and unresponsiveness, the institutions that serve inner cities confront in intensified form the crisis of legitimacy that afflicts the public sector and government throughout America. Take one telling example from education. In the late nineteenth and early twentieth centuries, visitors almost always commented on the orderliness of large urban schools. Discipline was more a problem within small country schools than within cities. (Edward Eggleston's *Hoosier Schoolmaster* is a vivid example of the problems of country school keeping.) Often it was young women with little training teaching classes of fifty or seventy-five students who maintained this order.[90] Today, not only order but violence against students and teachers stand out as serious problems within urban schools, and armed police sometimes guard their corridors. Yet classes are much smaller and teachers by and large more educated and experienced. Teachers no longer command respect by virtue of their position because the legitimacy of schools as institutions has collapsed.

As with other urban institutions, the politics of urban transformation exposed the historic contradictions built into urban school systems, which finally exploded in the 1960s. The principal contradictions were: the theory of democratic control and the practices of segregation, tracking, and unequal

[89] On the history of educational administrators, see David Tyack and Elizabeth Hansot, *Managers of Virtue: Public School Leadership in America, 1820–1890* (New York: Basic Books, 1982).

[90] Edward Eggleston, *The Hoosier Schoolmaster* (1871; reprint, New York: Hill and Wang, 1957); Tyack, *One Best System*, pp. 50–56.

resource distribution; the vocational promise of schooling and the inability of graduates to find good jobs; and the theory of public control and the reality of bureaucratic and professional governance. Attempts to assert community control represented one response to the crisis not only in education but in law enforcement as well, where protests against police brutality reflected the eruption of some of the same contradictions and a similar collapse of legitimacy. The story of urban politics can be framed in a similar way. Protest against its inaccessibility, inadequate performance, and unresponsiveness exploded in the same era largely as a result of historic contradictions mercilessly exposed in postindustrial cities. Urban government, always tarnished by an aura of incompetence and corruption, never garnered the esteem accorded public schools or other institutions. Still, its status fell even lower, eroding its tenuous legitimacy, pushing citizens toward community action, neighborhood protest, and other forms of a new urban politics, or further into cynical withdrawal and political apathy.[91]

Many institutions have deserted inner cities; the ones that remain are failing; along with city government, their legitimacy has collapsed. Perhaps the only viable institutions remaining in inner cities are churches. Although many congregations have abandoned inner cities, the ones that remain continue to command respect through their secular as well as religious activities. Institutional withdrawal and collapse not only rob inner cities of the services they need, they knock out the props that sustain a viable public life and the possibility of community. They destroy the basis of "civil society." Denuded of institutions, cities move ineluctably toward privatization and away from a public life, toward anomic individualism and away from community. As community becomes more elusive in inner cities, its restraints and satisfactions disappear, eroding the buffer between individuals and a consumer culture to which they lack access through legitimate means.[92]

Institutional failure, a degraded public life, and the collapse of community do not stop at the borders of inner cities. They diminish the lives of everyone. That is another reason why the problems of the underclass represent in intensified form transformations that are reshaping the rest of America. The renewal of public life and the rebuilding of community require the revitalization of urban institutions. Without a renewed public sphere, no policies directed toward family, work, or welfare will turn around the crisis within America's inner cities.

[91] See the chapter by Harvey Kantor and Barbara Brenzel; Katznelson and Weir, *Schooling for All*, offers a compelling account of this process.

[92] Jeremy Nowak et al., "Religious Institutions and Community Renewal" (research report prepared for the Pew Charitable Trusts, Philadelphia, 1989); Michael Walzer, "The Idea of Civil Society," *Dissent* (Spring 1991): 293–304.

Contributors

DAVID W. BARTELT is director of the Institute for Public Policy Studies and associate professor of geography and urban studies at Temple University. He is coauthor of *Philadelphia: Neighborhoods, Division, and Conflict in a Postindustrial City* (1991) and *Homelessness in Pennsylvania: How Can This Be?* (1989).

BARBARA BRENZEL is professor of education at Wellesley College. She is author of *Daughters of the State: A Social Portrait of the First Reform School for Girls in North America, 1856–1905* (1983) and of several articles on the history of women, education, and social reform.

THOMAS F. JACKSON is a doctoral candidate in history at Stanford University and is writing his dissertation, "Beyond Civil Rights: African-American Political Thought and Urban Poverty, 1960–1973." He will be a postdoctoral fellow at the Center for Urban Affairs and Policy Research at Northwestern University.

JACQUELINE JONES is Harry S Truman Professor of American Civilization at Brandeis University. She is author of numerous books and articles, including *The Dispossessed: America's Underclasses from the Civil War to the Present* (1992) and the award-winning *Labor of Love, Labor of Sorrow: Black Women, Work, and the Family from Slavery to the Present* (1985).

HARVEY KANTOR is associate professor of education at the University of Utah. He is author of *Learning to Earn: School, Work, and Vocational Reform in California, 1880–1930* (1988). He also edited (with David Tyack) *Work, Youth, and Schooling: Historical Perspectives on Vocationalism in the United States* (1982), and is currently writing a history of poverty, equal opportunity, and educational policy since World War II.

MICHAEL B. KATZ is Stanley I. Sheerr Professor of History, chair of the History Department, and co-director of the Urban Studies Program at the University of Pennsylvania. He is the author or editor of ten books on the history of education, social policy, and poverty, including *Poverty and Policy in American History* (1983), *In the Shadow of the Poorhouse: A Social History of Welfare in America* (1986), and *The Undeserving Poor: From the War on Poverty to the War on Welfare* (1989). He serves as archivist to the Social Science Research Council's Committee for Research on the Urban Underclass.

ROBIN D. G. KELLEY is associate professor of history and Afro-American studies at the University of Michigan. He is author of the award-winning *Hammer and Hoe: Alabama Communists during the Great Depression* (1990) and of numerous articles on labor, culture, and politics in the United States and Africa. His work in progress is "Native Sons and Daughters: The Black Urban Poor in Late Capitalism."

ANDREW T. MILLER is visiting assistant professor of African-American history at Union College. He recently completed a dissertation at the University of Pennsylvania, "Looking at African-American Families: Recognition and Reaction." He is the author of "Measuring Mulattoes: The Changing U.S. Racial Regime in Census and Society," *Journal of Interdisciplinary History* (forthcoming), and "Under the Same Roof: Differences in Racial and Ethnic Household and Family Structure in 1910," in Susan Watkins, ed., *After Ellis Island* (forthcoming).

SUZANNE MODEL is associate professor of sociology and associate director of the Social and Demographic Research Institute, University of Massachusetts, Amherst. She is author of numerous articles on racial and ethnic stratification and social mobility, and, under a three-year grant from the Russell Sage Foundation, is writing "The Great Ethnic Derby," a history of racial and ethnic inequality in New York.

ERIC H. MONKKONEN is professor of history at the University of California, Los Angeles. He is author of *America Becomes Urban: The Development of U.S. Cities and Towns* (1989), *The Police in Urban America, 1860–1920* (1981), *The Dangerous Class: Crime and Poverty in Columbus, Ohio, 1860–1885* (1978), and he edited *Walking to Work: Tramps in America, 1790–1935* (1984). He is engaged in a long-term study of homicide in the United States and England in the nineteenth and twentieth centuries.

KATHRYN M. NECKERMAN is assistant professor of sociology at Columbia University. Her University of Chicago dissertation examines "Education and Family Strategies: Black and Polish Youth in Chicago, 1910–1940." Neckerman's many articles include "'We'd Love to Hire Them But . . .' : The Meaning of Race for Employers," with Joleen Kirschenmann, in Paul Peterson and Christopher Jencks, eds., *The Urban Underclass* (1991); and "Family Structure, Black Unemployment, and American Social Policy," with Robert Aponte and William Julius Wilson, in Margaret Weir, Ann Shola Orloff, and Theda Skocpol, eds., *The Politics of Social Policy in the United States* (1988).

MARK J. STERN is professor of social work and of history at the University of Pennsylvania. His books include *Society and Family Strategy: Erie County, New York, 1850–1920* (1987), *Poverty and Dependency: Old Problems in a New World*, with June Axinn (1988), and *The Social Organization of Early Industrial Capitalism*, with Michael B. Katz and Michael Doucet (1983).

THOMAS J. SUGRUE is assistant professor of history at the University of Pennsylvania. He spent the 1990–91 academic year as a research fellow at the Brookings Institution. He is currently revising his Harvard dissertation, "The Origins of the Urban Crisis: Race, Industrial Decline, and Housing in Detroit, 1940–1960," for publication, and is working on a study of George Wallace voters, liberalism, and racial politics in the urban North.

JOE WILLIAM TROTTER, JR., is professor of history at Carnegie Mellon University. His publications include *Coal, Class, and Color: Blacks in Southern West Virginia, 1915–1932* (1991) and *Black Milwaukee: The Making of an Industrial Proletariat, 1915–1945* (1985). He is also editor of *The Great Migration in Historical Perspective: New Dimensions of Race, Class, and Gender* (1991). He is currently working on a study of black workers in twentieth-century Montgomery, Mobile, and Birmingham.

Name Index

Aaron, Henry J., 411n.24, 412n.26
Abada, G., 277n.52
Abbott, Grace, 355n.58
Abramowitz, Mimi, 293–94n.1
Acs, Gregory, 399n.80
Adams, Carolyn T., 125n.25, 126n.31, 128nn. 32–34, 130nn. 35–36, 133n.42, 136n.47, 139n.54, 148n.94, 149n.97
Adamson, Wendell M., 297n.4
Addams, Jane, 260, 362n.87
Albini, Joseph, 179n.33
Alger, Horatio, Jr., 357
Alinsky, Saul, 428
Allan, Emilie, 163n.7
Allen, Robert L., 431n.78
Allen, Walter R., 120n.9, 141n.64, 144n.79, 194n.1
Alonso, William, 232n.14
Altman, Irwin, 118n.1
Altschuler, Alan A., 389n.55, 426n.66
Amberg, Stephen, 104n.57
Anderson, Alan B., 423n.61, 426n.66
Anderson, Elijah, 55n.1, 56–57, 126n.27, 189n.50, 190n.53, 222n.3, 294n.2, 457n.38
Anderson, James, 122n.14
Anderson, James D., 37n.15
Anderson, Jervis, 183n.39
Anderson, Martin, 462n.55
Angus, David L., 202n.15
Anker, Laura, 203n.18
Antunes, G., 310n.35
Apgar, William C., Jr., 124nn. 16, 18, and 21, 132n.38
Arrington, Richard, Jr., 323, 329
Aschenbrenner, Joyce, 265–66n.32
Ashby, LeRoy, 358n.69, 359nn. 73 and 74
Asher, Robert, 103n.53
Attaway, William, 46n.30
Atwater, W. O., 36n.13
Auletta, Ken, 4–5, 16, 194n.1, 220n.1
Avery, Burneice, 113n.82
Axinn, June, 241n.26, 454n.31

Bach, Robert, 168n.18
Bacon, Edmund, 148n.92, 149n.95

Bailey, Barbara, 297n.4
Bailey, Thomas, 168n.17, 184n.42, 400n.83, 400–401n.84
Bains, Lee E., Jr., 318n.53, 319n.54
Bales, Jack, 357n.66
Baltzell, E. Digby, 261n.11
Bane, Mary Jo, 19n.43, 55n.1, 115n.89, 126n.27, 142n.71, 161n.3, 224n.6, 372–73n.16, 443n.7
Banfield, Edward, 13n.25
Bardolph, Richard, 80n.55
Barreau, Allen, 47n.32
Barret, Michele, 257n.5
Barrett, James R., 199–200n.11
Barrett, Michelle, 257n.5, 287n.77
Bartelt, David, 118n.1, 120n.6, 141n.67, 144n.81, 147n.88, 408n.12, 409n.17, 452n.26, 456n.36, 461nn. 52 and 53, 462n.55, 463n.57
Bartlett, Dana W., 349n.39
Bastian, Ann, 369n.7
Bauman, John F., 112n.76, 126n.29, 145n.84, 150nn. 102, 103, and 104, 151n.106, 463n.57
Bean, Frank, 161n.2
Beard, Rick, 92n.15
Beasley, R. W., 310n.35
Beaver, Patricia D., 47n.32
Bekombo-Priso, M., 277n.52
Bell, Daniel, 180n.35
Bell, Winifred, 11n.22, 460n.47
Bellingham, Bruce, 352n.49, 357n.64
Bellow, Saul, 3–4
Benham, L., 166n.13
Berg, Ivar, 396n.73
Berger, Mark C., 101n.49
Berke, Joel S., 374n.21, 386n.48
Berndt, Harry Edward, 427–28n.72
Berry, Jeffrey, 330n.78
Berry, Mary Frances, 77n.48, 259n.7, 284nn. 66 and 67, 286n.76
Berube, Maurice R., 389n.55
Bethel, Elizabeth Rauh, 35–36n.12
Bigham, Darrel E., 57–58n.7
Billinsley, Andrew, 263n.22, 278n.54
Binford, Henry, 94n.25

Subject Index

academic schools, 385
affirmative action, 165–66, 184
African Americans. *See* black community; black movement; black people; black workers
African Methodist Episcopal Church, 64, 65
African Methodist Episcopal Zion Church, 64
Afro-American League, 66
agency, 441–42
Agricultural Adjustment Administration, 41
Aid to Dependent Children (ADC), 11, 216, 459
Aid to Families with Dependent Children (AFDC): decline in value of, 241, 411; effectiveness of, 459–60
Alabama Black Liberation Front (ABLF), 327–29
Alabama Christian Movement for Human Rights (ACMHR), 317, 322–23
almshouses. *See* poorhouses
American Federation of Teachers (AFT), 390
American Missionary Association, 37
antidiscrimination legislation: effect of, 106, 371; ethnic niches resulting from, 165
antipoverty programs, 417–18
Appalachian whites: economic success of, 47, 453–54; job and housing experiences of, 49–50; migration of, 46–52
artisans: black people as, 31, 59–60, 71–72; decline of black and other, 59–60, 89–90, 92, 450

banks, black-owned, 36
Baptist Church, 64. *See also* National Baptist Convention
baths, 349
Birmingham, Ala.: post–World War II economy of, 312–30; resistance of black people in, 304–31; shift in racial composition in, 324–25
black community: infrapolitics of Birmingham's, 295–96, 300–302; intraracial conflict in, 66, 332; multiclass urban, 66; in Philadelphia, 126, 132–37; response in 1915–45 period, 76–80; transformation of spatial structure of, 58. *See also* ghetto/

ghettos; racial segregation; residential areas
black elites. *See* middle class
black middle class. *See* class discrimination; middle class
black movement: achievements of, 413, 415; in North (1960s), 424–30; resistance of, in Birmingham, 305–31; role of, in Community Action programs, 419–20; themes of, 414
black nationalist organizations, Birmingham, 327
Black Panther party, 425, 431
black people: under poverty line in Birmingham, 325; as undeserving poor, 10–11
black school movement: demands of, 388–91; opposition to, 390
black workers: discrimination against, by black middle class, 67; effect of deindustrialization on, 226, 230; and emergence of industrial working class, 70–72; during Great Depression, 296–97; lack of nineteenth-century mobility for, 451; as strikebreakers, 63, 72–73, 450. *See also* deproletarianization; discrimination
block grants, 151, 153
Brotherhood of Sleeping Car Porters, 78
Brown v. Board of Education, 374, 460
bureaucracy: in urban school systems, 387–91, 401; welfare rights groups protest against, 426–27. *See also* government workers; public sector

Carter administration, 154
Charity Organization Society, New York, 8, 449
Chicago Freedom Movement, 425, 434
child fosterage: in Africa, 277–78, 280; African-American, 268–69, 272, 275–79; in Caribbean, 277–78, 279–80; estimates of, from Census data, 269–72; in Euro-American families, 273, 275, 276–77; as replacement for orphanage, 355–56; in United States, 277–78
children: in household production, 199, 208–9; labor force participation of, 202, 244–49

Subject Index · 503

Kennedy administration, 414, 415, 460–61
Kerner Commission, 80
Keyes v. Denver School District No.1, 375n.23

labor force participation: of black women,
71–73, 170, 200, 208, 226, 229, 249; of
children, 202, 244–49; decline of black
men in, 397; of immigrants, 90; of urban
working-class women, 200–202, 210,
249–52; of women, 215–16. *See also* black
workers; immigrants; minority workers;
white workers
labor market: blacks restricted in Southern,
29–31, 33–34; competition between blacks
and Appalachian whites in, 46–52; competition between blacks and immigrants in,
28, 43–44, 450, 452; deproletarianization
for blacks in, 447–48; drop-outs from,
397–98; government role in restricting,
33–34; during Great Migration, 68–74; importance of education in urban, 392–93;
Johnson administration strategy for, 415;
marginalization in, 452–54; overrepresentation in, 164; in plantation South,
39–46; poor people in, 87- 88; racial discrimination in, 106, 400–401; segmentation for working-class men (1900–40) in,
209–10. *See also* black workers; immigrants; unemployment; white workers
labor mobility: limited black-worker, 110; of
nineteenth-century workers, 91, 450; in
plantation South, 39–46; shifting, in sharecropping system, 41–42
labor unions: commitment to blacks by UAW
and USWA, 106, 313; discrimination
against blacks by, 184; effect on work stability of, 97; employment policies of, 106–
7; exclusion of blacks by, 72; experience of
blacks joining, 67; organization of black
railroad workers, 183; policies for blacks of,
106, 313
landownership, post-bellum black, 35–36
Latinos, 22
Legal Services Corporation, 412, 464
legislation: antidiscrimination, 106, 165, 371;
creating mothers' pensions, 355; Housing
Acts (1949, 1974), 146, 151–52, 462

Magdalene Houses, 360–61
magnet schools, 385
male-headed families, 250

manufacturing sector: decline of, in urban
economy, 128, 138–39, 394, 399; growth
of, in suburbs, 394–95; replacement of urban, by services sector, 443–44
marginalization: of African Americans, 29,
31–33, 323–24, 452–54; defined, 452;
impact of, on urban areas, 443, 449–57; of
white workers, 454; of women workers,
196
Masons, 65
mass demonstrations, Birmingham (1963),
318
Mayor's Office of Citizens Assistance, Birmingham, 329
Medicaid/Medicare, 411, 465
Methodist churches, 64
middle class: attempt to mobilize, 415–16; as
beneficiaries of antipoverty programs, 417–
18; black, 58, 63–64, 66, 114–15, 311–
12, 446; development of suburban areas
by, 93–94; expansion and mobility of, 75;
social control in minority community by,
188
migrants: Appalachian whites as, 46–52; economic and spatial constraints on black,
101; Hispanic, 101
migration: of blacks, 100, 106, 126, 144, 150,
237, 370, 456; communities created by,
51–52; factors contributing to black, 44–
46, 58–59, 69, 451; impact of, on urban
areas, 443, 449–57; post–Civil War restriction to black, 451; from urban industrial
areas, 143–44. *See also* Great Migration
militant action, Birmingham, 327–28, 330
Milliken v. Bradley, 376, 385
minority workers: displacement of urban,
395; economic opportunity for urban, 392,
396–97; effect of shift to service sector for,
400; occupational opportunity for, 392–93;
returns on education for, 401
mortgage market: effect on segregation of,
141–42; government intervention in, 153,
461
Moynihan report (1965), 13, 57, 264
mutual aid: black societies for, 64–65, 432;
societies for, 76–78; in urban working-class
communities (1900), 202–3. *See also* fraternal societies

National Assessment of Educational Progress
(NAEP), 379–80

centration of, 18–19; factors altering urban, 100–101; gaps in history of, 86–87; government policies for, 408–9, 417, 461–63, 465–66; nineteenth-century, 61, 93; patterns of, 88–89, 101; research in, 14–15; rural, 446; spatial distribution of, 448; from unemployment, 91; urban, 56–57, 62, 115–16, 324, 372, 404–5, 444; vocabulary of, 6–7. *See also* culture of poverty; poor, the; poverty rate; shelter poverty
poverty paradox, 404
poverty rate: basis for, 231; for blacks (1949–79), 222–24; differences in urban and suburban, 372; of dual-earner families, 250; in 1930s and 40s, 233–34, 239; in 1960s and 70s, 238, 241–42, 372, 417; of over-sixty cohorts (1970s), 241, pretransfer, 232, 233 (fig.); of urban jobless (1950s), 237–38
private assistance: in Birmingham during Great Depression, 297; in urban black community, 64–65. *See also* mutual aid
prostitution, 79
public assistance: AFDC and General Assistance as, 459–60; effect of federal, 34–35; during Great Depression, 217; and restrictions for blacks in South, 76. *See also* poorhouses; public relief
public housing: beneficiaries of programs for, 409; in Birmingham, 313–14
public policy: effect of, on urban jobless family, 242–52; for housing, 113, 145–54. *See also* housing policy; public housing
public relief: in Birmingham during Great Depression, 297–301; in early 1900s, 203–4; indenture as, 254; indoor, 343; outdoor, 7, 204, 341, 343, 345. *See also* General Assistance; poorhouses
public sector: black employment in, 183–85; contraction of, 399. *See also* government workers

race riots. *See* riot/riots
racial discrimination: in Birmingham during World War II, 304–5; in labor market, 392, 400–401; in Northern industrial centers, 100
racial isolation, 375
racial repression, Birmingham, 305–9, 320, 330
racial segregation: defacto Northern, 66; effect of government policy on inner-city, 408–9; forces in urban, 110–14; in poorhouses and jails, 346; in post–World War II

Detroit, 101; schools to reduce urban, 385; during World War I, 58
racial steering, 133–34
racism: for African Americans, 447; differing degrees of, 332; directed toward African Americans, 10–11; in Northern economy, 63–68
Randolph (A. Philip) Institute, 433–34
Reagan administration, 154
redundancy of place, 122, 157
relief. *See* mutual aid; public relief
rent strikes, 427
research: in black movement, 423–24; in poverty, 14–15; in underclass, 18–21; in welfare and social-control institutions, 364–65
Residential Advisory Board v. Rizzo, 135n.45
residential areas: and Detroit's post–World War II segregation, 110; increased segregation of (1920–30), 74–75; increased segregation of black, 74; in industrializing cities, 92–95; nearly all black, 61–62; rise of all-black, 61–62; and segregation by poverty status and class, 87–88; and segregation in Northern cities, 61; trend toward deconcentration of, 93–94. *See also* ghetto/ghettos; suburban communities
restrictive covenants, 113, 371
riot/riots: in Birmingham (1963), 318–19; in Detroit, 111; in Philadelphia, 135; in 1960s, 422

San Antonio Independent School District v. Rodriguez, 387
schools: achievement and completion rates in suburban, 378–79; inner-city segregation of, 374–75; in southern black communities, 37–38. *See also* urban schools
segregation: of black communities, 120–21; court-induced reduction of, 375–76; different levels of urban, 142; factors affecting levels of, 144–45; in inner-city schools, 374–75; persistence of, for blacks, 110, 141, 145; persistence of urban, 124; post–Civil War, legalized, 458; unconstitutionality of, 460–61. *See also* racial segregation; residential areas
segregation ratio, Philadelphia, 126–28
self-activity, 295n.3
service sector: effect of increase in, 128; effect of shift to, 140, 400. *See also* white-collar sector
settlement houses, 361–63